GROWING A SOUL

GROWING A SOUL

The Story of A. FRANK SMITH

NORMAN W. SPELLMANN

SMU PRESS • DALLAS

Publication of this volume was made possible
through the sponsorship of
the Southwest, Texas, and Rio Grande Conferences
of the United Methodist Church

Library of Congress Cataloging in Publication Data

Spellmann, Norman W   1928-
    Growing a soul.

    Includes index.
    1. Smith, Angie Frank, 1889-1962. 2. Methodist
Church—Bishops—Biography. 3. Bishops—Texas—Biography.
4. Texas—Biography. I. Title.
BX8495.S574S63   287'.6'0924   78-20876
ISBN 0-870-74171-3

To My Father,

without whom I could not have begun—

and

To My Wife,

without whom I could not have completed

this biography

Contents

vii

Illustrations are grouped following page 210

Foreword

MEMBERS OF THE A. Frank Smith Biography Committee, whose names appear in the Preface, express deep satisfaction and great pride in presenting this distinctive volume. It is about Bishop Smith's incredible life and the enormous influence he had upon people, institutions, and issues, in both church and state, in a foundational era that now stretches into a measureless future.

All clergymen who participated in the work of the committee served most or all of their ministry under Bishop Smith's appointment. Every one of us is indebted to him not only for the opportunities he opened for expanding ministry but for the unfailing support he generously gave us. Each of us is certain that Bishop Smith was his friend and gave him undivided personal attention!

The ministers and laypersons with whom he was associated shared the same feelings toward Bishop Smith. He was especially gifted in singling out a person, in causing one to feel that he or she was the most important person in his concern, and in inspiring all of us to rise above mediocrity in life and ministry.

It has been the consuming purpose of the committee that Bishop Smith's biographer capture the genius of this extraordinary man. It is hoped that this scholarly biography will illuminate the life and ministry of this Bishop of the Church who "walked humbly with God" and "served the present age" out of the resources of a perceptive mind, a warmth and breadth of spirit, with flair and an abundance of good humor, and from the vantage point of a world view. He was a leader and developer of people and institutions par excellence.

The committee's selection of the biographer to fulfill its mandate and purpose was a fortunate one. Dr. Norman Woods Spellmann, a dedicated and trained church historian, has shown himself a distinguished practitioner of his craft through his years of research in preparation of the book and the careful and sensitive manner in which he has translated historical material into a memorable reading experience. This scholarly work has, in our judgment, captured the true quality and spirit of Bishop A. Frank Smith.

The committee is particularly proud of the close relationship and cooperation manifest between Southwestern University, Bishop Smith's first alma mater, and Southern Methodist University, to which he also gave unstintingly of his time and service. From the librarians of Southwestern and the Bridwell Library of Perkins School of Theology, Dr. Spellmann received full and enthusiastic support. It is particularly appropriate that the SMU Press is the publisher of this work. All of this dramatizes the fact that the academe of the church is uniquely prepared to gather, record, and preserve the precious research materials of its servants and to nourish, protect the freedom of, and affirm the role of the Christian scholar as no other institution is able to do.

Finally, the committee's sense of satisfaction is complete because it has received the encouragement and support of the ministers and laypersons from the Southwest, Texas, and Rio Grande Conferences, sponsors of this significant undertaking.

DURWOOD FLEMING

Southwestern University
Georgetown, Texas
March, 1979

Preface

The story of a movement, an organization, or an era is that which comprises history, and no other literature is of greater significance.
—BISHOP A. FRANK SMITH[1]

THE LIFE OF A. FRANK SMITH revolved around stories: stories that he delighted to tell, and stories of the development of Methodism and the Great Southwest. "The only reason anybody would be interested in my biography," he once said, "would be to read about these Methodist institutions of which I just happened to be a part. My life is just sort of a thread which ties them together. I have a speaking acquaintance with about fifty years of history, and some of these people around here got the notion that I was an epitome of this period."[2]

Anyone who would understand A. Frank Smith and evaluate his significance must listen carefully to both of these stories—the story of his personal relationships and that of the institutions he helped to mold—for both offer insights into the man and his career. While many of Frank Smith's stories have long since departed, along with many of his friends and colleagues, the story of his formative role in the evolution of many great institutions of Methodism is engraved permanently in Southwestern University, Southern Methodist University, the Methodist Hospital in Houston, the Methodist Home in Waco, the Board of Missions of The Methodist Church, and the Methodism of his beloved "Great Gulf Basin." To follow the career of A. Frank Smith is to trace the history of Texas Methodism in particular and of American Methodism in general through half a century.

The heart of this biography is a collection of recorded interviews with thirty-eight persons who have generously shared their memories of Bishop Smith. Although I cannot list all of their names here (see Appendix B), I must acknowledge my indebtedness to them for the wealth of information they gave me. The contributions of Bishop W. Angie Smith, Bishop Arthur J. Moore, and Dr. L. U. Spellman are the most extensive and vital to the value of this biography. The greatest treasure of all is the set of six hours of recorded interviews that Dr. Charles S. Braden made with Bishop Smith in January, 1962. Mrs. Smith joined her husband for the last hour of these priceless conversations. Before his untimely death, Dr. Braden also had collected valuable papers and documents related to Bishop Smith's life and career.

I am unable to find words adequate to express my appreciation to the bishop's family: A. Frank, Jr., William Randolph, Mrs. Donald (Betty) Griffin. Their cooperation, patience, and encouragement have been boundless. Frank and Randy have also read the entire manuscript.

The following persons have served as "critics" of certain chapters: Rev. C. A. West, Rev. L. U. Spellman, Mrs. J. N. R. Score, Dr. Bonneau P. Murphy, Dr. Walter N. Vernon, Rev. Alfredo Nañez, Rev. Stewart Clendenin, Rev. Monroe Vivion, Rev. D. Lawrence Landrum, Dr. William C. Finch, Dr. Durwood Fleming, Dr. Willis M. Tate, Dr. Joseph L. Allen, and Dr. Hatch W. Cummings, Jr.

I gratefully acknowledge the cooperation and assistance of Dr. Decherd Turner, head librarian, and Mrs. Kate Warnick, curator of the Methodist Historical Collection, of Bridwell Library, Perkins School of Theology, Southern Methodist University, for access to the papers of Bishops John M. Moore, Edwin D. Mouzon, Paul E. Martin, William C. Martin, and W. Kenneth Pope. The papers of Dr. J. N. R. Score for the period before his election as president of Southwestern University are also in Bridwell Library. Miss Phoebe Davis, secretary to Southern Methodist University, granted my requests for information from the Minutes of the SMU board of trustees and from the papers of presidents Umphrey Lee and Willis M. Tate.

At Southwestern University, I am indebted to Miss Marjorie Beech and Mrs. Dorthy Thomas for their assistance in searching the papers of presidents J. N. R. Score, William C. Finch, and Durwood Fleming. Mrs. Mildred Gervasi granted me access to the papers of Dean Claude Carr Cody in Cody Memorial Library.

I am especially grateful to the Bishop A. Frank Smith Biography Committee for choosing me to write this biography and for their patience and encouragement. Members of this committee were: Dr. Durwood Fleming, chairman; Rev. William M. Harris, vice-chairman; Rev. C. A. West, secretary; Rev. Donald E. Redmond, treasurer; Rev. Alfredo Nañez, the late Rev. Monroe Vivion, Rev. Elmer J. Hierholzer, and consultants Dr. H. Grady Hardin and Dr. Decherd Turner. Other members of the original committee were Rev. R. F. Curl, Rev. Sterling F. Wheeler, and Rev. Joe Z Tower.

Dr. Durwood Fleming, president of Southwestern University, and Dr. William B. Jones, vice president and provost, have given me wholehearted support, including a sabbatical and a leave of absence during the seven years I have devoted to this biography.

I gladly acknowledge the expertise of Margaret L. Hartley and Charlotte T. Whaley, editor and associate editor of Southern Methodist University Press, as well as the professional services of Allen Maxwell, director of the Press.

Finally, I wish to acknowledge the extensive assistance of my wife, Betty, in polishing and typing the manuscript, and in proofreading the galley and page proof.

NORMAN W. SPELLMANN

Southwestern University
Georgetown, Texas
February, 1979

GROWING A SOUL

1

"From Generation unto Generation"

FRANK SMITH took great pride in his ancestry. He was especially eager to tell the story of his paternal grandparents Thomas and Mary Christian, who came to Texas about 1830 with Stephen F. Austin's second colony. Frank's persistent pursuit of his ancestral heritage complemented his lifelong interest in Texas history.

One reason for Frank Smith's interest in the Thomas Christians was the fact that he could trace both Thomas's and Mary's ancestors into the seventeenth and eighteenth centuries. The Christian line reached back to William Christian (1608-1663), a governor of the Isle of Man, celebrated in Manx history as a martyr of popular rights and the subject of a ballad entitled "The Death of Brown-haired William."[1] The Christian line came to the New World through William's grandson Gilbert Christian, who brought his wife, a daughter, and three sons to William Penn's "holy experiment" in America in 1726. It is believed that they came from Ireland, where three of William's sons had fled after their father's execution.[2] Gilbert Christian and his family eventually settled on Christian's Creek in the Valley of Virginia in present-day Augusta County. William, the oldest son of these Irish emigrants, married Mary Campbell of the Virginia Campbells, later distinguished for their service in the American Revolution and for their prominence in the political affairs of

Virginia, North Carolina, Kentucky, and Tennessee. It was William and Mary's great-grandson Thomas who came to Texas.

William Christian was captain of the Virginia Rangers for many years, served as county judge of Augusta County, and was awarded several thousand acres of land in Kentucky for his role in the French and Indian wars. Too old to take an active part in the American Revolution, William did participate in a skirmish on Long Island Flats. William left his Kentucky land to his son Gilbert, who married and moved to that western territory about 1789—three years before Kentucky became a state. It is believed that Gilbert fought in the American Revolution.

All that Frank Smith knew of Benjamin Christian, son of Gilbert and Lucy Richards Christian, was that he married Eliza Ann Greenup and that they were the parents of Thomas Christian, who was his great-grandfather.[3]

Both Thomas Christian and his wife, Mary ("Polly") Buchanan, were born in 1795, he in Kentucky and she in Virginia. Mary's ancestry was Scotch-Irish, her mother having come from Scotland and her father's grandfather from Ireland. Soon after their marriage about 1820, Thomas and Mary Christian moved to Illinois and then on to Missouri, where they joined the last contingent of Stephen F. Austin's second colony headed for Texas.[4] They were known to be in Bastrop, the head of Austin's "Little Colony," in May, 1832, and it is possible that they arrived before November, 1831.[5]

According to an agreement with Austin, heads of families engaged in farming received a *labor* (173 acres) of land; those who raised cattle a *sitio* or league (4,428 acres); and those who followed both occupations a *labor* and a *sitio*.[6] Thomas Christian chose his headright from a site east of the present city of Austin where Elgin was later developed,[7] but he was delayed in taking possession of his land by hostile Indians. While the Christians waited in Bastrop (called Mina until 1837), their sixth child, Sarah ("Sallie") Buchanan Christian, was born on September 11, 1832. She was to be A. Frank Smith's grandmother.

Frustrated in his efforts to settle on his headright, Thomas Christian accepted an invitation from John Webber to join other colonists at his fortified settlement for mutual protection.[8] Two famous colonists, Josiah Wilbarger and Reuben Hornsby, had already moved onto their headrights in the general vicinity.[9] In August, 1833, Christian and Wilbarger went to Hornsby's Bend on the Colorado River, several miles east of the present city of Austin. There they met Strother, Haynie, and King, who joined them on an exploring expedition up Walnut Creek to the northwest.[10] On their return they stopped at Pecan Springs for lunch. Feeling safe within just a few miles of the Webber settlement, Christian, Wilbarger, and Strother unsaddled and staked their horses. King and Haynie, being more cautious, staked their horses with saddles and bridles on. Suddenly, a shower of arrows fell upon the five men, as a band of Comanche Indians attacked. Christian and Strother were severely wounded, and Wilbarger was also wounded while attempting to assist Christian. Seeing that Strother and Christian were mortally wounded and Wilbarger pierced in both legs by arrows, Haynie and King mounted their horses and fled.

The "Wilbarger Scalping" and Mrs. Hornsby's "dream" that saved Wilbarger are well known in Texas folklore, but few persons know the location of the historical monument marking the site.[11] The bodies of Thomas Christian and young Strother were buried somewhere on the Hornsby league.

Frank Smith took great pride in telling of his great-grandfather's scalping, and of the fact that both he and his brother, Bishop W. Angie Smith, later presided over the Oklahoma Indian Mission Conference, which included the Comanche tribe, for thirty-nine consecutive sessions.[12]

Two incidents in the life of Mary Christian had special significance for Frank Smith. In the Spring of 1835,[13] some eighteen months after Thomas Christian's death, a Methodist society was formed at Bastrop [Mina] by James Gilliland, a Methodist lay-preacher and exhorter. Among the eleven charter members of that society was Mrs. Thomas Christian.[14] Mary Buchanan had been a Methodist in Virginia before her marriage to Christian. When Gilliland came to Webber's settlement in 1835, looking for Methodists as well as other Protestants, he must have informed the lately widowed Mrs. Christian of his plans to organize a society at Bastrop. This small congregation was the foundation for the first Methodist church established within the bounds of what became the Southwest Texas Conference—where A. Frank Smith served pastorates at University Methodist Church in Austin and Laurel Heights Methodist Church in San Antonio and was presiding bishop for twenty-two years.[15]

The second incident also occurred at Bastrop some three years later, after Texas had declared her independence from Mexico. In mid-January, 1838, the Reverend Doctor Martin Ruter, superintendent of the Methodist missionary work in the Republic of Texas, heard that people in and near Bastrop were "perishing for lack of knowledge" of the Christian gospel and decided to visit them:

Three men, armed with rifles and well equipped, offered to accompany me and we all went together, though I carried no arms myself. I spent a Sabbath there, formed a society of fifteen members, and we returned without being molested. On the route we took we travelled 30 miles without seeing a habitation and, in that space, passed six graves of persons whom the Indians had murdered and robbed.[16]

Mary Buchanan Christian, who was living near Bastrop at this time, is believed to have been among those fifteen members thus officially organized into a Methodist church by Martin Ruter.[17]

During the year following her husband's death, Mrs. Christian and her six children were given shelter by the Reuben Hornsbys. In 1834 or '35 she married James ("Uncle Jimmie") Burleson,[18] who had been General Andrew Jackson's commissary in the battle of New Orleans before he settled near Bastrop in 1827. Although Burleson died in January, 1836, he left his widow (widowed for the second time in three years!) a home on his tract of land near Bastrop. Here Mrs. Mary Christian Burleson lived with her seven children[19] until she moved onto Thomas Christian's headright (north of Elgin) in 1840. In 1838, therefore, when Martin Ruter formed the society in Bastrop, she would have been Mrs. Mary Buchanan Christian Burleson.

Before her death in 1870, Mrs. Burleson gave the right-of-way for the Houston and Central Texas Railroad, which was built across her holdings, and sufficient land for a townsite, upon which Elgin was built.[20]

Frank Smith's paternal grandfather, John Summerfield Smith, was born in Tennessee in 1833—"the year the stars fell"[21]—at Chickasaw Bluffs where the city of Memphis now stands. John Smith came to Texas when he was about eighteen years old. As Frank Smith told it: "I do not know how nor why my grandfather came to Texas in 1851 nor how he got to Bastrop, but come he did and met and married Sarah Buchanan Christian, who had been only a few months old when her father Thomas Christian was killed."[22] Sarah was given considerable acreage upon her marriage to John Smith, who had such success in farming that he was one of the largest landowners in Bastrop County when Frank Smith came to know him. "I spent most of my summers after I entered college in my grandfather's home," Frank recalled, "and I came to know him well and to respect and love him devotedly."[23]

Besides being a successful farmer, John Smith was a "dowser" or water witch, locating water wells all over Bastrop County. Frank remembered a time when he tested his grandfather's skill by hiding a pan of water: "I have often seen him walking along holding a forked stick with a wet rag attached to its stem and have seen the two-pronged switch turn down and twist off in his hands as he would pass over the pan of water."[24]

A devout Methodist, John Smith was a class leader and a steward in the Elgin Methodist Church for fifty-five years. One of his most prized possessions was a set of Adam Clarke's *Bible Commentaries*, published in 1843 and bound in calfskin. He had given a hundred acres of land for that treasure. "My grandfather literally read those six volumes to pieces," commented Frank. "He considered no sermon worth its salt unless the preacher followed the interpretation of Adam Clarke."[25] Frank Smith was equally proud of these commentaries, which he inherited when his grandfather died in 1915. When Frank went to see him shortly before his death, John Smith repeated insistently, "Son, I do not want to die." When Frank asked, "Grandpa, are you afraid to die?" the old man retorted, "Oh, no, but I am reading about Isaiah in Adam Clarke's book, and I do not want to die till I have finished what I am reading."[26] Frank hoped that his grandfather got caught up on Isaiah before his time ran out.

Four sons and three daughters were born to John and Sarah Smith. William Angie, the youngest son, was born on May 28, 1862. Since this was during the Civil War, John Smith was serving with the Confederate commissary department. Rounding up cattle and driving them to the Mississippi, he delivered them to his counterpart east of the river. For a time following the war, he drove cattle up the long trail from Texas to the railhead in Kansas. Not interested in farming or in raising cattle, William Angie had a consuming ambition to be a lawyer. Because John Smith did not consider a college education important, he would not send his son to school, even though he was financially able to do so. To begin college, Willam Angie sold for a dollar an acre the two hundred acres of land he had inherited from his mother. With this $200 he set out for nearby Georgetown to enroll in Southwestern University. The relationship that he established between the Smith family and Southwestern was to continue beyond 1973 when Sherren Bess Smith, the Bishop's granddaughter enrolled there as a freshman.

Southwestern University had been established in Georgetown by the

Methodist Conferences in Texas in 1873 as "Texas Methodism's Central University,"[27] drawing together and extending the historic traditions of Rutersville, Wesleyan, McKenzie, and Soule colleges. Frank Smith was particularly proud of Southwestern's Rutersville heritage, because it began in the time (1840) of the Republic of Texas and was named in memory of Dr. Martin Ruter, the Methodist missionary who had formed the little society in Bastrop which included Smith's great-grandmother, Mary Christian Burleson. Of equal if not greater significance was the fact that William Angie Smith met his bride-to-be, Mary Elizabeth Marrs, at Southwestern University, just as Frank later met Bess Patience Crutchfield there in 1908.

On his mother's side of the family, Frank Smith could trace his ancestors only as far as his grandparents. Thomas Willis Marrs was born in Fayette County, Arkansas, on February 3, 1844. He was a cousin of Sam Houston. Frank Smith remembered from his childhood days in Georgetown that his mother and a granddaughter of Sam Houston called one another cousin. During Frank Smith's years in Houston (1922-1962), he and Mrs. Smith were always invited by Sam Houston descendants to join their family circle at the annual San Jacinto Day celebrations held at the San Jacinto Battlegrounds.[28]

Moving to Texas about 1859, the Marrs family settled in Blanco County. Young Thomas was soon carrying mail from Austin to various points in Blanco County. On more than one occasion he narrowly escaped from Comanche Indians, who still made raids within a few miles of Austin. Soon after the beginning of the Civil War, Thomas and his three brothers enlisted in the Confederate Army in Bowers' Company of Walker's Division. After the war, while visiting in Florence, a small community in northern Williamson County, Thomas met Miss Catherine Thompson. On September 12, 1866, they were married.[29]

Catherine Thompson was born in Alabama in 1850. Immediately after the Civil War her family fled the economic desolation and carpetbagger rule in Alabama and came to Texas. They settled near Florence, where Catherine's father began farming. Following her marriage to Thomas Marrs, Catherine moved with her husband into the village of Florence. Here Thomas built and operated the first store in the higher part of town, where the business district eventually developed. Three children were born to the young couple: Mary Elizabeth on October 20, 1867; Thomas Jefferson Benjamin Franklin in 1869; and William Park in 1878. In 1879 Thomas and Catherine moved to Georgetown, some twenty miles away, in order to give their children the advantages of a college education. There Thomas Marrs opened a grocery store, which he operated until his death in 1904. Frank Smith remembered it as the largest grocery store in Georgetown.

The Marrs family was devoutly Baptist. Thomas was converted in the Florence Baptist Church and baptized in 1872 by G. W. Barber, Sr., one of the pioneer preachers in Texas. When they moved to Georgetown, Thomas and Catherine became members of the Baptist Church there. Thomas was the Sunday school superintendent for many years. While visiting their grandparents in Georgetown, Frank and Angie Smith always attended the Baptist Sunday school.[30]

Frank retained fond memories of his grandfather Marrs: "As I think back upon him, I do not recall ever having known a kindlier, more loveable man. He was always in a happy frame of mind. He loved to hunt and fish. His friends were numbered by his acquaintances, and he was the idol of his grandchildren."[31]

Thomas Marrs wanted his children to have all available comforts. Long before Georgetown had a public water system, Marrs set up his own with running water in various rooms, including toilets, and even a bathtub. He ordered a square-style piano from New York, which was shipped by sea to Galveston and brought to Georgetown in a wagon. All three children were taught to sing and to play the banjo, guitar, and mandolin as well as the piano.

Mrs. Marrs was quieter and more reserved than her husband. An incessant worker in her flower gardens, she kept their yard blooming with flowers of all varieties in beds neatly lined with up-ended bricks. After her husband's death in 1904, she sold the grocery store and her home and lived with her daughter's family until her death in 1931.

The three Marrs children were sent to college. Franklin, the oldest son, quickly dropped his first three names and was called Frank for short. Frank Marrs took a business course at Southwestern University and then married. Soon he felt a call to preach and went back to school, earning degrees at Baylor University and Baptist Seminary in Louisville, Kentucky. While pastor of a Baptist church in Del Rio, Texas, he became interested in the Mexican people and in 1900 volunteered to go to Mexico as a Baptist missionary.

For thirty years Frank Marrs worked among the Mexican people, eventually becoming the supervisor of all Southern Baptist missionaries in Mexico. He also began the Southern Baptist mission in Chili. In later years both A. Frank and Angie Smith had opportunity as Methodist bishops to become personally acquainted with the fruits of their uncle's ministry when Frank presided over the Rio Grande Conference for twenty-two years and Angie was in charge of Methodist activities in Chili for a quadrennium. Speaking humorously but with an obvious sense of pride, Bishop Angie Smith declares: "The Baptists' work was so much better than ours that I was ashamed to tell them it was my uncle who had started the Baptist work."[32]

A. Frank Smith was named for this missionary uncle, although the "Angie" part of his name came from his father. Bishop Angie Smith's full name was William Angie Smith, Jr. Given half an opportunity, he will quickly explain how he and Frank received their respective names: "When Frank was born, my father was only willing to give him half of his name; but when I was born he saw the possibilities, and he gave me all of his name!"[33]

Mary Elizabeth Marrs, Frank Smith's mother, entered Southwestern University in the early 1880s.[34] Here she met Willam Angie Smith from Elgin, and friendship developed into courtship. William Smith soon realized that his dream of being a lawyer would never come true without financial help from his father. Seeking a shorter route toward a profession, he decided to leave Southwestern and go to a business college in Poughkeepsie, New York.[35] Immediately after receiving his business degree, William returned to Georgetown, where he found employment as a bookkeeper for a lumberyard. He married Mary Elizabeth Marrs in February, 1887.[36]

Six children were born to William and Mary Smith, but the last two did not survive infancy. Marrs Vernon was born in Georgetown on January 7, 1888. Soon afterward the little family moved to Elgin, where Mr. Smith worked in a general merchandise store. Here Angie Frank was born on the first day of November, 1889, near the site of his great-grandfather's headright. The combined influence of the Smith background of Methodism in Elgin and the birth of Frank brought about an important decision. Although raised as a Methodist, Willam Smith had never joined the church. Mary Smith, of course, was a Baptist—"a deep water Baptist," as Frank later described her.[37] Under these circumstances, Mrs. Smith suggested that they both join the Methodist Church in Elgin and have Frank baptized at the same time. If this decision to join the church had been made in Georgetown, where Thomas Marrs's influence was dominant, Frank Smith might have been brought up in the Baptist church.[38] For some reason, the Smiths moved back to Georgetown for a brief period; a third son was born there on October 31, 1891, and named for his grandfather, John Summerfield Smith.

Soon the family returned to Elgin, and Mr. Smith opened a general merchandise store of his own. Frank Smith's earliest memories were of Christmas in Elgin in 1892. "I have a clear picture of things in general," he recalled, "going to Sunday School, to father's store, wearing skirts and waists as little boys did in those days."[39] More distinctly Frank remembered the birth of Angie (William Angie, Jr.) on December 21, 1894. Considering how much the Smith family moved about, it is rather remarkable that Frank and Angie were both born in Elgin. But this was to be the pattern of their lives—one remarkable parallel after another. Both were born in Elgin and both were named Angie. Both planned to be lawyers, but both changed to the ministry in their senior years at Southwestern University. They won the same honors at Southwestern. They married girls with the same first name: Bess. Following distinguished careers as Methodist preachers, each was elected to the episcopacy; they were colleagues in the Council of Bishops for sixteen years.

The Smith family continued to move from place to place more often than a typical Methodist Preacher's family. In 1895 they were in Gonzales when Frank started kindergarten. Three years later they were in Bartlett, where their first and only daughter was born, Mary Ruth. In 1900 tragedy struck the family when little Mary Ruth died of typhoid fever. The Smiths had returned to Elgin because Mr. Smith's father and uncle wanted him to join them in the new venture of drilling an oil well. According to Frank Smith, both the continual moving and the drilling for oil were evidence of his father's restless ambition:

To recount these many moves leaves the impression that my father was a rolling stone, but not so. He was driven by a consuming ambition to achieve great things, and he was always looking for something better farther on. He was an unfailing success as a merchant. He operated on a cash basis and never borrowed a penny as long as I knew him. He had an idea that debt is a sin and that no real businessman would involve himself. This notion, of course, restricted him to a narrow range of operation. But even so, he made money in every business venture he ever attempted. He wanted to make big money and he thought his best chance was in oil, which was just coming into prominence at the turn of the century. So having accumulated enough to drill a well, a simple operation in those days, he would sell his store and spend a few months securing leases and "spudding-in" the well. Then would come weeks or months of drilling and always a dry hole. Then back to merchandising.[40]

After the death of their baby daughter and their failure to strike oil, the Smith family moved back to Georgetown. For the children Georgetown meant Grandfather Marrs and the Baptist Church. With a chuckle, Bishop Angie Smith remembers what happened when his parents tried to take him to the Methodist Sunday school: "I was crying and got out in the middle of the street and ran all the way home in order to go back to the Baptist Sunday School, because I'd always gone there with my grandfather."[41]

Another business practice of Mr. Smith's was that of buying bankrupt stores. When he heard of such a store, he would go to that town and place his bid for the merchandise. Then he would put on a big sale and sell everything he could. Whatever was left would be taken back to his home-base store. It was apparently for this reason that the Smiths left Georgetown and moved to Rogers.[42] It was in Rogers that Frank and Angie met and became friends with the Meachum sisters, Eldora and Sophie—a relationship that was to develop later at Southwestern University. Sophie Meachum concisely summarizes their friendship: "Frank and Angie didn't live in Rogers long enough to go to school, but we played croquet and waded in my aunt's water tank."[43]

After an equally brief period at Rosebud, the Smith family finally settled down in Corsicana for four years, 1903-1907. This community in east central Texas, the site of the state's first commercial oil field,[44] played a unique role in the development of the oil industry. As Texas historian Seymour Connor describes the situation:

Without doubt the most significant development in Texas during the early twentieth century was the explosive development of the oil industry. . . . The Corsicana boom is important not only because it was the first in Texas but also because . . . the first commercially practical refinery in Texas was built in Corsicana.[45]

Among the men who were first trained in oil production in Corsicana were Walter W. Fondren, "a subsequent founder and original director of Humble Oil & Refining Company," and the Hamill brothers, "who in 1909 drilled the discovery well at historic Spindletop on the Gulf Coast of eastern Texas."[46] Walter Fondren was just an independent driller when William Smith got to know him at Corsicana. It was not a close relationship, just two men interested in the same thing. When Frank Smith went to Houston about twenty years later as pastor of the First Methodist Church, however, Walter Fondren remembered Frank's father from drilling days at Corsicana. Mr. and Mrs. Fondren were to become two of the closest friends Frank and Bess Smith ever had.[47]

Unlike Walter Fondren, William Smith never did strike oil in producing amounts. Consistent with his earlier experiences, the four wells he drilled during these four years in Corsicana were all dry.[48] The reason Mr. Smith never found oil, as he learned too late, was that he always stopped drilling when he struck salt water. On almost every lease he drilled, large oil companies later went on down past the salt water and found producing wells. According to Frank Smith, "My father drilled the first well over in Liberty County where they have a big oil field now. They hit it exactly where he had tried. Everywhere he said there was oil, they found oil, but he knew nothing about depth."[49]

Despite Mr. Smith's many failures in drilling for oil, his family never suffered financially. For one thing, he ran his drilling operations the same way he ran his stores, never borrowing money. When he had saved enough to buy leases and drill another well, he would sell his store and go to work with his cable rig. Drilling in that fashion in those days only cost about 75 cents per foot.[50] And Mr. Smith always kept enough money in the bank to start over again in another store. As Angie Smith declares, "If my father did not have as much as $25,000 in the bank, he thought he was broke! He always made a good living as a merchant."[51] The facts do not support those who would picture Frank and Angie Smith as overcoming a background of poverty. "It was a frugal family," says Angie, "but we never knew such a thing as lacking something to eat or wear. We never knew want from that standpoint at all." To drive home his point he offers a description of one of their typical "old-fashioned" breakfasts as "composed of cereal, usually a dry cereal as well as oatmeal, and always fried chicken or steak, and always bacon and hot biscuits and toast, and two or three kinds of jelly and jam and preserves and such as that."[52]

If the family suffered, it was from lack of a close, intimate father-son relationship. "He was not a companionable person," Frank explained. "He never lived in one place long enough to become part of the community. He had no cronies and he never took part in social activities. I had vast respect for my father, but no warm affection. He gave his children no opportunity to be close to him."[53]

In the various communities where Mr. Smith lived, he was known as a religious man of strong principles, strictly honest in his business, a rather stern man who took no part in frivolities. Callie Blair (Mrs. Finis

Crutchfield, Sr.) remembers Mr. Smith in the Corsicana period: "My family went to every prayer-meeting on Wednesday nights. Mr. Smith and his wife were always there. He was a prayer-meeting-going father!"[54] And the Smith family was always in church on Sunday morning. This was particularly difficult for the boys because they had to work late on Saturday nights in their father's store. Angie explains, "Living as we did in the central section of the state, the big cotton section, Saturday night was one of the biggest nights in the store, and we would stay open until 11:30 or midnight every Saturday. But it was an absolute rule that we had to be up and in Sunday School the next morning without fail."[55]

Mr. Smith would not compromise his principles either for financial gain or to avoid loss. In a town with a large German population, the German farmers were some of his best customers at the store. One day, in the midst of a heated prohibition election, a group of these men came into the store to warn Mr. Smith that if he voted for prohibition they would never spend another nickel in his store. Mr. Smith ran them out of the store, declaring that he was going to vote the prohibition ticket and that he didn't care whether they ever came back or not![56]

Mr. Smith's policy was strictly "cash and carry." One day a neighbor who lived next door to the store came in for a spool of thread. "Mr. Smith, I want a spool of this thread," the woman said, "but I'll have to pay you the nickel later." Mr. Smith quickly reached into his pocket and handed her a coin. "Here's a nickel. Now you can pay me for the thread. If I let you have that on credit, then I can't honestly tell the next person to come in here that I have never done any business on credit." Angie, in recalling this incident, says that he didn't know at the time whether to be embarrassed or proud of his father. "If he had a principle, he absolutely lived by it and stuck to it, not varying one iota even though it might cost him profit or someone's trade."[57]

Mrs. Smith was exactly the opposite in temperament. "Mother was a bubbling extrovert," declared Frank. "She was happy and warm and affectionate, like her father:"[58] Also like her father, Mrs. Smith was a deeply religious person. She taught a Sunday School class and was president of the Woman's Missionary Society. Many times in the evenings she would play her big square piano and sing, and sometimes she would read the Bible to her sons. They did not have family prayers or a regular time for devotions. Frank summarized the situation: "My father always said the blessing before every meal, and I never knew him to be profane in speech, but ours was not the sort of pious home from which preachers are supposed to come."[59]

Corsicana was the largest place the Smiths had ever lived. As Frank said, "With a population of about 15,000 at that time, it possessed attractions and temptations to which I had never been subjected."[60] Among the attractions were the high school athletic teams. Frank played on the football team each fall and ran with the track squad in the spring. In his senior year he won two ribbons at a high school track meet in Waco, one for winning the quarter-mile dash and the other for a relay event.

Corsicana also offered greater opportunities for friendships. Frank played ball, dug caves, and hunted for treasure with the other boys his age. He knew many of the girls, too, as he wrote:

Girls seemed to be a part of the picture, wherever I was. . . . I always had a girl, someone more special than the others of the group. And I had more dates than would have been possible had it not been that dating was so inexpensive. The first motion picture shows, called nickelodeons, were just coming in—admission five cents; rollerskating was quite the vogue and admission to a skating rink with skates provided was twenty-five cents, sometimes only ten cents. Ice cream sodas were ten cents each, so a boy could take a girl out for a full evening's entertainment for fifty cents. More often boys and girls spent the evenings in the parlor or on the porch of the girl's home. Usually, there would be more than one couple present. We would play the piano, sing, make fudge or welch rarebit on a chafing dish, roll the rugs back and dance, and go home by eleven o'clock, having had a wonderful evening and having spent not a penny. . . . We had picnics, hay rides, dancing school and other diversions too numerous to mention. Those were happy wholesome days, and I was always in the middle of whatever was going on.[61]

At Sunday school Frank made two lifelong friends, Callie Blair and Beauford Jester. Although Callie was a year older, she and Frank had a few dates. According to Callie, there were several girls at Corsicana who were quite interested in Frank Smith, "but he didn't seem to want to settle down." Although he was "a pretty sporty dresser, he didn't have to dress up much to look real fine, we girls thought!"[62] Callie went on to Southwestern University and married Finis Crutchfield, one of Frank's closest friends.

Beauford Jester's father was superintendent of the Methodist Sunday school, and Frank cherished his relationship with the Jester family. He and Beauford were "great buddies" as boys, and their friendship continued into manhood. When Jester was elected governor of Texas in 1946, he asked Frank to give the prayer at his inauguration.[63] Three years later, when the governor died while still in office, Frank was asked to come back to Corsicana to hold his funeral in the First Methodist Church, where the two boys had become friends.

Frank Smith described himself as an omnivorous reader from childhood to maturity. Although there had been no public library in any of the small towns where the Smiths had lived, Mr. and Mrs. Smith supplied reading material for their boys. Frank read the *Youth's Companion* from the first page to the last every week. The family subscribed to *Woman's Home Companion* and the *Ladies Home Journal*, and around the turn of the century they added the *Saturday Evening Post* and *Argosy*, a magazine largely devoted to tales of outdoor adventure. One of Frank's first books, sent to him by an uncle, was *Beautiful Joe*, the story of a dog who had been cruelly abused but finally found a loving master. Frank loved that book. He also read the familiar boys' books: *Black Beauty*, *Tom Sawyer*, *Huckleberry Finn*, *Robinson Crusoe*, and *The Swiss Family Robinson*. His lifetime interest in history began with the reading of a series of books written by an English author, G. A. Henty, based on the exploits of Englishmen and the spread of the British Empire. He also read the Horatio Alger books. As a teenager, Frank became interested in the *Leatherstocking Tales* by James Fenimore Cooper:

I was tremendously enamoured of these stories and I reached a point where I could not sleep at night. I recall that my mother forbade my reading anything else for the time that had anything to do with Indians. She gave me *In His Steps* by Charles M. Sheldon, which impressed me greatly; she also gave me a book of illustrated Bible stories, which I read and re-read and still have in my possession.[64]

Because of their gaudy covers, the Frank Merriweather books were frowned upon by his parents. So Frank had to "bootleg" that series and read them on the sly. *Diamond Dick* was also on the forbidden list, but Frank soon lost interest in such books. The Frank Merriweather books, however, could well have been distributed through the Sunday schools, in Frank's opinion.

During his high school years Frank's interest turned more and more to biography and history: *Les Misérables*, *A Tale of Two Cities*, and Washington Irving's books, as well as those by Sir Walter Scott and John Esten Cooke.

I was not in any sense a bookworm, but I can recall sitting on the porch and reading many a morning or afternoon when the other boys were prowling about or hopping rides on freight trains. I can also remember lying on my back under the cradle of my baby sister and reading while I rocked her cradle. I always read a book or magazine while doing the churning for my mother, which was one of my household chores.[65]

Mr. Smith, who had wanted to be a lawyer, kept several lawbooks, including a thick volume by Blackstone. Frank commented: "My father told me that Blackstone was the basis of all our judicial proceedings, so I read this volume when I was fifteen. It was over my head, of course, but as I intended to be a lawyer, I figured that the sooner I tackled the fundamentals the better it would be for me later on."[66]

If the Smiths had remained in Corsicana, Frank would have gone to Baylor University. Mr. Smith knew President Brooks and had the greatest respect for him.[67] But in the fall of 1907 Mr. Smith bought a store in Taylor, Texas, and moved the family to a new home about twenty miles from Georgetown. Frank remained behind, perhaps to finish the football season. When the time came for Frank's departure, he went by the parsonage to say goodbye to the Whitehurst family. Paul Whitehurst and Frank had played on the football team together and developed a warm friendship before Paul died suddenly from injuries received in a game. After that tragedy the Whitehurst family practically adopted Frank. Callie Blair Crutchfield remembers how dearly the Whitehursts loved him: "Frank just made himself at home over there at the parsonage. He enjoyed their easy ways and thought an awful lot of them."[68] Naturally, Frank would want to spend his last hour in Corsicana with his "second family." When he had shared his plans for the future with them, Brother Whitehurst said: "I want to give you your church letter before you leave." "Thank you," Frank replied, "but I do not belong to the church." The Reverend James A. Whitehurst could not have been more dumbfounded. Since Frank had been secretary of the Sunday school and one of the most active young men in the church, everyone had assumed that he was a member. Knowing that Frank was leaving that night, the fatherly pastor said, "Come on over to the church with me right now, and I will give you the vows of the church at the altar." On that fall Sunday night in 1907, Frank Smith became a member of the Methodist church.[69]

"I have often thought," Frank later declared,

that I would perhaps never have joined the church had I not already belonged when I got to college. I can look back upon more than one incident in my life that was a turning point for me. This was one of them. If it did not sound presumptuous, I would say that an unseen force has seemed to intervene at crucial points in my life to keep me in the main stream and headed in the right direction.[70]

2

"Study to Show Thyself Approved"

ON THE FIRST DAY OF JANUARY, 1908, Frank Smith arrived in George-town, Texas, to enter Southwestern University. Following in the footsteps of his father, who had been the first of his family to attend college and to want to be a lawyer, Frank came with two distinct advantages: his father's blessing and his grandfather's support.[1]

"I secured room and board for $12.50 a month at the home of Mr. and Mrs. Mash Hardie, a groceryman," Frank later recalled. "My room-mate was Ben O. Wiley, a freshman from Greenville—an affable fellow, but quite a bookworm."[2]

On that first day, Frank met two persons who were to play important roles in his life, Bess Patience Crutchfield and Finis Crutchfield, who bore the same name but were not related. Bess Crutchfield clearly re-membered the occasion. She and a friend were sitting in the study hall of the old Prep School building, when a young man walked in wearing "patent leather buttoned shoes, a flowered vest, peg-topped trousers and carrying a derby hat. Of course, he caught our attention at once. Well, we just nearly died, we got so tickled. We couldn't take our eyes away because he was a right nice looking fellow."[3]

Describing the meeting, Frank recalled: "I saw Bess Crutchfield the first day I entered the old Prep Building. Instinctively I knew she was the girl I wanted for a college sweetheart. I wrote her a note to this effect a few days later, and she wrote back that she was already spoken for." According to Bess's memory, the note had a more tantalizing theme: "He wrote a note to me and said, 'I don't know whether I want you or Dot for my girl.' Dot was my friend. And I wrote back and said, 'Don't waste time on me, I'm mortgaged.' And then he started going with Dot."[5] Frank had the last laugh when he explained, "Not going with her, just looking at her. They [the dormitory matrons] didn't let you go with them. No, they wore uniforms and were chaperoned."[6] It was two years before Frank and Bess finally got together, as Frank put it, "after she had run through several mild flirtations and I had made eyes at more than one other girl. But in my heart I knew there was no other person for me."[7]

Having come to Southwestern a year earlier than Frank, Finis Crutchfield was well established on campus: a member of the Kappa Alpha fraternity, freshman class representative on the Council of Honor, and chairman of the YMCA membership committee.[8] Finis had heard about Frank Smith and had met him before Frank was "discovered" by any of the other fraternities. "One of our fellows came around the corner with this young man who had on a white vest, hair combed back, very important looking for a 'prep.' And I said, 'Who is this?' He answered, 'This is Frank Smith from Corsicana.' So we got acquainted right there."[9] Finis and Frank became close friends, a friendship they were to cherish and maintain for more than fifty years. As Bishop Angie Smith says, "Finis Crutchfield knows as much about Frank's college days as anyone, especially the early days."[10]

Frank soon had an opportunity to repay Finis for his assistance in getting him into the mainstream of college life, including membership in the Kappa Alpha fraternity. A student from Corsicana, Callie Blair, had attracted Finis's attention, but Finis had not been able to obtain a formal introduction. Shortly before a fraternity party, Finis sought Frank's help: "Frank, you're from Corsicana, and you have known Miss Blair for several years. Now, you don't have any special person to invite to our social, and I want you to invite Miss Blair for me, so that we can get acquainted." Agreeing to do so, Frank introduced Finis to his future wife, an act of which he was always proud.[11]

Since secondary education had not developed on a large scale in Texas at that time, the majority of students entering Southwestern University were required to spend several terms in the Fitting School (as the Prep was formally designated) to complete their preparation for college level work.[12] When Frank Smith entered the Fitting School in January, 1908,[13] there were almost as many students in the Prep School (257) as there were in the university (376).[14] Frank began a number of lifelong friendships: with Joseph Bartak, who was to have a distinguished career as a Methodist missionary in Czechoslovakia; Bess and Hallie Crutchfield; Otto Moerner, who was to become a prominent leader in Christian education; and Ruth P. Morgan, later Mrs. Ruth Morgan Ferguson, who was to return to Southwestern for a long tenure as the dean of women.

The Fitting School was located diagonally across University Avenue from the First Methodist Church in the "Old Campus," a ten-acre tract that also held Giddings Hall for men, five cottages built by the Annual Conferences of Texas, and the university's athletic field. The Fitting School Building, a three-story struture, housed a chapel, classrooms, the literary societies of the Fitting School, the YMCA Hall, and the Athletic Association rooms.[15] In this building Frank Smith met Bess Crutchfield, attended classes for five months, and began his activities in the YMCA. Unfortunately, the records of the Fitting School no longer exist. The faculty included Frank E. Burcham, principal and instructor in mathematics (whose basic math course Frank never did pass[16]); Miss Mary H. Howren, Latin; James E. Binkley, history; Dr. Claude Nichols, Greek; and John H. McGinnis, English, with whom Frank and Bess were to maintain a long friendship.[17]

Frank lived for four and a half years in the Kappa Alpha fraternity house, "a neat little cottage on the Prep School campus, consisting of two bedrooms with a chapter meeting room connecting them."[18] Sam Ayres, one of the outstanding athletes of his day, was Frank's first roommate. The KAs rated very high on campus for their strict academic and moral standards. As Finis Crutchfield says emphatically, "We gave demerits to the fellows that didn't keep up with the standard of the university."[19] Frank recalled that there were several older men in the fraternity who were preparing for the ministry and who helped set the tone. Scholarship was expected of every member.[20] When Angie came to the campus the year after Frank graduated (1912), the other fraternities were complaining that they were tired of buying scholarship medals and cups when the KAs always won them.[21]

Although both Frank's roommate, Sam Ayres, and his closest friend, Finis Crutchfield, were outstanding athletes, Frank did not participate in collegiate sports. "I had the build for it and was repeatedly urged by the coaches and players to do so, but my father prohibited it," Frank later explained. "He considered college football a dangerous game. In addition, I had no particular desire to do so. My extracurricular interests in college were in other fields, and I begrudged the time that football, baseball and track would consume." There was one physical activity that Frank did enjoy: "I learned to swim and dive quite well in the San Gabriel River, a lovely crystal-clear stream fed by springs on the outskirts of Georgetown."[22]

Aided by Frank's intention to become a lawyer, the literary or debating societies in the Fitting School led him into the area of oratory, where he was to excel. Finis Crutchfield remembered this new direction of interest: "Lots of times when we were out practicing the high jump or dashes, Frank was back there practicing for an oratorical contest."[23] Frank's first competition came in May at the end of the academic year. The three days following final examinations were set aside for contests, recitals, and student art exhibitions, beginning with the Fitting School Declamation Contest. Frank entered against nine other contestants and "won hands down!"[24] The title of Frank's medal-winning declamation was "The Speech that Made History."[25]

With the coming of summer, Frank learned what many college students experience: "I was never again a member of the family unit, save as a visitor for brief periods during summers and at Christmas time." Considering his rather formal relationship with his father,[26] it is not surprising that during the summer Frank spent more time at his grandfather Smith's home in Elgin than at home in Taylor.[27] As Hallie Crutchfield Pierce remembered, "Frank worshipped his grandfather, just worshipped him."[28]

According to the permanent records of Southwestern University, Frank Smith's official "date of entrance" was September 23, 1908, the beginning of his freshman year.[29] Continuing to live in the KA fraternity house on the "Old Campus," Frank now had to walk three blocks to the college campus, east of the Katy railroad tracks. The center of all academic and religious activities was the Main Building, "a stately structure built of white limestone, completed in 1900, said to be the most beautiful single school building in the South."[30]

The first floor of Old Main was shared by the departments of philosophy, chemistry, and physics, and by the gymnasium. The chapel dominated the second floor, with the society halls opening into the main floor of the chapel to give it a maximum seating capacity of about 1,500. "The first daily duty of all students," according to the university's regulations, "is that of attendance upon Chapel service. . . . The daily exercises in the institution are opened with religious services, consisting of a Scripture lesson, singing, and prayer." Concern for each student's moral and spiritual development included required attendance at Sunday morning church services, with student monitors appointed to check attendance and examine excuses. In order to maintain the proper decorum, the young women were marched to the First Methodist Church, two by two in long lines. A familiar sight on Sunday mornings along the ten blocks of University Avenue between the Women's Annex and the church was President Hyer or Dean Cody leading the group, with a properly forbidding chaperone guarding the rear of the procession. Callie Blair Crutchfield describes the implicit design: "Never to let a student go out of Southwestern who was not a Christian."[31]

The second major landmark of the college campus was the new men's dormitory, Mood Hall, completed just in time for the fall term of 1908. Built at a cost of some $70,000 in the same architectural style and limestone construction as the Main Building, Mood Hall was deemed "a worthy monument to the man who first conceived the idea of a central college for Texas Methodism," Dr. Francis Asbury Mood.[32] Although Frank Smith never lived in Mood Hall, many of his friends did.

Far more important to Bess Crutchfield was the Annex Building, or women's dormitory, two and a half blocks east of the Main Building, "crowning the greatest elevation about Georgetown." More than a dormitory, the Annex contained "a large auditorium, gymnasium, diningroom, parlors, society halls, rooms for elocution, art and music, and apartments for the Professor in charge of the Annex and the lady teachers."[33] This building became home for Bess and Hallie Crutchfield in 1899, when, following the death of their mother, the two girls came to Georgetown to live with their uncle, Dr. John R. Allen, "the Professor in charge of the Annex." Bess and Hallie lived with "Uncle John" and "Aunt Molly" on the fourth floor of the Annex until Dr. Allen bought a home on Laurel Street. Some time after Frank Smith came to Southwestern, the Allens and their nieces moved to a second home, which was located northeast of Mood Hall (approximately where the Martin Ruter Dormitory now stands).[34]

At that time, Georgetown had a population of about 3,500 people, to which the university added some 500 students during the September-through-May academic year. The Central Texas community was considered an ideal location for Texas Methodism's central university. "Free from the dissipations and distractions of the city," Georgetown had demonstrated "the excellence and feasibility of prohibition" for more than fifteen years.[35] Skeptics were soon convinced of the truth of such claims, as the following excerpts from a contemporary "Letter to the Editor" illustrate:

I came to Georgetown three months ago. . . . I was prejudiced against the University. Those prejudices are [now] gone, and my opinion of the school has been radically changed. . . . Georgetown is in many respects the best place I ever saw. The high moral tone, the warm-hearted people, their refined and cultured manners, and the earnest religious sentiment pervading and controlling the town, make this a very desirable place in which to live.

But the University is a marvel to me. Think of nearly half a thousand students in the town, creating no more stir or friction than if they were not here. Hard at work, . . . not loafing on the streets, and seen only when going for the mail, or to make necessary purchases at the stores. . . . Hen-roosts, calves, yard-gates and sign-boards are safe from disturbance, and there seems to be absolutely no friction between the citizens and the students.[36]

On Thursday morning, September 24, 1908, at the formal opening of the fall term, Frank Smith probably met for the first time Dr. Edwin DuBose Mouzon, who was to have a great influence on his life. Having just come to develop the newly created theological department, this distinguished Methodist minister was invited to deliver the opening address to the students. Along with many others, Frank must have been impressed by Mouzon's leaving the auspicious pastorate of San Antonio's Travis Park Methodist Church to accept a professorship at Southwestern University. Both the establishment of the new Department of Theology and the appointment of Dr. Mouzon to guide this pioneer effort in the education of future ministers had received considerable publicity in state and national Methodist publications.[37] Through a fascinating series of events and a remarkable parallel growth of careers, the lives of Edwin D. Mouzon and A. Frank Smith were to be closely related for more than a quarter of a century.

During his freshman year, Frank Smith also came under the influence of President Robert Stewart Hyer and Dean Claude Carr Cody. A native of Georgia, trained at Emory College, Hyer had come to Southwestern as professor of science in 1882. As a scientist, Hyer is best known for having experimented in wireless telegraphy as early as 1894 and

X ray in 1897. As president of Southwestern University since 1898, Hyer had raised admission standards, improved curriculum, strengthened the faculty, and established a medical school in Dallas. Under his leadership the Main Building, the Women's Annex, and Mood Hall were constructed. As an active layman in the Methodist Episcopal Church, South, he was a delegate to four General Conferences and a member of the General Board of Education.[38] President Hyer's respect for Frank Smith played a part in Smith's appointment to the University Church at Southern Methodist University in 1916, during Hyer's term as the first president of that university.[39]

Dean Claude Carr Cody's influence on Frank Smith was more personal. Although his field of specialization was mathematics, Dean Cody was a practicing historian. He helped organize the Texas Methodist Historical Association in 1909. As editor of the association's quarterly, he collected, preserved, and published important material concerning the history of Methodism in Texas. Cody contributed to Frank Smith's interest in and appreciation for this heritage.

Like Hyer, Cody was a native Georgian and an honor graduate of Emory College. Elected to the professorship of mathematics at Southwestern University in 1879, he was probably influential in bringing Hyer to Georgetown. After years of service as secretary and chairman of the faculty, Cody was appointed dean of the College of Science and Liberal Arts in 1906. As treasurer of the board of trustees and secretary of the board's executive committee, he played a significant role in policy making. A warmer man by nature than Dr. Hyer, Cody was beloved by his students and colleagues. In a tribute to Dean Cody, the student editor of the *Sou'wester* wrote: "It is not unusual to hear men say that they owe what they are to Prof. Cody and the Lord."[40]

For his freshman year classes, Frank Smith took English with Professor Albert S. Pegues, history with Professor Stephen H. Moore (affectionately called "Sleepy"), geology with Professor Randolph W. Tinsley, economics with Professor John R. Allen, and oratory with Miss Cora Lee Smith.[41] Pegues, Moore, Tinsley, and especially Allen were deeply religious men, who were genuinely interested in the spiritual development of their students. If they noticed a student missing from Sunday school or church, they quietly sought out that absentee during the following week.[42]

All students were encouraged to participate in the literary societies. These were student organizations, two for men and two for women, which featured training in competitive debate, public speaking, and parliamentary procedure. The members became fiercely loyal to their societies, and the high point of the year was the annual debate between the two men's societies at commencement. These experiences were especially valuable to those training for careers in law or the ministry. Frank Smith chose the Alamo Society, where he was associated with such future leaders as Finis Crutchfield, J. Frank Dobie, Neely G. Landrum, and Dan E. Root.

The most memorable event of the year for Frank Smith was the Freshman-Sophomore Declamation Contest held on the second day of the commencement activities, June 12, 1909. The ten contestants were chosen in a preliminary contest from among the twenty-five men in the freshman and sophomore classes who had the highest averages in oratory.[43] Harold G. Cooke, later president of McMurry College, was also one of the top ten. Frank cherished a lifelong friendship with Harold.[44] "The Fresh-Soph contest this year was excellent," J. Frank Dobie wrote for a Georgetown newspaper. "All the speakers had good selections and delivered them in an enthusiastic manner. The contest was very close and after careful consideration the medal was awarded to A. Frank Smith."[45] The title of Frank's medal-winning declamation was "Infirm of Purpose."

Since Frank lived in the KA fraternity house, his college expenses can only be estimated. If he had lived in Mood Hall, he would have paid between $158 and $180 a year for room and board, depending upon the size and location of the room. Tuition was $75 for the year, making the total cost for a year about $250.[46] Although his grandfather Smith was paying for his college education, Frank sought to contribute what he could, selling zithers (small musical instruments) during the summer of 1909.[47]

When Frank returned to Georgetown in the fall of 1909, he found the campus filled with a record-breaking enrollment of 331 in the College, 170 in the School of Fine Arts, and 229 in the Fittng School—a total of 730 students.[48] The new students included several persons who were to become influential in Frank Smith's life. Sawnie R. Aldredge of Dallas entered the sophomore class, transferring from Columbia Military Academy. Sawnie and Frank became such close friends that they planned to go to Harvard Law School and room together. Aldredge later became mayor of Dallas. Eugene R. Millis came as a freshman, beginning a friendship that was to develop later in Houston, when

Millis became a newspaper editor and Smith a pastor and then bishop. The "prep" class included Lois Craddock (later Mrs. J. J. Perkins), Hallie Crutchfield (Bess's younger sister), Julia Mouzon (Dr. Mouzon's daughter), Sophia Meachum (an old friend from Rogers), L. U. Spellmann, and Arthur R. Wilson (who later endowed a chair in religion at Southwestern).[49]

For his sophomore course, Frank continued taking English and history, began French, and added philosophy.[50] He probably took this second year of English with Assistant Professor John H. McGinnis, who had just "moved up" from the Fitting School faculty. Frank and Bess continued their friendship with John McGinnis until his death in 1960. An additional link in this relationship was Grace Gillett, a classmate and friend of Frank's and Bess's, whom McGinnis married shortly before he left Southwestern and went with Dr. Hyer to join the original faculty of Southern Methodist University in 1915.[51] Frank's philosophy professor, Dr. John R. Allen, probably had more influence on Frank than any other teacher at Southwestern. Besides the "parental" bond between Bess and her "Uncle John," Frank had two years of classes with Dr. Allen before he and Bess began going together, and he went to visit his professor on Laurel Street long before he went to visit Dr. Allen's niece.[52]

Frank Smith remembered one incident from his sophomore year with both embarrassment and amazement. A prominent United States senator from Mississippi came to the campus on a lecture tour to speak on the subject "Is the Negro a Human Being or an Animal?" The conclusion of the lecture was that the Negro is an animal. Frank said that he was embarrassed at the time "because Turner Van Hoose, our colored janitor, was sitting down there by the stove, keeping the stove warm and hearing what was said. But nobody got up and walked out, and I never heard it mentioned in a classroom." Frank was amazed by the incident "because Georgetown was the center of as much culture as could be found anywhere in Texas at that time. It was a community of an unusually high type of citizenry." Recalling the senator's lecture many years later, Smith declared: "Now just think how far we have come. The progress that has been made in my lifetime in the amelioration of racial injustice is unbelieveable. I thank God that I have lived long enough to see progress made and minds opened as they have not been before!"[53]

Bess Crutchfield begins to come into A. Frank Smith's life more frequently during the year 1909-10. Elected one of "Southwestern's Four Prettiest Girls" that year,[54] Bess had always had a number of boyfriends.

Now she was limiting her attention to two young men, A. Frank Smith and Arthur Henderson. Arthur, a ranch boy from Vancourt in West Texas, divided his time between playing football and ranching. In the fall he came to Southwestern to play football; in the spring he would return home for ranching.[55] Arthur was also a member of the Kappa Alpha fraternity. Fraternity brothers expected certain favors from each other, one favor being that of "looking after" a brother's girl friend. When Arthur finished the football season and was making arrangements to return to the ranch, he called on his "brother" Frank Smith to look after his girl friend, Bess Crutchfield. As Frank remembered the agreement: "Arthur said to me, 'I'm going to marry Bess, and I want you to take care of her while I'm gone.' And I did, and I always felt like a dog, but I didn't regret it. When he came back, I think he tried to pick up where he left off, but the race was too far gone. But he was a good sport about it."[56] Frank and Bess put their initials on the concrete sidewalk built in front of the Main Building in 1910, "one of the first strips laid in Georgetown."[57]

Bess, a talented violinist, had taken lessons before she was a college student. She was already a senior in the fine arts department in 1909-10, playing her senior recital just before Thanksgiving in the university auditorium.[58] She was also working toward a B.A. degree at the same time. While she was a senior in fine arts, she was also a sophomore along with Frank in the college.

Although Frank did not win any medals or prizes for oratorical contests in his sophomore year, he was chosen to participate in the Alamo Society's intermediate debate on the affirmative team. By a close three-to-two vote, the negative team won the debate concerning the resolution: "That the proposed Nicaragua Route offers more advantages than are offered by the Panama Route."[59] Nevertheless, Frank's prowess in public speaking was enough to gain him a place in yearbook humor:

A. Frank Smith, as every one knows, is a very eloquent youth, and he is seldom reluctant to exercise his oratorical powers. So, when the Glee Club boys had their picnic, Mr. Smith was called upon to say grace. . . . After making the usual invocation of blessings on the repast, thinking that the occasion demanded something further, he proceeded to expatiate on the grandeur of nature. When he had, in his most impressive manner, spoken a few sentences, he halted, stammered, then ended with this climactic expression: "And now, Oh Lord, bless this food and—and—heal the sick."[60]

The following joke on Bess Crutchfield appeared in the same yearbook:

Prof. McGinnis (in English A.): "Miss Crutchfield, what caused the death of Samson?"

Miss Bess Crutchfield: "The Philistines cut off his hair and it broke his heart, so he died."[61]

Sophomore Frank Smith's student activities included participation in the Prohibition League, the University Glee Club, and the YMCA, which he served as secretary. A new organization was the Camping Club, hilariously pictured in the *Sou'wester* as a group of student "Huck Finns and Tom Sawyers." Frank's highest honor of that year, if not of his entire college career, was his election in June as president of the Students' Association for the year 1910-11.[62]

During the summer of 1910, Frank Smith joined 127 of his classmates in summer school. While the permanent record shows his enrollment for this session, it does not indicate which class he took. Apparently he was trying to improve his record in freshman geometry, which had previously thwarted him.

The year 1910-11 began and ended with significant changes for Southwestern University, changes that laid stepping-stones along the path that Frank Smith could not yet anticipate. Professor Mouzon had been elected to the episcopacy of the Methodist Episcopal Church, South, the preceding spring. While this event temporarily removed one of the guiding influences of Frank's life, it brought about the introduction of a new guide, Frank Seay.

To fill the vacancy created by Mouzon's unexpected departure, President Hyer brought in two men with different backgrounds. Herbert Lee Gray was a mature teacher and an experienced missionary, having served in China, Mexico, and Cuba. A native of Georgia and a graduate of Emory College, Gray had done graduate work at Vanderbilt and at the University of Chicago under the great biblical scholar George Adam Smith. Frank Seay, the son of the late governor of Alabama, was a brilliant young scholar. He had earned his Master's degree at Southwestern in 1899 and followed that with a year at Harvard, a summer at the University of Chicago, and a year abroad at Halle, Berlin, and Oxford. Frank Seay had taught in the Fitting School the previous year and was now to be Gray's assistant in the Department of Theology.[63]

Frank Smith was still planning a career in law. The requirements for the B.A. degree allowed a student to choose between courses in philosophy and biblical literature, and Frank had chosen philosophy. He first came under Frank Seay's influence in the YMCA, where Seay was on the Faculty Advisory Committee and Frank Smith was a mission and Bible study leader. Each member of the faculty was responsible for a week's chapel services, and Seay was an experienced and able preacher.

His junior year brought Frank Smith new responsibilities. On the basis of his outstanding work in history, Frank was appointed student assistant to Professor Moore in the history department.[64] There were new demands upon his time and abilities as he assumed the duties of the president of the Students' Association and of an associate editor of the *Sou'wester*.

The school year 1910-11 also brought new friendships. Three former students, Robert L. Kurth of Lufkin, H. Bascom Watts of Tuxedo, and James M. Willson of Bridgeport returned to the campus. Kurth was the younger brother of Ernest L. Kurth (class of '05), longtime trustee of Southwestern University.[65] H. Bascom Watts later had a distinguished career as a Methodist preacher and in 1952 was elected to the episcopacy, serving eight years with A. Frank Smith on the Council of Bishops. James M. Willson, later of Floydada, Texas, was to become a strong supporter of Methodist higher education in Texas, serving as trustee at McMurry, SMU, Texas Wesleyan College, and Lydia Patterson Institute.[66]

New members of the freshman class (1910-11) included Fannie Dobie, younger sister of J. Frank Dobie; Eugene B. Germany, a future trustee of both Southwestern and SMU; and Harry Hughes, a fraternity brother who would be Frank Smith's roommate at Vanderbilt and his dear friend until Hughes's untimely death in 1922.[67] This was also the year when Margaret Root, sister of Dan, entered the Fitting School. A prominent Georgetown family, the Roots lived in a large home where Cody Memorial Library now stands. Margaret Root, who married Herman Brown, is memorialized by the Margaret Root Brown Professorship in Fine Arts at Southwestern. The Browns became longtime friends of Frank and Bess Smith.[68]

In his junior year, Frank continued previous work in English, history, and French, and added Spanish. Two foreign languages were required for the B.A. degree. Professor Ryland Fletcher Young, a native of Fayette County and a graduate of Southwestern University, taught both French and Spanish. Having come to Southwestern's faculty in 1880, he was second only to Dean Cody in length of tenure. Like Cody, Young was a man of deep piety, genuinely interested in his students.

One event in Frank's junior year overshadowed all others. On August

2, Bess Crutchfield accepted his fraternity pin, an act almost equivalent to engagement.[69] Engaged or not, Bess had to be in by 10:00 P.M. The Allens' bedroom was upstairs over the living room, so "Uncle John" would drop his shoes promptly at ten o'clock, a sign that it was time for Frank to leave. Nor could Frank and Bess go for buggy rides at night. Uncle John was very strict about such things.[70] He also frowned upon telephone calls to Bess and Hallie from young men. One day when Frank called, Dr. Allen answered. When Frank asked to speak to Bess, Dr. Allen objected and inquired about Frank's interest. Taken by surprise, Frank replied that he wanted to borrow a book. "Which book?" asked the experienced professor. After a moment of silence, Frank named the only book he could think of at the moment, *Quo Vadis*.[71]

Frank must have been an able antagonist for Dr. Allen, because their encounters were celebrated in the 1911 *Sou'wester*. In the cartoon section there is a picture of Dr. Allen lying in his bed greatly disturbed by a bad dream. Frank Smith's face appears in the dream. The caption explains: "Dr. Allen's mind works, Frankly, during the night as well as the day. It is Bes(t) but still it makes the Dr. have bad dreams." Frank was also the subject of a "Suggestion from the Annex Girls:" "Frank Smith would save shoe leather next year by taking up his abode at Dr. Allen's."[72]

On at least one occasion, Frank Smith became involved in sorority affairs. When Lois Craddock (later Mrs. J. J. Perkins) came to Southwestern, Bess Crutchfield was determined to pledge Lois for her sorority, Delta Delta Delta. Lois's roommate was Callie Blair, an old friend of Frank's from high school days in Corsicana. Callie was a member of Alpha Delta Pi, which had not yet extended an invitation to Lois. Callie still remembers the conversation:

Bess said to me, "Now, Callie, I know that you might want Lois in ADPi, but you all haven't said anything to her. We want her in our sorority. Will you rush her for us?" And I said, "Okay." So I went and talked to Lois, and I said: "Now that's a good sorority, Lois. And my sorority hasn't said anything to you." So Bess and Frank Smith made a date with Lois to take her to a ballgame. I remember that so well. Lois pledged Tri-Delt.[73]

Of the four and a half years that Frank Smith was a student at Southwestern University, his junior year was the busiest. Almost every month he was involved in some major event: the Alamo Society's "First Annual Open Session"; "A Trip to Mars," a musical stage show written and directed by Miss Bernice Long, perhaps the first such production permitted at Southwestern; "The Hero of the Gridiron: A College Comedy in Five Acts"; the annual concert of the glee club—further evidence of the diversity of Frank Smith's talents.[74] In December the Alamo Society paid special tribute to Frank, electing him to represent their society in the commencement debate against the rival San Jacinto Society for the coveted Brooks Prize. The five month's preparation period for the debate indicates the quality required of the contestants.

In April the faculty chose Frank as one of the four junior men to participate in the commencement oratorical contest. Even though he had a full month to prepare, he was already carrying a heavy load of responsibilities: final preparations with his teammate L. H. Robinson for the Brooks Prize Debate, last minute work on the *Sou'wester*, and the continuing demands made upon him as president of the Students' Association—not to mention the last round of exams to be graded for Professor Moore's history classes and preparation for his own final examinations! May 27 must have come all too soon under such circumstances, and Frank did not win the Junior Orator's Medal.[75]

These final weeks of the year 1910-11 were disturbed by the news of Dr. Hyer's election as the first president of Southern Methodist University. How would Hyer's departure affect Southwestern's future? Who would be the new president? Under Hyer's leadership the university had made major gains in many areas. Would these be jeopardized by his leaving? These and many other questions created new anxieties and added to the unrest that normally comes with the end of a school year. Frank Smith was drawn into the vortex of this emotional unrest during the commencement exercises. As the president of the Students' Association, he presented a gift from the student body to President Hyer at the conclusion of the baccalaureate address given by Hyer. J. Frank Dobie described the scene:

I have witnessed a few scenes of depth and sadness, I have read in the world's great literature many accounts of partings sincere and great, but nothing thus far has ever so affected me as the presentation of a pure gold locket, set with a crystal diamond (all of it simple) to Dr. Hyer, in the name of the student body by Frank Smith.[76]

Drama of a different nature had captured the hearts and minds of the audience in the university auditorium on the preceding Saturday evening, when graduating seniors, faculty and students, families and alumni gathered for the Brooks Prize Debate between teams representing the San

Jacinto and Alamo societies. The resolution to be debated was, "That the Responsibility of Institutions of Higher Learning to Ecclesiastical Organizations in Matters of Administrative and Educational Politics is Mutually Disadvantageous." Representing the Alamo Society, A. Frank Smith and Lem H. Robinson were assigned the negative position.[77] J. Frank Dobie's account captured the excitement of the contest:

> If you have never been thrilled by the splendid cheers and songs of those two societies as they sit on opposite sides of the galleries, if you have never hung on the words of each successive speaker, hoping, wishing, wondering, if your heart has never stopped beating to hear the decision of the judges, then you know not what this debate means. By a vote of four to one the Alamos, led by L. H. Robinson and Frank Smith, overcame the San Jacintos, led by J. G. Harrell and L. F. Sheffy.[78]

In the light of Frank Smith's extensive contribution to Christian higher education (see chapters 14 and 15), one is tempted to quote at length from this early affirmation. Since the entire typed manuscript is available in Bishop Smith's papers, however, his opening statement of purpose will suffice:

> . . . We grant to the secular institution that it has a distinct work to perform, yet we maintain that the church has just as distinct a part to play along educational lines and that its work cannot be performed by secular institutions. While the secular institution has for its primary object the training of the intellect, the church must, through its institutions of learning, cast such a moral and religious atmosphere about its students that the character of each will be molded according to that universal ideal of religion and advancement which it is the mission of the church to bring to mankind. . . . It is my purpose to bring before you three distinct phases of the question under discussion. First, the inherent right and duty of the church to educate and the special office she holds in the educational world. Second, the broadening influences in our churches, and their steadily decreasing sectarianism. Third, the advantages derived by the church through affiliation with education, and, through the church, by the world at large.[79]

Since Frank Smith won all of the other medals for oratory, why didn't he win the Junior Orator's Medal? It may be that pressing circumstances forced him to give priority to his preparation for the Brooks Prize Debate. Trying to give both projects equal time might have meant winning neither. Certainly the Brooks Prize was the more prestigious, and victory there meant glory for his society. Whatever the explanation,

Frank Smith listed the Brooks Prize among his most cherished achievements in college.[80]

After teaching French during the summer session, Frank Smith began
his senior year at Southwestern with vigor. Although he still lacked credit
in freshman geometry, he signed up for a full year (three courses) in
math with Dean Cody. Not only did he pass all three courses; he also
conquered trigonometry with a grade of 98. He completed his fourth
year in both English and history and finished the degree requirements
for Spanish and chemistry. He also served again as assistant to Professor
Moore in history.[81]

That elusive geometry requirement was finally settled in a manner
that produced a humorous sequel; at least Frank Smith considered it
amusing and enjoyed telling the tale at his own expense:

I never could pass in freshman geometry. I did not know the principles involved, and if the geometric figure changed from that which I had memorized
from the book, I was lost. I took more than one special examination in freshman geometry with no success. Near the end of my senior year the professor
of freshman math asked me if I were competing for academic honors, and
I told him "no." "Well," he said, "I'm going to give you a pass in freshman
geometry, so that you can graduate. I am ashamed to take any more money
from you for special examinations, and I am convinced that you can never
make a pass in this course."

When I went to Missouri eighteen years later as a bishop, to hold the
Missouri Conferences, I found this math professor teaching in Central College, our Methodist school in Missouri. He was always a lay delegate to
Annual Conference, and he took great delight in taking the floor each year
at some time during the session of the conference during the four years I
held that Conference, to tell with glee how thick-headed I was and that I
would not be at that moment in the presiding officer's chair had it not been
for him. He would always conclude with the statement: "I now know what it
takes to make a bishop; give him a pass in freshman math so he can graduate."[82]

During his senior year, Frank Smith was not as deeply involved in
extracurricular activities as he had been. The offices that he did hold
were appropriate to his senior status: editor-in-chief of the *Sou'wester*
and president of the Alamo Literary Society. Continuing his member-
ships in the Prohibition League and the YMCA, he added the Southwestern University Press Club.

Excitement had been building in Georgetown during the fall term
as announcements and invitations went out proclaiming the inauguration

ceremonies for President Charles M. Bishop. Not every student generation has an opportunity to participate in the pomp and circumstance
surrounding a presidential inauguration. The color and tradition involved
have roots in the period of the Renaissance. As Frank Smith had been
chosen to represent the student body at the departure of Dr. Hyer, he
was delegated to speak for his fellow students at the inaugural banquet
honoring Dr. Bishop. In a distinguished company of university presidents,
judges, and clergymen, Frank Smith sat at the head table and presented
his accolades.[83] According to a Georgetown newspaper, "The speech of
Mr. Frank Smith, representing the student body, was a model of its kind,
chaste and eloquent."[84] The editor of the exploits of the senior class,
writing in the *Sou'wester*, gave this more personal account: "Dec. 8.
Inaugural banquet. Mr. A. F. Smith makes speech, thus covering class
with glory. Was not very scared."[85]

December proved to be a special month for Frank and Bess. Bess
sketched the development in her diary:

On October the twenty-ninth, Frank asked me the one question, if I thought
enough of him to be engaged to him. I told him no. . . . I thought I would
wait until he had been to Harvard a year—but on Dec. 21, the KAs gave
a party, and out on the porch we talked it over . . . and that night I told
him *Yes*! I did some good old thinking before I said it. Then I went home
and thought nearly all night. Boys don't realize what it means to a girl.[86]

Whatever Frank's thoughts were at that time, in later years he could
never think of Southwestern apart from his courtship of Bess. "It was
there that I met Bess Crutchfield who was my college sweetheart," he
wrote fifty years later. "Because of her, the thought of Georgetown and
Southwestern is dearer to me than words can express."[87]

In early April of that year, 1912, Frank Smith and fellow members
of the University Press Club were hosts for a two-day meeting of the
Texas Intercollegiate Press Association. The editor of the *Sou'wester*
and one of the most capable public speakers in the Southwestern student
body, Frank was invited to participate in the program. As the last speaker
in a group of nine at an afternoon session, he had one of the most difficult positions on the schedule. Using humor to keep his audience awake
and attentive, Frank sought to arouse sympathy for "Lo, the Poor Editor."
Another participant in that afternoon program was Mr. Umphrey Lee
from Daniel Baker College, who spoke on the "Literary View of the
College Short Story."[88]

This was not Umphrey Lee's first visit to the Georgetown campus. Umphrey was a member of the Daniel Baker College debate squad and had met Frank Smith during debates between the two schools' teams. Once when Southwestern was host school, Frank arranged a blind date for Umphrey with a pretty sorority sister of Bess's, Mary Margaret Williams. The date turned out far better than anyone expected, and Umphrey and Mary Margaret were married in 1917. Frank never let his former debate opponent forget who had introduced him to his wife-to-be.[89]

Spring was revival time for Southwestern University, and the revivals were always held at the First Methodist Church. In comparison with those of previous years, the revival of 1912 was declared to be "one of the greatest revivals ever held in Georgetown." A major support for this claim was the fact that "eight young men yielded to the call to preach."[90] Dr. L. U. Spellmann clearly remembers the dramatic moment:

As was the custom in those days when a man had, as we said, "surrendered to the call to preach," he made his decision public in a church service. This was the way of announcing his intention. So in a revival meeting when a pastor preached on the "call to preach," he would close by saying: "If there is anyone here who feels the call to preach, let him come down the aisle and by coming down here make his public announcement of his decision." Well, old Brother Nelms made such a call. And in due and ancient form, they started singing the hymn. Frank Smith was down just a pew or two in front of me. And as the hymn began—he was about third from the aisle— Frank started moving out toward the aisle. And I'll never forget old Dr. Nelms—a brotherly man, and I imagine he had talked to Frank about it— as Frank started, he said with a great deal of emotion in his voice: "Come on down, come on down." And Frank walked down the aisle and gave the old man his hand. And this was his public announcement of his intention to enter the ministry. It made a rather profound impression on the student body and on Frank's friends who had not anticipated anything like this.[91]

Bess's entry in her diary—the only existing contemporary account—both dates the event and explains why she was not at the service.

On Friday, March 29, '12, Frank decided he would be a preacher and went up that morning. I didn't go to church because I knew I would act like a baby. Instead I stayed at home and cried & prayed that I might be able to help him all I could and would be better myself. I am so glad he decided to do it, but I fully realize what it means both to him and to me—and the responsibility involved. I am willing though to do my part and anything I can do to help him succeed. I know he will make as good [a] preacher as he would have a lawyer.[92]

How did it come about that this young man, who from his grammar school days had wanted to be a lawyer, should suddenly change his mind just six weeks before his graduation from college? This was not a sudden decision made under emotional stress but a public announcement of a decision reached over a long period of time. That a revival was under way at that very time was more or less coincidental. Once he had arrived at his decision, Frank wanted to make a public announcement, and the revival services offered a convenient opportunity. As he later explained: "Because I had been president of the student body, editor of the annual, and student assistant in history, I wanted to make a declaration before the student body."[93] With an obvious touch of humor, Bishop Smith remembered that Ashley Chappell, brother of Clovis, thought that he was responsible for Smith's decision to enter the ministry, since he was holding the college revival services at the First Methodist Church. "I asked the pastor to have a service called one morning for those who wanted to enter the ministry," Frank explained, "and Ashley went to his grave thinking that he had called me to the ministry. He had nothing to do with my going into the ministry."[94]

Frank stated clearly that the determinative influences in his decision had long been at work: "I look upon the fact that through home influence and a Christian college I was made to lead a moral life, and to be conscious of God's place in the affairs of every man as the determining influence in my call to the ministry."[95] As we have seen, Frank Smith had grown up in a family with a religious heritage. Just before he left home for his final year at Southwestern, his mother had given him a Bible in which she had inscribed in a strong hand: "May the teachings of this book be a blessing to your life. Study well. Mother. Aug., 1911."[96] This parental influence is best seen in his parents' response to Frank's decision. Knowing his father's delight in his determination to be a lawyer, Frank was naturally concerned about how Mr. Smith would react to his change of direction:

I wrote to my parents, thinking they would be amazed. My father had told me all my life, "Oh, you must be a lawyer, son." And to my amazement, I got a letter back from my father and one from my mother. She wrote at home; he wrote from the store. He said: "I have been expecting this. All I have to say is, make a good one. Be a good preacher." I had thought that he would express disappointment. And my mother wrote me and told me something she had never before told me. She said, "I knew you were going to be a preacher. When you were five weeks old, you had the measles. The doctor told me you were going to die. And I held you in my arms all day and prayed, and I committed you to the Lord. I promised the Lord that every day that I lived I would pray that you would be a preacher. I knew it was coming." But fortunately, she never had told me that before. I knew more than one boy in school with me whose mother had called him into the ministry. They got to college and rebelled. . . . I am glad my mother did not place me in such a position. Very wisely she never told me that until this happened. She expected it to be, however, and went to her grave believing that God had accepted her dedication and her prayers. I must confess that I never felt that this incident could have determined my career, but I never said this to my mother. And who knows?[97]

Not until many years later did Frank receive further insight into his father's response. While he had known for a long time that his father was "undoubtedly an unhappy and a disappointed man," Frank explained that he had never known why:

I think I may have found the answer not long before his death. His only surviving sister told me that he was called to preach and was under strong compulsion, but that he resolutely closed his mind to such a future. Instead, he expected to make a name for himself in law, always leading a clean and honorable life. Then, disappointed in his desire to be a lawyer, he determined to become a rich man. In this he likewise was disappointed, although he did live a clean and upright life. I believe this may have accounted for his restlessness and his living within himself. This could likewise account for his refusal to ever become an active layman in his church or to make close personal friends of his various pastors.[98]

When Frank asked his father if what his aunt had told him was true, his father replied, "Yes, son, the Lord threw a brick at me and I dodged it, but it hit two of my boys."[99] Frank's younger brother, Angie, who was still at home at that time (April, 1912), confirmed Frank's interpretation: "My father was very ambitious for Frank to be a lawyer. But genuinely, I think there was great elation on the part of my parents over Frank's decision."[100]

The person whose response was most important of all to Frank Smith was Bess Crutchfield. As Frank later explained: "Although I knew we were going to be married, I can't pinpoint the time she said she would marry me or when I asked her. But I knew it. And I felt that I ought to tell her I was thinking of going into the ministry." Bess's reply is a classic for preachers' wives: "Frank," she said, "I know that if you go into politics you could be governor or a U.S. Senator, but I had rather live in a circuit rider's parsonage than in the White House."[101]

According to Hallie Crutchfield, however, Frank's desire to preach was "something of a blow to Bess. I wouldn't say that she didn't want him to, but Bess did cry, even though it was short-lived."[102] On the other hand, Bess was one of those persons who needed a good cry in the process of adjusting to changes. Frank insisted that he would never have entered the ministry if Bess had been opposed.

If Bessie had said she didn't want to marry a preacher, I am very sure I would have dropped the idea. . . . I had not come to any final decision, and that would not be turning my back on the Lord. I could serve him elsewhere. It would have been fair to Bess and perfectly understood by the Lord. . . . If Bessie had said to me, "I just can't take a life like that," I would not have said, "I'll choose her instead of God." That would not have been it. . . . The call of God is for one's life, and the future course of that life is incidental to the call and the dedication. With all my heart I would have intended to be God's man had I gone into the law.[103]

In later life, Bess Smith added an interesting feature to the story of their engagement and of Frank's vocational decision:

I was so glad for Frank to go into the ministry. Frank had thought that he was going to be a lawyer. I don't know why I had the idea, but I had in my mind that lawyers were just out after the dollar and nothing else. So I told Frank when he first asked me to marry him: "Well, I'll just have to think about it." I didn't think I was fitted for public life. "You go on to Harvard. After you come back, then if you still feel the same way, maybe we can make a decision."[104]

In addition to his family's influence, Frank Smith also credited his experiences at Southwestern University with his decision to shift from law to ministry:

Southwestern was worth a great deal to me. When I went there I had no thought of entering the ministry. But somewhere along the road—I can't pinpoint any particular reason why—I became cognizant of the fact that a man is not his own. He is bought with a price, as the Scripture has it, and what he does should be with respect to the service he can render. . . . I turned to the ministry, not because of some Pauline experience, but rather with a feeling of regret that I wasn't able to carry out what I wanted to do [i.e., to go to law school]. I didn't want to be a preacher, but I knew I should do what I ought to do.[105]

When his old friend Edwin A. Hunter asked Bishop Smith to write an account of his call to preach for a book that Hunter was compiling, Smith prepared a more orderly account for publication:

I had reached the end of my college course; my next step would take me into specialized training in a professional school. . . . And then, from some un-bidden source in the early spring of that senior year, the thought came to me that it was I—A. Frank Smith—who had decided my future course, and with that thought came the question, "Has a man the right to make such a decision of his own accord?"—and the further question, "Would you be will-ing to abandon the law, if you believed God wanted you to do something else?" Within the area created by these two questions came my call to the ministry, and within this same area came my acceptance of the call—I could not get away from these two questions. I had to face them and answer them. . . . I had to believe that whatever I did later was God's will for me. . . . Gradually the certainty laid hold of me that I should preach. I canvassed my qualifications, my temperament, my attitudes, asking myself, with God's help, what I was best fitted to do. With no resisting of the convictions upon my part, I realized that my life work should be in the ministry. Had I decided to remain with the law, I could have believed profoundly that it was God's will for me to do so, and I would have entered upon a legal career feeling called of God to do so. . . . From this background [influence of home and a Christian college] came the questions above referred to and eventually my call and dedication to the Christian ministry.[106]

Frank Smith was concerned about popular misconceptions of the complete peace that was supposed to follow immediately upon accept-ance of a call to preach. He was enough of a student of both Scripture and church history to be skeptical about such claims. Recalling his own agonies, he declared:

I think I know something personally of what Jesus experienced in the wil-derness. The first several weeks after I came into the ministry were the bleakest, most miserable weeks I ever spent. I would wake up at night and feel like I was a lost soul. And I've gotten up and knelt down by the bed many a night and said, "Lord, I don't know what is the matter, but I am going to stick it out." And then the light began to break. I had a kind of feeling that when I got down there [at the altar of the church] and crossed the bridge that the light would come. But to my amazement, it got darker. And [the next day] I struck Frank Dobie down on the street, and he said: "You are the damnedest fool I ever saw. You have ruined a great lawyer to make a plug of a preacher." Well, a lot of them said that to me. And I felt like I had to say to myself, "You can succeed as a lawyer . . ." Over against that I put the humblest place in the church. "Now, are you willing to go in here and be the minister?" And until I was able to say that, I wasn't willing to make the choice. And I was just in a fog, but gradually light began to come, I think, after I had proved to myself and proved to the Lord that I meant business. But it wasn't any sudden revelation.[107]

Nor did Frank's inner agonizings go unnoticed by his fellow students. "During his senior year in college, Frank Smith fought one of the bitterest battles I ever saw a man fight," a classmate wrote. "I think that gradually there came to him a definite sense that he must give his life to the ministry of his Church. It was a battle. I doubt that he had thought of being or planned to be a preacher before that time."[108]

Who were the professors at Southwestern who might have been influential in Frank Smith's decision to enter the ministry? From the available evidence, one would have to place Professor Frank Seay among those most predominant. Eight years later, when Seay died during an influenza epidemic, Frank Smith wrote of him:

I am sure I shall never love another man more than I loved Frank Seay, and I am just as sure that no man will ever love me more than he did. He had a great influence on my life at a time when I was undecided just how to pitch it for the future. I think his greatest work consisted in giving to young men a sane, workable conception of the ministry as a life work. . . . He had faith in me, and was deeply interested in all that concerned me. . . . My life will always be richer and more fruitful because I knew him.[109]

Although Frank Smith did not mention other professors by name as being specifically related to his vocational decision, his brother and his classmates agree that the following were important influences in Frank's life at Southwestern: Dr. Robert S. Hyer, Dean Claude Carr Cody, and Professors John R. Allen, Stephen H. ("Sleepy") Moore, Albert S. Pegues, and Herbert L. Gray.[110] Frank would certainly have discussed the matter with his pastor at First Methodist Church, Rev. W. L. Nelms, regarding both the public announcement in the service and the procedure for Frank's license to preach.[111]

According to Finis and Callie (Blair) Crutchfield, who certainly knew as much about Frank Smith's early years at Southwestern University as anyone, Professor John McGinnis played a unique role in Frank's call to the ministry:

It was shortly after Frank came [to Southwestern] and joined the Kappa Alpha Fraternity that we all began to realize Frank's ability and what he could do. Dr. McGinnis and somebody else took Frank out buggy riding one after-

noon, and he told Frank, "Now I don't want you to be a lawyer, Frank, because you could be the greatest preacher in all of Texas if you would devote
yourself to that. You have great talent and you have great persuasive powers." I don't know what all he said, but that's the idea, that Frank would be
a great influence in the church. And Frank then began to think about it. So
we always said, kind of *sub rosa*, that John McGinnis called Frank to
preach.[112]

This claim of significance for McGinnis is consistently challenged, however, by Frank Smith's other classmates, his brother, and his sons. Such
an act was out of character for Professor McGinnis, as they remembered
him. None of them had ever heard McGinnis mentioned in relation to
Frank's call to preach, by Frank or anyone else.[113]

Now that Frank had declared his intention to enter the ministry, his
next step was to request the Quarterly Conference of Georgetown's First
Methodist Church to recommend him to the District Conference for
licensing as a Local Preacher. Upon receiving this recommendation at its
May meeting, the Georgetown District Conference authorized Frank
Smith "to preach the Gospel, according to the rules and regulations of
the Methodist Episcopal Church, South."[114]

In May the preliminary round for the Senior Oratorical Contest was
held to choose six senior men to compete on commencement morning.
The senior competition required that each contestant write his own oration, each presentation being judged on the quality of its composition as
well as its delivery. As the Brooks Prize was the crowning achievement
for debaters, winning the Trustees' Medal was the ultimate goal of
orators. When the six survivors of the elimination preliminaries were
announced on May 17, Frank Smith was among those advanced to the
final contest.[115]

Commencement exercises were held in the auditorium on the second
floor of Old Main on Monday, June 10, 1912, beginning with the
Senior Oratorical Contest at 9 o'clock. Frank Smith's oration, entitled
"Our Mission," was fourth in the series. The final speaker was Frank R.
Stanford, a fellow Alamo, who had won the Junior Orator's Medal in
1911, defeating Frank Smith.[116] The winner's name is a matter of record:
"At the Senior Commencement exercises . . . yesterday morning, in the
oratorical contest, A. Frank Smith of Mart won the trustees' prize, a
$50 gold watch."[117]

At the graduation exercises at 10 o'clock, A. Frank Smith received
the Bachelor of Arts Degree from Southwestern University. Among those

also graduating were Grace Gillett, Robert L. Kurth, Neely G. Landrum, and J. M. Willson.[118] One of Frank's classmates later wrote the following tribute:

Frank Smith was the natural leader of the student body at Georgetown while there in school. I do not know of a single man or woman who did not respect and love him. In fact, he meant almost as much in the life of the student body, as a student member of the school, as did the beloved Dr. C. C. Cody, as a faculty member of the institution. He won all kinds of medals, debating, oratorical; in fact, he won about all the medals that were offered and then some. I think one of Frank Smith's great secrets of success has been his willingness to help people. He was just that sort of a man in college. He was an honor student of the school, one of the most brilliant men I ever knew, but the thing that sticks with me more than his brilliance in his studies, and more than the fact that he was a natural leader in the student body, and that he was successful in winning medals and honors while at school, is that he was just a friend of the other students, and they loved him just as he loved them.[119]

For his part, Frank Smith was deeply grateful to Southwestern University. "Southwestern was worth a great deal to me, and I am a firm believer in the church putting its greatest emphasis in the small institution," he declared. "It is the smaller campus in which you have contact with the whole group where a man develops his individuality and his capabilities to a greater extent than you can if you are just lost in a large crowd. I was supremely happy at Southwestern."[120]

During the summer of 1912, Frank worked for the Hogg Organization for Higher Education, traveling over the state speaking in churches and schools. Announcements of his speaking schedule were published in area newspapers. "In those days higher education was looked upon askance," Bishop Angie Smith explains, "and the attempt was made to encourage young people to continue their education."[121] Speaking to such a wide variety of audiences and meeting people across the state should have been a valuable experience for a young ministerial student. That he learned about a style of life unknown in the sheltered confines of a church-related college is illustrated by the following extract from his travel diary:

Dallas, night of June 13th. Met this man in lobby of hotel, he was almost in delirium tremens, so drunk he was sober. He drunkenly addressed me and told me he was sick. He then told me he had been drunk for three days, and that he couldn't sleep. He had a pint bottle of whiskey at the time. I advised him to go home, and learned that he was a bachelor real estate man having appointments out in the city. I proposed to take him to the street car about two blocks away, and in great amazement he replied, "I don't want to be obligated to anybody. Why do you want to help me?" I insisted, so we started for the car. For the entire two blocks he continued to ask me who I was and why I was helping him. As we stood on the corner waiting for a car, he suddenly asked me if I were a Christian, saying he knew I must be from the way I had treated him. And then he asked me to pray for him just as he got in his car. Thus even to a drunken man, kindness and the fruits of Christ's spirit are plainly evident.[122]

Frank Smith might have been a small-town boy in a big city, but he was also a seasoned member of the Student Prohibition League and of the Young Men's Christian Association. Frank's brief account of this incident in Dallas illustrates how well he had learned to distinguish between the evils that men do and the image of God that remains, regardless of the sinful acts performed. From his professors and fellow students at Southwestern University, Frank Smith had come to understand the meaning of Paul's advice to the young minister, Timothy (2 Tim. 2:15): "Study to show thyself approved unto God, a workman that needeth not to be ashamed, rightly dividing the word of truth."

3

"Take the Sword of the Spirit, The Word of God"

IN SEPTEMBER, 1912, Frank Smith made the long train trip to Nashville, Tennessee, to begin his theological education at Vanderbilt University. His grandfather, John Summerfield Smith, who had paid for Frank's undergraduate work at Southwestern University, also paid for his professional training. Angie, who would be going to Southwestern that same year, recalls that Mr. Smith opened the big iron safe in his home to get the money he was giving Frank. "They didn't have banks of any strength in those days," Angie explains, "and besides nobody ever robbed. My grandfather reached in that safe—he must have had twenty-five thousand dollars just in currency—and counted out to Frank the money he would need. Grandfather was well-fixed."[1]

Since its opening in 1875, Vanderbilt University had been one of the foremost universities in the South. Under the wise direction of Bishop Holland N. McTyeire and Chancellor Landon Cabell Garland, systematic theological training and critical study of the Bible were firmly established.[2] According to John O. Gross, Vanderbilt's "theological school furnished for forty years just about all the professionally trained ministers for the Methodist Episcopal Church, South."[3]

When Frank Smith went to Vanderbilt in the fall of 1912, Dean Wilbur Fisk Tillett had developed one of the strongest theological

faculties in the nation: O. E. Brown, professor of biblical and ecclesiastical history; J. H. Stevenson, professor of Hebrew and Old Testament
exegesis; John A. Kern, professor of practical theology; Thomas Carter,
professor of New Testament Greek and exegesis; and Henry Beach
Carré, professor of biblical theology.[4] Dean Tillett, who was also professor of systematic theology, was one of Methodism's major theologians.[5]

Five of Frank Smith's classmates from Southwestern University had
preceded him to Vanderbilt, including his Brook's Prize debate partner,
Lem H. Robinson.[6] Nevertheless, Frank said, "I was advised not to go
there because it was a place of radicalism."[7] Such criticism was aimed
primarily at Dean Tillett and other members of the faculty who were
classed theologically as "Evangelical Liberals."[8] Although overzealous
critics charged them with the errors of modernism, the Vanderbilt theological faculty was clearly within that distinctly evangelical type of
liberalism which began with Horace Bushnell and came into full maturity before World War I. As described by the historians of American
Christianity, these particular liberals "were especially aware of a basic
Christological difference between their type of thought and that of those
left-wing liberals who took a strictly humanitarian view of Jesus. They
[evangelical liberals] endeavored to construct their systems of thought
in terms of the person and work of Jesus Christ."[9] On the other hand,
these Christocentric liberals insisted that Christian thought come to
terms with all aspects of modern knowledge, including the principle of
organic evolution and the historical-critical method of studying the
Bible.[10]

With Frank Smith's academic and personal experience at Southwestern University, he had no reason to fear Vanderbilt as "a place of
radicalism." He had been introduced to the principle of organic evolution by such staunch churchmen as Robert S. Hyer and Randolph W.
Tinsley. He had been taught the values of biblical criticism by ordained
Methodist scholars whom he greatly revered—Edwin D. Mouzon, Frank
Seay, and H. L. Gray. And, as he later explained, he had no reason to
fear "the faith-destroying teaching of Dr. Tillett":

One of the required courses for freshmen was Dean Tillett's "Personal Salvation." . . . I know of no one course that ever meant quite so much to me as
did this course, and there is no book I studied in college or seminary to
which I revert more often now than I do to *Personal Salvation*. . . . I never
troubled about the heresy of the Dean after I took this course under him.

And I troubled less about it after I came to know and to love the sweet spirit and humble devotion of the man himself.[11]

Vanderbilt University also came under attack by some Methodists for an alleged attempt to throw off the control of the Methodist Episcopal Church, South. When Frank went to Vanderbilt, there was a civil case pending before the Chancery Court of Tennessee to determine whether the university's trustees were to be elected by the board of trust of the university or by the General Conference. When the court decided in favor of the General Conference in February, 1913, the board of trust appealed the case to the Tennessee Supreme Court. The final ruling was not made until the month Frank was due to graduate.[12]

While at Vanderbilt, Frank Smith met three future bishops of the Methodist church, two of whom, Ju Sam Ryang of Korea and Juan Nicanor Pascoe of Mexico, were classmates. The third was Dr. John M. Moore, then home missionary secretary of the Methodist Episcopal Church, South, who lived with his wife on the Vanderbilt campus. Mrs. Moore was pianist for the Sunday school where Frank taught a class.[13] Moore was elected to the episcopacy in 1918. Ryang and Pascoe were elected in their respective native lands in 1930, which was also the year of Frank Smith's election. The coincidence of the three Vanderbilt classmates' being elected bishops in the same year was to attract considerable attention.[14]

The biblical department of Vanderbilt University, as the school of theology was then designated, was divided into nine "schools" or areas of study. Presumably, students were required to take at least one course in each area: Old Testatment Language and Literature, New Testament Language and Literature, Biblical Theology and English Exegesis, Church History, Systematic Theology, Practical Theology, Practical Sociology, Public Speaking, and Religious Education. The only surprises among Frank Smith's courses are the *omissions*. He took neither the Constitutional History of Methodism nor the History of Methodism. It is understandable that he was given credit in "Argumentation" for previous work taken at Southwestern University.[15]

In the fall of 1912, Bishop Walter Russell Lambuth, just back from his dramatic missionary journey in the Congo, came to the Vanderbilt campus to recruit volunteers for the new mission in Africa. Frank remembered how Bishop Lambuth "came to Wesley Hall and called a retreat over the week-end and laid it on the heart of every man: 'Will you be one who will go?' " Bishop Lambuth told the exciting story of his seven-hundred-mile trek into the Congo, accompanied by the brilliant scholar and teacher John Wesley Gilbert of the Colored Methodist Episcopal Church's Paine College. He described the welcome they had received from Chief Wembo-Nyama and their promise to him to establish a mission for his people. Frank responded to the challenge: "I took it to my heart, and I wrote a letter to Bessie. And I said, 'Are you willing to go to Africa?' And she wrote back at once, special delivery: 'I will be glad to go to Africa if you want to go.' " By the time Frank received this assurance, however, his zeal for the Congo mission had cooled. When the spirit-stirring young bishop left the campus, so did Frank's sense of urgency. "I felt not the least compulsion to go to Africa," he said later.[16]

While Frank and a fellow student were returning to Texas for the Christmas holidays in 1912, they met a woman on the train who had suffered great sorrow. Her twenty-one-year-old son had just died of spinal meningitis, and she was taking his body to the old home in Arkansas for burial. Since she had already lost her older son and her husband had died within the year, she had to face the ordeal of this son's death alone. Smith continued the account:

Her son didn't know her, she said, when she reached him. He didn't know that she had cried & prayed beside his bed. And then she said—and I shall never forget the expression on her face, its radiance & especially its look of assurance—"Oh, I thank God for resurrection & Jesus Christ who made it plain to us." . . .

Oh! how my heart went out to her, as I thought that surely here was one whose heart was utterly crushed, but then her wonderful faith & even [her] peace turned my pity to praise of God. . . . I could hardly keep back the tears as I thought of her thoughts of her Master, even in such times of grief. . . .

When it was almost time for her to leave the train, I went to her seat & told her goodbye, telling her that her faith had been worth a great deal to me. And she told me that she was going to pray that I might make a successful & useful man. The knowledge of that consecrated woman's prayers for me is an eternal comfort & incentive to me. Never have I seen greater faith in God's promises than she displayed.[17]

Several other instances sketched in Frank's student notebook show a sensitive and responsive young man, always eager to be helpful to strangers in need.[18] Following one such incident, Frank wrote down his reflections: "Unless engaged continually in some form of unselfish activity, one grows spiritually cold. Unless having something definite to pray for continually, one can't get into as close communion with God as would otherwise be the case."[19]

What did Frank Smith learn in the classroom at Vanderbilt? The only source of evidence that has survived from his student years is the above-mentioned notebook, a loose-leaf book small enough to fit into his coat pocket. Although its imitation leather cover is well worn, the contents are remarkably legible despite the years. While no professor would want to be judged solely by what goes into his students' notebooks, a student's class notes do offer an indication of what the student considered important enough to write down. During a class in homiletics, for instance, Frank Smith made this notation:

Only a few years ago our sermons were practically Bible stories. Our preachers took texts & preached on the times & lives of Moses, Daniel, Job &c., with only an occasional application to present day problems. We have now realized, however, that the beauty of our religion is the fact that it did not exist as an everyday reality only 2,000 yrs. ago, but that it affects each succeeding generation more & more closely. And with this realization has come the preaching from a modern standpoint: the applying of God's truths to our daily life and problems. . . . The world realizes more and more each decade that Christianity is the groundwork of our lives, whatever they may be, and that it is affecting the world and humanity more & more as time passes.[20]

Even though Frank's notes do not give the professor's name, they clearly indicate that he was being taught typical evangelical liberal theology. As defined by William J. McCutcheon, the evangelical liberal believed in "a concept of growth and continuity which expressed the idea of progress and envisioned the chief functions of the church to be ethical preaching and moral education."[21] These themes of growth and progress appear again and again in Frank's notes:

Every living thing must either grow or decay; it cannot stand still. So it is with our spiritual lives. We must either grow stronger or weaker in our faith and experiencing. . . . Constant diligence is necessary in order to keep ever on the upward path.

With each succeeding age, God reveals Himself and his works a little more distinctly to man. Our discoveries, inventions, &c. serve but to draw us nearer to our God, who through those means is becoming daily more manifest to us.

The evangelical liberal's confidence in this growth and progress was based, McCutcheon continues, on belief in "the immanence of God, the goodness of man, and man's freedom of will and inherent capacity for altruism."[22] The class notes illustrate these beliefs:

God has placed man here, in His image, to overcome sin of his own free will and when man finally reaches the ideal set by Christ for the life here on earth, man's mission on earth will be done. . . . We have a great destiny to perform.

We realize, as we struggle for the truth, and strive to lift ourselves and humanity, that God in his omniscience can look ahead and see the glories which lie ahead of us. . . . We are almost tempted to give up in despair when we think of the terribly slow process of man's mind, and of the growth necessary in order to achieve new and higher ideals. Then we remember God's presence, we remember that we have our work to do in preparing for the coming of the Kingdom. . . . The road stretches on and on & on; from each height gained a higher mount is seen before, and from this another and another, stretching on & on & up & up rising to the very throne of God Himself. We will not be able to travel *all* the road, but we must travel our part, & endeavor to carry mankind farther towards the goal.

Vanderbilt's liberal theologians were truly evangelical or "Christocentric" because they "endeavored to construct their systems of thought in terms of the person and work of Jesus Christ."[23]

Man is *not* born damned; he is born with the ability to sin, but also with the ability to be saved. When man first sinned, God did not damn the race. . . . Instead he showed his justice & also his love by giving his son to fulfill the law. . . . Christ offered to leave his home in heaven to suffer for man, and God allowed him to come to the earth as the propitiation of man's sins. . . . When we consider our unworthiness, & yet see what vast things God is doing for us, we are overwhelmed & must exclaim with Paul, "I have been saved thru the mercy of God alone, and the merit of our Lord Jesus Christ."

The business of the preacher is not simply to preach; it is to *live* his religion. Preaching with mere words is incidental, unless our lives preach continually. Christ did not tell simply of the Father, but he performed works. He made his life a living testimonial of his message.

Central among the presuppositions shared by liberal theologians, according to Claude Welch, was "the *liberal spirit*—the spirit of open-mindedness, of tolerance and humility, of devotion to truth wherever it might be found."[24] An illustration of this "liberal spirit" is found among Frank Smith's notes: "All truth is of God, and eternal. No truth can contradict another. They may seem to contradict but that is only because their full significance and real place has not been discovered, and the error lies, not in the truths but in man's interpretation of them."[25]

On one occasion Frank noted a statement made by a fellow student from Japan, T. Murata: "The only thing in existence that does not change is God's truth. The forms in which it is clothed will of necessity change as peoples move forward in their ideals & conceptions, but the great truth, the impelling motive, will never change." This concept of truth was not unique to liberal theologians, but it was characteristic of their particular interpretation of Christianity. The classic expression of this view, as Claude Welch indicated, is found in Harry Emerson Fosdick's phrase "abiding experiences set in changing categories."[26]

Liberal theology was not only taught in the classrooms at Vanderbilt but was also the subject of discussion in the Theological Club which met monthly in Wesley Hall. During the spring term of 1914, for example, liberal theology was featured in all three meetings held by the club. At the February session, Frank Smith presented a report on "Modern Liberalism." In March, Dean Tillett read a paper entitled "The New Emphasis in Theology." Dr. J. A. Kern closed the series in April with a study of "Personalism."[27]

During Frank Smith's senior year at Vanderbilt (1913-14) he roomed with Harry L. Hughes, his fraternity brother and Alamo Society colleague at Southwestern, who had graduated with the class of '13.[28] Harry had been a big brother to Angie Smith, helping him to get established and to follow in Frank's footsteps (KA fraternity, Alamo Society, etc.). As a trusted friend of Frank's, Harry would also have forwarded Frank's cause with Bess Crutchfield.[29]

Having completed her second Southwestern degree in June, 1913, Bess took a job teaching school in Blossom, Texas. Paul Martin, who lived in Blossom at that time, was dating one of Bess's students, Mildred Fryar, whom he later married. Martin remembers that Frank Smith came to Blossom to see Bess at Christmas time.[30] Frank also remembered the occasion distinctly, because the Methodist preacher there invited him to preach, and Frank had never preached a sermon. Frank later explained why he had not preached before then: "I never went out and preached over the week-end as so many of my seminary mates did. I had nothing to preach about, and I was trying a build a foundation for my active ministry as I read and studied and thought and prayed."[31] Knowing that the pastor would not let him escape with such a flimsy excuse, Frank prepared to preach his first sermon. "I got together something in a history thesis I had written and something else, and that was the only, sermon I had."[32] Bishop Paul Martin remembers that Sunday in Blossom as a very special day: "Bess gave a violin solo, and Hallie played the accompaniment for her. And Frank's sermon was a wonderful message for a young man. The community was well pleased. We knew then that he had all the qualities of greatness."[33]

Shortly after Frank returned to Nashville, he went to see a motion picture entitled *From the Manger to the Cross*:

It was a magnificent portrayal of our Lord's earthly ministry. Immense crowds saw the picture. Men and women wept during the passion and suffering of our Lord. I was struck with the appearance of a policeman who, with his 18 year old son & 15 yr. old daughter, was viewing the film. They were so intensely interested, he eagerly explaining every scene, that I watched them throughout the entire picture, almost 1½ hrs. I was deeply impressed with his deep interest & I felt that here was a devout Christian.[34]

Six weeks later Frank recognized the policeman's face in a Nashville newspaper. Officer Wright had been killed while involved in special training. From the article Frank learned that Wright had been an active member in one of the Nashville suburban churches.

His funeral attracted a crowd not more than half of whom could get into the building. Some of the most prominent businessmen of the city attended.
    This proved I was right in my first estimation of his character. . . . My point is that the true Christian man's life among his fellows will speak for itself—just as did patrolman Wright's actions and face tell me volumes concerning him that day in the picture show.[35]

During the spring term, Frank's interest in observing the faces of people around him proved useful when he joined a group of other senior theologs in street preaching. Apparently this project grew out of the students' classroom work with Professor C. Detweiler.[36] Frank's student notebook indicates that Detweiler had two basic themes: (1) "True character is the character that has been thru the fire & come out triumphant." Strong character is developed by "rubbing up against the evils of this world, not by shunning them." (2) Only the preacher who "knows all about vice personally can cope with it. We must get right down into the midst of the evil. . . . We must go down into the depths and taste the very dregs of this world's misery & sin, not to take part in it, but to rub up against it & know what it really is." "An abstract sermon on sin will not amount to the paper it is written on," Detweiler declared, "but a sermon straight from the shoulder, one that deals with the facts, one that makes the offenders mad enough to tar and feather the preacher, that is the kind of sermon that will accomplish something."[37]

The most obvious place to "get right down into the midst of evil" in Nashville was in the slums through the street preaching project.[38] Frank's notebook contains two entries that illustrate his method of observing in these projects and then drawing conclusions based on his observations. In the first of these he wrote:

While taking part in a street service in the slums of Nashville with a group of fellow students, I stepped over and spoke to a young fellow at the end of the crowd, who seemed to be intensely interested. He told me that he had tried to live a Christian life all the year before, and that he still held family prayers. But he realized that he was not sincere in his life. . . . A woman had been responsible for his downfall and, he said, "I was working with three Holiness preachers, but I was so much better than they that I just lost my faith. I realize, however, that my faith should have been fixed on something higher than they, and I am going to make a new start."

From this incident Frank concluded that a hypocrite's influence is awful, "worse, of course, if he pretends to be a preacher, but an awful blighting, lowering sin in any case & under any circumstances."[39]

The second incident reveals Frank Smith's humility as well as a greater depth of insight. Again the setting is a street service in the slums of Nashville:

I noticed two women kneeling and looking out from a window in the upper story of the building before which we were holding the services. . . . These were prostitute women who had rooms there. As the services progressed they seemed intensely interested, and before long they were both weeping bitterly. One of them came down and gave her hand in prayer.

These women have souls no matter how low they may have fallen, and they are capable of being reached. But the conditions of our social life are such that they are forever outcasts & cannot leave their lives of sin when they would. The world has no place for such a character. This condition of affairs should be changed. We should give the woman of this character a place in the world if she wishes to reform her life. We preach to these women, but we have no relief to offer them when they want to change their mode of living.[40]

Not only did Frank give more space to his reflections in this account, but also he penetrated beyond the success of the moment to the harsh realities of the future for the repentant women.

Frank's insight into the interrelationship between individuals and their social environment brought him into harmony with the "social gospel" movement.[41] Dedicated to the reconstruction of society in accord with the ideal of the kingdom of God, this distinctive expression of Protestantism's social conscience grew out of the "conviction that the well-being of men required the transformation of the social environment as well as the changing of individuals."[42] While John Wesley had held a similar conviction almost two centuries earlier, not until the late nineteenth century did a unique combination of circumstances bring about this emphasis in American Methodism.[43] As Robert M. Miller has indicated, liberal theology was one of these necessary circumstances.[44] Both northern and southern Methodists played significant roles in the social gospel movement. Bishop Eugene Russell Hendrix of the Methodist Episcopal Church, South, was the first president of the Federal Council of Churches, an organization that symbolized the social gospel's successful penetration of American Protestantism.[45] The General Conference of the Methodist Episcopal Church adopted a "Social Creed" in 1908; the southern church followed in 1914. A number of Methodism's outstanding social gospel leaders were trained at Vanderbilt.[46]

When asked later in life if he had been a social gospel preacher, Frank Smith replied: "I certainly was a social gospeler to the point that I felt we ought to integrate the Christian spirit into everything that was done. I was a great admirer of that man Rauschenbusch.[47] He came into his heyday when I was in seminary. I certainly advocated and supported all social movements and causes that could arise."[48] Entries like the following in Frank's student notebook support his memory of having been an advocate of the social gospel:

If we would control a nation for Christ, we must secure control of the forces that direct that nation. We are not working simply to drag the man from the gutter, but to remove the gutter itself.

God's omnipotence is in it all. The time will come when race cleavages will be swept away and men, instead of being united as a nation, will be united as a Christian brotherhood over all the earth.

Our reward in heaven depends upon our activities among our fellow men for the causes of God. . . . It is the part of Christians to become active workers in the Kingdom, & not just sit down and shout "Hallelujah, I feel good."

As evidence that men are realizing that Christianity "is for every day of the week & not just for Sunday, that it is for every business man & not just for the preacher," Frank pointed to the "Men and Religion Forward Movement" along with the YMCA and the "Layman's Movement."[49] His mentioning the first movement is significant because historians of the social gospel agree that "the high tide of general Protestant interest in the social gospel probably came with the 'Men and Religion Forward Movement' of 1911-1912."[50] While he was a student at Vanderbilt, Frank heard two of the leaders of these movements, John R. Mott and Washington Gladden, speak in the university chapel. Mott was the general secretary of the World Student Christian Federation, secretary of the International Committee of the YMCA, and chairman of the executive committee of the Student Volunteer Movement. Frank took careful notes on Mott's sermon, "Alone with God."[51] Generally recognized as "the father of the social gospel," Washington Gladden was the principal speaker at Commencement in 1913.[52]

The record of Frank Smith's theological training gives evidence that Dean Wilbur Fisk Tillett and his dedicated faculty took seriously the goal which they had set for themselves:

The whole end proposed to be accomplished by the Biblical Department is to furnish the Church with ministers who, in addition to a sound Christian experience, humble piety, and consecration to God, are well instructed in the Scriptures, sound in doctrine, refined but simple in manners, earnest, direct, and plain in the presentation of the truth, and ready for any field to which the Church may assign them.[53]

By coincidence, the conclusion of Frank Smith's theological education at Vanderbilt University was paralleled by final steps in the so-called "Vanderbilt Controversy"[54] (of which the civil case mentioned earlier, which was in the Tennessee courts all during Frank's years at the university, formed a part). As Bishop Ivan Lee Holt later wrote: "In the long history of the Methodist Episcopal Church, South, no controversy has aroused such bitterness as the Vanderbilt controversy. In one form or another it came before the General Conferences of 1898, 1906, 1910, and 1914. From 1905 to 1914 it was the major issue before the church."[55]

On March 21, 1914, the Tennessee Supreme Court handed down its decision concerning the legal rights of the Methodist Episcopal Church,

South, with regard to the control of Vanderbilt. Contrary to popular opinion, as Dr. John O. Gross writes, "the question of the university's affiliation with the church was not the question the court was asked to decide."[56] The principal issues in the case as determined by the court were two: whether the General Conference had the right to elect the members of the board of trust of the university, and whether the College of Bishops had visitorial powers and the right to veto the actions of the board.[57] Denying that the bishops had visitorial or veto powers, the court ruled that the board of trust was self-perpetuating. The only direct link that the church had with the university was the charter's requirement that "membership on the board of trust was contingent upon confirmation by the General Conference or its agent, the General Board of Education."[58] As Frank Smith summarized the decision in retrospect:

The General Conference said, "We have the right to nominate." But the court said, "No, you haven't. You only have the right to confirm or to refuse to confirm the nominees of the Board." Well, the General Conference in 1914 just pulled out and quit. . . . The General Conference, not Vanderbilt, pulled out. We have got as much claim to Vanderbilt as we ever had.[59]

Frank Smith was not alone in this judgment. "By a majority of eleven votes," lamented Vanderbilt's President Henry Nelson Snyder, "Methodism tossed away in a fever of blinding emotionalism the richest opportunity for educational service ever given to an ecclesiastical body in the South."[60] John O. Gross concurs:

By refusing to accept the only relationship that it had ever possessed, namely, the right to determine membership on the board of trust, the church permitted the university to pass into the hands of a private corporation. . . . Until the [General Conference] closed the chapter on Vanderbilt University the institution was unmistakably and unabashedly Methodist.[61]

The loss of Vanderbilt University, however, did not spell total defeat for Methodist higher education in the South. In fact, the sequel to the Vanderbilt story was another chapter for that book Frank Smith wanted someone to write "about the ways in which things that were apparently disasters turned into triumphs."[62] That sequel was the story of Southern Methodist University and of Emory University. While the General Conference (Oklahoma City, 1914) was still considering its relationship to Vanderbilt, many delegates began pushing for the creation of two new universities, one east of the Mississippi and one to the west. Before adjourning, the conference created a commission empowered to establish "an institution or institutions" with university status.[63]

Chartered in 1911 by the five annual conferences in Texas, Southern Methodist University extended its patron conferences in 1913 to include the two Oklahoma conferences and the New Mexico Conference. The action of the General Conference in 1914 opened the way for much greater expansion. On July 16, less than two months after the adjournment of the General Conference, the Educational Commission adopted Southern Methodist University "as the university west of the Mississippi River."[64] In the same month Asa Candler, brother of Bishop Warren A. Candler, offered a million dollars toward the establishment of a university in Atlanta, Georgia. Emory College in Atlanta was made the liberal arts division of the new Emory University. In a remarkably short time, the Educational Commission had—in Bishop Candler's words— "more than repaired the loss of Vanderbilt."[65]

When the candidates for degrees, faculty, and members of the board of trust gathered at Wesley Hall for the procession to the university chapel for Commencement in June, 1914, Frank Smith was not among the students in the graduating class. As he later explained,

I had an acute attack of appendicitis. I hadn't written my thesis, and I didn't take the final examination in one two-hour course. My trouble came at just that time. I was engaged to be married on the sixteenth day of June, and I already had my appointment. So I just pulled out, figuring I would get those two credits later. But I never got my degree. [66]

When Bess Crutchfield graduated from Southwestern University in June, 1913, one of her classmates wrote the following sketch of her: "Long ago it was predicted that Bess would make a name on the stage as a violinist, but now Bess is quite 'Frank' in saying that she is going home to be trained in the gentle art of domesticity. She would make a good preacher's wife for she *is* a 'good girl.' "[67] Bess Crutchfield never regretted her decision in choosing "domesticity" over a career as a violinist. Looking back over forty-seven years of marriage, she could think of only one change she would have made: "If I had it to do over again, I don't think I would want to be engaged for so many years." Sharing in this retrospection, Frank reminded Bess that they had had no choice in the matter: "That's all we could do. This matter of subsidizing your children and letting them get married early just hadn't come into vogue then. We had to wait until I got out of school and got a job." With a chuckle, the Bishop quickly added, "I wish it had; maybe we missed out on something."[68]

In late October or early November of 1913, Frank Smith wrote to Mr. Crutchfield asking for his permission to marry Bess. Mr. Crutchfield's reply is dated November 7, 1913:

Your letter was received yesterday—asking for Bess' hand in marriage. I will not say that I was surprised at its contents. . . . Yes, both wife and I are willing to give Bess' happiness into your keeping. And there is no one else that we would be so willing to trust her to. . . . Bess has a happy disposition and I am sure will make a loving wife and companion. Be kind to her always, and you can be sure of our love and blessing.[69]

By June, 1914, Frank was assured of an appointment and had completed his years in school.[70] The wedding date was set, and "at high noon" on Tuesday, June 16, 1914, A. Frank Smith and Bess Patience Crutchfield were united in marriage by Dr. John R. Allen in the First Methodist Church in Georgetown.[71] Hallie Crutchfield was maid of honor, and Angie Smith was best man. Bess's father had come down from Hope, Arkansas, to give his daughter in marriage. Harry Hughes, Frank's roommate at Vanderbilt and former fraternity brother at Southwestern, was also in the wedding party.[72] "Rev. and Mrs. Smith were expected to leave on the 1 o'clock northbound M. K. & T. train," according to a newspaper report, "but instead they slipped away from the crowd and in Mr. [Sawnie] Aldredge's touring car made the trip overland to Austin, where they took the train for Elgin."[73]

4

A Traveling Deacon: 1914-1916

"IF YOU HAVE AN APPOINTMENT of any sort, I would like to have it," wrote Frank Smith, finishing his last letter to the presiding elders on his list. As he later explained his state of mind: "About two months before school was out, I wrote to all the bishops and presiding elders in the Southern Methodist Church. If I had gotten an offer from Oregon or Utah or somewhere the Southern Methodists didn't amount to a hoot-in-a-whirlwind, I would have gone. I didn't know the difference."[1] What Frank Smith did know was that most of the annual conferences of the Methodist Episcopal Church, South, met in the fall, and it would be difficult for him to get an appointment in June when he graduated from Vanderbilt University. The first reply came from Brother Moss Weaver at Anadarko, Oklahoma, which was the Kiowa trading post and headquarters for the Indian Agency. "He wrote that that place was open and would pay me a thousand dollars a year: It had a parsonage with a few pieces of furniture in it. And I accepted." No sooner was that hastily written acceptance in the mail than a letter came from Bishop Edwin D. Mouzon. The preacher at Alto, Texas, was being moved in the middle of the year to fill an opening in Oklahoma. The bishop wanted to send Frank to the Methodist church in this East Texas milling town, which paid a salary of $1,200. Frank had known Mouzon at Southwestern University: "Al-

59

though I had never taken courses from him, I sat in on some of his classes and knew him well. So I wanted to go right now, and I wrote to Brother Weaver." Weaver wrote back, saying: "I won't release you. You have given your word and a preacher's word is his bond. And I can't get another preacher. However, if you will get somebody to take your place, who will agree to come to Anadarko, I will release you." Fortunately, Frank was able to find a seminary classmate to take his place in Oklahoma.[2]

"We just loved Alto," Mrs. Smith recalled. "It was wonderful: the people were so kind to us."[3] One person stood out in the Smiths' memories of Alto—Fred Florence. Although he was Jewish by faith, Fred attended the Methodist services and was often a guest at the parsonage. On one occasion when Hallie Crutchfield was visiting her sister and Frank in Alto, she met Fred Florence. With a twinkle in her eye, Hallie remembers the incident: "Believe it or not, I had a date with Fred Florence. We cut across a vacant lot and went to a picture show. I think there were very few young men there at the time, and he probably offered to take me. Fred loved Frank just like a brother."[4] Frank considered Fred "as close a friend as I ever had, a dear cherished friend through the years."[5]

Bishop Angie Smith, who later became a close friend of Fred Florence's, remembers a humorous aspect of the relationship between Frank and Fred:

Fred was the banker at Alto. One day he came to Frank and suggested that Frank establish a credit rating by borrowing and paying back a sum of money. Frank replied that he didn't know of anything he needed. "Don't you need some new clothes? What about a nice dress for Bess?" "No," said Frank, "we have everything we need. Even the horse and buggy are paid for." Finally the banker asked, "Do you own a typewriter?" Of course, Frank didn't, so Fred let Frank borrow the money to buy a good typewriter. He wanted Frank to have a good rating.[6]

Evidence of that typewriter purchase can be found in Frank's student notebook, which he continued to keep after leaving Vanderbilt. Not long after the anecdotes switch from Nashville to Alto, the entries abruptly change from handwritten to typewritten.[7]

The young preacher's first appointment was not without its problems. The initial difficulty, one familiar to beginning preachers, was what to preach on his first Sunday. Not having preached any sermons during the spring term, Frank turned in desperation to the sermon he had prepared at Blossom the preceding Christmas. "That was my opening sermon," he recalled, "but I didn't have anything to preach that night." A hasty search through the parsonage turned up a few copies of the *Homiletic Review* left by the previous preacher. "I got one of these down. I had never seen one before. When I found out what it was, I got me a sermon for that night. I always seemed to be one jump ahead. I never had time for seed corn to develop and grow."[8]

Another problem arose when several church members in Alto severely criticized the pastor and his wife for playing dominoes in the parsonage. "I could have gotten bitter about that," Frank remembered, "and fought back in anger. But I always thought it wise to avoid an actual fight if possible. So we just pulled down the shades and kept on playing dominoes."[9]

The former pastor at Alto had been an expert gardener. "That was the first thing I heard when I went to Alto," Frank remembered:

People were always saying, "Oh, Brother Smith, you should have seen what a perfect garden Brother Armstrong had. He was a great gardener." Well, I wondered how in the world I was going to compete with that man. I didn't want to plant peas and onions. So I decided that I would plant corn right up against the fence, and that was all I planted, so nobody could see that I didn't have a garden.[10]

Fall was annual conference time in Texas in those days. As Frank explained:

The old bishops would come down—the same bishop held all the conferences . . . and start at the West Texas Conference and move with the cotton. Come across to the Texas Conference; it always met on Thanksgiving Day. Then they would go to the Central Texas Conference and finally wind up at the North Texas.[11]

As Alto was in the Texas Conference, Frank went to Bay City, where Bishop J. H. McCoy was to hold the conference. Bishop McCoy thought that Alto paid too high a salary for a beginner and decided that Frank would have to move.[12] Since the only opening in the Texas Conference was a circuit, Frank decided to try the North Texas Conference, where Dr. John R. Allen was a member. That conference met in Denison during the first week of December.[13] Received "on trial" as a probationary member by the North Texas Conference, Frank Smith formally

began his ministerial career, which would last for forty-six years. Transferring into North Texas at the same time were two men with whom
Frank would be closely associated, Sam R. Hay and Walter N. Vernon.
Fortunately for Frank and Bess, one of the presiding elders had known
Bess and her parents since the time when they lived in Cameron. Frank
recalled the way his first regular appointment was made: "When Brother
W. F. Bryan, my first presiding elder, saw that they had me down for
just a dive up on the Red River, he said, 'I'm not going to let that young
couple go up there. I will take them over to Detroit.' So we were appointed to the Detroit Circuit."[14]

In the meantime Bess Smith, completely unaware of any possibility
of their leaving Alto, had decided to visit relatives while Frank attended
annual conference. After spending a few days with her father in Arkansas,
she went to Georgetown to see her Uncle John and Aunt Molly (the
John R. Allens). Bess remembered the distressing experience clearly:

When I got to Georgetown, I had a telegram from Frank. "Meet me in
Palestine. We have to move." Of course, we hadn't any idea of moving. The
people wanted us, and even the Baptists in Alto petitioned to have us returned. So I cried and I cried, and I said, "I should never have married a
Methodist preacher. Here we thought we loved these people and they loved
us, and we are going to move." I met Frank at Palestine, and when we got
to Alto they were having Sunday School. Of course, they hadn't expected
to see us. When we told them, they all started crying, and we started crying,
and we were all griefstricken. But anyway, we moved.[15]

Life on the Detroit Circuit was not as comfortable or as easy as it had
been at Alto. The salary was supposed to have been $800, which was
$400 less than they had received at Alto, but they received only $500
during that year, 1914-15. War had broken out in Europe in August,
and the people of Red River County were soon short of cash. What they
couldn't pay in money, though, they gave in other ways. Explaining the
arrangement, Frank said: "I had my books put out to so much in cash.
They couldn't sell their cotton, and they had no money, but they more
than fed us enough. I was left with about forty cords of firewood, at
$2.00 a cord, and a barn full of hay and maize."[16] During the year Bess's
sister came for a visit, from which she remembers a "social call":

These old ladies would come, smoking pipes and spitting in the fireplace.
When they left, I said, "Bess, how in the world can you stand it?" And she
said, "Oh Hallie, you can get used to anything. You'd love all of them."

They would bring peanuts and sweet potatoes and that sort of thing instead of money. But Frank and Bess just took it in their stride, and they made some fast friends in that little town. Bess was just a wonderful preacher's wife, adjusting herself to every need and every requirement. Frank's work always came first in her mind.[17]

One thing to which Bess Smith never did adjust was the method of taking a bath. "We had a well on the back porch," she explained, "and we had to draw the water. We had to build a fire in the woodstove in the kitchen and bring in the tin tub, pour the hot water, and take a bath that way. Consequently, we didn't have too many."[18]

Being a preacher's wife in Detroit called for an unusual type of diplomacy. As Frank said, "It was a 'Firm Foundation' kind of community, so they wouldn't allow a piano in the church. That would be too worldly." Some of the young people in the choir discovered that Mrs. Smith played the violin, and they begged her to play for them. Impressed with her musical ability, they soon elected her choir director. Bess remembered, "I couldn't carry a tune, so I told them that I was sorry but I couldn't direct their choir. Then I asked them if it would help any if I would lead with my violin. They thought it would. Well, I broke up nearly every violin string in that part of Texas trying to tune up my violin to that little old reed organ, it was so high pitched." It wasn't long before some of the men in the church "waited on" their pastor. They asked that Mrs. Smith please not play her violin in church any more, insisting that "the fiddle was the devil's instrument."[19]

How was Frank Smith's homiletical skill developing? A visitor to Detroit in May, 1915, wrote the following sketch of the young pastor:

We worshipped in the morning at the Methodist Church. The pastor, Rev. A. Frank Smith, preached. The whole discourse moved on a high plane of thinking. It had power; it had light; it had driving force; it was absolutely pleasing in its simplicity. . . . He compels attention. His countenance draws you. . . . His voice is of much softness, and yet of penetrating quality. . . . He has excellent preaching gifts, and it may not be too much to say that greater things may be expected from him in the years to come.[20]

Of all the Smiths' memories of Detroit, the most cherished was the birth of their first child, Angie Frank, Jr., on November 3, 1915. The first weeks of his life, however, brought restless nights and hours of frustrating anguish to Frank and Bess. The baby cried constantly, and nothing comforted him for long. Detroit's only medical care came from the widow of a country doctor. Her diagnosis was that the baby had colic, and she gave him a patent medicine called Peewee's, containing laudanum. This brought some relief.

The first week in December Frank had to attend his annual conference meeting in Bonham. While he was away, he left Bess and Frank, Jr. in Blossom with Bess's Aunt Rena, Mrs. H. E. Black.[21] Frank's presiding elder, Brother W. F. Bryan, had written that he had a nice appointment worked out for Frank at Ladonia. Since Ladonia was not far from Bonham, Frank left home early enough to make a quick inspection of his proposed appointment before going on to Bonham. "I got on the train," he remembered, "and went up to see Ladonia. It was a lovely church, with a dome up there. And they were going to pay $100 a month. I was delighted."[22] When Frank arrived in Bonham, however, he was called home. Frank, Jr. was much worse and Bess was afraid he was dying. By the time Frank could get to Blossom, the doctor there had discovered the original cause of the baby's troubles: he was tongue-tied and could not nurse properly. Not only was the baby starving to death; his stomach had also been badly burned by the medicine. Correcting the initial problem was relatively simple, but the burned stomach would require months to heal.[23]

Relieved that his baby son was finally receiving proper treatment, Frank Smith returned to Bonham. Now, however, there was disappointing news at the annual conference. Brother Bryan's plans had gone awry, and Frank would not be preaching in that lovely church "with the dome up there." Instead, Bishop McCoy was appointing him to Forest Avenue in Dallas. Some months earlier, when Brother Bryan had visited the Smiths in Detroit, he had asked Bess where she would like to go for their next appointment. "I don't care, Brother Bryan," she had replied, "just so it has a bathtub."[24] But the church on Forest Avenue did not even have a parsonage. Frank remembered his reaction:

Forest Avenue was a little wooden type [church] set at an angle over a mud hole on an unpaved street behind the fairgrounds. This fellow told me, "We're not going to move from here. If we move over on a paved street, people are going to drive up in automobiles and they will run us working-folks out. We are going to stay right here on this mud hole where they can't bother us." Since they had no parsonage, they had asked for a single man. . . . And they were going to send me to that.[25]

Before the North Texas Conference adjourned its session in Bonham,

Frank Smith was elected to deacon's orders and ordained by Bishop James H. McCoy. His election occurred on the second day of the conference, Thursday morning, December 2, 1915.[26] Since Frank had only been admitted on trial the year before, he was not eligible for deacon's orders as a traveling preacher. As a local preacher for five years, however, he was eligible for ordination as a local deacon.[27] Bishop McCoy held the ordination service on Sunday morning, December 5, after preaching to "an immense congregation."[28]

"I didn't want to go to Forest Avenue," Frank admitted. "But I went on and found a room for us with one of the members."[29] The move to Dallas did offer certain benefits. Since the new school of theology at Southern Methodist University had opened that fall, Frank could complete the course work left unfinished at Vanderbilt. To make the trip to the campus more convenient, Frank bought a bicycle and became a commuting student-pastor. This relationship to SMU also enabled Frank to renew many old friendships. Harry Hughes had married his Southwestern sweetheart, Eldora Meachum, and transferred to the new seminary.[30] There were six former Southwestern professors at SMU. Dr. Robert S. Hyer had come as president of the new university; Bishop Mouzon was acting dean of the School of Theology, and Frank Seay and Frank Reedy were teaching on that faculty; John H. McGinnis and John H. Reedy taught in the College of Liberal Arts.[31] Umphrey Lee, now in SMU's graduate school, was president of the student body;[32] and Paul Martin from Blossom was a freshman.[33]

Of far greater importance to Frank and Bess Smith, the move to Dallas may have saved the life of Frank, Jr. Although he was now able to nurse normally, his stomach continued to reject food because of the medicine burns. Having lost four pounds since birth, he now weighed only five pounds. Through Frank's friends at the university Dr. Minnie L. Maffitt, the medical director for women at SMU, heard of the baby's condition. Frank remembered that Dr. Maffitt

made up a prescription to give him every two hours, a mixture of three ounces of milk to twenty-seven ounces of water. That was just enough to sustain life, and that is all he could hold on his stomach. That medicine had taken the lining out of his stomach, and he would just throw milk right back up.[34]

Hallie, Bess's sister, recalls that Dr. Maffitt "literally used to come over there and fix his formula and give it to him to see his reaction. And she would take him three times a day to weigh him on the post office scales in Dallas Hall. She brought him through, and Bess gave her all the credit."[35]

After Frank Smith preached his first sermon at Forest Avenue Methodist Church on Sunday morning, December 13, 1915, the *Dallas Morning News* devoted sixteen column inches to the sermon under quarter-inch headlines: "REV. A. FRANK SMITH BEGINS NEW PASTORATE." Drawing upon I John 1:3-4 as his text,[36] the new pastor said, in part:

John tells of what he heard and saw; it was no matter of speculation with him, no process of abstract reasoning and argument by which he sought to prove the existence of Christ to his hearers. He simply tells his experience, relying wholly upon this to achieve the end desired. John assumes that Christianity appeals to the heart directly. To him knowledge is . . . the heart's inner certitude respecting that which satisfies its longings and hopes. John believes that this knowledge, which alone brings us into conscious possession of salvation, comes only through experience. . . . We may share this fellowship only through knowing Christ as the apostle knew him. And again, that if we do so know him, our fellowship is the same as that enjoyed by John, who even leaned upon his breast and talked with him after his resurrection. Wonderful, wonderful conception—that we of this twentieth century may know and possess such divine communion with our Lord! The Christian spirit knows no time limits, no racial distinctions; wherever and whenever men find him they have that divine fellowship in Christ. . . .

This fellowship appeals to all men in every walk of life. It may demand one thing of you and just the opposite of me, but in each of us must be the spirit of complete concentration and obedience to God's will.

John wrote that his joy might be complete. Aptly it is said that every Christian is a missionary. There is something within the converted man that compels him to take the message to others. Until John had done his best to reach all who might be reached his joy could not be complete. And neither can your Christian joy nor mine be complete until you and I have done everything within our power to reach those who might be reached.

May our mutual prayer and reconsecration pledge be found in those sweet lines: "O, Jesus, I have promised to serve thee to the end. . . ."[37]

This sermon shows the young preacher endeavoring to open the Word of God to his people. Beginning with his text, he seeks to explain the meaning in relation to its immediate context. He has matured considerably since that first Sunday in Alto.

In late January or early February of 1916, Frank Smith was appointed to a new Methodist congregation known as the University Church, meeting on the third floor of Dallas Hall at SMU for its Sunday services. The exact date is clouded by conflicting accounts. According to Frank Smith, writing forty years later, "In early February of 1916 a church was organized at the University, and I was made the pastor. Bess and I at once moved to the Campus, and lived in Rankin Hall."[38] An earlier date is given by Ivan Lee Holt, then serving as university chaplain, chairman of the School of Theology faculty, and professor of Hebrew and Old Testament interpretation.[39] In an article written for the *Texas Christian Advocate* (April 27, 1916) Holt stated:

The question of Church membership for our students and actual training of them in religious work in a Methodist Church organization seemed to those who were most interested such important matters that we finally decided to ask the presiding elder of the Dallas District to form a church organization. On the evening of January 28, such an organization was formed, after a sermon by Bishop Mouzon. Reverend A. Frank Smith was transferred from the Forest Avenue Church to be the first pastor of the University Church.[40]

This appointment brought an end to Frank's formal theological education. As he later explained, "Because we did not want the new church to seem to be a student appointment, Dr. Hyer and I thought it best for me to drop my courses, so that I might be the pastor of the church and not be a member of the student body. Therefore, I was in class only six weeks, did not complete a course and received no credit."[41]

Frank Smith's first sermon to his new university congregation on Sunday, February 13, made a profound impression on the students and faculty. "The new pastor is a university man and a finished orator and has a wonderful personality," said the account in the student newspaper. "He is sure to be a powerful factor in molding aright the religious life of the university. No university audience ever listened more attentively to a sermon than Sunday's audience listened to the words of Rev. Smith, and the sermon he preached was wonderfully adapted to the persons to whom he spoke."[42]

After speaking to rural or small town parishioners for a year and a half, the young preacher faced a unique challenge in preaching to an academic congregation. Not only was he facing a much younger and more intellectual audience, but he was also speaking to his former professors. What kind of sermon would be appropriate? Excerpts from this sermon published in the *Campus* offer an opportunity for comparison with Frank's earlier sermon. Pointing to the "Sermon on the Mount" as "a perfect message in the hands of a perfect messenger," Frank preached on "The Man with a Message":

Before a message will bear fruit or mean the most to the world there must be a direct need which the message must satisfy. The successful man is the one who shapes his life to meet the needs which will arise. The great men in the history of the world are those who have realized the needs of life and have grasped them. . . . The Old Testament itself is the story of the unfolding of universal need and the acceptance of this need by great characters led and inspired by God. Abraham was led by the vision of a need from the rest and peace of a happy settled life to the hardships and toil of a journey into an unknown land. Only such a vision could have led to such a sacrifice. . . .

The living and burning question with us is how are we meeting the needs of our everyday life. The message that fits itself to time and place is the message of power. Often, however, the spoken word is not the most powerful or the most effective message that can be delivered by man. Alone the message is useless. The life must back it every minute and every day. . . .

In life a man must choose the ideal and the life through which that ideal can best be reached and expressed. God calls men to law or to any other profession or vocation just as truly as he calls men to preach his word. Consecrate the life first to the ideal and truly choose the means of expressing this ideal, and a man's life is then shaped aright. . . .

We are reminded of the essentials of a good messenger. The messenger must be a pioneer. He must be the man who blazes the trail into an unknown country and one who leads his fellow man. Necessarily he must be ahead of his time. . . . The very fact that he is to be ahead of his time is a guarantee that he will be misunderstood. Often we have misunderstood a man only later to find that we love and prize that most of all which first we could not understand.

Man does not rise to an occasion. If he meets an occasion nobly and well it is because he had been living ready to meet the occasion. The messenger must have a vision. Abraham, Wesley, Luther or Christ would have been impossible without a vision. We of today must have the worldwide vision. This is necessary if we are to be of aid to our brother here and across the water. Our message must be from God, through us to men. Then our words will not be in vain.[43]

This sermon, changing from the biblical exposure previously emphasized to a more topical approach, presents Jesus as the ideal or example to be followed rather than as the Savior. The contrasts between faith and knowledge, between experienced reality and abstract reasoning, are replaced by an emphasis on man's need for a vision. Instead of a balanced affirmation or an interrelation of the two facets of evangelical liberalism, Smith's sermon is a move toward unfettered liberalism.

If a preaching service does not satisfy the requirements for formal existence, surely a quarterly conference marks the official reality of a

Methodist church. Dr. O. F. Sensabaugh, who was then the presiding
elder of the Dallas District, recalled the occasion: "We organized the
church in February following the opening of school. In a short time I
held the First Quarterly Conference with A. Frank Smith as pastor.
Sunday School Superintendent, Stewards and Trustees were elected, and
University Methodist Church was chosen as the name."[44] This historic
"First Quarterly Conference" was held on Monday night, February 21,
1916. In his report as pastor, Frank Smith noted that the list of charter
members already included 134 names. Since fifty or sixty persons who
intended to become charter members were yet to be received, the list was
being held open. Several of Frank's friends, former faculty and staff at
Southwstern University, were elected to offices in the new church. Frank
Reedy, who had been bursar at Southwestern, was elected Sunday school
superintendent and district steward. Frank's former English professor,
John McGinnis, was chosen assistant Sunday school superintendent and
secretary of the board of stewards.[45] President Hyer was also named to
the board of stewards,[46] and Umphrey Lee was one of the student assistant superintendents of the Sunday school.[47] Frank always attributed his
appointment to the University Church to the men he had known at
Southwestern University: "They all knew me: Dr. Hyer and John Mc-
Ginnis and Frank Seay and a half dozen of them that had come up from
Georgetown. They were going to have a student church and pay $100
a month. And they said, 'Let's get Frank Smith.' "[48]

In later years Smith enjoyed telling this story about Dr. Hyer:

Robert Stewart Hyer was a very remarkable man and a great scientist. Very
austere with a Van Dyke beard, he would walk around and smoke cigars in a
very dignified fashion. We called him "King Bob"—smoked cigars all of
the time. But when the General Conference of 1914 passed the provision
that preachers should agree to abstain from smoking, Dr. Hyer quit. As he
told me later, "I teach young preachers. If they can't smoke, I ought not to
smoke to set an example." When he resigned as President of S.M.U. in 1920
and gave full-time to his chair in Physics, however, he went out that very
day and bought himself a box of cigars.[49]

The young University Church pastor was on the front page of the
campus newspaper again in March: "A. Frank Smith preaches a great
sermon." Praised for having "already won a place in the hearts and
lives of the students," Smith was also commended for drawing a large
congregation on a "between-terms Sunday." The student reporter took
obvious delight in pointing out that the Dallas presiding elder had "not

permitted" visiting Bishop E. E. Hoss to preach that Sunday for fear
of an embarrassingly small attendance. Characterized as a sermon of
"a young man to young people, inspiring and helpful," Smith's message
dealt with the difficult text, "It is through chastening that ye endure."[50]

It is through chastening that the characters and best qualities in the lives of
men are tested and developed. But to the youthful person the idea of chastening is a repugnant one. . . . But chastening means more than mere trial.
There is a deeper significance. Traced to the Greek, the word also means
"to instruct." Then instruction and education have part in the chastening
process. . . . To be really educated one must pattern his life after some great
life and must be a student of some great principles. Jesus Christ is the great
life after which we may all pattern [our lives], and his teachings are the
words of eternal life which should become the educational principles in the
lives of young and old.[51]

In April recognition of the ministry performed by Frank Smith and
his newly organized congregation had spread to the pages of the *Texas
Christian Advocate.* "Texas Methodism is aware that University Church
is now an efficient organization," the editor affirmed,

with about two hundred members and active in all departments. . . . Rev. A.
Frank Smith, well known throughout Texas as one of the most prominent
young preachers of our Church, was made pastor and, with the assistance
of members of the Theological Department, is doing all that could possibly
be asked. . . . Great enthusiasm and zeal is [*sic*] being shown by the young
people.

The new church had even begun revival services under the leadership of
Dr. Paul Kern and Bishop Edwin D. Mouzon.[52]

To the watchful eye of the Dallas presiding elder, however, the
University Park area was not developing as rapidly as expected. Neigh-
boring Highland Park was expanding, and "leading Methodist families"
were locating there in large numbers. Sensabaugh saw that "something
must be done to give proper strength to the University Church." Submitting his plan to Bishop Mouzon and President Hyer, Sensabaugh
suggested that "the name of the church should be changed to Highland
Park Methodist Church and [either] a lot secured from the University
or one very near the southwest corner" of the campus. Encouraged at
this high level, the energetic elder then obtained the cooperation of Dr.
and Mrs. R. W. Baird, influential residents of Highland Park. While the
Bairds invited representatives of every Methodist family in that section,

Sensabaugh urged officials of the university to share in a meeting of interested persons at the Bairds' home "to talk over the matter fully." As Sensabaugh tells the story,

When we arrived, the room was crowded. I asked the Bishop [Mouzon] to lead us in prayer and preside. I then fully stated my plans and asked for a full and free discussion. After everyone present had an opportunity to speak, a vote was taken. By a large majority it was decided to make the change of name and proceed at once to secure a location either on the southwest corner of the campus or a lot near that place and proceed in the erection of a building that would temporarily house a congregation.[53]

Since the site "on the southwest corner of the campus" was part of the original one hundred acres given to SMU by Mrs. Alice T. Armstrong,[54] the trustees were not free to deed this property to the University/Highland Park Church. When President R. S. Hyer and Pastor A. Frank Smith explained the situation to Mrs. Armstrong, however, she readily agreed to release the land for the new church building.[55]

Even with the gift of land the proposed church would need substantial assistance to build the required facilities. Anticipating this necessity, Sensabaugh had already drawn up a comprehensive plan involving two other Dallas Methodist churches. Changes in downtown Dallas were making the location of First Methodist Church increasingly untenable. Since the most promising area for relocation was too near the prospering Trinity Methodist Church, and a simple merger of the two congregations would vacate the strategic downtown area Sensabaugh proposed a three-way merger that would produce two new churches. After conferring with the pastors of the three churches, Sensabaugh organized each quarterly conference to discuss the merger. Bishop Mouzon, invited by Sensabaugh with the concurrence of Bishop McCoy,[56] explained the situation to each conference "in a masterful way, as was his custom." Sensabaugh then "put the vote in each conference. There was a total vote of seventy-six: seventy for and six against."[57] Frank Smith described the arrangement:

Our little church on the campus . . . was merged in May 1916 with First Church, on Commerce St., and Trinity Church, on McKinney. Out of the merger came a new First Church, which used the old Trinity building for several years (while a new sanctuary was built on Ross Ave.), and Highland Park Church; the University Church and Trinity Church passed out of existence. I became the pastor of the Highland Park Church.[58]

According to a newspaper report, "The new First Church has made a substantial donation toward a . . . building for the University Church. A lot 210 x 210 feet has been secured for the University Church and a magnificent structure will be built there."[59] In the meantime, Burgin and Hay continued as pastors of their respective churches until Annual Conference met in November. This situation caused some confusion, for as late as September 4 Dr. Sam Hay was still making explanations to his board of stewards at First Methodist Church, as their minutes indicate:

Dr. Hay explained the status of this church since the union of First, Trinity and University churches. He said 1st Church was on a circuit composed of these 3 churches, with Dr. Burgin as Preach [sic] in charge, and Dr. Hay and Rev. Mr. Smith as Junior Preachers & this condition would continue until Annual Conference in November, each Church on a circuit having its own Board of Stewards. A new Board of Trustees has been elected by the combined Quarterly Conference, and all property of the three churches is now under the charge of this new Board of Trustees.[60]

When the North Texas Conference met in November, Burgin would become the pastor of the new First Methodist Church and Hay would be appointed the presiding elder of the Dallas District, succeeding Dr. Sensabaugh.[61]

With the close of the academic year 1915-16 and the coming of summer, Frank Smith "lost" the majority of his congregation at the University Church as the students went their respective ways until September. Doris Miller Johnson sketched the campus summer scene: "Once more the wild grasses grew shoulder high. Pedestrians shunned the walks and took to the middle of the streets that led to the university to avoid the leaning Johnson grass stalks. . . . With every stir of wind, a cloud of grasshoppers shifted from one weed patch to another. The area was still repeating the rural sounds of its farm origin."[62] Frank Smith and Bishop Mouzon crossed the area between Atkins Hall and Dallas Hall. Recalling that moment in later years, Frank said: "I remember Bishop Mouzon standing there and waving his hand over the Johnson grass out there and saying, 'Frank, our young preachers like you won't have to go east of the river now to get their theological training.' "[63] To recruit these young men as well as to boost Smith's salary during the lean summer months, Bishop Mouzon asked him to serve on the School of Theology staff.[64] Formal announcement was made in the *Texas Christian Advocate*:

During the summer months Rev. Frank Smith, pastor of the University Church, will act as Secretary of the faculty of the School of Theology. All letters of inquiry should be addressed to him by prospective students of this department. He will remain at the Univerity during the entire summer and will be pleased to answer all letters touching the terms and courses of next year's work. Brother Smith himself is a graduate in theology. We congratulate the faculty upon securing the services of so competent a man.[65]

Frank's description of the job was more colorful: "They gave me one hundred dollars a month during the summer to drum up students for the School of Theology. Bob Goodloe was my secretary. He knew how to work a typewriter, and we got off pretty well."[66]

When the SMU catalog for 1916-17 was published in June, 1916, Frank Smith was listed among the "University Faculty" as "University Pastor and Special Lecturer and Instructor in Religious Education." He was also included in the School of Theology faculty as "Special Lecturer and Instructor in Religious Efficiency, 1916-17."[67] Did Smith actually receive a faculty appointment and teach classes at SMU? There is no mention of this in any of his letters and papers. Any such plan was apparently nullified by Dr. Sensabaugh's proposal to expand the small University Church into the Highland Park Church, with its greater potential for growth in the rapidly developing Highland Park suburb of Dallas. Ordinarily such a fast-growing church would not be entrusted to so inexperienced a minister.

In late July Frank himself raised the question of his replacement as pastor of Highland Park Church with Bishop Mouzon and Frank Reedy, the bursar at SMU. Reedy explained the situation in a letter to Mouzon:

Smith has been a wonderful success out here. As you say, he has acted with a veteran's sagacity, and the spirit of leadership he has shown, even among these professors, is remarkable. Frankly, I have found more ability in him than I expected, and I never knew how I loved him until we have worked together through these delicate months.

Of course, I cannot expect anything else than that some more experienced man will be assigned to the University charge, and therefore expect Brother Smith to be given other work, but I believe that every official of the University would join me in a statement that his services have been fully satisfactory and that it would be a great disappointment if his new appointment should not have all the signs of a genuine promotion. Smith has led us through a very delicate period and with great skill.[68]

In September plans were being made that would bring about a significant change in Frank Smith's life, although he only learned of them later. Representing the University, Dr. Ivan Lee Holt, SMU's chaplain and chairman of the School of Theology faculty, was attending the Missouri Conference when he heard that Bishop Eugene R. Hendrix was looking for "the right man" to appoint to University City Church in St. Louis. A close friend of Bishop Hendrix's,[69] Holt himself had organized the University City Church ten years earlier. When the appropriate occasion arose, Dr. Holt recommended Frank Smith to Bishop Hendrix for that appointment. Thinking that Mouzon was Smith's bishop, Hendrix wrote to Mouzon asking him to release Frank Smith for the church in St. Louis.[70] Presumably, Bishop Mouzon forwarded Hendrix's letter to the bishop in charge of the North Texas Conference, James H. McCoy, and informed Holt of what had happened. On September 4, Dr. Holt replied to Bishop Mouzon:

Bishop Hendrix is very anxious for someone for University City. I note what you say about Frank Smith and there is not a doubt in my mind that something good will open up for him in Texas. I don't know of anything there that can possibly offer him the opportunity University City offers, and I knew he would meet the situation there. Hence my suggestion. Bishop Hendrix went so far as to ask me to write Frank and see whether he would come. But if it is your wish, I shall say nothing further to Frank about it. It is a splendid opportunity for him. Hope you have found your man for University Church, Austin.[71]

Holt's letter seems to be urging that Frank Smith be allowed to accept the University City Church appointment. Or is Holt subtly suggesting Smith for University Church, Austin? At any rate, Bishop Mouzon did appoint Frank Smith to the Austin church. According to Frank's later explanation, this appointment was due to "two ifs" getting together:

If Holt hadn't told Hendrix about me, and if Hendrix hadn't written to Mouzon asking for my release, I wouldn't have gone to University Church. [Smith believed] Mouzon had said, "If Hendrix is willing to take him to University City Church, St. Louis, I am willing to take him to University Church, Austin." And that is how it came about that I went to University Church, Austin.[72]

Even though Bishop Hendrix was the "Senior Bishop" in the College of Bishops of the Methodist Episcopal Church, South, it was Bishop Mouzon—and not Bishop Hendrix—who obtained Frank Smith's release from Bishop McCoy.[73] On Friday, October 20, 1916, Frank Smith was received by transfer from the North Texas Conference into the West Texas Conference, meeting in Uvalde, Texas.[74] The following morning, Bishop Mouzon read the historic question: "Who are admitted into full connection?" This solemn moment is related in the conference *Journal*:

The Bishop called to the Bar of the Conference those who were eligible for admission, having been two years on trial and having passed approved examinations. He addressed them with references to their privileges and duties, and propounded to them the disciplinary questions, which they answered satisfactorily. They were then admitted into full connection by vote of the Conference. They are: Milton Fly Hill, Harold S. Goodenough, George F. Harris, G. G. Smith, George Traylor Hester, and A. Frank Smith.[75]

The conference did not meet for business on Sunday but devoted the day to worship, with preaching services morning and night. The Committee on Public Worship received requests from the Protestant churches in Uvalde and assigned certain preachers to meet those requests. Frank Smith was assigned to the evening service at the Presbyterian Church. Having known Frank at Southwestern University, L. U. Spellman attended the Presbyterian service to hear his classmate preach. He remembers that evening vividly:

That morning Dr. C. W. Webdell, the pastor of Travis Park [the largest and most prestigious church in the conference] had preached there, orating and sprinkling stardust. Frank preached a rather short sermon, delivered in a quiet and modest manner. On the way back to the hotel where several were staying, Frank—a stranger and no doubt lonely—dropped in behind a group of the big boys. As he went along, he heard one of them say in a rather loud voice, "We had two services today. At one we had a great sermon and at the other a little prayer meeting talk." Frank told me about this years later after he was elected bishop. He joked about it, but I could still detect something of the pain it gave him at the time.[76]

Monday morning the conference was back at work. By tradition and requirement of the *Discipline* an annual conference performs the same tasks every year. One unusual item of business in 1916 had been sent down by the General Conference, a proposal that the conference lay leader and the district lay leaders become ex-officio members of the Annual Conference. The vote in the West Texas Conference was thirty in favor of the proposition and eighty-five opposed.[77] Since 1866 the Southern Methodists had permitted four lay delegates from each presiding elder's district "to be chosen in such manner as might be determined by each Annual Conference."[78] It was clear that the West Texas Conference still considered that number of lay delegates to be sufficient.[79]

At the close of the afternoon session, when Bishop Mouzon read the pastoral appointments for 1916-17, A. Frank Smith was appointed to the University Methodist Church in Austin, Texas. Under the headline "Rev. A. Frank Smith has fine record in work with students," the *Austin American* announced:

Rev. A. Frank Smith, new pastor of the University Methodist Church, comes to Austin from the University Church at Southern Methodist University at Dallas. He is a college bred man and has for the past six years been actively engaged in student work. Familiar as he is with the duties of an office which is calculated to form and mold the minds of some 800 Methodist college men and women, there is no doubt expressed but that he will make the University Church one of the best pastors that has ever served its congregation.[80]

5

A Time of Trial: University Methodist Church

IF THE PASTORATE of budding Highland Park Methodist Church on the Southern Methodist University campus had been a challenge to young Frank Smith, the responsibilities of being pastor to the thousand-member University Methodist Church in Austin staggered his imagination:

I was only twenty-six years old, two years out of the seminary, not yet an ordained elder, and I had been appointed to a well-established church with a congregation of over a thousand, composed of state officials, several justices of the higher courts, a former governor, deans and faculty members of rank, students and townspeople—a brilliant array of "eggheads" and "hoi polloi." And there I was, still wet behind the ears, green as a gourd.[1]

The difficulty of shepherding such a large and diverse congregation was vastly compounded by an extended and heated controversy created in large measure by the previous pastor, "Fightin' Bob" Shuler. According to Shuler, the issue was Prohibition. An ardent advocate of the anti-liquor crusade, Shuler demanded the unconditional support of this cause, especially of his church officials, as if zealous commitment to Prohibition were the sole mark of loyalty to the Methodist church. As members of the congregation explained the situation: "Anyone who didn't take an oath that he was a prohibitionist and so forth couldn't have any official

77

connection one way or the other. All of those who did not toe the line were just lopped off the Board. The church was split right down the middle."[2] Among those whom Shuler had alienated were former Governor Sayers; Judge Davidson, the chief justice of the Court of Criminal Appeals; Judge Rice, the chief justice of the court of civil appeals; and any number of college professors and others. Under these circumstances Frank Smith remembered:

My task was to bring harmony in place of dissension, to restore ousted leaders to official position, and to create an atmosphere, if possible, where the church could move forward. Mine was a task of trying to draw them together, and at the same time to try to escape being called a partisan of the "outs" that I was trying to bring back in.[4]

Having previously heard of the situation at University Methodist Church, Smith urged Bishop Mouzon not to send him there. "I did not want to go to University Church and begged the Bishop to send me to a small appointment where I could study and develop in normal fashion. But he was adamant, so I went."[5] Bishop Mouzon did not, however, leave Smith without his active support. Having served University Methodist Church some twenty years earlier, Mouzon still had a number of friends in that congregation. He wrote to them, urging that they return to their church and assist the newly appointed pastor in a combined effort at reconciliation. Unfortunately, Mouzon's well-intended efforts went awry. Recalling the experience years later still brought grief to Frank Smith:

Bob Shuler's crowd got hold of the fact that Mouzon had written, and they got the notion that I had been sent there to be partisan to that crowd and not to play ball with them. They just stood off and looked at me, and they said, "Now we pay the bills here, and that crowd quit." I remembered one woman that taught in the university. She looked me in the eye and said, "You are on trial here. You are just a kid and if you don't make good here, you are ruined for life. You are going to do as we say, or you are going to be branded." That's just how cold-blooded it was. And that is what I faced; it was agony of soul.[6]

Knowledge of the crisis at University Methodist Church soon spread across the state. People would stop Frank's father on the street and say to him: "Bishop Mouzon has ruined your son by sending him there to follow Bob Shuler in such a church."[7]

Yet it was in this critical situation that Frank Smith began to earn his reputation as a conciliator. His first opportunity came when Rev. Sterling Fisher, the presiding elder of the Austin District, presented him to his new congregation. As an Austin newspaper reported:

Rev. Mr. Smith expressed his appreciation of the opportunity for service in this pastorate. Referring to the University Methodist Church in Dallas, from which he came, he said: "I have left a great student body, a great church, and a great opportunity, but I feel that God has called me to a greater service here. I believe in prayer. If, in the beginning of this year, we will determine to use our common sense, and to have faith in prayer that God will add unto our store of it, no problem shall arise which we cannot solve. I expect to place my soul and life into this work, and you and I together shall win, and shall make this the greatest year we have known.[8]

That Frank Smith's desire to restore harmony to this divided congregation was warmly received is clear from the article's conclusion: "After the service, Mr. Smith was welcomed very heartily by the many members of his congregation." Bishop Mouzon wrote from Dallas: "You may be pleased to know that I received a very brotherly letter from Bob Shuler telling me that you had 'swept the decks.' I had also a good letter from Brother C. D. Rice, a very fine gentleman. I did not forget to pray for you the Sunday morning when you faced your new congregation. I rejoice that God was with you."[9]

A second opportunity for reconciliation came with an invitation to the office of former Governor Joseph D. Sayers. Both Sayers and John Summerfield Smith, Frank's paternal grandfather, had come to Texas in 1851 and had lived in Bastrop until the Civil War, when they served together in the Confederate Army. After serving as governor of Texas for two terms, 1898-1902, Sayers had remained in Austin and had been an active member of the University Methodist Church. Frank Smith recalled their conversation. Said Sayers:

Mr. Smith, I have called you down to my office to say to you that I would not sit under the preaching of a Methodist preacher who was not against the liquor traffic. I have been an anti-Prohibitionist from principle all my life, and I have never voted the Prohibition ticket. But I have never been under the influence of liquor in my life. Now Mr. Shuler says that he put me off the official board of his church because I was an anti-Prohibitionist. That is a lie. I quit Mr. Shuler because I did not approve of his antics. He would come up there on Sunday morning, having heard of some "carrying on" at a fraternity house the night before, and he would get up and call names and denounce them. One Sunday he got in a fight with the devil up there. He took off his coat, pitched it down on the pulpit seat, lay down on his stomach and stuck his neck over the edge [of the platform], shook his fist and dared the devil to come up and meet him. That is when I quit him. That is why I quit going to church, not because he left me off the board or anything else. But I want you to know that I can't respect you as a Methodist preacher unless you are for Prohibition.[10]

During that session with Sayers, Smith learned of a deeper cause of the conflict between Shuler and certain officers of the church. Before Shuler had come to Austin, he had been pastor of the Methodist Church in Temple, Texas, where he became friends with James E. Ferguson, a young lawyer-banker with political dreams.[11] After his appointment to University Methodist Church, Shuler wrote to Ferguson requesting a gift of $2,500 to install permanent pews in the galleries of the church. Shuler allegedly promised to attach plaques on the pews giving credit to Ferguson for his gift, thus supplying valuable publicity for future political campaigns. The gift was made and the pews were installed, giving the promised donor credit. With a chuckle Frank Smith recounted the ironical turn of events that followed:

Well, bless Pat, Ferguson up and announced for governor within a couple of years [1914] on an anti-Prohibition ticket. Shuler came out to the toenail against him, so Ferguson just published that letter about the pews. That blew Shuler straight up! He went to his board and demanded that they send Ferguson's $2,500 back to him. But the board members said, "We didn't ask for that gift, you did. He sent the money to you and the pews have been installed. It is not our obligation, and we are not going to return the $2,500." So Bob Shuler just began to throw them off the board right and left. Then these people made a plea to Bishop McCoy who was holding this conference to move Shuler, but McCoy wouldn't or couldn't move him. Fighting mad by then, Shuler came back that fourth year and just cleaned out that whole crowd.[12]

Although the Prohibition campaign was involved, the basic issue was the board's refusal to back Shuler in his fight with Ferguson. Shuler's opponents were not simply "wets."

That Frank Smith's diagnosis of the controversy was correct is confirmed by a statement that Shuler himself made to Smith on a later occasion. While in Austin to take part in a Prohibition rally, Shuler came to see Smith. As Smith remembered it, the conversation centered on Judge Steadman, formerly the chairman of the Board of Stewards of University Methodist Church, whom Shuler had forced to resign.

Bob Shuler said to me, "I hope you will put Judge Steadman back on your board. I deliberately insulted Judge Steadman. I slapped him in the face"—that's the way Shuler expressed it—"and compelled him to resign. He would not get off otherwise, and he said he would not support my policies. And no man can stay on my board unless he supports me. But Steadman is a good man, and I hope you will put him back on the board." And that was Bob's ticket: support him or resign![13]

By listening to the estranged members of the congregation, Frank Smith learned the nature of the forces that had divided his flock.

To restore harmony and unity among his parishioners, the young pastor sought to rebuild on the foundations of basic Christian doctrine. He had not forgotten the notation in his Vanderbilt notebook: "The only thing in existence that does not change is God's truth."[14] Through his weekly sermons, he proclaimed these eternal verities in forms understandable and compelling to his people. Preaching on Hebrews 3:14—"For we are made partakers unto the end"—he pointed out that this epistle "was written to those already converted, lest they should lapse into indifference." Rephrasing the text, he said: "If we hold the confidence with which we started, firm to the end, we shall see Christ."

Watch the trickle from a tiny spring as it drips from beneath a great rock and starts down the mountain side, a very small stream. You could easily dam it with your foot. But soon it is reinforced by other streams and growing ever larger, it furnishes power for the lights of great cities; it sends out irrigation streams and turns the wheels of many mills, giving employment to thousands of people. The ingenuity of man can no longer stem its tide as it flows out into the ocean. Then as vapor it is kissed up by the sun and falls again upon the land as refreshing rain. So in the Christian life, at first you are weak and uncertain; someone might have turned you aside very easily. But opportunity came to cast your vote on the right side; you had a chance to stand in the community for some good movement and as you grew you became rooted in right principles and actions. And, finally, your splendid strength has been kissed up by God's love to fall in showers of blessings upon all around you. No mature Christian can tell you how these things are done. They only know they have found Christ.[15]

On another occasion, Frank Smith preached about the call of every Christian to be a messenger for God.

Too commonly it is thought that the only people called of God are preachers and missionaries. Society can be revolutionized only when it is permeated with men and women who know that God has called them to the particular work which they are doing. In whatever the profession there is the opportunity of serving God. . . . Each of you has the privilege of choosing a profession. When you have found Christ's message for your life, establish an ideal and shape your life in accordance with it. . . . There can be no message without the realization of a need. Many of you here are students. We are all students in life. Education should bring to you a consciousness of the great world need, and should equip you to meet it. . . . There is need for a message which only you can give to the world. Do you feel that message? Are you in such close touch with Christ that you realize what message you are commissioned to give?[16]

"Three Characteristics of the Truly Christian Community" is the title of another sermon Frank Smith probably preached during this period. Only an indication of the text (Acts 21:5-6) and a bare outline have survived:

I. Christian Love and Fellowship
II. Realization of Divine Guidance
III. Complete Consecration of life to the Service of God.[17]

Even these three points indicate the preacher's effort to restore a God-centered fellowship as described in the Methodist ritual for church membership: "Brethren, the Church is of God, and will be preserved to the end of time, for the promotion of his worship and the due administration of his word and ordinances, the maintenance of Christian fellowship and discipline, the edification of believers, and the conversion of the world."[18]

On the other hand, Smith's efforts to revive unanimity among his people did not preclude his preaching on potentially controversial subjects. In words that could be applied to Shuler's revivalistic services, Smith declared:

I believe God looks down with disgust upon those who make a habit of "getting religion"—who make the profession of religion no more than walking down the aisle to shake hands with the preacher, or presenting themselves at the altar without the slightest intention of changing their lives. But my heart goes out to those earnest ones who fall three times a day, but rise and go on trying. My creed teaches that no matter how often you fall, you can try again. If we would pray for more grit and grace and leave off some of the emotion, we would be better Christians.[19]

As remembered by Mr. Hines H. Baker, who was a senior law student at the University of Texas in 1916-17, Frank Smith's "point of view was that you accomplish more with ease and smooth moving than you can by speaking out too strong. I suppose that's one reason they sent him to Austin to succeed Shuler."[20] Having attended Shuler's services at University Methodist Church as well as his Men's Sunday School Class at the YMCA, Baker capably compares the two ministers:

Frank Smith was altogether different from Bob Shuler. Shuler was a spectacular fellow that engaged in controversial preaching, a very positive fellow, a crusader. And I liked him. I didn't like some of the ways he did things, but I had to admire his courage and his forthright effort to meet the vices and evils of that day. Smith was an entirely different kind of preacher. He didn't seek out those issues. He preached on personal religious experience and the spiritual values that were to be derived from the relationship with God. Smith was above everything else interested in people and interested in their personal experience, the development of the best that they had in them. His ministry in the pulpit was directed that way.[21]

Speaking more specifically of Frank Smith's style of preaching, Mr. Baker remembers:

He was different from anything I'd ever heard before. He had a very attractive personality and a free and easy manner in the pulpit. That was one of the things that impressed me. He was not on fire in the sense of being a spell-binder or anything of that kind that you often found in the young preachers of that day. Even at his age then, he was philosophical and mature. He was a young man, only four or five years older than I, but to all appearances a much more mature man than his actual age would indicate. He was solid, his judgment was mature, his sermons marked him as a man of experience and knowledge, a spiritual person. I admired him greatly, enjoyed his sermons and appreciated his approach.[22]

Skilled and experienced in public speaking as he was, Frank Smith knew that preaching alone would not accomplish the reconciliation of his divided congregation. "I once heard an oration on 'The Magic of the Spoken Word,'" he told his parishioners, "and I thought that this was the greatest thing in life. But I have come to learn that the message lived is the most powerful and enduring of all."[23] In this area of personal relationships, the day-by-day living out of his Christian faith, the young pastor performed his most effective ministry. Singling out this characteristic of Frank Smith's, Mr. Baker recalls:

He had a tremendous interest in people. Usually he did something for the people he knew, and the fact that he did something for them made them real to him. Smith was a warm person, the kind of person who makes friends. He cultivated people, did things for them to show them his personal interest in them. A great many people were highly pleased with him after he was there a short while and became personally attached to him in a way that you could never quite become with Bob Shuler. You could become a militant with Shuler and enlist in his campaign, but they were different men, different in their motivation and in their thought processes. Smith appealed to the very best that was in you from the standpoint of doing things with and for people. His influence was the influence of a man you respected and admired and who gave you the definite feeling that he was personally interested in you. He was a fellow that people loved. I don't mean to say that he was "namby-pamby" or anything like that. He was vigorous, but he conducted himself in such a way that it was hard to get mad at him. He was a man of peace.[24]

Mr. Baker recalls one particular incident from the spring of 1917 as typical of Frank Smith's manner. By chance he met the pastor on the campus, just south of the University Methodist Church:

He spoke to me, he knew me, and he was, as always, very cordial and very much interested in knowing how I was getting along and what I was planning to do. He knew I was chairman of the Men's Council, for instance. It made me feel good to meet him on the campus, because he always had a cheerful word and he was interested in you and the things that you were interested in.[25]

Although Hines Baker made his initial profession of the Christian faith in Judge John C. Townes's Sunday school class at the University Baptist Church, he joined the University Methodist Church under A. Frank Smith. As Mr. Baker recalls that exciting and significant day in his life:

One Sunday morning in the spring of 1917, I made a confession of faith in Judge Townes's Sunday School Class, but I joined the church with Frank Smith that evening. Although a good part of my family were Baptists, including my brother Rex, I had been attending church services at University Methodist Church morning and evening with fair regularity. If I was going to be a church member, I wanted to be a Methodist. The Baptist pastor was hunting me all Sunday afternoon, but I evaded him and went to the Methodist Church and joined that church with Frank Smith.[26]

As Hines Baker moved up rapidly in the Humble Oil & Refining

Company in later years, eventually becoming its president in 1948, Bishop Smith publicly expressed with increasing pride the fact that he had taken Baker into the Methodist church. Although the bishop was famous for his remarkable memory, he forgot that he had not baptized the young law student, claiming on numerous occasions that Hines Baker was the first person he had baptized by immersion.[27] Although the bishop's account has become almost legendary, Mr. Baker describes how his baptism actually took place: "Bishop Smith told about baptizing me a number of times in churches or places where I was known, and he told about that experience in a very animated way. Actually, he was the one who was supposed to baptize me, but he caught a terrific cold. The occupant of the Bible Chair performed the ceremony."[28]

Another law student whom Frank Smith came to know that first year in Austin was Robert A. Shepherd, who later became a good friend in Houston. Mr. Shepherd remembers his impression of the young pastor of the University Methodist Church: "As I belonged to the Baptist Church at that time, I did not attend his church. A great many of my friends and classmates were Methodists, however, and I heard of Frank Smith frequently as an outstanding young minister and a friend and counsellor to the students who attended his services."[29]

Frank Smith especially enjoyed his relationships with the students who attended his Sunday school class, and he proudly followed the careers of these young men through the years. "I taught a class of Methodist students at ten o'clock in the University Y and then ran two blocks to the church for my eleven o'clock service," he recalled.

Some of my Sunday School boys became outstanding men. John Redditt, for instance, was a State Senator, Chairman of the Texas Highway Commission, and a member of the Board of Regents of the University of Texas. He has made a fortune in law and oil and is very active in the Methodist Church in Lufkin. Another was Lynn Landrum who became the "Columtator" of the *Dallas Morning News*. I totally disagreed with his usual views, but I never doubted his brilliance. Both of these men were in turn president of my class, and I could name many others who achieved success and became real churchmen.[30]

"Frank Smith's Sunday School Class was probably *the* Sunday School class of that time," John S. Redditt remembered. "We had over a hundred every Sunday. At that time the facilities at the University Methodist Church were very limited, and we had to go to the YMCA to find an auditorium large enough to handle this class." When asked about the particular appeal of Frank Smith's class, Mr. Redditt replied: "Well, he had a wonderful personality and knew how to get along with people. That was the greatest quality the man had, you know, and he was very well liked. And he made the class interesting. I enjoyed it very much." The fact that the class met in the YMCA made it easier for those not affiliated with any church to attend. "It was a Methodist class, but Smith didn't make it just Methodist. He had a tremendous appeal to all denominations." Looking back over his college days, Mr. Redditt praised three men who most influenced his life. "The Good Lord appointed some earthly angels to look after me: Judge Townes, the Dean of the Law School, Dr. Curry who directed the YMCA, and Frank Smith."[31]

While the pastor of University Methodist Church was striving to end conflict within his congregation, two controversies broke out that created new unrest in Austin, particularly for the two major groups of his church's membership: those related to the state government and those related to the University of Texas.

One center of contention was Governor James E. Ferguson. Soon after Ferguson's successful campaign for reelection in 1916, the state legislature began an investigation of persistent rumors of malfeasance circulating about the governor. Although Ferguson managed to evade this examination until the legislature adjourned, he immediately set off a new uproar by vetoing the biennial appropriation to the University of Texas. The governor was apparently striking back at the board of regents for its refusal to remove certain faculty members whom the governor found objectionable. Ferguson's opponents soon began efforts to impeach him. At least one member of Smith's congregation was directly involved in these proceedings: former Governor Joseph D. Sayers, who was one of the regents defying Ferguson. Could any member of such a congregation have avoided the turmoil surrounding the indictment of the governor by a Travis County Grand Jury in July and his impeachment by the House of Representatives in August, followed by the three-week trial before the Senate? Ferguson was not only removed from his office but was also barred forever from holding any other office of honor, trust, or profit in the state of Texas.[32]

The tensions created by World War I had been increasing each year of Frank Smith's ministry. Finally, on Good Friday morning, April 6, 1917, the United States Congress declared war on the German Empire. Many of the older students at the University of Texas rushed down to the recruitment office to volunteer for service in the United States Army. Mr. Hines Baker remembers the sudden zeal to sign up: "I remember that very well, because I was one of the first ones in, along with my brother Rex, George Petty and a number of other students from the law school. It became a very active thing during April and May."[33] For those who remained on the campus, officer training classes were begun as the university became the center of several military establishments. Even the University Methodist Church became involved in the war emergency training. "Since the University had no auditorium at that time," Smith explained, "university convocations and gatherings had been held frequently in the sanctuary of the University Church over the years. With the coming of the war, the sanctuary was in constant use with speakers from all over the world addressing the men in training."[34]

The impact of the war is reflected in Frank Smith's sermons as early as December, 1916.

As we pause this morning on this Christmas eve, let us take stock of ourselves. . . . As a people God has been singularly good to us. We can gather about our firesides in peace, with our loved ones near, and thank God for His goodness. Across the waters the third Christmas has dawned upon the greatest tragedy the world has ever seen, and literally millions of families will face this Christmas with the heart-breaking realization that the bread-winner of the family is occupying a grave "somewhere at the front." No American who thinks can enter into this season without a heart saddened and mellowed by the sorrows of the world all about us.[35]

In the Methodist tradition, the evaluation of the work of a minister and his church is carried out annually by the Fourth Quarterly Conference under the guidance of the presiding elder. Since the elected officials of the local church comprise this body, the Fourth Quarterly Conference is a formal type of self-study. The Reverend Sterling Fisher, the presiding elder of the Austin District, held such a conference at the University Methodist Church on Friday evening October 12, 1917, examining the first year of Frank Smith's pastoral leadership of that congregation. Financially, the grand total of expenditures had increased from $12,621 for the previous year to $15,711 for the year then ending.[36] One hundred and ninety new members had been added, including nineteen by profession of faith. Judge William E. Hawkins, associate justice of the Supreme Court of Texas, pleased with the reports of the year's work, moved that the secretary of the conference submit summaries of the reports for publication in the *Texas Christian Advocate* and the Austin newspapers. Included in that report was the following resolution which had been unanimously adopted:

Whereas, the conference year is now drawing to a close under the able leadership of our pastor, Rev. A. Frank Smith, the University Methodist Church is completing a year of successful work, in many respects one of the most successful in the Church's long history; and

Whereas, under the most trying circumstances of war, drouth, crop failures, University agitation, business depression and hard times generally, the work of the Church has gone bravely on, and the records of this year's work as reported in the Fourth Quarterly Conference show all reports up in full and in a most flattering condition; and

Whereas Brother Smith's labors among us have been blessed of God in that his preaching has found a ready response in the hearts of our members and his daily walk among us has been a source of inspiration and a help to us all, so that Brother Smith and his estimable wife have endeared themselves to us, and we desire their return; and

Whereas, in the year's labors our pastor has been ably seconded by our efficient and consecrated presiding elder, Rev. Sterling Fisher; now, therefore be it

Resolved, by the Fourth Quarterly Conference of University Methodist Church that we hereby express our appreciation and love for Brother Smith and Brother Fisher, and our utmost confidence in them, and we hereby memorialize the Bishop and his advisors and the Annual Conference to return to us for another year both Brother Smith and Brother Fisher to their respective places as pastor and presiding elder.

[Signed:] Robert E. Cofer, N. A. Rector, R. C. Lomax, Committee[37]

The young pastor also received high praises from his bishop during the meeting of the West Texas Conference in Corpus Christi the following week, according to an Austin paper.

When Mr. Smith gave the annual report of the University Methodist Church, Bishop Edwin D. Mouzon stated that it was the best report that had ever been given during any session. The work of his church is looked upon by Southern Methodism as the most important work in the conference and in the State. . . . Smith is considered by Bishop Mouzon to be one of the greatest leaders of young people in the Methodist ministry.[38]

Looking back on that first year in Austin, Frank Smith was not so enthusiastic about his success.

Somewhere in the Scripture, it says: "The Lord preserves the simple." I guess

the Lord watched over me, because I got by and had a good year. We went
on into our second year and we were getting along all right, except I felt
just like I was being par-boiled all the time. I got "gun-shy." If I was away
from home and got a telegram, I just knew something terrible had happened.
Every time I saw a Western Union boy, I would jump behind a telephone
post. I was so conscious of trying to hold things together.[39]

It was a new experience for Frank Smith to be reappointed to a
church. "I had five different appointments the first two years of my
ministry," he recalled.

I was always just one jump ahead. Engulfed in administrative work, I had
no time for seed corn to develop and grow. I never learned to sermonize;
I was just pitched out and had to learn to swim, and yet knowing that I was
going to preach next Sunday to college professors and Supreme Court Justices and so forth.[41]

Early in their second year in Austin, on January 30, 1918, Frank
and Bess's second child, Charles Allen Smith, was born. Becoming quite
ill during the last days of her pregnancy, Bess had to be rushed to the
hospital on very short notice. When Mrs. Smith recalled this experience
in later years, she emphasized the contrast between her reaction of intense anxiety and her husband's calm response:

As we rode over in the ambulance, I tried to tell Frank that I hadn't been as
good a wife as I wished that I could have been, talking about the way you
would imagine anybody would when they thought they might not come back
from the hospital. And I thought Frank would say, "Oh, Bess, you've been
wonderful." But he just said, "That's all right, honey, I'll meet you in heaven."
I could tell right then that he wasn't going to meet me in heaven right away.
He did come to see me every afternoon, however. He would sit there in the
room with me and read his books. We both have always treasured our books.
    Then, on the third day, during the coldest spell of that winter, there was
a big fire in the hospital. At 3 o'clock in the morning, I was awakened by
the sound of breaking glass and I heard someone say, "Come quick to the
hospital right back of the capitol." And then the girl across the hall from me
ran in and said, "Oh, Mrs. Smith, the hospital is on fire!" Of course, we
mothers all wanted our babies, and I started ringing for the nurse. Then an
old gentleman came in—he looked as if he might be a truck driver—and
asked me if I could walk. When I said no, he picked me up in his arms and
carried me down the hall. When we reached the top of the stairways, we
met a nurse who told us that our babies were all safe.
    Well, they took us across the street and put us in a house. There was an
epidemic of measles at the University, and you have never seen quite as

many measles cases in all your life. So all the measles cases and the surgical cases and everybody were just stacked up in this house, in the hall and in the parlor. The doctor had them put me down on a mattress on the floor. So I caught the attention of a nurse and said: "Would you call my husband and tell him that the hospital has burned and to come for us." It must have been four or five o'clock in the morning.

Well, Frank thought that somebody must be playing a joke on him on account of the new baby, and he started back to bed. But then, just to be sure, he called the doctor. "Oh, no," the doctor insisted, "the hospital hasn't burned. Someone is just trying to trick you." So Frank tried to go back to bed, but he couldn't sleep. Then he decided to call "Central"—you know how in that day you could just call Central and she would tell you everything. So Frank called Central and Central told him, "Yes, the hospital has burned, but all the patients are safe." We didn't have a car, so Frank had to call a taxi.

When he got there, I thought he would come throw himself on the mattress and hug the baby and hug me and say, "Oh, I'm so glad that you all are safe." But when Frank came to the door, he stopped and hesitated and said, "I lost a dozen books in that fire."[42]

When Mrs. Smith told that story, Bishop Smith always defended himself by saying, "The best way in the world to prevent hysteria is just to be normal."[43]

During his ministry in Austin, Frank Smith helped organize the first Wesley Bible Chair in Southern Methodism.[44] Approved by the five Methodist annual conferences in Texas in 1915, the Bible Chair began offering credit courses at the University of Texas in February, 1916, although it was not fully chartered until 1917.[45] Frank Smith and Senator R. E. Cofer, chairman of the board of stewards of the University Methodist Church, represented the West Texas Conference on the statewide board of trustees. Late in 1917 Smith was offered the position of director and teacher. Writing to his brother Angie, the young minister declared:

I am completely up in the air as to my plans for the future. I have a proposition to take the Bible Chair in connection with the University here. Mr. George Walling, one of my members, offers to erect a $50,000 plant if I will do so. It is one of the greatest opportunities, educationally, in our Church. Frank Seay,[46] Dr. Dobbs, Bishop Mouzon and others want me to take it. I am not certain about it, however. Dr. Bishop is turning heaven and earth to get me to come to Georgetown, and there is a tentative proposition at S.M.U. So I don't know what I will do. I have to decide in the next few weeks. By the first of February, anyway.[47]

In a significant exchange of letters with Bishop Mouzon extending over a period of several months, Frank Smith poured out his inmost feelings concerning his vocational goals along with his reflections on ministering to students in state schools. On May 22 he wrote to the bishop expressing his deep appreciation for "the confidence all of you seem to feel in me by tendering me the position [which] offers one of the greatest fields of service in the entire Church, and one that will type the way for the work at our other State Universities. I am overwhelmed," he continued,

when I realize the possibilities for our Church in our secular institutions, and also in the general student movement that is now beginning to assume shape, a field that has been almost wholly neglected in the past. . . . I believe that the work of identifying our students in these institutions with our Church, rather than allowing the Y organizations to wean them away, will be productive of untold good for the Methodists in the years to come.

Because of a long-held conviction that he would "eventually go into school work if the Lord opens the way," Smith had "proceeded on the assumption that this opportunity might be the providential leading of God." But he had had second thoughts:

I have gone into the problem as thoroughly as I could, and I have come to the conclusion, after months of thought and prayer, that I should not accept the Bible Chair. My honest conviction now is that I should not undertake this work. There are others who can do the work just as well as I, beyond a doubt, and who are really better equipped. . . . I want to remain for a while longer, at any rate, in the pastorate.[48]

Of far greater import was a second decision which had also been made "only after heart-searching and prayer just as conscientious as that affecting the other decision." In this same letter of May 22, Smith wrote to Mouzon:

I am going to ask for a change from University Church this Fall. Many things enter into this matter that cannot be adequately expressed in writing, naturally, but I think I can make my motives plain to you. Let me say, in the beginning, that there is no disposition upon the part of anyone in the church to have me moved. The church was never in better condition, our congregations are magnificent, and our finances are well up. All the people seem to be happy and contented. I feel that I have vindicated your confidence in me, in a measure at least, and I have to the best of my ability discharged my obligation to the Lord while here. As the situation now exists the old trouble is rapidly being forgotten. The people are working together harmoniously. We are on the eve of launching a campaign to pay off a good part of our indebtedness. . . . The church is just now at the place where it can enter into a magnificent period of progress. This being the state of affairs, I feel that I can leave the church with a clear conscience and with the road clear for my successor. The right man could come here just now and remain for years. . . . It will be just as easy, even easier, for me to move this Fall, than it will be two years hence at the close of my quadrennium.

Since the "supreme task of straightening out the tangle" had been accomplished, Smith felt "justified in considering the case from a personal viewpoint." Now his letter becomes intensely personal:

The past two years have been very trying ones to Bess and me. Our whole future depended upon whether we made it go here, and there was very little save criticism from the preachers of the State. And the situation here itself was extremely delicate; and rather than disappoint you we would have died in the breach. I have rarely known what it means to have any time at all with my family, day or night. The tense situation is being removed now, but the strenuosity of the pastorate increases rather than diminishes. Including a Bible class for the women, a Mission study class, my Sunday School class, the preaching and the numerous addresses, etc., demanded in a university community, together with what pastoral work I can get to, my existence is a mad rush. I have not had time to do anything with my fourth year Course of Study. I have had absolutely no opportunity to take up my correspondence work from Vanderbilt upon which my degree depends,[49] and I am particularly desirous of securing my degree.[50]

Although he found it "easier to preach now than ever before," Smith longed for "time for outside study and meditation and broadening" that did not come from his "regular sermonic studying." Convinced there was not a better appointment than University Methodist Church, "so far as prestige and rank are concerned," Frank Smith maintained that he was "not swayed by selfish motives in desiring a change." Nevertheless, he yearned for a more peaceful situation: "a place where I would have more normal conditions, where my opportunities would be all that I could grasp, where I would not have, of necessity, to make certain alignments in adjusting a row, as I have had to do here."[51]

Acknowledging that Bishop Mouzon had recently been assigned to supervise another episcopal area,[52] Smith concluded his letter with a moving appeal:

I realize that you are not my bishop this year, to my great disappointment, and I have gone at great length into this matter with you, not as my bishop, but as I would with my father, because I believe you will be personally interested. My decision not to take the Bible Chair is so closely bound up with this other decision that I could hardly go into one without going into the other.[53]

Toward the end of May Bishop Mouzon came to Austin to preach at First Methodist and University Methodist churches. Following a brief personal visit with Frank Smith, he discussed the situation at the University Church with several interested "brethren." Mouzon wrote to Smith on June 6 after his return to Dallas:

I have been thinking seriously about your situation in Austin and the conditions at University Church. I confess that conditions are much more serious than I had previously known. . . . You have done well at University Church. I hardly see how anyone could have done better. But after some further conversation with other brethren I have concluded that possibly I was asking too much of you when I suggested to you that you ought to remain another year or until the close of your quadrennium. If you feel about the matter now as you did when I talked with you I shall not insist on your remaining. I see plainly that there are still serious troubles in the church which will have to be handled very definitely, and that when this is done it is practically certain that there will be some further disturbances. I do not doubt that you could do this as well as anyone else, but I feel that it would be asking a little too much of you.[54]

Mouzon also expressed concern about Smith's health and urged him to "get a way for a short while. At least you might take your wife and babies and go to Georgetown for the Summer School of Theology."

Frank Smith's prompt reply to Bishop Mouzon further illustrates his profound respect for the bishop as well as his deep dependence upon Mouzon for guidance and support:

Your letter has made me very happy because of your expressed confidence in me and my work here. Your belief in me means more to me, I assure you, than you can ever know.

I am still of the opinion relative to my leaving University Church that I was when you were here. Bess and I wish to abide by your decision in the matter. If you had said you thought we should remain here, the matter would have been settled, so far as we are concerned, and we would have considered no other alternative whatsoever. Needless to say, however, we are both very glad that your decision is what it is. . . . This has been a heartbreaking task for the past two years.[55]

In response to Mouzon's urging him to take a vacation, Smith replied
with understandable pride that President Bishop had invited him to give
the commencement address at Southwestern University. "I shall try to
remain there for a day or so, at any rate, and meet the brethren and
attend some of the lectures."[56] To return to Georgetown only four years
after his own graduation to give the Commencement address must have
brought Frank Smith considerable pleasure. The following account of
his address appeared in the local newspaper:

Rev. A. Frank Smith of University Methodist Church, Austin, alumnus of
the University and winner of the Senior Oratorical Contest his Senior year,
among his host of other honors, delivered the address of the morning. He
spoke on "The Messenger," the need, the opportunity, the responsibility,
with special relation to the present war. He concluded by welcoming this
year's class into the fellowship of the Alumni of the University.[57]

Whatever tranquillity Frank Smith enjoyed in anticipating release
from the difficulties of his Austin pastorate was shattered in mid-July
when his new bishop came to town on a familiarization tour. William
Newman Ainsworth, a native Georgian just elected to the episcopacy and
assigned supervision of the Texas conferences, was considering residing
in the capital city. Austin Methodists eagerly greeted him with large
congregations, luncheons, and receptions. Following a personal conference with their distinguished guest, Frank sent this ardent plea to Bishop
Mouzon:

Bishop Ainsworth has just left Austin, and expects to be in Dallas tomorrow
and Thursday. . . . I talked very briefly with the Bishop concerning the situation at University Church; he seems to be of the opinion that I should remain here. I told him I was amenable to his wishes, of course, but wished to
express my desires in the matter. There were naturally many things that I
have discussed with you and that you understand here that I could not mention to Bishop Ainsworth. . . . I told him I had discussed the matter fully
with you, and that you understood the situation thoroughly, and asked him
to talk the matter over with you, which he said he would gladly do. I am
writing to request that you go over the problems with him; I will appreciate
it very much. If you both agree that I should return, I have not another word
to say. I am anxious that Bishop Ainsworth should not feel that irresponsi-
bility and lack of faith to my trust here is responsible for my desire to leave,
and I am sure you can explain the exact situation to him. . . . We are going
to appreciate and love Bishop Ainsworth, but that does not lessen our regret
that you are not with us again this year.[58]

Perhaps with unintentional foreboding Bishop Mouzon's prompt reply began, "My dear Brother," instead of the customary "My dear Frank."

> Bishop Ainsworth was in Dallas but he had only one day here and I got to see him for not more than an hour, and had little time to discuss any important matters with him. . . . I had no chance to say more than a few words to him about the pastorate of University Church. I could clearly see, however, that from his sizing up the situation in Austin he thought that you were exactly the man to remain there.[59]

Under these circumstances, Frank Smith was receptive to a special assignment in the United States Navy Chaplaincy that was offered to him by Secretary of the Navy Josephus Daniels. As Smith later explained his motivation:

> I felt I ought to go. I talked with Bishop Ainsworth about it, and Ainsworth said: "Well, I've known fellows that have tried to break into high-steepled churches, but you are the first I've ever known that tried to break out of one." . . . I felt a strong compulsion for going into the Chaplaincy, but I have often asked myself whether it was a desire to serve my country or to get away from that situation [at University Church] that made me want to go into the Chaplaincy.[60]

For more than a year the young pastor had watched the university students leave his congregation for duty with the armed forces. The College of Bishops had been urging ministers to volunteer as chaplains. Editorials in the *Texas Christian Advocate* declared it a matter of "paramount urgency" that the Methodist church extend her ministry to the men fighting "a mighty Crusade to destroy German militarism," and maintained that "the Church has no more imperative duty just now than the moral and spiritual safeguarding of the men in our camps and it should be a joy to our people to support our noble men who have left their comfortable charges for the army work."[61]

"I am very anxious to get into war work," Smith wrote to Dean W. F. Tillett in mid-September, 1918.

> I have a request from Mr. Josephus Daniels to come to Washington on the twentieth of this month, to receive appointment to a chaplaincy in the Navy. . . . I am of the opinion that my appointment is to come directly from the Sec'y of the Navy, and I desire a letter of recommendation from you that I may present to him. I will carry a letter from Bishop Mouzon, one from Dr.

R. S. Hyer, one from Governor Hobby of this State, and I desire one from you, most of all.[62]

In accord with this request Dean Tillett wrote to Secretary Daniels:

If I were called on to name the best half dozen young ministers in the Methodist Episcopal Church, South, for service in the office of chaplain in the army or navy of the U.S., I would place in that list the name of Rev. Frank Smith, of Austin, Texas. . . . Intellectually, morally, religiously and socially I consider him eminently fitted for effective and satisfactory service as a chaplain.[63]

In September Frank Smith made the long train trip to Washington, D.C., where he met with Secretary Daniels,[64] passed his physical examination at the Navy Yard,[65] and received his commission. Lieutenant (jg) A. Frank Smith, Chaplain Corps, U.S.N., then returned to Austin to say goodbye to his congregation. Shortly thereafter, he explained his new status to J. Richard Spann, who was soon to leave for Washington in quest of a similar appointment.

I went to Mr. Daniels when I reached Washington, and after we had concluded our arrangements, I carried a letter from him to Cap't Frazier stating that the Sec'y desired my appointment at once as a Chaplain. . . . I hold a Commission directly from Sec'y Daniels, and am on detached service, i.e. I am given greater freedom in my movements, and am going to do some special work for Mr. Daniels. I will hold the Commission of Jr. Lt. Every person who comes in under thirty-one years of age must come in as Acting Chaplain. . . . I am very happy over the prospects of the service I am going to be able to render.[66]

Shortly after Frank reached home, a severe influenza epidemic spread throughout Austin. Charles Allen, the Smiths' baby son, was among the first stricken. "We could get no medical attention," Frank remembered. "We had two soldier camps near Austin, and the boys were dying like flies. The doctors were just worked to death."[67] Bess's sister Hallie came down from Dallas to help out. She, too, remembered the impossible burden on the doctors:

From the parsonage on Salado Street, we could hear the coughing of the soldiers out in their tents on the lawn of Sealy Hospital. The doctor really at the last couldn't come to our baby because he was just burned out—that was the way he said it—he just could not come. But I don't think the baby would have lived anyway.[68]

Charles Allen Smith, not quite nine months old, died early Sunday morning, October 20.[69] "Baby died two-thirty this morning," Frank wired his father. "Funeral in Dallas eleven o'clock Monday morning. Will call you from Dallas."[70] As Hallie explained the situation: "We brought his body back to Dallas for burial because Bess and Frank had bought a lot at Greenwood Cemetery together with Uncle John and Aunt Mollie."[71] According to Frank, their plan had been that Bess and the children would live in Dallas with Hallie and George Pierce while Frank was in the chaplaincy. Now the death of little Charles and a "false armistice" changed everything. "When our baby died, I didn't want to go back anyway," Frank later explained. "So when that false armistice came on, I just rolled up my commission and mailed it back to them and told them goodbye, and that was the end of it. I wrote the Bishop that I had resigned my commission but preferred not to return to University Church."[72]

The tribulations and anguish associated with his Austin pastorate inevitably left their mark on Frank Smith. As one of his longtime friends recalls:

Frank once told me that when he was relieved of that appointment he literally sat down and cried of sheer relief. Nevertheless, I think the agony of soul that he suffered as a young man confronting an all but impossible situation was the fire that forged some of the characteristics that he carried through life.[73]

Since Bishop Edwin D. Mouzon had appointed Frank Smith to the University Methodist Church, his evaluation of Frank's ministry there may appropriately bring this chapter to its conclusion. On November 4, 1918, Mouzon wrote to his friend John A. Kerr, one of the leading laymen of Laurel Heights Methodist Church in San Antonio:

I am writing this matter in order to give you some idea of the kind of man Bishop Ainsworth has sent to Laurel Heights Church to be your pastor. Bro. A. Frank Smith is, I think, without doubt the strongest man of his age in Texas. Two years ago when University Church, Austin, was torn asunder, I looked the whole field over and sent Bro. Smith there.

He has done a notable work. He has accomplished even more than I had hoped for.[74] He would certainly have been returned to University Church but for the fact that he had accepted a commission as Chaplain in the navy and the Bishop had gone ahead and made arrangements to put Bro. Talley at University Church. Even then, if Bro. Smith had expressed a desire to return, the Bishop would have returned him, but as the Bishop had made arrangements for University Church, Bro. Smith thought it best not to be returned. He would have gone on into the navy but for the fact that peace is in sight, and it is evident that by going into the chaplaincy at this time he would have no opportunity to do anything toward the winning of the war.

You will find Bro. Smith to be a good preacher, an excellent pastor, and a most lovable man. His wife is one of our finest young women, brought up from infancy under the influences of our church and our schools.

I look for a continuation of the good work Bro. Felix Hill has been doing.

Your friend and brother,
EDWIN D. MOUZON[75]

6

Laurel Heights

"THE FIRST I KNEW of my appointment to Laurel Heights Church, San Antonio," Frank Smith recalled, "was when I read the appointments of the West Texas Conference in the *Dallas News*."[1] He and Bess were in Dallas for the funeral of their baby boy when the conference met in San Antonio on October 23-25, 1918.[2] As Frank remembered their ill-fated experience:

Mrs. Smith and I and our three-year old son returned at once to Austin to gather our few belongings for the move to San Antonio. My successor at University Church was already moving into the parsonage, so we stopped at the Driskill Hotel while in Austin. The second night I was struck before daylight with a violent attack of flu. I had a high fever by the time we caught the noon train for San Antonio. As soon as we reached there, we went right out to the parsonage, and I went to bed. Mrs. Smith secured a doctor at once, who put nurses on the case, and for weeks I hovered between life and death. It was mid-November when we reached San Antonio, and it was mid-February before I entered my pulpit.[3]

Only a fellow minister could adequately comprehend Frank Smith's overwhelming frustration during those long months of illness and convalescence or, once his strength began to return, his eager impatience.

99

Only a bishop could effectively admonish him to exercise prudence in taking up his tasks and responsibilities. Bishop Mouzon, who had experienced a similar crisis during his pastoral career, wrote to Frank in early January:

You have had your share of affliction this fall and winter, but I am sure that you have brought home to your heart the assurance that was given the Apostle: "My grace is sufficient for you. My strength is made perfect in weakness." Out of your affliction and illness in San Antonio good may come.

I recall how when I was sent as pastor to our Central Church in Kansas City, Missouri, just as I was beginning to get my hands on the situation I went down with pneumonia in both lungs and was desperately ill. This drew the membership of the church to me and their kindness drew me to them in such a way as to create some of the closest friendships of my life. My pastorate at Central Church, Kansas City, became in many ways one of the most fruitful pastorates of my ministry. I pray that your experience may have a like result.[4]

Bishop Mouzon's prayer was remarkably prophetic. "The people were wonderful to us during this interim, as well as afterward," Frank Smith remembered.[5] Thirty years later he wrote the following tribute:

I could not speak of Laurel Heights Church save in terms of appreciation and endearment. Mrs. Smith and I came to Laurel Heights in the first decade of its life and in our early ministry. Both of us were still in our twenties, and keenly conscious of our inexperience; but the people of Laurel Heights Church opened their arms and took us to their hearts. They acted as though they had the best minister in Methodism, and they loved us and bragged on us and spoiled us, until we had to do our best to deserve some small part of their faith and goodness, even though we knew we could never be all they said we were. Those were supremely happy and formative years. . . . We look back upon [them] as the golden years of our ministry, and as the period in which was laid the foundation upon which our entire subsequent ministry was built.[6]

The young pastor's recuperation may have been more rapid than he remembered. In early February Mr. John A. Kerr, the chairman of the board of stewards at Laurel Heights, wrote to Bishop Mouzon: "Frank Smith is making good at our Church. He is now recognized as the best preacher that we have ever had and is in every way gripping the hearts of our people. If he holds up as he is now going, he will lead our Church into its great place of usefulness."[7] By the middle of February, Smith's recovery could be celebrated at a reception welcoming the new parsonage family. "Practically the entire membership came to the reception, stayed the full time, and seemed to enjoy it immensely," Frank Smith wrote to Bishop Mouzon.

I am completely happy in my work here. The people are the most responsive and appreciative I have ever known, and they are coming to church. Our morning congregations fill the house. . . . Our evening congregations are larger than the morning congregations have been, so John Kerr and Brother West tell me. And each Sunday the crowds increase. They are already talking about opening the Sunday School room to accommodate the morning congregation. . . . The best thing about the whole situation is the fact that the people themselves are very enthusiastic.[8]

With typical humor, Frank added, "Bess actually says she likes it better here than in Dallas, and I did not think she would find a place this side of paradise of which she would say that."

Although her husband was regaining his health, Mrs. Smith had not been well since the birth of their second son.[9] For some reason she believed that she would die when she was twenty-eight years old. On the morning of her twenty-eighth birthday, during breakfast, she declared, "I'll never see another birthday." Without looking up from his breakfast, Frank replied, "Well, I'd better notify the undertaker and have him come out and take your measurements."

Now that didn't seem to faze her a bit. She just said, "All right, I won't live through this year." About a month or two after that, Bishop Mouzon got married again. Well, we had known the Mouzons and known them well in Georgetown. Bishop Mouzon married again about a year after the death of his first wife. Bessie got so mad, she said to me, "That's what you'd do. You wouldn't wait a year." Then she went to the dentist and found that she had a bad tooth draining into her system. Soon after that tooth was extracted, she was as chipper as ever.[10]

In most aspects the Laurel Heights Church differed from the University Church in Austin. Although it paid the same salary of $3,000, Laurel Heights had only 365 members, less than half the membership of University Church. The lovely $80,000 sanctuary of Laurel Heights was only nine years old—and debt free. It was a neighborhood church with a strong family atmosphere and a membership composed of doctors, lawyers, ranchmen, and a few retired people. As Frank remembered, "There was only one employed person in the congregation, an old bachelor hat salesman."[11] The homogeneous congregation had never known dissension. "After the strain, tensions and bereavement we had experienced at University Church," Frank declared, "those were glorious years for us."[12] The Laurel Heights congregation was also composed of a wealthier group of people than University Church; in fact, it was

the wealthiest and most influential church group in San Antonio and the wealthiest residential church in the Methodist Episcopal Church, South. My predecessor told me that one could stand on the parsonage porch and see the homes of eight millionaires, all members of Laurel Heights. A Catholic banker in San Antonio told me that the roster of the official board of Laurel Heights was financially stronger than the board of directors of any bank in the city.[14]

The only weakness the young pastor could see in his new church was its lack of financial organization. "There were no pledges and no budget. Members simply paid what they desired when they desired. No one worried because there was always money in the treasury." This situation gave Frank an "invaluable experience in dealing with people on that financial and social level and in trying to teach them churchmanship."[15]

In 1919 American Methodists united in the Centenary Movement to commemorate the beginning of Methodist missions. One aspect of the celebration was a financial campaign to undergird the Methodist missionary work, endangered by the economic effects of the war. As a member of the West Texas Conference Board of Missions, Frank Smith participated in the planning and execution of the program within that annual conference. He saw the opportunity that the Centenary Campaign offered for increasing the connectional consciousness of his congregation and for stimulating the growth of a sound financial structure in the church.

At Smith's insistence, Bishop Mouzon came to San Antonio in April to make the main address at the Preliminary Gift Banquet.[16] The following day Frank wrote his profound appreciation to the bishop: "The effects of your address are electrical. Your coming to San Antonio was worth thousands of dollars in actual money to the campaign."[17] Smith named two prominent men, friends of the bishop's, who had earlier termed the movement "inopportune" and would not support it:

Dick Terrell told me that you converted him last night. He says he is now willing to go anywhere in the District, at any time, to speak. And Mr. Kokernot said he counted that as the greatest address he had ever listened to. . . . You have a grip on these people that no one else has, and you have accomplished more for the Centenary Movement and for these local people than all the rest of us combined can do.[18]

In concluding this letter, Smith added a personal word that illustrates his relationship to Bishop Mouzon:

Your presence in our home was a benediction to us. You said one thing to me that did me lots of good and that I shall never forget. You said that you did a great deal of studying and made a great many sermons to "save your own soul." I am able to appreciate that just now, and I take courage from your experience.

All across the United States the Centenary Movement captured the imagination of American Methodists. According to one historian, "The magnificent Centenary Movement of the Methodist Episcopal Church and the Methodist Episcopal Church, South, is simply not comprehensible except in terms of devotion and sacrificial spirit of millions of Methodist laymen and women."[19] Dr. Elmer T. Clark declared, "It is well known that without this great advance movement our missionary work would doubtless have collapsed during the arduous days following the World War."[20] Under Frank Smith's pastoral leadership, Laurel Heights Methodist Church oversubscribed its quota four times. "This was the first challenge the church ever had," Smith said, "and from then on it met every demand with speed and joy."[21]

In the middle of October, 1919, when the West Texas Conference met in Austin, Frank Smith reported sixty-eight new members for Laurel Heights: twenty-three by profession of faith and forty-five by certificate of transfer. This raised the total membership over four hundred for the first time.[22]

Although the *Journal* of this conference held in 1919 states that A. Frank Smith was among the five "travelling preachers" who had been ordained elders, the careful reader will note the broader statement in the daily proceedings: "The report of the names of those ordained Elders and Deacons at this session, and of those certified by Bishop Ainsworth as ordained at other times and places was made."[23] Smith was one of those "ordained at other times and places." He had been *elected* to elder's orders by the preceding session of the West Texas Conference that met in South San Antonio,[24] but the death and funeral of his baby boy had prevented his attending that session and being ordained with his class. A remark found in Bishop Smith's personal daily journal, written thirty years later, clarifies the matter: "Came to Austin today. . . . At 5 p.m. I ordained Murray Dickson Deacon & Elder at University Church. He is a missionary to Bolivia. *I was ordained Elder at the same altar in 1918 by Bishop Ainsworth.*"[25] Under Methodist polity an annual conference must elect a person to deacon's or elder's orders before a bishop can ordain that person. Since Frank Smith had been elected to elder's orders in October, Bishop Ainsworth could ordain him at any convenient time thereafter.[26]

During the Smiths' second year in San Antonio, Bess's improved health allowed her to take a more active role in the church. She remembered working very hard that year: "I had charge of the Young Ladies' Missionary Society. I organized and had charge of the Sunday School and Church Orchestra. I taught a class in the Junior Department. I had charge of a circle and belonged to the Bluebirds." Dr. Minnie Maffitt, the physician at SMU who had saved Frank, Jr.'s life, came to visit the Smiths about this time. "She was quite a friend of ours," Mrs. Smith explained:

Dr. Maffitt was sitting with me in church, and someone came over and said, "Mrs. Smith, we want you to have charge of one of our departments down in the Sunday School." Dr. Maffitt looked at me, and after the lady left she said, "If I ever catch you having charge of anything, I'll never be your friend again. It might have been necessary in the past, but now this is a large church, and there are many people who are capable of doing the work. You shouldn't do it."[27]

Mrs. Smith, a talented musician, found new opportunities in San Antonio to play her violin. She was first violinist in the Tuesday Music Club Octette and a welcome member of the string section of the San Antonio Symphony. Both Frank and Bess were drawn into the leading social groups of the city. "We were wined and dined in the homes of these people sometimes for weeks at a stretch with never an evening off," Frank recalled,

and we became members of the Army-Civilian Club, an exclusive and highly influential group in San Antonio. The chief function of the pastor of Laurel Heights was to represent the most influential group of laymen in San Antonio in any and all civic and social affairs. In 1919 I made the main address for the first Armistice Day celebration, held in front of the Alamo with all the military forces in and around San Antonio participating.[28]

Another influenza epidemic broke out in Texas in January and February of 1920. In San Antonio the situation became so critical that a quarantine was put on all public meetings, including church services, for two weeks. In Dallas the epidemic was equally severe, claiming the life of one of Frank Smith's dearest friends, Professor Frank Seay.[29] Writing to Bishop Mouzon, Frank declared:

> I shall never have a greater shock than I received when Mrs. Seay's telegram came to me Saturday night at ten o'clock, saying that her husband was dead. I did not even know that he was sick. Bess was in bed with influenza at the time, or I would have gone to Dallas for the funeral Sunday.
> I am sure I shall never love another man more than I did Frank Seay, and I am just as sure that no man will ever love me more than he did. He was a great influence on my life at a time when I was undecided just how to pitch it for the future. I think his greatest work consisted in giving to young men a sane, workable conception of the ministry as a life work. . . . He had faith in me and was deeply interested in all that concerned me. Too, he confided in me. . . . My life will always be richer and more fruitful because I knew him. I shall miss him more than I can now realize.[30]

Frank's younger brother, Angie, a student in Seay's classes at SMU's School of Theology at that time, remembers the close relationship between Frank and Dr. Seay: "Of the men who influenced Frank at Southwestern University, the one man above all others was Frank Seay. . . . And later at S.M.U., Frank Seay had a tremendous influence on Frank's life. Frank Seay was as close to Frank as anyone could possibly be. And Frank was devoted to Seay."[31]

Despite recurrent flu epidemics and drought conditions, Laurel Heights Methodist Church continued to thrive. In a letter to Bishop Mouzon, Frank Smith wrote: "Even tho' you are not the Bishop technically in charge of my congregation, I always feel, and shall ever feel, that I want to make an occasional report to you of the work we are doing." The outstanding characteristic of his parishioners was their constant seeking of opportunities to express their love and appreciation for the pastor and his family. As evidence of this constant care, Frank noted that the parsonage was being repainted and their bedrooms repapered, that the congregation taxed the capacity of the sanctuary each Sunday, that he had been assured an assistant the next year, and that his salary had been raised to $4,500, "putting us on a par with Travis Park."[32] A budget had been set up, pledges secured by the stewards, and offerings were three times as large as they had ever been before.

With the financial structure of the church more firmly established, Smith was now concentrating on churchmanship. "I have felt that the one great thing our people needed here was a connectional consciousness," he wrote Mouzon. Two current projects were aimed at correcting this situation. The West Texas Woman's Missionary Conference had accepted an invitation to meet at Laurel Heights in May, and the College of Bishops was considering an invitation to hold its fall meeting there. "Our people are greatly enthused over the idea of entertaining the College," Smith continued. "I hope you will exert your influence to have them come here. We will entertain all who will accept such entertainment in our best homes, and the church will provide entertainment for all others who prefer to go to the hotels. The meetings of the College would be held in Laurel Heights Church."[33]

His report to Mouzon shows that Frank was especially proud of the increasing membership of his congregation:

We have had a considerably larger number of accessions this first six months than we had the whole of last year. Indeed, never has Laurel Heights had so many accessions in a year, as we have had these six months. Almost half of them have been on profession of faith. Fifteen have been children from the Sunday School; all the others have been adults.

"We have had no special series of meetings," he emphasized in conclusion, "but have received them all at the regular services."[34]

Angie Smith, who earned a considerable reputation as an evangelist, once asked his brother how he took in more new members on profession of faith every year than many of the preachers who depended upon evangelistic services and annual revivals for their new members. "I pick out ten or twelve outstanding men and women of the city, the leading people in the community," Frank replied, "and I seek to win them personally. Then the crowd follows. When you win a particular leader, there are certain groups of people that will follow." "Now this is the ability that Frank had," Angie explains; "he had that ability to pick those leaders and to win them."[35]

During the spring of 1920 Arthur Moore, a general evangelist from Georgia, came to San Antonio to hold a two-week revival meeting at Travis Park Methodist Church. In that brief time Frank and Arthur Moore began a friendship that quickly developed into a bond of mutual affection. As Arthur Moore recalls, "Before that meeting was over we found ourselves congenial with each other. We seemed to have melted and just went into each other's lives almost immediately."[36] After returning home to Georgia, Arthur wrote to Frank indicating in his initial greeting one way in which the friendship found common ground: "My dear Frank: I hope you are out on the 'fairway' shooting a 45 by now."[37] Turning to more serious matters, Arthur confided:

> I am giving the matter of coming to Texas some very serious thought. I am tired of "gadding about." My children are growing up and I feel that I owe it to my family to settle down where I can be with them a little more. What would be the attitude of the preachers out there toward a transfer? I would not care to go anywhere and not feel that I was welcome. Write me freely how you feel about it. . . .
>
> I am hoping to see you when I go to Lubbock and San Angelo in August and September. . . . Let me hear from you. I learned to love you much.[38]

Apparently Bishop Ainsworth was also thinking of Arthur Moore and Texas, for in September, while the evangelist was in San Angelo, Texas, he received a telegram from the bishop. Moore describes the scene in his autobiography: "I happened to be at lunch with a company of preachers when Western Union brought this message to me. It said simply, "I am transferring you from the South Georgia Conference to the West Texas Conference, and I expect to appoint you as minister of the Travis Park Church, San Antonio."[39] With 1,750 members, Travis Park Methodist Episcopal Church, South, was the largest congregation in the West Texas Conference.

Although Arthur Moore had been in the Methodist ministry for eleven years, for eight of those years he had served as conference missionary in South Georgia or as an approved general evangelist. "I'd never had an appointment to a church except six small country churches," he recalls:

Frank and I were both just boy preachers, carrying very heavy responsibilities. We had come into big appointments early, but we had sense enough to know it. Mouzon had been very good to Frank and Ainsworth to me. Yet we were not haughty over it; we were humbled by it, and we just gave ourselves to the service of our people. We were just absorbed in trying to be good Methodist preachers and pastors to our people. Frank had more pastoral experience than I had, and I turned to him often for very serious counsel as to how to deal with problems and always found him a wise advisor.[40]

The Smith and Moore families discovered the same congeniality, often going for long rides together in the country or taking a trip to Corpus Christi. On many occasions Dr. Felix Hill and his family would share in this fellowship. Hill was the presiding elder of the San Antonio District. "He became our confidant," Moore remembers, "more or less our 'father-in-God.' " Sometimes the three families would drive to Kerrville to visit Angie Smith and his new bride.[41]

In a city the size of San Antonio, with a population of about 142,000 served by thirteen Methodist churches and several Methodist-related institutions, Frank Smith and Arthur Moore had no difficulty finding projects at which they could work together. Both of the young pastors served on the boards of Westmoreland College, the Methodist school in San Antonio; Wesleyan Institute, which trained pastors for the Mexican conference; and the Texas Mission Home and Training School. "Frank and I always went to preachers' meetings on Monday morning," Arthur says, "and then out to dinner together. We'd go to the hospitals in the afternoon to call on our sick members. We found in each other a complementing partner. We relied on each other. Anything I tried to do, Frank helped me; and if I could help him, of course I did."[42]

One major project that Arthur Moore and Frank Smith initiated was aimed at strengthening the Protestant image and spirit in San Antonio. As Arthur explains, "San Antonio had been dominated by the Roman Catholics from the beginning. We wanted to unite the Protestants of the city in a great show of strength."

We formed a Protestant Committee and planned a great weekend of speeches climaxed by a parade in downtown San Antonio. That was a daring thing. The churches made floats symbolizing our Protestant heritage. We organized our people, marched down Houston Street for half a mile, went over to Commerce Street and back around for nearly two miles. The parade took over two hours to pass by. The military people estimated our people at 38,000. It was a parade! It gave us more Protestant solidarity than we had ever had, and it put new life into all our churches—Presbyterian, Baptist, Methodist. Frank and I were both involved in that celebration. Incidentally, we didn't design it for that purpose, but at the next election we elected a Protestant mayor.[43]

While they devoted the major portion of their time to their respective churches and to Methodist institutions in San Antonio, Smith and Moore were neither narrowly Methodist nor exclusively Protestant in their interests and activities. Arthur Moore especially remembers their friendship with Arthur Drossarts, the archbishop of the Roman Catholic

diocese of San Antonio. "Frank and I used to go around and have breakfast with Drossarts. We had a fraternity that kept us in touch with
each other, even in that early day." They also maintained friendly relations with the rabbi of the Jewish temple near Laurel Heights. "Frank
and I both preached for him on Friday nights from time to time," Arthur
reminisces. "I think we both played a humble but steady part in bet-
tering relations between the different groups, including our Jewish
brethren."[44]

These interfaith friendships ran counter to the prevailing trend in
the Texas of the early 1920s, which were the years of the revival of
the Ku Klux Klan in the state. As Charles Alexander has described the
boosters of this new version of the Klan:

They were shrewd enough to realize that the wartime hostility toward everything which did not conform to a formalized conception of Americanism
had turned into postwar hysteria—hysteria which featured a revival of anti-
Catholicism; the growth of anti-Semitism; fear for the maintenance of white
supremacy; acceleration of the campaign to restrict foreign immigration;
and anxiety over the presence of Bolsheviks, anarchists, and "radicals" in
general. The Klan also portrayed itself as a crusader for "law and order" and
the protector of virtuous womanhood and orthodox Protestant moral standards—abstinence from alcoholic beverages, premarital chastity, marital fidelity,
respect for parental authority. From all these prejudices and fears the Kleagles
(Klan organizers) were to select and apply the ones that were most effica-
cious in the particular area they were "kluxing," as propaganda work for the
Klan came to be called.[45]

In contrast to the Klan of the Civil War Reconstruction period, "The
Klan of the twenties was an enemy not only of Negroes but of Catholics,
Jews, radicals, immigrants, bootleggers, moral offenders, habitual crimi-
nals, modernist theologians, and assorted other types."[46] Although anti-
Catholicism and anti-Semitism were important in the kluxing of the
Southwest, Alexander shows that "primary responsibility for the Klan's
rise in Texas must be attributed to the white Protestant citizen's reaction
against the postwar crime wave and the supposed moral breakdown
spreading over the state."[47]

The condition of lawlessness and looseness which frightened the white
Protestant Texan was most prevalent in the cities, especially those experiencing rapid growth. . . . As a result the Klan achieved its greatest strength
and its most notable successes in the booming cities of the Southwest. In
Texas the hooded fraternity gained partial or complete control of every major

city with the exception of San Antonio and Galveston. . . . By the end of 1921 the Klan in Texas occupied a position of power and influence unequaled in any other state.[48]

In San Antonio, where the population had rocketed from 96,614 in 1910 to 161,379 in 1920, the first Klan chapter was organized in November, 1920.[49]

Another distinguishing characteristic of the Klan in Texas in the twenties was the high quality and social level of its initial members. According to David Chalmers, "the Klan's first recruits literally constituted a Who's Who of business, the professions, and patriotism."[50] The assumption that only riffraff and fanatics belonged to the Klan is groundless. The membership of the order was remarkably diverse, including bankers, businessmen, salesmen, physicians, lawyers, ministers, university professors, mechanics, farmers, and day laborers.[51] "A lot of good people got caught up in it," Arthur Moore recalls; "the Klan just swept through the elected, high-placed officials. It was not easy to stay out of it."[52] Frank Smith's statement that "many leading preachers were early members of the Klan"[53] is supported by historical studies. The first Grand Dragon of the Realm of Texas was a Protestant Episcopal minister, and many clergymen served as Klan lecturers.[54] "A strikingly large number of Protestant pastors responded favorably to the Klan's continual overtures," Alexander claims. Arthur Moore tells of a "church visitation" made by members of the Klan at Lampasas, Texas, where the West Texas Conference was meeting in October, 1922: "On the last night I preached and at the close of the service, much to my surprise, they came in, about fifty of them, robed and hooded, and gave the church or the preacher—somebody, not me!—a gift of money. That was their way of getting publicity."[55]

Southern churchmen, according to Professor Robert W. Sledge, were particularly susceptible to the appeal of the Klan because of their traditional view of the church as "spiritual"—that is, the church's legitimate concerns were limited to the personal or individual aspects of religion and morality as opposed to those of a social, economic, political, or cultural nature. The role of the church was to proclaim the gospel to individuals, nothing more. "Like Southern womanhood," Sledge writes, "the Church was exalted, supported and protected so long as it kept to its proper sphere." This concept of the role of the "Church-as-spiritual left churchmen no other means of enforcing the ethic they preached than some kind of movement like the Klan, officially unrelated to the Church and unofficially pervaded by the Church's terminology and ideas." Since Protestant churches could exhort but not enforce moral purity, "the members and their pastors easily turned to an existing organization outside the Church for *action*."[56] "A Frankenstein's monster for Southern Protestantism," Sledge calls the Klan, "born of the union of Protestantism's moral commitment and its shackling concept of Church-as-spiritual." He concludes, "The Klan was an illegitimate and accidental offspring of the dichotomy, and an offspring that was alarmingly beyond Church control."[57]

In its early days the Klan's public image in Texas was not one primarily of anti-Catholicism, anti-Semitism, and anti-radicalism. Rather, the Kleagles attempted to sell the Klan as "an aggressive defender of 'one hundred per cent Americanism,' a white-robed and hooded band of super-patriots."[58] Frank Smith was repelled by this image, declaring: "I am just naturally afraid of a super-patriot, and there is no more detestable, no worse type of superiority complex than a pious superiority complex. They wind up being as intolerant as the devil himself."[59] Although strong pressure was put upon him by prominent men in San Antonio, Smith did not join the Klan or allow the Klan to enter his church services.[60]

Frank Smith and Arthur Moore were not alone, of course, in opposing the Klan. Several bishops of the Methodist Episcopal Church, South, denounced the Klan. These included William F. McMurry, Edwin D. Mouzon, and William N. Ainsworth.[61] Ainsworth, a native of Georgia who had been Frank Smith's bishop for four years, wrote in the *Dallas Morning News*: "We have indeed fallen upon days of degeneracy if the Christian ministry has allied itself with the Ku Klux Klan and debased the pulpit by defense of its methods."[62] Bishop Mouzon was equally opposed to ministers belonging to the Klan. In August, 1922, he wrote: "I have been greatly distressed over the growth of the Ku Klux Klan in Texas and Oklahoma and nothing has distressed me so much as the fact that so many of our preachers have been misguided and have gone into this organization."[63]

The defensive temper of the 1920s, reacting against the "unfamiliar terrain of diversity and change in which there lurked a thousand threats to the older orthodoxies,"[64] expressed itself by demanding conformity not only to a conservative moral code but also to a conservative Protestant orthodoxy. Fundamentalism, as the movement became known, reduced Christian theology to five essential points: the verbal inerrancy of the Bible, the deity and virgin birth of Christ, the substitutionary atonement, the physical resurrection of Christ, and his bodily return to earth.[65] Some historians insist that "the fundamentalists were distinguished less by their theology, which many others shared, than by their posture of relentless hostility toward any deviation."[66]

Frank Smith was as opposed to rigidity as he was to controversy. "As we have passed from being pretty largely a pastoral or an agrarian people to being an industrial section," he explained,

the chief problem we have had is to teach people to live together, to adjust themselves, to keep the windows open toward new breezes. I never saw a question come up in my life that I didn't see two or three other alternatives. I was never one to whoop it up for some particular facet of some movement. A man can get so enthused about one side that he can actually develop a spirit of hatred and bitterness in his heart because of his advocacy of one side or the other.[67]

Rev. L. U. Spellman recalls that "Frank's policy was to look at all sides of a question. If he saw little or no merit in one side or the other, he could at least appreciate *why* some men thought or fought as they did. He didn't like rabid controversy, nor did he appreciate extremists whatever their cause."[68]

One of the causes of the Fundamentalist-Modernist controversy, according to Norman Furniss, was "the conservatives' conviction that modernism and evolution, in questioning their cherished doctrines, would destroy Christianity as a moral force in the nation."[69] This concern for conformity to a conservative moral code was a point of confluence for Fundamentalism and the Ku Klux Klan.[70] Modernism was practically a synonym for historical or higher criticism of the Bible. The infallible Bible formed the broad foundation of the Fundamentalist's pyramid of theological doctrines, each belief upheld by the one below. To tamper with any one block of that base might cause the collapse of the entire structure.[71]

When Professor John A. Rice of SMU's seminary faculty wrote a book on the Old Testament,[72] he was sharply attacked by the Rev. J. Frank Norris, pastor of Fort Worth's First Baptist Church, for denying the doctrine of scriptural infallibility.[73] According to the president of Southern Methodist University, Dr. H. A. Boaz, "For some reason the objections raised by Dr. Norris took strong hold on our Methodist pastors in Texas [who demanded] the resignation of Dr. Rice from the faculty of the University. . . . At some of the annual conferences there was considerable excitement over what was to be done. It was a delicate and difficult situation."[74]

Beginning in the spring of 1921, the pages of the *Texas Christian Advocate* reverberated with a battle of words over Professor Rice's book.[75] Dr. Rice's students and others contributed effective letters defending the professor's character and scholarship, but Bishop Edwin D. Mouzon's supporting statement carried the most weight with Frank Smith, as his letter to Mouzon clearly shows:

After reading your article in last week's *Advocate* I must write just a word to say that . . . each chapter should be published in our *Advocates* in various sections of the Church. . . . I have never read anything quite so illuminating and satisfying and convincing as is your statement of Methodism's position. I do hope that you will be placed for the next few years so that you can do some writing. You are able to do it, and I believe that responsibility rests upon you just now, as it does upon no other person in the Church.[76]

Since Smith did not participate in these verbal battles published in the church's papers, his viewpoint can often be found only in the public statements of his champions, especially Bishop Mouzon.

As a member of the executive committee of SMU's board of trustees that approved Rice's appointment as professor of Old Testament literature, Bishop Mouzon was in a position to speak with additional authority concerning the controversy centering on Rice's book. Not only was Rice's view of the Old Testament "the view of all Old Testament scholars at the present time," Mouzon declared, but also his faith was "true to the great doctrines of Methodism."[77] On the other hand, Bishop Mouzon did not give his unqualified approval to everything in Rice's book, as the following statement demonstrates:

I have whenever I have been spoken to about Dr. Rice's book, expressed my great regret at certain things contained therein and to Dr. Rice, personally, I have expressed my surprise and my regret at some things contained in his book. However, . . . my attitude to all such questions is as follows: Is a man loyal to Jesus Christ? Does he believe in him as the Son of God and the Savior of the world? Does he believe in salvation through faith in Him alone? Has he himself an experience of salvation? Is he living the life that a Christian ought to live? If an affirmative answer can be given to these questions,

my attitude has been that we would allow him considerable latitude in discussing philosophical and historical questions.[78]

Frank Smith was in full accord with such an irenic spirit.

In another article Bishop Mouzon summarized his "Methodist objections to Fundamentalism" in six points:

I object to Fundamentalism because it confuses scriptural doctrines with things
that are not; . . . because it insists on "creed" rather than on "faith" and
"the Christian life;" . . . because of its unchristian intolerance; . . . because
of its stress on the purely individualistic aspects of the gospel to the exclu-
sion and denial of the social application of the teachings of Jesus; . . . because
of its misleading methods of propaganda; . . . because of its sowing of dissension among the Churches.[79]

Mouzon concluded his rejection of fundamentalism by publishing—
as Frank Smith had urged him to do—a booklet entitled *Fundamentals
of Methodism*. In discussing the Methodist view of the Bible, he emphasizes a distinction drawn by the Protestant Reformers between "the
word of God and the Scripture which *contains* or *presents* that word."
Mouzon continues,

It is the unanimous declaration of the Reformers that Scripture is Scripture
because it gives us that knowledge of God and of his will which is necessary
for salvation; because it presents to the eye of faith God himself personally
manifesting himself in Christ. It is this presentation of God himself and
of his will for our salvation which is infallible and authoritative.[80]

Although it did not attract the attention that converged on the controversy concerning Rice's book, another Fundamentalist-instigated skirmish in 1921 involved Professor H. L. Gray at Southwestern University.
As Arthur Moore recalls, "Gray, a very beloved professor at Southwestern, had written or made some statements that seemed to be liberal
for that time. He was a member of the West Texas Conference, where
he came under considerable criticism."[81]

When the West Texas Conference met in San Antonio in October,
1921, before the Rice affair had been settled, "a resolution from certain
laymen of the conference" was presented for adoption during a business
session. The daily journal of the conference does not further identify
the nature of the resolution, but it does sketch the heated debate and
parliamentary maneuvers that followed. When neither the resolution's

supporters nor its opponents could gain a majority, its supporters moved for referral to the Committee on Lay Activities. Opponents of the resolution narrowly succeeded in sending the resolution to the Board of Education, where Professor Gray would receive a more sympathetic hearing. Arthur Moore was president of the board; John A. Kerr, chairman of Frank Smith's board at Laurel Heights, was vice-president; Gray himself was secretary; and Frank Smith was a member. At least two of the other members were trustees at Southwestern University.[82]

Arthur Moore recounts Smith's advocacy of Dr. Gray: "I remember when they were buzzing around about Gray's liberalism, Frank stood at his side and defended him. Frank said, 'This is a good man, and you are not going to censure him. There's room in this family for different viewpoints.' "[83] That evening, at the next session of the conference, Moore presented the following report from the Board of Education:

Inasmuch as there has been considerable agitation among our people that has seemed to indicate fear and anxiety concerning our faith and teachings as a church;

And whereas, our church has always regarded the Holy Scriptures as the Word of God, inspired in that unique sense in which no other literature, ancient or modern, is inspired, and that they are the one infallible, authoritative and final revelation of divine truth to the world.

1st. We wish to express our firm faith in and allegiance to, the Bible as the inspired Word of God as taught and earnestly contended for by our fathers in Methodism down through the years.

2nd. We do not believe that our holy Christianity has suffered or ever can suffer from the discovery of truth, and we wish it understood that we do not in the least degree discourage thorough, reverent and constructive scholarship and extensive research. We welcome devout scholarship and investigation, but we repudiate that so-called scholarship which goes to the extent of assailing or calling in question the divine origin and integrity of the Holy Scriptures.

3rd. We also re-affirm our disciplinary attitude toward the Scriptures and unreservedly call for wholesome teachings upon this subject from all, both preachers and teachers.[84]

The conference adopted this report without further debate.

Professor Rice was not so fortunate as his colleague at Southwestern University. Despite the support of Bishop Mouzon, faculty colleagues, and students, Rice finally concluded that he should resign his professorship at SMU. The day before Dr. Rice's resignation was announced in the *Texas Christian Advocate*, Bishop Mouzon wrote to Frank Smith:

"I have appointed Dr. Rice to Okmulgee in the East Oklahoma Conference, a fine Church among fine people, with parsonage and a salary of $5,000. . . . the storm will subside I trust."[85]

As noted earlier, the crucial issue in the fundamentalist controversy concerned the significance or authority of the Bible as a whole. Does that authority reside in the Bible because each and every word was literally dictated by God, as the Fundamentalists claimed? Or does the Bible's significance derive from God's unique revelation of himself through those human words, as Dr. John A. Rice affirmed?[86]

In his preaching at Laurel Heights Methodist Church, Frank Smith sought to be a biblical preacher. "I always used a text," he recalled in later years, "and I always found it powerfully stimulating."

I loved to draw analogies between scriptural events and happenings and apply it to the day. I just took to that. I couldn't keep from using a text to save my life. That was my authority. The Bible is a man's authority for standing up there in the pulpit. He is the representative of God. . . . I always had the pulpit Bible open before me, and I handled it with reverence to let the people be conscious of the fact that that is where I got my authority. I tried to create that atmosphere and feeling that this was the word of God and I was there to reveal the word of God, to open the word of God to the people. . . . My one thought was to help people grow their souls, to have the mind that was in Christ Jesus. I tried to keep my feet on that base, "Jesus Christ, the same yesterday, today and forever."[87]

Seeking to classify himself in relation to the fundamentalist controversy, Frank Smith said, "I counted myself more of a liberal than a conservative. I'd say that I was a conservative liberal. I was a liberal with conservative tendencies."[88] Arthur Moore remembers Frank as being "intellectually and theologically ahead of his day." "Frank had a good balance," Moore recalls. "He was out front and much more hospitable to new ideas and new demands."

At Laurel Heights Frank was thought of as a great preacher who had a love for people, and therefore he was both a good pastor and a good preacher. He got both of them in the same skin. . . . Frank and I were entirely different in our methods. I had been ten or twelve years in full-time evangelistic work. I'd storm the gates and call for mourners. Frank was more polished than that. According to a story that went around, there was a certain lady who went to hear Frank preach every Sunday morning at Laurel Heights, and then she'd come down and hear me preach at Travis Park that night. She said, "When I hear Dr. Smith preach, I go away feeling like I am undoubtedly the best woman in San Antonio. But after I hear Brother Moore preach Sunday night, I'm afraid the Devil will get me before I can get home."[89]

Frank Smith's correspondence during these years with Dean Paul Kern of SMU's School of Theology illustrates one way Smith kept up to date "theologically and intellectually." Before preparing a series of sermons on the Apostle Paul, for instance, Smith asked Kern to recommend the best books written about Paul.[90] Smith was also an avid reader of the *Christian Century*, one of the major voices of liberal Protestantism. He even tried to persuade Bishop Mouzon to subscribe to the *Century*.[91]

One of the few weaknesses that Frank Smith found at Laurel Heights Methodist Church was, as we have seen, the lack of churchmanship and sense of Methodist connectionalism. In his efforts to instill a distinctive Methodist identity in his people, Smith discovered one group that required special attention. These were the young women for whom the Missionary Society had little appeal. Although these ladies attended church and Sunday school regularly, they were not attracted by the traditional Methodist woman's organization. Angie Smith described them as

the young society women who do all the work in the comunity chest drives, the heart association, the Junior League crowd, the horse show crowd. They have got to have expression. Frank was trying to reach them for something besides coming and sitting down on Sunday morning. Well, Frank organized what he called The Blue Bird Society[92]

These young women of Laurel Heights Methodist Church soon won recognition in the *Texas Christian Advocate* for their work with the San Antonio Mission Home and Training School, Methodism's ministry to unwed mothers:

Rev. Frank Smith vowed if the Lord let him live this year, he would help the Home. The young matrons of his Church formed the "Blue Bird Society" which has indeed brought happiness, contributing baby clothes, etc., besides papering and renovating five rooms and two halls, making the house more like a home.[93]

Such projects did not prevent the young pastor and his wife from giving the regular Missionary Society its full share of their attention, as illustrated in the following tribute: "Rev. A. Frank Smith and Mrs. Smith are very much loved in Laurel Heights. Bro. Smith gave the Bible lessons to the society during the year, wonderful lessons of help and inspiration. Under their leadership the Church and the Society are growing."[94]

The people of Laurel Heights were expressing their appreciation to Frank and Bess Smith in a number of ways. In January, 1922, Frank wrote to Bishop Mouzon, "This fourth year has started out better than any of the preceding—our prayer meetings and evening services are better attended than ever before. Some of the members got together and presented us with a new car for a Xmas present. San Antonio becomes more attractive every year."[95] After Easter Smith wrote again:

You will be glad to know that I received a class of seventy-one into the church on profession of faith. Laurel Heights has never received more than forty-three on profession of faith during any entire year heretofore. This year we have received seventy-one by profession, and of course more will be received before the year shall close. You will also be glad to learn that we paid more than five thousand dollars on the Centenary Pay-Up Drive, bringing us above our sixty per cent on pledge, and more than two hundred per cent paid on our original quota.[96]

When the General Conference of the Methodist Episcopal Church, South, met in Hot Springs, Arkansas, in May, 1922, Frank Smith and Arthur Moore decided to attend the first week. Since they were able to obtain clergy passes from the railroad, their expenses wre nominal. On Wednesday morning, May 3, as Frank and Arthur watched from the visitors' gallery, Bishop Warren A. Candler called the conference to order and conducted the opening devotional service. Seven bishops participated in this service. When the secretary of the conference called the roll of bishops, thirteen responded.[97]

Three major issues faced by this General Conference concerned matters that would be of increasing interest to Frank Smith and Arthur Moore in the years ahead. One of these came from a continuing movement to limit the power of the episcopacy. Those advocating such a limitation sought to make the presiding eldership elective by the annual conferences rather than appointive by the bishops—an issue that was at least a hundred years old.[98] A more direct measure was proposed which would require bishops to be elected for a specific number of years, changing a lifetime episcopacy into a term episcopacy. During the year leading

up to the General Conference at Hot Springs, the correspondence section
of the weekly *Nashville Christian Advocate* had bristled with debate over
these proposals.[99] Bishop Mouzon wrote to Frank Smith, declaring that
such a term episcopacy was no episcopacy at all:

If some men had their way, as is indicated in the memorial being adopted by
a number of the Annual Conferences looking toward the election of Bishops
for a term of four years, there would not be any Bishops at all in the Church,
and there would be no sense in calling such men Bishops. Rather than pass
a measure of that kind, it would be better outright to abolish the Episcopacy
and elect certain representative men as Presiding Elders.[100]

Although seven annual conferences sent memorials requesting the General Conference "to provide suitable legislation for the election of bishops
for a specified number of years, they being subject to re-election," a
majority of the delegates rejected the proposal.[101]

Unification with the Northern Methodists was a second issue before
the General Conference in 1922. Since 1876 off-and-on negotiations for
such a union had been conducted, and the General Conference of the
Methodist Episcopal Church had just rejected a plan proposed by a
joint commission. Southern opponents of union, therefore, argued that
all negotiations should cease. The situation was saved when Ivan Lee
Holt, whom Frank Smith had known at SMU, and a group of pro-union
delegates maneuvered the leader of the opposition, Judge John S. Candler
of Atlanta, into proposing a compromise measure on the floor of the
conference.[102]

The third issue debated in 1922, of more immediate interest to Frank
Smith, was whether or not a pastor could be reappointed to the same
church for more than the traditional limit of four consecutive years.
Smith was then more than halfway through his fourth year at Laurel
Heights. In 1918 the General Conference had authorized the bishops
to make an exception to the four-year limit "where a Quarterly Conference shall request and a majority of the presiding elders shall concur
by ballot."[103] Four years of experience with this legislation had convinced
the bishops that it was bad for all concerned. As they stated their position in the Episcopal Address, "We have given this provision a fair
trial and feel constrained to report that in the main it works embarrassment to congregations, pastors, presiding elders, and bishops."[104] Nevertheless, after considerable debate, the delegates were only willing to relieve "embarrassment to congregations," for they continued the exception:

"When a majority of the presiding elders shall concur by ballot, the bishop may appoint a preacher to a pastoral charge for more than four consecutive years."[105]

A highlight of a General Conference session was the election and consecration of new bishops. Since five bishops had died during the quadrennium,[106] the conference decided to elect five additional bishops. Voting was by written ballots without nominations, the election continuing until one person received a simple majority. While the votes were being counted, the conference proceeded through its agenda. Frank Smith remembered the exciting moment when the report of the first ballot was given:

Arthur Moore and I were sitting up in the balcony together. And, bless Pat, when they read out who had votes, they read out, "A. F. Smith, ten votes." And Arthur turned to me and said, "Where are my votes?" Well, I learned later that Mr. John Kerr, the chairman of my board at Laurel Heights and the leader of the Lay Delegation of the West Texas Conference, had gone around and got his crowd to give me a complimentary vote for Bishop. Mr. Kerr just wanted to get my name in the pot. I disappeared on the second ballot.[107]

Arthur Moore explains: "We were so young and really so innocent as far as political performance goes. It never occurred to us that either one of us would ever be a bishop. We had no such ambition at all."[108]

Two of the five bishops elected in 1922 were to influence Frank Smith's life in the immediate future. James Edward Dickey, elected on the second ballot, would be given supervision of the West Texas Conference as part of his initial assignment. Samuel Ross Hay, elected on the third ballot, would be leaving First Methodist Church in Houston, one of the largest congregations in Southern Methodism. Within ten days Bishop John M. Moore would request Bishop Dickey to release A. Frank Smith for appointment to First Church, Houston.[109] Frank Smith described the following swift succession of events:

I went back home and told my folks, "They have taken me off the time limit, and I don't have to move. I want to stay ten years!" So they said, "We are going to have a party next Wednesday night and welcome you and Sister Smith back."

On Wednesday afternoon I got a call from the presiding elder in Houston about five o'clock. "This is George Davis," he said; "do you want to come to First Church, Houston?" "Why," I said, "of course, I want to go to

First Church, Houston." "Well," he said, "you are appointed." "Wait a minute," I said. "What are you talking about?" He said, "Bishop Moore has been down here and has met with the board. He tried to get you but couldn't. He is on the train headed for New York going back to Brazil to wind up his work down there. He told me to call you and tell you that you are appointed to First Church, Houston. Get your release from Bishop Dickey."

And an hour later we went over there to the reception where they were going to welcome us to stay another ten years and told them I was gone; I wasn't their preacher. It was a mournful occasion. Bessie cried every day till we left, but she did that with every appointment we served.[110]

Smith had mixed feelings about going to Houston: "I dreaded the idea of being the pastor of a great downtown church," he recalled. "Many of the pastors of the downtown churches of that day were rather sensational, and I thought you had to carry on that kind of business."[111] Arthur Moore remembers that Frank came to him for advice:

Frank was concerned about his style of preaching, not to popularize in any cheapening sense, but to be a little more of a man of the people. Sam Hay had been at First Church, Houston. Hay was a kind of rough and tumble preacher.[112] And I had certain books that had been helpful to me in my effort to speak to my people. I had a book of sermons by Sam Chadwick, a famous English Methodist preacher who had been head of Cliff College, a popular theological school where they trained Methodist preachers after the order of that time. And Chadwick had greatly stimulated my life and ministry. So I said, "Frank, read this."[113]

Frank also expressed his uneasiness to Bishop Mouzon, whom he considered "my father in the Gospel."[114] Mouzon said,

Frank, you go over there and be yourself. Don't try to imitate somebody else or try any of those stunts which are foreign to your temperament. You would be unhappy about it, and your people would know it was superficial and a pretense. If you can't succeed by being natural, you can go somewhere else and save your self-respect.[115]

Frank Smith thought that Bishop Mouzon had been responsible, at least in part, for his significant promotion to the First Methodist Episcopal Church, South, in Houston. In a letter to Mouzon dated May 29, he wrote:

I am quite certain that you had a deal to do with my appointment to Houston. I must express my deep appreciation for your confidence. If I can ever repay in some measure the great debt I owe you, it will be the joy of my life.

You will recall when I came to San Antonio, you told me to get R. L. Bell, Jno. W. Kokernot, and Mrs. Hal Browne into the church and my stay here would be profitable, if I did nothing else. You will be happy to know that on yesterday, my last Sunday here, I received all three of these into the church.[116]

Declining any credit, Mouzon replied:

You are mistaken in thinking I am responsible for your appointment at First Church, Houston; charge that up to Bishop Moore. He did mention it to me and I gave my approval, so you see I am not the only Bishop who thinks well of you. I expect you to have a great pastorate in Houston. Whatsoever else you may do, live close to God and always be sure of your personal relation to Jesus Christ. I am saying this just because I love you and not because I feel that there is any real occasion for me to exhort you after this fashion.[117]

Frank Smith's standing in San Antonio was indicated by the number and size of the gatherings held in his honor before he left that city for his new pastorate in Houston. The largest farewell was held at Travis Park Methodist Church under the guidance of Arthur Moore, with the combined congregations of Laurel Heights and Travis Park "taxing the capacity of the auditorium" of the downtown church. According to a newspaper account of the meeting, prominent civic and church leaders gave the speeches of tribute and farewell:

Mayor O. B. Black recalled his school days at Southwestern University when he was a fellow student with Mr. Smith and . . . lauded his friend as a strong leader who has taught San Antonio many things for the betterment of the city for God and humanity.

Nat M. Washer was a speaker for the Kiwanis Club, of which the departing minister is a member. . . .

Dr. Felix R. Hill, president of Westmoreland College, spoke a farewell message for the ministry of the city. The Rev. Mr. Smith has gripped San Antonio and every club in the city by his influence, the speaker said. . . .

John A. Kerr spoke for the Laurel Heights Methodist Church and told of the affection the congregation has for their departing minister.[118]

While this Sunday evening farewell was "filled with mirth and humorous and friendly jokes passing between the pastors and lay leaders,"[119] the treatment given Frank Smith by the San Antonio Kiwanis Club the following Friday was packed with pranks. Shortly after the weekly luncheon began in the ballroom of the Gunter Hotel, a police-

man came in and "arrested" Frank on a charge of speeding. To keep
the officer from taking away their "guest of honor," Arthur Moore and
Bishop Capers "posted bond" for Frank. Then Moore announced that he
had received a telegram from Mr. John T. Scott, the chairman of the
Official Board of First Methodist Church in Houston:

We the Official Board and Membership of First Methodist Church, Houston,
appeal to you to help us prevent Smith coming here as pastor. We understand, reliable authority, he belongs to that class super pious parsons. Carries
long face wears white tie and long coat and never cracks a joke. Our church
one of largest in Nation and we need first class men. Understand there is
opening at New Braunfels. Use your influence have Smith sent there.[120]

To help Frank improve his punctuality in keeping appointments, the
Kiwanians presented him with a "watch" that turned out to be an alarm
clock on a chain. The secretary of the club then read another telegram
just "received" from Washington, D.C.:

Please notify A. Frank Smith of his unanimous election to the Ancient and
United Order of Independent Bone Heads. We have three classes of membership: Honorary, Elective and Natural Born. In Smith's case we waive all
examination and elect him to life membership as a Natural Born. Reason
for our action, his choice of Houston over San Antonio as home. Mr. Smith
will have as his close associates the society of Mr. Ford's Peace-ship Party and
Dr. C. Cook of North Pole fame. With all these the bump of progress is a
dimple.

E. Z. MARK,
Worthy Grand Snarl[121]

According to a newspaper account, after "the departing minister expressed
himself briefly on the value of his Kiwanis associations and his sadness
at leaving," Arthur Moore "then invited everybody 'to file by to the
accompaniment of soft music and take one last look at the remains.' "[122]

Frank Smith's love for San Antonio is clearly shown in a "farewell
address" he gave at the Salesmanship Club. Speaking on "The Romantic
History of San Antonio," Smith sketched the story of the city from the
earliest days of French and Spanish rule to the present:

You must go back with me to the days of Louis XIV in France, before
George Washington was born, to find the early history of San Antonio. There
have even been found traces of civilization here when Columbus discovered
America, for the Indians first made San Pedro Springs the location for their
council fires. . . .

San Antonians should often visit San Jose and Concepcion Missions and with bared heads stand and commune with the spirits of the past and in imagination picture the scenes in which Indians and priests mingled in a young civilization. . . .

Every Texan should go to the old Governor's Palace and gaze at the door through which Moses Austin passed when he obtained the permit which allowed the white colonists to settle here. San Antonio must never allow the old Governor's Palace to be destroyed. It is next in importance in Texas and San Antonio history to the Alamo. . . .

San Antonio is different and it ought to be different, for we tread the soil made famous and sacred by the blood of Travis, Crockett, Bonham and Milam. Grant and Lee bid each other farewell here not to meet again until they came to Appomatox Court House. Here came Lanier, seeking health, and while he was here he composed some of the sweetest lyrics and wrote one of the best histories of San Antonio. Here also came O. Henry, seeking health with better success, and Theodore Roosevelt to train for the Spanish-American War. Then the soldiers of the 90th Division went from here to victory.

Here the virile, liberty-loving Anglo-Saxon mingles with the romantic Spaniard, and the city over which six flags have flown is all the more loyal to the American flag for having known the influence of the other five.[123]

San Antonio had indeed become an enduring part of Frank Smith's life. His sense of belonging in the community and of appreciating its uniqueness is clearly communicated in this address.

"The coming of A. Frank Smith to Laurel Heights in 1918," wrote that church's historians, "was an event of strategic importance. During his three and one-half years at this church, membership increased from 365 to 573 and the budget was practically doubled."

A few weeks before his transfer to First Methodist Church at Houston, he recorded with obvious satisfaction this final report: "This has been a good quarter in every respect. The largest ingathering this church has ever known has occurred during this quarter. There have been eighty-one additions to the church—sixty-three upon profession of faith and eighteen by certificate." However, above and beyond these measurable assets, A. Frank Smith left his imprint of spirituality on the hearts and lives of the people of Laurel Heights Church and it will never be erased.[124]

John A. Kerr wrote to Bishop Mouzon: "Frank is on his way to Houston [and] Laurel Hgts. members are in mourning. No preacher was ever loved more than these members loved Frank."[125]

Laurel Heights Methodist Church also held a unique place in Frank

Smith's memory. Many years later, writing to a close friend, Smith declared:

Laurel Heights Church means more to me than any other pastorate. It did something for me that no other church I ever served did. It put my feet on the ground and gave me a poise and direction that have never deserted me. I count the years spent there as the happiest and most productive in all my ministry."[126]

7

"The Great Gulf Basin"

"I CAME TO HOUSTON and preached my first sermon on June 4, 1922,"
Frank Smith recalled. "I had a full house and a warm reception. I returned to San Antonio, we packed our belongings, and Mrs. Smith, Frank
and I drove to Houston."[1] A more complete account appeared in a
Houston newspaper:

> Dr. A. Frank Smith, new pastor of the First Methodist Church, was given
> a royal welcome when he appeared for his first service at the church yester-
> day morning. The congregation, now the largest in Southern Methodism,
> filled the great auditorium and the several galleries.
> J. T. Scott, chairman of the board of stewards, . . . presented Dr. Smith.
> . . . The whole congregation rose in greeting him. . . .
> At the conclusion of the service practically the whole congregation came
> forward to greet in person the new pastor . . . and Dr. Smith was visibly
> affected by the ovation accorded him. . . .
> In his sermon[2] Dr. Smith sustained the reputation that had preceded him
> for being a pulpit orator of unusual ability. It was apparent that with his
> polished manner, his wonderful voice and the deep spiritual tone of his
> thought he caught the fancy of the big congregation from the start, and by
> the conclusion of his address many were heard to say that the bishop had
> made an ideal appointment in sending Dr. Smith to First Church.[3]

Houston's First Methodist Church claimed a rich heritage, reaching

126

back to 1837, when Methodist missionaries first came to Houston. This heritage inevitably intertwined with that of the Republic of Texas, for Houston was named for General Sam Houston and located just sixteen miles up Buffalo Bayou from the San Jacinto battlefield, where General Houston's army had won Texas independence on April 21, 1836. In the fall of 1836 the first Texas congress designated Houston the temporary capital city of the Republic.[4] Within a year (Sunday, December 17, 1837), Dr. Martin Ruter, the superintendent of the Texas Mission, and Rev. Littleton Fowler formed "a Sunday School Society" in "Congress Hall" in the village of Houston.[5] The first Methodist Church in Houston was organized in the senate chamber of that same capitol building in April, 1839, by the Rev. Jesse Hord.[6]

By 1922 Houston had developed a population of more than 150,000, second in size in the state only to San Antonio. With its deep-water ship channel and its extensive railroad connections, Houston was establishing its reputation as "the perennial boom town of twentieth-century Texas."[7] The decade of the twenties—embracing Smith's eight-year pastorate at First Church—would be a period of fantastic development. Formerly a distribution center with its prosperity primarily dependent on the handling of cargoes destined for other places, Houston then began its industrial development. By 1925 the depth of the channel had been increased to thirty feet to accommodate large tankers, opening the way for vast expansion of oil refineries. A four-million-dollar bond issue passed in 1922 financed construction of new wharves, a grain elevator, an additional channel railway, and other improvements. Cotton exports, the historic base of the area's prosperity, increased from 771,894 bales in 1922 to 2,069,792 in 1930. The ten-year burst is summarized by one historian:

By 1930 Houstonians could look back on a decade of fantastic port development. Not only had the Port of Houston surpassed all of its Texas rivals, but it ranked third in foreign exports in the United States, being surpassed only by New York and Los Angeles. Almost eighty shipping lines called regularly at the Port carrying in that year 15,057,360 tons of cargo valued at $500 million. Moreover, the industrial complex that lined the channel had grown each year until more than forty industries lay below the Turning Basin, and more than twenty-five above. In the same period, the city of Houston had grown from third to first in size in the state and to second in size in the South.[8]

First Methodist Church had maintained a parallel growth with

Houston. In 1922, with a membership of 3,000 and a salary of $7,500, it led Southern Methodism. "I early discovered," Frank Smith recalled, "that First Church was the dominant religious organization in the city in its impact upon the community."

The thing that made First Church's ministry during the twenties of such tremendous impact was the spirit and morale of the membership and the loyalty, pride and progressiveness and drive of the leaders. Many of the outstanding citizens in Houston were in First Church: lawyers, doctors, bankers, and business men. The presidents of the four largest banks in Houston were stewards in First Church. I found a ready response from these leaders, as well as from the rank and file among the members.[9]

The chairman of the board of stewards was John T. Scott, president of the First National Bank. A leading layman, Judge James A. Elkins, was president of the City National Bank and a senior partner in the law firm of Vinson, Elkins and Wood, which was to become one of the nation's largest law firms.[10] Samuel F. Carter, president of the Lumberman's National Bank, was active on First Church's board of stewards. Jesse H. Jones, another Methodist layman, was unchallenged as "Mr. Houston" for at least thirty years "through his control of a giant real estate empire stretching from Texas to New York, his banking connections, his insurance and investment companies and his newspaper, the *Houston Chronicle*."[11] In 1932, two years after Frank Smith was elected a Methodist bishop, Jones began thirteen years of public service in Washington with the Reconstruction Finance Corporation and in 1940 became President Roosevelt's Secretary of Commerce.[12] Jones's "most trusted lieutenant and right-hand man," Fred J. Heyne, was Sunday School Superintendent at First Methodist Church and an ardent admirer of his new pastor.[13]

Another layman at First Church, a close friend of Frank Smith's, was William Lockhart Clayton, whose Anderson, Clayton and Company built the largest private terminal on the Houston ship channel in 1923 for its cotton business. According to Jesse Jones, Will Clayton was "one of the sagest Americans both in foreign trade and in diplomacy, a gentleman who built up the world's largest firm of cotton merchants before beginning his distinguished government service career as Assistant Secretary of Commerce and later Under-Secretary of State."[14] Among the lawyers, Hines H. Baker, who had joined Humble Oil & Refining Co.'s legal department in 1919, was teaching a Sunday school class at First

Church. As noted earlier, Frank Smith received Baker into the University Methodist Church in Austin.[15] This renewed friendship developed in depth and mutual admiration over the years. Dr. Marvin Lee Graves, the son of a Methodist minister and a graduate of Southwestern University (Class of '85), became the Smiths' family physician.

"I was just thirty-two years old when I landed here," Smith explained, "and I must say, to my amazement, I got along all right."

> From the beginning we had great crowds. The morning service, which reveals the strength of any church, was a formal, dignified service—thought to be a little "high church" by some of the faithful. The evening service was of a free and informal nature, though never sensational, and drew people from all sections of the city. There was little or no program, however, save Sunday preaching and pastoral calls. The day of big programs, missionary, hospital and educational specials was yet to come.[16]

To say that Smith's adjustment to his new appointment was purely routine, however, would be misleading. It was not an easy task for a man in his early thirties to follow as successful and popular a minister as Sam Hay was. Having served appointments in Houston, Hay was well known throughout the city. After four years as pastor of Shearn Memorial, he became presiding elder of the Houston District and then organized the South End Church, which later became St. Paul's. His appointment to First Church in 1919 was his fourth assignment in Houston. Speaking about Frank Smith's beginning at First Church, one prominent member of that congregation explained:

> Dr. Smith did not make the mistake of trying to tear down what Bishop Hay had been doing during the years of his pastorate. He was not jealous of all the popularity that had been Bishop Hay's. He knew that the people who most loved Sam Hay would love him, and that the people who had been most loyal to the church in the years past would be most loyal to the church under its new administration. Such an attitude was bound to bring success, and the splendid life and growth of the church under Bishop Hay continued under A Frank Smith.[17]

Bishop Hay played a significant role in making that transition a smooth one, Frank Smith insisted. He wrote to Bishop Mouzon: "We have received a most cordial welcome from the people of First Church. Bishop Hay remained here for six weeks after my arrival and did all he could to smooth the way for me. There was not a discordant note, so far as I can discover."[18] In fact, Hay was one of the first to commend Smith on his new appointment: "I want to congratulate you and also the First Methodist Church of Houston. The Bishop has made a wise appointment, and in every way it meets with my approval. . . . Nothing will give me more pleasure than to aid you all I can in getting your start in this great Church."[19]

Sam Hay had received a salary of $7,500 at First Church, whereas Smith had received $5,000 at Laurel Heights. Since Hay was an older man and far more experienced, some of the stewards at First Church thought that Smith should be paid less. If they paid their new pastor $6,000 that would be a substantial raise for him. Then, later on, as Smith matured, they could show their appreciation by raising the salary back up to the $7,500 figure. John T. Scott, the chairman of the board, objected:

Not on your life! We're bringing a man here to be the pastor of the First Methodist Church. If he is capable of filling his predecessor's shoes, he is worth as much as his predecessor. If he isn't, we don't want him at all. We're not going to cut him back and tell the world that we want a man here who is not as good as the man we had.[20]

There was certainly no question in the mind of Bishop John M. Moore that Frank Smith was the right man for First Methodist Church in Houston. Knowing that the young pastor would be challenged as never before in his ministry, Moore wrote the following letter of encouragement:

I think you appreciate the fact that you now have the opportunity of your life. You must use every means possible of making yourself a good minister of Jesus Christ. Remember that you must preach, make sermons that count and deliver them with all the heart, skill and power that you can command. Do not let any office work use up the hours that you should have for study. Many men in these large places go to the office first in the morning, but my advice is to go first to the study and let nothing take you out until you have finished your task there. Give yourself to the pastoral work and to promoting the larger interests of the community Christianity. I am sure you know exactly what to do. The trouble will be in letting somebody cut down your ideal and change your program. I believe in you thoroughly and your success in all the work of the church will delight me.[21]

One expression of confidence that Frank Smith particularly cherished came from his friend Paul Kern, dean of the School of Theology at

SMU. "Allow me to present my congratulations together with a few expressions of sympathy," Kern wrote.

> I might think the job was too big for you if I did not recall that you had successfully handled every big responsibility into which you have ever been called. Surely now you have come into a place of tremendous leadership and I trust that power may be given to you adequate to your enlarged field of usefulness.[22]

Apparently, some of the preachers of the Texas Conference were not pleased with Smith's appointment. One of them, a man holding a position of leadership in the conference, sent the following protest to Bishop John M. Moore:

> . . . That the appointment of Frank Smith to First Church, Houston, was a great mistake is putting it mildly, both for the church and the conference. . . .
> There is a feeling not only of disappointment among the preachers of the conference but in many places, much stronger than that, it amounts to resentment and indignation. There are a dozen men in the conference that could have filled the place as well, or better, than the man you sent there. If you had to go outside of the conference why did you take a man of only seven years in conference instead of some man of experience and outstanding ability? There would not have been the same feeling if you had done that. . . .
> There is another side to this appointment: it is known that you did not consult the presiding elders of the conference outside of one man. That was another mistake. Also it is believed that another bishop was largely responsible for the appointment. The members of the conference resent that also.[23]

Ironically, Bishop Moore was accompanying Bishop Dobbs on an episcopal visitation in South America at this time, having requested Bishop Mouzon to take care of all matters pertaining to his district. One can only guess at the consternation that struck the protesting brother's heart when he received Mouzon's letter explaining the above circumstances. "I have before me your letter of July," Mouzon began, "in which you have some things to say touching the appointment of Brother Frank Smith to First Church, Houston."

> It is not necessary, neither would it be proper, for me to have much to say concerning the criticisms which you make of that appointment. There is one statement in your letter, however, to which it may be proper for me to make some reply. You write, "It is believed that another Bishop was largely responsible for the appointment." I am quite sure that you are in

error at that point. Bishop Moore has a head of his own and, while you will find that he advises freely with brethren, he does his own thinking. The one reason why I am replying to this statement in your letter is because it is generally known that Frank Smith loves me as a son loves his father and that I, and my children, look upon him almost as if he were one of our family. Now, at no time did I mention Frank Smith's name to Bishop Moore in connection with this appointment. It came as a surprise to me when Bishop Moore told me that, after consultation with brethren, he had decided to make that appointment. I had nothing at all to do with the making of his appointment. I will add, however, that the appointment meets with my approval and, if I am not mistaken, of others in the College of Bishops.[24]

Such resentment toward Frank Smith was limited to a minority of the ministers and was not typical of those in Houston, according to Bishop William C. Martin. Appointed to Grace Church in 1921, Martin remembers the first appearance Smith made at the weekly meetings of the Houston Methodist pastors:

We met every Monday morning in those days down at First Church. All of us were very eager to meet the new pastor. I had never met him before, although I had heard a great deal about him as all of us had who were aware of the more prominent ministers of the Methodist Church. We gathered in our assembly room well ahead of time. I shall never forget the moment of Frank's entrance. We were immediately aware, even though we had not seen him or met him before, we were aware that we were in the presence of a man of unusual gifts. He had all the appearances and all the expressions of assurance of himself, his mission, his ministry. We had no difficulty in realizing that we were all very fortunate in having him as our leading pastor in the city.[25]

During the four years that they were fellow pastors in Houston, Martin and Smith saw a great deal of each other. On the basis of that relationship, Martin characterizes Smith's early ministry in Houston:

In accordance with my basic memory of the man, there was no one point at which he stood out in spectacular fashion. He was a good preacher, interesting, and a man who dealt with the vital concerns of the Gospel and its application to everyday life. He was also a good pastor, and he was concerned about the administrative side of the life of the church. There just seemed to be a sound balance in his ministry embracing all that I regarded as being essential to a well-rounded pastoral ministry.[26]

Frank Smith's correspondence with Bishop Edwin D. Mouzon offers periodic glimpses of the young man's pastoral pilgrimage. Writing to Mouzon early in his fourth month in Houston, Smith reported:

Our congregations this summer, the people tell me, have been the largest summer congregations First Church has ever had, and the leading men on the Board tell me that the church has never been in finer shape. The membership is growing rapidly, the people are loyal and contented. First Church has a great grip upon the life of the city.[27]

Being the pastor of such a great church was having its effect on Frank Smith:

I feel that the Lord is going to bless us wonderfully in this pastorate. I have occasion every Sunday to think of what you said about my needing a pulpit where it would be necessary for me to call penitents. Already this difference is proving a blessing to my own life. Rarely a service passes that I do not receive men and women into the church on profession of faith, following the altar call.[28]

Seven months later, Smith wrote again:

Our congregations fill the house, galleries included, at every service—the house seats about two thousand. On Easter Sunday I received 275 into church membership and baptized more than sixty infants. As you said [it would] the opportunity & necessity of calling penitents at every service has made me over. Never a Sunday & rarely a service but that they come.[29]

The demands of such exciting success became a threat to Frank Smith's general well-being, as he implies in the following letter to Mouzon:

Last summer we came here the first of June, and I have been away only two Sundays since, once at the Summer School and once during Annual Conference, so I am feeling the need for a little relaxation. I do not know how to take a vacation, however: I have never taken one since I have been preaching. There is nothing that I think of that I care to do, particularly, and when I am away from home, I am wondering if everything is going all right. I find I would be better off at home than trying to "vacate."[30]

While the relationship between A. Frank Smith and Edwin D. Mouzon had been of ever increasing significance in Frank's life since they first met at Southwestern University in 1908,[31] this bond of affection became particularly clear in their correspondence during Frank's early years in Houston. In September, 1922, Frank wrote: "I feel that something has been neglected if I fail to make an occasional report to you concerning my work. I may never receive another appointment at your hands, but you will always be 'my bishop,' and I take pride in feeling that you will always be interested in my work."[32] That Mouzon appreciated and anticipated these "occasional reports" is apparent in his reply: "I have been wondering what was the matter with you that you did not write me. I was indeed glad to get your letter and to learn from you personally that everything was moving along nicely with you at First Church."[33] On another occasion, Mouzon declared: "I am always glad to hear from you, for you know how much I love you."[34]

Although Frank was always formal in his salutations—"My Dear Bishop Mouzon"—he usually closed his letters with "Affectionately yours." When matters concerning either family were discussed, Frank concluded, "Love to all of you" or "Bess joins me in love to all of you." In one instance, he used a phrase that became characteristic of his personal letters years later: "All the family would join me in love to all of you if they knew of my writing." Mouzon's daughter, Hattie, was seriously ill during this period, and Frank shared in the bishop's anxieties as well as in his rejoicing when Hattie miraculously recovered. He seems to have been much like a "big brother" to the bishop's children. "Carlisle greatly appreciated your note congratulating him on his success in school," Mouzon wrote on one occasion.[35]

In addition to special occasions, Frank Smith always sent greetings to Bishop Mouzon on his birthday and at Christmas. Replying to such a telegram on his fifty-fourth birthday, Mouzon wrote: "It was certainly thoughtful of you to remember that I had a birthday, although I confess that these birthdays are beginning to get a little serious."[36]

Complementing the father-son nature of their relationship, Bishop Mouzon's influence on Frank Smith was also a motivating force vocationally. As Smith declared: "I have said before and repeat that you have been the greatest inspiration my ministry has known. To merit your respect and affection is my continual endeavor."[37]

Perhaps the most serious problem that Frank Smith faced in his first year in Houston was the disruptive influence of the Ku Klux Klan. "The Klan was riding high," he recalled, "and had been the deciding factor in most of the city and county elections held just as I got to Houston. I was faced with a community tension of heroic proportions."[38] Since

its organization in October, 1920, the "Sam Houston Klan No. 1"—
the first Klan chapter organized in Texas—had gained strength rapidly.
Klansmen running for office in Harris County, according to the *Houston
Post*, had scored notable victories, either winning clear nominations or
entering the runoff.[39]

The chief of police and most of the Houston police were members
of the Klan. Without interference, Klansmen engaged in such extralegal
practices as tapping telephones over the city, intercepting messages at
the telegraph offices, and maintaining spies in the city post offices.[40]
Finally, the opponents of the Klan managed to plant a spy within the
Klan's meeting. Regardless of the efforts of the Klan's leadership to
change their meeting places, the spy managed to get into every meeting.
Bishop Will Martin remembers how very amusing it was "to those of us
who were not of the Klan." "The next day after every weekly meeting
of the Klan, the *Houston Chronicle* would publish a full account of what
went on, even calling the names of those who said such-and-such. Now
my dear friend, Brother ———, was a klansman and he was quoted
more than once. In fact, there were a number of Methodist preachers
who were in the Klan."[41] As Frank Smith learned, "Marcellus E. Foster,
the founder, publisher and editor of the *Chronicle*—Houston's first and
largest afternoon paper—was the medium of publicity through whom
those opposing the Klan operated. Using his initials, "MEFO," Foster
had a regular column in the *Chronicle*. "I came to know him well," Smith
explained, "and was associated with him in many ways. He was a brilliant and forceful personality."[42]

Frank Smith's immediate concern was to keep the Klan from splitting
his congregation.

I had both the Kleagle[43] of the Klan and the judge who was attacking them
most steadily here in my church, and they tried to bring it into the board.
I let it be definitely understood that this issue was not to enter our board
meetings or any other organization of our church and that no hooded figures
would be allowed to enter First Church. I said, "I can tell you one thing.
If any group with sheets shows up here at the door to march down the aisle,
I am going to stop them in their tracks." And I said to these two leaders:
"Gentlemen, you two men are in good standing in this church. I am going
to appoint both of you on the collection committee, and I want you to walk
down the aisle together on Sunday and take up the collection." Well, they did
it, and it took the steam out of them just like the hare-lipped fellow who
married a hare-lipped woman. When asked if he ever kissed his wife, he
replied: "Yeth, but I don't get much thnap out of it." Well, they couldn't

get much "thnap" out of jumping on each other during the week because Sunday morning they would be walking down the aisle together.[44]

Smith also credited John T. Scott for his help during that crisis. "We got through that with a minimum of difficulty because I had a sound, level-headed man as chairman of the board. He just wouldn't tolerate any of that thing coming in one way or another."[45]

Unfortunately, the matter was not that easily avoided. In August, the *Houston Chronicle* came out with headlines announcing: "PRESIDENT OF FIRST METHODIST CHURCH MEN'S BIBLE CLASS ASKED TO RESIGN, HOLDS KU KLUX KLAN 'RESPONSIBLE.' "[46] According to the newspaper article, Sunday School Superintendent L. L. Nelms had requested that George E. B. Peddy, an assistant criminal district attorney and chairman of the Ferguson headquarters for South Texas, resign the presidency of the Men's Bible Class because of his support of former governor James E. Ferguson's candidacy for the U.S. Senate. Peddy, in turn, accused Nelms and certain other members of the Bible class of being members or sympathizers of the Ku Klux Klan. Ferguson's opponent in the political race was Earle B. Mayfield, acknowledged candidate of the Klan. Ferguson was anathema to the Klan and Texas prohibitionists, not only because he had been impeached and removed from office as governor in 1917,[47] but also because he favored modifying the Volstead Act so as to permit the manufacture and sales of light wines and beer.[48] Mayfield's narrow victory over Ferguson in the Democratic primary runoff election in August—described as "one of the most vitriolic struggles in the history of a state long characterized by turbulent politics"[49]—triggered a statewide convention of disgruntled Democrats and opponents of the Klan who formed the "Independent Democrats of Texas" and nominated Frank Smith's Men's Bible Class President George E. B. Peddy to run against Mayfield in the November general election. This final campaign was marked by "an amazing series of filing of protests, injunctions, appeals, hearings, trials and rulings which must have made the voters dizzy in regard to the candidates' eligibility."[50] Since Peddy's suporters had to "write in" his name on their ballots, Mayfield had an overwhelming advantage and won by a two-thirds majority.

Such a prolonged and bitter political campaign must have been a trying ordeal for Frank Smith as he sought to maintain unity and concord in his congregation at First Methodist Church. "In the midst of this spirit of tension, religious and racial bigotry, and hysteria," he recalled, I preached the power of God to save, Sunday after Sunday."[51]

While Houston was still suffering through the religious and racial unrest caused by the Ku Klux Klan, Frank Smith discovered an opportunity for First Methodist Church to make a practical contribution and an effective witness to brotherhood. Through his friend Dr. Henry Barnston, rabbi of Houston's Temple Beth Israel, Smith learned that this Jewish congregation was facing a crisis. Having decided to build larger facilities on a new location, they were being forced to vacate their old temple before the new one was completed. Smith took up the matter with the chairman of his board, John T. Scott. "Out of that discussion," he recalled, "there came a sudden determination to invite Beth Israel to hold services in First Church."

The Ku Klux Klan was waning but still very active in the community. Mr. Scott and I decided it would not be wise to take the matter to the Board for discussion, but rather that we had better issue the invitation ourselves and assume full responsibility for it. This we did, and Rabbi Barnston gratefully accepted. Nobody in First Church or Beth Israel knew anything about it till it was formally announced. Some of the saints in both groups were scandalized and horrified, but it was a *fait accompli* before they heard about it. Instead of being with us for the anticipated three months, however, they were with us for eighteen months—and at no service cost to them whatsoever.[52]

"We received very severe criticism from some of our folks," Smith remembered, "and so did the Rabbi. But we passed right along." Then he added with a chuckle, "That's when the Jews adopted me."[53]

Sharing the same facilities for Christian and Jewish services was a relatively simple matter during ordinary seasons. First Church was a Jewish temple Friday night and Saturday morning, a Methodist church on Sundays. Special seasons called for greater care in scheduling, however—Easter, for example. The special Easter musical program presented by the First Methodist Church choir had attained such a wide reputation among Houstonians that the sanctuary could not accommodate the crowds. It became necessary for the choir to repeat the same program on the following Sunday evening. For this particular Easter, the choir had hung a large illuminated cross over the organ pipes. Since the special choral program was to be presented the following Sunday evening, no one thought of removing the six-foot illuminated cross. As Frank Smith later recalled, he received a telephone call on Monday night from an obviously distressed rabbi.

"Now, Dr. Smith, I am embarrassed to call you about this," Dr. Barnston began, "but we went down there tonight to have our Passover Services and there was an illuminated cross right up over my head. That didn't bother me, but some of the good sisters of Israel nearly died. Can we turn off the illumination?"

"Dr. Barnston," Smith replied, "we owe you an apology. That's not a Christian Church this week, that's your Jewish Temple, and we ought to have taken that down. I'll come down early in the morning and see to it."

"Oh, no," Barnston insisted, "I'll have our sexton take care of it."

When Smith arrived at the church early the next morning, the janitors were busily removing the cross, uneasily assisted by Sexton Keller. "Ah, Dr. Smith," said Keller, "these narrow Jews! They talk like the cross has something to do with Jesus Christ. Any fool knows that the cross originated in Switzerland years before Jesus was born."[54]

Speaking of the constructive impact that the Methodists' invitation to Congregation Beth Israel had on Houston, Smith explained:

That act electrified the community. The prestige and influence of First Church was enhanced beyond expression in this city and far beyond by this fraternal gesture. *Time* magazine even gave a half-page spread to it. Beyond a doubt this was a tremendous factor toward healing the wounds made during the preceding years. In later years Beth Israel was the home for months of St. Paul's [Methodist] Church when it was building out on South Main and likewise of the First Presbyterian Church when it relocated.[55]

On March 8, 1925, when the cornerstone for the new Temple Beth Israel was laid, the principal speakers for the dedication services included Rabbi Henry Cohen of Galveston, Rabbi David Lefkowitz of Dallas, and Rev. A. Frank Smith. According to a newspaper report of the occasion:

Dr. A. Frank Smith took the stand after the visitors had made their addresses and made a short impromptu talk. He congratulated the congregation of Temple Beth Israel on their new temple and expressed his good will. He also remarked on the three great contributions the Jews have made toward the progress of the world—the idea of a universal God, the establishment of a monogamous social life and the handing down of the Ten Commandments, upon which the whole legal structure of the world is based.[56]

"The consistently cordial attitude of your church and yourself throughout the period of Beth Israel's homelessness," Rabbi Barnston wrote to Dr. Smith, "has done more towards cementing the ties that should bind us than any other incident I can recall during my 25 years service in Houston. May God bless you."[57] As a continuing expression of their gratitude, the congregation of Temple Beth Israel still sends flowers to First Methodist Church each Christmas.[58]

Another major contribution to the restoration of brotherhood and interfaith fellowship was made through the annual men's banquet at the First Methodist Church. These dinners had been held for a number of years as strictly a Methodist affair. Frank Smith saw the possibility of making a constructive counteraction to the influence of the Klan by turning these fellowship dinners into brotherhood banquets. As Howard Grimes sketches this significant development in his history of First Methodist Church:

In an attempt to offset the post-war hysteria which had turned especially toward Jews and Catholics, the committee invited a number of Jewish and Catholic laymen to the affair in 1924 [and] the Brotherhood Banquet became definitely inter-religious in character. No doubt many anticipated widespread opposition.[59]

Mrs. J. N. R. Score, whose husband became pastor at St. Paul's Methodist Church in 1926, remembers the public amazement when the Roman Catholic Bishop from Galveston was one of the guest speakers. "That was just almost an unheard of thing in those days."[60]

Frank Smith explained the unique nature and attraction of these Brotherhood Banquets:

We allocated three-fourths of the tickets to general purchase by the men of First Church and kept the other fourth for special guests invited by the church: Catholic and Jew, both clerical and lay, and prominent persons in Houston and outside. We brought prominent speakers—governors and cabinet members, congressmen and senators, university presidents, and supreme court justices. The affair caught on like a prairie fire. Men sought tickets from outside Houston and from other states. From around two hundred or two hundred fifty the attendance grew to a thousand or more within a couple of years. From the head table Catholics, Jews and Protestants discussed freely the issues of the day. An atmosphere was created that men revelled in; divisions were healed. Friendships were formed that never could have come about through any other medium. Enough of clean, wholesome fun was injected to keep the programs lively. It was frequently said by visitors that no such gathering could be found anywhere else in the land. Those men's meetings at First Church did more than words can portray to create a spirit of good will and cooperation in Houston and made First Church the pride of the entire rapidly expanding city.[61]

The following comments written by the influential and respected editor of the *Houston Chronicle*, Marcellus E. Foster, support Frank Smith's evaluation of the dinners:

The banquet last night was a credit to a great church. There were assembled over 500 men representing every faith and every denomination in Houston. While it was a Methodist banquet, the guests included Jews, Catholics, Baptists, Presbyterians, Christians, and Unitarians. There was a spirit of good fellowship, harmony and high resolve. It proved that men who are leaders in the business and professional life of Houston are among the church members of the city. We congratulate Dr. Frank A. [*sic*] Smith on that testimonial of brotherly love and his desire to bring together those who have faith, regardless of creeds.[62]

Bishop Will Martin, who spent three years in Houston during those troublesome times, considers Frank Smith's role in the development of the Brotherhood Banquets "a significant element in Frank's ministry in Houston," and "indicative of the man's spirit."[63] Hines Baker, who attended many of the annual banquets, remembers them as "the big event of the year" and "a good occasion for interchange of ideas and fellowship, a unique fellowship that grew out of Frank Smith's regard for people, an attitude of warmth and brotherhood." He also remembers that Smith "got more fun out of it than anybody."[64]

Hines Baker was actively involved in another expression of Frank Smith's spirit of generosity and cooperativeness. A former German-speaking Methodist congregation was being moved from downtown on McKinney Street out into the Montrose area, which had become the elite section of Houston. "They didn't have quite the approach to the people out there that was needed," Baker recalls, "and the pastor sent out a call for experienced laymen to share in the organization of this new church, Bering Memorial." Frank Smith knew that two of his most capable young men lived in that neighborhood—Hines Baker and George Howard, both of whom had been members of Smith's congregation at University Methodist Church in Austin and were now lawyers in the Humble organization. "I had been teaching a mixed class down at First Methodist Church and George was also actively involved," Baker explains, "and Dr. Smith told us that we ought to go out there and help them."

He recommended me for Sunday School Superintendent and George for teacher of the men's class. And we moved our membership out there and put our lives into it. We spent night after night canvassing that area. It was an inspiration being in a church with those German families. Now that's the kind of man Smith was. He would send his own people out into another area to help start a new church. He was not a narrow person in any sense of the word.[65]

Bering Memorial was not the only Methodist church in Houston to benefit from Frank Smith's leadership at First Church, according to a report in the *Texas Christian Advocate* in 1923:

In Houston all of the Methodist Churches glory in First Church's achievements, because of the helpful, unselfish spirit manifested by Frank Smith's great high-powered organization which is ever extending the helping hand towards the advancement of every other Methodist Church in the city, as well as co-operating most heartily in every interdenominational Christian movement.[66]

A note in the First Church bulletin for November 30, 1924, states that "four dollars in every five raised in First Church last year went to the interests and enterprises of others."[67]

Another example of Frank Smith's practical flexibility and broad churchmanship was the Blue Bird Circle. As Smith later explained: "A group of young matrons in First Church would not join the Missionary Society, but I found that they were receptive to an organization that would support local projects, especially work among children."[68] With the approval and assistance of the president of First Methodist's Missionary Society, the pastor arranged for a meeting in March, 1923. According to a history of the circle:

A group of fifteen young matrons in short, tubular, "flapper" dresses and boyish bobbed coiffures attended the organizational meeting in the home of Mrs. John T. Scott, who, along with Mrs. S. F. Carter, served as honorary advisors. . . . The name "Blue Bird Circle" was Dr. Smith's choice because the blue bird symbolizes happiness and because the members wished to be bound together in a circle of love and good will.[69]

Smith conducted a devotional at the circle's biweekly meetings and assisted them in choosing their first charitable project: the Young Women's Cooperative Home, a "home-away-from-home" for students and employed girls, sponsored by the Methodist Women's Board of the Houston

District. Donating clothing and furnishings, arranging entertainment
and parties, the young women helped the home for a number of years.
As a courtesy to the men of First Methodist Church, circle members
served as waitresses for the annual men's banquets. In May, 1927, the
Blue Birds organized a day nursery for children of working mothers in
the industrial Cottage Grove section of Houston. The following year
the circle opened Blue Bird House in a small building on Main Street
adjacent to First Methodist Church for their gift shop and lending library. It was decided to make the Blue Birds interdenominational, and
the organization grew rapidly, attaining a membership of 130 by 1930
—Smith's last year at First Church.[70] In the words of Kenneth Pope,
pastor of First Methodist Church in later years:

The Blue Bird Circle was Frank's way of catching the interest of those
young women who weren't interested in the Missionary Society. It was the
difference between the social-secular mind which had some good to give
and the more pietistic devotional mind of the church. Frank simply reached
out and gave an avenue of expression for these less devotionally minded
young women.[71]

Another accomplishment of Frank Smith's ministry at First Methodist Church was the planning and building of a new Sunday school
building. In April, 1923, in a letter to Bishop Mouzon, Smith reported:
"Our Sunday School has practically doubled during the past twelve
months. We are averaging fourteen hundred each Sunday and growing
rapidly. On Easter Sunday, we had 2,157 actually present in classes."[72]
At the board of stewards meeting in September, "Brother Smith stated
that the project nearest his heart was the proposed Sunday School building: one that will be a community center and one from which the influence of Methodism will radiate for generations."[73] In October Houston
newspapers reported:

A new Sunday school building to cost $150,000 and equipped to care for
5,000 Sunday school scholars is to be erected during the coming conference
year by the First Methodist Church of Houston. . . . The campaign for funds
to erect the building will be inaugurated perhaps in January, officials of the
church state.[74]

These announcements proved to be premature, for construction did
not begin until 1928. By that time the plans had been considerably expanded, as indicated in Smith's letter to Bishop Mouzon written in May
of that year:

We are actively engaged in the construction of our Educational Building, which is to be completed in the early Fall. It is to be six stories in height, with a full basement in addition. It not only embodies every facility for modern Sunday School work, but is to be finished with materials of the highest possible type. In construction and appearance it will bear comparison with a college building or a modern office building. It is costing us $350,000. At the same time, we are to spend $50,000 on our present church structure, renovating it and enlarging the auditorium by some six hundred sittings.[75]

If the young pastor was in danger of inordinate pride in the new building and facilities, the following letter from Bishop John M. Moore would have brought him back to earth:

I congratulate you upon the completion of your new Education Building. I see you spent $425,000. That is a lot of money. I hope the major portion has been collected from the members. Most of our big churches are becoming helpless by reason of their own demands and to live selfishly is to live poorly, for churches as well as individuals. I am sure that you have done what you could to avoid this.[76]

Frank Smith's fostering of the relationship between First Church and Houston is apparent in the announcement of the opening of the new building:

On next Friday evening, 11 January [1929], from 7:30 to 10:30 o'clock, the membership of First Methodist Church will be at home to the citizenship of Houston at the Church, commemorating the completion of the Educational Building and the renovation of the church auditorium. The affair will be altogether informal with no program provided, the purpose being that the people of Houston may have the opportunity of inspecting the buildings.[77]

Despite a recent bout of pneumonia, Dr. Smith stood in the patio and greeted the hundreds of people who came for the official opening— including, according to a newspaper report: "Methodists, Baptists, Presbyterians, Lutherans, Episcopalians, Catholics, Jews, Christian Scientists, Christians, Unitarians, Spiritualists, agnostics, infidels, and others."[78]

Of all the Methodist institutions in Houston, the one that received Frank Smith's deepest commitment through the years was the Methodist Hospital. Several years before Smith came to Houston, Dr. O. L. Norsworthy, a prominent member of First Methodist Church, had offered to give his hospital to the Texas Conference if they would add to it and operate it. As pastor of the leading church in that conference, Frank Smith became involved in the raising of funds to build the new unit required by the agreement with Dr. Norsworthy.[79] In mid-February, 1923, a dramatic announcement was published in the *Houston Evening Post*:

Marking a new epoch in the annals of Methodism in Texas, the first hospital ever to be owned and operated by the church in this State, will be formally opened for service in Houston within the next three months. The first unit of the new construction, which is now nearing completion, is a handsome five-story structure built of reinforced concrete and dark red brick with stone finish.[80]

Adjoining the new $230,000 hospital on Rosalie Avenue and scheduled for completion at the same time, the Sarah Francella Bell home—"for the aged and infirm widows of Methodist preachers in the Texas Conference"—would be served by the hospital's staff. According to the newspaper article, the hospital would be "under the general supervision of a strong board of laymen residing within the bounds of the [Texas] Conference."[81]

Among the trustees who were members of First Methodist Church were the president of the board, John T. Scott; the treasurer, S. F. Carter; and at least two others: Judge J. A. Elkins and W. L. Clayton. Although not listed among the clergy on the board at that time, Frank Smith did take an increasingly active role in the development of the hospital, according to Mrs. Walter W. Fondren.[82] Shortly after the hospital opened in June, 1924, the *Texas Christian Advocate* reported: "The recent opening of the Methodist Hospital in Houston was only made possible by the raising in an incredibly short space of time $40,000 by Dr. A. Frank Smith and Dr. C. M. Bishop, pastors of First Church and St. Paul's respectively. . . . First Church raised $22,500 of the $40,000 and St. Paul's $17,500."[83]

"My father believed in the Methodist Church being an institutional church," A. Frank Smith, Jr. explains, "and to have a hospital here supported by the church was one of the things he thought the church should do."[84] "Dr. Smith was always deeply interested in the Methodist Hospital," Hines Baker agrees. "First Church, as the leading church in the community, gave him a responsibility for all city-wide projects of moment. He was looked to as the leader downtown, and he filled that position with grace and judgment and poise."[85]

The role that Frank Smith played in the development and support of the Houston City Board of Missions and Church Extension can only be surmised. After seven years of apparent inactivity, the board was re-organized in 1921 by the presiding elder of the Houston District, George W. Davis. Walter W. Fondren was elected president, and a goal of $2,400 was set for mission work for the coming year.[86] The first meeting of the board that Smith might have attended was held on November 3, 1922. At that time John T. Scott was elected president, and the budget increased to $10,000. A citywide campaign for funds was launched in mid-January, according to a newspaper report, and First Methodist Church oversubscribed its quota on the first day.[87] That year, 1923, was a record-breaking year for First Methodist Church. As Frank Smith wrote to Bishop Mouzon in November:

You will be glad to know that we are concluding the greatest year First Church has ever experienced. Every department is active and enthusiastic. We have had above five hundred additions, more than two hundred [of these] on profession of faith. We have raised above $100,000. We are having an average attendance of three hundred at prayer meeting. The Sunday School runs from 1350 to 1500 every Sunday, and the church is filled, with chairs in the aisles, for each of the Sunday preaching services.[88]

The total given to the city mission board that year was $4,350.[89] Almost forty years later, Frank Smith still remembered "how thrilled we all were the first year First Church raised $100,000 for all purposes. That was something for Ripley ["Believe It or Not"]: We just simply threw out our chests; we were doing things in a big way."[90]

Beginning in 1924, First Methodist Church included a regular amount in its annual budget for the City Board of Missions: 1924 and 1925, $2,500; 1926, $3,000; 1927, $4,000; 1928, $4,500; and 1929, $3,450.[91] Mr. Scott continued as president of the city board as well as chairman of First Church's board of stewards through these years. Obviously, much of the credit for First Methodist Church's support of the City Board of Missions and Church Extension belongs to him.

Frank Smith and John T. Scott did not always agree, particularly concerning the pastor's salary. At the end of Smith's first year at First Methodist Church, his salary was raised to $8,000. For 1924-25, the board increased the amount to $9,000. Smith immediately protested: "Brethren, you ought not to do that, you ought not to pay that at all. We don't pay salaries like that." In response to this objection from their pastor, the stewards returned the salary to $8,000. "The next time I dropped in at the bank, as I would do every few days," Smith recalled, "Mr. Scott just gave me a working over." He said to Smith,

"Now, Brother Frank, I know what you had in mind, but you are meddling in something that is none of your business. You have no right to come down and demand that we pay you a certain amount, and you have no right to interfere if we want to pay you more. It's worth something to the First Methodist Church for it to be known that they have a preacher who's worth $9,000, more than any other preacher in this town is getting. If you don't want to take the money, bring it down here and put it in the bank or take it out here and throw it in the bayou if you want to. But we have a right to pay you what we want to, and it is none of your business. You preachers come and go, but we are setting this standard for the First Methodist Church."[92]

When the board raised his salary to $10,000 for 1925-26, Smith had learned his lesson and did not object. Somewhat to his embarrassment, however, the news of the salary increase was announced in the next day's paper: "DR. A. FRANK SMITH HAS SALARY RAISED—FIRST METHODIST CHURCH PASTOR WILL RECEIVE $10,000 PER YEAR." As a new member of the church's board, H. Lee Millis—"an old school mate of ours at Southwestern and the son of a Methodist preacher"—had participated in the unanimous vote to raise Smith's salary. Then Mr. Millis, who also happened to be the editor-in-chief of the *Houston Post*, went home and wrote an account of the board meeting for his paper. Among other things, Millis reported:

It is said that no other church in Southern Methodism is now paying a larger salary to its pastor than the First Methodist Church of Houston will pay during the coming year. Only one or two other churches in the connection pay as much. . . . Dr. Smith is one of the youngest of the Methodist pastors in the larger pulpits, still being less than 40 years of age. His reputation as a pulpit orator and pastoral administrator is Southwide.[93]

A few weeks later, with the arrival of Christmas, the young pastor had almost forgotten his embarrassment over the salary-raise headlines when he received a beautiful gift from a distinguished member of Congregation Beth Israel who often attended Sunday night services at First Methodist Church. The enclosed gift card read: "Season's Greetings and Happy New Year." Then there was a handwritten personal note: "Dear

Doctor, I am glad that your church has met your terms and that you are not going to leave us."[94]

Throughout the 1920s John T. Scott was "Mr. Methodist Layman" in Houston. He was chairman of the board of stewards at First Methodist Church, president of the board of trustees of Methodist Hospital and of the Sarah Francella Bell Home, and chairman of the City Board of Missions and Church Extension. Such dominance of leadership was not an unmixed blessing. An experience that Hines Baker remembers illustrates the problem in relation to the First Methodist Church. Shortly after Mr. Baker had transferred his membership from First Methodist to Bering Memorial to help give guidance to that new church, he was elected lay-leader of the Houston District, primarily through the influence of his former pastor, A. Frank Smith.

The first assignment Baker received in his new position was to organize Wesley Fellowships in the local churches of his district. The purpose of these fellowships was to attract and develop the leadership potential of the younger laymen in the churches. "I thought it was a great idea," Mr. Baker recalls. "We couldn't rely on the old leaders always: we had to educate and develop young men to take these places of leadership and responsibility." His initial opportunity to present this new Wesley Fellowship program was at the weekly Monday morning preachers' meeting, held in the Men's Bible Class room at First Methodist Church. In these familiar surroundings where he had taught for a number of years, Baker sought to interest the ministers in the new Board of Lay Activities program. "I tried to present it as clearly as I could, emphasizing the necessity of developing the future leaders in the church, future people to carry the load," Baker explains. "To my amazement Bishop Sam Hay and Frank Smith—the two men I naturally looked to for support—turned a cold-shoulder to it. They rebuffed me, and I was discouraged and disheartened. The 'Wesley Fellowship' program looked to me like the main thing I could do to be really effective as District Lay-Leader."

Later that week Baker went by First Church to talk to Smith. "Frank, I don't understand your position toward the new program," he began.

I've been a member of your church, and I have seen young men just floating around. You have your leaders and they are carrying the responsibility, and these younger men have no place to go, nothing to do, no planned program for them to enlist them actively in the work. You have a big church and they just get lost in the shuffle. I know you can have a larger number of

effective men in there. You have some diligent young men with high potential that are busy in the church. They are the people that ought to be
on the board.

When he remembers that conversation now, Mr. Baker laughs at himself:

I talked pretty strongly for just a kid lawyer, but I was really discouraged
when the two top men wouldn't support the recognized program of the
Lay Board of the church. And I was amazed at the answer he gave me. We
back-filled around on it, and then he said: "Well, I'll tell you, Hines, we've
got just so many places on our Board that we've got to fill. We have these
older men who are busy. I'd have to put some of these aggressive young men
on the board if they were doing this work, and I don't want to do that."

As Baker tries to understand Smith's reasoning, he suggests that
Smith was probably deferring to Bishop Hay. "Smith had succeeded
Hay at First Church, and Hay was his bishop. I don't think that Bishop
Hay wanted to encourage this new program." Baker concludes:

Smith had to be a practical administrator, of course. I suppose that as you
wag along with the church set-up and get a smoothly moving thing, you
endanger it when you introduce some of these ambitious fellows filled with
fire and a desire to do something. He just had so many offices. I guess he
didn't know what else to do except send his young men out to help somebody
else, as he sent George Howard and me to Bering.[95]

Frank Smith's eight years as pastor of Houston's First Methodist
Church were filled with memorable experiences and achievements. Certain occasions were of such significance to him and his ministry that
they must be given some attention here.

In June, 1923, Frank Smith was awarded his alma mater's highest
honor, the Doctor of Divinity degree. Southwestern University was also
celebrating her Golden Jubilee, and a number of extras were added to
the festivities—with an emphasis on Houston. Bishop John M. Moore,
of the Texas Conference, gave the baccalaureate sermon. Dr. Paul W.
Horn, earlier superintendent of Houston's public schools for seventeen
years, was inaugurated as the university's sixth president. Dr. William
States Jacob, pastor of Houston's First Presbyterian Church, delivered
the commencement address. Under the direction of Miss Laura Kuykendall, the students presented a "gigantic historical pageant, 'The Spirit of
Southwestern,' in the style of the annual May Fete."[96] The six-day cele-

bration reached its climax on Friday, June 8, with the commencement exercises and the granting of degrees.[97] H. Lee Millis, Frank's former classmate at Southwestern, caught the meaning of the event for "Doctor Smith":

Heartiest congratulations upon the signal honor old Southwestern has bestowed upon you. No recipient of this degree was ever more deserving of it. It is a splendid recognition of your services and ability by those who know you best. . . . How proud of you I am, and how greatly honored I have always felt at having been a school mate of yours. We boys always regarded you as a remarkably gifted man, intellectually, spiritually, and oratorically, but the best of it all is the splendid spirit in which you have accepted the responsibility that goes with the possession of these unusual gifts, and the great use to which you are putting them.[98]

In September, three months later, Mrs. John R. Allen died after a long illness. The Allens, "Uncle John and Aunt Mollie," had reared and educated Bess and Hallie after the girls' mother died in 1899.[99] In the tribute that Dr. Smith wrote, he emphasized Mrs. Allen's motherly nature:

In 1892 Mrs. Allen became Matron of the Ladies' Annex [at Southwestern University], a position which she retained for sixteen years. And it was here that her greatest work was done. She became literally mother to hundreds of girls who had broken their home ties and gone away to school. All over the Southland today they call her blessed for the individual and unselfish care she bestowed upon each one as they passed from youth into womanhood. . . . Mrs. Allen was never blessed with children of her own, but she was mother to hundreds. . . . Those of us who watched beside her during [her last days], caught a vision of our Lord not before revealed to us, as we saw her spirit grow stronger as the sands of life ran to their close. . . . At noon, on Thursday, September 13, 1923, the silver cord was loosed, the golden pitcher was broken and she had entered into the presence of her Lord. On Friday afternoon, . . . just as the sun was setting we laid her body away, beneath a mountain of flowers in Greenwood Cemetery . . . to await the Resurrection Morn. And as we looked up from the newly made mound into the heavens, tinged already with the lengthening shadows of the coming night, we could see through the darkness the expanding light of a new day, destined never to grow old, in that land "Where no storms ever beat on the glittering strand and the years of eternity roll." I loved Mrs. Allen, she was my mother. My life here is nobler and heaven is nearer and dearer because she lived and loved me.[100]

The year 1924 was one of new life and new experiences. On February 14, St. Valentine's Day, Elizabeth Ann was born to the Smiths. Having had two sons, they had been hoping for a daughter. With fatherly pride, Dr. Smith wrote to Bishop Mouzon: "Bess and the baby are both doing splendidly. We all send love to all of you."[101]

In September the church bought a new home for the expanding parsonage family on Yoakum Boulevard, a lovely residential section of Houston. The Fondrens' home was across on the next street, Montrose.[102] As described by Dr. Smith, this "beautiful home, costing $30,000, gives us a parsonage in keeping with the church plant."[103] As an indication of his appreciation, Smith had new letterheads printed using the parsonage address.

In November, 1924, First Methodist Church became the first congregation in the city to broadcast a church service over Houston's first radio station. As Dr. Smith explained:

That was in the day of radio's infancy, of the crystal receiving sets. The chief interest was to receive cards from various sections of the country saying that we were being "picked up" in Atlanta or Spokane or by some ship at sea. It was things like this that made First Church *the* church of Houston. People generally felt that First Church belonged to the whole community.[104]

Of all the honors and tributes that A. Frank Smith ever received, the one that he must have cherished the most was a letter from his father dated "Austin, Tex., 12/12/25":

DEAR SON:

I met Mr. Flowers from Elgin on the street here today and he said some prominent man of Houston had said recently when at his hotel in Elgin that you was the best preacher in Houston, and had more friends than anyone of any denomination in the city. I am mighty glad to have such reports of your work, and hope your popularity may develop very rapidly.

Just wanted you to know we are all much pleased at such reports of your work.

Love for all—Father
W A SMITH[105]

During the 1925 session of the Texas Conference, Dr. Smith was elected a delegate to the General Conference for the first time. Of the other four ministers elected on the first ballot, J. W. Mills and L. B. Elrod were presiding elders and Dr. James Kilgore was a professor in the School of Theology at SMU.[106] Bishop Mouzon immediately sent his commendation: "I wish to congratulate you on your election to the General Conference. I should have been personally disappointed if this had not taken place."[107]

The major event of the year 1926 was the General Conference of the Methodist Episcopal Church, South, which was held in Memphis, Tennessee, in May. For some reason, Dr. Smith did not arrive until the third day.[108] Besides serving on the Committee on Publishing Interests, he was engaged in the daily routine of the business sessions. As a courtesy, Bishop Hay called upon him to lead the conference in prayer at one session.[109] The most noteworthy act of this General Conference was a new regulation on lay representation in the annual conferences, calling for one lay delegate from each pastoral charge. This General Conference also continued the possibility of unification with Northern Methodism by requesting the College of Bishops to appoint a new commission.

The most unusual event of 1927 for Dr. Smith was the family vacation at Chautauqua Park, Boulder, Colorado, lasting the entire month of August.[110] Except for "a little vacation" spent at Colorado Springs in August, 1923,[111] this was the first time in thirteen years that the Smiths had a real vacation. As the children remember, it was also the last until the summer of 1935.[112]

Beginning in mid-January, 1928, one event—and a cluster of closely related proceedings—dominated the thoughts of Houstonians and eventually captured the attention of a majority of the people across the nation: the choice of Houston as the site of the Democratic National Convention and the almost certain nomination of Al Smith as the Democratic candidate for President of the United States. Dr. Smith's reply to Bishop James Cannon's inquiry about lodging during the convention illustrates both aspects of the excitement:

It is a keen disappointment to my wife and myself that we cannot have you in our home while you are here for the Convention. Every spare bed we have, however, and even space for cots has already been claimed by our numerous Texas relatives and friends who do not propose to lose this opportunity of a lifetime to see a political convention. I must confess that I was not enthused when I learned it was coming here. However, Al Smith will not find the stage set for him down here unless he brings in enough Tammanyites to create a mock atmosphere. Texas, and especially Houston, is pronouncedly dry and anti-Smith.[113]

Southern Democrats—and that generally included the bishops, minis-

ters, and members of the Methodist Episcopal Church, South—were
convinced that they could not carry the "Solid South" without a platform
dedicated to the enforcement of the Volstead Act and a candidate pledged
to that "dry plank." Fear that Al Smith was a threat to prohibition
aroused strong opposition to the New York governor's nomination.
While his Roman Catholic background was a factor, the evidence does
not support the charge that prohibition was merely a cloak for religious
bigotry.[114] As Bishop John M. Moore wrote in mid-May to Dr. Smith:
"I will never vote for Al Smith. If he is nominated I shall do everything
within my power to bring about his defeat in November. His nomination
would be an open affront to the moral and religious leadership of the
South if not to the nation."[115]

Given this kind of opposition to Al Smith before the convention, one
can understand the outrage among Southern Democrats when the governor—after his candidacy was secure—shattered the compromise based
upon his pledge to support the dry plank in the Democratic party's platform. "I have never seen such widespread revolt against any nominee
as is to be found in Texas today against [Al] Smith," Dr. Smith declared.

His candidacy is an affront to everything the South holds dear. . . . A refusal upon the part of the South to support Smith, to the extent of giving
our Electoral Vote to Hoover, would be the greatest victory we have
achieved since the Civil War left us prostrate. And it would do more for
Prohibition and the cause of moral righteousness than can be estimated.[116]

Just such a strategy was adopted by more than two thousand anti-Smith
Democrats meeting at Asheville, North Carolina, in July. Methodist
Bishops James Cannon, Horace M. DuBose, Edwin D. Mouzon, and
probably John M. Moore participated in the "Asheville Rebellion," Cannon being elected national chairman.[117]

As Dr. Smith and his colleagues predicted, the "Solid South" split
apart in the November election. Hoover carried seven of the twelve
southern states and a majority of the region's popular and electoral
votes.[118] "Now that the election is over," Dr. Smith wrote to Bishop
Mouzon, "I wish to express again the great debt we all owe to you and
others among our leaders for your clear and unequivocal attitude on
the great moral issue, which was paramount in the recent campaign."

No finer spectacle has even been afforded in American political life than
that of the rising of our Southern people above party allegiance, with all

the pressure of newspapers and politicians to the contrary, to the call of high idealism. This election marks the beginning of a new day for America and especially the South, in things political. . . . History has been made during the past summer and fall, and I am profoundly grateful for the fact that through the vision and courage of certain of our leaders, Methodism had a large part in that making.[119]

The year 1928 was an unusually busy one for Dr. Smith, the vast majority of his memories of that year being more pleasant than the "Al Smith business." If the thought of becoming a bishop had not entered his mind before, it was presented to him in February. The Reverend P. R. Knickerbocker, who preceded Sam Hay at First Church, Houston, and had since been appointed pastor of Church Street Church in Knoxville, Tennessee, wrote to Dr. Smith:

You are doing a marvelous work and I am hoping [that] at the next General Conference you are going to be made one of our Bishops. We are thinking of it very seriously over here East of the Mississippi River. I had Bishop DuBose to dinner with me a couple of days ago, and he said he considered you the best available material in the Church for that office.[120]

Other friends were doing more than thinking and talking about Dr. Smith's qualifications for the Methodist episcopacy. Arthur Moore and Luther Bridgers, in order to introduce Smith to Georgia Methodists, persuaded President William F. Quillian of Macon's Wesleyan College to invite Smith to give the Commencement Literary Address for that "oldest chartered woman's college in the United States."[121] "I hope you can accept this invitation," Bridgers wrote.

I know you will shine and bring great inspiration at Wesleyan. While you are up there I want you to speak to the Atlanta Preachers' Meeting. Now, Frank, trust my judgment as you do my intention for I will not do the unwise thing. I think I am conversant with the fine points of prudence. I love you so devotedly and believe in you so strongly.[122]

The success of Dr. Smith's appearances in Georgia is confirmed by a letter to him from Bishop Warren A. Candler in June: "My Dear Brother Smith—I am sorry I was out of the City [Atlanta] on May 27th, and thereby missed seeing you. It would have been a joy to grasp your hand and to have heard your voice. I hear good things of your work at Wesleyan College, which gives me much pleasure but no surprise."[123]

Startling announcements continued throughout that year. "I have the pleasure of informing you," Bishop John M. Moore wrote in early May, "that the Bishops have elected you a member of the Commission on Constitution provided for by the last General Conference."[124] This was a formal notice which Moore wrote as secretary of the College of Bishops. A week later, he sent a much more personal message:

It was a real pleasure to have you elected on the Commission on Constitution. Bishop Hay and I agreed beforehand that we would nominate you and H. E. Jackson and insist on the election of the two, and we won much to our joy. This will be an interesting experience for you. I am sure you will make a very close study of the whole matter. You will find it valuable to you in the future.[125]

Bishop Warren A. Candler called the commission together for an organizational meeting on August 21. Composed of three bishops, six traveling elders, and six laymen, this commission was charged with the responsibility of preparing "a Constitution for the consideration of the next General Conference,"[126] which would meet in May, 1930. With only two years to perform its task, the commission was expected to do what the Joint Commissions on Unification had been unable to do in seven or more years. Two constitutions prepared by joint commissions had failed to win approval.[127] The Southern General Conference, during the session Dr. Smith had attended as a delegate of the Texas Conference in 1926, refused to accept yet another constitution presented to it by a special commission established in 1922.[128] At least the new commission had before it three constitutions which had failed to gain approval. What would both churches accept?

Dr. A. Frank Smith did not attend the initial meeting of the Commission on Constitution in August, 1928. On the thirtieth day of July, William Randolph Smith was born into the parsonage family. That happy event brought messages of congratulations from both of Frank Smith's episcopal mentors, Bishop Edwin D. Mouzon and Bishop John M. Moore.[129]

Dr. Smith's active involvement in the commission's work began in November when the Committee on Judicial Council and Amendments met in Memphis. This was his initiation into "the really valuable knowledge of the fundamentals of our government" that Bishop Moore was so concerned that he acquire.[130] Under the chairmanship of Bishop U. V. W. Darlington, this was a small working committee of two lawyers

—Judge M. E. Lawson of Missouri and the Hon. D. C. Roper of Washington, D.C., and two clergymen—Dr. A. F. Watkins of Mississippi and Dr. Smith.[131]

One other startling announcement that Dr. Smith received in 1928 should be mentioned. In mid-July, L. W. Dean, writing on behalf of the board of trustees of Southwestern University, wrote:

In the opinion of all the former students of this institution with whom I have had opportunity to discuss the matter, you are the man we need to take the helm at Southwestern, as its President. . . . We need you at Southwestern, and I am writing now to know if you would consider the acceptance of the Presidency of our Institution.[132]

That Dr. Smith declined promptly is clear from the fact that Mr. Dean wrote again four days later: "I wish you might reconsider the matter of accepting the Presidency of Southwestern. . . . I do not believe there is anything you can do for your Church or for this State that would have such far reaching and beneficial effect as the service you might render as President of this Institution."[133]

The dramatic events and experiences during the year 1928 were to be followed by still more excitement. Early in January, 1929, a letter from Bishop Mouzon indicated that Dr. Smith was still being considered for the episcopacy. "I see Felix Hill often at the crossroads of the Church, Memphis," Mouzon wrote. "Hill is interested in new bishops, talks of Arthur Moore and you and Kern. But I mustn't write about such things."[134]

Dr. Smith's reply to Mouzon reveals his strong sense of responsibility to his family and his ministry in Houston as well as his high esteem for the episcopacy of Methodism:

Your reference to Felix Hill and his interest in the forthcoming General Conference is in keeping with what he has said to me more than once. No man could appreciate the Episcopacy more than I; our very existence as a connectional organization depends upon our keeping our Episcopacy inviolate. And our Bishops must be, by common consent, our biggest men, our best men, our greatest preachers. And as a pastor, I am profoundly convinced that our Bishops should be relieved of most of the routine duties to which they are now subject, so that they might be allowed to magnify their preaching gifts, and their spiritual leadership. And I fully appreciate the high honor done me when my name is mentioned in this connection. However, if there were any possibility of my name ever being seriously considered in this way, the time for that is far removed. I have little children, I should be at home for the next several years; and I feel that I have been here just long enough to begin to enter into a ministry reaching beyond my immediate congregation and denomination. By every gift and grace of heart and mind, Paul Kern is qualified for the Episcopacy, and I am hoping that he will be the Texas man elected next year.[135]

There were also those "west of the River" who were working for Dr. Smith's election. Dr. J. N. R. Score, who had been appointed to St. Paul's Methodist Church in Houston in 1926, was particularly active. Following the election of delegates to the 1930 General Conference, Score shared the good news with Bishop Mouzon that "Brother Frank Smith leads the Texas Conference delegation [having] received one-hundred ninety-seven votes of the two hundred twenty-eight cast. This letter is simply to recall to your mind the conversation I had with you at Lake Junaluska. Certain friends in the East tell me that Frank is being spoken of most favorably. Please say a good word for Frank whenever you can," Score urged. "I need not tell you how splendid he is. He is in every way qualified for the highest honor and responsibility our church can give."[136]

In mid-July, 1929, Bishop Warren A. Candler, the "Senior Bishop" of the Methodist Episcopal Church, South, wrote to Dr. Smith to see if he would be interested in a church in Candler's area. "I would be glad to have you at Galloway Memorial Church in Jackson, Miss., the capital of the State. . . . It is the greatest Church in the State & not far from Millsaps College."[137] Evidently Smith had written to Bishop Candler earlier expressing a "wish to have more contact with the Central South." Candler believed that Smith "would like the people and they would like you and be blessed by your ministry." If Smith were interested in Galloway Memorial, Candler would initiate his transfer to that annual conference. Of course, if Frank Smith had accepted a transfer to the Mississippi Conference in 1929, he would not have been elected a bishop in 1930.

Ever since his appointment to First Church, Houston, in 1922, Dr. Smith had been trying to persuade Bishop Mouzon to come for a week or more of preaching. As often as the invitation was extended, just as often did Mouzon regretfully decline. Finally, in December, 1929, Mouzon brought the dream to reality. "Your coming is the high point in all my ministry," Smith exclaimed, "and that one thing which I have most desired since I began preaching."[138] In writing to Mrs. Mouzon just after Bishop Mouzon had preached that week of services, Dr. Smith confided to her:

> To have Bishop Mouzon preach for a week in my pulpit was the realization of a hope that I have cherished ever since I have had a pulpit. And the memory and inspiration of his wonderful messages, and of my personal association with him during these days he was here, will ever remain among the most precious of all my experiences.[139]

Dr. A. Frank Smith's pastorate at First Methodist Church in Houston came to a close in May, 1930. Eight years earlier, as we have seen, he had been appointed to that great church to succeed Dr. Sam R. Hay, who had been elected to the episcopate of Southern Methodism. Dr. Smith's pastorate was also terminated by his election to be a bishop in the Methodist Episcopal Church, South. He was the fourth pastor of First Methodist Church to be so honored.[140]

"Figures and statistics are revealing," Frank Smith said on more than one occasion, "but they cannot portray the soul of a church."[141] Yet even a brief comparison of the statistical tables for First Methodist Church, Houston, for the eight years of Dr. Smith's pastorate there reveals a remarkable growth and development. The total budget for the church increased from $73,095 in 1922 to $104,051 in 1930. For the years 1928 and 1929, the budgets totaled $173,886 and $150,226 respectively.[142] From a membership of 3,050 in November, 1922, the congregation grew to a membership of 5,015 in November, 1930. During those eight years, the church averaged more than five hundred new members every year, with two hundred joining by profession of faith annually. As Dr. J. N. R. Score, Smith's colleague in Houston for four years, pointed out: "During at least three of those eight years, First Methodist Church was the leading church in the entire Southern Methodist denomination in additions on profession of faith. No man's ministry can year after year bear such fruits unless the preacher's heart is that of a true evangelist of Jesus Christ.[143]

8

Pastor and Preacher

"IN MY PREACHING, I sought to drive a nail and brad it. I always preached for a verdict of complete surrender to the Lord. I always stressed the fundamental verities and tried to create in my people 'the mind that was in Christ Jesus.' "[1] In these words A. Frank Smith sought to depict his homiletical goal. He believed that his particular style of preaching had been more a matter of the press of circumstances than of any objective weighting of the merits of the various styles. "I never learned to sermonize," he explained. "I was just pitched out and had to swim. From my first sermon at Alto to the day I left the pastorate, I was just one jump ahead. I had no time for seed corn to develop and grow."[2]

Even if Frank Smith had experienced a more favorable combination of circumstances, he would probably have developed the same style of preaching because of his two basic criteria: "versatility and effectiveness at the moment."[3] "From the beginning I was determined that I would not read my sermons nor rely upon notes," he recalled.

I had a passion to communicate my message and to look my congregation in the face while I preached. I would never have forsaken that determination even though I had found leisure to write. Furthermore, I had no particular desire to major in the pulpit if it would lead to poorly discharging the responsibilities which always seemed to face me. This does not mean that I simply "fired from the hip." I never faced a congregation in my life without knowing exactly what my line of thought was to be, how I was to start, and where and when I was to conclude. I had my outline burned into my mind before I ever stood upon my feet. I memorized my line of thought, but the verbiage came from the inspiration of the moment as I established rapport with my listeners.[4]

The only time that Frank Smith completely wrote out a sermon was when it was needed for publication, and then he only wrote it out after he had delivered it. "It never even remotely occurred to me that I might ever have a volume of sermons printed," he declared. In Dr. Smith's understanding, sermons were prepared with a particular congregation in mind. The greatness of a sermon could only be judged in relation to that congregation in which it had been preached. "Great preaching," he said, "rests ultimately upon its effect upon the hearers, the community of the faithful."[5]

The one sermon that Dr. Smith is definitely known to have repeated several times during his career as a pastor is entitled "The Man with a Message." It was his opening sermon at the University Church in Dallas (February 13, 1916), at the University Church in Austin (November 5, 1916), and at First Church, Houston (June 4, 1922). He also gave it as a baccalaureate sermon at Brackenridge High School in San Antonio (January 22, 1922). Although he was a relative stranger in each of these situations, he was not contradicting his basic principle that sermons are to be prepared for a particular congregation. On three of the four occasions, Smith was clearly preaching this sermon as a means of introducing himself to his new congregation. "The Man with a Message," therefore, takes on special significance. While it may not be typical of his sermons as a whole, it is one that he obviously valued. This sermon is also helpful in illustrating Smith's manner of adapting his sermons to his hearers or to a special occasion. In three of the four instances of his preaching this sermon, a newspaper reporter took sufficient notes to make a comparison possible. For the presentation to the congregation of First Methodist Church in Houston, we have the actual manuscript that Dr. Smith preached from, written out almost word for word.

The first (SMU) and second (Austin) versions of the sermon were adapted to their respective university congregations, as may be seen in the careful defining of terms and the concern for vocational decisions.

By "man" is meant here personality—that which vitalizes and creates. By "message" is meant not news or information, but song, story, deed—anything that has an influence. There can be no message without the realization of a need. There is no success in a life that is not planned to meet some need. The foresighted man of affairs looks to see where some need will arise, and prepares himself to meet that need. . . .

Many of you here are students. We are all students in life. Education should bring to you a consciousness of the great world needs and equip you to meet them. . . .

Each of you has the privilege of choosing a profession. When you have found Christ's message for your life, establish an ideal and shape your life in accordance with it. . . . In whatever profession there is the opportunity of serving God. . . .

Where these university versions of the sermon mention only "the professions," the third or baccalaureate version adds "the businessman or woman" to the vocational options. The fourth version, prepared for the largely adult congregation of First Church, Houston, omits this section on vocational choices altogether.

An illustration concerning Carlyle's lack of appreciation for his wife during her lifetime, added to the second version of the sermon where a majority of the congregation would be married, is omitted from the third version which was aimed at high school seniors. Smith also omitted reference to the great Protestant preachers—Luther, Wesley, and Moody —from the baccalaureate sermon, presumably because of the high percentage of Roman Catholics likely to be present in such a secular gathering in San Antonio,[6] the other versions being addressed to Methodist congregations.

In the later accounts of the sermon, the preacher is more adept in his use of descriptive language. The rather lean language of the first version becomes complex in the second and third and even ornate in the third and fourth versions.

When speaking to the high school or largely college-age congregations, Smith emphasized the inevitability of the "messenger's" being misunderstood. He tempered this point for the conflict-torn congregation in Austin: "To carry his message may bring misunderstanding."

Dr. Smith's objection to Fundamentalism's dependence upon dogmatic formulations ("quibbling over outworn formulas and incidental statements"), given relatively little emphasis in the two 1916 versions of the sermon, receives more sustained presentation in the 1922 version. In order to have time to develop this theme more fully without extending his sermon, Dr. Smith cut out a section of the previous versions concerning God's revelation through nature. With the skill of a diplomat, he declared: "I hold devoutly to the faith of the fathers, and I want none other than the religion of my dear mother. But this calls for a spiritual interpretation, and an application for my own day, not one having to do with methods and verbal statements."

A comparison of the four versions of "The Man with a Message" also shows that Frank Smith's theology was becoming more sophisticated. "The message that is needed" shifts from one that is "high and ennobling" in the earlier versions to one that is "of divine authority." Told to "pitch your life upon a lofty plane" in the former sermons, the "messengers" are admonished "to live continuously in the realm of the divine" in the later versions. "Vitalized by the transforming power of an uplifting ideal" becomes "vitalized and thrilled by the transforming power of fellowship with the divine." Finally, it is interesting to note that man's need of redemption and new life through Jesus Christ is emphatically affirmed in the later versions of the sermon, while in the earliest version Christ is seemingly just another man of vision along with Abraham and Elijah, Luther and Wesley.

During Dr. Smith's eight-year pastorate in Houston, at least fourteen of his sermons were reported in the local newspapers. Ten of these sermons were preached on Sunday mornings at First Church, three on Sunday evenings, and the other a midday Lenten sermon given at Christ Church (Episcopal). Fifty sermons in manuscript form have survived in Smith's papers from this period. When he declared in later years that he never wrote his sermons, he was apparently speaking of his practice after he became a bishop in 1930. One hundred manuscript sermons that survive from the thirty years of his episcopacy are generally in outline form. The fifty Houston sermons and twenty-nine from the Laurel Heights period, however, are almost completely written out. The fourteen sermons reported in the newspapers and the fifty manuscript sermons may not be considered an adequate base for an analysis of Dr. Smith's preaching at First Church, but they do offer glimpses of the kind of preaching he presented to his Houston congregation.

These sermons show that Dr. Smith generally preached topical rather than textual sermons. Of the fifty manuscript sermons, only five are textual. In topical sermons the outline is determined by the particular subject, problem, or issue rather than by the text from the Bible. The purpose of the text in these sermons is to support the position taken by the preacher. In a sermon primarily addressed to the businessmen in his congregation, for example, Dr. Smith declared: "It is not good for business for businessmen to become so engrossed in their material affairs that they neglect giving attention to aesthetic and spiritual things."[7] In support of this proposition, Dr. Smith took his text from the Old Testament book of I Kings: "As thy servant was busy here and there, he was gone." These words were the answer of a man assigned to guard a prisoner during a battle, trying to explain why his prisoner had escaped. "The one supreme concern was that the prisoner should be guarded," Dr. Smith stated, "but while the servant fussed about, his chief responsibility was neglected and slipped through his fingers." Having given "the setting for the text," he announced that he would apply the text "to modern conditions *without further reference to the original occurrence.*"[8] He then began the body of his sermon with a strategic affirmation:

I, for one, rejoice in the power of achievement of the modern man. . . . The modern businessman is too often maligned for his selfishness and lack of sympathy. He may appear, at times, to be "hard boiled," for life is grim and earnest with him. But in the final analysis, there is no greater influence in the world today than the Christian businessman. His heart is responsive and his attitude is sympathetic.[9]

Dr. Smith was reflecting the tenor of his times in making such a statement. "Businessmen were at the apex of their public esteem in these golden years before the Crash," historian Sydney E. Ahlstrom writes, "and there was a pervasive tendency to identify religion with the business-oriented values of the American way of life."[10] The association of religion and business was one of the most significant phenomena of the day, according to the biographer of the '20s, Frederick Lewis Allen. "So frequent was the use of the Bible to point the lessons of business and of business to point the lessons of the Bible that it was sometimes difficult to determine which was supposed to gain the most from the association. . . . Business had become almost the national religion of America."[11] Nevertheless, Dr. Smith maintained a clear distinction and priority in his sermon:

His [the Christian businessman's] heart is responsive and his attitude is sympathetic, but he is busy, busy, busy, as we all are. We are so busy that it is impossible to meet every demand made upon us, and consequently life becomes a constant matter of choosing. . . . These choices are necessary, but a proper standard of value in choosing must be maintained. . . . It is all wrong to be so busy about business and social interests that there is no time for aesthetic and spiritual things.

Upon what does business and the social order rest, anyway? Why, upon the spiritual integrity of people, of course. Were it not for faith and character and morality, your business could not last for twenty-four hours. And faith and character and morality . . . come only through the development of man's spiritual nature. . . . Business has its place—all honor to it—but it must never stand between an individual and his worship of God the Father . . .

We all have responsibilities: to live means to bear a fair share of the common burden. But it is so easy to become burdened with trifles. The supreme responsibility of every person is the development of a well rounded life, the fitting of his soul to dwell in the Father's house as becomes one made in God's image.[12]

Dr. Smith's civic-mindedness, mentioned in the preceding chapter, also appears in his sermons. In another of his topical sermons, Dr. Smith drew the biblical base from two passages, one from Genesis and the other from Revelation. "The Bible begins in a garden [Genesis 3] and ends in a city [Revelation 21], and this has ever been a parable of life," he stated. "The trend of every people has always been from the country to the city." Houston, in the 1920s, was one of the fastest growing cities in the nation. Instead of blaming the nation's ills on her multiplying urban centers, as the Ku Klux Klan did, Dr. Smith pointed to the cities as opportunities for Christian ministry.

Writing, art, science, astronomy, architecture, literature and the theater are all products of the city, but even as the strength of every civilization has been gauged by the life of its cities, so has the downfall of every civilization come through the corruption of life in its cities. Herein is to be found both inspiration and warning for us today. . . . We are destined to be a nation of city dwellers. Only the Christianizing of our cities will preserve us from the fate of nations that have grown great and died in the past. But with the principles of Jesus Christ dominating our thoughts and practice, no words can describe the achievements that may come to us through the inspiration and cooperative endeavor that life in a highly organized city affords.[13]

Appealing to his fellow citizens' civic pride and love for Houston— which he so obviously shared—Dr. Smith declared: "Houston is destined to be one of the great cities of America, but Houston will be a great city only as the integrity of her citizens makes life safe and property secure." As the city needs the ethical guidance and strength of Chris-

tianity, so also do Christians need the "social contact and personal association" of the city "to develop and express the distinctive Christian
virtues." Rejecting the idea that Christianity is a withdrawal from the
world, Dr. Smith affirmed that "the Christian message is essentially a
social message. Everything connected with the Christian religion pro-
claims the fact that it is to dominate the social order and revolutionize
the community in which Christians live."[14]

Dr. Smith preached other sermons in which the biblical text was a
more determining factor. In a baccalaureate sermon (May 31, 1925)
based on Phil. 3:13-14—"Brethren, I count not myself to have appre-
hended; but this one thing I do, forgetting those things which are behind, and reaching forth unto those things which are before, I press
toward the mark for the prize of the high calling of God in Christ
Jesus"—he saw the Apostle Paul indicating "three conditions necessary
to successful living: first, relationship to the past; second, relationship
to the future; third, possession of a definite goal." Restating his text, Dr.
Smith began his interpretation of the first condition: "Forgetting the
things which are behind."

Youth is usually too prone to discard the past, and a fine distinction must
be observed here. There are some things about the past that must be clearly
recognized. In the first place, one must never have a contempt for the past.
Its methods may be antiquated, but its spirit is heroic and precious. It provided the stage for the accomplishments of countless multitudes, and we are
where we are today because of the past.

With his abiding appreciation of historic traditions and achievements,
Frank Smith was simply unable to follow the Apostle's explicit statement
by recommending an unconditional forgetting of the past.

Likewise, one must never discard the sentiment connected with the past.
Most of life's sentiments takes root in the past, and life would be a dreary
proposition without this sentiment. Sentiment is necessary to high and holy
living. The blessed memories of old homes and old loves and old faiths will
make nobler and purer the homes and loves and faiths of today.

Having made his own view clear, Dr. Smith returned to the exposition
of his text.

While recognizing the past in this way, one must, nevertheless, realize that
the past is gone forever. The past is not to enslave you. No man living in

the past is qualified for the present. The task of the present generation is to incarnate the spirit and the best of the past in modern methods and applications. Live in the present and for the future.

Frank Smith's eminently pragmatic viewpoint was not blurred by sentiment for the past. Warning his young listeners not to assume that "all that is old is orthodoxy and whatever is new is heresy," he declared that "age has nothing to do with orthodoxy. Truth and service determine orthodoxy. The needs and opportunities of each generation must determine the application of truth."

The Apostle's second requirement for successful living, Dr. Smith continued, is "Reaching forth to those things which are before with anticipation and expectation."

Picture an athlete on a cinder track, straining every muscle to get ahead. Be a progressive, believe that the best is yet to be. Live in an atmosphere of expectancy. Great doers have always been great believers and men and women of vision. The world wants leaders with eyes able to read the future and who believe absolutely in the glorious outcome of life.

The third requirement is having a definite objective, "pressing on toward the mark."

The Apostle knew what his goal was . . . realization of the divine in his own life. For you it can mean no less if the journey is to be worth while. You were placed here for a purpose, . . . to make the world a better place in which to live and to develop a soul for eternity. . . . The nature of the goal will determine the nature of the life lived in reaching the goal. Success is measured by the spirit of endeavor and not by material achievements.[15]

Many of Dr. Smith's sermons have this same traditional three-point pattern. For a communion sermon he chose three sayings of Jesus: John 16:7, Luke 11:9, and Matt. 7:14. To counter the "cynical philosophy" of H. L. Mencken, he discussed three exponents of "the *real* 'old-time religion'": Abraham, Moses, and Jesus. In a "Mother's Day" sermon, he spoke of three meanings of marriage: union of hearts, union of lives, union of character. Entering the Kingdom of God, according to another of Dr. Smith's sermons, calls for three qualifications: (1) "Except your righteousness exceed that of the scribes and Pharisees, . . ." (Matt. 5:20); (2) "Except ye repent, . . ." (Luke 13:3); and (3) "Except ye become as little childen, . . ." (Matt. 18:3). A sermon on "The Parable of the

Sower" characterizes three types of people whose response to Jesus is inadequate: the indifferent, the shallow, and the worldly. Fathers attending a "Father and Son Night" service were challenged to instill within their sons through personal example three qualities: character, thrift, and religion. On a Christmas Sunday, he preached on three meanings of Jesus' birth: "he came to teach men how to live; he came that men's sins might be forgiven; and he came to relate this life to the life to come."[16]

The communion sermon mentioned above illustrates Dr. Smith's use of Scripture in his preaching. Three sayings of Jesus are examined in a comparison and contrast pattern, preparatory to the Sacrament of the Lord's Supper: "It is expedient for you that I go away" (John 16:7); "Ask and ye shall receive, seek and ye shall find, knock and it shall be opened unto you" (Luke 11:9); and "Strait is the gate and narrow the way which leadeth unto life" (Matt. 7:14). Beginning with the contrasting elements, Dr. Smith indicated that each of these three passages occurs in a different Gospel, each represents a different period in Jesus' ministry, and each "bears an obvious meaning all together different from the meaning of the others." On the other hand, Dr. Smith continued, each of the three passages has a "secondary meaning [which] binds them together and gives them the meaning I wish to use this morning." Each "insists on man's dependence upon God and the necessity of man's realizing this dependence before spiritual resources are available to him."

The passage from the Fourth Gospel, Dr. Smith explained, emphasizes the necessity of Jesus' going away in the flesh,

else his followers would never enter into the fullness of a spiritual experience. So long as Jesus was with them they looked to him personally, as a child in the home depends upon its parents. They had no occasion to develop a self-reliance possible only when they were thrown upon their own resources and realized that of themselves they could do nothing, and so called upon their Lord for strength.[17]

This necessity of man's realizing his own helplessness before he can receive spiritual strength is also taught by the second saying, "Ask and ye shall receive." Jesus' third declaration means that "only whole-souled consecration to Him would lead to life eternal." Such consecration grows only from a keen sense of one's need of Jesus and the lack in one's life without him.

So I find a common view of man's relation to God in all three sayings of

Jesus. And it is that necessity of our dependence upon God that I wish you to bear in mind as you approach the Lord's Table this morning. . . . If you are perplexed and troubled, if you are discouraged with the result of your endeavors, you are in the best possible frame of mind to throw yourself completely upon Jesus. . . . If you are grieved and your heart is heavy and you realize neither your possessions nor anything earthly can bring you comfort, "Draw near with faith." The Holy Comforter is waiting to receive you.[18]

No preacher lightly takes on "the three great problems faced by the human race," not even if he does so in the name of the Apostle Paul. A sermon of this nature should reveal a preacher at his best, offering valuable insights into his mature thinking and illuminating his grasp of the Christian faith. While one would wish for a word-for-word transcript of such a sermon preached by Dr. A. Frank Smith, only a newspaper account is available.[19] These three great problems faced by the human race, according to Dr. Smith, are sin, grief, and death. As the basis for his sermon, he selected three passages from the letters of the Apostle Paul: "For I know whom I have believed and am persuaded that he is able to keep that which I have committed unto him against that day" (2 Tim. 1:12); "We know that all things work together for good to them that love God" (Rom. 8:28); and "For we know that, if our earthly house of this tabernacle were dissolved, we have a building of God, a house not made with hands, eternal in the heavens" (2 Cor. 5:1). According to Dr. Smith, these three statements are "a definite, positive expression of belief in a personal Savior, in a loving Father, and in eternal life." These three great affirmations form the foundation upon which Paul addresses "the three great problems faced by the human race: sin, grief, and death. Over against the first, Paul places a Savior. Over against the second, he places providential care, or a loving Father. Over against the third, he offers immortality."[20]

Sin is the greatest world problem. Volumes have been written about it. Men have not been able to understand down the ages why God has permitted sin to remain in the world. . . . Often men have become cynical and despaired of an answer. Sin has always been rampant. No wonder men have become despondent after these hundreds of thousands of years of fighting it. Paul, too, might have become cynical if he had dwelt upon sin alone. But he was interested in a remedy for sin. He focused his attention on a plan of salvation from sin. He found it in his own experience. . . . Paul could give assurance that Christ was able to save from sin because he had experienced a transformation in his own life. As he reminded his hearers, he had among sinners been himself the chief.[21]

Paul was not alone in this assurance, Dr. Smith continued, citing the similar experiences of "Zacchaeus, the cheat; the scarlet woman; the dying thief on the cross; and the innumerable others that look down from heaven this morning. The greatest discovery any individual can make is that Jesus is his savior."

To counter the second great problem, "grief and worry," said Dr. Smith, Paul pointed to "the providential care of a loving Father." Reminding his congregation of Paul's personal tribulations, Dr. Smith continued:

There were many things in Paul's life that did not appear to be working for the good of anybody. He was estranged from his family, cast out from his people, he was often imprisoned, mercilessly beaten, and even thrown to the lions in the arena. If anybody ever had reason to doubt that things work out for the best, it was Paul. Yet Paul was content to wait to know until he should know as he was known, "persuaded that neither death, nor life, nor angels, nor principalities, nor powers, nor things present, nor things to come, nor height, nor depth, nor any other creature, shall be able to separate us from the love of God, which is in Christ Jesus our Lord."[22]

The third giant agony of human existence is the ever-present challenge of death. As a pastor, Dr. Smith was often asked: "Why was this young man or that young mother taken?" "There are many things we do not understand," he confessed.

Paul did not understand the grave, but he did know that the grave is not the end. When death does come to our loved ones or to us, however, we know, with Paul, that "we have a building of God, a house not made with hands, eternal in the heavens." You will not have much peace in this life, until you come to believe that.[23]

The Christmas sermon that Dr. Smith preached at First Methodist Church, Houston, as reported in a local paper, is of interest for several reasons. Advent congregations expect sermons of much sentiment and emotion. A Christmas Eve sermon preached by Smith at University Church, Austin, was described, for instance, as "teeming with the beauty and holiness of the day; the story of the Star of Bethlehem was touchingly told."[24] This Christmas sermon in Houston, however, stands in striking contrast. "Christmas must mean more than mere good cheer to the Christian," Dr. Smith declared. "It must be a time when the meaning of Jesus' birth comes home to us anew."[25]

To elucidate the significance of Christmas, Dr. Smith discussed three meanings of the coming of Christmas. The celebration of Jesus' birth takes on unique importance for the Christian "because Jesus came to teach men how to live," he stated as his first point.

In the final analysis, success or failure in life can only be judged in terms of human association. Without the opportunity to develop either generosity or selfishness, courage or cowardice, man can neither succeed nor fail in a moral sense. One develops these things only through association with other human beings. . . . We are all individual parts of a great whole, and Jesus said that men could live only as they practiced unselfishness, and that life must be told in terms of unselfish action.

It was Frank Smith's nature to emphasize the positive and constructive side of things. Knowing that people tend to think of the Christian ideal of life as one that demands self-sacrifice and resignation, he insisted that

this is not Jesus' teaching. Instead of self-sacrifice, let us rather say self-expression; instead of 'submitting to the will of God,' let us rather 'spring to the will of God,' gladly conforming ourselves to His demands as the only basis upon which we can exist with our fellow men and develop our character. The world discovered long ago that life is real and beautiful only as the spirit of Jesus is obeyed.

Lest anyone in the congregation think that the preacher was presenting some kind of "boot-strap religion," Dr. Smith declared that "right living alone never saved any man; it isn't enough that you are now trying to live right." Referring to the "Rich Young Ruler" (Luke 18:18) as "exemplary in his personal life," he continued:

I doubt if any person here today is as careful to keep all the commandments as was he, yet he lacked one thing, the spirit of complete consecration to God. . . . Just one thing he lacked, and all his righteous living along other lines could not hide his lack there. And so with you this morning; if you are not perfect now, you need a Savior. If you have ever sinned in your life, you need forgiveness. This embraces us all. . . . You need forgiveness and you need a Savior. Your heart can't be satisfied until you have sought and obtained forgiveness. That is true with respect to your relation to your fellow man whom you have wronged. It is infinitely more true with respect to your relation to your God whom you have wronged. And you have such a Savior in Jesus. "They shall call His name Jesus, for He shall save the people from their sins."

This passage attracts attention because it appears in a Christmas sermon preached in the 1920s. Protestant ministers did not ordinarily give much attention to man's sinfulness and need of salvation in Christmas sermons, especially during those years of "Protestant acculturation."[26] Frederick Lewis Allen characterized the '20s as an era when millions of Americans devoted their attention to "a series of tremendous trifles."[27] Frank Smith, in this Christmas sermon, was certainly not typical of the time.

That "Jesus came to relate this life to the life to come" is the third emphasis in Dr. Smith's sermon on the significance of Christmas. "Having taught us how to be forgiven of our sins, and how to live here," he said, "Jesus has gone into the next and larger room of the mansion of His Father, there to prepare for our coming."

Jesus taught that life is one, that eternity begins here, that death is a change but not a break. . . . To the Christian, as to Jesus, death is but the opening into a larger and fuller life, merely an incident in a normal experience. It was Jean Valjean, the immortal character in *Les Misérables*, who cried as the cold dew of death gathered upon his brow, "It is nothing to die, it is an awful thing not to have lived." This is the Christian experience.

This passage beautifully illustrates one of the formative principles of American liberal theology: "emphasis upon the principle of continuity."[28] Since eternity begins in this life, death is not a break but only a change or an opening into a more complete life. American liberals characteristically interpreted the future life as "immortality of the soul" rather than as "resurrection of the body."[29]

Dr. Smith concluded his Christmas sermon on a strong note of assurance to his congregation:

I do not know your circumstances this morning, but I do know that you have been disappointed and buffeted in life's journey. And I do know that there is a tug at the heart strings from that land "Where no storms ever beat on that glittering strand and the years of eternity roll." And I do know that you have life left this morning, that your sins may be forgiven, and that you may begin now the life you will live through eternity with your Lord.

Only in this closing personal appeal did he permit a moment of sentimentality. Having addressed the body of his sermon to his congregation's rational understanding, he sought the additional motivating power of their emotions to gain the desired act of commitment.

This sermon on "The Significance of Christmas," in summary, is an interesting combination of the unexpected and the predictable. Within the context of both its immediate and larger settings, it is unique in its unsentimental and realistic approach to the meaning of Christmas. Avoiding the traditional patterns of beautiful symbols and poetic fancies usually associated with Christmas, Dr. Smith sought to portray the significance of the coming of Jesus Christ in terms of salvation from sin and death. On the other hand, reflecting the influence of his theological training at Vanderbilt and of his chief mentors, Bishops Mouzon and Moore, Dr. Smith predictably couched much of his sermon in the terminology and thought patterns of American liberal theology. In evading simple classification, this sermon is characteristic of the man who preached it. Although he was certainly a man of his times, he prized spontaneity and versatility above conformity to any pattern.

As noted earlier in this chapter, Frank Smith believed that the value of a sermon "rests ultimately upon its effect upon those who hear it." "Effectiveness at the moment" was one of his basic criteria in judging preaching. Although there are many persons still living who heard Dr. Smith preach while he was pastor of First Methodist Church in Houston, their memories of his preaching have been influenced by the interval of more than forty-five years. Inevitably, the memories of his preaching as a pastor have been intertwined with more recent impressions of his preaching during his thirty years as a bishop. How fortunate it is, therefore, that an evaluation of Dr. Smith's preaching was written in 1930, soon after he left First Methodist Church, by his close friend and fellow pastor for four years, Dr. J. N. R. Score. As a highly regarded preacher in Southern Methodism, Dr. Score was eminently qualified to make such an appraisal.

Beginning with the spectacular growth of First Methodist Church during Frank Smith's eight-year pastorate there, Dr. Score wrote:

From a church of some three thousand members, the First Methodist Church in Houston grew to a membership of five thousand. . . . During [at least] three of the eight years of his pastorate the First Methodist Church was the leading church in the entire Southern Methodist denomination in additions on profession of faith. No man's ministry can year after year bear such fruits unless the preacher's heart is that of a true evangelist of Jesus Christ.

. . . Any man who can preach to the same congregation for a period of eight years and have his congregation almost double in numerical strength and find his crowds the last year of the eight greater than the first year must have a mind of great versatility and originality. . . . He is a man of unusually keen insight. He possesses the ability of turning a phrase and giving it new meaning. He can take an ordinary drab subject and bring it to newness and freshness. . . . He is a man of unusual breadth of mind. We are referring to the rich mental experience—a mind, which is at home in various fields. . . . His friends are continually astonished not only at the breadth of his acquaintance with the thought of mankind, but at his deep insight into the problems raised and questions asked in various fields of mental endeavor. This breadth of mind has made him a preacher of unusual attractiveness to a great multitude of people. . . . Here in Houston, "Dr. Smith's crowd" was drawn from all walks of life, from all social positions, and from all sections of the city. This fact alone testifies to the human appeal and the winsomeness of his presentation of his message. . . . One of the leading businessmen in Houston said publicly about Dr. Smith that one of the "distinguishing characteristics of his ministry had been the large number of men who had not only attended his services and heard him preach, but had been actively engaged in the work of the Church because of the virility of his character, of the masculine appeal of the Gospel that he preached." . . . We can think of no preacher to whom we would rather listen Sunday after Sunday, or day after day. Never have we heard him speak but that we came away with a sense of having received something of definite value for personal living. . . . Frank Smith's preaching deals with the great fundamental urges of the human soul. It deals always with the tried and tested elements of the message of the Christ and the revelation of God that is to be found in Christ. It has always been his aim to present the truth in such a fashion that it could be assimiliated and used by his hearers.[30]

Although A. Frank Smith enjoyed preaching and worked diligently to attain his full potential as a preacher, he believed that being a pastor was equally important. "I had no desire to major in the pulpit if it would lead to poorly discharging the responsibilities which always seemed to face me. I came into the ministry to be a pastor," he explained, "and I wanted to be a pastor to the people. I wanted to love them and I wanted them to love me."[31]

Two letters that Dr. Smith received from members of his congregation illustrate his success in combining his pastoral and preaching ministries. "I like to have you as my pastor for several reasons," Judge Langston G. King wrote. "I enjoy your sermons very much; but just lots of preachers can preach good sermons. We have come to know you not only as a good preacher, but as a man with human understanding and human sympathy. I believe you understand people better than any minister I ever knew."[32] Another prominent Houston citizen, W. P. Hobby, wrote to thank Dr. Smith for his "beautiful words and the comforting manner" with which Smith had conducted his wife's funeral. "I am especially glad it was you because of her fondness for you and because of the many messages from your pulpit that gave her hope and cheered her life."[33]

Throughout his parish ministry Dr. Smith sought to be a pastor to all of his people, not just to a part of his congregation.

I never failed to declare myself on moral issues and I never hesitated to take sides when it came, but I did not denounce the other side of what I was doing. They were children of God. . . . You don't have to create divisions in order to stand for something. If people are good people, you can stand for what you want, and they will still love you. It's the way you go about it that is important. It's when you get personal that you start a row. . . . Each member of the congregation ought to be able to say, "That's my preacher," or "that's my preacher's wife," and feel comfortable in their presence.[34]

Dr. Smith applied the same guideline to friendships within the congregation. "We have made it a point never to have close friends," he stated. "We were friends to all of them." The Smiths, for example, never went on vacation trips with another family or even with a group of families. "I'm sure that people who did that had royal good times, but I think it is not a good idea for a preacher to be identified with a certain segment of his congregation and not with others." The Smiths had many friends, but there was no select circle who had a standing invitation to drop in and make themselves at home at the parsonage. "We tried to be pastor to the whole congregation," Dr. Smith insisted, "and not of some certain set."[35]

It is almost unbelievable that Frank Smith considered himself a timid person. With reference to pastoral calling, Dr. Smith said: "I did a lot of calling, made the regular rounds, but it was hard for me. People might laugh when it is said, but I am timid. It's hard for me." Praising his wife for her supporting role, he continued:

Now Bessie is a natural born visitor. She never saw a stranger. She likes crowds. If it's a dog fight, she wants to go to it. If it's a fire, she wants to jump on the firetruck and go along. So between us, we got around. Bessie would meet the folks and I would go along. Well, I looked important anyway. I mean I could put on a solemn look while she was with the people.[36]

Naturally this reaction to crowds troubled the pastor, so he brought up
the matter with their family doctor, Dr. Marvin L. Graves, whose father
was a Methodist minister. Frank Smith later recalled the conversation:

I said, "Doctor, it troubles me to think that I'm a preacher and yet people
irritate me in crowds." "That's perfectly natural," he replied, "that's nature
trying to assert itself. You spend your life in crowds, and when you don't
have to be in a crowd, you don't want to be in one. You want to run away
from it. That's perfectly natural. If you were a hermit and never saw anybody, you'd probably want to get in with somebody if you had a chance.
But you work in your parish with crowds all the time. and you don't want
to go there when you don't have to. It isn't dislike of the people."

"I do like people," Frank Smith insisted. "I love people and I want to
be kind. I've always wanted folks to feel that I was trying to be kind.
I never had any other desire but just simply to try to help people grow
their souls and fit themselves for the Kingdom of God."[37]

One of the most widely appreciated ways in which Frank Smith expressed his interest and concern in people—church members and non-
members alike—was the letters he wrote to them. As Hines H. Baker
explains:

My wife and I received any number of letters from him [Dr. Smith] that
gave us the definite feeling that he had a personal interest in us. If something occurred, an advancement for me in the organization or something I
did in the community, he would write a note expressing appreciation and
so forth. When our oldest boy made Phi Beta Kappa at the university, we
got a very nice letter from Dr. Smith. But he didn't just take an interest
in his own church members. We had a fellow here in our organization
[Humble Oil & Refining Co.] who was a strong Catholic. He had several
letters from Dr. Smith in connection with various honors or achievements
of his children. Things of that kind that evidenced his concern for people
was one of the reasons he had such potent influence.[38]

People who spent much time with A. Frank Smith remember that
he carried a little packet of white 3" x 5" note cards in his pocket. If he
heard about an illness, an honor, or something that concerned a church
member or a friend, he would make a brief note to himself as a reminder
to write that person a letter at the first opportunity. "Frank Smith had
a great concern to thank somebody for something they had done, to
compliment them or to bathe their wounded feelings," Bishop Arthur
Moore remembers. "He was always out on the street of life helping

people, understanding their sorrows, or sharing their joys."[39] One such
letter was written to a couple who had recently lost their little daughter.
The grieving parents replied: "Dear Dr. Smith, Your beautiful letter
of sympathy has brought us more comfort than we can tell you. It has
helped and strengthened us greatly, because we know how fully you
understand our sorrow."[40]

Many years later, in a chapter he contributed to a book on *The
Ministry*, Frank Smith pointed out "the value of letter writing of the
right sort":

What a rich field there is for the discriminating person who knows when
to send a note of sympathy, or a word of commendation to a public official
who is doing a faithful job, or a word of felicitation to the one who has
been promoted by his company. A brief note at the right time is doubly
appreciated, and the writer is never forgotten.[41]

Another way in which Dr. Smith was a pastor to his people involved
Christian stewardship. He was always seeking appropriate channels for
philanthropic giving. While nurturing this expression of Christian love,
he would find particular cases of need that would especially appeal to
the donor. In one such instance, he enabled W. L. Clayton to establish
a scholarship fund to keep a young preacher from the Texas Conference
in SMU's School of Theology. T. Walter Moore had been "praying
and working [his] way through school for six years" but had come to
the end of his resources two years short of attaining his B.D. degree.[42]
Through Mr. Clayton's gift, the young man was enabled to complete his
theological education. Since then, the Reverend T. Walter Moore has
served as a pastor in the Texas Conference for more than forty-five years.[43]
Dr. Stewart Clendenin, who was a friend of Moore's and had just joined
the Texas Conference "on trial" in 1927, still remembers how impressed
he was by Dr. Smith's thoughtfulness and timely aid. "That was my first
knowledge of Dr. Smith and the kind of man he was," Dr. Clendenin
explains. "Of course, we young preachers thought Dr. Smith was a great
man for helping a struggling student to finish seminary."[44]

Another strong point in Dr. Smith's pastoral ministry was his administrative ability. "We never saw him flustered," Dr. Score declared,
"never saw him in a hurry, never saw him panicky." One basis for this
serenity was Frank Smith's "ability to set up and use an organization."

Many men find the addition of assistants and the bringing in of new members in their staffs a decided disadvantage. They find that each new assistant adds additional responsibility to their work because they try to supervise even the details of their assistant's work. It was not so with Frank Smith. The men and women who composed his corps of assistants at the First Methodist Church were given the broad outlines of program and were shown their personal responsibilities. They were co-laborers with the pastor of the church. They understood what he wanted done and that each would be allowed to do his work in his own way. The result was a fine *esprit de corps*, the development of personal initiative in the work of his assistants, and in the accomplishment of the tasks to be done.[45]

This is not to say, however, that Dr. Smith was complacent or unaware of shortcomings. Dr. Monroe Vivion remembers that Frank Smith worried because he couldn't find meaningful ways for all the new members to participate in the life and activities of First Church.

Houston was growing by leaps and bounds, and everybody who came to Houston wanted to join First Church because Frank Smith was so widely known and admired and respected. He had a good pastorate, but he was worried about so many folks joining the church that he couldn't put them to work. I heard him make the statement that from the time he came to First Church in '22 to the time he left in '30, there had not beeen a 10 percent change in the leadership of the church. He considered it a tragedy that he had been unable to work more of the new members into the life of the church.[46]

Dr. Smith's concerned awareness of this problem is just further evidence in support of Dr. Score's belief that "Frank Smith has always had the heart of a true pastor."

He has always been at the beck and call of those who needed him. No problem in the life of any of his people has been too small to demand his careful attention. We have known him to stay all day long at a hospital just to be near and to talk and give comfort to someone who was in distress because of the serious illness of a loved one. . . . During the four years it was our privilege to serve side by side with Frank Smith as a brother pastor in the same city, we came to believe that one of the reasons for his success was the combination of social graces that he possesses. He gave of himself not only in the pulpit, not only in his office, not only in the sick room, but he gave generously of himself in the social life of his people. Small wonder that he was so beloved.[47]

9

"Now Called to the Work and Ministry of a Bishop"

"THIS IS A VERY SOLEMN BUSINESS," Bishop Hiram Abiff Boaz advised the delegates to the twenty-first General Conference of the Methodist Episcopal Church, South, convened in Dallas's First Methodist Church. "Before we proceed with the first ballot for bishops, we will sing a hymn and have a word of prayer."[1] Addressing his prayer to the delegates as much as to God, Bishop Edwin D. Mouzon stated the traditional Methodist interpretation of the way bishops are chosen:

Almighty God, . . . We believe that thou dost lay thy hand upon men and call them into the ministry. We believe that men do not take this upon themselves. . . . O Lord, we have come to a critical hour in the history of the Church. We need men moved upon by the Spirit of God, free from selfishness, loyal to Jesus Christ, filled with the Holy Spirit, with faces turned toward the morning. . . . O God of our fathers, Spirit of the Living God, do thou thyself set apart to this high service the men of thy choosing. We ask it in Jesus' name. Amen.[2]

Earlier, in their formal address to the delegates, the College of Bishops had requested the election of additional bishops. "In view of the fact that no new bishops have been elected for eight years and the further fact that three active bishops have passed away since any were elected, we suggest that the episcopacy be strengthened to such extent as seems wise to the General Conference."[3] The General Conference, however, was sharply divided concerning the wisdom of "strengthening the episcopacy." The Committee on Episcopacy submitted a majority report recommending the election of three new bishops, and a minority report insisting that it was "unnecessary and unadvisable to elect any additional bishops at this session."[4] The arguments presented during the floor debate on these two reports comprise an interesting glimpse of Southern Methodism's view of episcopacy as well as of the developing struggle between the bishops and the executive secretaries of the general boards—polity questions that would be of concern to A. Frank Smith for the next thirty years.

Led by A. J. Lamar, one of the powerful publishing agents of the church; O. E. Goddard, secretary of the Foreign Department of the Board of Missions; and E. B. Chappell, editor of Sunday School Publications—the minority argued that "thirteen effective bishops [were] sufficient to do the work of the Church . . . if the present bishops do a man's job and take a sufficient number of Conferences to keep them busy."[5] They also emphasized the "widespread discontent within our Church with the expense of our present superintendency." Goddard concluded the minority case with an emotional appeal portraying the requests for help coming from Brazil, Africa, and China:

And here we are facing needs enough to make a man grow gray overnight, talking about spending $100,000 [during the quadrennium] for episcopal supervision that we do not need, with a cry coming from all these foreign fields enough to break a man's heart, that we cannot supply. Hear me today, from the depths of my soul, elect no new bishops.[6]

Chiding the previous speakers for their "financial wail," Frank S. Onderdonk, the pioneer of Methodist missionary work in Mexico, declared:

There are requests coming in from all over the Church for a more aggressive episcopal leadership. . . . If I sense the times in which we live, with new legislation which we are putting on . . . and this tremendous demand for leadership in evangelism, . . . it seems imperative that the Church have today some younger men who can join their older colleagues on the present college of bishops and go out and meet this new day and put on this program.[7]

Attacking the economy argument more directly, Judge D. C. Roper of the Baltimore Conference asked: "shall we lay the stress on finances or on leadership?" If the board secretaries wished to cut expenses, he suggested, "It seems to me that you might well consider reducing the expenses attaching to your numerous boards, not only by reducing the number of such boards, but by giving these boards more work rather than your bishops more work." Roper continued, "Are we not laying stress at the wrong place? . . . If you will strengthen this college of bishops so as to bring this message of spirituality to a larger number of groups of people throughout this country, you need not worry about your finances."[8] As chairman of the Committee on Episcopacy, F. P. Culver (a clerical delegate from the Central Texas Conference) had the last word, returning to the fundamental question:

How many bishops we need depends upon what you want a bishop for. If we go back to the days of 1886 and 1890, perhaps we have a sufficient number. But if we remember that we are living in 1930, it is an entirely different proposition. . . . We want leaders in the field, not merely executives in the bishopric. . . . During this quadrennium, when we are planning a forward movement in evangelism, where there ought to be a kindling of the fires of evangelistic fervor all over our Church, we ought to have a proper leadership.[9]

When the final vote was taken, 251 delegates favored the election of three new bishops, overcoming an impressive opposition of 147.[10]

The first ballot for bishops was taken on Tuesday morning, May 20. Proceeding in the historic manner—without nomination, a simple majority being sufficient for election—the delegates cast their votes and then continued with the scheduled business until the tellers returned. Pending matters were then suspended while the results were announced and another ballot was taken. Arthur Moore and Paul Kern, after leading on the first two ballots, were elected on the third. Although Frank Smith was in seventh place with only eighty votes on the first ballot, he quickly rose to fifth place with 132 votes on the third ballot, just behind Dr. T. D. Ellis and Dr. Forney Hutchinson. Moore and Kern, receiving 233 and 227 respectively, were well above the 217 required for election. On the fourth and fifth ballots Smith fell far behind, receiving 84 and 58 votes.[11] This was to be expected, as Smith later explained:

They had already elected one man from Texas, Paul Kern at Travis Park, and Arthur Moore's shirt-tail was still wet from crossing the Mississippi. They counted him a Texan. . . . And there was no reason why I should have been elected. I was only forty years old, had just built the educational building and renovated the inside of the church with a big indebtedness and the depression coming on. My youngest child was only a year and a half old, and Mrs. Smith was not well. I was rather glad that they did pass me by.[12]

A sixth ballot was taken just before adjournment that day, but the votes were ordered sealed for the night (presumably to avoid rumors or premature news leaks). "I remember taking a long drive with Frank," Arthur Moore recalls, "and commiserating with him that I had been elected and he hadn't. 'Well, Frank, it looks like it's not going to be you this time.' 'Yes,' he said, 'I'll go back and have a good pastorate.' "[13]

When the General Conference convened the next morning, Dr. Forney Hutchinson immediately requested permission to make a personal statement. Since Hutchinson had been in a close race with Dr. T. D. Ellis for the one remaining position, he had no difficulty gaining everyone's attention. He said, in part:

I never in my life wanted to be a bishop, and the closer I get to it the less fascinating it is. Over in my native state there was a boy who got into trouble. The lawyer he engaged told him, "You have a bad case, son." "I know I have, and that is why I am getting a good lawyer." "But you face the electric chair." "Yes, sir, but facing it isn't what I'm worrying about. What I want to do is to keep from sitting down in it." . . .

[Since] I do not know the result of the last ballot taken in our effort to elect a bishop, my statement must cover either of two possibilities. After much prayer and careful consideration, I must request, in the event that there is no election, that those who have been voting for me do so no more. If, on the other hand, I have been elected, I must respectfully decline to accept.[14]

When the results of the sixth ballot were announced, Hutchinson had moved ahead of Dr. Ellis and to within eleven votes of election. Smith had dropped to twenty votes. There was still no election on the seventh ballot, but the distribution of the votes shifted radically. Of the 199 votes for Hutchinson on the previous report, Dr. Ellis received only thirteen, increasing his total to 190, but Dr. Smith's total jumped back up to 112. On the eighth ballot Smith rose to 161 while Ellis fell to 172. "At about 12:15 o'clock, just as the General Conference was getting ready to adjourn the morning session," according to Dr. J. N. R. Score, "the secretary read the report of the ninth ballot: 'Ballots cast, 440; necessary to elect, 221. . . . T. D. Ellis, 129; A. Frank Smith, 240. A. Frank Smith has received a majority of the votes cast.' "[15] The *Journal* continues:

The Chair [Bishop Warren A. Candler] announced that A. Frank Smith, having received a majority of the votes cast, is elected a bishop of the Methodist Episcopal Church, South. Bishops Darlington and Hay, at the request of the Chair, conducted Bishop Elect A. Frank Smith to the platform and presented him to the conference amid great applause.[16]

How can this sudden change be explained? On the sixth ballot, taken late Tuesday afternoon, Frank Smith had received only twenty votes. Yet, before noon on the following day, he was elected on the ninth ballot with more votes than either of the two other bishops elect had received. Dr. Score, who had been actively supporting Dr. Smith,[17] explains:

From the close of the Texas Annual Conference in November when Frank Smith was elected to lead his delegation to the opening of the General Conference in Dallas in May, one heard the name of A. Frank Smith repeatedly. It was generally conceded by those who knew the sentiment of the Church at large that he was sure of election, if not in 1930, certainly in 1934. Of all the men who were discussed for the Episcopacy, he seemed to be the only man who was not being opposed by some group or faction.[18]

There was also considerable activity by other supporters, especially in the course of Tuesday evening, Bishop Martin remembers:

W. F. Bryan had a lot to do with that election. Bryan had been Frank's presiding elder when Frank was at Detroit and admired Frank very much. Now Frank and Arthur [Moore] both told me this. Bryan found out that Forney Hutchinson was not going to accept it. There were enough people across the church that had Frank in mind that W. F. Bryan could turn that thing around.[19]

Bishop Angie Smith believes that John W. Barton, former publishing agent, had played a significant role. "Barton came to me and said, 'If Forney Hutchinson isn't elected on this [sixth] ballot, I have twenty-five men who have agreed to change to Frank.' Forney withdrew his name, and Frank began to jump and went right on in."[20] Mr. John T. Scott, longtime chairman of the board at First Church, Houston, is also said to have been actively involved in Frank Smith's election.[21]

On the other hand, Mrs. Smith was not at all pleased with the prospect of her husband's becoming a bishop. She later explained:

I didn't want Frank to be elected. It was for selfish reasons. The children were small, and I felt like it would break up the home. So that morning when Frank's vote started rising, I got up and left the church. My sister, Hallie, and I rode all around through Highland Park, and I was just crying and weeping. Finally, at noontime, we came back to the church, and the election was over. Then I regretted that I had missed seeing them escort him to the platform and all that.[22]

Frank described her reaction:

I came out of the door of the church, and Bess was just sitting in the car. When she saw me, she broke out into a loud boo-hoo. That's the first time I'd seen her since I was elected.[23] . . . That was Wednesday, and the Consecration Service was set for Thursday evening. Bessie and I talked it over. I could have pulled out as one of our men had done in 1922 after he was elected. But she said, "Frank, we didn't seek this. Providence must be in it. Whether we wanted it or not, the Lord will take care of us if we go into it right."[24]

Gathering in the sanctuary of Dallas's First Methodist Church, "the Conference convened at 8 P.M., Thursday, May 22, 1930, in special consecration session with the Senior Bishop, Warren A. Candler, in the chair." After the sermon by Bishop Collins Denny, the bishops elect were presented for consecration. For this very personal experience, Frank chose his brother Angie and "Uncle John," Professor J. R. Allen, as his presenting elders. Then, as stated in the *Journal* of the Conference:

Bishop Candler led in the imposition of hands upon Bishop Elect Smith, assisted by Bishops Mouzon, DuBose, Cannon and Hay, and the presenting elders.

Bishop Mouzon gave the exhortation and presented a copy of the Holy Scriptures to each of the newly consecrated bishops.

Bishop John M. Moore, Secretary of the College of Bishops, presented to each of the newly consecrated bishops his ordination parchment.[25]

How fitting that Bishops Mouzon and Moore had these particular roles in the service! Above all others, these two men had been most influential in Frank Smith's life. Now they would be his senior colleagues in the College of Bishops.

There was another facet of Frank Smith's role in the General Conference of 1930 that should not be overlooked. This was the so-called "Cannon Controversy." In the first instance, Frank Smith was drawn into this unfortunate episode through his membership on the Committee on Episcopacy. The criticism of Bishop Cannon doubtless resulted from a wide spectrum of motivation. While some of his defenders suspected a sinister Roman Catholic plot, others blamed the antiprohibition forces. As the zealous chairman of the church's Board of Temperance and Social Service, Bishop Cannon had earned the epithet "the Dry Messiah." Still others attributed the bishop's plight to political enemies, saying that Cannon had offended the democratic sensibilities of southerners by supporting Hoover instead of Al Smith in the 1928 presidential election. Whatever the critics' grounds, the specific charge brought against Bishop Cannon in 1930 was "playing the stock market." Complaints were presented to the Committee on Episcopacy "against the ministerial character of Bishop James Cannon, Jr., touching his alleged speculations in the stock market."[26] Perhaps the most prestigious of all the committees of the General Conference, the Committee on Episcopacy was composed primarily of the leaders of the respective delegations.[27] Bishop Arthur Moore recalls the tension-filled committee meeting:

Frank was over in the corner. Controversy troubled him. He was whittling with his pen knife on a stick of wood. And one old layman said to me, "That fellow over in the corner doesn't do anything but whittle." I was trying to help Bishop Cannon express some regret, and I said, "Bishop Cannon, you have had two or three years to think this over. You do regret all of this, don't you?" He replied, "I do regret that I lost my money and that my judgment was poor." Frank loved to tease me about that. And the committee voted forty-nine to four, I think it was, to try Bishop Cannon. And that night there was great consternation. No bishop had ever been put on trial. But the next day Cannon made a very abject apology to the whole General Conference and took that instead of a trial.

Then the report got out that other bishops had been dabbling in the stock market. It suddenly became a major sin. One by one, these bishops, all of them old men, got up to tell the General Conference that they had not gambled. Finally, everyone had spoken except Bishop Candler. He was the great Georgia man. He didn't like all of that, but he had to say something, so he got up. There was a rumor out that he was rich on Coca Cola stock, which was not true. But he got up, and there was a painful silence. "The only stock I ever owned. . . ." and he paused to let that soak in. They thought they were going to hear a confession, I guess. "The only stock I ever owned was a heifer cow, and she went dry." And that was the end of the Cannon controversy.[28]

Unfortunately, there was one further attempt to embarrass Bishop Cannon. A day or two after Frank Smith had been elected a bishop, the Committee on Temperance and Social Service submitted its nominations for the new board for the ensuing quadrennium, including the name of Bishop James Cannon, Jr. Ordinarily, such nominations were automatically accepted. In this instance, however, the chairman of the committee, Josephus Daniels, gave notice "for himself and others of the minority that they would dissent from some of these nominations."[29] An attempt was made to cut off the implied attack on Bishop Cannon by calling the previous question, but the defensive move failed to gain the required majority. A motion was then made and seconded "that the name of Bishop Elect A. Frank Smith be substituted for that of Bishop James Cannon, Jr. as Chairman of the Board."[30] According to Bishop Arthur Moore, "Frank didn't want it, and he didn't want to be Cannon's opponent, but he couldn't help it. These men were making a determined effort to take Bishop Cannon off of the Board."[31] The emotional intensity of the debate —and therefore the embarrassment to Frank Smith—is clearly illustrated in the following exchange:

W. A. NEWELL: The Board of Temperance and Social Service speaks for the morals of our Church. It is our voice: [but] for a long while it has been the voice of one man. If this one man is continued upon the board, his voice will continue to be the voice of the Methodist Church on moral questions. . . . If we send this man out again to speak for us—not upon what men have charged him with, not upon those charges which his enemies have turned in to this body—but of his own confession we will send a man out to speak for us whom everyone of us will have to apologize for. . . . I beg you, and so move, that we substitute the name of Bishop A. Frank Smith, the last elected bishop and the one who received the highest number of votes—that we substitute the name of Bishop A. Frank Smith for the name of Bishop Cannon on this board. . . .
BOB SHULER: Back of this movement to displace Bishop Cannon is one of the most iniquitous conspiracies that has ever come about in civilization. It is not that the wets are interested in the matter of gambling. They are interested in unhorsing a man who, if he remains in the saddle, will unhorse them for all time. . . . The hour has come when we should rise above any personality and make a mighty stroke for civic decency in the United States of America, in the name of our Saviour.[32]

At one point the presiding bishop attempted to cool the temper of the engagement. "May the Chair rise to a question of parliamentary situation?" he said. "It occurs to the Chair that everybody is out of order. Brethren, will you hear the Chair for just a moment? Let us remember that this is God's work and that we are God's children in the presence of God."[33] When the previous question was finally ordered, a large majority requested a roll call vote so that each delegate's vote became a public record. The amendment to substitute the name of Bishop Smith for the name of Bishop Cannon failed by a vote of 134 yeas to 259 nays.[34]

Bishop A. Frank Smith's first episcopal assignment was to five annual conferences: the Missouri, the Southwest Missouri, the St. Louis, the Oklahoma, and the Indian Mission in Oklahoma.[35] As he later recalled, "We didn't know if we were going to be sent to China or to California. But Bishop Hay interposed, and we were sent to Missouri and Oklahoma."[36] Arthur Moore explains how assignments were made "in those days":

The College of Bishops made its own assignments in those days. They'd have a committee that went by rotation, five men, and they made the episcopal assignments. Frank and Paul and I were the "back-benchers," the "freshmen," and we accepted it. We got our appointments without much consultation. They just said, "This is it." It was the old Methodist idea— you got your marching orders. So they sent Paul Kern to China, Frank went to Missouri, and I went to the far West. Seniority was a much bigger item then, and ordinarily the bishop elected last would be sent to the foreign field. Well, Frank and Bess had a little baby, and their daughter was having severe ear trouble. Sam Hay was on the committee, and he knew that Frank ought not to leave his family or to take them to China. Frank's appointment to Missouri was determined somewhat by his daughter's illness, though he never wanted you to say that. He thought it was preferential treatment, which he didn't want. He didn't ask for it.[37]

Arthur Moore also remembers that "Frank took a little criticism, nothing serious, because he continued to live in Houston and didn't move into his area."[38] Actually, Frank Smith had little choice in the matter, but this was not known even by his friends. He expected to live in Oklahoma City, as indicated in the 1930 *Discipline*'s list of bishops' addresses.[39] His brother, Angie, explains the circumstances:

Bishops lived anywhere they wanted to then. And Frank and Bess went to Oklahoma with no other intention than living in Oklahoma, either to rent or buy. And a certain very prominent minister, whose name I shall not call, said to them, "We would prefer that you remain in Houston. We really prefer that our bishop not live in Oklahoma."[40]

Frank, Jr., then fifteen years old, still recalls the family's driving on that long trip:

Right after Dad was elected Bishop, it was stated that we were going to move away. And some of my friends had parties for me, and I never did move. It was kind of embarrassing. But we took a trip, drove up through Oklahoma, looked around Oklahoma City, and contacted real estate people looking for a house. Then we went up through Missouri, Springfield and across to Central College. They never did find a place they wanted, so they came back down here since there was no residence rule.[41]

One reason the family didn't move to Missouri was that Bishop W. F. McMurry chose to continue living at Central College at Fayette, Missouri,[42] although he had been assigned conferences in Illinois, Kentucky, and Virginia. Bishop Smith's sensitivity on the subject was still apparent years later:

I was sent to Missouri and Oklahoma. Bishop McMurry remained in Missouri. A bishop could live where he chose then. Then, in Oklahoma, Forney Hutchinson told me outright, "Well, no, we don't want any bishops up here. We never have had any, and we don't need any." So I just sort of from day to day stayed on in Houston. That is how I remained on here, but people said, "Frank Smith wouldn't leave Houston to go to heaven." That wasn't true. It was just a set of circumstances.[43]

For this first quadrennium, 1930-34, Bishop Smith was also appointed by the College of Bishops to the Board of Lay Activities with Bishop H. A. Boaz, and to the Commission on the Revision of the Hymnal along with Bishops W. A. Candler, John M. Moore, Sam R. Hay, and U. V. W. Darlington. This was apparently the beginning of the close friendship that developed between Bishop Smith and Bishop Darlington through the following years.

After the adjournment of the General Conference, while Oklahoma City was still their presumed destination, the Smiths returned to Houston to say their farewells. Many letters of congratulation awaited the young bishop. A message from Bishop Edwin H. Hughes of the Methodist Episcopal Church is representative:

I know you well enough to believe you will render your Church and our dear Lord very real service in the episcopacy. Likewise, I know you well enough to believe that you will join with us in overwhelming our unworthy sectionalism so that in due season we may have a continental Methodism that represents God's will for our two great churches.[44]

Bishop Smith's reply to Will Martin reveals his care in responding to these messages of congratulation as well as his amazement over the recent events:

My dear Friend: No letter has come to me which is more deeply appreciated than is yours. I have admired and loved you since first I knew you, and the years and the miles can never change that feeling upon my part. I only hope and pray that the day may not be far distant when our paths will cross, and that I may have the privilege of fellowship with you and of laboring with you in the work of the Church.

I do not know what it is all about yet, but I do hope and pray as I enter upon this new relationship that I may be able to render some small service to the Kingdom in these changing years. Pray for me.[45]

Smith became Martin's bishop in 1934, and Martin became Smith's colleague when he was elected among the next group of bishops in 1938.

The following excerpt is from a two-page letter sent by a Sunday school class and cherished by Bishop Smith as an expression of appreciation from a church group:

We are happy in the honor you have brought our Church and to our City, but we shall sadly miss you. We are [grateful] for the many beautiful things which we have heard you say in the pulpit that you filled with such reverence, sincerity and earnestness. . . . You have lived among us with a gracious dignity and a singleness of purpose and unselfishness that has been inspiring. . . . We shall always hope that you may come back to see us and that you may live in Houston again someday. . . . The Philathea Class, Alice Spence, Secretary.[46]

"CITY UNITES IN TRIBUTE TO BISHOP SMITH," declared a front-page article in the *Houston Chronicle.* "The heart of a city . . . was poured out in touching tributes Thursday night to Bishop A. Frank Smith at the Knife and Fork Club dinner, attended by 500 persons in the ballroom of the Rice Hotel." The article provides impressive documentation of Frank Smith's city-wide ministry and of the community's deep respect for him as a person:

Rev. Harry G. Knowles, pastor of the First Christian Church, called Doctor Smith "the bishop of all the churches of Houston . . . By his candor and frankness and out of the richness of his experience, he has won us all. He has been everybody's friend, everybody's pastor." . . .

The leader of the Jewish churches in Houston, Rabbi Henry Barnston, told Bishop Smith, "I pray that your children will have the great influence upon men that you have had." . . .

Father Jerome A. Rapp of Sacred Heart Church said, "I have known him for a long time [as] the servant of a tender conscience. . . . His has been a life of extraordinary usefulness." . . .

William Strauss, representing the Episcopalians, remarked, "He has helped to set a higher standard in charity work." . . .

Ross S. Sterling (Publisher of the *Post-Dispatch* and former President of Humble Oil & Refining Co.) declared, "He has won the hearts of all of us." . . .

Jesse Jones, "Houston is making a real sacrifice in giving you to the larger work of your church. You have made Houston a better place in which to live. You have caused many of us to have greater respect for your church, and especially you have made the men of your congregation take a real interest in their church." . . .

Dr. J. N. R. Score, pastor of Houston's newest church, St. Paul's Methodist, said, "Doctor Smith in his eight years here has walked with business leaders, with social leaders, with the intellectual leaders of this greatest of cities in Texas—without losing the common touch. His is a great heart." . . .

John T. Scott, of the First National Bank and long-time chairman of the Board at First Methodist Church, declared, "We do not see how we can let Frank Smith go. His going is a great personal loss to me and to thousands of others. I want him to know that he carries with him the love and esteem and the prayers of an entire city." . . .

Bishop Sam R. Hay said, "Frank Smith is leaving to do more work and receive less pay. He is entering the realm of administration where there will be less affection and love. I know in the years to come, Frank, you will long for your congregation again." . . .

Bishop Smith then spoke briefly. "It is hard to leave. It is hard to say goodbye. Mrs. Smith and I appreciate this dinner and all the things you have said about us . . . and the happiness of these eight years. . . . Half of our married life has been spent here. Two of our children were born here. . . . We shall always call this home. God bless all of you."[47]

Since his annual conferences were not scheduled to meet until September, Bishop Smith devoted the summer months of 1930 to becoming acquainted with his preachers and their churches. As a result he was away from home for weeks on end. He sketched his procedure as follows: "I would go up and stay for a week at the head of a district in a county seat and preach every night. Then we would radiate out to the circuits during the daytime and bring the people together, just trying to uphold the morale. They had no money, but they did have plenty to eat. Lovely people."[48] The people of Missouri were impressed by such commitment, as the following report indicates:

This is perhaps the first time that a bishop has traveled throughout the bounds of the Sedalia District, touching every one of the 14 counties included in the district and holding services in each congregation in the district. Surely there is no more devoted and consecrated bishop in our church than A. Frank Smith. But few men have the physical strength to stand the labors to which he gives himself.[49]

These long absences from home were difficult for Mrs. Smith and the children. On one occasion when Bishop Smith had been away in Missouri for two weeks, he had just one day at home before leaving for a meeting in Atlanta. "When I came into the upstairs living room," he remembered, "I noticed that Lula didn't speak to me. Lula, a colored woman, had been with us so long she was part of the family. She practically raised the children."

Lula was sweeping and acted like she hadn't seen me come in, but she mumbled loud enough for me to hear, "It's a terrible thing for the children to be raised without a father." Then our daughter, Betty, ran into the room, and Bess told her that I was going to Atlanta the next day. Betty said, "Daddy, are you going to leave again tomorrow?" And Lula whirled around and said, "Child, you haven't got a daddy. You just got a road lizard for a daddy!" And she kept right on sweeping.[50]

The change was almost too much for Mrs. Smith. "For the first six weeks after Frank started being away all the time," she recalled, "I would cry when he came home, and I would cry when he left. He would be gone up to three weeks at a time." "It was hard on Bess," the Bishop agreed. "We had been married sixteen years when I was elected, and I don't reckon I had been away from home but sixteen nights in all those years."[51]

To meet this crisis, Frank and Bess worked out several schemes. The first was for him to make regular long-distance telephone calls. "Frank called home every night," Mrs. Smith explained. "Now, that sounds like an extravagance, but it was the only method we had of keeping in touch. And he wrote me every day, and to the children almost every time he wrote me." "I called home every night for selfish reasons," Frank commented. "There is no lonelier place in the world than a hotel room. And I would call up and hear her voice, and it always gave me a lift. I felt the world was all right." "Our phone bill was enormous," Bess added, "but we felt like it was worth it." "I don't know any better investment we ever made," Frank agreed.[52]

Another defense against loneliness that Mrs. Smith developed was to plan things with the children that they could all do together when their father returned. Frank, Jr. recalls one such instance:

Mother liked to play tricks. It was just basic to her nature. Right after Dad had been elected bishop, he was feeling pretty good about it. So while he was up in Missouri preaching for a week, Mother and I worked out a plan. I had a microphone that could be plugged into the back of a radio. Take out a tube and plug this thing in. You could cut out the set and broadcast. So when Dad got back, he and Mother were in the upstairs sitting room listening to something on the radio—one of those great big sets with a round speaker on top. I was downstairs in the study with my microphone, and I began to read the script Mother and I had written.

"We interrupt this program to welcome to our broadcasting system a new station in Joplin, Missouri. The announcer will come on and give us a report of events there this past week."

When Dad heard that, he said, "Listen to this, listen to this, Bessie; that's where I have been. They have a new station up there." He thought they might say something about him or his preaching.

"One of the principal events of the week has been the visit of our new bishop. While we were glad to have this young man, he still has a long way to go."

Well, it just killed him. He couldn't believe it. He said to Mother, "Why, that's going all over the country!" Dad just kept on like that until Mother couldn't hold it any longer. Finally she told him what we had done. But he fell for it, hook, line and sinker.[53]

A third effort Mrs. Smith made to deal with her loneliness was the Gem Pickle Company. "I just finally decided one day, 'This is a life-time thing, and I can't spend my whole life crying.' So I started keeping busy."

A friend of mine, Mildred Nelms Conover, and I went into the pickle business. For a few years we made the best pickles on the market. We didn't make any money out of it, but it was a lot of fun. We sold them through the stores, all the grocery stores here and in Galveston and in Beaumont. And we sold them to the hotels. We started out at home, but then our business grew and we were receiving orders for dozens of cases. Well, we couldn't very well take care of that at home. Mildred had a relative who lived out of town, and we moved everything out there. We took everybody along. My father lived with us; we'd take poppa along. We'd take the maid. We'd take anybody who would go and cut pickles. And we were just so occupied because we'd have to go out and solicit business and then go out and deliver. Finally, I got so busy that my children were wearing safety pins where buttons should have been, and I just had to quit. Mildred didn't want to do it alone, so the Gem Pickle Company dissolved.[54]

The only time that Bishop Smith raised any question about the Gem Pickle Company was when "Amos and Andy" entered the picture. While the famous radio team was at the height of its popularity, they visited Houston. Randy, the youngest of the Smith children, remembers the occasion: "Mother and 'Miz Mildred' decided that they were going to give some of their pickles to Amos and Andy. They drove down to the Lamar Hotel, asked to see them, and presented them with a bottle of those crazy pickles. Dad was just beside himself. He couldn't believe it."[55]

As a bishop of the Methodist Episcopal Church, South, A. Frank Smith presided over his first annual conference when he convened the Missouri Annual Conference in Columbia, Missouri, on September 3, 1930. Organized in 1816 by Bishop William McKendree, the Missouri was the oldest conference west of the Mississippi River. According to the official *Journal*, "Bishop Smith greeted the conference most cordially as he began the routine work of the session. His remarks were brotherly and felicitous."[56] An example of this brotherly spirit is found in the "Minutes" toward the end of the first day's business: "On Bishop Smith's suggestion a message of greeting was sent to Bishop and Mrs. McMurry expressing appreciation of Bishop McMurry's superintendency of our conference and his great labors at Central College."[57] Bishop McMurry had enjoyed great popularity presiding over the Missouri Conference for the preceding eight years, winning special praise for his administrative ability as president of Missouri Methodism's Central College for six of those years. Succeeding such an effective and beloved leader would not be easy, but Frank Smith knew how to share in appropriate praise to his predecessors.[58]

Dr. J. N. R. Score, present as a visitor at the Missouri Conference session, wrote the following account of Bishop Smith's initial experience:

We found there just what we had expected to find, a sane, well-balanced, calm, brotherly man, presiding in an assembly of brethren. He began his ministry as a Bishop by telling the brethren of the Missouri Conference that

it was their conference, not his. He gave them to understand that he was
their servant and friend. As I watched the administration of the conference,
I saw undergraduates on small circuits, super-annuated preachers, and strong
men in the leading appointments of the conference banded together as
brethren and each shown the same brotherly consideration, kindness and
courtesy. During the two days I was there, Frank Smith worked at least
nineteen hours a day. In addition to the work in the conference room and
the cabinet session, he made half a dozen addresses, interviewed personally
half of the men in the conference. When I left to return home, he already
was calling most of the younger men of the conference by their first names.
. . . A man of the conference . . . told me that Bishop Smith's knowledge
of conference problems and his grasp of the situation was nothing short of
phenomenal.[59]

Dr. Score was, of course, a close friend of Bishop Smith's. But other accounts, written by more objective observers, are equally full of praise
for the new bishop. The editor of the *Arkansas Methodist* gave this
favorable evaluation:

It was a pleasure to find that Bishop Smith had won all hearts by his democratic spirit and Christian courtesy and the profound respect of all by his
capable handling of the business of the Conference. With the ease of a
practiced parliamentarian he presided and expedited business, but neglected
nothing and gave ample time to all important interests. His sermon Sunday
morning was an appropriate and timely masterpiece of sermonic eloquence
—one of the best I have ever heard on such an occasion. He threw more life
into the ritual of ordination than is usual. This propitious start for our
youngest and newest bishop augurs well for the future of Methodism. He is
evidently the kind of bishop needed for these momentous and perplexing
days.[60]

A member of the Oklahoma Conference, who had gone up to the session
of the Missouri Conference to "scout" their new bishop, reported in the
Oklahoma Methodist:

Holding his first Conference, Bishop A. Frank Smith presided with proper
dignity and becoming ease. . . . Bishop Smith "caught" us all with his
cordiality, his wit and pleasantries, his tact and fairness in presiding, his
fine spirit of comradeship, the earnestness of his message. Our Bishop
Bishops well.[61]

That Bishop Smith's initial success was no flash in the pan is shown
by yet another favorable report written two months later, after he had

completed his first round of conferences. In his "Observations at the Oklahoma Conference," the editor of the Nashville *Christian Advocate* stated:

This was the fourth Conference over which Bishop A. Frank Smith has presided; the other three were those in Missouri. Throughout his episcopal district he holds the admiration and confidence of ministers and laymen. He is found to be a brother beloved, a poised parliamentarian, a wise counselor, a strong preacher, a trustworthy guardian and authority in the adjudgment of the appointments. He does not have to learn how to be a bishop; he already knows, and his work gives the highest satisfaction.[62]

Of all the generous praise he received, Frank Smith most appreciated the letter from his mentor, Bishop Edwin D. Mouzon: "I have taken personal pride in the manner in which you have entered upon your new responsibilities. The reports that come to me are just such reports as I had expected to get with reference to you and your work in the office of a Bishop."[63]

While a father-son relationship was shared by Bishop Mouzon and Frank Smith for twenty years, a fundamental shift in the nature of that bond is shown in the letters exchanged between the two bishops during the months from July through October, 1930. In early July Bishop Mouzon wrote to Smith about a certain preacher who had "closed all doors against himself here in North Carolina. It would be tragic for him to be forced to locate this fall. He ought to have one more chance." Mouzon then suggested several possible exchanges they could make. Prompt action was urgent since Mouzon was soon leaving for Brazil.[64]

Assuring Mouzon of his desire to help Brother ——————— and to cooperate "at all times in the solving of any problems you may have," Smith firmly but politely replied, "I am wondering, however, if it would be the wise thing for me to bring Brother ——————— to Oklahoma; and, if he is brought, whether it would be wise to bring him this year." In three pages of single-spaced typing, Smith then detailed the reasons for negative answers to both questions. "I have stated the various angles of this case as I see them," Smith concluded; "what is your frank opinion of the matter?"[65]

"My dear Frank," Mouzon replied, "I thank you for your letter. I fully appreciate your position. I think you are wise in your decision. We will let the matter stand. . . . I cannot ask another Bishop to assume responsibilities which are my own. . . . Your friend and brother."[66]

While Mouzon may have used this closing previously, the two men came nearer to a "friend and brother" relationship after this exchange of letters.

When the time for his fall conferences was at hand, Bishop Mouzon was not willing after all to "let the matter stand" with relation to Brother ———————. Smith had written in September asking Mouzon's advice on certain problems with which Mouzon was familiar. Given that opportunity, Mouzon sent the requested information and included the following comment: "I could wish the way would open for you to take ———————. I mean to send him back to [his present appointment], but he is as restless as he can be and will never be satisfied again with what he can get in this part of the world. But as I wrote you before, the responsibility is mine and I am not asking you to relieve me."[67] Despite Mouzon's disclaimer, he is once more applying pressure—intentionally or unintentionally—on Smith to take Brother ———————. That Smith interpreted the letter in this fashion is clear from his reply: "I want to assure that I would gladly take ——————— if it were possible, if for no other reason than that you have asked me to do so. . . . It will be impossible for me to use him this year, however, due to conditions that obtain at this time." After sketching these "conditions," Smith played his trump: "Even if things were wide open, it would be unwise for ——————— to return to Ardmore. I went to Ardmore and looked into the situation there. He has a few friends who are moving heaven and earth to get him appointed there, and he is in constant communication with them, advising them what steps to take. . . . If it should become possible for me to use ——————— another year, and under a different set of circumstances, I will gladly do so."[68] That closed the matter.

Changes in the plan of episcopal supervision, if any, were ordinarily made at the spring meeting of the College of Bishops, usually held in Nashville. Bishop Arthur Moore recalled the 1932 session:

Bishop Denny, an austere man but very friendly towards me, came by and said, "Arthur, we're going to send you to Oklahoma." Frank was sitting across the room, so I went back and told him, "Frank, I'm going to succeed you in Oklahoma." "Oh," he said, "where am I going?" He was so surprised, I had to laugh. "The Lord only knows where you are going!" Then the committee came in and read our appointments. They gave Frank Illinois in place of Oklahoma and reassigned him to the three conferences in Missouri and the Indian Mission.[69]

This minor change in Bishop Smith's assignment was typical of that year's schedule. Since the General Conference at Dallas had recommended more frequent shifting of the bishops, the College of Bishops issued a statement of explanation: "In view of the many problems created by the present economic situation, involving the future of many of our institutions, . . . the College of Bishops felt that a minimum of changes should be made."[70] Along with so many others, the bishops were feeling the crunch of the Depression. Bishop Angie Smith recalls that there were no funds to pay for the College of Bishops' meeting expenses in those years. "As a result," he said,

the bishops had to go where a local church could furnish rooms for their meeting and where they could be entertained by the local people. I was pastor of First Methodist Church in Shreveport, and we invited them to hold their winter meeting [1932] at First Church. Conditions were so bad financially that the bishops in that meeting took a voluntary cut of $1,000 in their salaries, from $6,000 back to $5,000.[71]

The following year, according to Bishop Arthur Moore, "the Episcopal Fund from which we received our salaries and traveling allowances was totally depleted. There was no provision for securing a loan to pay the bishops' salaries. So, throughout the year of 1933, we were without any salary whatsoever."[72] The bishops all signed a joint note to secure a loan to pay their living expenses.[73]

The financial crisis did not prevent Bishop Smith from traveling throughout his episcopal district. During the winter and spring of 1932, for example, references to his travels constantly appear in the columns of the respective *Advocates*. After reporting a series of meetings that Bishop Smith held in January, the Richmond *Christian Advocate* noted that "he had been at home only three days in five weeks."[74] The news reports indicate that Bishop Smith scheduled as many conferences or speaking engagements as possible during his trips. Within three days in March, he preached at six District Conferences in Missouri.[75] In April he was in the Southwest Missouri Conference. On Sunday, April 24, he preached at Joplin in the morning, at Carthage in the afternoon, and at Neosho in the evening. The next day he preached the opening sermon for the Woman's Missionary Conference held at Nevada, Missouri.[76] By the end of the quadrennium, Bishop Smith could report: "I have had the privilege of preaching in more than 150 different churches in Missouri, and in some of them more than a dozen times each."[77] Such activity, as well as the quality of Bishop Smith's preaching, soon caught the attention of the Northern Methodists' *Central Christian Advocate*:

As a leader of the churches, Bishop A. Frank Smith has won his way. As a preacher he is a master of assemblies, in no hurry but piling up boulders of thought, an emphatic but not noisy delivery, facing his entire congregation, floor and gallery, and not staring absent-mindedly at some corner of the ceiling or some other corner of the floor. He reaches his goal and immediately concludes. Epigrams are sufficiently plentiful, but they mark proofs and climaxes and none exist for their own sake. That they built the faith and devotion of the people was demonstrated by the fact that in the presence of a rainstorm one day and the next stinging cold, his congregation grew and ended with a great hearing.[78]

During these early years of Frank Smith's episcopal career, he chanced to run into an old cowboy who had known him as a youngster. "What are you doing now, Frank?" asked the cowboy.

"I'm in the ministry," Frank replied.

"Well, I'll be derned!" the cowboy declared, obviously surprised. "Where's your church, Frank?"

"I don't have just one church now," Frank explained. "I'm a bishop and I have oversight of a great many churches."

"Well, I'll be damned!"[79]

In his first quadrennium as a bishop of the Methodist Episcopal Church, South, A. Frank Smith supervised four annual conferences through the entire period: the Indian Mission in Oklahoma and the three conferences in Missouri—the St. Louis, the Southwest Missouri, and the Missouri. He held the Oklahoma Conference the first two years, 1930-31, and the Illinois Conference during the last two, 1932-33. The following resolution is representative of the appreciation he received as the quadrennium came to a close: "We have greatly enjoyed the presence and administration of Bishop A. Frank Smith during this quadrennium; his unfailing kindness and patience, his brotherliness, and his great preaching have won for him an abiding place in the hearts of Missouri Methodist preachers and laymen alike."[80]

What effect did this high office, accompanied by so much praise, have on Frank Smith? According to Dr. J. N. R. Score, "The honor which has been given him, the high office to which he has been elected [has] in no way changed his attitude to life or to his ministry. He is still the brother beloved."[81]

What kind of bishop would Frank Smith become? As indicated by these early years, what was his potential? Dr. J. N. R. Score predicted:

Frank Smith will never be a dictator. Frank Smith will never be an autocrat. Frank Smith will always be a brother. He may make mistakes, but they will be mistakes of the head and not of the heart. He will be a wise, sane administrator. And if life gives him a span of years in which to invest his ministry in the Church he loves, history will write him down as one of the truly great men produced by our Church.[82]

10

A Watershed in Episcopal
Administration: 1934-1938

A PERSISTENT MOVEMENT to diminish the power of the episcopacy of southern Methodism crested during the sessions of the General Conference meeting in Jackson, Mississippi, in 1934. Although this movement was part of a broad spectrum of democratizing trends within the Methodist Episcopal Church, South, extending back into the nineteenth century,[1] its most recent manifestation focused on "term episcopacy"—electing bishops for a limited term of years rather than for life. It was humorously referred to as the "French Revolution" after George C. French, a clerical delegate from the North Texas Conference who had led the movement during the General Conference held in Dallas in 1930.

Anticipating a renewal of the cry for "term episcopacy" in 1934, the bishops devoted several pages of their Episcopal Address to a defense of life tenure, a tradition in American Methodism since its origins in 1784. Bishop John M. Moore, designated by the College of Bishops to read the address at the opening of the conference, clearly stated the traditional position:

[Mr. Wesley's] conception of the episcopacy was that of a presiding, directive, administrative superintendent with life tenure bestowed by the ceremony of ordination. . . . It has always taken ordination as well as election to create bishops, and ordination has never been given for a term of years. Ordination is an act to confirm permanency. . . . When it comes to democracy, the primary and essential principle is representativeness, and this is fully observed in our entire system of government, including the choosing of bishops. The fact of life tenure does not destroy the representativeness of the episcopacy any more than it does that of the Supreme Court of the United States.[2]

Not only did Frank Smith sign his name to this address along with the other bishops, but also he wrote a note of "deep personal appreciation" to Bishop Moore "for the invaluable service you rendered our Methodism in one of the most critical hours of her history through your scholarly, penetrating and comprehensive grasp of the issue of the hour, as revealed in the Episcopal Address."[3] In a more vigorous expression of his own viewpoint, Smith had previously written to Bishop Mouzon, "The more I see of the difficulties that confront a Bishop, the more I wonder how our 'democratic' brethren who need no Bishops would solve these problems. When the episcopacy goes, *or is limited*, the itinerancy [*sic*] will go, or at any rate have to be made into a form of diluted congregationalism."[4]

Agreeing with the bishops, the Committee on Episcopacy recommended "nonconcurrence" for six memorials[5] presented to it which asked for a limited term of office for bishops. As soon as this report was properly before the conference, however, George French moved to reject the recommendation of the committee and to set "a fixed term of years" for bishops. A lengthy debate, marked by lively parliamentary stratagems, ensued.[6]

Bishop Arthur Moore remembers how dismayed he was by the strength of the "termites" attack—an epithet publicly acknowledged by the leaders of the movement. Moore sought out his colleague Paul Kern and said, "Paul, I'm going to quit! I don't want to be a radical, but I don't know why we should take all this abuse. We didn't need to give up good churches to get kicked in the pants. Would you quit?"

"Yes," Kern replied. "I'll quit."

"Well, let's go get Frank."[7]

Later, when the three young bishops were discussing the pending legislation, Bishop Moore stated rather emphatically that if term episcopacy came in, he would resign the office rather than submit himself to an on-and-off policy with the accompanying accusations of "running for office" and "courting favor" and to other pressures that were sure to follow. "If there is no pastorate open to me, I can go back where I started and hold revival meetings for the brethren."

Echoing his colleague's sentiments, including the determination to resign, Bishop Kern recalled his numerous years as a college professor: "If I can't get a church, I can go back to teaching school."

After a few moments of silence, Bishop Smith declared his position: "Well, I don't have enough religion to hold revivals, and I'm not smart enough to teach school. I'll just have to stay in and be a bishop."[8]

These three men were especially concerned about the changes proposed in 1934, because they were the youngest members of the College of Bishops. Elected in 1930, they were just beginning their episcopal careers, which had brought drastic changes in their lives during the past four years. All three had been pastors of large city churches where each had received a high salary for that day—$10,000. As a bishop, however, each received only $6,000. Instead of the spacious parsonage provided him as a pastor, each bishop received $2,000 to pay for his housing, secretarial, and traveling expenses.[9] Since the other bishops were well beyond their prime, these three "freshmen" had to carry far more than their share of the vast assignments and staggering responsibilities. Arthur Moore later explained their plight:

We had lost five bishops by death and retirement during the quadrennium 1930-34; we had only eleven bishops left for active service in a college that almost always numbered sixteen. . . . I fully expected the General Conference to elect some new bishops . . . but they said, "We can't pay the bishops we have. Why elect more?" . . . The financial depression sweeping across the nation seriously reduced the income of the church. The Episcopal Fund from which we received our salaries and traveling allowances was totally depleted. There was no provision for securing a loan to pay the bishops' salaries. So throughout the year 1933, we were without any salary whatsoever.[10]

But Bishop Moore clearly recalled how Frank Smith's response to their despair "put an end to the only episcopal rebellion I have ever been mixed up in. But that's Frank, always calm and philosophical, full of common sense. That's a good illustration of his wisdom."[11]

Besides the qualities Bishop Moore pointed out, this anecdote reveals four dominant characteristics of A. Frank Smith: his quick sense of humor, his conciliatory spirit, his commitment to the Methodist church, and his persistent humility. As will be seen in this and later chapters, these qualities enabled Bishop Smith to be an agent of reconciliation on many occasions during the difficult years leading up to the unification of the three branches of American Methodism in 1939 and in the equally challenging years of making that union effective.

What became of the "French revolution"? On Friday, May 4—the day after Frank Smith had "put down" the "episcopal rebellion"—the General Conference resumed its deliberation on "term episcopacy."[12] The position of those favoring the election of bishops for a limited number of years was succinctly stated by George C. French:

My main contention is this: the position of our honored chief pastors is an office and an office only. It is not an order. . . . The essence of the Episcopacy lies in the power in the hands of the man that occupies that office. . . . That office is in disrepute because too many men who have occupied that office are willing, too frequently, to exercise, recklessly, autocratic power. . . . I do not believe it is safe to put that much authority in any man's hands for life.[13]

In response to the historical arguments presented by the bishops in the "Episcopal Address,"[14] Forney Hutchinson put forward the other principal argument for "term episcopacy":

These historic approaches make no appeal to me, frankly. All argument about what has been leaves me cold. [Laughter and applause] We are not operating in John Wesley's day. . . . We are operating in this day and our legislation is to be for this generation and not for the generations gone. That this [present system] was entirely proper at another age, I do not question, but it will not be proper and expedient and acceptable to the church that is coming.[15]

The defenders of "the plan of our itinerant general superintendency" avoided the theological question of ministerial orders, emphasizing rather the constitutional protection of the episcopacy. Nolan B. Harmon of the Baltimore Conference declared:

For 150 years Episcopal Methodism has been organized with the highly centralized power in the hands of its College or Board of Bishops. Our church has been triumphant under that leadership. . . . Our founding fathers . . . wrote [into] the constitution of the church in 1808 . . . "They [the General Conference] shall not change or alter any part or rule of our government so as to do away with Episcopacy or destroy the plan of our itinerant general superintendency." . . . If you pass this resolution . . . the Episcopacy shall be at the control of the General Conference completely.[16]

Judge John S. Candler of the North Georgia Conference was the only speaker to mention the question of orders, but his basic point was constitutional:

I have been trained to believe for sixty years that this is a constitutional question, and that our College of Bishops make up an order. . . . To adopt the motion . . . is to surrender every position that was taken by the greatest men in our church in 1844 . . . who drew those articles of separation. . . . If you are to do away with the itinerant system, let us come out flat-footedly and go into the Presbyterian or Congregational Church.[17]

A careful study of the hundreds of words in the debate over "term episcopacy" leads one to the rather uncomplimentary conclusion that both sides were basically arguing expediency rather than constitutional or ministerial orders. The chairman of the Committee on Episcopacy, in his closing summary, unashamedly based his case on expediency:

I argue for the life tenure of Episcopacy not because of anything that was contained in the Episcopal Address. . . . I am just too ignorant of those things to agree that the Episcopacy is anything but an office in Methodism. . . . But I do think, for the sake of expediency, we ought to have a life tenure. I might find a great many illustrations, but I suppose almost everyone will agree with me that the United States Courts are very much superior to our state and city courts. . . . The men on the bench of the United States Courts are removed from the temptation of yielding to popular whim and mob violence, and I want my bishop to be relieved from the temptation of playing to the crowd and yielding to the mob.[18]

When at last the vote was taken, the proposal for "term episcopacy" failed to carry, receiving 131 votes for and 252 against.[19]

In a number of ways, this General Conference did further define the office and nature of the episcopacy, providing some limitation. A provision was adopted to enable twenty or more traveling elders to bring a bishop to trial before the Committee on Episcopacy as being "unacceptable, inefficient, or lacking in adaptation to the office . . . so as to be no longer useful in the work." Upon recommendation of the committee, the General Conference could "retire" that bishop without his consent, "returning him to membership as a traveling elder in the Annual Conference of which he was last a member."[20] This is really removal from office rather than retirement, as the last phrase makes clear. A bishop who retired because of age or for any other reason was still considered a bishop.

To eliminate any problems related to terminology, the General Conference ordered that the *Discipline* and the *Ritual* be changed, substituting the term "consecration" for "ordination" with reference to bishops —with the implication that the episcopacy is an office and not a third order of the ministry.[21]

No longer could the bishops live wherever they chose. The General Conference instructed its Committee on Episcopacy to designate, after consultation with the bishops, a certain city in each episcopal district as the site of the bishop's residence. Thereafter, when the College of Bishops assigned a bishop to a particular episcopal district, that bishop would "be required to live within his district" in the city so designated.[22]

No longer could the College of Bishops serve as a "Supreme Court." Following a constitutional amendment passed by the preceding General Conference and approved by the annual conferences, this General Conference formed a Judicial Council and elected its first members—a major change and a clear limitation to episcopal power.[23]

In another far-reaching move, the General Conference passed and sent to the annual conferences for their adoption a constitutional amendment limiting the term of the presiding elder's office to four years. The bishops could not reappoint a man to another term as presiding elder until that man had served at least four years "in some other relation."[24]

In his informative examination of "The Moving Tide of Change" in Southern Methodism (1918-1938), Professor Robert Sledge explains:

The changes that were made (by the General Conferences of 1930 and 1934) indicated in concrete form that a genuine change of mood had come over the M. E. Church, South. More precisely, they showed the passing of an older conservative generation in favor of a younger generation reflecting the reform impulses of the twentieth century. . . . The decade of the 1930's saw the consummation of that progressive victory through enactments of law, elections of personnel, and acquisition of moral and intellectual leadership.[25]

In basic agreement with Professor Sledge, Bishop William C. Martin places greater emphasis on the role played by Bishops Arthur Moore, Paul Kern, and Frank Smith. "The three men who were elected in 1930 in Dallas gave a new image to the episcopacy," Bishop Martin maintains. "There was a decided turning point, a water-shed in episcopal administration."

From that time on, there was a decided relaxing in the manner of making

and announcing appointments. The old closed-cabinet began to move out.
Now, Bishops Moore and Mouzon had been more relaxed at that point than
some of the other bishops such as Darlington, Denny and Candler. But there
came to be, under the leadership of these men—Moore, Kern and Smith—
without any fanfare of trumpets about it, just a changed attitude toward the
way a bishop should treat his brethren in the cabinet or in the conference.
. . . The Disciplinary requirement for consultation [before appointment]
came about through the brotherly regard which these three men had for the
men around the cabinet table and for every member of the conference. It
just began to feed out that way. And Frank Smith was certainly one of the
most influential in that development.[26]

The Plan of Episcopal Visitation for 1934-35 assigned Bishop A.
Frank Smith to the Eleventh District, which included the Texas, North
Texas, Oklahoma, and Indian Mission conferences.[27] His assignment to
the North Texas Conference moved Bishop Smith to reminisce. "I
count it a high privilege to be connected again with the old North
Texas Conference which I joined in the beginning," he wrote to Will
Martin, "and to renew fellowship with you brethren whom I have
known and loved through these many years."[28] There were, however,
obvious difficulties in this assignment. The conference had suffered a
serious division during the preceding three or four years, when "a bitter
rift developed among leading members of the conference that split the
conference wide open—from bishop to circuit preacher."[29] Most recently, "some seventy or seventy-five" members of the conference wrote
letters to the General Conference charging Bishop Boaz with maladminis-
tration. Although the Committee on Episcopacy, after hearing the complaints, took no action against Bishop Boaz, the College of Bishops did
change his assignment.[30]

In characteristic manner, Bishop Smith "worked to heal the divisions and to set the conference back onto its primary task of ministering to the world."[31] Although he considered the difficulty to be basically
a struggle for place and power, Bishop Smith explained the circumstances as follows: "North Texas had some of the strongest preachers
in Texas, and being a relatively small conference, there was not room
to move the preachers around satisfactorily."[32] As Bishop William C.
Martin—pastor of Dallas's First Church from 1931 to 1938—recalls:
"Frank Smith was brotherly, altogether understanding of the problem
that confronted the pastoral ministry of those days, having been for so
long a time in the pastorate himself."[33]

It is interesting to note that Bishop Smith finally began using a letterhead of his own in 1934 after his assignment to Houston. During the uncertainty of his first quadrennium,[34] Bishop and Mrs. Smith had decided to rent a house in Houston.[35] Throughout that four-year period Bishop Smith wrote his letters on borrowed letterheads, their headings depending upon where he was when he wrote. When he succeeded Bishop Boaz in the Texas Conference, he moved his family into the new episcopal residence in Houston at 2308 Southmore Boulevard.[36] The earliest surviving letter that Bishop Smith wrote on his new letterhead is, appropriately, addressed to Bishop Edwin D. Mouzon.[37]

The "Bishops' Crusade" was the most demanding project undertaken by the College of Bishops and the Methodist Episcopal Church, South, during the quadrennium 1934-38. While in session in Jackson, Mississippi, in May, 1934, the General Conference requested "our Bishops to lead the Church in a movement for the full payment of benevolences and that stress be placed upon the spiritual values in these funds."[38] On the closing day of the conference, Bishop John M. Moore announced that the College of Bishops had appointed A. Frank Smith "to lead a Church-wide movement in behalf of the benevolences."[39] This was the inauspicious beginning of what Bishop Arthur Moore would later call "one of Frank Smith's most significant contributions to the general Church."[40] At the time, however, the bishops were skeptical about the success of any kind of financial drive, since the Depression still held the entire nation in its grip. Perhaps later in the quadrennium there might be something possible in a purely spiritual movement. Bishop Smith began thinking about a churchwide celebration of the bicentennial of "John Wesley's spiritual birthday coming up on May 24th, 1938."[41]

In the meantime, the bishops were far more concerned about the financial disaster threatening the extensive foreign mission enterprise of Southern Methodism. The onslaught of the Depression had been so rapid that the average yearly income of the Board of Missions was reduced by more than half in three years' time. Although the board had drastically reduced its work in every field, it was unable to pull back as rapidly as its income declined, and it was forced to go into debt to prevent the collapse of a program developed through nearly a century of sacrifice and struggle. This indebtedness would seriously handicap the church's missionary operations for a decade. When the College of Bishops met in Nashville in May, 1936, they resolved to rescue the Board of Missions from this stifling debt. According to the official minutes, "Bishop Boaz moved, and Bishop Kern seconded the motion, that the Bishops approve the movement to pay the debt of the Board of Missions, that Bishop Arthur J. Moore be made the Director of the movement, and that a commission be appointed to cooperate with Bishop Moore."[42] The necessary interrelationship of this new program and the one under Bishop Smith's direction became obvious, as the minutes indicate:

Bishop Smith made some remarks regarding the Bishops' Crusade. He suggested that definite action upon the proposed plans be postponed until Bishop Arthur J. Moore returns [from Africa] for the set-up of the Mission Movement. It was voted to approve the plan in principle but defer action upon the details until Bishop Smith and Bishop Moore could confer.[43]

When Bishop Moore returned to the United States in August, 1936, he and Bishop Smith drew up a combined program for presentation to a large group which would be representative of the entire church. As Bihop Moore recalls:

Frank and I decided to put on a Crusade—that was our idea and our word—with two sections: one devoted to missionary cultivation and paying off that debt, the other devoted to the deepening of the spiritual life. . . . There was a period in there, first of all because we were younger and had physical stamina and because we had fresh ideas, when we almost called the shots in the Church, South. Frank, Paul and I not only provided the ideas, but we did the drudgery. The other bishops were older, too old for it.[44]

At an early point Dr. Elmer T. Clark, the editor of *World Outlook*, was brought into the planning. "Elmer Clark was the creative man in the Board of Missions," explains Bishop Moore. "He did a lot of things for us. A very versatile man, he was invaluable in planning, in creating literature, and in developing publicity."[45] These plans were then presented to a combined meeting of representatives from all the annual conferences and the College of Bishops, held in Nashville in September, and received their enthusiastic approval.[46]

As described in *World Outlook*, the "Bishops' Crusade"

is a two-year enterprise of a spiritual nature, initiated and led by the College of Bishops, and having two phases or sections.

The first section, directed by Bishop Arthur J. Moore, is called the Missionary Forward Movement. Its purpose is to make the church vitally missionary and evangelistic in spirit and attitude and to pay our missionary debt so that the entire income of the Board of Missions may be applied to our work in the fields.

The second section, directed by Bishop A. Frank Smith, is called the Aldersgate Commemoration. Its purpose is wholly spiritual: it will re-emphasize the primary Methodist principle of personal religious experience in the lives of Methodist people.[47]

The mighty campaign was launched in an unprecedented manner at the General Missionary Council which met in New Orleans in early January, 1937. Never before had all of the bishops of the Methodist Episcopal Church, South, appeared on a program together. In addition to nine major addresses per day for two days, there were special rallies for youth, for women, and for the black Methodists. Bishop Smith and Dr. E. Stanley Jones addressed the "mass meeting of colored people."[48]

To present the movement to the leaders of all the annual conferences, a series of one-day "Missionary Rallies" was held in forty-four carefully selected cities across the nation "in the greatest missionary mobilization Methodism has ever known."[49] "We divided the bishops into two sections," Bishop Moore explained, "and everyone of them spoke at least at one rally. Kern and Ainsworth took a team West of the [Mississippi] River, and Frank and I led in the East." A team of six would speak at each rally: "the two team leaders, at least one other Bishop, a missionary secretary, a woman, and at least one outstanding National from one of our fields"—as it was stated in the now quaint words of the *Pastor's Manual*. Beginning on January 12, 1937, with the Kern-Ainsworth team in Memphis and the Moore-Smith team in Washington, D.C., the teams held four rallies a week (Monday through Thursday) for five and six weeks respectively. "We'd preach all day," Bishop Moore recalled, "take a sleeper out on a midnight train and wake up in the morning at our next rally city. It was a long grueling experience, but Frank and I stayed with it."[50]

One important quality favoring the young bishops was the sense of humor they shared. "After our night meeting," Bishop Moore remembered, "we would have to wait for our sleeper until midnight. So we'd gather around in the station and tell stories on each other."

I remember when we were in Charlotte, North Carolina, at the beginning of the second week. Frank would speak at ten and I would speak at eleven. An old layman, sort of a camp-follower of mine, came to hear me speak—but he heard Frank. Frank had a whiz of a sermon. So between the two hours, he said to me: "Brother Arthur, you must do your best. That old man who just spoke is mighty nigh as good as you are." I'd kid Frank about that, because I was a year older than he was.

Frank and I had an arrangement with Paul Kern, who was leading the team in the West. Every night we would exchange reports by telegram of the day's crowd, their spirit, and the collection. So Paul ran into some foul weather out in Oklahoma while Frank and I were having good crowds. Our collections were running twice what his were. Then we hit Mobile and we got a little handful of money, about $700, and we wired Paul the facts. Back came his telegram in reply: "Thank God for Mobile."[51]

There were also times of sorrow during those six weeks of missionary rallies. On February 6, as the fourth week ended, Bishop Smith received word that Dr. John R. Allen had died in Dallas. Smith just had time to reach Dallas to hold the funeral service and to be with Bess and Hallie when they laid Uncle John's body to rest beside Mrs. Allen's grave —in the same cemetery where Bess and Frank's baby boy was buried twenty years earlier.[52] In a moving tribute to Dr. Allen, Bishop Smith declared:

As one of his former pupils who early fell under the charm of his spirit, as a member of his family who held him in vast respect and loved him with steadfast devotion, I give testimony to the radiance of his life, the purity of his soul; and with that great multitude whose lives he touched, only and always for the good, I thank God that he lived, that though dead, he yet speaketh, and that some day we shall join him in the Father's house.[53]

No sooner had Bishop Smith rejoined his colleagues in Tennessee than death struck another dear friend. As the bishop himself wrote:

As the Bishops' Crusade team in the East boarded the train in Chattanooga on the evening of February 10th, we received word of the sudden death of Bishop Edwin D. Mouzon only a few moments before at his home in Charlotte, North Carolina. He was to have joined us the next day in Roanoke, Virginia, for a Crusade meeting.

I turned back for his funeral in Dallas, and somehow it seemed perfectly natural that I should have had some connection with Bishop Mouzon in his last days, for he had been so much a part of my life from my youth onward. I entered Southwestern University as a freshman the same day that he became a professor in that institution; I was often in his home during my college days, and he had much to do with my decision to give myself to the ministry. He had become a Bishop in the Church when I finished my theological work in Vanderbilt and he gave me my first appointment. Later I was to receive other appointments at his hands, and for a time I was the pastor of his family.

After becoming his colleague in the College of Bishops, I was privileged to share a common interest and task with him that ripened the associations of earlier years into a relationship precious beyond words to me. The last three weeks of his life we were together in the Bishops' Crusade. I shall treasure the memories of those days to the end of the way.[54]

The culmination of the Missionary Forward Movement came on the twenty-third and twenty-fifth of April, 1937, with a churchwide celebration of the beginning of Southern Methodist Missions. These days were chosen, according to the publicity materials, because "they mark the eighty-ninth anniversary of the sailing of Charles Taylor and Benjamin Jenkins—our very first foreign missionaries—for China." On Friday evening, April 23, the *Pastor's Manual* declared, "there is to be a dinner in every Southern Methodist Church, at which an appropriate program will be presented." Featuring a dramatization of the historic sailing of the two missionaries—"simple enough for presentation in any church"—the prescribed program reached its climax as Bishop Arthur Moore's voice was broadcast on radio stations all across the South.[55] A free-will offering concluded the evening's program. On Sunday each Methodist preacher would have his moment to share in the creation of missionary zeal. "The occasion should inspire a sermon of unusual power," the *Manual* prescribed. "Let the pulpits of Methodism ring with the message."

In early May, when the Board of Missions met in Nashville, Bishop John M. Moore—as president of the board—announced that "due to the Bishops' Crusade, the Board of Missions was back on a cash basis."[56] Later that month, reporting through the Nashville *Christian Advocate*, Bishop Arthur Moore wrote: "After carefully canvassing the returns, the Bishops are convinced that not less than $400,000 has been given by the Church for its missionary work." Continuing, he declared:

The depression indebtedness of the Board of Missions can now be liquidated. New missionaries can sail forth to fill up the ranks so sadly depleted in the last eight years. All departments of work can be strengthened and the morale of our missionary personnel will be vitalized. . . . We finish but to begin. We have closed the missionary forward movement only to launch out again in the mightiest spiritual enterprise the Church has known for a generation. . . . My colleague, Bishop A. Frank Smith, has a more difficult and delicate task than that which we have just accomplished. Whatever may be our successes in organization and work, they are but superficial and temporary unless the Church renews its consecration and is re-endowed with the passion and power which comes only from a personal relationship to Jesus Christ.[57]

The Aldersgate Commemoration, under the direction of Bishop A. Frank Smith, began in 1937. In a letter to Dr. Score, Bishop Smith described his feelings about this enterprise:

When I think of the possibilities of our Aldersgate Commemoration and what a let-down it will be if nothing comes of it, I am scared to death, but when I realize how eager and expectant the Church undoubtedly is, I am certain that nothing can prevent a great spiritual awakening all over the Church next year. There are evidences of interest on all sides that amaze me, really.[58]

Three months later, in May, 1937, Smith wrote again to Score:

I have put in the hardest summer's work this year I have ever done, and I am trying to get everything in shape for the *Crusade* before I leave. I have gone over every line that will appear in the Crusade material, the plan, guide book, etc. What I have not written outright, I have largely revised, trying to get harmony and cohesion in the whole setup. I believe every agency in the Church is properly represented, and that they are all co-operating heartily.[59]

Bishop Smith intended that each conference would freely choose to participate in the Commemoration and adopt goals appropriate to its needs and capacity. Each bishop accepted responsibility for appointing a committee in each of his annual conferences to present the Aldersgate Commemoration for adoption. In the West Texas Conference, for example, Bishop Boaz appointed J. Grady Timmons, pastor of Travis Park—the conference's most prestigious pulpit—to chair the Aldersgate Committee. The report of the committee was made an "order of the day" and the "leading" ministers and laymen spoke in its favor. The conference recorded its "determined support of the Aldersgate Commemoration in every possible way" and pledged "whole-hearted co-operation to our Bishops, and especially to Bishop A. Frank Smith, Director of the Commemoration." Seven goals "for our own Conference" were adopted:

1. A more vital experience of religion in the heart of every preacher and local church official and teacher, and a general religious awakening in every congregation.
2. The reception of not less than 4,000 members, 10 per cent of our membership, into our Church on profession of faith during the coming Conference year.

A. Frank Smith in his senior year, 1911-12, at Southwestern University.

Old building of the "Prep" School, Southwestern University, ca. 1908.

A. Frank Smith, Bess Crutchfield Smith, and A. Frank Smith, Jr., in 1922.

A. Frank Smith at the time of his appointment as pastor of First Methodist Church, Houston, in 1922.

The Smith family on the day of Frank, Jr.'s marriage, June 12, 1939. Left to right: Betty, Randy, Bishop Smith, Mrs. Smith, and Frank, Jr.

Bishops A. Frank Smith and W. Angie Smith at the unveiling of a plaque honoring them at Elgin, Texas, in June, 1944.

Mrs. W. W. Fondren and Bishop Smith at the dedication of the Fondren Science Building, SMU, May 10, 1950.

Bishop Smith, as chairman of the SMU Board of Trustees, with President Umphrey Lee and members of the board, November 10, 1950.

Bishop Smith at the Los Angeles Airport on his way to Hawaii in 1950.

Mrs. J. J. Perkins, Mr. Perkins, and Bishop Smith at the presentation of the Perkins School of Theology buildings at SMU in February, 1951.

Bishop and Mrs. Smith aboard the *Queen Mary* in April, 1953.

Bishop Smith with President and Mrs. Umphrey Lee, Vice-President Willis M. Tate, and other distinguished guests, at the groundbreaking for the Umphrey Lee Student Center at SMU, October 30, 1953.

Bishop and Mrs. Smith at a dinner honoring him on his twentieth anniversary as presiding bishop of the Texas Conference, March 15, 1954.

Bishop Smith, Umphrey Lee, and Mrs. Smith on the bishop's birthday, November 1, 1956.

Bishop Smith at the consecration of Eugene Frank as a
bishop, in New Orleans, July
1, 1956.

Bishop Smith honoring Mrs.
W. W. Fondren, then second
vice-president of the Methodist Board of Hospitals and
Homes, for her cooperation
in the work of the board, at
its 1956 annual meeting, held
in Chicago.

Bishops A. Frank Smith and
W. Angie Smith at the fall
meeting of the Council of
Bishops in Phoenix, Arizona,
November 18, 1959.

Bishop Smith at work, ca.
1960.

Service of presentation and dedication of communion ware at the chapel of the Methodist Hospital, Houston, in 1960. Left to right: Chaplain Elton Stephenson; Dr. Durwood Fleming, president of Southwestern University; Mr. Z. V. Donigan, donor of the communion ware; Bishop Smith; Mrs. C. A. Dwyer, a leader in the hospital's volunteer programs; and Mr. Ted Bowen, then Administrator at the hospital.

The Methodist Hospital, Houston: original building.

Mrs. A. Frank Smith.

Bishop A. Frank Smith.

3. An increase of 10,000 in enrollment and attendance in the Church Schools of the Conference.

4. An intensified program of education . . . looking toward a deepening of our sense of responsibility for accepting and paying the whole of our benevolent askings.

5. The adoption of a definite set of objectives . . . [by] each charge. . . .

6. A cultivation movement in every Church, using the literature provided and recommended by the College of Bishops . . . informing all our people in Methodist history, doctrines, and work.

7. Cooperation, according to the plans now outlined and later to be announced by the College of Bishops, in every part of the Aldersgate Commemoration.[60]

Convinced that "major responsibility for promoting the Commemoration rests on the Conference Aldersgate Committees," Bishop Smith asked the College of Bishops to give them special attention. Immediately following the meeting of the College in December, each bishop called together all of the presiding elders and members of the conference committees in his episcopal district.[61]

The intensive cultivation began in January, 1938. Since one of the goals of the Bishops' Crusade was to strengthen the church's basic structures, Bishop Smith worked primarily through the connectional channels. During the first week of January, retreats were held for the pastors in every district throughout the church. "These Retreats are expected to generate a spiritual enthusiasm and power which will insure the larger success of the Aldersgate Commemoration," Bishop Smith explained. "Nothing of the kind has ever been undertaken on a similar scale in our Church before."[62] On the same day that the preachers met, the women of the missionary societies gathered for their own districtwide retreats. Bishop Frank Smith's diplomatic skill is to be seen in the choice of Miss Daisy Davies, Superintendent of Spiritual Life of the Woman's Missionary Council, to organize these meetings for the women. Also, through the cooperation of the Board of Missions Department of Education and Promotion, a special study book was prepared by Dr. W. T. Watkins, professor of church history at Emory University. Entitled *Out of Aldersgate*, this book was designed for use in a variety of settings: the district meetings, college student groups, or the "School of Missions" to be held in every congregation. "The most notable piece of literature prepared for the Commemoration," according to Bishop Smith, was produced by special arrangement with the Methodists in England:

"a large poster, reproducing in full size and exact colors the famous Salisbury portrait of John Wesley." Painted to commemorate the union of British Methodism in 1934, the picture belonged to the Wesleyan Museum in London and had never been reproduced in the United States. "The plates are being made in London from the original painting and under the personal supervision of Mr. Salisbury," Bishop Smith explained, "and these posters will be sent to pastors in January or February."[63]

"After the district retreats," Bishop Smith continued, "the most important matter before us is the success of the District Aldersgate Institutes." "In a fine spirit of cooperation, the Board of Missions has turned over to the Commemoration the regular district missionary institutes. Presiding elders and conference committees are urged to secure the largest possible attendance and to devote the entire day to the Commemoration."[64]

Believing that "nothing can permanently happen in the Church that does not [also] happen in the schools and colleges of the Church," Bishop Smith commissioned the Department of Schools and Colleges of the General Board of Education to plan and carry through preaching missions to Methodist students "as a major part of the Aldersgate Commemoration."[65] During the months of February and March, these "Aldersgate Christian Missions" were held on the campuses of eighty-five church-related and state-supported colleges and universities. According to one report, "Student groups are making definite plans for the mission through retreats, forum and discussion groups, special vesper and chapel services on the theme and the study of selected literature."[66]

In addition to drawing upon these existing structures within the church, Bishop Smith organized a series of inspirational mass rallies in over forty cities from coast to coast.[67] While there were no continuing teams as in the first phase of the Bishops' Crusade, at least one bishop and one general board secretary spoke at each of these rallies. To stimulate congregational singing, Bishop Smith arranged for such famous song leaders as Homer Rodeheaver to direct the singing at each rally.[68] Securing forty dates for these meetings that would not conflict with other important matters was one of the most difficult problems facing the director. As Bishop Smith wrote to Dr. Will Martin,

I wish it were possible to get the message and plan of the Aldersgate Commemoration across without the regional meetings. They will take eight weeks, and coming just before the General Conference, it makes it quite difficult.

But the Church is demanding them, and I know of no other way to create the interest and unity that is necessary to the best result.[69]

As Bishop Arthur Moore had used the General Missionary Council meeting at New Orleans to "kick off" the Missionary Forward Movement, Bishop Smith asked the council to devote its 1938 session to the Aldersgate bicentennial. Savannah, Georgia, was chosen as the site for the council, since that was the only city in the United States having historical association with John Wesley.[70] According to advance publicity: "In a very real sense, the spiritual preparation for [John Wesley's] heart-warming experience was in the city of Savannah, Ga., where Mr. Wesley spent two years immediately preceding the Aldersgate awakening."[71]

Planned around the theme of "The Primacy of Personal Religious Experience in the Life and Work of Methodism," the four-day meeting (January 11-14) offered participants a variety of presentations. The mornings were devoted to addresses "delivered by outstanding American Methodists on themes growing out of Mr. Wesley's heart-warming experience." In the afternoons, Dr. Paul N. Garber, professor of church history at Duke University, gave lecture tours "to the spots in and about Savannah made sacred by the personal presence of Mr. Wesley." At 5:30 each evening Dr. Henry C. Morrison, President of Asbury College, conducted "old fashioned Methodist Class and Testimony Meetings." The night meetings, held in the spacious Savannah Auditorium, featured the most famous speakers on the program: Bishop Ralph S. Cushman and Dr. Merton S. Rice of the Methodist Episcopal Church; Dean Umphrey Lee of Vanderbilt's School of Religion and Dr. Edwin Lewis of Drew University; Dr. Charles C. Selecman and Dr. Ivan Lee Holt of Southern Methodism; and the governors of Georgia and Tennessee. Bishop Frank Smith's sense of balance is evident in his choice of those giving the morning addresses: Miss Daisy Davies of the Woman's Missionary Council; Mrs. Fred B. Fisher, former missionary in India; Dr. James H. Straughn, president of the General Conference of the Methodist Protestant Church; three university presidents—Henry N. Snyder of Wofford, Harvey W. Cox of Emory, and William Preston Few of Duke; two secretaries from the Board of Missions, Dr. W. G. Cram and Dr. Elmer T. Clark; and four of the southern bishops (two older and two younger): John M. Moore, U. V. W. Darlington, Paul B. Kern, and A. Frank Smith.[72]

Few men had a greater appreciation for the treasures of the historical past than Frank Smith, but he was concerned lest the Aldersgate Commemoration be *only* a historical memorial. In his address entitled "The Recurrence of Aldersgate in the Twentieth Century," he stated:

Men differ and will continue to differ in their interpretation of Wesley's Aldersgate experience. . . . If it be viewed as an isolated experience, real but unique, not again to be repeated, we gaze upon it as upon the light streaming from a long dead sun, bathed in the heat once generated but hopelessly certain that the heat must come to an end. But if this experience be looked upon as one of the many occasions upon which God in overwhelming fashion transformed the soul of a man, then from the vantage ground of this twentieth century Aldersgate is as radiance from a living sun, obscured now and then by lowering clouds but yet abiding with its life-giving warmth, again to be experienced.[73]

This same concern is emphasized in a special "Address to the Church" sent out by the College of Bishops in early February:

We seek no idolatry of a dead tradition. We would not worship the past, but rather serve the present. With no garlands would we embellish the tombs of the prophets. We would speak a living voice. . . . Our task today is to capture for our generation those dynamic and ageless realities which in all centuries have been mediated out of the heart of God through Jesus Christ to the searching spirits of men.[74]

After preaching twice a day for eight days in First Church, Birmingham, where his brother Angie was pastor, serving as the major speaker in several regional rallies from Birmingham to Phoenix, and participating in numerous others, Bishop Smith was able to report to the College of Bishops on March 31 that the second phase of the Bishops' Crusade was meeting with enthusiastic response all across the church.[75]

The last mass meeting related to the Aldersgate Commemoration was held Sunday afternoon, May 1, during the sessions of the General Conference in Birmingham. Dean Lynn Harold Hough of Drew Theological Seminary and Bishop A. Frank Smith gave the major addresses.[76] According to one report, "The General Conference was deeply influenced by the Aldersgate Commemoration. The Aldersgate session on the afternoon of May first was the spiritual high point of the Conference."[77]

As Director of the Aldersgate phase of the Bishops' Crusade, Bishop Smith addressed one final challenge to the church on May 20:

We are a united Methodism now, 8,000,000 strong, the greatest Protestant body that ever existed on this earth. That strength must be mobilized . . . for the conquest of this nation in the name of Christ.

The Aldersgate Commemoration has already accomplished much. It has not only created a new spirit but has actually made us more successful in our work. I have received reports from a large majority of our presiding elders covering this Aldersgate year through Easter. These reports are thrilling. We are not counting noses or gathering statistics [because] the Commemoration is a spiritual movement, intended to bring a new sense of God to all our people. More efficient work is indicated by these reports:

We have thus far in 1938 had 1,000 more revivals than were held during the same period of 1937.

Thus far in 1938, there have been 24,000 more members joining our churches on profession of faith than was true of the same period last year.

Through Easter of 1938, the new increase in the membership of our Churches was 38,000 more than the net increase through Easter of 1937.

Our Churches have paid $250,000 more on their benevolences this year than they paid during the same period last year. . . .

Now let us go forward to Aldersgate. Let every preacher set aside Aldersgate week and observe the two Sundays and the evening of Tuesday, May 24, as great spiritual occasions. . . . This movement must be carried on until every congregation on May 24th experiences a spiritual transformation, sweeping us into the mightiest revival movement Methodism has ever known.[78]

The special program for "Aldersgate Week," mailed out to all pastors and published in the *Advocates*, is an illustration of the thoroughness of Bishop Smith's planning. The program is also an interesting mirror of the times. "We are in the midst of a revival of interest in public worship," declared a contributor to the *Southwestern Christian Advocate*. "We are just beginning to realize the deep spiritual significance of a properly ordered service of worship and the part it plays in the spiritual quickening and the religious culture of the soul."[79] The 1934 revision of the Course of Study included for the first time a book dealing exclusively with worship and another book discussing the theological nature of the sacraments: G. W. Fisk's *The Recovery of Worship* and E. B. Chappell's *The Church and Its Sacraments*.[80] For the two Sundays included in "Aldersgate Week," Bishop Smith suggested sermon topics and gave related information. For the "Aldersgate Day" observance he furnished a detailed "Order of Service":

Theme: "Coming to Our Own Aldersgate"
This service should be held in the evening in *every church*. . . . Every Meth-

odist should seek the "warm heart" this night; they should find God, secure
a personal experience of religion, and rededicate themselves to Christ and
the Church. . . .
Order of Service:
I. Silent Prayer. Enter the church silently and reverently. Let there be no
talking or irrelevant distractions of any kind.
II. "Break Thou the Bread of Life."
III. Sacrament of the Lord's Supper.
IV. "Amazing Grace."
V. Scripture Reading: "The Way to Emmaus."
VI. Hymn: "O for a Thousand Tongues to Sing."
VII. Readings from the Writings of John Wesley, without comment.
VIII. Hymn: "How Shall My Wondering Soul Begin?"
IX. The Story of Aldersgate. In not more than ten minutes relate simply
and impressively the story of Wesley's "heart-warming" two hundred years
ago tonight.
X. Testimony Service.
XI. Altar Service. At exactly 8:45 P.M., the moment of Wesley's experience,
while all [are] kneeling, read Mr. Wesley's statement beginning with, "In
the evening, I went very unwillingly to a society in Aldersgate Street."
XII. Spontaneous Prayers.
XIII. Benediction—the people still kneeling.[81]

The centrality of the Sacrament of the Lord's Supper is noteworthy in
this service. John Wesley was listening to a reading from Martin Luther,
not participating in the Eucharist, when his heart was "strangely
warmed."[82] Bishop Smith's intention is shown in the combination of
the two hymns and the passage from Luke's Gospel. In the first two
lines of the two stanzas of "Break Thou the Bread of Life," the emphasis is upon Jesus' words in the Fourth Gospel which reveal the
sacramental meaning of the "sign" of the "Feeding of the Five Thousand": "And Jesus said unto them, I am the bread of life . . ." The words
of the hymn echo, "Break Thou the bread of life, Dear Lord, to me, /As
Thou didst break the loaves beside the sea." Bishop Smith's use of the
passage from Luke—"The Way to Emmaus"—as the Scripture Reading
supports such an interpretation, for it was only when Jesus "took bread,
and blessed it, and brake, and gave it to them [that] their eyes were
opened, and they knew him." (Luke 24:30-31.)

"Amazing Grace," the second hymn in the recommended "Order of
Service," is fitting for the theme chosen by Bishop Smith: "Coming to
Our Own Aldersgate." Here, too, the "Program for Aldersgate Week"
seems to mirror for us the distinctive developments in Methodism

which occurred in the 1930s. One of the major trends noted by historians of Methodist thought is a "rediscovery of John Wesley" during this decade. "In the 1930's," Wiliam J. McCutcheon writes, "no fewer than four major American publications centered upon the life and thought of John Wesley."[83] One of the four was *John Wesley and Modern Religion*, written in 1936 by Dr. Umphrey Lee, a close friend of A. Frank Smith's since their college days[84] and the first speaker at the Savannah nationwide rally. Lee's study was significant, in part, for its "rediscovery" of Wesley's high conception of the Lord's Supper.[85]

According to the "Program," the Sunday after Aldersgate Day was to be an integral part of the celebration. "Personal religious experience is worthless and will not endure unless it finds instant and constant expression in activity," Bishop Smith pointed out. "Note how John Wesley's personal experience almost immediately transformed him into a flaming evangelist, an incessant worker, an ecclesiastical statesman, and a social reformer."[86] Every Methodist preacher, therefore, should preach on the theme, "The Implications of Aldersgate." If any brother had difficulty preparing such a sermon, Bishop Smith suggested five points: "(1) constant work to bring others to Christ; (2) a knowledge of and loyalty to Methodist history, doctrine, polity, and spirit; (3) a liberal support of the Church and its institutions; (4) a flaming missionary passion; and (5) moral living and social righteousness."[87]

Looking back from the perspective of a third of a century later, Bishop Arthur Moore summed up Bishop Smith's role in the Aldersgate Commemoration:

As I evaluate Frank's total contribution to the general Church, next to his superb leadership of the Division of Home Missions would be his masterful leading of the Aldersgate Year of the Bishops' Crusade. I've been bragged on a lot because I got the money and got the missionaries turned around. Frank's contribution has never received adequate recognition. But the whole movement, in both the missionary side and in the deepening of the spiritual life, I honestly think, issued in a new epoch in the Southern Church. Frank's leadership in the field of personal religion was a very constructive and lasting contribution.[88]

11

The Unification of American
Methodism

"MY PART IN UNIFICATION was just to carry on what the others had begun," Frank Smith explained with characteristic modesty. "When Bishop Mouzon died in 1937, I was placed on the Commission in his place for the concluding two years. They hadn't really tied anything up when I came on, but all the wheels were in motion."[1]

Actually, Smith had been actively supporting the movement toward the reunification[2] of Methodism in America since the early 1920s. When the northern Methodists adopted a plan of union in 1924, Smith immediately wrote to Bishop Edwin D. Mouzon, "All of us down this way are overjoyed at the action taken by the Springfield Conference on Unification. When the special session of our General Conference is called, I hope to be present and see us take the vote which will forge the final link in the chain."[3]

The special session of the General Conference of the Methodist Episcopal Church, South (Chattanooga, July, 1924) did indeed accept the same plan of union by an overwhelming vote (297 to 75), but the "forging of the final link" required a three-fourths majority approval by the delegates to the annual conferences—tabulated collectively, not by the respective annual conferences. The effort to capture these votes, pro and con, led to "the bitterest battle the M. E. Church, South ever fought within its own ranks."[4] Through their own heated partisan leadership some of the bishops set the tone. As Bishop Mouzon wrote to Frank Smith, "The enormous amount of agitation and ill will stirred up by the Anti-Unificationist Bishops distresses me more than anything in my life."[5]

Before leaving Chattanooga, the opponents of union began to form an extensive organization led by Bishops Warren A. Candler, Collins Denny, and William A. Ainsworth. Within a month, "The Friends of Unification" were gathering their forces under the leadership of Bishops Edwin D. Mouzon, James Cannon, Jr., John M. Moore, William F. McMurray, and Horace M. DuBose. Strikingly similar in structure, the two organizations each had a central committee, annual conference committees, and district chairmen. Considerable sums of money were raised to support their respective propaganda campaigns. Frank Smith's correspondence with Bishop Mouzon indicates his participation. Smith wrote:

Bro. R. W. Adams told me yesterday that he had recently heard from you relative to the need for additional finances for unification publicity. I wrote Bishop Moore last week, in response to a letter from him, to draw on me personally for $200 for this cause when a note falls due representing money he has advanced. Were you writing Adams about additional money or for money to cover that already used? I want to try to get some for you if you need it.[6]

Dr. Smith was also listed among the "Great City Pastors" supporting unification, according to a famous article, "Who's Who in Unification," by Dr. Charles C. Selecman.[7] While the minutes of the "Friends of Unification" meetings list a "Dr. A. F. Smith" among the ministerial members, this was probably Dr. Alfred Franklin Smith, editor of the *Nashville Christian Advocate.*[8]

When the annual conferences met in the late summer and fall of 1925, it soon became apparent that the plan of union would not receive a constitutional majority. The final tabulation showed a vote of 4,528 for and 4,108 against the adoption of the proposed plan—a majority, but not the required three-fourths of all the votes cast.[9] "The defeat of unification and the manner in which it was defeated," Bishop Mouzon later told his younger daughter, "was the greatest spiritual tragedy of my life."[10]

Painful as it was to friends of unification, the defeat in 1925 proved to be no more than what Bishop John M. Moore called "a detour" in

The Long Road to Methodist Union.[11] By 1930 a series of negotiations had begun which led to the formation of The Methodist Church, a union of the Methodist Episcopal Church, the Methodist Episcopal Church, South, and the Methodist Protestant Church, in 1939. One major factor facilitating this union, according to Methodist historians, was "the increase in cooperative enterprise after 1930, when a series of major projects and celebrations, undertaken jointly, showed American Methodists that they had less to fear from one another than they had supposed."[12]

Bishop A. Frank Smith was actively involved in each of these "cooperative enterprises." In 1930 he was appointed to the Commission on the Revision of the Hymnal.[13] The northern Methodists had begun work on a new hymnal in 1928, and the two groups now formed a Joint Commission. The following year (1931), the Methodist Protestants joined the common task. The northern and southern Methodists were each represented by five bishops, five ministers, and five laymen. The Methodist Protestants were represented by their president, John C. Broomfield, and five ministers.[14] Due to "some disturbing but unfounded rumors abroad," the secretary of the commission, Dr. Fitzgerald S. Parker, sought to "reassure any fearful saints of the soundness of doctrine" in the new hymnal,

and of the strictness with which the music will be held to true standards of our congregational worship. We are fortunate in having on the Commission men eminent in letters and musicians of unquestioned ability, beside others who are able to judge of the value of a hymn from the standpoint of a worshipping congregation. . . . With ten bishops on the Commission, there is no need to fear radicalism of any kind.[15]

As Bishop Smith recalled, the rumors were not completely unfounded:

Some of the fellows were throwing a whole lot of John and Charles Wesley's hymns to the wind. Joseph M. M. Gray and Henry Hitt Crane wanted to delete every hymn that had the word blood in it, every one. Well, old Dean Wilbur Fisk Tillet got up and almost tearfully pleaded for the faith of the fathers. Now that was ironical, because the old Bishops of the southern Church had refused to reappoint Tillet as Dean of Vanderbilt after the "Vanderbilt row"—as we commonly called it—because he was looked upon as a turncoat and especially erratic theologically.[16]

The work of the three groups was generally conciliatory. Bishop Edwin

Holt Hughes declared in 1923, "Scatter the mood of our meetings over the three Methodisms and unification will arrive with holy speed! All this points forward, as we trust, to the merging influence of a Common Hymnal."[17] By 1934 all three branches of American Methodism had adopted the hymnal produced by the Joint Commission. Published in 1935, the new hymnal provided the three participating churches with another common bond.[18]

Bishop A. Frank Smith also took part in the Sixth Ecumenical Conference held in Atlanta, Georgia, in October, 1931.[19] "Representing all the diversified bodies of Methodists which had sprung up throughout the world," delegates and visitors came not only from all across the English-speaking world but also from Europe, Asia, and Latin and South America.[20] "The spirit of union was manifest throughout the session," declared the editor of the *Texas Christian Advocate*. "The fine fellowship of the Conference, together with a new recognition of common tasks and obligations, brought the question of union forward in the thinking of all."[21]

From these and other favorable influences,[22] the movement toward union gathered momentum. In 1934, the General Conference of the Methodist Episcopal Church, South appointed a Commission on Interdenominational Relations and Church Union. This commission, together with similar groups already established by the Methodist Episcopal and the Methodist Protestant churches, formed the Joint Commission. Bishop Smith recalled that he had hoped to be on the southern commission, "but Arthur Moore wanted to be on that, and as Bishops he was my senior, so he was appointed."[23]

The Joint Commission released its completed Plan of Union late in 1935, and the General Conferences of the Methodist Episcopal Church and the Methodist Protestant Church overwhelmingly adopted the Plan in the spring of 1936. Each church then submitted the Plan to its annual conferences in the fall. These developments, particularly the strong affirmative margins, were watched with deep interest in the South. Some southerners wondered whether there might not be some way to speed up the process.[24] The College of Bishops of the southern church discussed the question at its December meeting and decided to submit the Plan of Union to the annual conferences in 1937 so that the 1938 southern General Conference could complete the unification process.[25]

Once again the opponents of Methodist union went to work in their continuing efforts to "save Southern Methodism." Hoping to repeat their successful strategy of 1925, they aimed their propaganda at the lay delegates to the respective annual conferences. Although he had been forced to retire because of age in 1934, Bishop Collins Denny continued to be the most feared spokesman of the opposition to union. "Bishop Denny's pamphlet and articles have troubled and unsettled many of our leading and best members," wrote Judge John T. Ellison of Alabama to Bishop John M. Moore.[26] The intensity of feeling against Bishop Denny is apparent in a letter Bishop Moore received from Bishop James Cannon:

I am sending a copy of Bishop Denny's statement in the *Times-Dispatch* this morning. . . . Let us hope that all the counsel of Ahithophel will come to naught, and that he will saddle his ass and ride back to his home not to hang himself, but to remain quiet; but, however, he has worked himself up with the hope that he will become the great and historically recognized champion who defeated the Plan of Union, even though it would be indicated that a great majority of the Church is wayward enough to desire to carry out such an ungodly scheme.[27]

Although Bishop A. Frank Smith disagreed with Bishop Denny, he tried to maintain a brotherly relationship with him, as the following letter from Bishop Denny illustrates.

MY DEAR FRANK,

Not to speak of an official right belonging to me as one of the bishops of the Church, it was altogether in harmony with your brotherly feelings to do me the favor to instruct the secretaries of your Conferences to send me lists of the lay delegates to those Conferences. I regret to tell you that Bishop John M. Moore did not do me the courtesy even to acknowledge my request, that while Bishop Boaz acknowledged the letter I wrote him he told me in short order that I could write to his secretaries, when a postal card from him would have brought these lists, and that my old student Paul Kern not only refused to send me the lists but rebuked me for writing anything touching this Plan [of Union]. . . .

Mrs. Denny joins me in love to that dear Wife of yours, and to yourself. So long as I have a home, she and you will be welcome, and I hope we may have the privilege to entertain you.

Affectionately,
COLLINS DENNY[28]

When the annual conferences of Southern Methodism had voted on the Plan of Union, with a majority of more than 85 percent in favor of adoption, the center of attention shifted to the General Conference to begin in Birmingham, Alabama, on April 28, 1938.[29] Realizing they could not prevent the conference from adopting the Plan of Union, the opponents determined to challenge the legality of the whole procedure. That the members of the Southern Commission were aware of this strategy is made clear by the following letter to Bishop John M. Moore from Judge J. T. Ellison, dated February 5, 1938:

Bishop A. Frank Smith told me in Birmingham Wednesday that Bishop Denny said to him that when the General Conference adopted the Plan of Union it would be enjoined within 24 hours from the time it was passed. . . . There can be no question but there will be a determined effort to prevent Methodism from going into a United Church.[30]

Trained as a lawyer and experienced as an editor of six editions of the *Discipline* of Southern Methodism, Bishop Denny was known to be a skilled church lawyer and an able parliamentarian.[31]

To counter the legal attack upon the Plan of Union, the southern commissioners prepared a twofold defense. Immediately following the adoption of the Plan by the General Conference, the Judicial Council would be asked to determine the legality of the Plan and of the manner of its adoption.[32]

The second line of defense would be to obtain the services of an able core of respected lawyers to be prepared for any civil court action later. As Judge Ellison reported to Bishop John M. Moore, "Bishop Smith said that when the constitutionality of the Plan was referred to the Judicial Council, Bishop Denny would appear before that body with an elaborate brief. We should be equally as well prepared to properly present our side of the question." In Judge Ellison's opinion, "Judge H. H. White and Judge J. Morgan Stevens are two of the ablest ecclesiastical lawyers in our Church and both are from the deep South, the section of the Church from which they should come."[33] Knowing of these preparations, Bishop Smith could confidently write to his friend Bishop Frederick Deland Leete (of the northern church):

I cannot believe that the "antis" can make much headway at Birmingham. Our course is very clear, viz.—to give the largest possible majority for the Plan and proceed with plans for the convening of the Uniting Conference, leaving it to the opposition to do what they will with respect to court action.[34]

When the General Conference convened in Birmingham in late

April, 1938, the carefully marshaled forces favoring union conclusively defeated all opposition.[35] While the voting was still in progress, Bishop John M. Moore announced that the College of Bishops was requesting the Judicial Council "to determine the legality of the act of the General Conference . . . and of the actions of the Annual Conferences . . . in the ratification and adoption of the Plan of Union, and whether or not the said union and Plan of Union have been legally authorized."[36] Within a few moments, the secretaries handed their official tally to Bishop Cannon, who then announced to the conference: "We have the report on the resolution which was presented to you to be voted upon. The vote is 26, no; 434, aye." The delegates burst into "prolonged applause,"[37] but any celebration had to await the report from the Judicial Council.

After five days of suspense,[38] Judge Martin E. Lawson, chairman of the Judicial Council, presented the report to the General Conference. It was a lengthy and highly technical document. Only after Judge Lawson had been reading for fifteen or twenty minutes did he come to the first clear indication of the council's decision: "It is further urged that the General Conference, in its action in 1906, was acting in a judicial capacity and that the constitutionality of the method by which the footnote was added in 1922 is *res adjudicata*. With this contention we do not agree."[39] When Judge Lawson read "with this contention we do not agree," Bishop John M. Moore's face "lighted up like a sunrise, and the delegates—as if they had been awaiting some signal—responded with a roar of approval."[40] The Judicial Council was declaring that the Plan of Union had been legally adopted and that the union of the three churches was legally authorized.

The final step in the constitutional process, according to the *Discipline* of the Methodist Episcopal Church, South, was the official pronouncement by the College of Bishops which was made on Wednesday afternoon, May 4, while Bishop A. Frank Smith was presiding.[41]

. . . We, the College of Bishops, do hereby announce and declare that the said Plan of Union of the Methodist Episcopal Church, the Methodist Episcopal Church, South, and the Methodist Protestant Church has been legally and constitutionally adopted by the Methodist Episcopal Church, South.[42]

During the succeeding year, Bishop Smith was involved in two major efforts designed to further the reconciliation of the long-divided branches of Methodism. In late November of 1938, the southern College of Bishops invited the northern Board of Bishops and leaders of the Methodist Protestant Church to Nashville for informal discussions and fellowship. At a banquet "in honor of the Bishops of American Methodism on the occasion of their first joint meeting since 1844," representatives of the three churches presented appropriate words of welcome before the two major addresses. Bishop Edwin Holt Hughes, Senior Bishop of the Methodist Episcopal Church, spoke on "American Methodism: a Preview and a Prophecy." Instead of having their own Senior Bishop, U. V. W. Darlington, give the other featured speech, the southern bishops asked Bishop A. Frank Smith to make that important address. His subject was "Southern Methodism Greets a United Church."[43]

The southern Methodists devoted their General Missionary Council to a presentation of Unification. The four-day meeting featured the three cochairmen of the Joint Commission on Unification: Bishop Edwin Holt Hughes, Bishop John M. Moore, and Dr. James H. Straughn. The leaders of northern Methodism's Boards of Foreign and Home Missions, Evangelism, and Education and of the Woman's Foreign and Home Missionary Societies were also invited to speak to the large gathering of southern Methodists. Bishop Smith was scheduled to speak on "United Methodism and the Future," the theme of the closing session.[44] On the preceding evening, however, it was announced "that due to the death of Mr. W. W. Fondren, a dear friend of Bishop Smith, the Bishop would not take his place on the program Friday morning."[45]

As we have seen, Bishop A. Frank Smith became a member of the Commission on Interdenominational Relations and Church Union in 1938. The death of Bishop Mouzon in 1937 and the retirement of Bishop Ainsworth in 1938 left two vacancies on the Southern Methodist Commission. Smith replaced Mouzon, and newly elected Bishop Ivan Lee Holt succeeded Ainsworth.[46]

The immediate task of the Joint Commission was to prepare for the "Uniting Conference," called for by the Plan of Union, to be held at Kansas City, Missouri, April 26 to May 10, 1939. Meeting in Evanston, Illinois, on June 30, 1938, the Joint Commission chose the famous "Two Hundred"—including all members of the Joint Commission—who were to produce the prospectus for a new *Discipline* by combining and harmonizing the *Disciplines* of the three churches.[47] The old *Disciplines* were divided into eight sections, and a separate committee was formed to prepare each section.

Bishop A. Frank Smith shared the leadership of the Committee on Membership and Temporal Economy with Bishop Frederick D. Leete of the northern church and Dr. Leonard B. Smith of the Methodist Protestant Church.[48] The care with which Bishop Smith maintained the balance of authority with his cochairmen is reflected in his correspondence with Bishop Leete. On August 9, 1938, Smith wrote:

MY DEAR BISHOP LEETE:
    The Reverend W. F. Bryan, the Pastor of First Church, Galveston, is Chairman of our Commission on Budget of our Church. He has written to me asking whether it might be permissible for him to sit in on our Committee Meetings in Memphis in early September, in view of his connection with the Commission on Budget.
    I have written to him that such will not be possible, as we should have to let in anyone who wishes to come if we throw the meeting open to any save Committee members. I have not told him that I am writing to you about this matter, but I am wondering if an exception may not be made in his case, or if it would not be safer to stick to our rule.[49]

When Bishop Leete replied in the negative, Smith immediately responded, "I think you are exactly right in your position with reference to the coming of Dr. Bryan. . . . I agree with you that embarrassing complications might arise if our meetings were thrown open to other than the duly accredited members of the Committee."[50]

After two or three meetings and many weeks of difficult and exacting work, the eight committees submitted their harmonizations to the Joint Commission in January, 1939. For an entire week, Bishop John M. Moore reported, the commission "carefully reviewed, revised, and passed upon every page of every report. The amended reports were printed in a volume immediately, and the *Prospectus of the Discipline* was in the hands of every delegate to the Uniting Conference by March 15."[51]

In that same month, Bishop Smith wrote to Bishop Leete: "Seven weeks only, and we shall gather at Kansas City. I can hardly believe that we have come this far and with so little friction and with such sustained enthusiasm. It augurs well for the days ahead that such is the case."[52]

The Uniting Conference met in Kansas City, Missouri, beginning on April 26, 1939. Following a communion service in a nearby Episcopal cathedral, the nine hundred delegates—led by the three cochairmen of the Joint Commission and fifty-two of the bishops of the uniting churches—marched in solemn procession to the Municipal Auditorium, where the business sessions were to be held.[53] Bishop Smith sent pictures from the Kansas City newspapers to his children back in Houston. On a picture showing the long line winding from the cathedral to the auditorium, the bishop has written in the word "ME" with an arrow pointing to a tiny figure in the procession.[54] Another picture displays a panoramic view of the interior of the auditorium showing the four thousand delegates and visitors facing the stage, where the assembled bishops are seated. Again Bishop Smith has indicated himself by drawing an arrow above an almost indistinguishable dot.[55]

According to the provisions of the Plan of Union the Uniting Conference had five duties to perform:

1. To harmonize and combine the rules and regulations as found in the *Disciplines* of the three Churches relating to membership, the Conferences, the ministry, judicial administration, and temporal economy.

2. To harmonize and combine the Rituals of the three Churches.

3. To provide for the unification, co-ordination, and correlation of the connectional missionary, educational, and benevolent boards and societies of the three Churches.

4. To provide for the unification, co-ordination, and correlation of the publishing interests of the three Churches.

5. To provide a plan for the control and safeguarding of all permanent funds and other property interests of the three Churches and the interests of those persons and causes for which these funds were established.[56]

Bishop A. Frank Smith was involved in the achievement of four of these five assigned tasks.

As already noted, Bishop Smith was cochairman of the committee that prepared the large section of the *Discipline* on "Membership and Temporal Economy," which included all matters related to church membership, the local church (official board, stewards, trustees, etc.), church property, church finances (general and local), and lay activities.[57] "Bishop Leete was ill," Frank Smith recalled, "so I had to serve as chairman at all of our meetings. And there was a good deal of straightening out to be done."

We were working out all those things that had to do with the creating of the World Service Commission and all the other differences of approach that we had. For instance, we had a fixed budget in the Church, South, that could not be changed. In the M. E. Church, they could change it at will any year. They could lift the apportionment going to the Board of Missions and put it over against the Board of Temperance if they wanted to, or vice-versa.

There was a great deal of unhappiness about that particular point, so we came out with the proposal that the budget be fixed for a quadrennium and that it could not be changed save upon a majority vote of the World Service Commission and three-fourths of the bishops concurring.[58]

It was difficult to harmonize the previous practices of the three churches and still please all those involved, Smith remembered.

The northern Church provided that when a Bishop retired he should not have a pension from the Church but should go back to his annual confer-ence from which he had been elected and receive whatever pension they were paying. Well, at Unification, we provided that in The Methodist Church it should be a part of the World Service Commission and that a special committee handle those affairs. There was considerable fear upon the part of some of the old-timers among the northern Bishops. Titus Lowe and [unidentifiable name] came together, and they said: "Why that World Serv-ice Commission won't have any interest in a Bishop who's done." And I said to them, "According to the rules we have here, the World Service Com-mission is set up upon nomination by the Bishops, and surely the men they nominate are going to be men who will be sensible and kind and brotherly." And it worked out splendidly.[59]

Bishop Arthur Moore claimed that Frank Smith solved a problem that had been plaguing the northern Methodist publishing house.

The three Churches were trying to clear all indebtedness before Union, but the M. E. Church had bought a big printing plant outside of New York at Dobbs Ferry. It was an enormous thing, and it proved to be a problem child. It was too expensive. They had a big debt as a result of buying that plant. Frank, with his usual diplomacy, went to see Jesse Jones who was then the chairman of the RFC [and Secretary of Commerce]. Mr. Jones helped them find a buyer for that property at Dobbs Ferry and relieved the northern Publishing House of that indebtedness.[60]

"Perhaps the most conspicuous thing [in Unification] that Frank did," Bishop Arthur Moore declared, "was his Presidency of the Council of Bishops."[61] According to the Plan of Union:

There shall be a Council of Bishops composed of all the Bishops. . . .[62] The Council shall meet at least once a year and plan for the general oversight and promotion of the temporal and spiritual interests of the entire Church and for carrying into effect the rules, regulations, and responsibilities pre-scribed and enjoined by the General Conference, and in accord with the provisions set forth in this Plan of Union.[63]

While neither the northern Board of Bishops nor the southern College of Bishops had constitutional standing, the Plan of Union made the Council of Bishops an essential part of The Methodist Church. In his definitive study of the organization of The Methodist Church, Nolan B. Harmon explained the significance of this new arrangement:

This recognition and establishment of the Council of Bishops as an integral whole thus gives official status to a true general superintendency which now inheres, not in any one bishop but in the bishops organized as a council. . . . To a certain extent this collective power of the bishops is, or can be, more powerful than was the joint action of either of the former groups of bishops. . . . [Those] bishops met with each other as individuals to plan their work, and while they formed an organization of their own, their joint action was scarcely more than the sum of their individual might. . . . Now, however, in the Plan of Union, the Council of Bishops is recognized constitutionally, and to it is frankly mandated episcopal oversight over the whole church. It must, and does, exercise over the whole connection its joint and complete superintendency.[64]

"The Council of Bishops will be the chief agency in making union a continuing and living power," Bishop John M. Moore wrote.

The General Conference is too occasional and too variable in membership and too lacking in personal knowledge and understanding to be a cementing power. Its principal function is legislative, and its pronouncements at times may be spectacular, but the Council of Bishops by incessant labors and conscientious, toilsome administration will keep the foundations secure and thereby build enduring structures. The Methodist Church has untold possibilities for Christ's kingdom in and through its Council of Bishops.[65]

"It was a great tribute to Frank that he was chosen to be the first President of the Council of Bishops," Bishop Arthur Moore declared. "They wanted a man who could speak to every other man in there, [one] that wasn't tagged as being pro this or pro that."[66] Bishop William C. Martin, who was also a member of the council when Frank Smith was elected, agrees:

That is an indication of how deeply loved Frank was. It is indicative of the sense of confidence that he had generated by his presence and statements that he had made on questions then under consideration. Those of us who knew him best and loved him most were grateful that the whole Council should have looked to him for that place of leadership. And he filled it, as he did everything else that he was asked to do by the Church, with grace and dignity and effectiveness.[67]

During the transitional year including the Uniting Conference and the first General Conference of The Methodist Church, the two senior Bishops, Edwin Holt Hughes and U. V. W. Darlington, served as co-chairmen of the Council of Bishops.[68] As Bishop Smith explained: "I was elected the first President[69] of the Council of Bishops in Atlantic City in 1940, and Bromley Oxnam was elected Secretary. We served through the rest of 1940 and 1941. Then, thereafter, there was a change once a year so that we served for the two meetings of the Bishops, spring and fall."[70]

As the first president of the Council of Bishops, Bishop Smith had no guidelines or precedents to follow. His task was difficult and sometimes personally painful, as he remembered:

We had to work out our system of rules, and we had a pretty rough time of it. These old-time Bishops, North and South, would get up and talk about anything, anything at all. So Bromley [Oxnam] said to me, "Let's work out an agenda." Bromley's just the last word in getting things down. "If you will call them down, I will present the agenda and we'll make them follow it." One time Bishop Hughes jumped up and began to talk about something way out on the periphera. And I said, "Bishop Hughes, you are out of order. You can't do that." That is the only time he flared up at me. I was very fond of Bishop Hughes. He said, "You young fellows have got things streamlined here so much that you've streamlined out the brotherhood in the interest of efficiency." And he sat down with his feelings obviously hurt.[71]

Bishop Smith later regretted one regulation that he had helped to establish.

We had several retired Bishops who talked continually and then would make a motion about anything in the world. So Bromley said to me, "Let's adopt a rule that retired Bishops can't vote." We adopted [that rule] when we met in Atlantic City in the fall of 1940, and then we put it into effect when we met at the Cloisters on Sea Island, Georgia, in the fall of 1941, the same week as Pearl Harbor. And I ruled that if a man could not vote, he could not make a motion. Then when Bishop Richardson of Philadelphia succeeded me as President of the Council, he wouldn't adopt that rule. He let them make motions and so forth. But it was our rule, and we could change it if we wanted to. Then the General Conference—perhaps in 1948—came along and wrote it into the *Discipline* that a retired Bishop cannot vote in the

Council. They made a law out of what was merely a rule of the Council. . . .
Now it's in the *Discipline* and only the General Conference can change it.[72]

The immediate problem facing Bishop Smith, according to Bishop
Arthur Moore, was the great diversity of minds and methods represented
in the council of sixty-two Bishops.[73]

Here was a top-flight challenge: directing a body of men, nearly all of whom
were individualists, accustomed to giving orders—to weld them into a
working organization and maintain harmony. Frank knew how to keep
personalities from clashing. More than once I have seen two or more Bishops
moving on head-on collision routes, and Frank would detour somebody and
get a consensus. Bromley Oxnam was a high-grade organizer. You didn't
have to prompt Bromley; you had to restrain him. Straughn felt he had to
preserve and defend the Methodist Protestant way, but Frank knew how to
keep him happy and to keep Bromley from running off the reservation. If
there was disagreement, Frank was the middle-man, not slapping someone
down, but balancing with wisdom and without making anybody feel that he
had lost his side of the cause. Frank taught us to laugh it off and get on
with the work.[74]

There was one interim problem relating to the bishops of The
Methodist Church that the Uniting Conference had difficulty solving:
"The effective Bishops shall be assigned for service to the various Jurisdictional Conferences by the Uniting Conference."[75] Henceforth, in the
united church, bishops would be elected by the Jurisdictional Conferences, and the bishops of each jurisdiction would then "arrange the
Plan of Episcopal Supervision of the Annual Conferences within their
respective territories."[76] In the meantime, someone must assign the present bishops to the newly created jurisdictions.

After extensive debate and considerable parliamentary maneuvering
regarding whether these assignments were to be made by a special com-
mittee(and if so, how it was to be constituted) or by the regular Committee on Ministry and Judicial Administration, the task was finally
entrusted to the latter.[77] When that committee presented its report for
adoption by the conference, it not only had assigned the bishops to the
various jurisdictions but also had assigned the bishops to certain residence
cities, as had been the practice in the Methodist Episcopal Church. A
distinguished southern leader challenged the authority of both the committee and the conference to assign bishops to residences, and the whole
matter was referred to the Committee on Judiciary for a decision.[78]

Four days later the Judiciary Committee reported that it had found "a provision in the Appendix of the *Discipline* of the Methodist Episcopal Church, which, by custom, usage, and judicial decision at least has had all the force and power of law." While admitting that this provision was "subject to debate as the basis for legislation," the committee, nevertheless, regarded "the pressing of the question of power as unwise" and recommended

that this Uniting Conference proceed to make a schedule of assignments of the effective Bishops, not only to the respective Jurisdictions, but also to Episcopal residences, and that the Bishops be requested to accept such assignments, subject only to such adjustments and modifications as the Council of Bishops may deem wise.[79]

To prevent difficulty in the future, the conference adopted legislation drawing a distinction between "Episcopal Areas" (the annual conferences over which the bishop would preside) and "Episcopal Residences" (the particular city in which he would live): "Each Jurisdictional Conference may fix the Episcopal Residences within its Jurisdiction and assign the Bishops to the same. The Bishops of the Jurisdiction shall fix the boundaries of the Episcopal Areas."[80]

In the meantime a substantial rumor had been making the rounds concerning Bishop Smith's assignment. According to a report in the *Houston Post*:

Possibility that Bishop A. Frank Smith of Houston would be transferred from Texas to New York loomed Friday, as reports spread that the committee on assignment of bishops had under consideration a plan to send the Houston bishop to the Northeastern Jurisdiction, and fix Syracuse, N.Y., as his official residence. Requests for Bishop Smith came from leaders in the Northern Church, it is said, who have been favorably impressed with his record and personality.[81]

When the Committee on Ministry and Judicial Administration reported the "Assignment of Bishops to Jurisdictions and to Residences" on May 8, however, Bishop A. Frank Smith was assigned to Houston in the South Central Jurisdiction.[82] Three days later the bishops announced their assignments to the areas. Bishop Smith's "Houston Area" included five annual conferences: the Oklahoma Indian Mission, the Southwest Mexican, the Southwest Texas, the Texas, and the Louisiana.[83] This was basically the same as the Fifth Episcopal District to which the College of Bishops of the southern church had appointed Bishop Smith for 1938-39.[84] Although the new Southwest Texas Conference was the same geographical area, it now included the former Methodist Protestant and the former Methodist Episcopal Church charges within those boundaries. The new Southwest Mexican Conference included all the Spanish-language work in Texas and New Mexico.[85]

An editorial in the *Houston Post* passed the good news along to its readers:

Highly gratifying to Methodists in particular and the people of Houston in general is the announcement that the uniting conference of Methodism at Kansas City has reassigned Bishop A. Frank Smith to this episcopal area of the new Methodist church, which assures his continued residence in this city.

No other minister of the Methodist denomination who has ever served in this area has won more devoted friends among the people generally, or exercised a wider and more wholesome influence upon the life of the city, than has Bishop Smith. . . .

The people of this section—not Methodists alone—have come to feel that Bishop Smith belongs to them. He has built himself into the hearts of the people, and entrenched himself in their confidence in such degree that he is a power for good in the life of this community and this State which is fully appreciated. In this chaotic and critical time, he is needed here.[86]

Bishop A. Frank Smith also played a significant role in the fourth task assigned to the Uniting Conference, which was "to provide for the unification, co-ordination, and correlation of the connectional . . . boards and societies of the three Churches."[87] The area which presented the most difficulty was that of bringing together the various boards and agencies related to the missionary work of the three branches of American Methodism.[88] Frank Smith was to devote the remaining twenty-two years of his episcopal career to this monumental task.

Although Bishop Smith would play an important role in implementing the design of Methodist union, he never forgot that Bishop John M. Moore had made unification possible.[89] Addressing an assembly honoring Moore, Smith commended him for "his infinite labors, his amazingly wide range of interests, his scholarship, his administrative genius, and his ecumenical spirit. . . . American Methodism is peculiarly indebted to [Bishop] Moore for his consummate leadership in the field of Unification."[90] Smith also acknowledged his personal indebtedness to Bishop Moore:

You have been a constant inspiration to multitudes of us younger men, and your spirit and example will be a constant incentive to us thru the remainder of our days. . . . I am increasingly grateful for the fact that my own life was brought into a relationship with you early in my ministry, and I shall hold you in affectionate esteem and gratitude to the end of the way.[91]

12

The Board of Missions Story

"THE GREATEST AND MOST DIFFICULT TASK of Unification," Bishop A. Frank Smith declared, "was the creation of a unified Board of Missions. Each Church had its own system and method."[1] Thirteen separate missionary agencies of the three uniting churches were to be combined: seven from the Methodist Episcopal Church; five from the Methodist Episcopal Church, South; and one from the Methodist Protestant Church.[2] Unable to reach a consensus, the Joint Commission submitted three different plans to the Uniting Conference: (1) three boards, as recommended by the preparatory committee;[3] (2) a unified board with four divisions, as recommended by the Executive Committee of the Board of Missions of the southern Methodists;[4] and (3) a unified board with three divisions, as recommended by the Committee on Policy and Programs of the Board of Foreign Missions of the northern Methodists.[5]

The General Standing Committee on Missions received these three plans and proceeded to draw up a unified board proposal based on a compromise between the second and third plans.[6] There would be just one board, the Board of Missions and Church Extension, but it would be composed of three relatively autonomous divisions—Foreign Missions, Home Missions and Church Extension, Woman's Christian Service—and a Joint

Division of Education and Cultivation. As Dr. John R. Mott, the chairman of this committee, explained:

We have tried to conserve all of the values contained in our past and in our present organizations. . . . We have [also] been most anxious to get away from old categories where we could and chart some new courses. . . . We have tried to present a plan and a process that will foster united planning and unified action. . . . We have tried to maintain the maximum of autonomy —and at the same time—a united front with mutually supporting divisions. There have got to be great acts of trust in one another.[7]

Each of the old agencies had its loyal advocates who resisted change. "Some of the elderly [board] secretaries found it hard to give up the idea of running their part of the board as they had always done," Bishop Arthur Moore recalls. "To see their beloved organization disappear into a larger and more unified structure was not their idea of progress."[8]

Since the members of the proposed board were to be elected by the yet to be formed Jurisdictional Conferences, the delegates accepted the hastily prepared and admittedly imperfect plan knowing that there would be time for further improvements. During the period between the Uniting Conference and the organizing of the new board, the old boards were authorized to continue their former functions. In the meantime a Joint Committee of fifty-seven representatives from the respective agencies was formed "to secure cooperation between the Boards, and in order to assist in administering the total program under their care, and in order to suggest further steps for the merger and administration of the Board of Missions and Church Extension of The Methodist Church."[9] While Bishop A. Frank Smith is widely known for his leadership of Methodism's Home Missions enterprise, he has not received proper recognition for the masterful leadership he gave to this Joint Committee that completed the combining of the thirteen separate missionary agencies. As Bishop Smith later recalled:

Bishop Broomfield of the Methodist Protestants, Bishop McConnell of the M. E. Church and I were appointed as the three bishops. Broomfield and McConnell didn't take any particular interest in it and fell by the wayside, and I became chairman of the whole. We met every few weeks since there was so much work to be done. And we had our rumpuses. It wasn't North and South or black and white, it was men and women. That is where we had our rumpuses. I remember when we met at St. Paul's Church in Atlantic City, just before the General Conference [1940] opened, to jubilate and say we had done it. And everybody got up and said they loved everybody else.

Mrs. Evelyn Riley Nicholson, who was President of the Woman's Foreign Missionary Society of the M. E. Church, said: "When I taught in Cornell College, I dictated a letter once to my secretary. And I said, 'cooperation without capitulation is difficult.' But when my secretary brought me the letter to sign, it said 'cooperation without decapitation is difficult.'" And then she sat down. That was her contribution to our love-feast.[10]

A comparison of the description of the Board of Missions and Church Extension in the *Journal* of the Uniting Conference with that in the *Journal* of the 1940 General Conference shows that the greatest change recommended by Bishop Smith's committee was one of strengthening the unity of the board and lessening the autonomy of the three divisions. The paragraphs stating the "Authority" of the divisions in the 1939 *Journal* declared: "The Division shall have authority to regulate its own proceedings; . . ." The 1940 paragraphs state that the divisions "shall have authority to make By-Laws in harmony with the Charter and Constitution of the Board and of its Divisions; to regulate its own proceedings in harmony with its By-Laws; . . ."[11] In the 1939 *Journal* the divisions elect their own officers and make appropriations. In the 1940 *Journal* the divisions nominate their officers to be elected by the board and recommend appropriations to the board.[12] The term of office of the executive secretary of each division is not stated in the original document but is set at four years (subject to reelection) in the revision.[13] Bishop Smith explained to the General Conference:

By painstaking application and conscientious consideration of the intricate issues created by the unification of separate Missionary Boards and Agencies into one composite Board . . . your Committee sought to conserve all essential values as well as to meet the reasonable expectations of every foreign and home missionary and church extension interest involved. . . . Despite divergent viewpoints on vital issues, the discussions were characterized by mutual consideration and a common purpose to prepare the way for an effective and fruitful functioning of this composite missionary agency of united Methodism.[14]

The initial members of the Board of Missions and Church Extension of The Methodist Church—elected by their respective Jurisdictional Conferences soon after the First General Conference—gathered at the Hotel La Salle in Chicago on July 23, 1940. The board's voting membership totaled 123, including "all Effective Bishops resident in the United States."[15] There were also 46 "Advisory Members."[16] Emphasizing their common heritage, Bishop Charles Selecman, the appointed convener, reminded the assembly that they were meeting on the 200th anniversary of John Wesley's formal opening of the Foundry meeting house in London, and read the passage from Wesley's *Journal* for July 23, 1740.[17] Selecman's remarks were doubly appropriate, for they helped to counter the mood of many of the members. As Bishop Arthur Moore recalls: "Everything was in a state of flux, and everybody was watching to see that his own interests were not left out—old loyalties were present with all of us."[18]

As the organizing process continued, Bishop Moore was elected president of the board; Bishop Smith, president of the Division of Home Missions and Church Extension; Bishop Francis J. McConnell, president of the Division of Foreign Missions; and Mrs. J. D. Bragg, president of the Woman's Division of Christian Service.[19] The three division presidents were *ex officio* vice-presidents of the board.

As president of the Division of Home Missions and Church Extension, Bishop A. Frank Smith presided over a board of managers having sixty-three members: fourteen bishops, ten ministers, ten laymen, thirteen women, four youth, and twelve "Advisory Members."[20] The division was charged with "the general supervision and administration of the work of Home Missions and Church Extension in the United States of America, Alaska, Hawaii, Puerto Rico, and the Dominican Republic; and administration of all [funds] contributed and established for the work of Church Extension."[21] Through its Section of Home Missions, the division maintained a total of almost 5,600 missionaries and deaconesses in the "home field"[22] under the direct supervision of the executive secretary, Dr. E. D. Kohlstedt, and of the four department superintendents (City Work, Town and County Work, Negro Work, and Goodwill Industries). The other section, Church Extension, had two executive secretaries: Dr. T. D. Ellis in the Louisville office and Fred W. Mueller in the Philadelphia office. Ellis and his assistant, W. V. Cropper, administered the work in the Southeastern and South Central Jurisdictions; Mueller and his assistant, H. C. Leonard, had the other four Jurisdictions: Northeastern, North Central, Western, and Central.[23]

"Church Extension," according to Dr. Bonneau P. Murphy, "was concerned primarily with the thrust for new congregations and the accumulation of a loan fund, to make incentive grants to churches, and for the administration of special emergency funds for the restoration of property after hurricanes and floods."[24] The tremendous size of the work carried out through the Church Extension Section is illustrated by a report made at that first meeting of the division: "Funds now amounting to over $10,000,000 are in the hands of the Division for the work of building new sanctuaries and saving those that are in difficulty."[25]

As the first president of the new division, Bishop A. Frank Smith faced two immediately pressing challenges. On the one hand, he had to guide a newly created agency. "To appreciate this chapter in Frank's life," Bishop Arthur Moore insists, "you have to understand the newness and the terrific responsibility which followed the adoption of Unification."

It's far easier to meet in a great conference and vote for union than it is to implement it. We had to organize from the ground up. Someone had to take those plans and implement them and work out the actual structure. . . . In any formative situation, it's progressive and yet tempered courage that counts most. Frank was strong at that point on how to move ahead when the way was not too clear. . . . The annual reports [of the board] reveal the enormous amounts of business, financial and otherwise, that went on in that Division; but they don't show you Frank's wisdom and back-of-the-scenes suggestions of how to get around a roadblock. . . . What he did at the point of establishing a working organization and making it function was about as creative and decisive a contribution as he ever made.[26]

The second challenge was to bring into being a new Division of Home Missions and Church Extension without destroying the old secretaries with whom he had to work. Dr. E. D. Kohlstedt had served as executive secretary of the Board of Missions and Church Extension of the Methodist Episcopal Church since 1927.[27] Dr. T. D. Ellis held an even longer tenure as secretary of the southern Board of Church Extension, having been in that office since 1922.[28] "Frank had in those uniting elements men who had been secretaries of Home Missions and of Church Extension for a long time," Bishop Moore explains,

very strong men who thought they ought to preserve their old methods. The old secretaries, bless their hearts, felt that the way they had been doing it must be preserved as though their way was the Ark of the Lord. But Frank, with great patience and wisdom, knew how to find the middle ground between their old ideas and the new needs.[29]

The relationship with Dr. T. D. Ellis was particularly sensitive. In the episcopal election in 1930, when Frank Smith was elected, Dr. Ellis had been running well ahead in the voting, coming within thirty-three votes of election on the sixth ballot. On that ballot, Ellis received 157 more votes than Smith, only to see Dr. Smith skyrocket to election on the ninth ballot.[30] "Tom Ellis was a disappointed man at Dallas," Bishop Arthur Moore remembers. "They dropped Tom and picked up Frank. [So] Frank was outwardly eager to be kind to Dr. Ellis ever after that."[31] Dr. Ellis was not always an easy man to get along with, as Bishop Smith learned: "He was a very positive, driving kind of fellow. In the Board he interpreted just any question as opposition. You were either for him or against him."[32]

Dr. Bonneau P. Murphy, who joined the staff of the division in 1941 as associate secretary under Dr. Ellis in the Louisville office, remembers the situation:

Tom Ellis had been a great leader in the church, a delegate to every General Conference since 1910, and the "floor leader" of the pro-union delegates at Birmingham [1938]. But he was accustomed to having his way. When he would come to his board with a recommendation, he would say to them, "Now you do this or accept my resignation." This is the kind of thing that "Bishop Frank" had to overcome.[33]

Bishop Arthur Moore, as president of the entire Board of Missions, appreciated Smith's ability to work with Dr. Ellis and Dr. Kohlstedt. "Frank took these men—older than himself, long-experienced, and determined to preserve what they thought was the best method—and developed a synthesis," Moore recalls. "I've never seen Frank's wisdom and quietness and ability to coordinate play a more important role than it did in the organization and management of that division."[34]

Through his role as the presiding officer of the Division of Home Missions and Church Extension, Bishop Smith sought to develop a sense of unity and responsibility among the members. " 'Bishop Frank' had a wonderful way of presiding at meetings," Dr. Murphy declares.

He could bring the group into unity of purpose by reminding them that they were representatives of their people. "Now the reason the people of Oklahoma have confidence in the Division," he would say, "is that you are up here, Mr. Newton. You speak out and you represent them. Then when you go back, you interpret what was done and said here."[35]

The minutes of the organizational meeting at the beginning of a quadrennium contain this passage: "Bishop Smith called to the attention of the new members of the Division that they are a very small handful, representing the whole church. This puts upon all members a heavy responsibility and necessity of becoming acquainted with the work of the Board so they can speak intelligently back home."[36] Another passage shows how Bishop Smith often shared helpful historical background with the members:

Bishop Smith made a statement on the Missionary and Church Extension organizations in the three Churches previous to unification in 1939, and cited some of the difficulties attendant upon merging the different methods of former organizations in the present organization. He called attention to the study committee set up by the Division more than a year ago and the resulting changes in the Constitution governing the Division as passed by the General Conference.[37]

"'Bishop Frank' had a fine way of turning a tense situation around by telling a humorous story," Dr. Murphy remembers. "He had a warm, personal, friendly approach to everyone, always commending people."[38] As the minutes of one meeting note: "Bishop Smith spoke of the recent honor which has come to Dr. Martin Essex of this Division, superintendent of schools in Akron, Ohio, who has recently been named president-elect of the American Association of School Administrators."[39] At the close of a four-year series of meetings, "Bishop Smith paid tribute to the members of the Board who have labored faithfully during this quadrennium for the work of the Division, noting that many of them would not meet again as a Board."[40]

Smith was especially concerned to praise retiring staff members in the presence of the division members or before the entire board whenever possible. When W. J. Elliott retired as treasurer of the division in 1948, Bishop Smith "voiced high praise of the thirty years of loyal and efficient service to the Church by Mr. Elliott" and commended him as "a most remarkable analyst of figures—one who puts romance into arithmetic, whose figures come alive and represent people and causes." In presenting a check to Mr. Elliott, Bishop Smith said: "You may exchange this for something else, but you cannot spend it, for it is bound by love to the hearts of your many friends."[41]

As president of the division, Bishop Smith was far more than just a presiding officer at annual meetings. According to Bishop Moore, Smith "gave assistance at the secretarial level and helped them work out their

formulas and problems."[42] The staff expressed their appreciation for
Smith's guidance as a matter of public record in the minutes of the
January, 1956, meeting of the division: "We want to record our grateful appreciation for the wise, discerning and understanding leadership
our president, Bishop A. Frank Smith, has given to the administration
of the work of this Division. We who serve consider our relationship
with him a choice privilege in Christian fellowship and service."[43]

Dr. Bonneau Murphy, who was on the division staff for nineteen of
Bishop Smith's twenty years as president, remembers that Bishop Smith
helped him "with a good many difficult situations."[44] Murphy particularly appreciated Bishop Smith's assistance in the merging of the two
old corporations which had held the invested funds for the church extension work of the northern and southern churches: the Philadelphia Corporation and the Louisville Corporation. "That was a long, arduous and
very difficult process," Dr. Murphy recalls. "It took twenty-five years to
get those two corporate entities merged and their assets transferred. This
was a point at which Frank Smith had a great contribution to make. He
had a legal mind, and he was especially good during that time when I
was having to struggle with the lawyers over interpretation of the legal
aspects of those trust funds."[45]

Resistance to merger was strong in both offices: it came from Fred
W. Mueller in the Philadelphia office and from T. D. Ellis and later
Walter V. Cropper in the Louisville office. As Bishop G. Bromley Oxnam
complained to Bishop Smith four years after the unification of the three
churches, "There is a good deal of feeling abroad concerning what many
believe to be the refusal of both our Board [Philadelphia] and the
Louisville Board to move to New York, as was ordered by the General
Conference."[46] Whatever the cause of the delay,[47] it was not until 1956
that the church extension work was unified in one office [Philadelphia]
with one executive secretary, Dr. Murphy.[48] Bishop Smith's obvious relief
and gratitude are noted in the minutes of the January, 1957, meeting of
the board: "Bishop Smith spoke warmly of Dr. Murphy and his part in
the eventual union of the Kentucky and Pennsylvania Corporation offices
in Philadelphia. Bishop Smith voiced his pride 'beyond the point of
expression' in being a part of the work of this Division."[49]

Full compliance with the will of the General Conference did not
come until September 1, 1959, when Bishop Smith signed the papers
for the "merger of the Board of Home Missions of the Methodist Episcopal Church (a Pennsylvania corporation) with the Division of Na-

tional Missions of the Board of Missions of The Methodist Church (a New York corporation)." With the caption "A Historic Event," pictures of Bishop Smith signing the documents were sent out to all Methodist periodicals.[50] Soon afterward Smith wrote to Murphy: "You and Gleith [Mrs. Murphy] have done more to cement union at its most critical point than any other person or persons, regardless of number. And you have done it by exhibiting the love and good will which animate all you do and think. I am tremendously proud of the Murphys."[51]

Bishop Smith also assisted the staff members with the proposals and recommendations which they presented to the division through its various committees. As Dr. Murphy explains:

We had committees of different types: a committee on home missions, a committee on church extension, an administrative committee, a financial committee. And all of these committees funneled in recommendations to the executive committee or sometimes to the entire Division. Now every staff member who had anything of importance to put before a committee would talk with "Bishop Frank" about it in advance, because he was on all of these committees and very often was elected chairman of the major ones. So our proposals would come to these committees where he was *ex officio* a member or sometimes presiding. And if it looked as if a recommendation was going to provoke controversy, he would decide whether to put it forward and with what strategy. Sometimes he would go talk to the people that he knew would be negative on some of these things we wanted to do. Sometimes he wouldn't press it, or he wouldn't present it. He would wait, sometimes for a number of years. Maybe that person would no longer be around. But all of us utilized his leadership, especially if it involved financial matters.[52]

Difficulties with the staff convinced Bishop Smith and Bishop Moore that the Division of Home Missions and Church Extension must have a single executive officer. The more aggressive and unified leadership of the Division of Foreign Missions was another contributing factor. As Bishop Arthur Moore explained: "Kohlstedt was a good man, but an older man and not a match for 'Diff' [Dr. Ralph E. Diffendorfer] when there needed to be a match. You had to be on your toes or somebody else would run around you. So Frank brought in some new blood to be as vigorous as the Division of Foreign Missions."[53] The retirement of Dr. Kohlstedt and Dr. Fred Mueller in 1944 offered the opportunity for more changes in the division's staff. A letter from Bishop Smith to Dr. Alfredo Nañez at this time offers valuable insights into the significance of these staff developments.

My Dear Brother Nañez:

To my very great disappointment and regret, I am not going to get to go to Mexico City for the Laymen's Meeting in September. Dr. Kohlstedt and Dr. F. W. Mueller of the New York and Philadelphia offices of the Division of Home Missions and Church Extension are both retiring this year, because of age. The Board of Missions at its organizational meeting in Chicago last week, gave the Home Division permission to elect three Executive Secretaries at the meeting of the Executive Committee in New York in September. We are to elect an Executive Secretary for the Division as a whole, and two sectional Executive Secretaries, one for Home Missions and one for Church Extension, Philadelphia Office.

Since I was reelected Chairman of the Division, naturally I am responsible for these elections, and the welfare of the entire Division for the next quadrennium depends upon what is done in New York in September. . . .

If it were not for the crucial nature of this meeting in New York, I would cut this session of the Executive Committee and go to Mexico. . . . [However] I feel that I can render more service to the Mexican work by seeing that no mistake is made in these elections to the Board Secretaryships, than I can by going to the meeting in Mexico City.

I have written at length about this so that you can explain to the members of the Conference why I did not go. It grieves me greatly, but I am sure the brethren will understand.

Cordially yours,
A. Frank Smith[54]

Bishop Smith was mistaken at one point—perhaps wishful thinking. The Organization Meeting in July authorized the election of *four* executive secretaries: "an Executive Secretary of the Division of Home Missions and Church Extension and three Executive Secretaries to be allocated as follows: one Executive Secretary for the Section of Home Missions and two Executive Secretaries for the Section of Church Extension, one for the Philadelphia Office and one for the Louisville Office."[55] In short, Church Extension was to continue divided. Dr. Earl R. Brown, pastor of Cleveland's First Methodist Church, was chosen to lead the division.[56] Dr. Clarence W. Lokey succeeded Dr. Kohlstedt in Home Missions.[57] Dr. W. Vernon Middleton, former executive secretary of the Philadelphia Missionary and Church Extension Society, succeeded Dr. Mueller as head of the Church Extension office in Philadelphia. Dr. Walter V. Cropper continued as executive secretary of the Louisville office with Dr. Bonneau Murphy as his associate secretary.[58]

"Frank drew around himself these strong new men," Bishop Moore observes, "and made that division a real power."[59] With his "challenging and brilliant leadership," Dr. Earl R. Brown directed the division with distinction for thirteen years. The relationship between Dr. Brown and Bishop Smith was marked by mutual respect and affection. They worked together easily and closely. Bishops in other agencies envied Bishop Smith for having such a capable and cooperative executive, and other secretaries told Dr. Brown how fortunate he was to have Bishop Smith to work with.[60] When Brown retired in 1957, his colleagues paid him the following tribute, which illuminates Bishop Smith's choice of Brown for this key role:

In a unique manner Dr. Brown endeared himself to us as a leader, a co-worker, and a brother in Christ. Our discouragements and delays he shared with us and like a proud father rejoiced in the successes of the members of the staff. His constancy of purpose and his steadfast emphasis upon human worth and dignity revealed to us the spark of the divine with which we are all endowed. . . . The underprivileged, the handicapped and the needy were his special concern. . . . He dared to dream great programs for this Division. . . . The memory of his sense of humor and his ability to cause us to laugh at our own follies will sustain us through many difficult situations. . . . We shall always be better men and women because Dr. Earl R. Brown passed down our way and walked into our hearts.[61]

Dr. Vernon Middleton became known as an able administrator and "one of the great secretaries of the Board" during his twelve years in the Philadelphia office. After filling in a year as executive secretary for Home Missions, he was chosen to succeed Dr. Brown as general secretary of the division in 1957. Elected a bishop in 1960, he continued his commitment to church extension until his untimely death in 1965.[62] The first man that Bishop Smith brought to the staff of the Division, Dr. Bonneau P. Murphy, unified the Louisville and Philadelphia offices in 1956, as we have seen, and served twelve years as the first executive secretary of all Church Extension work.

Bishop Smith also attracted to the Board of Missions such wealthy and experienced Methodist laymen as Mr. J. J. Perkins, the philanthropist oilman from Wichita Falls, Texas. Aggressive businessmen did not always understand the board's need for their participation, as the following letter from Smith to Mr. Perkins indicates.

DEAR BROTHER JOE:

I have the copy of your letter to Bishop Moore. I am sure you are too modest in saying that you are worth nothing to the Board of Missions.

Naturally the details of the work have to be prepared in advance by the Secretaries, just as Dr. Lee prepares his report to the SMU Board—but the members of the Board make possible the carrying out of these plans and the Secretaries have no support or direction save as they get it from the Board. You and Lois have meant much to the whole set up. The members all know who you are and how much you mean to the Church. What you have done makes possible the program of the Board. Without preachers and missionaries there could be no Board or program. When people give their money and then come in person to the meetings it makes an incalculable contribution.

I hope you will not insist upon resigning. . . . I nominated you for the Board in 1940 and in 1944 and 1948. I do not wish to nominate anyone to take your place.

I am on my way to the Bishops' Council and then to Buck Hill Falls. I will see you there.

Yours,
A. FRANK SMITH[63]

Lois Craddock (Mrs. Perkins) and Frank Smith had been friends since their student days at Southwestern University.[64] Naturally, Mrs. Perkins always accompanied her husband to the board meetings. "We went to those meetings for a good many years," she remembers. "They were very interesting, and you met such fine people from all over the world. I never did enjoy anything as much as going to Buck Hill Falls and to those meetings."[65] During one of the annual sessions, while the new missionaries were being commissioned, Bishop Smith was sitting next to Mrs. Perkins. "She turned to me," he recalled, "and said, 'I never will get over the hurt in my heart that I did not get to be a missionary.' And I said, 'Lois, think how *much more good you have done by sending them out. It is providential that you didn't.*' "[66]

Mr. and Mrs. Perkins responded to the immediate needs of missionaries as well as to the appeal for long-range investments. On one occasion, at the suggestion of Bishop Smith, they purchased automobiles for two Chinese bishops to use in this country during speaking tours. Unfortunately, Bishops Chen and Kaung were unable to take the cars back to China with them because of the deterioration of relationships between the Chinese and United States governments.[67]

Bishop Smith's role in attracting substantial donations to the work of the Board of Missions was, according to Dr. Murphy, a very subtle one. " 'Bishop Frank' just put the bug in their ear," he explains. "Sometimes he would say to these people, 'Now this is an important project,' or 'If you were to show your interest in this endeavor by supporting it, others would be stimulated to contribute.' But mostly, I think, people gave because of their affection for 'Bishop Frank' or because of their confidence in his judgment. That was the key to the whole thing."[68]

Although Bishop Smith's policy in personnel relations was generally one of patience and even, if necessary, long suffering, he could take a firm hand. " 'Bishop Frank' was not the kind of person to just go in and whack 'em on their heads," Dr. Murphy recalls. "He wanted to win them by gaining their confidence and persuading them."[69] There was one executive secretary in the division, however, who persisted in testing his power against that of Bishop Smith—or any other bishop, for that matter. Walter V. Cropper, who succeeded Dr. T. D. Ellis as head of the Louisville office, "tried to carry forward that same independent attitude," according to Dr. Murphy. "In one meeting, I remember, one of the bishops raised a certain question with Cropper. But Cropper replied: 'Just keep your shirt on.' Imagine anyone uttering a thing like that to a bishop in a public meeting of an agency of the church."[70] Explaining the events leading up to Cropper's "showdown" with Bishop Smith, Murphy continues:

When the Division made a loan to a local congregation, we took a lien on the local property which was called a trust agreement. Now we gave $20,000 to a Wesley Foundation church project in Tucson, Arizona, and we took the usual lien. Later that church wanted to re-locate, and they requested that we put the lien out on the new property. Cropper took the position that they just ought to pay it, because they were selling the property. The *Discipline* said "it [the lien] *may* be transferred," and I felt like it ought to be transferred. So Frank and Arthur Moore got together with Cropper at the annual meeting, where this thing had come to a head, and they told him that he could transfer this lien or they didn't have to re-nominate him. They put it just that boldly.[71]

Since Murphy was Cropper's assistant in the Louisville office at that time, the two bishops—presumably to prevent any kind of retaliation—gave Murphy a new assignment as assistant to the general executive secretary of the division, whose office was in New York.[72] Bishop Smith wrote to the suddenly itinerant Murphy: "Dear Bonneau: There are few men with whom I have been associated as long or as intimately as I have been with you and none of whom I appreciate or love more. You have dignified and magnified the program of the Church wherever you have gone, and I have taken great pride in your ministry as well as in your fellowship. Blessings on you and yours. Affectionately, A. Frank Smith.''[73]

Another way in which Bishop Smith contributed to the development of the newly created Board of Missions and Church Extension was in the work of the executive committee. In the beginning the committee included the officers of the board and of the divisions as well as the executive secretaries and the staff members—about thirty people—and it had all the authority of the annual board meeting except in appropriations.[74] Bishop Arthur Moore describes the work of the executive committee:

The executive committee met quarterly, and we had many called meetings, especially in those early years when we were building the structure of our work. And it took a lot of time, because we had those strong-minded secretaries and some equally strong-minded women. You had to let everyone talk out. Frank had remarkable patience, more than I did. He'd wait till the right time and suggest something that would move us ahead. His ability to get men and women of differing viewpoints to meet in the middle of the ground was, in my opinion, as great a service as he rendered at any time.[75]

On the basis of this confidence, Bishop Moore—as president of the board —always asked Bishop Smith to preside in his absence. A letter from Moore to Smith in February, 1946, illustrates their relationship.

DEAR FRANK:
. . . When you get to the March meeting of the Executive [Committee] of the Board of Missions and Church Extension, will you please preside for me. Miss Welch will have all the details in hand. . . . Once again let me tell you of my deep affection. We have walked side by side in a wonderful intimacy for a long time. As for me, I want it to grow deeper and stronger until we are together in the Father's house.
God bless you and Bess,
ARTHUR MOORE[76]

Bishop William C. Martin, who was a member of the executive committee from 1956 to 1960, characterizes Bishop Smith's impact in the committee meetings:

Frank did a masterful job in his efforts to keep things moving together. There was something about the man that created a sense of confidence. He didn't have to stand on a soap-box and shout. Just the bare announcement of his convictions carried great weight. He thought things through pretty carefully before he spoke, and it took a lot of force to unsettle him.[77]

Even Bishop G. Bromley Oxnam (president of the Foreign Division, 1944-1952), who was renowned for his incisive intellect, declared to Bishop Smith, "I have such great respect for you and what you are doing that my own reaction is to vote in favor of anything that you propose."[78]

This is not to say that all was peaceful and placid in the executive committee meetings once the old secretaries retired. Rev. A. W. Martin, a very strong leader in the board and a member of the committee from the beginning, was "outspoken about everything," according to Dr. Bonneau Murphy. "'Bishop Frank's' handling of A. W. Martin was really a marvel of strategy and approach and understanding, but mostly behind the scenes. Martin would come back into the meeting with a little different feeling about the business before us."[79]

Perhaps one of the most rigorous debates that ever occurred within the executive committee concerned the invested funds of the respective divisions. Shortly after Bishop Oxnam was elected president of the Foreign Division, he began to discover how much money the various corporations had in capital. As Dr. Murphy remembers, "Bishop Oxnam conceived the idea that we should get all of that [capital] under the direction of the whole board to be utilized as leverage for great board projects."[80] Bishop Oxnam expressed his concern in these words:

All I had in mind was to request our attorney to give us information enough to act intelligently in the matter of the approximately $11,000,000 in trust invested by the Pennsylvania and the Kentucky Corporations. . . . No one regards the Trust Agreements as more binding than I do. I have always insisted that we live up not only to the letter of the Agreement, but to the intent of the donor insofar as that is known. I have heard, though, that a considerable proportion of these funds are undesignated and could be used to build many churches in this important period, if the Board so desires. Are we in the banking business or are we in the church extension business?[81]

Bishop Smith was determined to defend the autonomy of the divisions at this point, however, and, according to Dr. Murphy, had things very carefully organized.

"Bishop Frank's" strategy was to get the women opposed. He convinced them that they were the ones who were going to lose because they had big assets. Now Bishop Oxnam was accustomed to winning every battle he fought, but he sure got snowed under in that one. When it came down to the wire, "Bishop Frank" just said, "Maybe we ought to let the ladies comment on this." Oxnam was really amazed that they didn't see the logic of his position and just go along with it.[82]

Just after the meeting, Oxnam wrote Smith a letter of apology and explanation:

MY DEAR FRANK:

. . . I am terribly embarrassed if there were any misunderstanding concerning the intent of my motion. . . . There was no thought of criticism and no thought of questioning the Division of Home Missions. . . . Of course, I should have talked this over in advance, but had no opportunity to do it. Your more than generous references to me at the meeting touched me deeply. In fact, I was quite embarrassed because I do not deserve them; but to think you hold such an opinion heartens me far more than I can say.[83]

Historically speaking, Methodist bishops are described as "itinerant General Superintendents." All of them include the holding of annual conferences in their itineraries, but Bishop A. Frank Smith's relationship to the Board of Missions greatly increased the extent of his travels. The executive committee meetings were held in New York City: at 150 Fifth Avenue in the Methodist Publishing House building, then in various hotels, and finally at 475 Riverside Drive in the new Inter-Church Center.[84] The round trip from Houston in those days would take a week, even if the meeting lasted only one day. "Frank would get on the train in Houston," Bishop Angie Smith recalls, "and write letters all the way to New York. Whenever we met on a train, and we traveled a lot together, I never saw him that he did not have a stack of letters about that high to mail at the next post office, wherever he was. And wherever I go, people will say to me, 'I have a letter from your brother, Frank.' And it's always written in longhand and headed 'En Route.' "[85]

Bishop Smith's constant journeys to the meetings of the executive committee made him a well-known figure on the railroads between Houston and New York City. Bishop Ivan Lee Holt told of riding a train across Texas when the man next to him struck up a conversation. Presently this man asked Holt what he did, and Holt replied that he was a bishop of the Methodist church. "Why, how can that be?" the man asked. "There's only one Methodist bishop, and he's A. Frank Smith."[86]

Inevitably, many of Bishop Smith's favorite stories had to do with railroads. For example, he was changing trains in St. Louis and went into the station to get a shoe shine. "Good mornin', Gen'ral!" the shine boy greeted him. "A good morning to you, too, but I'm not a general," Smith responded. "Well, what are you then?" "I'm a bishop in the Methodist Church." "Oh," the boy nodded, "I knew you's the head man whatever you's in."[87]

As president of the Division of Home Missions and Church Extension, Bishop Smith also had to travel outside the continental United States to Alaska, Hawaii, and Puerto Rico. These destinations eventually forced him into the "air age." "Bishop Smith never would fly if he could avoid it," Bishop Kenneth Pope declares. "In the first place, it went against his demeanor, his mode of living. He couldn't write letters on an airplane. He said to me one time, 'When I ride on the train I can be by myself; when I ride on a plane, I can't do anything. Somebody shows up that I know, and I have to get into a conversation.'"[88] One flight apparently caused the bishop special concern: the flight to Hawaii. Flying over land was one thing, but flying over water was quite another. Bishop Pope remembers how preoccupied Bishop Smith became as the date of his departure drew near.

When something got hold of Frank Smith, he could yaw and heave, inhale and exhale over it more than anyone you ever saw. He really put out an atmosphere over that particular flight. Well, just as Bishop Smith was going into the Rice Hotel one day, a cemetery lot salesman met him. "Bishop, I've been wanting to talk with you. With all your experience, I'm sure you know most of the circumstances, but I've been wanting to talk with you about a cemetery lot." Frank was nervous anyhow, and he said, "Yes, I have a trip coming up in a few days, but if that airplane falls into the Pacific Ocean the last thing I'll need is a cemetery lot."[89]

Bishop Smith made a much longer overseas trip in 1953, but he apparently undertook it in place of Arthur Moore, and it was related to the Council of Bishops as much as to the Board of Missions.[90] The primary occasion for the voyage was the request for an American Methodist bishop to assist in the consecration of a successor to the retiring bishop of the Northern European Central Conference.[91] Sailing from New York in February, Bishop and Mrs. Smith were able to tour several countries before attending the conference in Helsinki, Finland.[92] As Bishop Smith reported "to all our Texas Methodist family":

Mrs. Smith and I have had a wonderful trip thus far. We spent ten days in Italy; then we were in Athens, Istanbul, Beirut, Jerusalem, and Cairo, before coming to Helsinki. We will have some time in Austria, Switzerland, France, and England, and we sail for home on April 23.[93] This is both a business and a pleasure trip. I am commissioned to do certain things for the church apart from the Helsinki Conference. We have found everything interesting and rewarding—but the best part of the entire journey will be getting home again.[94]

It was fortunate that Bishop and Mrs. Smith were able to enjoy such a lovely trip at this time, for Mrs. Smith suffered a severe heart attack two months after their return. A letter from Bishop Smith to his dear friend Bishop Will Martin states the situation: "Bess is doing well. She has had no company and must be in the hospital for a long time, but we hope for a full recovery. To know that you and Sallie are 'standing by' helps more than I can say."[95] Although it was recorded nine years later, the following account of Mrs. Smith's sudden illness reveals not only the depth of the relationship between Frank and Bess but also the indomitable sense of humor which they shared in moments of crisis.

Bishop Smith: When Bessie had her first attack in 1953, I just happened to be at home. I was completely overcome it was such a shock. But Bessie said to me, "Remember our thirty-nine years together."

Mrs. Smith: I was lying there on the bed waiting for the ambulance to come, and Frank came to the bed and he was crying. And he said, "I never did think you'd go before I did." I thought it was one of the sweetest things and I appreciated it, but I couldn't help but be amused. And I said, "Well, Frank, I haven't gone yet."[96]

Since the first General Conference in 1792, American Methodists have increasingly thought and planned quadrennially. Every General Conference is a time of beginning anew. The members and officers of the Board of Missions and Church Extension were elected in accord with this four-year pattern. Although the other officers of the division were changed each quadrennium, Bishop Smith was reelected by acclamation in 1944, 1948, 1952, and 1956.[97] The Division of Foreign Missions had three different presidents during the same period. Only Bishop Arthur Moore remained in office as long as Bishop Smith did. As Bishop Moore frankly said of the twenty-year period: "From then [1940] until we retired, we went to every meeting together, we had adjoining rooms whenever possible, we had a table just for the two of us, and together—I guess I could say—dominated the Board of Missions and directed its activities."[98]

Bishop Moore's sweeping observation did not, however, include the Woman's Division of Christian Service. Moore himself admitted that "the women more or less had their own show," one reason being that "they really had in those days more income than the rest of us."[99] According to Dr. Bonneau Murphy, Frank Smith didn't dominate the Woman's Division either. Murphy recites the following episode as a case in point.

I remember one incident when we were having a rather tense time with the representatives of the various divisions, espcially the Woman's Division. They were creating some problems by wanting to hold on to their money. Mrs. J. D. Bragg, then President of the Woman's Division, was called out to the phone. While she was gone, "Bishop Frank" said to the group: "Now I am sure that the Woman's Division will be agreeable to this proposal to make this approach to the unification of our work." Then Mrs. Bragg came back, and Bishop Smith said, "Mrs. Bragg, I have just indicated that I thought the Woman's Division would support this unity proposal." And she said, "Well, the Woman's Division will *not* support that, Bishop!" So "Bishop Frank" quickly said, "What I meant to say was that I was doubtful that the women would support it."[100]

The women were afraid their division would be liquidated, but as Dr. Murphy explains: "Nobody wanted to liquidate them, because they would bring in ten or twelve million dollars a year. But Frank and Arthur wanted all the Divisions to learn to live together in harmony and unity of purpose, and those two men did accomplish that."[101] Bishop Smith believed there was greater strength in a unified ongoing program than in spectacular campaigns. As World War II was drawing to a close, Smith declared: "I want to see the [Methodist] Church take the lead among the American Churches in a big post-war program, but I had rather we would maintain our annual giving at an increased level than to have one huge lump-sum campaign."[102]

Bishop Moore also remembers several instances when Bishop Smith unintentionally "offended the good sisters" of the Woman's Division. One of these occurred when Moore was preparing to leave for Africa with Miss Sallie Lou McKinnon, a secretary of foreign work in the Woman's Division. "Miss McKinnon and I had supervision of many of these fields," Moore explains. "We greatly admired her, but she was a very domineering woman. Meaning to be funny, Frank asked me, 'Are you going into the jungle with that woman? If you do, you'll come out with a ring in your nose!' And Miss McKinnon heard him, and she was mad as hops. Frank had to apologize about the ring in my nose."[103] Given half a chance, Bishop Moore can think of many humorous stories about Frank Smith.

When the women of the board spoke about Bishop Smith, they commended him for his understanding as well as for his sense of humor. A group of women from his Episcopal Area who were members of the board paid Bishop Smith the following tribute:

We have especially appreciated Bishop Smith's understanding of the Woman's Division. In fact, we affirm that he is a man who understands women. He understands our viewpoint and responds to our way of thinking. We recall that a young woman welcomed him to the annual meeting after his return from Hawaii with a kiss of greeting—Hawaiian style! The next morning he apologized to the meeting for not shaving. Said he, "I just didn't want to shave off the lipstick." He has his ways of congratulating us women! [104]

The greatest contribution that Bishop A. Frank Smith made, according to Dr. Bonneau Murphy, was his "molding the National Division into a service agency."

The great burden of his approach to missions and connectional work was that these agencies were the servants of the Church, and that we won good will for the benevolences of the Church by the way we conducted ourselves in our relations with the local church and with the conferences and districts. This was the constant burden of his message to the staff of the Board and especially to the National Division. . . . He urged us to spend all the time we could in the field where we could practice the servant role as well as bring the mission concept to the people. . . . "Bishop Frank" would say to me: "Now when you go down to Church A, you may be the only representative of the general work of the Church that they will ever see. Their attitude toward benevolences may be made in large measure by what they think about you and the way you conduct yourself." . . . That's why we like to be known as "Brother Murphy" or "Brother Andrus." We didn't even sign titles on our correspondence. He wanted us to create a spirit of good will and understanding. . . . And he exemplified in his relations with us those things that he urged upon us. He was always quick to be available, and he wasn't ashamed to say to people, "I love you." That wasn't any facade; coming from him, you knew he meant it. It was personal. [105]

During the fall of 1959 the staff of the Division of National Missions began preparations for a special celebration of Bishop Smith's twenty-year presidency of the division. Dr. Vernon Middleton, the general secretary, wrote to all the members of the entire Board of Missions:

DEAR FRIENDS:
. . . Ever since Methodist union the Division of National Missions has had but one presiding officer, Bishop A. Frank Smith. Since Bishop Smith will retire at the meeting of the South Central Jurisdiction in July, this Annual Meeting [January 19-22, 1960] will be his last.
We are now planning to set aside an evening of the Annual Meeting to honor him, and one of the things we would like to do is to present him with a book of testimonial letters . . .

In addition, some of us would like very much to make a more tangible presentation. . . . If you care to participate in this gift please send your check . . .[106]

As chairman of the program committee, Dr. Bonneau Murphy developed an imaginative presentation of Bishop Smith's life and career with an appropriate mixture of historical fact, humor, and sentiment. These affectionate plans were jeopardized in a frightening manner on Christmas Day when Bishop Smith suffered a sudden stroke. Writing to Alfredo Nañez on New Year's Day, Smith briefly sketched the attack:

A spasm of a small blood vessel in my brain on Christmas morning left my left leg useless for a few days. It is back to normal now, but the doctors feel that it is best to take precautions against a possible return of the trouble. I am in "confinement" by their orders for three weeks. I have no reason to anticipate further trouble, but I shall follow the doctors' advice both now and in the days ahead.[107]

Nine days later Bishop Smith wrote to Dr. Murphy, in reassuring longhand: "Dear Bonneau: Your wonderful letter would make me well if nothing else did, and I thank you for it. . . . You are a great comfort and blessing to me. . . . Tests revealed no permanent damage, but the doctors insist that I cancel everything for three weeks. My leg is normal and I feel fine. I will see you at Buck Hill Falls."[108]

Bishop Smith's recovery continued so that he was able to attend the twentieth annual meeting of the Board of Missions. The second evening, January 20, was entirely devoted to honoring Bishop Smith. Under the chairmanship of Bonneau Murphy, the staff had prepared an entertaining presentation featuring a series of thirteen large cartoons depicting significant episodes in the bishop's life and career and a humorous commentary read by Dr. Gordon Gould. At appropriate places in the story, representatives from the various areas of the division's ministry gave personal testimonials concerning Bishop Smith's contributions. The minutes of the division give this impressive summary:

The Rev. Taro Goto, of the Pacific Japanese Provisional Annual Conference, dwelt on Bishop Smith's concern for Japanese-Americans in the west. The Rev. Matthew Botone, of the Oklahoma Indian Mission, presented to the bishop a beautiful headdress made of American eagle feathers, a woven blanket, and moccasins. Bishop Arthur J. Moore, representing the Board of Missions, told of his forty-year intimacy with Bishop Smith and of his sterling qualities. The Rev. Luis C. Gomez, district superintendent in the Rio Grande Conference, represented the Latin-American work, the Rev. Tomas Rico Soltero the Puerto Rico Provisional Annual Conference, and Dr. Harry S. Komuro, the Hawaiian Mission. Miss Isabel Kennedy, in true Hawaiian style, presented Bishop Smith with an orchid lei. The Rev. Fred P. McGinnis represented the Alaska Mission, Mrs. J. Fount Tillman, the Woman's Division of Christian Service, Bishop Roy H. Short, the Joint Section of Education and Cultivation, and Bishop Richard C. Raines the Division of World Missions.

Dr. W. Vernon Middleton, representing the staff of the Division, gave Bishop Smith a handsomely bound book of letters from scores of well-wishers. Mr. H. Conwell Snoke presented a check for $1,000, saying he had handled many checks of much larger amounts but none so freighted with love and affection. Dr. Earl R. Brown, former general executive secretary of the Division, spoke on the subject, "The Best Is Yet to Be."

Bishop Smith made gracious response to the speeches and expressed his deep gratitude for his privilege in having been connected with the Division and its various fields of work.[109]

Mr. Norman G. Byar, the staff artist who drew the cartoons, also prepared a clever cover for the printed program, a caricature of Bishop Smith doodling on a piece of paper while presiding over a meeting. Samples of Bishop Smith's doodles decorated the margins of the cover.

At the business session the following morning, the members of the division declared their gratitude to Bishop Smith in a formal resolution for the minutes and gave him a standing ovation. The resolution states, in part:

Bishop A. Frank Smith, . . . the Division has seen your appreciation of those who have built the foundation in the past and given us our heritage. In these two decades you have given enviable direction. . . . Quick to respond and defend your position, you were just as quick to show courtesy to those of contrary views. You have mingled in good humor to relieve tedium in business sessions. Yours is a spirit large and expansive. . . . We move into the new decade confident we shall build better for having had you as our episcopal leader.[110]

Bishop Smith's response to these acts of commendation is best seen in his letter to Dr. Murphy:

I simply can't find the words to say what is in my heart. The party was perfect, and I am indebted to all who had a part in its planning and execution. The tributes were far too generous and the size of the check overwhelmed me. To you especially am I indebted for this never to be forgotten occasion, and I shall treasure in memory its every moment so long as I live. Your leadership in the Division and the Board has been an inspiration to me and a tower of strength to the Division. My love and prayers shall abide with you and Gleith and your children so long as I live.[111]

13

National Missions: Three
Special Concerns

DURING THE THIRTY YEARS that A. Frank Smith served as a Methodist bishop, he developed an enduring commitment to the ministry of National or Home Missions. Beginning with his assignment to the Indian Mission in 1930, he supervised the Methodist work among the American Indians in Oklahoma for fourteen years. For twenty-two years he presided over the Spanish-speaking conference in Texas, which is now known as the Rio Grande Conference. As the bishop of the Texas Conference for twenty-six years, he was closely engaged in the development of a program of church extension in the Houston metropolitan area. During the twenty years of his presidency of the Division of Home Missions and Church Extension, Bishop Smith was in a unique position to focus the vast financial resources and professional skills of The Methodist Church upon these three areas.

The Indian Mission in Oklahoma was reorganized[1] in 1918 by Bishop Edwin D. Mouzon. When Bishop A. Frank Smith arrived to preside over the twelfth annual session of the mission in September, 1930, the conference reported 2,600 members gathered in twenty-seven pastoral charges, organized in three districts covering an area four hundred miles long and two hundred miles wide.[2]

To the southeast are the Choctaw and Chickashaw Nations, which comprise the Choctaw District. Nearer the central part of the state are the Creek, Seminole, and Euchee Nations, which form the Creek District. To the southwest are the Kiowa and Comanche Nations, which comprise the Kiowa District.[3]

Fifteen of the twenty-seven pastoral charges were circuits with four or five "preaching points" on each circuit. Twelve of these places had no buildings, and the average value of the sixty-five "houses of worship" was just twelve hundred dollars. There were only seven parsonages for the thirty-two preachers and three presiding elders. These parsonages were valued at less than two thousand dollars each.[4] The superintendent of the mission, Rev. William U. Witt, described the condition of the people:

Of the one hundred and twenty-five thousand Indians in Oklahoma—almost half of the Indian population of the United States—there are said to be thirty-two tribes, each speaking a different language. The very large majority of these do not have a written language, and many of the older Indians cannot read or write or speak the English language. . . . Most of the Indians are now, or have been, wards of the government, driven hither and thither by the whims of the white man [since] the dark and tragic decade [1829-39] of the removal of the Indian tribes [from the southeastern U.S.] to the wilderness west of the Mississippi . . . those tribes who followed the "trail of tears" as they left their comfortable homes in the East, by order of the government, to go to [what] became the Indian Territory. . . . The vast majority of them are confronted with an enforced poverty. . . . A few of the Indians do have "oil money" which is handled by the government, but in most cases it has proved to be a curse rather than a blessing because of the continual hounding of grafting and bootlegging white men. The Church rarely sees any of it. . . . Exploitation and grafting in high places has impoverished these Indians and weakened their confidence in those to whom they have a right to look for help and guidance.[5]

After learning that the Indian pastors were paid an annual salary averaging a little over a hundred dollars apiece, Bishop Smith reported to the Board of Missions: "The Indian Work is purely a labor of love."[6] One pastor in the Choctaw District, for example, was too poor to pay traveling fare, so he walked his circuit—about 240 miles each month.[7] Bishop Smith also deplored the lack of facilities for training Indian preachers. He believed that the mission's greatest need was a special Indian training school with a definite program for training young ministers and Christian workers.[8] According to a report in 1937:

Lack of an educated and efficient leadership is perhaps our most serious handicap. Only one of our thirty-one pastors, from the common acceptation of the term, can be said to be educated. Most of them never attempt to preach in English [although] many of our young people do not speak or understand their native tongue.[9]

By the time of Unification in 1939, however, there were encouraging indications of progress. Five young Indian ministers were enrolled in the Department of Theology at SMU, four of these supported by the Board of Missions (M.E., South) and the fifth by a university scholarship.[10] There were six more "houses of worship" than in 1930 and ten more parsonages. Many other church buildings and parsonages had been repaired and improved. Membership now stood at 3,230, a net increase of 630. The annual gathering of the mission was attended by 1,400, Superintendent Witt reported, and "was never more inspiring. Bishop Smith, who is greatly loved by our Indian constituency, was at his best and exhorted and encouraged the great throngs of Indians in a most helpful way."[11] That Witt accurately expressed the Indians' appreciation for Bishop Smith is illustrated by the following resolution adopted by the mission in 1938:

To Bishop A. Frank Smith, our beloved bishop, we wish to record our very great pleasure and rare benediction in [your] coming again in our midst and we trust and pray for at least another quadrennium. You understand our delicate problems and great needs as perhaps no other Bishop has known. Your love for us and abiding interest so manifestly expressed in your sincere efforts to advance our Mission have been a constant inspiration and always a perennial blessing to us. Your coming has brought a rich store of helpful information and wise counsel and a blessed fellowship that has stirred the best there is within us with appreciation. We desire to assure you, Bishop Smith, that every member of the Mission does love you with a sincere brotherly and profound appreciation, infinitely beyond the expression of our feeble words. We pledge you our hands and hearts for the future.[12]

During the last four years of Bishop A. Frank Smith's supervision of the Indian Mission, he was also president of the Division of Home Missions and Church Extension of The Methodist Church. Working with Dr. Bonneau P. Murphy and the Louisville Church Extension Office, Bishop Smith was able to increase the amount of aid for the Indians. As Dr. Murphy remembers, "Bishop Smith wanted to get things moving in church extension for both the Rio Grande Conference and the Indian Mission, and we worked together in a most effective way in those two mission areas."

The condition of the properties in the Rio Grande and in the Indian Mission conferences was nothing short of disaster. One of the important things we did was to hire a builder, as part of the staff, who spent full-time helping local congregations to plan for and construct church buildings and parsonages.[13]

Since the United States had become involved in World War II, the shortage of construction materials and the restrictions of a wartime economy greatly limited the amount of work that could be done. Nevertheless, policies and patterns of procedure worked out during this period were to succeed beyond all expectations in the postwar years.

When Bishop Smith's fourteen-year presidency of the Indian Mission ended in 1944, he wrote to W. U. Witt, the superintendent of the mission: "I will always love the Indians above all other conferences, and shall remember you personally in my daily prayers. I will keep in touch with you thru the Board of Missions, and probably see more of you than I have under the old arrangement."[14] The bishop assigned to succeed Bishop Smith was his younger brother, W. Angie Smith, who had just been elected by the South Central Jurisdiction.[15] In his letter to Witt, Bishop Frank Smith went on to say, "If Angie doesn't do to suit you and the brethren, we will superannuate him immediately, or perhaps scalp him."[16] Apparently Bishop Angie Smith did "suit" the Indian Mission, for he remained the bishop of that conference for twenty-five years. He often declared, "After Frank's fourteen years, I was the bishop for twenty-five annual conferences, so for thirty-nine years the Indian Mission did not know there were any other bishops—and I never did tell them any different!"[17]

Bishop Frank Smith's humorous remark about scalping Angie had two references. Their great-grandfather, Thomas Christian, had been scalped by Comanches in 1833—a story that either of the Smith brothers would tell given half a chance.[18] There is also a story that once when Frank made the appointments for the Indian Mission, some of the Indian preachers complained that they had been hurt. One of them said to him: "Bishop, our forefathers scalped your forefather; now you scalp us!"[19]

Many "Frank and Angie" stories were based on the brother bishops' unparalleled episcopal supervision of the Indian Mission.[20] When Frank was honored for his fourteen years as bishop of the conference, he was given a beautiful chief's headdress made of eagle feathers. When Angie was honored for his twenty-five years, he was given a handsome saddle. "Well," explained Frank, "they have honored us in relation to that part of the anatomy which we respectively used the most."[21]

Witt's final report as superintendent of the Indian Mission in 1944, coinciding with the close of Frank Smith's episcopal supervision of the Oklahoma Indians, indicates the condition of affairs at that time:

I have seen our loved Indian Mission grow from 2,594 members to 4,019 members reported a year ago. During these nineteen years we received 4,161 members, the majority of these on profession of faith. Then we had two districts with twenty-three pastoral charges; now we have three districts with forty-two charges. . . . We are now established in fourteen tribes whereas twenty years ago, we worked among only six tribes. . . . Our advancement in organization and in Christian education has been far more marked than our growth in membership. The standards of education [sic] equipment, both of our members and ministers, have been remarkably lifted through institutes, district leadership training schools, and workers' councils. Also, we are beginning to reap benefits from a few scholarships which enabled young ministers to attend the School of Theology, Southern Methodist University, and East Central College, Ada, Oklahoma. These were made possible by the Board of Missions and Church Extension.[22]

Affirming that their mission had made "continued and satisfactory progress" under the presidency of Bishop Smith during the past fourteen years "in the face of troublesome and almost insuperable problems," the Indians unanimously adopted a resolution requesting the College of Bishops of the South Central Jurisdiction to reassign Bishop Smith to the Indian Mission. The resolution stated, in part:

Whereas, the quadrennium of the presidency of Bishop A. Frank Smith will end in the spring of 1944; . . .
Whereas Bishop Smith is so universally loved by the members and friends of the Indian Mission and is by gifts, training and character so eminently fitted for the delicate task, which he has so signally accomplished by his forceful and illuminating addresses and by his wise and brotherly counsel in his administration of the business of the Mission; . . .
Therefore, . . . we sincerely trust that in your wisdom and in the providence of God he may be returned to us for another quadrennium.[23]

Smith was not reassigned to the mission, however, and in September, 1944, he wrote the following letter to the Indian Mission Conference:

MY DEAR BROTHERS AND SISTERS:

... I am lonely today, in that I am not preparing to go to the Indian Conference, as I have done each September since 1930. My heart is glad, however, in the memories I have of each of you, and in the certainty I have that the Mission will go steadily forward to greater and greater achievements.

The fifteen conference sessions I spent with you were occasions of great joy and spiritual inspiration to me. The Mission has grown steadily under the direction of Brother Witt, Brother Etchieson, and the consecrated leaders of the various tribes. I am eager and determined to see that the Board of Missions strengthens the support of the pastoral charges, and enterprises a building program over the conference. I shall not be content till this is done.

You will be happy under the administration of the Bishop in charge of the Oklahoma conferences. I have known him a long time. He is a man of consecration, ability, and deep love for his fellow man. Under his leadership the Mission will go forward to its greatest accomplishments. (Incidentally, your new Bishop happens to be my younger brother. If he doesn't behave himself, just let me know. I will attend to him like I used to, a long time ago.)

May the Lord bless you all. Please remember me in your prayers, as I do you. I hope to visit you one of these days.

Sincerely and affectionately yours,
A. FRANK SMITH[24]

During the quadrennium 1944 to 1948 American Methodism entered a period of phenomenal growth, not only in membership but also in benevolences. Total contributions for all benevolent purposes increased from $8 million in 1940 to $80 million in 1960.[25] The first step in this renaissance of Christian stewardship was the quadrennial program, adopted by the 1944 General Conference, known as "The Crusade for Christ," of which one aspect was "a Church-wide effort to raise as a special fund a sum not less than $25,000,000" to alleviate the suffering of war victims and to rehabilitate and extend the work of the church at home and abroad. Of that $25 million, more than $4,800,000 was assigned for Home Missions and Church Extension.[26]

Of far greater significance to the Indian Mission and the Rio Grande Conference, however, was "The Advance for Christ and His Church" (1948-1952), which introduced "Advance Specials." As one Methodist historian explains:

General benevolence apportionments were set at a higher level, but far more significant in terms of financial undergirding was the response to the plan for Advance Specials, which permitted a local church to select a particular project to which it would give money over and above its apportion-

ment. In the first year of operation—1948-1949—this device yielded about
$2 million. . . . This change in the giving pattern reflected the desire of
persons and churches to contribute more directly to specific causes with which
they had a fairly immediate connection, rather than to general benevolence
funds.[27]

"When the Advance for Christ and the Week of Dedication programs
came along," Dr. Bonneau Murphy states, "we made special efforts to
put in funds for new congregations and new buildings in the Rio Grande
Conference and the Indian Mission. I suppose we must have put forty
or fifty thousand dollars a year into the churches and parsonages of the
Indian Mission."

Bishop Smith would work with the District Superintendents to designate
the strategic center in the various districts to emphasize in a given year. We
always got a fine building constructed because our builder would go down
and work with the local people, getting architectural plans to fit their needs,
and getting the Anglos interested in this building and their contributions.

The other major construction project carried out in the Indian Mission was on the district level. "Bishop Frank wanted to build training
centers in each district," Dr. Murphy recalls, "and finally we were able
to build three or four of those district centers."[28] The need for these
centers was created by two basic characteristics of the Oklahoma Indians:
their tribal style of life and their enthusiastic response to revivalistic
services. The annual reports of the superintendent indicate that district
as well as annual meetings drew crowds in the hundreds. Eight hundred
people attended the Choctaw District Conference in 1932, where the
host congregation had only a small church building, twenty by twenty-
four feet. "We built eight brush arbors, one of them an immense affair,"
Superintendent Witt reported, "and we slept on God's green carpet
underneath the blue canopy of heaven."[29] In his 1937 report, Witt explained: "The district conferences are old-fashioned, heart-searching,
soul-stirring and saving camp meetings with business sessions sandwiched
in. Our Indian brethren still believe in mass evangelism and make all
their services intensely evangelistic."[30] Annual meetings of the mission
were similar to the district meetings, except more than a thousand
attended. "They'd bring their tents and camp by tribes, each tribe doing
its own cooking," Dr. Murphy remembers:

In those days, of course, the woods were the restrooms: the men would go to one side of the road and the women to the other. Bishop Frank and I would usually stay in a nearby motel. Then we built the district centers. We'd build a big tabernacle for meetings and services, surrounded by tribal centers furnished with kitchens and serving places, sleeping areas with restrooms and showers. Many of the Indians stayed in these tribal centers, but some of them wanted to camp out in their tents.[31]

Finally, the division and the Advance program undergirded the salaries of the Indian pastors. From an average salary of $500 in 1944, the combined effort raised minimum salaries to $1,800 in 1958 and up to $2,000 in 1960. Bishop Angie Smith and his Oklahoma Conference were major donors in this increase, contributing almost $54,000 through Advance Specials in 1959.[32]

Encouraged by this financial assistance and continuing support from the division and the annual conferences, the Indian Mission grew rapidly. In 1952 the new Superintendent, Dewey Etchieson, reported, "This quadrennium marks the greatest period of growth in the history of the Oklahoma Indian Mission. Programs of visitation evangelism, coupled with revivals in every charge have resulted in a twenty-five per cent increase in membership on profession of faith. . . . Our present membership of 5,781 is the highest in our history."[33] At the time of Bishop Frank Smith's retirement as president of the division in 1960, Etchieson announced with obvious pride:

This has been a grand year for the Indian Mission. Three new churches and five new preaching places have been established. . . . Our work has grown and spread across such a wide geographical area that it has become necessary to establish a new district [which] will serve our churches on each side of the Oklahoma-Kansas line. . . . The Mission this year received 479 on profession of faith, the largest number we have ever received on profession of faith in any one year. . . . A new record was set in World Service giving, $2,338, [and] a new high has also been reached in local giving to pastors' salaries, $17,366. . . . Our Pastors School was the best attended one we have had, with an enrollment of 65. . . . Two of our young men are entering National Methodist Theological Seminary, Kansas City, Missouri. . . . Principally from Week of Dedication sources, we have completed six new parsonages and two new church buildings this year at a cost of $53,700. . . . Of the thirty-two tribes in Oklahoma, The Methodist Church has work among sixteen. Our total membership is over 6,000. . . . We have risen from the struggling efforts of a few to a mighty army of God, bursting the boundaries of Oklahoma both to the north and south and determined by the grace of God to spread the Gospel of Christ among all Indians.[34]

At that point, Bishop Smith must have exclaimed with feeling, "Amen!"

When the Texas Mexican Conference of the Methodist Episcopal Church, South,[35] met at Edinburg, Texas, in October, 1938, it had a new bishop: A. Frank Smith. When Bishop Smith arrived at the railroad station, he was met by the two presiding elders of the conference, Rev. Alfredo Nañez and Rev. Frank Ramos, neither of whom had known him before. As Dr. Nañez now recalls that moment:

We were overwhelmed by his personality and did not know what to say. Finally, Frank [Ramos] started talking about Brother Allbritton, the pastor of First Methodist Church in Edinburg, who had told us a few minutes before that he was sixty or more, yet his hair was black as coal. "Ah, don't believe that," said Bishop Smith; "he dyes his hair." With that, the ice was broken, and we started a relationship memorable and precious.[36]

At that time the Texas Mexican Conference had 4,513 members gathered in fifty-eight societies, which were organized into thirty-six pastoral charges. There were forty-four churches and thirty parsonages.[37] Of the thirty-nine men to be appointed as pastors, nine were "Supplies," three were "Assistant Pastors," and one was a student.[38] Uncertain as to the new bishop's way of making appointments, the two presiding elders anxiously awaited some indication of procedure. "Tuesday and Wednesday passed, and the bishop did not say a word about appointments," Dr. Nañez recalls.

Frank and I did not know what to do. Finally, on Thursday afternoon, the bishop asked, "Are the appointments ready?" "Ready?", we replied, "you have to appoint us first." "Well," the bishop declared, "if I had wanted to move you, I would have told you long before I came to Edinburg, so make the appointments." That night we had them ready for his approval.[39]

This initial experience proved to be typical of Bishop Smith's practice in the Mexican Conference. Bishop Smith did not speak Spanish and could not know his Mexican pastors as well as he did his Anglo pastors, but it was not his style to make the appointments himself. "He wanted the cabinet to have that responsibility," Dr. Nañez explains. "He would sit and listen to us argue, and when we were in accord, then he would make the appointments."[40]

In 1939, the Uniting Conference created the Southwest Mexican Conference, which combined "all the Spanish-language work in Texas and New Mexico."[41] In July, after he had been assigned to organize and supervise this new conference, Bishop Smith wrote to Bishop William C. Martin, whose Western Mexican Conference had previously included the Spanish-speaking work west of the Pecos River. Smith's letter illustrates his concern for the feelings of the pastors and members involved in the change:

The Texas Mexican Conference is scheduled to meet in Dallas on October 12, but I [think] that the Conference should meet in El Paso in connection with the El Paso District of the Western Mexican Conference. . . . I do not wish to visit a hardship upon you, but it is my very definite opinion that you should be present when this merger is effected. El Paso is in the Western Mexican Conference. I would not feel free to suggest to the brethren there that the Texas Mexican Conference meet there unless you should take it up with the local brethren and get their reaction. Furthermore, there are some local problems centering about the District Superintendents of the Texas Mexican Conference and the probable necessity of setting up a third district following the merger, out of what has been [included in] your Conference, would make it better all around if you were on hand. As you know, the Mexicans are a proud and sensitive race. I think the presence of both Bishops at that meeting would give them great satisfaction.[42]

For some reason the El Paso location was not feasible, and Bishop Smith organized the new Southwest Mexican Conference in Dallas in early November. It began with three districts, 55 pastoral charges, 6,364 members, and property valued at $302,165.[43] As the years passed, an increasing number of the pastors and members of the conference were native or naturalized citizens of the United States, and the conference requested that its name be changed by the South Central Jurisdictional Conference meeting in El Paso in 1948. As Bishop Smith explained, "Those people said, 'We are not Mexicans from Mexico. We are Latin Americans.' "[44] The new name, Rio Grande Conference, honors the annual conference of the Methodist Episcopal Church, South, that appointed the first missionary to the Spanish-speaking people living in the Rio Grande Valley in Texas in 1859.[45]

Leaders of the Rio Grande Conference credit Bishop Smith with major contributions in two areas: ministerial education and property improvement. In both instances, Smith's position as president of the Division of Home Missions and Church Extension was crucial.

For many years Spanish-speaking workers were trained at Wesleyan Institute in San Antonio and at Lydia Patterson Institute in El Paso.

With the rapidly rising requirements for the ministry, however, these schools were financially unable to operate above the high school level.[46] Considerable help at the college level was made available when Bishop Smith recommended that the Board of Missions "lease Wesleyan Institute property to Trinity University for ten years in return for scholarships for Latin American students."[47] By 1943 the Board of Missions was making $1,100 available annually in a special scholarship fund.[48] Josué Gonzales was one of the first to receive such financial assistance, and Bishop Smith added his own personal encouragement: "I am glad you are going to SMU. You will enjoy your work, and the Lord has great things in store for you in the ministry. After you get started there you will find things to do to provide all the support you will need. Keep in touch with me from time to time."[49]

In 1945 Bishop Smith and Dr. Alfredo Nañez, the executive secretary of the Rio Grande Conference, were finally able to work out a systematic program with the combined support of Southern Methodist University's Perkins School of Theology and the Board of Missions. As chairman of SMU's board of trustees (since 1938), Bishop Smith invited Bishop Guerra of Mexico and Dr. Nañez to come to Dallas to meet with Dr. Umphrey Lee, president of SMU, and Dean Eugene B. Hawk and Dr. Robert W. Goodloe of the School of Theology. A special program for Spanish-speaking ministry was planned, and Rev. Ben O. Hill, former executive secretary of the Texas Mexican Conference, was appointed to be in charge of the program.[50] Bishop Smith then took the proposal to the Board of Missions, as the minutes of the Annual Meeting indicate:

At the present time, the chief difficulty which we face [in the Spanish-speaking work] is securing acceptable pastoral leadership. We desperately need a place where a young man, and sometimes an older one, can find Biblical and theological training, even though he is not yet a college graduate. An increasing number of young men are looking to full college and theological training; and yet we must make provision for a group of men who are not able to meet the full qualifications. With this in mind, . . . a committee named by Bishop A. Frank Smith to begin such training is recommending that a group of ministerial candidates be brought to Southern Methodist University, and that a Spanish-speaking teacher be assigned them as counsellor and guide. A small appropriation is being set aside for this purpose.[51]

In 1947 Bishop Guerra wrote to Smith proudly announcing arrangements "for Bishop John N. Pascoe to teach in the School of Theology

[SMU] for one quarter, thus initiating a new era in the history of educational relationships between our two Churches." Guerra continued: "Since I know you have backed this idea and have always been an ardent supporter of our Mexican church and people, I wish to express my gratitude for your growing interest in our work."[52] Subsequent correspondence between Bishop Smith and Dr. Nañez documents Smith's continuing interest in this project. In 1953, for example, Smith wrote:

I have been given definite assurance that the Board of Missions will continue to put the $4,000 per year in your project. . . . Dr. Schisler said the Board of Education would give $1,000.00 per year. . . . I am going to see Dr. Curl and Don Redmond next week about this same matter. I feel confident the Southwest Texas Conference will make a contribution annually sufficient to bring your budget to the $6,200.00 you desire.[53]

The other major contribution that Bishop Smith made to the development of the Rio Grande Conference was in the area of property development. "All of our buildings were dilapidated when he became our bishop," Dr. Nañez remembers, "and he determined to improve the physical condition of the conference. During his years with us, the face of our Conference was completely transformed."[54] The statistical records illustrate the tremendous increase. When Bishop Smith organized the Southwest Mexican Conference in 1939, the total property value was $302,165. In 1960, when Bishop Smith retired, the total value of the conference's property was $3,446,497.[55] Dr. Nañez explains how Bishop Smith brought this about:

The National Division, through its Advance Specials, contributed a great deal. The local Anglo churches and the adjoining Anglo conferences responded generously. And the Rio Grande Conference did all it could. Somehow Bishop Smith was able to appeal to the leadership of the conference in a very fine and positive way. And the leadership of the conference responded by working.
    Dr. Kohlstedt, Dr. Middleton, and Dr. Brown didn't know anything about our work, but Bishop Smith—as President of the Division—interested the executives of the Board in our conference. He was instrumental in convincing them that this was an important piece of work, so they began working for us all over the connection. That was very crucial. Our work would not be what it is today if he had not been the leader of the National Division for such a long time.
    Bishop Smith did a great deal to put our conference on the map. Wherever he went, he talked about the Rio Grande Conference, so that

when he retired all the Church was aware of the Spanish-speaking work.

Bishop Smith worked with Bonneau Murphy, and Dr. Murphy tried his best to help us in every way. Through his efforts, we were able to get these three groups together to build many churches and parsonages. The majority of the churches and parsonages we have now were built during that period.[56]

Understandably, the Rio Grande Conference loved and appreciated Frank Smith and Bonneau Murphy. As Dr. Nañez wrote to Dr. Murphy on one occasion: "You and Bishop Smith believed in this work long before the Church in general was aware of it. Your interest and vision had much to do with this tremendous change, and for this our Conference will be always thankful to God."[57]

Bishop Smith's influence in the executive committee of the Board of Missions, noted in the preceding chapter,[58] was of vital significance, according to Dr. Nañez:

Bishop Smith was more than a presiding officer, for he had a way of doing things. When he wanted something to be done, he would not bring it to the Board. He would bring it to the executive committee. And the executive committee could not say no to the bishop; he was such a tremendous personality. That was his style, and he was very powerful there because he was very hard to refuse. You couldn't say no to him, that's all.[59]

According to Dr. Bonneau Murphy, Bishop Smith also had his way of working with the Rio Grande Conference:

When Bishop Frank first came there, they felt that they were just the last limb on the tree. Their minimum salaries were so low that a man could scarcely support his family. And Bishop Frank tried to give them confidence. The Board of Missions helped through the National Division to raise the minimum salaries through the years until it was more representative. Bishop Frank always had great patience as a presiding officer, but I think that he showed more patience and more consideration of the brethren in the Rio Grande Conference. Some of them would want to speak in Spanish, for instance, and he didn't understand a lot of Spanish. So he would have someone interpret for him, right at his ear, when they were talking, so he could understand what was being said. I think he tried to stimulate that conference to do better planning and its leaders to be responsible.[60]

As Smith wrote to Nañez in 1943: "I have high hopes that we are well on the road toward establishing a minimum salary *in keeping with the dignity of the Conference* and the needs of our preachers."[61]

In 1948 Bishop Smith persuaded the Board of Missions to establish a new department—the Department of Spanish-speaking and Indian Work in the Southwest—with an office in San Antonio, Texas. Dr. Clarence W. Lokey, former executive secretary of the Home Missions Section, was appointed superintendent. In his first report to the division, Dr. Lokey declared, "The increased effectiveness of closer contact with the work has more than justified this new plan of administration."[62] As supporting evidence, he listed a number of special gifts obtained, totaling some $121,000—including Miss Anna Kelsey's gift of $90,000 for a church and parsonage in Corpus Christi. At that time, the Rio Grande Conference had twenty-one self-supporting charges and fifty-one mission charges.[63]

Bishop Smith was deeply interested in Lydia Patterson Institute, the school for Latin Americans in El Paso.[64] Even before the institute closed its department of ministerial training,[65] Bishop Smith recognized the necessity of reorganizing the school and incorporating it with a responsible board of trustees. "With the help of Bishop Frank, we were able to get the South Central Jurisdiction behind the Institute," Dr. Bonneau Murphy recalls. "Our organization of finance and field service conducted a financial campaign to get that organization on its feet."[66] By 1956 the following report could be made:

Lydia Patterson Institute, with buildings recently renovated at a cost of over $85,000, is now chartered in the State of Texas and operates under a Board of Trustees elected (one minister and one layman) from each of the Annual Conferences of Texas and New Mexico. With this strong local leadership the institution has been able to serve the people more effectively.[67]

In 1960, the year of Bishop Smith's retirement, the Spanish-speaking Work Committee reported: "Through the past year a total of $164,465.20 has been secured through solicitation of the [San Antonio] office." Of this amount, $65,000 was directed for salaries, $53,000 for buildings, $7,600 for Lydia Patterson Institute, and $38,400 was undirected. On the basis of this Advance Special giving, the minimum salary support was raised to $2,200 for an approved supply pastor and $2,400 for a conference member giving full time to his work. For its part, the Rio Grande Conference accepted half of the support of its conference executive secretary and set up a Committee on Minimum Salary Support "through which the conference will begin to share more in the support of the weaker and mission charges."[68] That the pastors and members had attained a considerable sense of confidence and dignity, as desired by Bishop Smith, is indicated by the traditional Methodist "rule of thumb": since 1940—in two decades—membership had increased from 6,430 to 14,447; pastoral support from $10,346 to $126,909; World Service and Conference Benevolences from $4,870 to $21,537; and the total collected for all causes from $41,331 to $333,108.[69]

Because of Bishop Smith's many contributions to the Spanish-speaking ministry, the Methodist Church of Mexico awarded him its Medal of Merit. Bishop Eleazar Guerra came to San Antonio and made the presentation during the 1953 session of the Southwest Texas Conference, Accompanying Bishop Guerra were two leaders of the Mexican church who had been classmates with Bishop Smith at Vanderbilt University: Rev. Juan Pascoe, the first bishop of Iglesia Metodista de Mexico, and Dr. Milton C. Davis, a teacher for thirty-five years in the theological schools of Mexico.[70]

Not only did Bishop Smith seek to build a corporate sense of pride and achievement among the Rio Grande pastors; he also attempted to assist them individually to gain an appropriate sense of self-esteem. His personal letters to them were especially effective in this endeavor. Writing to one of the district superintendents, he said in part: "My dear Brother Ramos: . . . I am mighty proud of the record made by your District. Please thank your people and preachers for me and be assured of my appreciation to you personally. With every good wish, I am cordially yours, A. Frank Smith."[71] When one of the senior leaders retired, Bishop Smith wrote to him as follows:

We missed you tremendously at the Conference. You have meant more than you realize to the development of the Rio Grande Conference, and your influence will never lose its power. I have felt a sense of security and well-being across these twenty-two years in the knowledge of your steady hand and decisive influence as you kept things on an even keel ever looking forward. I love you and my every memory of you is a gracious and happy one. Blessings always upon you and your dear wife and your loved ones.

Affectionately,
A. FRANK SMITH[72]

Upon hearing of the death of a pastor's wife, Smith sent this expression of his concern:

I am deeply grieved to learn of the passing of your dear wife. She was a radiant Christian soul and the entire Conference will miss her inexpressibly. While my heart goes out to you in sympathy, at the same time I rejoice in your hope of seeing her again in the Father's house. Please assure all the loved ones of my abiding sympathy and continuing prayers.[73]

In 1953, while Bishop Smith was in Europe on an assignment for the Council of Bishops, he asked Dr. Alfredo Nañez to send him a copy of the Rio Grande Conference *Journal* so he might write a note to all the pastors. Apparently, he wrote to all of them from Rome.[74]

Bishop Smith gave the Rio Grande pastors a sense of stability and security through his practice of placing the career or personal needs of a pastor above the desire of a congregation when a choice was necessary. Dr. Nañez recalls the following instance:

We were meeting in Fort Worth one year, and the wife of one of the young preachers who didn't know Bishop Smith very well came to me. "Brother Nañez, the Superintendent insists that we must move because he needs my husband in another place. But I am expecting a child very soon, and I don't know how to tell that to the bishop." "Oh," I said, "just go tell him what you have told me." So she went and said, "Bishop, we would like to stay here for another year for personal reasons. I am going to have a child in a few weeks." "Well, of course you will stay here," Bishop Smith assured her. To him, a person was important. A preacher or his wife was very, very important, and he would go to the very end to protect that preacher in the conference. He would always stand by the man who was in need. He said to me, "Well, the Church is of God and it is going to continue whether a pastor stays or moves. If this man's family needs to be protected, this man is going to stay." That's the way he was.[75]

On another occasion, a congregation's wish to have a new pastor brought the following reply from Bishop Smith, addressed to the leading layman in the congregation:

I am writing to you, and through you to the other members of ———— church who spoke to me before conference about their desire for a change in pastors. . . .

I want to assure you of my appreciation of the gravity of the situation at ————, and of my respect for those who came to see me. . . .

As you doubtless know, I talked at length with Brother ————, and with three laymen from ———— who were at the conference. . . . My conversations with Brother ———— were altogether upon the basis of what was the wise thing to do, both for him and the church. He told me that he positively expects to retire in two years, and that his plans are made to that end. I was told by his laymen that he is not well enough, at his age, to enter upon a new pastorate. Brother ——— assured me that he would willingly go wherever he was sent. I told him that I would say to his people that he expects to retire within two years, and I further said to him that I hoped he would carry no resentment in his heart because certain of his members thought a change desirable, but rather, that he would make of these last years the best of his entire ministry. He said that such was his desire and purpose.

After weighing all factors involved, I have returned Brother ——— to ———, and I believe that such was the wise thing to do. My action did not imply indifference to the representatives of those desiring a change, nor did it mean that conditions should continue indefinitely at ——— as they are now. It did mean, however, that a church is not helped if, in the solving of one problem, another as great or greater is created.

I am confident that those desiring a change would not be happy to see Brother ——— forced into an earlier retirement than he had planned, . . . or placed in a situation that would affect his health. I do not imply that Brother ——— was returned because he is a sick man, nor that he was returned simply because he promised to retire in two years. He was returned to be the pastor of ——— with no restrictions involved or implied. But at the same time, it is but just and Christian to recognize that certain factors do affect his decision.

I have gone over this entire situation with Dr. Nañez who can elaborate upon the matter as a whole far better than I can in a letter. . . .

I trust and believe that all of you who talked to me, as well as others in the church who share your feelings, will loyally continue your support of your Church and pastor, and I further trust and believe that together you and Brother ——— will make of the next two years the finest that ——— has ever known.

Most sincerely yours,
A. FRANK SMITH[76]

Bishop Smith's relationship to the Rio Grande Conference was greatly influenced by his association with Dr. Nañez, the executive secretary of the conference's Board of Education from 1939 to 1959. Throughout their long alliance, Smith gave Nañez continuing praise for his contributions to the development of the conference, as the following excerpts from their correspondence indicate. In 1943, Bishop Smith wrote: "I think we had a most successful session of the Conference. . . . I am increasingly appreciative of the fine service you are rendering to the Conference. You are doing a work that is more necessary to the future welfare of the Conference than any other work that can be done."[77]

In order to keep the Rio Grande Conference in the mainstream of

Methodist programs as well as to make the conference more widely known, Bishop Smith enabled Dr. Nañez to attend all of the significant meetings of the church. "Because he wanted the conference to be known, he got me invited to all kinds of meetings," Nañez explains. "I was constantly relating the Spanish-speaking work."[78] In 1945, for example, Smith encouraged Nañez to attend an evangelism meeting in Albion, Michigan:

Dr. Dawson Bryan tells me this will be one of the most significant meetings ever held in our Church. The outstanding men from the Church will be there. The whole question of evangelism for the modern day will be discussed, as well as the next phase of the Crusade. . . . The Area Crusade Fund and the General Commission will care for your expenses. . . . I deeply appreciate your fine leadership and the farsighted vision with which you are directing the thinking and the affairs of the conference.[79]

Detecting considerable unrest in the Rio Grande Conference in the early 1920s, Dr. Nañez wrote to Bishop Smith offering to resign as executive secretary:

Having given so many years to this work, Mrs. Nañez and I certainly do not want to do the least thing to bring dissension and we are ready and willing to do our part, since the whole difficulty seems to revolve around us. . . . Your kindness and loyalty to me have gone beyond what I deserve and I prize them very dearly in my heart, but I think it is imperative to see this whole thing dispassionately for the good of the Conference, regardless of personalities.[80]

Bishop Smith's reply reaffirmed his confidence in Dr. Nañez:

I appreciate your fine spirit and attitude. The Rio Grande Conference owes more to you and your wife than can be expressed in words. You have always placed the welfare of the Conference ahead of every other consideration.

The Conference continues to grow, and I would like to believe that any internal feelings are the result of growing pains. I do not see why people who have the same aim, as surely as our leaders in the Conference have, cannot find a ground for mutual cooperation in so far as methods are concerned.

You have always been very cooperative in all the dealings I have had with you, and you have had but one aim, and that has been the welfare of the Conference. I believe we can find a way out, by the Lord's help, and I do not believe that your work or influence need be curtailed in the least.

. . . I am delighted that you are going to the General Conference. No

Conference will have worthier or more intelligent representation than will
the Rio Grande.[81]

Bishop and executive secretary weathered the storm. As Nañez himself
said in another context, "When it came to persons, Bishop Smith would
be loyal to that person to the end."[82]

Dr. Alfredo Nañez is a man of rare talents and abilities, as all who
have known and worked with him testify. He was the first member of
the Rio Grande Conference (Southwest Mexican or Texas Mexican included) to earn both college and seminary degrees. He received an
honorary Doctor of Divinity degree from his alma mater, Southwestern
University, in 1950. He has edited two Spanish editions of *The Methodist
Hymnal* and of the Methodist Ritual.[83] At Bishop Smith's insistence he
remained as executive secretary until 1959, having served twenty years
in that position of leadership with distinction. No one was more appreciative of Dr. Nañez than Bishop A. Frank Smith. Having appointed
Nañez to a district in the Rio Grande Conference in 1959, Smith wrote:

It gives me great satisfaction to see you back in the Cabinet before I leave
the Area. . . . The growth and development of the Conference and the
people generally is a source of great pride and joy to all of us who have
known the work and the people across the years. To you, in no small measure,
must go credit for much of this achievement.[84]

As noted in the preceding chapter,[85] the Division of National Missions and the Board of Missions honored Bishop Smith upon his retirement as president and vice-president, respectively, at the Annual Meeting in 1960. Speaking on behalf of the Rio Grande Conference was
Rev. Luis C. Gomez, superintendent of the Southern District, who had
been a student pastor at Texas Tech in October, 1938, when Bishop
Smith first presided over the Texas Mexican Conference at Edinburg.[86]
He paid the following tribute to Bishop Smith:

As Latin American Methodists in Texas and New Mexico, we can say that
practically all that we are we owe to our beloved Bishop A. Frank Smith.
He has given us twenty-two years of his life. He came and found us crawling
like children. He has helped us to get on our feet in all the phases of life.
For his guidance and concern for our conference, we are thankful.

Bishop Smith has been patient, understanding, kind, friendly, and firm with
us. He has laughed with us when we have been happy, and he has suffered
along with us when we have faced difficulties and great problems. . . . He

has been a great spiritual leader, a great friend of our people, and a devoted and consecrated Bishop. We all love him. We thank God for Bishop A. Frank Smith.[87]

There have been four distinct periods in the history of organized Methodist missions in Houston in this century, according to Walter W. Armstrong: (1) 1913-19??: the Society whose records apparently disappeared after 1914; (2) 1921-1937: the reorganized "Houston City Board of Missions and Church Extension"; (3) 1937-1942: the "Laymen's Board"; and (4) 1942 to the present.[88] A Frank Smith was an active participant in the second period[89] and was to be even more closely involved in the third and fourth.

As Bishop Kenneth Pope says, "Houston doesn't grow; it explodes!"[90] Between 1920 and 1930, the population of Houston increased 111.4 percent. During the 1930s—the "Depression Years"—it increased only 31.5 percent. World War II and full-scale industrialization started the boom again, and the 1940s saw an increase of 55 percent. In the 1950s Houston added another 56 percent to its population. Between 1930 and 1960, the years of A. Frank Smith's episcopacy, Houston grew from 292,352 people to 938,219—or 1,243,156 if the entire metropolitan area is included.[91] By way of contrast, the population of the entire state of Texas increased only 20 percent per decade between 1900 and 1952.[92]

The current and future development of the "Great Gulf Basin" was one of Bishop Smith's favorite topics of conversation. "Bessie says I have one tune and two notes," he admitted. "One is the 'Great Gulf Basin' and the other is 'Growing a Soul.' "[93] "Frank Smith took a very active interest in church extension," explains Dr. Bonneau Murphy, "because his own area was in a constant state of development. And he pushed church extension in his area, realizing that if he didn't make the future, the future would overwhelm him."[94] Dr. L. U. Spellman offers the following perspective:

The rim of the Gulf was the southern and eastern boundary of the area where Frank Smith spent his mature life. This vast industrial complex was still in its infancy when he began his ministry, but he foresaw its potential. He also saw the need for the church to match its growth and to influence its development.[95]

In his brief history of the movement, Walter Armstrong writes:

What may be called the modern era in Houston Methodist Missionary effort began in 1937 when Bishop A. Frank Smith, Presiding Elder H. M. Whaling, Jr., and Raymond P. Elledge applied for a charter for the "Houston District, Methodist Episcopal Church, South, Board of Missions and Church Extension, Incorporated."[96]

Armstrong traces this renewed effort to "some correspondence" between Elledge, Whaling, and Hines H. Baker "about the need of, and plans for, a better organization of Methodist forces in the city."[97] It was no coincidence that Elledge and Baker were members of Bering Methodist Church, where, along with Loyal Nelms, they had helped revitalize an older church. Baker and Nelms—and perhaps Elledge, too—had been members of First Methodist Church in Houston when A. Frank Smith was pastor there. As we have seen, Smith had urged some of his most capable young laymen to transfer their church membership to Bering to enable that congregation to attract and hold many of the new families moving into that area of Houston in the 1920s.[98] "Smith prevailed upon these laymen," says Dr. Durwood Fleming, "to go out to Bering to take leadership in that church. They got a taste of what it means to be in church extension and became enamored with spreading the church out into the city and doing it in an organized fashion."[99]

By 1937, Baker recalls, "the old City Board of Missions was just a body collecting a certain amount of money to pay the conference claims for the churches that couldn't meet them, things of that kind. It was not an aggressive body."

We moved that it be reorganized [he continues] as a District Board of Missions and Church Extension, with the idea that we would establish a sound program of founding new churches. We would not found a new church unless it bore promise of succeeding. We would give support by helping them to acquire a real church site, not just a corner lot, but a large enough site that they could start in a position to build the ultimate plant that they needed on that site. I had contact with Bishop Smith in connection with all the organization and early work with that.[100]

When the Houston District Conference met in 1937, Elledge—"a very clear-eyed, brilliant lawyer"[101]—presented a charter and bylaws which became the basis for a reorganized Board of Missions: a board of directors composed of fifteen laymen, elected by the District Conference in three classes, each class serving a three-year term, with the bishop of the Texas Conference and the presiding elder of the Houston District as ex-officio members. On Elledge's nomination, the following were elected as the original directors: Marcus Greer, Fred J. Heyne, J. E. Josey, Jr., R. J. Beard, John T. Scott, to serve one year; A. D. Simpson, Hugh Watson, J. O. Webb, Ewing Werlein, John B. Williams, two years; and Hines H. Baker, R. L. Cole, E. L. Crain, Raymond P. Elledge, and Walter W. Fondren, three years. As Armstrong declares, "Perhaps no more distinguished company of men have been gathered into one undertaking in the history of this city."[102] Without taking away any of the credit for the revitalizing of the board from Elledge, it must be pointed out that these were also men who had been closely associated with A. Frank Smith for many years. As Dr. Durwood Fleming says,

Bishop Smith always walked among the big men with great ease. He extracted from these men a confidence. They believed in Frank Smith's integrity; they believed in his spirit. He knew what was going on in Houston, and he had that great sensibility about the church getting in on the ground floor. However it came about, he was encouraging the formation of a Houston Board of Church Extension.[103]

Under the chairmanship of Hines H. Baker, this board organized three new churches and constructed eleven buildings during its first year, earning feature coverage in the *Houston Post*. Bishop Smith was quoted as saying, "This building program in the Houston District sets a record for the number of edifices under construction at one time in one District in the Methodist Episcopal Church, South."[104]

When the Mission Board was restructured in June, 1943, Elledge— who had served as president for four and a half years—reported that the board had given financial aid to twenty-six churches, had sponsored the organization and building of six new congregations, and had raised or received over $39,000 since 1937.[105]

The Elledge or "Laymen's Board" was not organized in accord with the *Discipline* of The Methodist Church, being deliberately designed to exclude any clergy participation and not accountable to any body other than itself. Elledge himself had stated publicly, "We are convinced that such a Board cannot be successful unless it is independent of the clergy," arguing that preachers are not safe guides in economic and business matters and should confine their activities to "spiritual matters."[106] How could Bishop Smith have given his support to such an organization? As Smith described himself:

I am a pragmatist if I can be one without sacrificing principle for expediency. Our only object is to get ahead and to get ahead in a way that will work. There is no need in laying down a pattern and never being able to get the material to fit the pattern. You have got to alter your pattern to fit the material, especially when you're working with people. A pattern is nothing but a method, and if one method doesn't work, use another method that does work, as long as you don't sacrifice the principle.[107]

The old City Board was not meeting the needs of the day. The economy of the Houston area had recovered sufficiently from the depression to support a more aggressive program. With his great faith in the Methodist system and his confidence that "things will work out eventually," Bishop Smith was apparently willing to support the "Laymen's Board," believing that corrections could be made later on. Furthermore, most of these men were his trusted personal friends.

The later restructuring of this board was a work of art in human relations. When the district superintendent, Dr. H. M. Whaling, was elected editor of the *Texas Christian Advocate*, Bishop Smith appointed the beloved elder statesman, Dr. W. F. Bryan, to the district. With the coming of Dr. Bryan, Armstrong writes, "there was an increased demand for a reorganization of the Board." He continues:

Under the wise guidance of Dr. W. F. Bryan, the District Conference adopted a new constitution in 1943, changing the membership of the Board to include the Bishop in charge, the District Superintendent, the pastor of each church in the district, and one layman from each pastoral charge plus an additional layman for each 500 members over a basic 500 in each church. . . . This Constitution also set up an Executive Committee of the Board to carry on the details of the program, composed of the Bishop, the District Superintendent, five pastors and ten laymen from the churches of the district, the officers and Executive Committee to be elected at the annual meeting of the whole Board.[108]

When the more representative and greatly enlarged board met for its organization, the members appreciatively elected Elledge as chairman of the Executive Committee. Claud B. Hamill, the wealthy oilman, was elected president of the board, and Fred J. Heyne, who had been a member of every board since 1913, "was again elected treasurer." Other distinguished laymen on the Executive Committee were Walter L. Goldston and O'Banion Williams.[109]

An increasingly frustrating problem facing the board was that of inadequate funds to purchase choice sites in new residential developments which were constantly being projected in the metropolitan area. Unless such purchases were made immediately after the opening of a development, the price of the land usually became prohibitive. Since 1937 the board had operated on a budget supported half-and-half by "askings" from the churches in the district and by private donations. In that year, the churches' share of the $6,000 budget was based on "ability to pay": 25¢ per member from the three larger churches, First, St. Paul's and Bering; 15¢ per member from Grace and St. John's; and 10¢ per member from each of the other twenty-two churches in the district. As the needs became more apparent and urgent, the churches were asked to raise an increasing amount, reaching $14,485 in 1949-50. By establishing a standard rate of one dollar per member annually, the board was receiving $29,753 from the churches in 1952-53. Although the special gifts brought the annual budget to nearly $60,000, this still was not enough money. "Almost every meeting discussed the need for more money to meet the demands of growth in the city," Armstrong writes.[110]

Meanwhile, the Houston District had grown to such size that it was divided in 1951 into two districts. Bishop Smith appointed Stanley Carter and Stewart Clendenin as the district superintendents. Dr. Clendenin explains:

Stanley took care of the education program because he was trained in that area, and I took the lead in the Board of Missions business. I told the group one night that we were so far behind that we needed right then a half million dollars to catch up. After the meeting, Mr. Bob Smith walked out with Kenneth Pope and declared, "You've got a visionary for a District Superintendent. He's as crazy as he can be!" But Bob Smith himself told me later how right I was and that I was seeing what they all eventually came to see.[111]

At the semiannual meeting of the board in October, 1951, Dr. Clendenin urged the board to raise $500,000, one half to be used as a revolving loan fund and the other half to be granted as gifts to those churches unable to repay the board. The board approved the proposal and asked the Finance Committee to submit a plan for raising such a fund. It was not until August, 1953, that Judge J. W. Mills, as chairman of the Committee on Promotion, presented a plan to the Executive Committee:

a plan to raise $500,000 in five years by selling 2,000 shares, each share to pay $10 three times a year, thus providing an extra $60,000 annually above all other Board funds for setting up new churches and helping the weaker and struggling congregations. Bishop A. Frank Smith gave strong approval to the proposal and the Executive Committee voted approval and set aside $2,500 for campaign expenses.[112]

The plan was then presented to the October meeting of the full board. Bishop Smith again spoke in favor of the proposal:

In the more than thirty years that I have lived in Houston, I have witnessed some remarkable movements and events in the civic and religious life of this vibrant, throbbing metropolis. . . . The story of the amazing expansion of the Methodist Church inspires and brings courage and satisfaction to every informed Methodist in this great city. Glorious as are past achievements, however, none have had the sweep and vision of the proposal now being made, to launch a movement and create an organization that will match the material growth of Houston with a corresponding spiritual development. . . . We are now proposing to assume that responsibility—and to make of it an opportunity and a privilege. Because I know Houston Methodism, I know it will be done.[113]

On the motion of Ben K. Bering and E. C. Scurlock, the board unanimously adopted the plan.[114] "Bishop Smith had a way of making people believe in themselves," according to Abe Pounds, conference treasurer of the Texas Conference from 1922 to 1972. "He'd get up and make them believe that they could do it. I think that's the reason the Texas Conference made such great achievement under this administration."[115]

In December the executive committee approved the name "Room-to-Grow" instead of the earlier designation "Houston Five-Year Plan" and appointed a special "Room-to-Grow" Promotion Committee: J. W. Mills, Durwood Fleming, Kenneth Pope, W. N. Blanton, Dunbar Chambers, Neal Cannon, Frank Sharp, L. L. Nelms, and the two district superintendents, Stewart Clendenin and Stanley Carter.[116] "We earmarked every bit of this 'Room-to-Grow' money for new property—church sites and parsonages—but none of it was to go for salaries or salary supplement," Dr. Clendenin explains.

When I first came on this district in 1950, the Mission Board was a very strong group within the city, but this was when it really began to boom out because we had some capital to work with. Those laymen on the Board were strictly first-class, but the one who really pushed the thing was Bishop Smith. He encouraged people to plan things, and when you came in with your proposal, he would help you refine it.[117]

"Bishop Smith always did have the idea of expanding that district board," Dr. Monroe Vivion agrees; "he always had an eye to the future. He was supportive when Stewart Clendenin and Stanley Carter were the district superintendents, always encouraging them in that kind of thing."[118] While praising the Board of Missions and Church Extension of the Houston Districts as "the strong arm of the expanding church," the *Texas Christian Advocate* declared:

The inspiration of Methodism's expansion [in Houston] is Bishop A. Frank Smith, who came as pastor to First Church, Houston, in 1922. Elected a bishop in 1930, he was assigned to the Houston area in 1934. His vision and his emphasis upon a serving church for 30 years has kept the churches, old and new, "other church" minded.[119]

The reference to Bishop Smith's having been pastor of Houston's First Methodist Church is fully appropriate in an account of his influence on that city's Board of Missions. It was during his pastorate at First Church that Frank Smith came into the lives of so many men who were shaping and would shape the future of Houston. Mention has already been made of Hines H. Baker, the first chairman of the "Laymen's Board," who was just a lawyer in the Legal Department of Humble Oil & Refining Company in the 1920s. In 1937 Baker became a director on Humble's board, and in 1948 he was elected president of the company.[120]

Walter L. Goldston, an independent oilman, had been a member of First Church during Smith's pastorate and was a close friend of the family. It was Goldston who had an elevator installed in the episcopal residence on Kirby Drive for Mrs. Smith's convenience after her heart attack in 1953.[121] A member of the board's executive committee for two terms (1943-44, 1947-48), he also served as president for two years (1944-45, 1945-46). On at least three occasions, Goldston gave sums of $10,000 to the board for various special projects.[122]

Another member of First Church in the 1920s, Frank Sharp, a real estate developer, became an active participant in the board in 1944. Within a decade, he gave a building for the Industrial Acres church (Jacinto City), built the Golden Acres church, and gave sites at Forest Oaks, Oak Forest, and Scenic Woods (Love). He also served two terms as vice-president of the board (1956-57, 1957-58).[123] "Mr. Sharp was what I'd call a good substantial churchman," Dr. Clendenin declares. "When I was superintendent of this district [Houston-West], no one was more generous in pointing to land and helping with the purchase, and lending money to struggling churches. Mr. Sharp was right along with Mr. Walter Goldston and Mr. Bob Smith, men of that caliber."[124]

Three men who had been Sunday school superintendents at First Church during Frank Smith's pastorate there became leaders in the Houston Mission Board: Fred J. Heyne, Loyal L. Nelms, and William N. Blanton. As noted earlier, Heyne was Jesse Jones's "right hand man," especially during Jones's thirteen years in Washington as head of the RFC.[125] "Loved and honored in Houston and Houston Methodism," Armstrong writes, "Fred J. Heyne's services place him in the top echelon of Methodist laymen in the city."[126] Bishop Smith deeply cherished his long friendship with Fred Heyne.[127]

Loyal L. Nelms, the president of Wessendorf-Nelms Tool Company, also enjoyed a great reputation in Houston. After serving two terms as vice-president of the board, Nelms was president during the first two years of the "Room-to-Grow" program.[128] St. Luke's Methodist Church was "organized" in the Nelmses' living room. Bishop Smith was particularly proud of this new church.[129]

W. N. ("Bill") Blanton, longtime executive director of the Houston Chamber of Commerce and a commissioner of the Port Commission beginning in 1953,[130] gave invaluable service to the Houston Board of Missions. Between Blanton and the real estate developers on the board —men like Frank Sharp and R. E. ("Bob") Smith—the board had as accurate a projection of where and when the city of Houston was growing as was available. Blanton was the first president of the board following the adoption of a new charter and bylaws in 1951. Under this new charter, the board was called "the Houston Methodist Board of Missions" and a board of directors replaced the former Executive Committee. Blanton continued to serve on this new board of directors for four years and was also a member of the special "Room-to-Grow" Promotion Committee.[131] "Bill Blanton knew Bishop Smith like few men do," Dr. Durwood Fleming says.[132]

Of all the oustanding men associated with the Houston Board of Missions, Mr. E. C. ("Eddie") Scurlock received the highest praise from Bishop W. Angie Smith:

When Frank was Bishop in Houston, he [Scurlock] said to Frank upon one occasion: "Pick out any location where you believe a Methodist Church is going to be needed, and I will buy that piece of property and hold it. And any time you want to put a Methodist Church there, no matter what the

price is by then, I will sell it to you for the original price." Now I don't
know of any Bishop anywhere who had that kind of privilege.[133]

Bishop Frank Smith also greatly appreciated Scurlock's generous support:

I married Eddie Scurlock when he couldn't afford to send his collar to the
laundry, but he has made a lot of money in the oil business. Now his chief
interest is in giving it away. I was riding along with him one day in a
private airplane, and I said: "Eddie, why don't you get a plane of your
own?" "I don't need a plane," he said, "I can borrow one whenever I need it.
Why, I could build five churches for what this plane would cost me." And
he has built half a dozen churches around here.[134]

Scurlock was a member of the Executive Committee of the Houston
Board of Missions in 1952-1953, vice-president in 1958-1959, and was
the president at the time of Bishop Smith's retirement. Beginning while
Scurlock was president, annual bus tours were organized to view the
various "Room-to-Grow" sites throughout the metropolitan area, with
the pastor and one layman from each church in the city invited to
participate.[135]

R. E. ("Bob") Smith completes the group of these men who were
so closely related to Bishop A. Frank Smith in the Houston Board of
Missions. There was a strong bond of mutual admiration between the
two. "Bob Smith is a very fine gentleman; he believes in the brotherhood of man and practices it," Bishop Smith declared.

In the early days before Bob got started in the oil business, he was a prize-
fighter. Today [1962] he's probably the wealthiest man in town and said
to be one of the fifteen richest men in America. His wife used to be one of
my Sunday School girls when I was pastor of University Church, Austin.
She devotes all of her time now to caring for the afflicted children out there
[at the hospital]. They have a lovely home but live very simply. Bob is a
very active Methodist layman. You will see him every Sunday morning
down at First Church [Houston] handing out bulletins at the door. When
Kenneth Pope was there—he was very fond of Kenneth—he said, "I stand
at the door to welcome the people as they come in, and then I stand there
to console them as they go out." That's Bob Smith![136]

According to R. A. Shepherd, who has known Bob Smith ever since
"those rough and tough days in the Mexia oil fields" in the 1920s,
"Bob Smith greatly admired Bishop Smith and gave him his friendship
and confidence."[137] Smith was a member of the Directors of the Board
of Missions for two terms, 1959-60 and 1960-61.[138]

Speaking of the Houston Mission Board and these leaders, Dr. Durwood Fleming declares, "Bishop Smith was behind the whole thing. He would make all of the important meetings and be there to give that final word of encouragement and his blessings. Then these guys would go out and work their hearts out—and give!"[139] Bishop Smith was justly proud of them: "When I came to Houston in 1922, there were eight Methodist Churches here. Now [1962] we have ninety-four. Of course, the city has expanded, but our church has more than kept pace with the population growth."[140]

14

Southwestern University

"THE COMMITTED LIFE COMES FIRST, but we cannot stop with that," Bishop A. Frank Smith declared, speaking to a nationwide radio audience on the "Methodist Hour" series.

We who call ourselves Christian cannot tell a needy world of the power of God in human life, unless and until we stand forth as Exhibit A in proof of that power. Here the Church begins, and here it stands or falls. We must also be prepared to give a "reason for the faith within us." . . . The strength of the Protestant is his right to individual choice and private judgment, [yet] without instruction the right of choice becomes a liability and private judgment becomes forlorn individualism, without balance and devoid of power. . . . There is no more pressing problem facing the Church today than this obligation to make intelligent and effective Christians of its members. . . . We must teach our people, [and] this calls for cooperation in home, Sunday School, pulpit and college.[1]

Because Bishop Smith appreciated the unique contribution of the church-related university, he gladly served on the boards of trustees of six Methodist institutions of higher education: American University, Oklahoma City University, Southern Methodist University, Southwestern University, Lon Morris College, and Scarritt College. His commitment to

287

the church-related schools is well illustrated by his role as a trustee of Southwestern University.

When Bishop Smith became a member of Southwestern's board of trustees in 1933,[2] the university faced a financial crisis. In January, 1925, the women's dormitory was destroyed by fire. Unable to raise the necessary funds for a new and larger dormitory and the purchase of additional land, the trustees were compelled to borrow $300,000.[3] As the university's historian, Professor Ralph Wood Jones, writes, "There can be no argument with the necessity for the transaction; however, during the next ten years [the indebtedness] hung as a mill-stone of ever-increasing weight around the university's neck from which it barely escaped the flood of financial disaster."[4] Although the faculty had taken a 35 percent reduction in salaries over the preceding two years, 1931 and 1932, the university's indebtedness still stood at $363,000 when Smith became a member of the board. Student enrollment was less than 300, having dropped 42 percent in five years. In the spring of 1934, when the university was least able to face it, the Southern Association of Colleges' survey committee visited the campus and recommended that Southwestern be placed on probation for lack of endowment and low teacher salaries. As if all these difficulties were not enough, several Methodist educational commissions recommended the relocation of Southwestern in San Antonio.[5]

In the spring of 1936, Bishop Smith received a suggestion that he call on Harry Carothers Wiess, then president of Humble Oil & Refining Company.[6] As the bishop recalled in a characteristically detailed manner:

I went to see Mr. Wiess. I had known him since we were boys together. In fact, his mother, Louisa Elizabeth Carothers, and my mother went to school together in Georgetown before she married Captain William Wiess of Beaumont. Captain Wiess was a trustee at Southwestern later on. So I went to see Mr. Wiess, and he said: "Yes, my mother wants to make a significant gift to Southwestern University, but I don't know if the school is secure or not. I don't want her to give it to a school that is going to go under." Well, I called W. E. Orgain of Beaumont, former chairman of the Southwestern board and a long time friend of Harry Wiess, told him we'd meet at 10 o'clock, and we went to see Harry Wiess. We told him that we thought they ought to make their gift on the condition of our paying off the debt. Then he called up their family attorney, Mr. Frank Andrews—he called him "Captain Frank." Now Frank Andrews was the son of a Baptist preacher and went to Southwestern along with my father and mother. He stood up with them, as they said in those days, when they were married. He lived in my mother's home for a while as a boy and worked for his board when he was going to school. And he had become an outstanding man here [in Houston]. Andrews, Street and Logan is still the name of the firm. "Well," he [Wiess] said, "Captain Frank tells me that he believes Southwestern University has sent more men of distinction out of Texas than any other school, not excluding the State University. When Captain Frank said that, that's enough for me. Now, I want to know, how are you going to keep the university alive?" We told him we would get out and raise the money to pay off the indebtedness.[7]

About the same time (mid-April), as part of a financial campaign for Southwestern University, two other gentlemen also called on Mr. Wiess: Dr. J. N. R. Score, former pastor of St. Paul's Methodist Church in Houston, and Dr. John W. Bergin, recently elected president of Southwestern. In a letter to Board President Dr. Claude C. Cody, Jr., Score wrote:

During the course of the conversation Mr. Wiess mentioned Mr. Frank Andrews three times, and . . . it occurred to me that doubtless he will talk to Mr. Andrews about Southwestern. . . . I believe a conference with Mr. Andrews before Mr. Wiess talks to him would be very valuable.

Dr. Bergin and I had the impression . . . that there was strong probability that as much as five or ten thousand dollars might be given on the sixty-five thousand dollar campaign, and that it was not impossible within the next few months for Mr. Wiess to perhaps assume the revised debt on the Woman's Building and name that building in honor of his father and mother.[8]

Perhaps the Smith/Orgain call was made in hopes of obtaining the larger gift from Mr. Wiess.[9] Whatever the sequence of the two visits to Mr. Wiess, the Wiess gift did materialize. On June 26, 1936, Mrs. Wiess conveyed to Mr. Andrews, as trustee, one thousand shares of Humble Oil and Refining Company stock, one thousand shares of Montgomery Ward and Company stock, and one hundred shares of Air Reduction Company stock—a total value of approximately $110,000. The conditions of the gift were stated in the trust agreement:

If Southwestern University discharges and satisfies its debt . . . generally known and referred to as the "Woman's Building Debt," and its indebtedness to faculty members and various persons . . . now estimated to be $60,000, without the use of any part of its present endowment funds or assets, and in addition thereto shall have received and have in hand new money or its equivalent in stocks or securities of bona fide and marketable paper in a sum of not less than $40,000 on or before the first day of March, 1937, the Trustee acting hereunder shall transfer and deliver to Southwestern University the stocks and securities hereby conveyed and all income therefrom; . . . to be used by said University for educational purposes only.[10]

"As soon as the agreement was formally signed," according to the university board of trustees minutes, "Bishop Smith immediately notified the Chairman of the Finance Committee, the President of the University, and the Chairman of the Board."[11] Mrs. Wiess died on July 7, less than two weeks after signing the trust agreement.

Although there was an understanding with the Wiesses[12] that there would be no public campaign to meet the terms of the gift, Bishop Smith did make the following statement in the July issue of the *Southwestern University Bulletin*:

The chief function of the Church in the field of higher education has always been realized best in the small college. All over the nation such institutions, of all denominations, have demonstrated this fact. Nowhere has any Church college more completely done the work it should do than has Southwestern University. Her past speaks for itself. And the complexities of modern life make such an institution more necessary than ever before. The future of our Methodism in Texas necessitates the maintaining of Southwestern. I know of no investment anywhere that can be more constructive or far-reaching than an investment in Southwestern University.[13]

By the beginning of 1937, Southwestern's total debt had increased to almost $500,000. A settlement of this half-million-dollar debt for only $105,000 was arranged by J. M. West, chairman of the Finance Committee, Dr. C. C. Cody, Jr., board president, Bishop John M. Moore, and Bishop Smith.[14] The Southwestern trustees still had to raise $145,000 before March 1, 1937, including the $40,000 of "new money" for endowment required by the trust agreement. This was a substantial sum for those financially tight times.

Bishop Smith took an active role in raising this $145,000. "Dr. J. W. Bergin was in my office today," Smith wrote to Dr. Score in mid-November. "We are trying to corral Mr. West into making a commitment concerning the paying of the debt at Georgetown. I am to see him tomorrow morning."[15] In early March Smith informed Score of the success of the campaign, including the "corralling" of Mr. West.

MY DEAR RUSSELL:
We have gotten over the line on the Southwestern proposition, with

several thousand dollars to spare. The formal decision is to be made on next Wednesday by the South Texas Commercial Bank, and until that time we are making no announcement. However, there is no question as to our having met the conditions of the Wiess bequest. We are all very happy over the outcome, and of course, this means a new day for the School.

. . . I went to Washington to see Mr. [Jesse] Jones and got $7,500.00. Mr. West gave me $32,500.00, and the rest was picked up here, there and yonder. We raised $85,000.00 in cash and $40,000.00 in notes for the endowment.[16]

The list of donors, although never made public,[17] should include the faculty, who had been "extremely generous in cancelling the amounts [approximately $30,000] due them by the University [when] they were given to understand that the school would from now on pay them promptly the full amounts of salaries as they accrued."[18]

By the time of the formal announcement of the Wiess gift (March 15, 1937), the value of the bequest had increased from $110,000 to $160,000.[19] In an accompanying interview, Bishop Smith stated: "Southwestern, as a result of the reception of the gift from Mrs. Wiess, is now clear of debt and has a productive endowment fund of approximately $600,000. The institution is in better financial condition than ever before in its history."[20] Ralph Wood Jones sees this "miraculous financial transformation" as the turning-point in the life of the university. "Beginning the year with a debt in excess of a half a million dollars, the school was debt free by June with a firm endowment of almost $600,000. The resurgence of the university can be dated from this time."[21] On the motion of Bishop Smith, the College of Bishops formally expressed "the hearty appreciation of the entire Church" to Mr. Wiess:

The College of Bishops of the Methodist Episcopal Church, South, in annual session in Nashville, Tennessee, has heard with much interest and gratification the full story of the generous gift to Southwestern University made by your sainted mother and yourself. It is our conviction that you made possible the saving of this noble old Institution.[22]

That Bishop Smith's role in securing the crucial Wiess gift was recognized is apparent in the letters he received at the time. Responding to a letter of congratulations from the bishop, Judge W. E. Orgain wrote:

You are entirely too generous in your conception of my part in contributing to the making of the Wiess gift and the final successful efforts to meet the terms thereof. As I have often said to Claude Cody and others, while there were many who had to do with the final result and without whom it could not have been accomplished, yet the situation never would have been, and having been, never would have been concluded without you. I think you were the factor in bringing about the gift and your determination to take advantage of it was an inspiration to all.[23]

Dr. J. W. Bergin, president of Southwestern University, also praised Bishop Smith: "Bishop, the renewed devotion of Mr. West, Judge Orgain and many others is due to your masterful ability in negotiating men. Thank you again."[24] Among those who had been invited to share in removing the university's indebtedness was Jesse H. Jones, who expressed his appreciation to his "close personal friend," Bishop Smith: "It was a pleasure to be of some small help in the very big thing you have done for [Southwestern]."[25] Having received the first of his many honorary degrees from Southwestern, Jones maintained an active interest in the university and endowed a scholarship fund for students there.[26]

Bishop Smith, on the other hand, recognized the part that Dr. J. N. R. Score had played in obtaining the Wiess gift: "I feel that your visit to Mr. Wiess and the placing in his mind of this project last spring is more responsible than any other one factor for this gift, and you will have an abiding satisfaction through the years in all that will come to Southwestern as the result of this gift."[27]

Encouraged by having met successfully the challenge of the Wiess gift, Dr. Cody and several other trustees who lived in Houston decided to complete the raising of funds for the proposed Cody Memorial Library.[28] President Bergin, in the letter of thanks to Bishop Smith quoted above, wrote:

I've been talking to Mr. Page, an outstanding architect of Austin. . . . Mr. Page asks about the plans for the Library. . . . [He] remarks "that if we had half of the money, we could build the first unit." The Library should cost around $100,000. We have $30,000. We can get $20,000 IF we could "Break Dirt" or something like that on June 8!"[29]

Bishop Smith told the story of Cody Memorial Library—a story he obviously enjoyed telling:

They [Dr. Cody and other trustees living in Houston] decided they would work out an agreement with the city of Georgetown, which had no library, and the P.W.A. Southwestern could say: "We will give you the site for it on the University campus, and then you can lease it back to us for a dollar a year for 99 years or something like that. We will put 33 or 35 thousand dollars in it and get the P.W.A. to give you the other $65,000." I went up to Washington to talk with Mr. Jesse Jones, who at that time was head of the Reconstruction Finance Corporation.[30] I sat by his desk and he called Mr. Ickes[31] and told him he would like to get this appropriation granted. And Ickes told him he wouldn't do it. I could not hear Ickes, but I could hear Jones. He and Mr. Ickes had no love for one another, absolutely none.[32] And Jones said, "Mr. Secretary, I have never asked you for anything before, but things are constantly coming across my desk that you are asking for. I have a request from you right now on my desk asking the RFC for a million dollars or more. If you do not give me this, I will not give you what you are asking for." And he hung up. He turned to me and said: "Go on back to your hotel and wait. We'll let it stew for a while."

Well, I went back to the Dodge Hotel where I always stayed, up close to the capitol. My train was to leave about 6 o'clock. About 4 the phone rang, and Mr. Jones said, "You can catch your train. We have squared it." So I came back in jubilation and told the folks about it, and we all jubilated together.[33]

Then, about a week later, they got notice that it was all off and would not be granted at all. So they said to me, "Go back up there and see what went wrong, Frank, for heaven's sake." Well, I decided I had better get in touch with Senator Morris Sheppard, whom I knew. He had been in Congress and in the Senate for a long time and had a lot of influence. I called Senator Sheppard, but they said he was in Texarkana where he lived. So I took the train to Texarkana. As I got off the train there and walked into the station, I saw Sheppard standing at the ticket window. I didn't let him see me; I just went right back and got on the train again. I gave them my pass and claimed the same berth and went on to St. Louis.

The next morning, between DeSoto and St. Louis, about thirty miles out—an hour's run in those days—I sent word in to Sheppard. He and Mrs. Sheppard had a drawing room in the same car I was in. And he bounced out in a minute: "Bishop, what can I do for you?" And I told him the story. "The whole thing is legitimate, as the City of Georgetown will tell you." "Why, of course, it's legitimate," he said. "Now, I have a Military Affairs Committee meeting in the morning, but you can see this man. If you have any trouble, let me know and I'll come by."

Well, when we got into Washington the next morning, I went over to the man's office. He was a Philadelphia lawyer, literally, one of those young fellows and a "New Dealer." And he said very positively and dogmatically, "Bishop, we are not going to grant this." And I said, "Why not?" And he waved a newspaper clipping and said, "It is our definite policy not to make grants to church institutions. This clipping says the grant has been made to

Southwestern University, and a Baptist college over in North Carolina has sent us a protest. Anyway, your name is Smith and the Mayor of Georgetown is named Smith. Is there any connection there?" "None whatsoever," I said, "except back to the time of Adam." And he said, "Well, I'm sorry, but we have rescinded the grant." Right at that moment the door popped open and in came Senator Sheppard. This fellow jumped up—nearly turned over his chair—"How are you, Senator?" Then Sheppard turned to me and said: "Bishop, I thought I'd better come by here on the way over to my committee meeting." And this fellow said, "What can I do for you, Senator?" "I just came by here to tell you to give my good friend Bishop Smith anything he wants." And he walked out the door saying, "Let me know, Bishop."

Well, this fellow said, "All right, Bishop, we'll sign the papers." And I said, "Why, you just said you couldn't do that." "Oh," he said, "Mr. Ickes says that Senator Sheppard is the most honest man he has ever known in public life, and for us to grant every request he makes without any investigation or question. Since the Senator has said to give you what you want, we'll sign the papers." And that's the way we got the library at Southwestern![34]

According to the *Williamson County Sun,* a number of persons had been working on the library project. Georgetown Mayor M. F. Smith received a long distance telephone call and three telegrams in two days' time, December 22 and 23, 1938. On the first day, a telegram came from Bishop A. Frank Smith "who was in Washington working in behalf of the project": "Allotment just granted. Matter closed. Secretary Ickes is notifying Ft. Worth today."[35] That same day the young congressman from the 10th district, Lyndon B. Johnson, called from Washington. On the twenty-third, both Texas senators—Morris Sheppard and Tom Connally—wired Mayor Smith concerning the Public Works Administration's allotment of $36,000 "for the Georgetown library project."[36] Fortunately, Georgetown had already raised its $44,000 share for the $80,000 building, because the law establishing the PWA required that actual construction on all PWA projects be under way by January 1, 1939. City officials were hard pressed to meet the deadline, but Mayor Smith broke ground for Cody Memorial Library on Saturday morning, December 31, at 10:00 A.M., assisted by Dr. J. C. Godbey, Southwestern professor and city alderman, and I. J. McCook, business manager for the university. Construction of the foundation began that afternoon.[37]

In October—while the furniture and fixtures were being installed in the completed library building—the university honored Bishop and Mrs. Smith at its "Dinner of the Golden Bowl," an annual social event honoring prominent alumni.[38] Bishop Smith gave the major address at the formal opening of Cody Memorial Library on November 26, 1939. The City Council and the University joined to make this a special occasion.[39]

On February 11, 1942, the board of trustees of Southwestern University met in Georgetown to receive the unanimous recommendation of its nominating committee that Dr. John Nelson Russell Score be elected president of the university to succeed retiring Dr. J. W. Bergin.[40] Although Bishop Smith had not been a member of the six-man selection committee,[41] he worked for his close friend's nomination, as Smith's daily journal and the correspondence between the two men imply.[42] When Score learned that he was being considered by the committee, he wrote to Smith concerning the attitude of Dr. Claude Carr Cody, Jr., chairman of the board at Southwestern. Because of his deep respect and affection for Dr. Cody, Score did not think he should accept the position unless Cody was favorable.[43] Smith replied:

I have just returned home and have not seen Dr. Cody. I expect to see him at once. . . . I will let you know my impression as to his attitude when I talk with him. I have a profound conviction as to what ought to be done at Southwestern, and I shall be keenly disappointed if it does not work out in that fashion.[44]

Early in January, Bishop Smith noted in his daily journal: "Had lunch with Cody at the Empire Room. I talked to him about Score for the Presidency of Southwestern. He is not particularly enthusiastic."[45] After two more meetings with Cody failed to gain his active support, Smith called Dr. Score. "I told him," he wrote in his journal, "he should take the place if elected, regardless of Claude—Cody will fall in line after Score gets on the ground."[46]

In the meantime, the trustees of Central College in Fayette, Missouri, had begun serious discussions with Dr. Score about becoming their president. "Score called me this morning," Smith noted in his journal. "He is just back from meeting the Trustees Committee of Central College. They want him to take the job and he is much interested. It will be a shame to lose him from Southwestern—if we do." The bishop had no intention of losing. The next day he went to see two other members of the Southwestern committee: Judge Tom McCullough in Dallas and Dr. Paul Quillian, pastor of First Church, Houston. "They will vote for Score," he wrote triumphantly.[47]

Dr. Score was unanimously elected. His words in a letter to Frank Smith show that he recognized the role that Smith had played:

My dear Frank: First of all, let me thank you for your presence and for what you said and did yesterday at Georgetown. You got away without my seeing you and having the privilege of saying to you in person what is so inadequate in a letter. I know something of what you did yesterday and through the weeks that have passed, and I do appreciate it and hope you will never have reason to feel that you were mistaken in what you have said and done.[48]

Having assisted in the selection of Dr. Score, Bishop Smith actively supported the new president and shared in the guidance of his alma mater. He never missed an opportunity to assure Score of Dr. Cody's growing confidence in him. "I have seen Claude since the meeting," he wrote, "and he is highly pleased. The reaction I get on all sides is enthusiastic."[49] A few months later, Smith sent another letter: "Saw Claude last nite. He remarked again that 'Score is doing a swell job.' "[50] Bishop Smith was virtually a third power teamed with the president and the board chairman, as a letter from Dr. Cody to Score indicates: "Would it be convenient for you to come to Houston February 27 for the purpose of discussing the finances of Southwestern with Bishop Smith and myself? At this meeting we could decide what to do, how to do it and what each one of us would attempt to do."[51] When Dr. Score sought Bishop Smith's assistance in countering the dwindling of student enrollment caused by World War II, Smith replied, "I am, of course, eager to help in any plan that will get the names of the students going away to college. If a letter to each pastor is the best plan, I will gladly send such a letter."[52] Within a month Bishop Smith had written every pastor in his episcopal area:

This is a testing time for the church and its institutions, and especially for the church college. The income from endowments is down and student bodies are greatly reduced because of war conditions. . . . Methodism has maintained colleges and universities from her beginning, and the long and honorable history of those institutions demands the respect and support of our people. Not only the church itself, but civilization today and tomorrow needs the influence of the church and of religion in the field of higher education.

I will appreciate it if you will read this letter to your people and lay this matter upon their hearts. Then upon the enclosed card, write the names of the boys and girls who intend to go to college next year. . . . *It is my purpose to write a short letter to every student whose name is sent to me,* asking him or her to consider one of our church colleges.

Be assured of my appreciation and that of our colleges, for your co-operation.[53]

President Score and Bishop Smith were not always successful in their efforts on behalf of Southwestern University. During the spring and summer of 1942 they spent many hours seeking to persuade Dr. Charles H. Harris of Fort Worth to relate his proposed school for nurses to Southwestern. Although both men were hopeful, these endeavors were ultimately fruitless.[54]

The formal ceremonies for the inauguration of Dr. Score as the tenth president of Southwestern University took place on October 6, 1942. The *Williamson County Sun* called the occasion "almost pageantry in its brilliance and splendor."[55] Bishop Smith recorded his delight over the events of the day:

Bess and I drove to Georgetown early this morning [from Austin] for the Inauguration of J. N. R. Score to the presidency of Southwestern University. A perfect day—and a most representative crowd. I presided at the service held in the new gymnasium. Bishops Holt, Selecman and Boaz were in the service. Gov. Stevenson was present. Score made a great address. He has every prospect of a great administration. . . . We met many old friends, and it was a happy occasion.[56]

Knowing that Dr. Score had devoted his scholarship and liturgical skills to the preparation of the text for the inaugural ceremony, Frank Smith sent his congratulations: "My dear Russell: The inauguration was flawless."[57] "If the Inauguration was flawless," Score replied, "it was because you were presiding. You did it nobly. You know, of course, how much I appreciate the fact that you and Bessie were here."[58]

Nevertheless, there was one flaw in the ceremony. At the conclusion of the singing of the "Alma Mater," the band director—instead of waiting for Bishop Smith to give the benediction—immediately began leading the University Band in the recessional march. "Poor Tom Johnson," Score explained, "was distressed beyond measure about not letting you say the benediction. That was about his last official act for Southwestern, as he has been called to the Army."[59] Angie Smith could not allow such an opportunity for a joke at Frank's expense to pass. As Score reported to Frank, "Angie tried to console me about Tom Johnson's not letting you give the benediction. He did so by saying that the look on your face was worth the confusion—that you looked as though the Second Coming had arrived and you had been left."[60]

In his Inaugural Address, Dr. Score called for a number of new buildings for the university: "a Chapel, a Student Union Building, a University Auditorium, a new Science Building, a new Boys' Dormitory, and other buildings to house the necessary life of a modern university."[61] Bishop A. Frank Smith played a significant role in bringing each of these proposed facilities into being. The chapel required the most persistent efforts and imaginative measures, primarily because of the extreme limitations imposed by wartime conditions and the related inflation. When completed in 1950, the chapel was not only the first major building to be constructed at Southwestern in a decade,[62] but also the keystone of the master plan for the future campus. Of greater significance, the chapel served as the stimulus for a series of major gifts to the university.

Shortly after the announcement of his election as president of Southwestern University, Dr. Score received a note of congratulation from Mrs. J. J. Perkins, unconsciously hinting at great things to come.

So many of your friends have told me that you will make Southwestern a wonderful president. . . . I had classes under Bishop Mouzon, Dr. Barcus, Dr. Cody, etc. When I attended graduating exercises last June, the spirits of all those men permeated the *old worn-out Chapel*. I still think of it as Chapel, for it was there we listened to their religious teachings every morning. I said to myself, . . . "There will always be a Southwestern."

I want you and Mrs. Score to know that I still have a deep feeling and interest in the school and my thoughts and prayers are with you.

Sincerely,

LOIS PERKINS[63]

Conversations with Mr. and Mrs. Perkins continued through the spring and summer. By early fall, Dr. Score was able to inform Dr. Cody:

The matter of a gift from Mr. and Mrs. J. J. Perkins seems to be coming to a head rapidly. . . . Mrs. Perkins has told Bishop Smith, Dr. Paul Martin [her pastor], Mrs. Score and myself that she was going to do something for Southwestern right away. . . . I have an engagement with them [in] November.[64]

As Mrs. Perkins recalls the origin of their gift to Southwestern, she and Mr. Perkins had gone to Georgetown for some occasion at which Bishop Smith was to speak:

Frank was up preaching in the old chapel, and Bess and I were sitting together. We got to laughing because the old pew shook every time we moved. It would go like this and then like that. We really couldn't move, and we said, "This seat is going to fall down with us before Frank gets through preaching!" Well, when my husband and I were coming home, I told him about the old seats and how it needed to be done over. Then I said, "Joe, I wish they had a nice chapel at Southwestern. It's a shame they don't have a place to have these meetings." Now my husband was a man of very few words, and he didn't say anything. But that night when we got home, he called Dr. Score and said, "Dr. Score, what do you need more than anything else down there?" And Dr. Score said, "We need a chapel, Mr. Perkins." And my husband said, "Well, get an architect who knows his business, and we will give you the money." Just like that! That's the way my husband did things.[65]

The correspondence between Dr. Score and Bishop Smith discloses the significance of Smith's help in securing the Perkinses' gift. In a lengthy letter dated October 28, Score wrote in part:

My dear Frank: I have been thinking about the proposal to be made to our friends whom you are going to see Friday. . . . Frankly, I do not know what to say to you and am, therefore, going to think out loud, relying—as I have these past sixteen years—on your ability to see the other side of the question and on your good judgment. . . . While I think endowments are our greatest need at the present time, I am also of the opinion that our friends would be less interested in such a gift than they would be in building some new building. . . . I know that the good lady involved is more interested in a Chapel than in anything else, and my opinion is that is what we should ask for at the present time.[66]

Eventually, after Dr. Score had been to see the Perkinses again, the Wichita Falls philanthropists declared their intentions. As Bishop Smith wrote in his journal: "A letter from Score this afternoon brought word that Mr. and Mrs. Perkins will give $75,000 for a Chapel in Georgetown. Bess and I called the Perkinses tonight and talked to them about their gift. They are certainly doing a lot of good with their money."[67] Amid the rejoicing, however, Bishop Smith became aware of a difference of opinion between Dr. Score and Mr. Perkins. Mr. Perkins stated his position in a letter to Smith dated November 23:

When Dr. Score mentioned the question of a Chapel, he said it would cost anywhere from $125,000 to $200,000. . . . I told him that $75,000 was the maximum we would want to put into this building and furnishings. With the native stone easily available, I believe that a very acceptable building could be put up for a maximum of $60,000, leaving $15,000 for an organ and furnishings.[68]

On the basis of his experience in building four churches—"ranging in price from $250,000 to $900,000"[69]—Score had estimated the cost of the desired building at $200,000. "I honestly believe," he wrote to Smith,

that we can build the Chapel we need for about $125,000. This would reserve $40,000 for the organ and other furnishings and $35,000 as a permanent endowment fund for the building. While the income of this money would provide less than the normal scale of depreciation, I believe it would be sufficient to care for the building. . . . We could very easily go out of business if we spent our endowment income in keeping up buildings given to us.[70]

Enclosing a copy of Mr. Perkins's letter and a copy of his reply, Dr. Score wrote again to Bishop Smith, "I believe this is a good beginning and that *you can handle it so that we will get the money we need for this Chapel.* I feel that I have gone about as far as I can go in the matter."[71]

Knowing Score and Perkins as well as he did, Bishop Smith believed that he could serve as a mediator, and he endeavored to keep the two men in conversation until something acceptable to both could be worked out.[72] In a letter to Score, Smith sketched his role in the continuing dialogue:

The best approach on the money matter is to see that they [the Perkinses] visualize the entire set up and then realize that $75,000 cannot do the job. When I see them next Thursday, I will talk about what a fine thing they have done. . . . Fortunately, you cannot build for some time, and we will be able to have time to [talk] with them.[73]

Differences also developed over the proposed manner of formal announcement of the Perkinses' gift. As Mr. Perkins wrote to both Bishop Smith and Dr. Score, "You have our entire permission to make this announcement in any way you want to make it at any time you want to make it—just so you do not place us in the center of the proposition. Neither of us care for the publicity that would attend this kind of occasion."[74] "He means every word of this," Smith advised Score, "but the wise thing to do is to get them to Georgetown if at all possible for an announcement dinner." With a bit of wartime humor, he added, "The only flaw is that gas rationing may prevent anyone from coming, the Perkinses included."[75]

In response to the persistent efforts of Dr. Score and Bishop Smith, Mr. and Mrs. Perkins finally agreed to come to the campus for an announcement banquet. The event would be publicized, in accord with the Perkinses' request, as the Annual Williamson County Southwestern Ex-Students Association Banquet, and Bishop Smith was featured as the speaker of the evening.[76]

On Tuesday, April 13, 1943, Bishop Smith wrote in his journal:

Bess and I drove to Georgetown today. . . . I never have seen the bluebonnets as thick nor as rich in color as they are this year. At seven o'clock there was a banquet in the Woman's Building honoring Mr. and Mrs. J. J. Perkins who announced a gift of $75,000 with which to erect Lois Craddock Perkins Chapel on the campus. I made the main speech. This was the sixth time I have spoken when the Perkinses have made a gift to a Methodist institution. Saw many old friends after dinner.[77]

According to a newspaper account, Bishop Smith "paid high tribute to Mr. and Mrs. Perkins by pointing out that this is one in a long and impressive list of gifts they have made to Texas Methodism. Commenting on the history of Southwestern, Bishop Smith said: 'This Chapel is significant of the things for which this institution stands.' "[78]

In the fall of 1943 the faculty and trustees of Southwestern University sought to express their great appreciation for Mr. and Mrs. Perkins by electing them to receive honorary degrees. Although Mr. Perkins was highly pleased at such an honor for his wife, he was clearly upset about the whole idea in relation to himself.[79] Pointing out that Bishop Smith had spoken on behalf of the proposal in the board of trustees meeting, Score urged Mr. Perkins to "speak to Frank Smith about the matter before making your final decision."[80] Score also appealed directly to Bishop Smith for help: "I don't know [Mr. Perkins] well enough to know exactly how to proceed, and I know you do."[81] "I think you have written Mr. Perkins a fine letter," Smith reassured Dr. Score, "and I would just go ahead upon the assumption that he will be there to receive his degree. I fully expected him to say what he has said, but I also fully expect him to show up when the time comes. I am enclosing a copy of my letter to Mr. Perkins."[82]

Bishop Smith's soothing letter to Mr. Perkins is a classic example of his ability in personal relationships.

My Dear Brother Joe:

I know exactly how you feel about the matter of your honorary degree, but I am very clear in my mind to the effect that you should by all means accept this degree. In the first place, you are in every way worthy of the distinction. Such a degree is granted in recognition of high character and of outstanding service to one's fellowman. I have not known at any time a worthier recipient of such a degree than are you.

In the second place, it will mean much to Texas Methodism for you to receive this degree. . . . For you to receive this recognition at the hands of an Institution of the Church which you have loved and served so well through these many years, will bring great satisfaction to all our people.

In the third place, it will mean much to Southwestern University for you to receive this degree. . . . I expect to be on hand to see you receive your degree next June. And I am certain in advance that no degree ever presented by that great old Institution will ever be received with more grace or worn with more humility and distinction than the degree granted to you.

With every good wish, I am

Cordially yours,
A. Frank Smith[83]

On June 19, 1944, during the commencement exercises, Southwestern University conferred the honorary Doctor of Humane Letters degree upon Mr. and Mrs. J. J. Perkins.[84] Mr. Perkins still felt that his degree was "a misfit." "No one, however, could attend a service such as this and not become thrilled over it," he declared to Dr. Score.[85]

Mrs. Perkins remembers an incident of a completely different nature that occurred during the commencement ceremonies:

Mr. Perkins and I, along with the others receiving honorary degrees, were seated on the stage of the old Chapel with Dr. Cody and Bishop Angie Smith. I was sitting over here, Dr. Cody [next], and then Angie. Frank was up giving the commencement address, and Dr. Cody went to sleep. I had to sit just way over this way to keep him from falling. Someone wrote Angie a note that said, "Wake up Dr. Cody." And Angie wrote back, "Let Frank wake him up, he put him to sleep."[86]

Although the Perkinses completed their pledge of $75,000 for the new chapel at Southwestern University in December, 1944,[87] no one could be certain when actual construction would begin. While wartime building restrictions were lifted at the end of the war in 1945, wartime inflation continued unabated. The cost of construction skyrocketed. Bishop Smith discussed these problems with Mr. Perkins early in May, 1948, during the sessions of the General Conference held in Boston.

Apparently Dr. Score and Bishop Smith had agreed that they must ask the Perkinses for another $75,000 if there was to be any hope for a chapel.[88] On Sunday, May 16, Smith made the following entry in his daily journal:

Russell Score called from Georgetown tonite to say that Mr. J. J. Perkins had written him that he would give $75,000 in addition to his first gift of that amount to insure the building of the Lois Perkins Chapel at once on the Southwestern campus. I talked to Mr. Perkins about this at Boston—at first [he was] luke warm—he later became enthusiastic. This building will mark a new day in the history of S.U.[89]

The "new day" was, however, farther away than it appeared. When bids were received, they ranged from a low of $329,000 to $400,000![90] The architect was sent back to his drawing board to see what cuts could be made to reduce the cost substantially.

Of greater immediate concern to Bishop Smith was Mr. Perkins's complaint, "Somehow or other I cannot hit it off too well with Dr. Score. I presume I am more to blame than he is."[91] Smith believed that the relationship between Mr. Perkins and Dr. Score was vital to the future of Southwestern University. Although he knew both men to be strong-minded, distinctive individuals, he sought to keep them working together. These men were his close friends, and he drew upon his exceptional perception of each to bring them into mutual understanding. "I have been rather closely associated with Dr. Score for twenty-five years," he wrote to "Brother Joe," "and I long ago came to a definite conclusion about him."

He is as capable a man, as brainy and as versatile a man as I have ever known. He has an indomitable will and determination. . . . Score is a brilliant fellow, and a very demanding person. . . . I listen to what he has to say, but I do my own thinking. When one says "yes" or "no" to him, that ends it. The things he wants done are worthy; he is a remarkable administrator and deeply consecrated. He is going to make Southwestern the outstanding small college in Methodism. . . . Southwestern is destined to become a very remarkable school, especially as a feeder for Perkins School of Theology, and I believe the Lois Craddock Perkins Chapel will mark a turning point for that school as the Perkins gift at S.M.U. did in Dallas.[92]

When the final round of bids was opened on August 26, 1949, the lowest was $187,175—or $35,175 more than the "final" amount given by the Perkinses.[93] In the meantime, Dr. Score had entered the Methodist Hospital in Houston with a heart condition.[94] On August 27 Bishop Smith wrote the following entry in his daily journal: "Went to see Score tonite. He & Dr. Cody want me to go to Wichita Falls to see the Perkinses about the Chapel situation at S.U. Fruitless errand, I fear." Succeeding entries tell the story:

Thursday, September 1, 1949: Drove to Wichita Falls this morn. Went to Mr. Perkins' office. . . . Told Mr. Perkins the Chapel at S.U. cannot be built with money he gave. Must have $50,000 more. He manifested interest. I believe he will do something eventually. . . .

Monday, September 5, 1949: Mr. Perkins called this morning & said he would give the extra money to build Chapel, provided the University would finish [sic] it. Also, provided he did not have to give more than $40,000 extra. I called Score & Cody—then Perkins. He will let me know in a day or two what he will do exactly.

Wednesday, September 7, 1949: Letter from Perkins this morn says he will give $39,000 more & finish Chapel at S.U.—great news.[95]

This last entry leaves a great deal unsaid. As a matter of fact, Mr. Perkins wrote *four* letters to Bishop Smith on September 6. One, a three-page businesslike document, is addressed to Dr. Score and to Bishop Smith:

GENTLEMEN:
 . . . Bishop Smith was here the other day and we were talking things out and it looks like you will never be able to finish the chapel unless we put a little more money into it. . . . If we put up this extra $39,000 we would put it up with the definite agreement and understanding that Southwestern would take care of the furnishings, including organ, pews, etc., in whatever way you might deem expedient and proper. I am sure these furnishings would be furnished by individuals and not by the University itself. . . . May I say that . . . what I have agreed to do in this letter is more of a sacrifice than any [contribution] which I have undertaken. . . .
                                          Yours very sincerely,
                                          J. J. PERKINS[96]

Bishop Smith's reply is a remarkable document, illustrating both his frankness and his diplomacy:

MY DEAR BROTHER JOE:
 . . . You are a marvel in expressing yourself forcefully and logically, and with a minimum of words. This letter leaves no doubt as to your feelings. . . .

I have worked rather closely with you and Lois for a good many years. I have never known you to be arbitrary on anything; you have always sought the judgment of all concerned before making your decisions on any matter. . . .

I can only repeat what I said to both of you yesterday [by telephone] about your Southwestern proposal. It is wonderful. No building has been erected there for ten years. The building of the Chapel will bring new life to the Institution, and it will be a lovely structure, thoroughly representative of the name it will bear. . . .

Southwestern is . . . in the best shape of any small college within the bounds of the former M. E. Church, South, as to size of student body, standing of the institution, and future prospects. The largest life service group in any college in Methodism is there, and this school will always be the chief feeder for Perkins School of Theology. . . .

Our love to you all,
A. FRANK SMITH[97]

A week later the bishop was traveling from Philadelphia to St. Louis, but his mind was on the Perkinses and Dr. Score. He wrote to his friend:

Mr. Perkins has sent me copies of his letters to you & Claude [Cody], & I have had two letters from Mrs. Perkins written within the past week. You will not think me presumptuous in urging the extreme desirability of sending Mr. Perkins everything you have on the Chapel building prospect—& if you can think of anything to ask his advice about, so much the better. He will tell you to exercise your own judgment, but to be asked will please him. Tell him every detail of your contract, etc. . . .

Do what the doctors say. And you know a lot of us are knocking daily at the door of that Great Physician.[98]

September 21 and 22, 1949, were historic days for Southwestern University. On Wednesday, the twenty-first, the contract was signed for the construction of the Lois Craddock Perkins Chapel. Since Dr. Score was unable to leave his bed, the signing took place in the President's Home. As Score wrote to Mr. Perkins:

We signed the contract yesterday in due and ancient form, the architect, the University attorney, Dr. McCook the Business Manager, and the contractor coming to my bedroom. . . . Tell Mrs. Perkins that they are meeting this morning in the Chapel she remembers so well and will march in a body to the site and have the ground breaking ceremony.[99]

Acting in behalf of her husband, Mrs. Score turned the first shovel of dirt at the festivities.[100]

Four days later, as if he had denied death until the chapel was be-gun, Dr. Score died.[101] "He was my dearest friend," Frank Smith wrote in his daily journal. "Bess and I will drive up tomorrow. I have the funeral. Last year at this time Paul [Quillian] and Russell were here—now they are both gone—who is next?"[102] At four o'clock the following afternoon, reading the Methodist Ritual that Dr. Score had helped revise, Bishop Smith led the last rites for his longtime friend in the sanctuary of the First Methodist Church in Georgetown.[103]

As Bishop Smith had assured Mr. and Mrs. Perkins, the public an-nouncement of their gift to Southwestern University and plans for building the new chapel did appear to influence other philanthropists to make generous contributions to the school. The bishop informed Mr. Perkins of one such major gift in the fall of 1948:

Perhaps Dr. Score told you of the anonymous gift of a large block of oil stock from a former student of Southwestern, a gift that will run above a hundred thousand dollars. The gift was made through the man's attorney [who] said that the man had refused to give to Southwestern in the past and that he had made this gift and would make others because he had become convinced by recent happenings that Southwestern was on sound ground financially. My prediction is that when the Chapel begins to go up other large gifts will be made, and the ball will begin to roll.[104]

Even with the momentum of the Perkinses' gift, significant donations did not materialize without effort. Bishop Smith's correspondence with President Score discloses the kind of cooperation they developed. In mid-July, 1945, for instance, Smith had given Score a progress report on his activities. "I still have high hopes about the matter I am working on here in Houston," he wrote. "It is something that cannot be rushed, but I think [it] is in good shape at this stage of the game. When the proper time arrives, I will have you pay a personal visit to the brother con-cerned."[105]

When the financial campaign "for a greater Southwestern" was launched, Bishop Smith issued a formal statement for publicity purposes:

No more significant event has ever taken place in Texas Methodism than the launching of this campaign. Southwestern holds a place unique in the affec-tion of and [in] service rendered to Southern Methodism. Never has its des-tiny been so secure and its future so radiant as today. . . . As an alumnus and a bishop in Texas, I pledge my undivided support to you and Southwestern.[106]

Bishop Smith's extensive personal relationships were a great asset. In a letter congratulating Dr. Score for "a most significant contribution" from Mr. Will E. Orgain, Smith commented: "His family and my family are intermarried, and we have known one another since early boyhood. He talks freely to me about his desires and purposes."[107] "For goodness sakes," Score replied, "is there any family in Texas besides mine with which you are not connected? You and Bessie are the beatinest people I ever saw. You are related to everybody either by blood, or by marriage, or else you went to school with them, or as a final possibility you know some dirt about them."[108]

Bishop Smith's friendship with Jesse H. Jones proved to be of value to Southwestern University on more than one occasion.[109] In the spring of 1945, Dr. Score went to Washington to talk to Mr. Jones about Southwestern's Navy Unit. "Mr. Jones was very helpful," Score reported to Smith. "I spent more than two hours with him. He mentioned, by the way, that he had received a lovely letter from you, and with a kind of catch in his voice he said, 'Brother Score, the Bishop will never know how I appreciated it.' And then he said, 'You know, I think he is one of our biggest men.' "[110] Several months later, while in Washington for a meeting of the Chaplains' Commission, Bishop Smith talked with Mr. Jones about contributing to the "Campaign for a Greater Southwestern."[111] After returning to Houston, Smith informed Score that Jones was "thinking in terms of doing *now* some things that we discussed together when I saw him in Washington."[112] In accord with his promise, Jones established the Jesse H. Jones and Mary Gibbs Jones Scholarships.[113] Recognizing Bishop Smith's role in these and other gifts to Southwestern, Dr. Claude C. Cody, Jr., longtime chairman of Southwestern's trustees, wrote to Smith, "Your continued interest, loyalty and service to Southwestern University through the years has been its most valuable asset. You have done things for the University that no one else could have done, not once but many times."[114]

Perhaps the most significant part of the financial foundation that President Score laid for Southwestern University was the McManus gift. In May, 1949, Fred McManus, a personal friend of Dr. Score, proposed to sell his W-K-M Company—a Houston firm valued at $5 million— to Southwestern and four other institutions:

The sale was to be accomplished without any investment of funds by the five beneficiaries: payments for stock purchases were to be made from annual profits at the rate of 70 per cent until the stock was paid out. Thereafter, the disposition of the company or its assets would be the concern of the new owners.[115]

When Bishop Smith first heard of this proposal, he was fearful that it might be "one of those 'evade taxes' propositions."[116] Three of the institutions declined to participate; but Southwestern officials consulted with the Bureau of Internal Revenue and were assured of the complete legality of the matter. As in the instance of the contract for the Perkins Chapel construction, the papers for the W-K-M transaction were brought to Dr. Score's bedside for his signature less than a week before his death. When the company was sold in 1955, Southwestern University received more than three million dollars for permanent endowment.[117]

Bishop Smith's involvement in Southwestern's development did not decrease after Dr. Score's death. Within a week of the board's appointment of Dr. William C. Finch[118] as acting president, Smith assured the former administrative assistant of his full support: "Dear Bill:—I am delighted over your taking the post of acting President. I want to talk with you as soon as possible about several things. . . . I hope you can get to Wichita Falls before long for a visit with the Perkins. . . . Please command me whenever and wherever I can help you in any fashion."[119]

The Lois Perkins Chapel was dedicated on November 13, 1950, with Bishop A. Frank Smith delivering the dedicatory address.[120] Paying tribute to Mr. and Mrs. Perkins, Bishop Smith said, "A place of worship justifies the right to believe. This chapel is a symbol representing Mr. and Mrs. Perkins' sense of duty, stewardship and love for God and one's fellowman."[121]

In characteristic fashion, Bishop Smith wrote a letter to the Perkinses expressing his personal appreciation to them and stating his views on the significance of their gift:

My Dear Lois and Bro. Joe:—Without delay I must say to you again that the dedication of the Lois Perkins Chapel was the outstanding event in the entire history of Southwestern University—and your presence there and participation in the program made the occasion perfect. . . .

The Chapel is beautiful and it will henceforth be the heart of the University. Every function will be held there and every student will be in it for Chapel each week. . . . The Chapel will be the hub about which the rest of the campus will revolve. . . . It is a wonderful thing for the Perkins name to be on that campus and especially as the Lois Perkins Chapel. . . .

Love to all,
A. FRANK SMITH[122]

The Perkins family has continued its interest in Southwestern University. In 1951, Mr. and Mrs. Charles Prothro gave the stained glass windows in the nave of the Lois Perkins Chapel which celebrate the "Protestant Evangelical heritage" of the university.[123] Three years later, Mr. and Mrs. Perkins gave a three-manual Aeolian-Skinner organ for the chapel.[124]

Another major building on the Southwestern campus that was funded during Dr. Score's administration, though it was not built until 1954, is the Fondren Science Hall. In early February, 1946, when Mrs. Walter W. Fondren announced her gift of a science building to Southern Methodist University, Dr. Score wrote to Bishop Smith: "I rejoice with you, Umphrey Lee and with Southern Methodist University in Mrs. Fondren's gift. If you will help me now with Mrs. Fondren, I feel that we have an excellent chance to get her to duplicate her gift here."[125] That the combined efforts of Dr. Score and Bishop Smith were successful is confirmed by a brief but dramatic notation in Smith's daily journal: "Talked to Mrs. Fondren. She has made [a] $500,000 gift to Southwestern for a Science Building."[126] Mrs. Fondren's gift was in the form of a stock-loan program requiring a number of years for maturity, unfortunately denying Dr. Score the satisfaction of seeing the impressive three-story white limestone structure.[127]

Dr. William C. Finch could not draw upon the close relationships of a prominent pastor like Dr. Score, but Bishop Smith worked with Southwestern's new president to overcome this disadvantage.[128] During an interval between ministers at St. Paul's Church in Houston, for example, Bishop Smith arranged for President-elect Finch to be guest preacher for that distinguished congregation of which Mrs. Fondren was a member.[129] Of even greater significance, when Dr. Finch was having difficulty persuading a reluctant Mrs. Fondren to attend the dedication ceremonies of the Fondren Science Hall,[130] Bishop Smith responded to his appeal for assistance as follows: "Dear Bill:—I saw Mrs. Fondren in Dallas last Friday. She told me she didn't know whether she would be in Georgetown on the 17th or not. I told her it would be an outrage if she were not there and that she had to come. She later told me for you and me to arrange the program. I think she will be there."[131]

Four days later Finch reported a completely changed situation: "I called Mrs. Fondren and had a very pleasant visit with her over the phone, the most pleasant in two years. . . . I appreciate more than I can say your helpfulness with Mrs. Fondren. She indicated she will drive up Monday morning." Requesting that Bishop Smith make the formal presentation of Mrs. Fondren at the dedication ceremony, Dr. Finch predicted, "I am sure you will say in a manner as no one else can, the things that need to be said concerning Mrs. Fondren and her support of Southwestern and the other Methodist institutions and years of dedicated stewardship which she and her husband so well represent."[132]

Mrs. Fondren did attend the dedication ceremonies on May 17, and —as Bishop Smith later reported—she was "highly pleased with . . . the program, and the attention that was paid to her."[133] Bishop Smith played a large part in focusing attention on Mrs. Fondren: he took twenty-nine minutes to introduce her! "It was an exciting introduction," Bishop Kenneth Copeland remembers, "and nobody was bored with that twenty-nine minutes."[134]

In accord with Mrs. Fondren's wishes, three plaques were placed in the building in appreciation for those who had enabled her to make this gift to Southwestern: Walter W. Fondren, her husband, who was one of the founders of the Humble Company; Dr. J. N. R. Score, who had been their pastor in Houston and was president at the time of her decision to make the gift; and Bishop and Mrs. A. Frank Smith, her dear friends, who were alumni of the university.[135]

Although they were included in the plans for "a Greater Southwestern" drawn up during Dr. Score's presidency, three other buildings of major significance to the university are credited to Dr. Finch's administration: the Alma Thomas Fine Arts Center, the Martin Ruter Dormitory, and the Bishops' Memorial Union. The role that Bishop Smith played in relation to each of these capital gifts is disclosed in his correspondence with President Finch.

In March, 1950, while he was still "acting president," Dr. Finch sought the assistance of Bishop Smith in nurturing the interest of a potential donor in Austin. "Through the good offices of Ted Richardson, my former student and our graduate," Finch explained, "I have been cultivating Mrs. Alma Thomas who is a member of Mr. Richardson's church." After sketching the pertinent developments to date, Finch continued,

Ted feels that you have a tremendous influence with Mrs. Thomas and that she will be guided in her giving by your advice and suggestions. I am wondering if you would be willing to let me arrange a luncheon or some other meeting with Mrs. Thomas for the two of us and that together, we might talk to her concerning Southwestern and her relationship to it.[136]

Bishop Smith responded enthusiastically to Dr. Finch's appeal, but he recommended a more cautious approach:

I have a feeling that . . . Mrs. Thomas may be a possible Patron Saint for Southwestern. . . . I believe it will be better for you to proceed a little further with Mrs. Thomas alone. . . . I shall make it a point to see her. Let us keep our approach coordinated, so that each may supplement the other and toward a common end. . . . Keep me informed as to anything I may do at any time to help out anywhere. I am eager to be of service.[137]

These cooperative efforts were eventually successful; the following January Mrs. Thomas established the Alma Thomas Foundation for the School of Fine Arts. "This is a gift of mineral rights which have been producing twenty to twenty-four thousand dollars a year," Dr. Finch informed Bishop Smith. "I expect that it will be the equivalent of a quarter to a half million dollar gift to the University . . . assuring the future of our growing School of Fine Arts."[138]

In the meantime, the inadequacy of men's housing at the university was becoming a critical problem. "We are losing students each year at Southwestern because our dormitory facilities are not attractive enough," Dr. Finch declared to Bishop Smith. Since they were having no success in persuading any of their prospective donors to give a men's dormitory, Finch sought the bishop's support in asking the annual conferences of Texas Methodism to raise a million dollars to be shared by the Wesley Foundations and the Methodist colleges in the state. "While I am not at all unaware of the many demands on you of other interests," Finch wrote, "I do not feel that I over-exaggerate the part that I know you could have in helping us here at Southwestern."[139] The Southwest Texas, Texas, and Central Texas Conferences soon joined in a cooperative campaign, pledging a minimum of $250,000 for the proposed Martin Ruter Dormitory.[140]

Having the funds for the construction of the two buildings in hand enabled the university to obtain more favorable bids. With understandable pride, Dr. Finch wrote to Bishop Smith, "We will sign contracts for the Alma Thomas Fine Arts Center and the Martin Ruter Dormitory tomorrow at eleven o'clock, with the sum . . . being approximately

$750,000, the largest construction figure in the history of the University."[141] Dr. Finch gratefully acknowledged Bishop Smith's assistance in attaining these goals. In the midst of this particular campaign, for example, he wrote to Smith, "I certainly want to say to you how much I have appreciated your support of the University and how heavily I count on the weight of your influence and the wisdom of your judgment in the development of the program here at the University."[142]

Bishop Smith's contribution to the Bishops' Memorial Union was of a different nature. This half-million-dollar building was dedicated to the six Methodist bishops who had been associated with Southwestern University as students or faculty: Sam R. Hay, '89; H. A. Boaz, '07; A. Frank Smith, '12; W. Angie Smith, '17; H. Bascom Watts, '13; and Edwin D. Mouzon, who taught theology there in 1908-10.[143] Whereas Bishop Smith had been personally engaged in the cultivation of donors for the other buildings, now funds were being sought to honor him and his episcopal colleagues. As Dr. Finch stated in a letter to Smith, "I want to ask Mr. Jesse Jones to share in this program in honor of his close friendship with you across these last twenty-five years."[144] The list of major donors reads like a "Who's Who in Texas Methodism" of that time: the Brown Foundation, Edgar W. Brown, Jr., the West Foundation, Houston Endowment, Inc. [Jesse Jones], Mr. and Mrs. E. L. Kurth, J. H. Kurth, Jr., Mr. and Mrs. E. B. Germany, the Fair Foundation, Mr. and Mrs. Charles G. Heyne, Mr. and Mrs. Fred J. Heyne, Mr. and Mrs. J. J. Perkins, Charles N. Prothro, Rev. and Mrs. W. W. Conerly, Mrs. S. W. Henderson, W. R. Nicholson, Mr. and Mrs. J. D. Wheeler, Mrs. C. W. Hall, Dr. and Mrs. William C. Finch, "and numerous other ex-students and faculty."[145]

As an active member of Southwestern's board of trustees, Bishop Smith had known of the developing plans for a union building. He first learned of the special designation from Dr. Finch in early January, 1953. Replying to Finch's letter, Smith declared, "No greater distinction can come to one of us than to be connected in some fashion with one of the buildings at Southwestern. As you well know and as I have often said to you, that is where my heart is even though my activities have been, in largest part, with another institution."[146]

In dedication services, the donor ordinarily presents the buildings to the chairman of the board of trustees. For the dedication of the Bishops' Memorial Union, however, the chairman of the board, Mr. John D. Wheeler, presented the building to Bishop A. Frank Smith.[147]

Although Bishop Smith retired in 1960, he did not cease to be involved in the affairs of his Alma Mater. In the fall of that year, when he learned that Vanderbilt University was considering Dr. Finch for the deanship of its Divinity School, Smith encouraged both sides of the negotiations. As he explained to Finch:

I know of no reason whatsoever for your leaving Southwestern; . . . but I believe that this opportunity at Vanderbilt will be challenging to you. . . .

Harvie Branscombe called me from Nashville some weeks ago and told me that he was very favorably disposed toward inviting you to become the Dean of the School of Religion. I told him that he could look the church over and not find a better man for the place than you are. You will recall that I mentioned Vanderbilt to you in our conversation here at my home a few months ago, and I am delighted to see this come about. I say this with full knowledge of the loss we all will suffer here in Texas. You have done a magnificent job and you have advanced Southwestern from a struggling small college up to a place of preeminence in Methodism and in the academic world. . . .

You will have a great administration there [at Vanderbilt], and you will love Nashville. Our love and our blessings will follow you.[148]

After thirty years of making appointments, no bishop could think of moving a preacher without also thinking of a possible successor. So, in this instance, Bishop Smith would naturally have someone in mind. "I do not know who is in the picture as your successor," he wrote to Dr. Finch, "[but] without being presumptuous, I want to suggest Durwood Fleming as a man amply fitted to assume responsibilities you lay aside."

Durwood and Lurline [he continued] have social graces of extraordinary capacity. He has done a magnificent job here, both as pastor, preacher and administrator. No Methodist preacher in this city has greater influence than he has, and his contacts with men and women of means is phenomenal. He is in his fifteenth year at St. Luke's Church and insofar as I am able to judge, he could stay another fifteen years. But . . . I have a feeling he would welcome an opportunity to go to Southwestern.[149]

In the meantime, Bishop Smith had been talking to Fleming. Although almost two decades have now passed since that conversation, President Fleming still remembers—with a profound sense of awe— what Bishop Smith said to him:

On the first Friday of February, 1961, Bishop Smith and I had a funeral service together. When I got into the car, he said: "Did you know that Bill Finch is leaving Southwestern?" "Well," I replied, "I have just read it." "Yes," Bishop Smith continued, "and I think you ought to go." And all the way out to the cemetery, which was a long distance, he was talking and I was listening. I couldn't believe what I was hearing, but I could tell that he had done a lot of talking. That's the way he was: he'd just start with an idea and start talking to people. He set these things into motion and they just carried you on. He didn't press me about it. He simply said to me: "Don't talk about it to anybody; just let it happen."[150]

A year later, when President-elect Fleming requested Bishop Smith to participate in his inauguration as president of Southwestern University, Smith gratefully accepted. "I certainly plan to be there," he wrote. "My only suggestion is that you give me a very brief and minor part on the program." Smith then closed his letter with this amazing statement, which encapsulates his influential role in the guidance of Southwestern University: "Incidentally, I have participated in the Induction of your five immediate predecessors in that office."[151]

15

Southern Methodist University

FOR TWENTY-SIX YEARS Bishop A. Frank Smith was involved in the direction and development of Southern Methodist University. As a trustee representing "the Church at Large," Bishop Smith attended his first meeting of the SMU Board of Trustees on June 4, 1934.[1] Among the two dozen men gathered in the office of President Charles C. Selecman that Monday afternoon, Smith recognized many of the prominent laymen and ministers from the five-state constituency of the university, including R. W. Fair of Tyler, Walter W. Fondren of Houston, Judge John E. Hickman of Eastland, Henry E. Jackson of San Angelo, J. J. Perkins of Wichita Falls, J. M. Willson of Floydada, Rev. Ivan Lee Holt of St. Louis, Rev. W. C. Martin of Dallas, and Rev. W. Angie Smith of Shreveport, his brother. Two other bishops were also trustees: Hiram A. Boaz, former president of SMU, and John M. Moore, chairman of the board.

The following year, on December 2, 1935,[2] Mr. and Mrs. Fondren gave the university 6,600 shares of Humble Oil Company stock for a library building. Although Bishop Smith had not been involved in the Fondrens' decision, he greatly enjoyed telling the story of their original offer.

Mr. and Mrs. Fondren, who always knew their own business and didn't need anyone to tell them what they wanted to do, came up to Dallas and completely surprised President Selecman with their intention to build a library for Southern Methodist University. Mr. Fondren, one of the most lovable characters who ever lived, told me later: "My wife and I came up here expecting to give $650,000. I asked President Selecman how much it would take to build a library. After some hesitation, he said that $400,000 would build a fine library. 'Well,' I said, 'we will give you $400,000'—and then I went back to the hotel and told my wife that I had made $250,000 since I left her that morning!"[3]

The election of seven new bishops by the General Conference of the Methodist Episcopal Church, South, in May, 1938, brought about dramatic changes at SMU, immediately affecting university president Charles C. Selecman and trustees Ivan Lee Holt and William C. Martin. Selecman was assigned to the conferences in Oklahoma and Arkansas. Martin was sent to the California and northwestern conferences. Holt was given the North Texas, Central Texas, Northwest Texas, and New Mexico conferences. Retiring Bishop John M. Moore, who had been chairman of the SMU board since 1932, was asked to devote his energies to the imminent unification of the three branches of American Methodism. Consequently, the SMU board met in June without a chairman or a chief executive officer.

Since Bishop Holt had just been appointed to the Dallas area and had been a trustee since 1918, Frank Smith thought Holt should be elected to succeed Bishop Moore as chairman of the SMU board.[4] J. J. Perkins was supporting Frank McNeny, the vice-chairman, but Selecman persuaded "Brother Joe" to vote for Frank Smith.[5] As Bishop Smith recalled the meeting: "Someone nominated Bishop Holt, . . . and Henry Jackson nominated me as chairman. When the votes came in, however, I was elected, and I took the chair at once."[6]

Bishop Smith appointed a committee to search for a new president to be elected by the board in November. In the meantime, "Acting President" Eugene B. Hawk, dean of the School of Theology, would run the university.

Although several candidates were mentioned in rumors during the succeeding months, none seemed to have a sure nomination. By the time the board met to receive the committee's report, faculty and staff found routine work increasingly difficult. Mrs. Loretta Hawkins, then secretary to the president, remembers the mounting excitement. Finally Bishop Smith came out of the meeting room and asked where he could find a telephone to make a confidential call. After a few moments, Smith returned, thanked her for her assistance, and went back into the board meeting without giving her any hint as to the board's decision. Then her telephone rang, and she learned the secret. "Could you tell me," asked the operator, "who just made that call to Dean Umphrey Lee in Nashville, Tennessee?"[7] Later, when the board adjourned, Bishop Smith dictated the official letter to Dean Lee:

The Board of Trustees of Southern Methodist University met in called session today, November 7, 1938, and after considering at length the several names presented by the Committee on Nominations for the Presidency of the University, you were made the choice of the Board by unanimous action. It gives us great joy in behalf of the Board to convey this information to you, and we bespeak for you and the University a magnificent Administration in the years to come, and may they be many.

Sincerely yours,
A. FRANK SMITH
Chairman, Board of Trustees
LAYTON H. BAILEY
Secretary, Board of Trustees[8]

Smith's pleasure was understandable, for he had known Umphrey Lee for many years. As college students they had been debate opponents, and Frank had introduced Umphrey to the future Mrs. Lee. When Frank was pastor of the University Church at SMU, Umphrey was a graduate student and president of the student body.[9] Dr. Lee was also well known and admired in the SMU community, for he had been pastor of Highland Park Methodist Church from 1923 to 1936 and had taught homiletics in the School of Theology from 1927 to 1933. For his part, Lee stated that he would never have accepted the presidency of SMU if Smith had not been chairman of the board.[10]

At the formal inaugural ceremonies for President Lee, Bishop Smith declared his faith in Southern Methodist University and his vision of the institution's role:

This occasion assumes particular significance, in the first place, because Southern Methodist University has come of age, nearing the twenty-fifth anniversary of its opening date. It is possessed of magnificent properties. It has developed an intellectual character which commands the respect of the academic world. . . . In the next place, this occasion is of particular significance because of the future. The world is being recast. Attitudes and methods which must serve economic, social and political areas perhaps for generations to come are even now being poured. The policy of isolation and indifference for individuals and for nations is henceforth and forever untenable. We are members of one another. . . . Only upon that assumption can the world look for that morrow which is its rightful heritage, and that day can come only through men and women possessed of trained minds, of social conscience, who are rooted in the spiritual verities. To the creating of that mind and that conscience this institution is dedicated. Amidst the needs of a changing day, this institution will rise to its best.

Then, addressing both Lee and the audience, Smith asserted his respect for the president-elect:

This occasion is of peculiar significance because of you [Umphrey Lee]. Born of the parsonage, bred to the ministry, preacher and prophet, you reveal in your character the redemptive processes of divine grace. Through the diligent exercise of your intellectual gifts you have won commendation in the realm of scholarship. Through the application of common sense, motivated by love for your fellowman, you speak and act as one having authority and men heed your counsel and gladly follow you. . . . With boundless faith and pride, Southern Methodist University commits to you, her own and most illustrious son, her traditions, her honor, her future, her life. May our Heavenly Father direct you in thought and deed, even as you shall direct the destinies of this institution.[11]

    Bishop Smith might well have mentioned another favorable portent for the university's future: the prospect of increasing patronage. Reporting on a "very satisfactory conversation" with J. J. Perkins in December, 1940, Smith informed President Lee that "Joe Perkins has definitely decided what he is going to do at the University." Smith's letter illustrates not only the bishop's well-informed grasp of the university's current needs, but also his understanding of Mr. Perkins's way of doing things.

[Mr. Perkins] wants to build a Field House. He has $75,000.00 now available and would like to build it for that much money. I told him I thought it would cost at least $150,000.00. . . . My guess is that he may propose to you $75,000.00, but if you hold out for $150,000.00 you can get it. He is willing to put the latter amount in it if necessary, but he does not want the work to start until the money is all in hand. . . . If we let him hold up the project until he has brought all the money in, there is always the possibility that something may happen to cause him to change his mind. On the other hand, if he once starts construction, he will have to see it through. . . . If he does not come down to see you before long about this Field House matter, you let me know, and I will take it up with him again.[12]

Lee immediately replied that Mr. Perkins had indeed proposed giving the university $75,000.00 for a Field House. "I want your advice about pressing him for the other $75,000," he added, "as I think it will cost that much."[13] The accuracy of Smith's prediction was apparent at the next meeting of the SMU board [June 3, 1941] when Mr. Perkins "announced that he and Mrs. Perkins desired to make a gift of $150,000 to the University for a new Gymnasium."[14] Construction began in October, just two months before Pearl Harbor and the entry of the United States into World War II.

Despite wartime building restrictions, the Perkins Gymnasium was completed before the 1942-43 academic year. The trustees and the university administration designed a dedication service that would attract a large crowd and praise physical fitness, philanthropy, and patriotism in a Christian context.[15] Approximately three thousand students and visitors, including five bishops and fifty district superintendents, gathered on campus for the ceremonies.[16] "A most representative group of Methodists from all of Texas was present," Bishop Smith wrote in his daily journal. "It was a delightful affair."[17] As he introduced Mr. and Mrs. Perkins, the bishop declared:

Southern Methodist University, from every blade of grass on the campus to the magnificent tiles of the memorial buildings, is vindication of the proper use of the American right to create wealth. Selfishly exploited wealth creates false standards, sows seeds of ruin and revolution; properly executed, it makes possible institutions and philanthropies, and by Christian character it produces the highest type of manhood and womanhood conceivable in our social order.[18]

Mr. Perkins listened with a smile, then rose and responded: "I appreciate all you have said about the great philanthropist; but I tell you right now, this Federal Income Tax is making philanthropists out of a lot of us."[19]

Bishop Smith's chairmanship of SMU's board of trustees was not always a matter of presiding over pleasant occasions. There were also times of tension and conflict of opinion between men of goodwill. One such instance developed within the executive committee of the board.

Early in January, 1942, President Lee came to Houston to discuss the matter with Bishop Smith. To avoid interruption, the two men went for a ride. "We drove for three hours," Smith noted in his daily journal: "Umphrey is troubled because Frank McNeny, chairman of the executive committee, has asked Karl Hoblitzelle and Fred Florence to be on the executive committee. Others on the committee [are opposed] and a row is in prospect. We've got to head it off someway."[20] The situation was particularly difficult for the bishop because the two were prominent Dallas businessmen, and Fred Florence was also a longtime friend of Smith's from their days at Alto.[21] McNeny and his supporters persisted in bringing up the matter at each meeting of the executive committee and of the board throughout 1942, but they were not able to gain a majority vote.[22] The executive committee finally worked out a compromise that was accepted by the trustees at their midwinter meeting in January, 1943. The board's bylaws were amended to permit the addition of three members to the executive committee. "A fine meeting," Bishop Smith wrote in his daily journal. "We put Florence, Hoblitzelle, and F. O. Burns on executive committee & S. B. Perkins—elder brother of Joe—on the Board."[23] Mr. Florence promptly sent a letter of appreciation to Bishop Smith:

As I look back through the years to the time when I first had the great pleasure of knowing you, it brings me so much happiness to realize that now once again you and I shall have this closer association together. You may be sure the opportunity to serve the institution with which you are connected will challenge me to my very best efforts.[24]

"Fred Florence loved Frank like a brother," according to George Pierce, "and Frank was responsible for Fred's love for the University. I don't think there's any question about that. Fred Florence did an awful lot for the University, but he wasn't the type to put it in banner headlines. He just did it, and people never knew what he did."[25] SMU's trustees soon saw the wisdom of adding Fred Florence to the board's executive committee. Within a year they declared their appreciation to the Dallas banker for giving "his personal time and assistance in the solicitation of funds for the Sustaining Fund Campaign."[26]

In the spring of 1944 the trustees of Southern Methodist University proposed a financial campaign "to raise a capital sum of $5,000,000 for endowment of the University."[27] As Bishop Smith later recalled, the campaign almost sank before it was launched:

Umphrey raised the question in the board, and Mr. Perkins got up and said: "Well, I will give $50,000 and that is all." Nobody else said they would do anything, and the board adjourned. Umphrey said to me: "Our campaign is dead. We won't even have a funeral. It's just dead. If Mr. Perkins is not going to give more than $50,000 we won't get off the ground." But as Joe Perkins and I walked over to Snider Hall where we were to have lunch, he said to me: "I am going to make a million dollars, and I don't know what to do with it. I have done about all I am going to do down at the Methodist Home and I am about through up here. I am going to reopen Burkburnett Field[28] and recycle some wells. It is going to make me a million dollars." So I said: "Mr. Perkins, I am glad you brought this up because there is something I have wanted to talk to you about. You ought to give that million dollars here to establish a school of theology." "Why," he said, "they have a building over there [Kirby Hall]. I would give something for scholarships, but they don't need any more buildings." And I said: "Oh, it could be more than that." Now we knew that Bishop [John M.] Moore was trying to raise a million dollars for a school of theology [at SMU].[29] So I said, "Mr. Perkins, you are the man who ought to do that." Well, he went on home, but he called me that night. "Lois is interested in that. Write me some letters and tell me what you have in mind."[30]

A brief notation in Bishop Smith's daily journal dates the above conversation and confirms its basic accuracy: "Tuesday, April 11, 1944 [Dallas] ... J. J. Perkins & I talked together. I am urging him to give $1,000,000 to School of Theology and let us name it Perkins School of Religion. I believe he is interested."[31]

Bishop Smith did not allow Mr. Perkins to forget this conversation. Immediately after lunch that day, Smith went to see Umphrey Lee. "Umphrey," he said, "here is our chance to get our school of theology." The two men agreed to have an architect prepare a drawing of the proposed school of theology, built around old Kirby Hall [now Florence Hall] on the northwest corner of the campus, including a chapel and dormitories.[32]

In the meantime, Bishop Smith wrote a number of letters to Mr. Perkins. "I must have written him a half dozen or more," he later recalled, "telling him what was involved and that the school would be called Perkins." At that point, Mr. Perkins objected, declaring that he did not want the school named for him. But Bishop Smith persisted. "It will mean something, Mr. Perkins. You exemplify in your life the very things that the school of theology stands for. The Perkins men and women will be all over the church, and the Perkins name will represent what you believe in."[33]

Bishop Smith also emphasized Mrs. Perkins's influence on her husband. "Lois directed his thinking. He always says that he doesn't do anything without her approval. She has steered his thinking in more than one instance."[34] As an example, Smith cited the following conversation:

Mr. Perkins came up to the General Conference at Kansas City in 1944 and told us that he would give [SMU] $350,000 of Tidewater Oil stock. But Lois said to me, "Don't you let him do that. It is not enough." And we kept our peace. I didn't tell Mr. Perkins that we would not take it. We just held things back and told Mr. Perkins we would see.[35]

Bishop Smith's daily journal contains several additional significant details:

Tonight [May 2, 1944] we had a dinner party at the hotel for the Perkinses and a few friends. I have been talking to him for some time about endowing the [SMU] school of theology and letting us name it for him. He and his wife told me tonite that they wanted to do that, giving $3,000,000 to start and *probably two or three millions later.* If this goes thru, it will be the biggest thing that ever happened to SMU.[36]

As soon as the bishop returned to Houston from the General Conference, he wrote to the Perkinses, describing the far-reaching implications of their proposed gift to SMU but keeping the letter on a warmly personal level.

The high point of the General Conference for me was not in anything the Conference did, but in the conversations I had with you and Lois about the School of Theology. That is a dream of years of mine, and the most wonderful thing that could happen to the University, and to the ministry of the Southwest as long as the Methodist Church lives. To know that it can be worked out so that Perkins and Trained Ministers will be synonymous in the thinking of future generations is the most appropriate cause for rejoicing I know.

I spent two days in Dallas on the way home, going over matters at length with Mark Lemmon, who is working on some plans, and also with Dr. Lee and Dean Hawk, who are collecting some data I want to go over with you and Lois . . . so you can get a picture of the overall possibilities with which this project is so full.

Bess joins me in love to you both.[37]

The original plan was for Bishop Smith to take the architect's watercolor sketch to the Perkinses' home in Wichita Falls as soon as the picture was available. At the last moment, however, Smith decided that the forthcoming Jurisdictional Conference would be a more favorable setting.[38]

Another indication of the bishop's careful guidance of this process of cultivation was his continual effort to keep key persons informed of developments.[39] On May 26, for instance, before discussing the anticipated gift to the school of theology at a noon meeting with the executive committee of the SMU board, Smith arrived in Dallas early enough to talk with two influential trustee-members of the committee. "After breakfast I walked up to the 1st Natl Bank & had a talk with Gene McElvaney about the Perkins proposition," he noted in his journal. "I then went to Frank McNeny's office & spent a couple of hours with him, discussing the same project. They are both enthusiastic over the idea."[40]

Events at the South Central Jurisdictional Conference in Tulsa, Oklahoma, in June brought the dream of a Perkins School of Theology still closer to reality. On Tuesday afernoon, June 13, the delegates decided to choose only two new bishops. After leading on the first ballot, W. Angie Smith was elected on the second. "I am exceedingly happy," Frank Smith wrote in his daily journal; "Angie has 24 years to go and will make a great Bishop."[41] Paul Martin—who had been the Perkinses' pastor since 1938 and an SMU trustee since 1933—was receiving enough votes to be a slight possibility for the other bishop.

Later that same afternoon, Smith continued, "Umphrey [Lee], Paul Martin and I had a conference with Mr. and Mrs. Perkins. They announced their intention of giving $1,000,000 cash to the School of Theology, probably within 60 days. That is great news."[42] Smith subsequently recalled that the announcement had been made in the Perkinses' hotel room: "He [Perkins] called us up to his room, my wife and me, Umphrey and his wife, Paul and his wife. And he said, 'Lois and I have talked it over and have decided to give a million dollars to the school of theology.' "[43] Paul Martin considers this meeting to be "the time in which the project definitely came into being, although the matter had been under discussion for some time."[44]

The following afternoon, Bishop Smith arranged for Mr. Perkins to share in a unique experience. Traditionally, two bishops escort a newly elected bishop to the platform for formal presentation immediately after his election. When it became clear that Paul Martin would be elected, Bishops Ivan Lee Holt and A. Frank Smith were chosen to be his escorts. Knowing that Mr. Perkins dearly loved Paul Martin and had worked diligently for his election, Bishop Smith arranged for Mr. Perkins to take his place as one of the escorts. "It was breaking precedent," Bishop Smith later explained, "but there was no law against it. And it meant much more to Mr. Perkins than it would to anyone else."[45] Smith's interpretation is confirmed by a letter from Mr. Perkins. "Thank you for your willingness to step aside and let me act as one of the escorts of our new Bishop up to the platform," the grateful layman wrote. "I wanted to do this very much indeed. I know it was only through your kindness that I was permitted to do this."[46]

Through that summer and fall, while Mr. and Mrs. Perkins were deciding the exact amount of their proposed gift, Bishop Smith frequently reassured them of his "consuming interest in the project" and of his certainty that it would "determine the leadership of Methodism and the entire Southwest."[47] Finally, in late December, Perkins informed Smith that he had taken the first step in a complex transaction that eventually would be worth approximately $1,300,000 to "the Endowment Fund for the Theological Department at Southern Methodist University."[48] "I would appreciate your assistance," Perkins requested, "in outlining an agreement with Southern Methodist University covering this gift for the Endowment Fund and placing such restrictions on its use as might be best, everything considered."[49]

On January 4, Bishop Smith joined President Lee and Dean Hawk in an all-day task of "working out the provisions of the Perkinses' gift."[50] Lee and Smith then drove to Wichita Falls that night to present these detailed plans to the Perkinses the next morning. Mr. Perkins accepted their recommendations, but Mrs. Perkins insisted that there be no public announcement of the gift. Bishop Smith apparently needed all his renowned powers of persuasion to convince her of the values of an announcement not only at the midwinter board meeting but also at a special convocation[51]—both to be scheduled during Ministers' Week at SMU.

At eleven o'clock on February 6, 1945, in the presence of all forty trustees and numerous special guests gathered in the Board Room of the Perkins Hall of Administration,[52] Mr. and Mrs. Perkins presented the university with a gift of $1,350,000 "to establish the Perkins Endowment Fund for the support of the School of Theology."[53] Bishop Paul Martin moved the adoption of a resolution changing the name of the school to Perkins School of Theology. "It was a high and holy hour," Bishop Smith declared. "No such gift was ever made to a school of theology in the South."[54]

That evening, at a special convocation held in McFarlin Auditorium, the drama was repeated for the benefit of an enthusiastically appreciative audience of hundreds of ministers from across the eight-state South Central Jurisdiction. "Despite the [wartime] travel ban a big crowd of preachers is here," Bishop Smith noted with obvious delight.[55] Mr. Perkins, repeating the explanation he had given to the trustees that morning, again acknowledged Bishop Smith's guidance of their decision: "Bishop Smith got me off in a corner some time ago and told me about the school of theology. I was impressed, and when I got home I talked it over with my wife. We came to the conclusion the school needed $3,000,000."[56] With understandable pride, Smith wrote in his daily journal: "Mr. Perkins told Board & crowd tonite that I had first given him idea concerning gift to School of Theology."[57] Mrs. Perkins later added her tribute in a personal letter: "Bishop Smith . . . This was your thought and your dream and if it had not been for you, we may never have given the money—and I am so happy that we did give it."[58]

In the meantime two major issues developed which were to have far-reaching significance for the future of the school of theology. As the chairman of the SMU board and as a close friend of the Perkinses, Bishop A. Frank Smith was vitally involved in working out solutions for both of these problems.

During the Spring of 1947, Bishop John M. Moore suggested to Bishop Smith and Mr. Perkins that the four-acre site on the northwest corner of the SMU campus was too confining for the proposed school of theology.[59] Mr. Perkins, having stood on the campus in front of Dallas Hall and envisioned the planned quadrangle for himself, did not agree with Bishop Moore.[60] Not one to be easily discouraged, Moore prepared a six-page carefully documented argument detailing the limitations of the four-acre site and the advantages of a twenty-one-acre site on the southwest corner of the campus adjoining Highland Park Methodist Church.[61] Moore mailed his treatise to Mr. Perkins, with copies to President Lee, Dean Hawk, and Bishop Smith. Mr. Perkins immediately wrote to Bishop Smith: "I have read Bishop Moore's letter with very considerable interest. . . . I would like to have your frank expression concerning what he has had to say."[62]

Before replying to "Brother Joe," Smith took the Zephyr to Dallas and "went over plans with Umphrey Lee . . . on Perkins School of Theology buildings."[63] Bishop Smith then called Mr. Perkins and proposed a "summit meeting" at the forthcoming Ecumenical Conference to be held in Springfield, Massachusetts, later that month.[64]

By mid-September Bishop Smith could send word to Bishop Moore that brought "great joy and exultation" to the elder statesman. "Your letter from New York is a marvelous revelation," Moore responded, "giving me new assurance that only the full plot of ground would be *in keeping with what you have guided Mr. and Mrs. Perkins to do.* He now wants a great school and is willing to make it so." With profound gratitude Moore concluded: "You have rendered a service that far exceeds anything the rest of us have done or could have done. Some day it will all come out in shining recognition. I give you my heartiest congratulations and my blessing."[65]

Credit must be given to Bishop Paul E. Martin for his part in encouraging the Perkinses to accept Bishop Moore's recommendation. Bishop Martin recalls making a special trip to Wichita Falls, at Bishop Moore's insistence, to show Mr. and Mrs. Perkins Moore's detailed drawings contrasting the two sites.[66]

The prospect of building on a different and much larger site raised a number of serious questions which Lee, Hawk, and others at SMU quickly called to Bishop Smith's attention. Assuming the continued use of Kirby Hall, the Perkinses had given a million dollars to add a chapel and two dormitories and another million to endow the school of theology.[67] As President Lee explained: "If we simply build [the three buildings] on the new site, they will not only look skimpy, but they will not meet our needs. We must have a classroom building and we badly need more dormitory space [for married students] and a library."[68] Dean Hawk urged Smith to persuade Mr. Perkins "to take some of the money he has planned to put in endowment and make possible an outstanding physical plant. . . . You are the one man to influence these good people in their investment."[69] Everyone, it seems, was looking to Bishop Smith to work another miracle at Springfield.

Delayed seven years beyond its customary decennial schedule by global conflict, the Seventh Ecumenical Methodist Conference convened in Springfield, Massachusetts, on September 24, 1947, with extraordinary fanfare. Reconciliation, renewal, and reorganization were the themes of this historic session.[70] Springfield also became symbolic of another major step in the series of decisions coincidentally made at major Methodist conferences that culminated in the creation of the Perkins School of Theology. "Umphrey [Lee], Hawk & I talked with Mr. & Mrs. Perkins concerning the *enlarged* plans for Perkins School of Theology," Bishop Smith noted in his daily journal. "The proposal is to move to a site between McFarlin Auditorium & Highland Park Church & build the complete plant at a cost of two million dollars."[71] Although Mrs. Perkins characteristically had insisted from the beginning, "It is not for us to say where the school should be built; it is not our school,"[72] Bishop Smith, President Lee, and Dean Hawk would not have decided anything contrary to the Perkinses' opinion. When the "Bishops of the S[outh] C[entral] Jurisdiction & trustees of SMU who are here met at lunch to discuss proposed removal of Perkins School of Theology" the next day, the decision had already been made.[73] As Bishop Smith wrote in his daily journal, "Talked to Mr. Perkins just before starting to train. He is enthusiastic about the enlarged program for the School of Theology."[74]

The Committee on the School of Theology[75] met on October 10 and agreed to recommend to the board that the seminary be built on the larger site. A special meeting of the board was then called for October 31 to receive the committee's report. "Board of Trustees met at SMU in called session at ten o'clock," Bishop Smith noted in his daily journal. "Very important meeting. Authorized . . . the relocation of Perkins School of Theology upon a new and enlarged site. This probably guarantees the future of Perkins as the best housed & best endowed school of theology in Methodism."[76] As the bishop wrote to Mr. and Mrs. Perkins following the formal groundbreaking ceremonies:

Never before has an entire school within a University been erected at the same time, and never before has a School of Theology been equipped physically and undergirded with endowment at the same time. You have done at Perkins within the span of a few years what it usually takes a generation or a century to accomplish. And above all, you have given our School of Theology a name that stands for everything the Church stands for.[77]

"This is one of the nicest letters we have ever received," Mr. Perkins replied, "and coming from you makes us appreciate it all the more." There was one aspect of "last Wednesday's activities" that displeased him, however: "I did not have four buildings to name instead of three. If I had had the fourth building I am quite certain that you could guess who it would have been named for."[78] That fourth building became a reality at the fall board meeting when Mr. Perkins announced an additional gift of $450,000 to SMU to build a men's dormitory in the Perkins quadrangle in honor of Bishop A. Frank Smith.[79] By the time of the dedication of the Perkins School of Theology in February, 1951, the Perkinses had increased their giving to a total of more than five million dollars, two million for buildings and three million for endowment.[80]

A second major issue that required a skillful solution and greatly affected the future of Perkins School of Theology was the racial integration of the student body. As early as 1946 special afternoon classes were held for Negro students in Kirby Hall, but credit for such courses could be obtained only by transferring to Gammon Theological Seminary in Georgia or some other school that trained Negro ministers. Later on, Negroes were permitted to attend regular classes as auditors.[81] In May, 1948, responding to a request from a trustee of both institutions, the SMU board "expressed its interest" in assisting in the training of some of the ministerial students of the Texas College for Negroes. Bishop Smith, as chairman of the board, was authorized "to appoint a committee to survey the needs of the University for a far-reaching program over a period of years."[82] In 1950 the board approved "admission of Negroes to the School of Theology . . . if, as and when it seems to be timely and proper to the administration."[83] The seminary student council responded by establishing a scholarship fund for Negro students, raised almost one thousand dollars among the student body, and discreetly informed the presidents of Negro Methodist colleges of this symbol of welcome.[84]

In the fall of 1952, five Negroes enrolled in the seminary, making Perkins the first southern Methodist school of theology to desegregate.[85] There was no public announcement of the board's action or of the students' presence. As Merrimon Cuninggim, who had been appointed dean of the school in 1951, later explained, "A policy of no publicity can give important protection to a program of desegregation in its early stages."[86] Due to the careful planning and cooperation carried out by the entire seminary community, the Negro students fully entered into all the usual activities of the seminary campus: living in the dormitory, eating in the seminary dining hall, participating in intramural sports or singing with the "Seminary Singers." As the fall semester passed without incident, some of the white students invited the Negro students to be their roommates in the spring. When word of this latter arrangement reached a prominent member of the SMU board from East Texas, serious opposition developed. As Bishop Smith recalled:

We were gathering for a Board meeting and this trustee showed me a paper which he was going to present to the Board demanding that we evict those Negro boys from the [seminary] dormitory immediately because the Board had never voted on that—which they hadn't. And I said, "Why Mr. ———, we can't do that. We do things through committees here. We will refer that to the Committee on the School of Theology." And he said, "All right, just so I know that it is taken care of. I know a million dollars you are going to lose if you don't do it." Fortunately, Paul Martin, who was chairman of the Committee on the School of Theology, was in South America. But when the fall came and the Negroes were back in the dormitory,[87] Mr. ——— (a fine old gentleman), began to get restless again. He was being prodded from different sources. Finally, he got to Mr. Perkins. I was in San Antonio, and Umphrey Lee's wife reached me by telephone at the airport. Now this was while Umphrey was recovering from his heart attack. So Mary Lee said to me, "I want Umphrey to resign as president. Mr. Perkins has called him about those [Negro] men in the dormitory. And Umphrey's doctor says that if he gets under pressure he will blow a gasket and have a stroke." So I said, "Mary, just tell Umphrey to keep steady, and I'll be up there tomorrow."[88] But I changed right then and there from the Houston plane to a Dallas plane and went out to see Umphrey. And I told him, "Umphrey, there's nothing to get excited about here. Mr. ——— just has Mr. Perkins stirred up." So I went up [to Witchita Falls] to see Mr. Perkins. And I said, "Mr. Perkins, Paul [Martin] is still in South America, and we will have to wait until he comes back because he is chairman of this committee." I didn't want to cause any trouble, of course, but I said, "I think you are too sore about this." And he said: "The board never voted on it. We voted to give them their degrees, but we didn't vote on housing"—which they hadn't. Then Merrimon Cuninggim came down [to Houston] to see me. And I told him, "Merrimon, if J. J. Perkins asks the Board to oust those boys, they are going to do it. I'll tell you the way it is going to be. They are not going to vote to throw the boys out. They are going to say we never agreed to let them in. And they are going to spank somebody for letting them in." And Merrimon offered to resign, and he said: "When I came here, I was told that they were to receive credit, and I supposed they could be housed."[89] And I said, "Well, I think it is fortunate that you did. I don't think we ever would have gotten a vote through [the Board]. But since they [the Negro students] are there, it will create a great deal more consternation to throw them out than it would to refuse to let them in. We face a fact, and this is probably the best way to handle it."[90]

In his "Reflections," Bishop Paul Martin describes what happened when he returned from his overseas visitation at Christmas [1953]:

Bishop Smith, President Lee and Dean Cuninggim convinced me that they believed I could help to resolve the difficult situation. My wife and I spent part of the Christmas holidays in Wichita Falls with our dear friends. One evening, Mr. Perkins, in the direct fashion that always characterized him, asked me, "Do you believe that if this matter is not settled in an amicable manner, it will hurt the University?" I replied in the affirmative. Then he simply but sincerely said, "That is the only consideration. The University must rise above any hurt feelings that can develop. The School of Theology is our first love."[91]

The Committee on the School of Theology, now that its chairman was back in the country, met to see if any recommendation should be made to the board concerning the housing of the Negro students. As Bishop Smith recalled: "When the Committee met in Dallas, Mrs. Perkins very tactfully yet very definitely expressed herself, and that was the end of it. We told Mr. ———— that the board committee had refused to take any action, and he didn't press it any further."[92]

The Perkinses were not SMU's only benefactors, of course. From 1938, when Bishop Smith became chairman of SMU's board, until the dedication of Perkins School of Theology in 1951, the total assets of the university had trebled, from just under seven million dollars to twenty-four million. The campus had grown from twelve buildings to twenty-eight.[93] In addition to the Perkinses' gift, Bishop Smith was personally involved in two major developments: the Fondren Science Building and the new Law School quadrangle.

Bishop Smith's friendship with the Fondrens was different from his relationship with the Perkinses. Since their college days at Southwestern, Frank and Bess had been good friends with Lois Craddock, while Joe Perkins was only included later. The Smiths and the Fondrens became acquainted in Houston when Frank was the influential pastor of First Methodist Church and Walter Fondren a vice-president of the Humble Oil & Refining Company. The Fondrens were members of St. Paul's Methodist Church, but their interests were not limited to that congregation. For many years Mr. Fondren led the Texas Conference lay delegation to General Conference, and Mrs. Fondren always accompanied him. The Smiths and the Fondrens were neighbors for several years. "We had the same house number, 3410," Mrs. Fondren explains. "We lived on Montrose and they lived on Yoakum. People used to ask me if the Smiths lived behind us, but I always said, 'no, we lived in front of them!' "[94] The Fondrens, like the Perkinses, always planned their major stewardship giving together. After Mr. Fondren's death in 1939, Mrs. Fondren sought to carry out the visions they had shared.[95] It was at this point that Bishop Smith became her trusted guide. According to Dr. Willis Tate, Mrs. Fondren looked to Bishop Smith for advice because of his friendship with her husband: "Mrs. Fondren was very high on Bishop Smith, and he had a lot of influence on her. I think it goes back to Mrs. Fondren trying to do what Mr. Fondren would have done if he had still been alive. Bishop Smith was constantly interpreting that because of what he knew about Mr. Fondren."[96]

Bishop Smith's public statements concerning Mrs. Fondren's gift of one million dollars for a science building for SMU support Dr. Tate's interpretation. Shortly after Mrs. Fondren announced her gift,[97] Bishop Smith declared:

Southern Methodist University is honored in having the Fondren name indestructibly preserved upon its campus and in its future activities. . . . The Fondren family is Christian in the highest sense, personally and collectively, privately and publicly. They exemplify within themselves the ideals and faith upon which the University is builded. Mr. W. W. Fondren, in his lifetime an outstanding success in the business world, together with Mrs. Fondren created large wealth, erected a Christian home, reared a Christian family and dedicated themselves and their all to God and their fellow men.[98]

Four years later, speaking at the dedication of the Fondren Science Building, Bishop Smith stated:

Precious memories are ours here today. We bear in memory a gentle person, who though absent in the flesh is here in the spirit—W. W. Fondren, who was an exemplification of modest, unassuming Christian discipleship, an inspiration to all who knew him and an example for all who were to follow after him. His devoted companion, Mrs. Fondren, has given herself unstintedly since he went away to carrying out certain projects they had in mind together. And though she is here alone this afternoon for this dedication, there comes to a climax that which was conceived while he was here and in which he participates.[99]

As we have seen, A. Frank Smith had a lifelong interest in the legal profession. When the seminary was moved from the northwest corner of the SMU campus, the board designated that area for the Law School quadrangle and the Southwestern Legal Center. Bishop Smith helped negotiate a financial arrangement with the Southwestern Legal Foundation and Mrs. Harper Kirby whereby Kirby Hall was released for use of the Legal Center and the Law School and a new Kirby Hall built on the new seminary site.[100] To refurbish the twenty-five-year-old building, Karl Hoblitzelle contributed a quarter of a million dollars with the understanding that the building would be renamed in honor of Fred F. Florence.[101] Florence was president of the Republic National Bank of Dallas, while Hoblitzelle was chairman of that bank's board of directors.[102] They were also members of the executive committee of SMU's board, and both were friends of Bishop Smith's. At the dedication of Florence Hall in 1951, Smith recalled his long association with Florence:

Thirty-seven years ago in a little village in the piney woods of East Texas, I came out of the seminary to go to my first circuit as a Methodist preacher. The banker of the town was the cashier, teller and janitor . . . a young man named Fred Florence. He persuaded me, against my better judgment, to borrow money from him. I have never been out of debt since. We began then an association that has deepened across the years and ripened since we have reached maturity. It gives me great pleasure . . . that the name of Fred F. Florence is to be ever perpetuated in one of the buildings on this campus.[103]

"I know of no place I had rather [this honor] would come to me," Florence replied with equal warmth and affection, "than at S. M. U.—a place where your heart and interests have been for so many years. Helen and I have the deepest devotion for you and your dear sweet wife, and we regard our friendship with you as one of the richest blessings God has bestowed upon us."[104]

As chairman of the board of trustees of Southern Methodist University, Bishop Smith gave such leadership in times of crisis that he became a symbol of both conciliation and strength. Administrators praised him for the depth of his understanding, the certainty of his support, and the skill of his diplomacy. "Let me tell you again how much I appreciate having you as the one to head up this organization," President Lee wrote to Smith in 1943. "You know how to take things, make them go smoothly, and direct the Board's thinking so that there is no waste of time in useless argument."[105] Two years later, when the wholesale liquor dealers of Dallas created a controversy by giving

$30,000 to SMU, Lee requested an emergency meeting of the executive committee to decide what to do with the money. The unsolicited gift was returned, and Dean Hawk wrote to Smith: "We were certainly delighted that you were here the other day when the storm broke. You have an inimitable way of saying, 'Peace, be still.' "[106] On another occasion Hawk declared: "I have never known any man whose influence and leadership in a board of trustees is so outstanding as is yours. . . . You have become the individual to whom we make reference when difficult situations arise."[107] Dean Robert G. Storey of SMU's Law School also praised Bishop Smith for having "been a source of inspiration in what we are trying to do and accomplish in the Legal Center."[108]

The most critical time of trial during Bishop Smith's twenty-two years as board chairman came during President Lee's illness in 1953 and 1954. After Lee "suffered a slight occlusion of the heart" in April, the executive committee shifted most of Lee's responsibilities to Vice President Willis M. Tate.[109] Besides the controversy that arose at that time over housing Negro students in the seminary dormitory, there was also the Beaty dilemma.

A professor at SMU for thirty-four years and chairman of the English department for thirteen, John Owen Beaty had a long tenure as "a self-appointed guardian of SMU's moral, political, and religious climate."[110] The difficulty was caused by Dr. Beaty's book *The Iron Curtain over America*, first published in December, 1951.[111] Under other circumstances the book might have gone unnoticed, but this was the era of Senator McCarthy's communist inquisition. The *Reader's Digest* published Stanley High's "Methodism's Pink Fringe" in February, 1950; the House Committee on Un-American Activities produced its "Review of the Methodist Federation for Social Action" in February, 1952; and the Houston-based "Committee for the Preservation of Methodism" attacked "communism" in Methodist church school literature as well as in the Federation.[112] On the one hand, Beaty's book was an embarrassment because professional communist-hunters with nationwide constituencies endorsed and praised the book for five months, from February through June, 1952.[113] On the other hand, the book was a source of chagrin because of its anti-Semitism and its misleading documentation. History Professor Paul F. Boller, Jr. described Beaty's *Iron Curtain over America* as "a dreary performance, full of distortions, omissions, and half-truths [that] shows not the slightest understanding of either modern history or the dynamics of Soviet communism."[114] Seven SMU law professors denounced it as "based on spurious doctrines and bigoted theories of racial and religious prejudice."[115]

When *Southwest Review* assistant editor Margaret L. Hartley favorably reviewed Ralph Lord Roy's *Apostles of Discord*—which characterized Beaty's work as "footnoted hate," "the most extensive piece of anti-Semitic literature in the history of America's racist movement," and "a composite of distorted half-truths and positive falsehoods,"[116]—Professor Beaty responded with an eight-page pamphlet entitled "How to Capture a University." "The attack upon me by the *Southwest Review*," Beaty charged, "is merely one of many manifestations of the effort of a certain powerful non-Christian element in our population to dominate Southern Methodist University." In addition to the "publishing interests of the University," Beaty continued, "those hostile to Christian civilization are concentrating upon its preacher training ["B'nai B'rith, an organization often referred to as the 'Jewish Gestapo,' has bought its way into a Christian School of Theology for seventy-five dollars!"], upon its teacher training, and upon the book-selling agency of the University." He declared the whole university suspect for cooperating with Temple Emanu-El in the Community Course series and with the National Conference of Christians and Jews on a summer human relations workshop.[117]

Under his doctor's orders not to get involved in stress situations, President Lee issued a public statement on February 13, 1954:

> . . . the pamphlet is being referred to the Board of Trustees for their study and for such action as they may see fit to take. This is being done because some of the implications of the pamphlet are in opposition to the known and published principles of The Methodist Church, which owns the University. . . . Furthermore, there are insinuations concerning which the Board will be requested to ask for specific charges.[118]

Beaty countered by mailing approximately three thousand copies of his "How to Capture a University" to parents of SMU students.[119] As an education correspondent for *Time* magazine succinctly commented: "Of all the professors the university has ever had, none has proved more embarrassing than friendly Dr. Beaty."[120]

On Thursday, March 11, 1954, Umphrey Lee addressed a formal letter to Bishop Smith:

> . . . For nearly a year I have done what I could to get into condition to resume my normal activities. My doctor now advises me that I must be free

from administrative responsibility for a year, and that after a year I shall probably not be able to work more than part time. This leaves me with no alternative. . . . Therefore, I am asking you, my long-time friend, to submit my resignation to the Board of Trustees of Southern Methodist University.[121]

Apparently Bishop Smith helped to persuade Lee to resign: such is the implication of a letter to Bishop Smith from Lee's physician written the following week:

I know you will be happy to find out that we have let Dr. Lee go out home, his blood pressure has returned to a safe point. Let me take this opportunity to thank you for the great service you rendered our friend and my patient, in getting him out of what I felt was a dangerous situation. I know we could have never done this so satisfactorily without your guiding help.[122]

"Many people, including Mrs. Lee," according to Lee's biographers, "believed that [Beaty's] attacks contributed to Dr. Lee's declining health and eventual resignation."[123]

Although Bishop Smith had informed the trustees that he would present Lee's resignation to the regular board meeting scheduled for May 6,[124] he convened a special meeting of the board on March 30. After receiving President Lee's resignation "with deep regrets," the board created a new position and named Dr. Lee "Chancellor of the University . . . with ex officio membership on the Executive Committee but without administrative responsibilities."[125] A lengthy explanatory statement was prepared "for the minutes, the press *and Doctor Lee.*"[126] When Lee asked Bishop Smith what a chancellor was supposed to do, the bishop replied: "Just walk across the campus and try to look benevolent."[127]

After the board had established a special committee to submit nominations for a new president to its May 6 meeting, Bishop Smith presented President Lee's referral of Dr. Beaty's "How to Capture a University" to the board for its action. Following a period of discussion, the board decided to send a letter to everyone who had received a pamphlet from Beaty. Emphasizing that Beaty had continued to distribute his pamphlet after President Lee's public statement that the whole matter was being referred to the board, the letter pledged that "a competent committee from the Board of Trustees is making full and searching inquiry into each of the charges made in Professor Beaty's paper and will report its findings to the Board of Trustees at the meeting on May

6th."[128] The letter was signed by Bishop Smith as chairman of the board, by Eugene McElvaney as chairman of the executive committee, and by Layton W. Bailey as secretary of the board. In order to assure all concerned that a "full and searching inquiry" would be made, Bishop Smith was authorized to appoint a committee "without limitation of membership on the Board." The trustees were clearly aware that Beaty had strong support from such Dallas organizations as the Public Affairs Luncheon Club.[129]

Bishop Smith's selections for the Beaty committee indicate his grasp of the pertinent power structures and his tactical influence on the eventual report. He chose five laymen, one bishop, and one minister, with himself ex officio. For the chairman he named D. A. Hulcy, the president of Lone Star Gas Company, who came from an old Dallas family of the cotton aristocracy and was not a member of the board.[130] As vice-chairman, Smith named J. M. Willson of Floydada, an SMU trustee since 1933, delegate to numerous General Conferences, donor of lectureships at twenty-two colleges in seven states, and past president of the West Texas Chamber of Commerce. The others were Floyd B. James, a trustee from Ruston, Louisiana; S. J. Hay, a member of the executive committee and president of the Great National Life Insurance Company; Bishop H. Bascom Watts of Lincoln, Nebraska; Dr. W. W. Ward, a prominent Methodist minister and longtime trustee from the Central Texas Conference; and J. S. Bridwell, Wichita Falls oilman, a trustee since 1939 and the donor of Bridwell Library. An impeccable panel of judges from any point of view!

A general sigh of relief accompanied the adjournment of this special meeting of the board of trustees, and Bishop Smith received praise for his guiding role: "There is a distinct uplift this morning in the spirit of all of us," declared Mrs. Loretta Hawkins, the assistant to the president. "It was an inspiration to observe the marvellous way in which you brought the Board to a realization of the University's needs and to the fine feeling of understanding with which they all left."[131] Smith even received praise from retired Bishop H. A. Boaz thanking Smith for *preventing* Bishop Selecman and himself—both former presidents of SMU—from coming before the board with a complaint about another matter. "You were wiser than I in that case," the old bishop conceded.[132]

Bishop Smith had given up keeping his daily journal by this time, but he clearly stated his position on the Beaty affair in a letter to Mrs. Hawkins, dated April 12:

It is my conviction that the Board should not only answer the Beaty charges but in addition should issue a dignified but positive statement on our own, leaving no ambiguity and no impression that we are on the defensive. We should not allow this sniping from the sidelines to go unnoticed. Our sustentation in Dallas is crippled next year unless we take a positive stand and stick to it.[133]

As directed, the Beaty Committee reported to the board on May 6. Having investigated Beaty's allegations, received testimony from Beaty and other appropriate parties, and examined Beaty's documentation, they declared, in part:

1. The material facts do not bear out the allegations made by Doctor Beaty in his pamphlets.
2. It is deplorable that Doctor Beaty, an employee of the University, failed to present his allegations to the administrative officers . . . instead, he presented his allegations to the students, patrons, and the press.

In so doing, Beaty had violated a bylaw passed by the board in 1933, after he had written letters to trustees and to many Methodist ministers protesting the retention on the university's faculty of a professor whom he considered subversive. The bylaw provided for the dismissal of any faculty member who presented grievances about the university to anyone but the president. Although the trustees could have dismissed Beaty on this ground, they chose to deny him the martyr's role. They restated the ideals and aims of the university—Bishop Smith's "positive statement"—and recommended that Beaty resign since he was "out of harmony with these principles and unable to support these ideals."[134] To this day the staff members of the *Southwest Review* credit Bishop Smith with saving their jobs in the Beaty crisis.[135]

By far the most important act of the board of trustees that Thursday in May, 1954, was the election of Willis McDonald Tate to the presidency of Southern Methodist University,[136] an office he was to hold for nineteen years.

"Bishop Smith was a great influence on my decision to come to SMU as Assistant Dean of Students in 1945," Dr. Tate recalls.[137] After several years as assistant to Dr. Paul Quillian at First Church, Houston, Tate was offered a series of attractive positions, including the one at SMU. He sought the counsel of Bishop Smith. "Well, Willis, if you stay at First Church, you will have a fine position as a layman. If you go to

SMU you will have a career and a profession."[138] This word of advice
proved to be prophetic. Nine years later Smith was the first to inform
Tate that he would be elected president of SMU. "About a day before
the Board was to meet," Tate still remembers with a sense of awe, "Bishop
Smith called and asked if I'd go to breakfast with him. And he told me
that they were going to recommend me for President."

How would the new president and the bishop work together? Umphrey Lee and Frank Smith had evolved an effective relationship as president and board chairman. Umphrey Lee's friends and associates thought
of him as a distinguished scholar, author, and preacher, a man who
thrived on harmony, avoided controversy, and disliked making difficult
decisions. As a result, it was sometimes necessary for the chairman of the
board to make a decision or perform some function ordinarily considered
to be the president's responsibility.[139] Tate, who had nine years' experience
in President Lee's administrative staff, recalls that Bishop Smith was considered "the firmest of us around here."

When there came a time when he had to step in and be tough, he could
really take them apart. I've seen him operate around here. You have evidence
of those folks whom he had to straighten out or get rid of. He had much
more talent and stomach for that than Umphrey Lee did. While Bishop Smith
didn't come around administering with a big stick, he was a symbol of
stability.[140]

Willis Tate was a layman, an All-American football player for the
"Mustangs," a trained administrator, and a more aggressive person than
Lee. Lee and Smith were the same age, whereas Tate was twenty-three
years younger than Bishop Smith. When asked to compare Smith's relationships with the two presidents, Tate responds:

Lee and Smith were long-time friends from their college days. Bishop Smith
was like a brother-image to Lee; he was more of a father-image to me. The
brother could step in in some ways that he didn't as a father, because his
son was running the business. He led me to believe that my function was
to get the job done. The more aggressive I was the more pleased he was.
I think Lee shared with him more of his problems and worried more about
some problems that I did.[141]

Dr. Tate especially emphasizes the freedom and encouragement *to be*
the president that Bishop Smith and the board gave him.

He never interfered with any administrative decision. He never failed to assume an active role in the solution of a problem that was his responsibility or on which I asked his help. It wasn't necessary to get his permission for anything because I understood and had faith in his backing as long as I was conscientious. Even if I was wrong, he'd back me publicly. He once told me that it was a good thing for the chairman of the board to live in Houston, because he obviously couldn't do anything down there. . . . I am sure that he took more abuse and took more pressure and answered more letters than I know about, but he never complained to me about it.[142]

The most intense abuse and pressure that President Tate and Bishop Smith faced arose when the SMU Student Center Forum Committee invited John Gates—who had recently resigned as editor of the *Daily Worker* and as a member of the Communist Party—to participate in a panel discussion with an FBI counterspy and three SMU professors. In the face of a storm of protest, Tate stood behind the right of the student committee to invite Gates as part of its case study of communism.[143] Some of the bitterest attacks came from longtime friends of Bishop Smith from the Houston area.[144] At the height of the protests, Tate wrote to Smith:

This is just a "love note" to tell you how deeply I appreciate your insight and courage in supporting me during this crisis. My great regret is that you and other good friends of the University must suffer in time and abuse as we are forced to stand by a principle. . . . I pray this will not harm the University and in the long run I trust it will help people to know what a Christian university must do and be.[145]

On another occasion, Tate wrote to Smith: "Your confidence in me is what motivates my best."[146] Tate believes that this was the secret of Bishop Smith's greatness: "his investment in the encouragement and development of people." "Bishop Smith gave people the freedom and encouragement and inspiration—and sometimes the discipline—that was necessary for their fulfillment," Tate explains.[147]

If Dr. Tate had any complaint about Bishop Smith as the chairman of SMU's board of trustees it was in the area of solicitation. "He never was very good at raising money for SMU," Dr. Tate says. "In fact, some of us almost accused him at times of protecting his donors rather than exploiting them for the University." Although Tate quickly acknowledges that Bishop Smith's friendship with the Perkinses and the Fondrens and others was "an asset to the University," he is convinced that Smith "simply did not want to do any kind of overt money raising."[148] A statement from one of Bishop Smith's letters to President Tate in 1955 illustrates the bishop's position:

Mrs. Fondren spoke to me about the possibility of Mr. [Jesse] Jones giving a half million dollars for the completion of the Coliseum. I have consistently made it a practice thru all these years in Houston not to solicit Methodist individuals for money, for specific gifts. Rather, have I cultivated their interest in the Church and her institutions, keeping before them certain needs as they exist. . . . I say this in order to say that I feel that this matter of the Coliseum is in a different category, because of Mr. Jones' age and because his name is not connected with anything about the University. He has always said to me that he did not want his name on a building, and no building he has erected bears his name. However, I am going to see whether he may be interested in the Coliseum proposal. I would guess that the prospect is not rosy, but I shall go into it fully with him.[149]

Smith, as usual, knew his man: Jones was not interested.

In fairness to President Tate, two further incidents should be mentioned. When the Fondren Foundation gave an additional $50,000 beyond its original grant of $550,000 for a Health Center at SMU "so that the building may be completed," Tate immediately shared this good news with Bishop Smith: "I know you had a hand in this matter, and I just wanted you to know of our victory."[150] About the same time [July, 1959], Tate asked Bishop Smith to consider a "post-retirement" position with the university. "So much needs to be done in the field of development and interpretation, and no one is better suited or more capable than you," Tate declared. "Our needs in realizing our dream, *such as endowment and project grants*, must be faced and met. This you could help us do on your own terms."[151] "Bess and I are deeply appreciative of your all-too-generous words and proposal," Smith replied:

I am eager to do anything possible, so long as I am able to creep about, for Southern Methodist University, and I expect to seek opportunities to that end . . . but I will do just as much for the University from the sidelines as I could do with an official position, and I would feel that an official relationship would be an imposition upon the University.[152]

At 9:00 o'clock on Friday morning, November 4, 1960, Bishop A. Frank Smith called to order his last meeting of the board of trustees of Southern Methodist University, ending his twenty-two years of chairmanship. Because of the large number of special guests, the meeting was held in Lois Perkins Auditorium in Selecman Hall. The first order of business sounded the only contrasting note to the otherwise dominant theme of grateful ovation: Bishop Paul E. Martin presented a resolution in memory of J. J. Perkins, who had died in September. A moving moment in the meeting came when Bishop Smith issued a special welcome to Mrs. Perkins as she assumed the trustee-at-large place created through the death of her husband. "She, herself, has said that she cannot take her husband's place," Bishop Smith commented, "but Mrs. Perkins will take her own place and this Board is honored to welcome her as a new member."[153]

Upon the election of Eugene McElvaney as chairman and Bishop Paul E. Martin as vice-chairman, Bishop Smith surrendered the chair to his successor, expressing his great respect for these two new officers and his personal gratitude for the privilege of serving the board for twenty-two years. As one of his first acts as chairman, Mr. McElvaney announced "a ceremony, the performance of which may never be equaled before this Board of Trustees." Bishop William C. Martin then presented a book of letters written by the members of the board to Bishop Smith. President Tate presented to Bishop Smith a silver plaque bearing the signatures of all the present members and officers of the board.[154] This plaque is on permanent display in the "A. Frank Smith Texana Room" in Fondren Library.[155] The following portion of President Tate's letter serves as an example of these messages of appreciation:

During the critical and formative years of Southern Methodist University, your vision, insight and leadership have guided the institution to eminence and fulfillment. . . . During its crises you have proven to be the bulwark of strength and stability. . . . Surely no man has had more influence in the destiny of this university and, truly, its stature is the shadow of your own dedication.

You have been the intimate friend and advisor to each of its presidents. . . . None realized better than I do their dependence on your contagious faith and vision. . . . My most personal decisions have been made with your generous counsel, and it was your faith in me and your willingness to stand by me that gave me courage to attempt the presidency.

WILLIS M. TATE[156]

It was not only at the time of his retirement that Bishop Smith was honored. He also received three significant honors while he was still chairman. In 1953 the faculty of the Perkins School of Theology chose him to be the Fondren Lecturer for Ministers' Week in 1955.[157] Bishops

John M. Moore and Edwin D. Mouzon, Frank Smith's avowed mentors, had appeared in this distinguished lectureship founded by Mr. and Mrs. Fondren in 1919. Approximately two thousand ministers from the eight states of the South Central Jurisdiction would hear Bishop Smith deliver his four lectures in McFarlin Auditorium. In the spring of 1956 Texas Gamma Chapter of Phi Beta Kappa (SMU) elected Bishop Smith an honorary member "in recognition and appreciation of [his] long and valued service to the cause of liberal education."[158] That same year Smith received a substantially different kind of recognition—but one no less cherished—from the eighty-nine-year-old former president of Southern Methodist University, Bishop Hiram A. Boaz, who wrote:

During your presidency of the Board of Trustees of S.M.U. the University has made its greatest growth, and that growth has largely been due to your wise leadership. . . . I have watched you with as much interest as if you were my own younger brother. You are an ideal BISHOP. You look like a bishop, you walk and talk like a bishop, and above all you preach like a bishop! You will go down in history as one of the great bishops of Methodism. You have my hearty congratulations.[159]

16

Bishop Smith and His People

"I KNOW THESE MEN," Bishop A. Frank Smith declared, speaking of the ministers of the Texas Conference of The Methodist Church. "Over four hundred men joined this conference 'on trial' during the twenty-seven years that I have had it. Three-fourths of the preachers of this conference have never known any other bishop except me."[1] If Bishop Smith had included the Southwest Texas Conference in his summary, he could have claimed an additional 189 preachers who had not served under any other bishop, or approximately 56 percent of the effective members of that annual conference in 1960.[2] Forty-eight ministers in the Texas and forty in the Southwest Texas conferences shared the entire term of Bishop Smith's episcopal supervision in their respective conferences.

One Texas Conference veteran recalls the closeness and informality of Bishop Smith's relationship with his preachers: "He was my bishop for nearly thirty years, and I felt as close to him as I did my own family."[3] Even in later years, the bishop retained that ability to be at ease with his preachers and their families. Walton Gardner remembers when Bishop Smith came to dinner at their parsonage in Texas City in 1955:

Right after lunch my little boy David was playing with his baton and asked Bishop Smith to play with him. "Bishop, I'd like to have a parade." "All

343

right," the bishop said, and he and Mrs. Smith got in line behind David. And they marched around the dining room and the kitchen and through the living room and out on the front porch and down the sidewalk. I can see the bishop going along, kind of prancing with his arms going like this. And after Bishop Smith got home, he wrote David a letter and thanked him for asking him to be in his parade.[4]

A pastor who served under Bishop Smith in both the Southwest Texas and Texas conferences was impressed by Smith's interest: "It seemed as though nothing was unimportant to him respecting the pastors and their families."[5] Ministers and laymen alike cherished the handwritten notes of congratulation, encouragement, or sympathy that Bishop Smith wrote to them.

Even in those conferences which Bishop Smith held for only one quadrennium, he quickly gained a remarkable acquaintance with his people. "I was in his cabinet in North Texas," Bishop Paul E. Martin explains, "and in those days [1934-38] a bishop had much larger areas. But when you brought up a man, he knew whom you were talking about. Frank had four conferences—the North Texas, the Texas, the Oklahoma, and the Indian Mission—but he knew the preachers and their families and could call them by name."[6] Evidence that Bishop Smith thrived on these personal relationships can be found in his daily journal. After recounting a round of five district conferences in three days, Smith exclaimed: "I wish I could spend all my time out among the people of my area." Even when the Smiths were on a rare vacation, the bishop took time to write. During their first trip to Europe, he spent most of a day in Brussels "writing post cards to the preachers." In 1953 he sent greetings from Rome.[7]

On the other hand, Bishop Smith sought to avoid the potential dangers of favoritism. "When I became a bishop," he once stated, "we entered into a lonely existence. We've never had intimate friends."

In a way a bishop can't be intimate with anyone. The moment it appears that he is unusually friendly with a certain person, the chances are that person will expect special favors. Then there are those who want to know what the bishop is saying about this or that, and it is dangerous business if they are able to quote you. . . . Now we haven't been unfriendly. We have certainly gone to as many of their homes as we could and have had association with them, but we have tried to be friends to all our people. There wasn't any one crowd nor any one person that could be singled out and said he's closer to the bishop than anyone else.[8]

"I always told my preachers, 'Talk to me about anything that's on
your mind or heart,' and they did," Bishop Smith declared. "And they
would come and talk to me about their family troubles, the difficulties
they were having in their churches, and what-have-you. I never wanted
them to do anything except to feel that I had a brotherly interest."⁹
If any one term adequately characterizes Bishop Smith's relationship to
his people, "brotherly" is that word. In 1931 Dr. J. N. R. Score described
Bishop Smith's presiding over his first annual conference as "a brotherly
man presiding in an assembly of brethren." Predicting that Smith would
never become a dictator or an autocrat, Score declared: "Frank Smith
will always be a brother."¹⁰

Three years later when Bishop Smith was assigned the North Texas
Conference, a former Texas Conference colleague found him to be
"altogether brotherly, understanding of the problems that confronted the
pastoral ministry of that day."¹¹ In 1945 a pastor returning to Bishop
Smith's area commended him for "maintaining the fine brotherly spirit
that you showed in the early days of your administration."¹² A decade
later, in his twenty-fourth year as a bishop, Smith still received such
praise when a veteran of the West Texas Conference declared to him:
"I always marvel at how you do it: one meeting after another, one problem after another, but always poised, unselfish, considerate, kind, tolerant,
and brotherly."¹³ Bishop W. Kenneth Pope recalls a beautiful example
of Smith's brotherly spirit at work. A young bishop, facing the problem
of how to deal with one of his men caught in an incident of "out and
out immorality," turned to Bishop Smith for advice. "Now Frank could
have been judgmental and suggested ways of throwing that preacher
out of the church," Pope commented, "but the first thing he said was:
'Remember, this man is your brother.' "¹⁴

Bishop A. Frank Smith did indeed seek to establish a fraternal relationship with his preachers, but always as an *elder* brother, not superior,
but always senior. He never ceased to be "the Bishop." While he was
"Frank" to his episcopal colleagues and to those who knew him well
before 1930, to many others he was "Bishop Frank."¹⁵ As Monroe Vivion,
a longtime friend and close associate of Smith's, says: "He knew he was
the bishop. And the bishop is the bishop. He didn't have to tell anybody
nor prove it. He just was the bishop."¹⁶ Consciously or not, those who
speak of Bishop Smith's brotherliness are generally comparing him with
the more austere and often autocratic bishops of the Southern Methodist
Church: Edwin D. Mouzon, John M. Moore, and H. A. Boaz.¹⁷

This elder brother image appears in a number of ways. Although Bishop Smith was known as a delightful conversationalist, he also knew how to dominate conversations. "He didn't hold a conversation with you; he talked and you listened," Kenneth Pope recalls. "I remember going up to Lakeview with him many times. As soon as he opened the car door, he would say: 'Good morning, brethren.' And not a word would be spoken, except by him, until we got there. If he had been dull, it would have been terrible, but he wasn't."[18] Lawrence Landrum, who chauffeured Bishop Smith about over the Galveston and Beaumont districts during his two terms on Smith's cabinets, agrees: "On these long automobile rides, he would start talking and talk for an hour without stopping, especially if you had something you wanted to say to him, and he didn't want you to say it."[19]

L. U. Spellman remembers an incident that became the basis of a widely repeated satirical tribute to one aspect of Bishop Smith's elder brother image—his "arm-around-the-shoulder" persuasiveness.

In the making of appointments Frank Smith had a great way of soothing the feelings of a disappointed pastor, making him feel that his appointment was not only adequate but also a real opportunity for service. One afternoon while we were making appointments in the cabinet room in the St. Anthony Hotel, a preacher came storming into the room, greatly agitated. "Where is that bishop?" he demanded. "He has me lined up for ———— and I am not going there. I mean to tell him so." We ushered him into the bishop's room and closed the door. Twenty minutes later he came out much subdued and mollified. "All right, put me down," he said, "I'll go." But at the door he paused for a final word. "That man ought not be a bishop. He should be the chaplain of a penitentiary. He could put his big arm around a condemned criminal, walk down 'Death Row' with him, and by the time they got to the electric chair have that fellow convinced that he had volunteered for the good of the country."[20]

In more technical terms, Bishop Smith did not conceive of the episcopacy as a third order of ministry, but he certainly thought of a bishop as *primus inter pares*—first among equals. He was offended, for example, when the Judicial Council ruled that a bishop could no longer transfer a preacher from his home conference to another without the preacher's consent. "Now that is certainly invading the prerogative of the episcopacy," Bishop Smith declared.

I used to say to the men who were being received into an annual conference,

"You are eligible to serve in any conference in Methodism in this country with the consent of the two bishops involved." Now his membership is tied down to one annual conference, and you can't move him out of there unless he is willing to go. Why, the next step in that logic would be that a bishop cannot bring a man into a conference unless the conference agrees.[21]

Did Bishop Smith ever exercise that authority to transfer a preacher against his will? "Just one time," he admitted, "I lifted a man arbitrarily out of one conference and took him to another conference I was holding, because he was going to split his church wide open." As Smith recalled the incident, the preacher had declared that he was going to throw certain leading men out of his church because they had opposed him. When the preacher persisted despite a direct warning, the bishop intervened. "I told him, 'I am going to transfer you out of this conference.' And he said, 'I won't go.' And I said, 'You will go, too, you will have to go.'" Even at that, Bishop Smith gave the preacher a choice: "Now you can go back and tell your friends that you are being thrown out, or you can tell them that you have a great opportunity over there and that you are going gladly."[22] This exercise of "arbitrary" power had a happy ending, as Bishop Smith later noted in his daily journal: "Brother ———, whom I moved last year from ——— against his will, is having a great time here."[23]

The men who served two or more terms in Bishop Smith's cabinets generally agree that the bishop never exploited his office. He was more likely to err on the side of leniency than of heavy-handedness. L. U. Spellman, a presiding elder seasoned under both Bishop John M. Moore and Bishop H. A. Boaz before Smith appointed him to the Corpus Christi, San Antonio, and Kerrville districts, describes Smith's practice:

Regarding the episcopacy, I think Bishop Smith saw himself as a leader but certainly not as a driver, a brother rather than a superior officer. He was a supervisor of church affairs but not a "law giver." When I once urged him to use his authority to deal with an unruly brother on the grounds that he had been given authority by the church for this purpose, he replied: "Lou, the more authority the church puts in your hands, the more careful you must be in the exercise of that power."[24]

Under similar circumstances Smith told Stewart Clendenin, "Authority is like money in a savings account: the more you use it the less you have, and the less you use it the more you have."[25] Spellman believes that the bishop was humbled by the size of the office. "He knew the authority of the office, but he did not deem it a position in which to be officious. In casual conversation he was more inclined to belittle himself than to exalt his abilities."[26] Smith enjoyed, for example, quoting a comparison made by Bishop W. J. Nold of the Catholic Diocese of Galveston. After the two bishops had been discussing their respective responsibilities, Bishop Nold said, "Bishop Smith, do you know the difference between you as a bishop and me as a bishop? When I tell my people to go to hell, they go!"[27] Always skilled at improving a humorous story, Bishop Smith adapted Bishop Nold's comment into a distinction between a Catholic bishop and his brother, Bishop W. Angie Smith. "The Catholic bishop tells his folks to do so and so or they will go to hell. Angie tells his folks to do so and so, and they tell him to go to hell."[28]

Closely related to Bishop Smith's brotherly spirit was his ability to listen to and to understand his preachers' problems. Three letters represent a multitude of examples found in the bishop's correspondence. In 1946 the pastor of a relatively small church wrote to Bishop Smith:

Thank you for your sympathetic understanding and handling of my case. I shall never forget, and you will never know what your kind words did for me the day I talked with you. . . . You were very busy and must have been crowded for time, yet you gave me all the time that was needed to state my desires, and your words of brotherly sympathy were like balm to my sorely wounded spirit.[29]

Another pastor who had apparently spoken in anger to the bishop wrote:

Please forgive the unkind remarks of the past that should not have been made and were made only under tension. You listened most kindly and understandingly and from that day our attitude toward you was changed. Never again did we feel that you were not interested. Few people could have taken the remarks in the wonderful way in which you did. It took a truly big person to do it.[30]

The third letter was written by a district superintendent in 1948, at the end of Smith's four-year presidency of the Central Texas Conference:

We are greatly grieved to give up our connection with you. . . . You were not only competent and capable as an administrator, but above all you were Christ's man, greatly beloved. I cannot imagine any person in our Conference, young or old, rich or poor, who did not feel perfectly free to come to

you with the problem in hand, and certain that he would have a hearing. . . .
You have been a great leader for us, and your administration will long linger
in the loving appreciation of the ministry and membership of the Central
Texas Conference.[31]

Kenneth Copeland declared that Bishop Smith "always found time
to let a preacher who was hurting come in and talk with him." In 1955
a fire destroyed the inside of the sanctuary of Travis Park Methodist
Church during Dr. Copeland's pastorate there. As Copeland described
his reaction to that devastating event:

I knew that we had to rebuild or move and build brand new. Either way,
it meant a long financial campaign. I had never been a builder of churches,
and I really faced my moment of greatest frustration. So I called Bishop
Smith and asked if Catherine and I could come down to see him. We set a
day, and Catherine and I drove down to Houston. And I said, "Bishop, this
is the first time in my life that I have really wanted to run." . . . And I'll
never forget: he stood up and put that large hand on my shoulder and said:
"Now, Kenneth, let me just say something to you. You have laymen in
your church and on your board who know more about raising money and
architectural drawings and building than you will ever need to know. That's
not your business. You advise with them about the religious significance of
the building, but your main job is to hold that congregation together. It's
your business to love them, preach to them, pastor them, and advise with
your committees. If you do that, they will build the church." Well, I went
back convinced that I was going to prove that his judgment was right if it
killed me. And it didn't kill me, and his judgment was right. That was a
crisis point at which he very gently, very lovingly and tenderly held me in
check. I had no need to run.[32]

According to the witness of more than one pastor, Bishop Smith
would kneel in prayer with his men when the circumstances were appropriate. "Too few times have I told you what you mean to me," one
minister wrote to the bishop. "From the time you knelt in prayer with
me in my study at ———— to this good hour, you have been a great stay
and bulwark of my faith, and I am truly grateful to you for your ministry to me."[33]

Another pastor, faced with a difficult decision, went to see Bishop
Smith. "We sat down and talked," the pastor recalls, "going up and
down both sides of the thing and trying to look at it objectively. And
then the bishop said, 'Let's have prayer together.' And we knelt there
and he put his arm around me, and we prayed together. That just shows

how deeply concerned Bishop Smith was about the lives of his preachers and our sense of accomplishment and of purpose."[34]

The situation was somewhat different in the Southwest Texas Conference. "Bishop Smith was not often available to the pastors of our conference for intimate personal advice or pastoral counseling," according to Dr. L. U. Spellman. Because of the great distances involved, the pastors usually took their troubles to their district superintendents. Bishop Smith did what he could by correspondence or, in emergencies, by long distance telephone. "I recall instances of letters from Bishop Smith," Spellman explains, "telling me of getting letters from men in my district who needed or wanted his counsel. He would tell me that he had written them in order that I might follow through or at least be apprised of his effort to assist."[35] Even in the Texas Conference, Bishop Smith expected the district superintendents to be the primary source of counseling for the pastors.[36]

Ask any number of Bishop Smith's close associates where the bishop's office was, and they will usually reply: "In his coat pocket on a pack of three-by-five cards." The bishop always kept a supply of these cards and several flat-shaped heavy lead pencils handy. During meetings, conversations, telephone calls, or riding in a car, he could conveniently make a quick notation of someone he needed to see or call, an idea for a sermon, or some other reminder. Instead of an office Bishop Smith often used the mezzanine floor of the Lamar Hotel or the lobby of the Rice Hotel as a meeting place in Houston.[37] His having such a "movable office" was not for the lack of options. In 1942, for example, Dr. Paul Quillian offered to provide an office and a secretary at First Methodist Church at the church's expense. The bishop declined, noting in his daily journal: "I appreciate it, but told him I had not been able to work things out so as to need a secretary for full time. I wish I could do so, it would lighten my load."[38]

One reason Bishop Smith gave for such an informal arrangement was that his travels kept him out of town except for four or five days a month. Also, the bishop desired to maintain an element of privacy for his callers —privacy that would not be possible in an ordinary office and reception room, much less at his study in the episcopal residence. Even the mezzanine of the Lamar Hotel sometimes failed to protect confidential matters, as Dr. Stewart Clendenin recalls:

One time Bishop Smith's timing was a little off when I went in to see him.

As I came in, I met my district superintendent, Dick Swain, as he was going out. And I asked the bishop what Dick was up to, not realizing that I was putting him on the spot. He didn't want to answer my question, and he wouldn't make up something. Yet he was too kind to tell me to mind my own business.[39]

By 1944 Bishop Smith had accepted the offer of a study at First Methodist Church. According to a young pastor who visited the bishop there, it was a makeshift arrangement at best. "There was nothing in the office but a little old desk and two or three chairs. He didn't even have a telephone. When he wanted to communicate with a secretary, he'd tap on a waterpipe."[40] Even though in 1945 Dr. Dawson Bryan "fixed up a study and office" for Bishop Smith at St. Paul's Methodist Church, the bishop never changed his loosely structured style. In 1947 Mrs. Smith gave her husband a dictaphone, and from then on he dictated a large part of his correspondence.[41]

"The District Superintendent is the key man in any successful program," Bishop Smith declared. "To the degree that he takes a matter to heart and does something about it, to that degree any Methodist program will succeed."[42] Given this high estimation of the position, how did Bishop Smith choose his district superintendents? What qualifications did he desire in these men who made up his cabinet? Some people still remember an annual conference when Bishop Smith declared just before reading the appointments: "Now I understand that there has been criticism of some of the appointments of district superintendents. I just want to say to you [the assembled clergy and lay delegates] that I would put the devil himself on a district if I thought it would help the church."[43] In this obvious instance of hyperbolizing, Bishop Smith was declaring one of his guiding principles in choosing his cabinet: the good of the church has priority over all other considerations. The men whom the bishop then proceeded to appoint to the district superintendency may have wished he had chosen a more flattering metaphor, but they couldn't argue with his basic point. Years later Bishop Smith used similar language to state a second principle: "I believe that if a man has shown by his ability that he has a right to be on a district, even though he was the devil himself, he's got a right to be on a district." On this occasion Smith immediately went on to qualify his exaggeration and to explain his intention: "I shouldn't say devil because he wouldn't have the character. But whether or not a man likes the bishop, whether or not he happens to see through the same knothole as the bishop, his personal feelings ought not to be considered."[44] In other words, a man's demonstrated ability is more important than his congeniality with the bishop.

In their characterizations of his actual practice in choosing his district superintendents, Bishop Smith's former cabinet members emphasize practicality. In the Texas Conference, for example, Dr. Lawrence Landrum says that Bishop Smith sought to maintain a balanced cabinet: "young and old, both sides of any political factions that might exist. . . . I don't think he let personality enter into consideration, but he sought to balance the cabinet to attain a consensus. He kept it balanced so that he could retain control."[45] As Dr. Stewart Clendenin succinctly reports: "Bishop Smith did not get all of his he-coons up the same tree."[46] Dr. Monroe Vivion agrees that balance was one of Smith's major concerns:

The bishop would look over the field and try to pick men that he thought could do the job, but he always matched them up pretty well. He wouldn't let either of the groups run the conference. Once in awhile he would appoint younger men: Neal Cannon and I were in our thirties. But he liked the idea of a man retiring off of the district. That would leave him a wide open appointment, which enabled him to move other folks up and to keep an experienced leadership in the cabinet at the same time.[47]

"There was more party spirit in the Central Texas Conference than in the others," according to Bishop Will Martin, who succeeded Bishop Smith in that conference in 1948. "There was quite a rift in that conference with very few men who weren't pro this or against that. Frank had to keep things pretty much in balance, and he did a good job of it."[48]

In the Southwest Texas Conference, the situation was somewhat better. "During the twenty-two years that Bishop Smith presided over our conference, we had no deep factions," Dr. L. U. Spellman explains; "but he kept a very well balanced cabinet regarding other differences: liberal and conservative, or North and South after Union [1939]. I think he named John Deschner because he was one of the strongest men coming to us from the M. E. Church."

Another difference in this conference was Bishop Smith's practice of direct exchanges in appointing his district superintendents. If a man coming off a district was appointed to "First Church," for example, the pastor at "First Church" would be appointed to succeed that particular superintendent. "When I complained that this policy of direct exchange sometimes tied his hands," Spellman recalls, "Frank said that a pastor lifted to make room for the district superintendent coming off the cabinet might feel it a reflection on his ability if he were not given the appointment as superintendent." Bishop Smith also used this direct exchange of appointments to keep the retiring district superintendent from being "jittery about where he will go. The average D. S. isn't worth a whoop his last year," Smith declared, "because he is trying to find a place for himself ."[49]

A third practice that Bishop Smith sometimes followed in the Southwest Texas Conference was appointing a man to a district to broaden his viewpoint. If a man who had real potential had become too one-sided in his theology, too extreme in his criticism of the church, or otherwise unappreciative of connectional polity, Bishop Smith might appoint him to the cabinet as an education in mainstream Methodism. Although there was obvious risk in such a policy, Spellman believes that Bishop Smith brought several men into strong leadership in this manner.[50]

Regardless of differences between the respective annual conferences, Bishop Smith wanted men on his cabinets who would carry out their responsibilities and not always come back to him with problems they should handle themselves. "The reason I like to have Lou Spellman in the cabinet," Smith once said, "is that when I put him on a district I can go on and forget about it. He'll take care of it. I have had some fellows that run to me, write to me or phone every time they stump their toe."[51] "Bishop Smith sent a man to a district and expected him to do his job unless there were unusual circumstances," Monroe Vivion says. "And he nearly always stood beside his district superintendent: whatever he did was right as far as the church was concerned."[52] Bishop Slater sums up the matter:

Bishop Smith's basic philosophy was to try to put the right man in the right place and expect that man to do the work. He had a fundamental respect for the men he placed in positions of leadership and he believed in them. He let them know that he believed in them, he expected them to do the job, and he didn't expect to interfere with them unnecessarily.[53]

The actual appointment of a district superintendent was generally more complicated than any other appointment. As Bishop Smith explained:

When a preacher realizes that he is never going to hold one of the top-flight appointments, his next best bet to get what he thinks is the recognition he wants is to go on a district. So they come to me and want to be superintendents, and I tell them frankly: "Well, there are eight men who want to go on this district and there can't but one go."[54]

The following notations in Bishop Smith's daily journal illustrate both the problems involved and the possible satisfactions that might come in choosing a district superintendent:

Tuesday, April 7, 1942: Spent entire day at office seeing various men. It is now time to make the appointment of a D. S. for Houston [District], and the brethren all have "notions." Dr. ———— spent a couple of hours with me; he does not want Brother ———— on the Houston District chiefly for political reasons. Dr. ———— knows the men and the conference, but his advice is always motivated by political considerations. . . .

Saturday, April 11, 1942: A perfect day. I met Dr. W. F. Bryan this morning in my office and notified him he would be the next D. S. on the Houston Dist. He was my first Presiding Elder when I joined the N. Tex. conf. on trial 28 yrs. ago next fall. And now I am able to make him exceedingly happy by appointing him here for his last two years. He retires in 1944. . . .

When asked by a newspaper reporter how appointments were made, Bishop Smith replied "with a twinkle in his eye": "It's easy. All we have to do is see that the congregations don't get preachers they don't want and that the preachers don't get congregations they don't want."[55] In a more serious vein, the bishop once wrote to one of his preachers: "I wish I could hold one conference and know that every man got just what he wanted and that every church got just what it wanted. Of course, such a situation as that will never happen this side of heaven itself, for circumstances and people are of such diverse types."[56] Of all the duties and responsibilities that A. Frank Smith carried in his thirty years as a bishop in the Methodist church, the making of appointments was the one that gave him "the greatest pain and worry." As he said following his retirement, "That was the chief relief to me when I was relieved from the travelling episcopacy: I no longer had to say, 'You go here and you go there.' "[57]

Part of the agony of making appointments grew out of Bishop Smith's sensitivity to the feelings of his preachers. He wanted them to share their preferences and aspirations with him; but as Lawrence Landrum recalls, "Bishop Smith had a hard time refusing anybody anything. He was so fond of people and didn't want to hurt anyone. He would always go a long way around to keep from offending anyone. And he bent over backwards to be sure he was being fair with everybody."[58] Such sensitivity was compounded, of course, in the Texas and Southwest Texas conferences where Bishop Smith had known his pastors for so many years. "Why, I have known some of these men since they were children," Smith exclaimed; "and when you can't give one as good an appointment as you have given another, they want to know why. And if they don't come, their wives do."[59]

Bishop Paul Martin recalls his impression of Frank Smith's great concern for his preachers when he was in Smith's cabinet in the North Texas Conference. "At first it worried me that we took such an awfully long time making appointments. Many times we were up until two o'clock in the morning," Martin recalls. "Then I came to see that it was part of Frank's consideration for everyone. Instead of saying, 'Well, this just can't be done,' Frank would say, 'Let's look into this thing one more time.' I do not know whether it made for any better appointments, but it certainly meant full consideration for a man and his family."[60] W. F. Bryan, who was a presiding elder or district superintendent for seventeen years in three different annual conferences and served in the cabinet with several bishops, declared: "I have often said to many of our preachers that [Frank Smith] was more patient and concerned in the Cabinet that every preacher should be given careful consideration in his appointment than any bishop I ever worked with."[61]

Another reason for the length of time Bishop Smith required for making appointments is suggested by L. U. Spellman. "Frank Smith was very deliberate and unhurried in making appointments, frequently talking at length about matters we thought extraneous. We were somewhat closer to our problems and doubtless over-eager to get to the job," Spellman explains. "I have seen a new cabinet member in his first meeting waiting with his pencil gripped in his hand, ready to write, while Frank talked on and on of matters far and wide."[62] Monroe Vivion agrees: "The bishop was a past-master at getting the mind of a group away from the immediate situation, especially if things were a little tense. And everything stopped while he was talking, too."[63] On one occasion the Southwest Texas cabinet, finding time on their hands during a general meeting at Mt. Wesley, "stole a meeting" on the bishop and put in a long day's work. "When Smith caught on," Spellman confesses, "we assured him our meeting was largely accidental. His only remark was that had he known it, he might have been able to meet with us."[64]

Bishop Smith encouraged his preachers and laymen to come to see him about appointments. These interviews were time-consuming and often trying, as the bishop's daily journal illustrates:

Sunday, September 23, 1945: After dinner the pulpit committee from 1st Church, ——— came to see me to ask for Brother ——— who had been supply pastor. I told them "No." They got mad. I'll see them later.

Monday, October 8, 1945: Spent entire day at office at St. Paul's seeing preachers and laymen. . . .

Tuesday, October 9, 1945: Spent day in interviews at office again. This is a tiresome business. . . .

Wednesday, October 10, 1945: Spent day at Church seeing people. . . . A delegation from ——— came to ask for a new preacher tonite. They are not an agreeable bunch. . . . I am completely exhausted.

There were times, understandably, when the bishop did not want to discuss appointments; however, he was not always successful in evading the subject.

Sunday, Sept. 8, 1946: Left Houston on the aft. train instead of the morning train yesterday in order to avoid the special cars carrying the Dist. Supts. to Grand Rapids. When I changed at St. Louis, I found the two cars on the Chicago train. They had missed the early train. So I had 5 hours of conferences with D. S.'s.

Monday, Sept. 9, 1946: Left Chicago for Grand Rapids. About 300 men bound for the meeting on this train. Again I had my hands full. I do not like to travel with a crowd of preachers from my area, especially D. S.'s. They want to talk shop continuously & it is exhausting.

In order to have more time for individual conferences with his preachers and laymen, Bishop Smith eventually adopted the practice of appointing cabinet chairmen and leaving much of the detailed work to his cabinets. "During my final four years on his cabinet," Lawrence Landrum recalls, "Bishop Smith wasn't present at more than half a dozen cabinet sessions. Now, he always had two or three or four appointments that he wanted to make. 'Make these first,' he would say to us, 'and then fit the others in around them.' "[65] Over in the Southwest Texas Conference, the bishop held his private conferences in a room adjoining the cabinet room in order to be more readily available. "While we sometimes thought that we could get more work done in Frank's absence," Dr. Spellman remembers, "when we got into one of our frequent 'dead ends' in making appointments, he would come in and, after the most meager briefing, suggest two or three moves that would completely break up the log jam." Repeatedly amazed at the number of related appointments that Bishop Smith could hold in mind and see through to a logical arrangement, Spellman suggests an explanation: "He must have known the individual members of the conference much better than we sometimes supposed and had men in mind for certain places."[66]

Laymen also played a role in the appointment-making process. Bishop Smith knew at least one layman in most of the churches in his episcopal area and frequently sought their judgment in matters dealing with their respective churches. "That was his great method," Dr. Landrum believes. "If the bishop was going to make an appointment to Longview, for instance, he'd get in touch with Mr. Nicholson. At Tyler, it would be Mr. R. W. Fair."[67] This man or woman would be the bishop's point of contact. Dr. Spellman recalls, however, that Bishop Smith did not necessarily make the appointments according to the wishes of these trusted persons. "The bishop listened to them, and sometimes it made a good deal of difference, but he didn't always give them the preacher they wanted."[68] Sometimes it was the other way around, according to Dr. Monroe Vivion: "Instead of taking their judgment about what they wanted, he would sell them what he wanted."[69] Dr. Stewart Clendenin explains how this was done. "The bishop would expose the man to the laymen, commend the preacher to them, and then 'let them choose.' Given the opportunity, Bishop Smith could pretty well persuade them that this was the preacher they ought to have."[70] Such persuasion, of course, depended in the first place upon the widespread trust and appreciation that laymen had for Bishop Smith. The following passage is typical of any number of letters in Bishop Smith's correspondence which illustrate this confidence:

Dear Bishop Smith: Please accept my personal thanks and those of the committee to whom you were most generous in giving audience on a matter of importance to this Church. Your keen understanding, your open-mindedness, and your Christian generosity in seeing the problem and offering us such sincere assurance of a workable plan were deeply appreciated. . . .[71]

Despite Bishop Smith's preference for an unhurried pace, the process of making appointments always accelerated with the approach of the last day of an annual conference. Lawrence Landrum describes the customary pattern:

Bishop Smith would talk with people off and on for thirty to sixty days before conference, always leaving things in a nebulous state until the day before adjournment. Then he would get the cabinet together around a table, take off his coat and his shoes and undo his tie, and we'd make appointments, sometimes all night long. Then, if there was anything left, we'd meet right up to the time for the reading of the appointments.[72]

On such occasions, of course, the bishop would have to ask a trusted lieutenant to preside over the sessions of the conference while he and the cabinet were out. The following notations in Bishop Smith's daily journal are typical of his descriptions of adjournment days:

Friday, October 23, 1942: I opened the [Southwest Texas] conference this morning, then put Dr. Heinsohn in the chair while I met several persons and cleared up some last minute appointments. At about twelve-thirty I read the appointments.

Friday, November 6, 1942: Dawson Bryan presided at the [Texas] conference session this morning while I met with the cabinet at the Rice [Hotel]. We completed the appointments by mid-afternoon and I read them at four o'clock.

What happened if something went wrong with an appointment? How did Bishop Smith deal with pastor-parish conflict? On the one hand, he generally held the pastor responsible. "Where there is trouble in a church," Smith declared, "three-fourths of it is the preacher. He may not have started it, but he could have stopped it." The greatest danger was letting one's personal feelings get in the way:

If a pastor says, "you can't say that to me" or "you can't do this or that," the matter becomes personal and the breech is widened. A pastor has got to be two different people. One is what he is professionally, the other is his personal feelings. For his personal feelings, let him cry on his wife's shoulder. Let her bustle up and say what she is going to do to anyone who talks like that to her husband. But as far as he is related to that church member, his personal feelings ought not to enter into it at all.[73]

The characteristic that Bishop Smith most valued in a preacher, according to Dr. Monroe Vivion, was "common sense, learning to deal with people." "I've heard him say again and again," Vivion recalls, "that ninety-five per cent of the problems in a local church are because the preacher didn't know how to get along with folks. It wasn't because he was a poor preacher. It wasn't because he did this or that. He just didn't have the ability to relate to his people."[74]

On the other hand, Bishop Smith's first concern in pastor-parish conflicts was to save the pastor. "Every Methodist preacher has the right to make an ass of himself at least once in his ministry," the bishop often declared.[75] The veterans of Smith's cabinets agree that the bishop always did his best to protect the interests of the pastor, to see that he got another chance. "He took the side of the preacher," Dr. Landrum explains, "because he believed that the church could get over any hurt, but the preacher could not."[76] And Dr. Vivion adds: "Bishop Smith's philosophy was that if you damage a preacher, you've injured all the churches where he will serve the rest of his life. But if you happen to damage a church, they'll get over it when the next preacher comes." Vivion believes that the bishop was overly solicitous toward the preachers and didn't give the churches enough consideration.[77] Dr. Spellman agrees that Bishop Smith "bent over backwards for men who were in trouble. It was part of his compassionate way of trying to help a man out of a tight spot."[78]

A. Frank Smith lived and worked in the middle of the road without apology. "Deliberation was Frank's trademark," says L. U. Spellman, "and I think his strength as a bishop was that he stayed in character in the exercise of his office. He was noted for looking at all sides of a question before he spoke or acted." A story about Bishop Smith and "Mr. Sam" Rayburn that still circulates in Texas describes the bishop and the congressman driving through the country where a snow white horse was grazing beside the highway. "Frank, that sure is a white horse!" "Well, Sam, it is white on *this* side."[79]

Bishop Smith's deliberateness helped him to establish and maintain brotherly relationships within his annual conferences. "If Frank saw a battle coming up in a cabinet meeting," Finis Crutchfield recalls, "he would say, 'Well, we'll pass over that for the time.' Then he would go on to something else until he could approach the problem from another angle and carry his point that way."[80] In the Central Texas Conference, where party spirit had been particularly divisive, Bishop Smith labored to bring about reconciliation. After Smith's first year, the superintendent of the Weatherford District wrote to him:

Strife and contention have receded, and goodwill and brotherly esteem are at the forefront. You deserve credit for a great deal of this change of attitude, and I want to express at once my admiration and appreciation for your gracious, brotherly Christian spirit exhibited in your presiding, in meetings with the brethren and in all of the cabinet work.[81]

Three years later, toward the end of Smith's quadrennium of supervision over that conference, the superintendent of the Brownwood District wrote to him:

It has been a great blessing to me to have been in your cabinet and to have had close fellowship with you. You have been so fair and impartial. You have done your best to work in peace and harmony in our conference. . . . You are not only a great Churchman but a great statesman as well. You have by your life and example condemned that which was small and local until no one could be associated with you without being a bigger and better man.[82]

Although Bishop Smith disliked conflict and avoided it whenever he could, there were times when his efforts to hold to the middle of the road thrust him into the crossfire. The most heartbreaking of these dilemmas swirled out of the controversy over alleged communist infiltration of The Methodist Church in the late 1940s and early 1950s.

Early Saturday morning, December 27, 1947, a reporter from the *Houston Press* called Bishop Smith for a statement concerning an article that paper had carried Friday afternoon about the Methodist Federation for Social Action.[83] Scripps-Howard staff writer Frederick Woltman,[84] assigned to cover the Federation's meeting in Kansas City, was predicting:

The prestige of the Methodist Church will be used here [Kansas City] this weekend to furnish a national sounding board for Communists and fellow travelers to expound the gospel of the Communist line. . . . If the Federation and its scheduled speakers run true to form, the Soviet dictatorship will be extolled, America's foreign policy will be castigated, Yugoslavia's Communist dictator Tito will be gently whitewashed and Chiang Kai-Shek will be denounced.[85]

"The Methodist Federation is a voluntary organization," the bishop responded, "and is not officially an agency or an adjunct of The Methodist Church and draws no support from the church." "As far as I know, the organization is interested merely in social and economic questions and has no political objectives or activities," he continued. "It was in existence long before the word 'Communist' was coined, and . . . has never been associated with Communist leanings of any description."[86]

Although Bishop Smith left Houston that Monday for a national Methodist youth conference in Cleveland, he kept a careful eye on the continuing newspaper reports: "The *Houston Press* has an inflammatory article today about the meeting of the Meth. Federation—also an editorial."[87] Tuesday's article was even worse: "Another article in the *Press* has set the local [Houston] people wild. Talked to B. [Bessie], & F. Jr. [Frank, Jr.] called me. Laymen there want a statement from the Bishops."[88]

This urgent request of the Houston laymen for the Council of Bishops "to publicly disavow the Federation"[89] placed Bishop Smith in a difficult situation. He knew that seventeen of the bishops—approximately one-third—including "Paul Kern, Will Martin, and possibly [Ivan Lee] Holt"[90] were members of the Federation. He knew that the Episcopal Address to the forthcoming General Conference included a vigorous defense of the church's freedom to proclaim the Gospel and a denunciation of "reactionary forces [that] strive to discredit our ministers by labeling them 'communists.' "[91] As the bishop himself wrote to one of his preachers, "We can't become victims of a red baiting hysteria that brands every liberal as a Red and a traitor."[92] Smith also knew that a special committee, appointed by the Council of Bishops at the request of the 1944 General Conference, would recommend that the 1948 General Conference create a "Commission for Social Action."[93] It would be inappropriate, therefore, for the council to issue any statement that might be seen as an infringement of the prerogatives of the General Conference. Smith decided not to ask the Council of Bishops for a statement but to treat the matter as a problem within his own Episcopal Area and issue a statement himself.[94]

After spending "a good part" of the next day "preparing a statement for the *Press* on the Kansas City meeting,"[95] Bishop Smith sent his carefully worded declaration to the Houston district superintendent with the stipulation that it be given only to the *Houston Press*, which had printed the Federation stories.[96]

Because of certain publicity attending upon a meeting of the Methodist Federation for Social Action in Kansas City recently, it is due the public and The Methodist Church that a statement of fact be made:

First: The Methodist Church imposes no restrictions upon the social, economic or political views of its members, each of whom has absolute freedom of thought and expression. . . .

Second: No Methodist and no group can speak for The Methodist Church save the delegated General Conference.

Third: The Methodist Federation for Social Action is not now, and never has been, an agency or adjunct of The Methodist Church. Its opinions are those of its members. . . .

Fourth: Any word spoken or any action taken by individuals or any group calling themselves "Methodist," whether at Kansas City or elsewhere, that might be reasonably construed as being subversive or disloyal, or that might discredit American democracy and exalt atheistic communism, or any other totalitarian philosophy, is to be deplored, and has my unreserved condemnation.[97]

Two days later, when he arrived in New York City for a Board of Missions meeting, Bishop Smith received an encouraging telegram from Houston:

Heartiest congratulations to you for your clear, forceful and statesmanlike presentation . . . as carried in the afternoon papers. . . . Affectionate regards,
DEE SIMPSON[98]

As the president of Jesse Jones's Texas Bank of Commerce, Simpson was an appropriate spokesman for the Houston laymen who had been distressed by the newspaper reports concerning the Methodist Federation.

Bishop Smith was amazed the next day to see his statement on the front page of the New York World Telegram: "I presume it is in every Scripps-Howard paper in the country!"[99] Surprise soon turned to disappointment because "the interpretation of the papers made it appear that I had attacked the Federation."[100] Under the headline, "Methodist Bishop Disowns Group Which Praised Reds," the New York World Telegram announced "Bishop Smith's condemnation of the Federation and its Kansas City meeting" in "a biting statement" which "smacked the Federation's anti-United States actions."[101] "It was not my purpose to denounce the Methodist Federation in my statement," Bishop Smith explained in a letter to Bishop Frederick D. Leete:

I issued my statement to meet an acute local situation here in Houston. Our people had never heard of the Federation before, and when they read the Woltman stories . . . and especially that 17 Bishops belonged to the group, they were simply paralyzed. . . . I waited a few days to see if anyone connected with the Federation would say anything, and when nothing was forthcoming, I made what I believed and still believe to be a statement of fact.[102]

In a similar letter, Smith wrote at length to his old mentor, Bishop John M. Moore:

I have no desire to attack the Federation, and I did not do so in my statement. . . . It is said that they have some 4,000 members in all [although] only some seventy-five attended the Kansas City meeting, four of them Bishops. I am sure most of these members are as dependable Americans and Methodists as are you and I. . . . It is my belief that the 17 Bishops who have allowed their names to be associated with the group should have spoken at once, either denying the Woltman implications or repudiating the Kansas City action. Since not a one of them said anything, I had to speak for the sake of our Methodist people here in Houston. . . . I have had a surprisingly large number of letters from prominent Methodists, lay and clerical, all over the country, expressing relief and appreciation that something had been said to let the country know that this was not an official agency of the Church at Kansas City.[103]

On the other hand, Bishop Smith also received severe criticism. "Some of the leaders of the Methodist Federation have issued a blistering attack upon me, charging me with impugning the character of the Bishops in the Federation, and linking me with the reactionary social and political elements in the South."[104] One letter the bishop received was so bitter that he still found it painful to discuss fourteen years later. "A New Testament scholar wrote me a two page letter," Smith recalled, "saying that I was a disgrace to the ministry and that I ought to be deposed from the episcopacy. He just turned loose on me something unbelievable. He said I was worse than Senator Bilbo and 'Pappy' O'Daniel together!"[105] There was even tension in the Council of Bishops over the matter. Bishop Smith, speaking at the orientation for the thirteen new bishops elected in 1948, advised them against identifying with fringe groups, since bishops represent the entire church as well as the council. Bishop James Baker, an officer of the Federation, was greatly offended. "Bishop Baker hotly defended *his practice* of sticking *my* neck out," Smith noted in his daily journal.[106]

When asked if he was sorry that he had gotten involved, Bishop Smith replied: "Although this statement caused me considerable distress, I do not regret having issued it. I would do it again under similar circumstances, but I do not rejoice over the misinterpretation it occasioned from both sides."[107]

Much to Bishop Smith's grief, the controversy over alleged communist infiltration of The Methodist Church not only continued but greatly increased during the next five years. Methodism's agony mirrored the anguish that racked the entire nation. In his perceptive study, *The Crucial Decade: America, 1945-1955*, Eric F. Goldman interprets the turmoil of these years as a response to "the Half-Century of Revolution," that period of accelerating change which began in the 1890s and culminated in the "New Dealism" of the Roosevelt era.

No nation can go through such rapid change in its domestic life without backing up an enormous amount of puzzlement, resentment, and outright opposition. Revolutions provoke counter-revolutions; drastic change, a weariness of change. . . . Rancor spurted out from all regions of the country and from a dozen different groups, each with its own special resentment. . . . But the most powerful thrust of discontent came from one readily identifiable group, the men and women who had come to be called conservatives and who now emphatically did not want to conserve the existing America.[108]

Although deeply rooted in American history, popular fear of radicalism has been associated with fear of Russian communism since the Bolshevik Revolution. Anxieties about the "Red menace" to American institutions attained new heights as the "cold war" developed after World War II. Goldman cites the Eightieth Congress, elected in the Republican sweep of 1946 and led by Senator Robert A. Taft, as a representative offspring of the combination of the conservative response to the "Half-Century of Revolution" and the anti-Communist persuasion. Impatient after sixteen years without influence over national affairs, this coalition of conservatives took over the legislative branch of government with a determination to dismantle bureaucratic control of the economy, to restore levelheaded businessmen to positions of leadership, and to "ferret out" the Communists in the State Department, in labor unions, and in the motion picture industry. "Any irritation with domestic New Dealism was stoked by the Communist threat," according to Goldman, and this resulted in "a tendency to denounce anything associated with the different or disturbing as part of a Communist conspiracy."

The joining of New Dealism and Communism in a troubled American mind was easy, almost axiomatic. Was it not the New Dealers, like the Communists, who talked of uplifting the masses, fighting against the businessman, establishing economic controls over society, questioning the traditional in every part of living? Was it not the reformers at home who had called during the war for linking hands with the Bolsheviks abroad? . . . It was not really the Russian and Chinese Communists but American Reds who had brought the crisis and who now direly threatened the truly American way of living and thinking.[109]

Since the angry conservatives were not always scrupulously careful to distinguish between liberals and Communists, they sometimes seemed to say that subversion and social reform were the same thing.[110] The House Committee on Un-American Activities, for example, issued a pamphlet in 1948 entitled *100 Things You Ought to Know about Communism and Religion*. Written in a question-and-answer form, the pamphlet had the appearance of objectivity.[111]

> Do Communist propagandists ever actually get before church groups as speakers? Yes. For example, the head of the Communist Party, on one occasion at least, spoke at Union Theological Seminary in New York City.
> Is the Y.M.C.A. a Communist target? Yes. So is the Y.W.C.A. Also, church groups such as the Epworth League.

At its December meeting, the Methodist Council of Bishops issued a strong denunciation of the Un-American Activities Committee. "Replete with distortions and innuendos," the report of the committee "creates the impression that the churches have been infiltrated by communists and that responsible leaders of the churches follow the party line," the bishops stated. "We expressly deny that communism has infiltrated our churches. . . . We reject communism, its materialism, its method of classwar, its use of dictatorship, its fallacious economics, and its false theory of social development." Concerning the committee's procedures, they declared: "The publishing of falsehood concerning individuals who have never been interviewed, who have had no opportunity to refute allegations, in a word, for a body to act as court, jury and executioner, without the individual or organization concerned being heard, is contrary to American tradition and in effect is to jeopardize our freedom." More specifically, the bishops pointed out that the Epworth League had "not been in existence during the last nine years," a glaring example of "the incompetency of the [Committee's] investigators." "We cannot and will not remain silent," the bishops concluded, "when confronted by practices at once un-American and a threat to a free church in a free society."[112]

Neither the members of the House Committee on Un-American Activities nor the American people seemed to be able to hear what the bishops were saying: the daily news was increasingly filled with a tide of evidence pointing to the "communist menace." In August, 1949, the State Department conceded the failure of American policy in China. In September President Truman announced that the Soviet Union had exploded its first nuclear bomb. In October eleven leaders of the American Communist Party were convicted of conspiring to overthrow the U.S. government. In December Chiang Kai-Shek and the Nationalist Chinese government fled to Formosa. In January, 1950, Alger Hiss was convicted of perjury. In February Senator Joseph R. McCarthy made his famous Wheeling, West Virginia, allegation of Communists in the U.S. State Department.[113]

February was also the month of the *Reader's Digest* article, "Methodism's Pink Fringe," aimed at the Methodist Federation for Social Action by one of the magazine's editors, Stanley High. High's primary objection was that the Federation "carries on against our American economic system" in the name of "America's largest and most powerful Protestant church." "To condemn the American economic system as unchristian" is "to discredit America at home and abroad" and "to promote conclusions which give aid and comfort to the Communists." Much of the article repeats Frederick Woltman's newspaper articles on the Federation's Kansas City meeting; but as a Methodist minister's son and a former candidate for this church's ministry, High knew how to get around the customary defense that the Federation was not an official Methodist agency. "The Federation's national offices are housed in the official Methodist building in New York City," he emphasized, "and the Federation's executive secretary maintains his standing as a Methodist minister by virtue of the official approval of his position by the presiding bishop at every meeting of the annual conference to which he belongs."[114]

For months Methodists were busy responding. Hundreds of sermons were preached; dozens of articles were printed in Methodist periodicals; the Board of Publications asked the Federation to move out of the Methodist Building; and Bishop G. Bromley Oxnam wrote a reply, which the *Reader's Digest* would not publish.[115] In late February a group of Houston Methodist laymen met with Bishop Smith to discuss High's allegations. "Some of the best men we had in Houston were greatly agitated over this article in the *Reader's Digest*," the bishop later recalled. "I knew that [Bishop] James Baker and others were heart and soul in that movement and that the charges made by High were too preposterous. But these men read that stuff, and they thought their church had sold them down the river. That Stanley High did more harm than you could ever imagine."[116]

The Council of Bishops devoted parts of three days out of their five-day spring meeting to a discussion of the High article and a formal response to it. Bishop Smith was one of six bishops chosen to draw up a statement to be sent by the council to all Methodist ministers.[117] This message gave no comfort to individualistic pietism. Beginning with a strong emphasis on "pride in Methodism's pioneering achievements in the field of social action," the bishops reaffirmed their commitment to "a free pulpit" as well as their rejection of communism. Without giving any recognition to the High article, they referred to "recently received communications from devoted and loyal Methodists in many sections of the church" inquiring about the relation of the Methodist Federation to The Methodist Church. In order to "clarify in the public mind the independent nature of the Federation," the bishops "recommended to the Federation's membership that the word 'Methodist' be dropped from its title." Although they acknowledged the Federation's "notable contributions to social justice" in the past, the bishops "deplored and sharply disagreed with certain positions taken and statements published of late in the Federation's official *Bulletin*." Their message concludes with a warning and a challenge:

We Methodists must not allow hysteria and fear to rob us of our confidence in our leadership nor divert us from our task. We therefore summon both ourselves and our people to a new consciousness of God's power; to quickened insight [into] human need; to a more constructive Christian statesmanship through which the Gospel may be preached . . . with a thorough-going application of its ethic to all the affairs of the world's life.[118]

In accord with the February request of the Houston laymen, Bishop Smith appointed a committee, consisting of four district superintendents and six laymen, to draft a memorial to be submitted to the Texas Conference in June. Smith appointed Hines H. Baker as chairman. According to a member of the committee, Dr. Lawrence Landrum, "Bishop Smith wanted us to draw up a conciliatory resolution. He came to two or three of our meetings, but he didn't participate."[119] Apparently unable to arrive at a consensus, the committee simply placed contradictory, if not mutually exclusive, paragraphs side by side in the "wherefore" section of the memorial. This was followed by these specific resolutions:

1. We commend the recent pronouncement of the Council of Bishops with respect to the Methodist Federation for Social Action . . . and request the Federation promptly to drop the word Methodist from its name.

2. We condemn any individual or organization that would seek to use The Methodist Church or any of its literature, groups, agencies, or programs for the promotion of socialism or communism ["as economic or political systems"].

3. . . . We call on those responsible for the preparation of our Church literature, for the selection of speakers at youth conferences and of teachers in seminaries and leaders in other fields of Church activity to exercise renewed vigilance in searching the background and beliefs of writers, speakers, teachers, and Church leaders in order to prevent abuse and to make our Church literature and all teachings conform to the views and beliefs of Methodism and to the mind and spirit of Christ.[120]

The passage of this memorial by the Texas Conference did not achieve the desired goals of the Houston laymen. The Federation persisted in using "Methodist" in its title, and Federation members continued writing material for Methodist church school literature that was deemed "Marxist" by the laymen. Therefore, they created an organization "to effectuate the objectives and purposes of the Memorial."[121] On December 19, 1950, a group of forty-two Methodist laymen, "appointed by the official boards of several Houston Churches," formed the Committee for the Preservation of Methodism. In April the committee published the first edition of its booklet entitled *Is There a Pink Fringe in The Methodist Church?*, intended to show how the Federation was attempting "to use the [Methodist] Church and its agencies as a propaganda vehicle for spreading socialistic and communistic ideas." Methodists, the committee insisted, should either resign their positions of leadership in the Federation or their offices in The Methodist Church. "This is what distressed me," Bishop Smith explained. "These were good men, men who were young with me, and we had grown old together here, and I had looked forward to the time when they would be our leaders in the church —and they had gotten led off by this 'Pink Fringe' business."[122]

The Committee for the Preservation of Methodism and their publications drew Bishop Smith personally into a continuing confrontation that caused him great agony. "There were already too many people shouting on both sides of the question," Smith commented to a friend, "to the neglect of other matters that needed to be done."[123] Just as the Houston businessmen were offended by charges that capitalism and the American system of free enterprise were un-Christian, so also were the staunch advocates of the "Social Gospel" offended when accused of "insidious and undercover efforts to undermine the fundamental principles upon which free democracy is builded" and of "spreading socialistic and communistic ideas which are utterly foreign to the fundamental beliefs of our denomination."[124] Bishop Smith's friends and colleagues on the Council of Bishops asked why the Houston laymen quoted *100 Things You Should Know about Communism and Religion* after the council had exposed it.

Folks I knew called me from all over the church [Bishop Smith declared] wanting me to denounce these men here. "Why," they said, "these men have put out this pamphlet with a pink fringe around the edge, and they have listed the names of all those who have ever been identified with the Methodist Federation in any way, just like the Un-American Activities Committee!" And they said to me, "They are your men, you are down there with them. You are evidently in full sympathy with what they are doing." And I said, "No, I will not denounce them. These are good men who love the church, and we are going to save them for the church." And they said, "By your silence you are siding with them." And I said, "A whole lot of liberals have brought this on themselves." And we did not denounce [the Houston men].[125]

Bishop Kenneth Pope, who was then [1949-1960] pastor of the First Methodist Church in Houston, believes that "the genuineness of Bishop Smith's pastoral heart was one of the greatest forces that prevented an out-and-out impossible explosion in Houston."

There was real travail in the early fifties. And the pressures of suspicion, uncertainty and frustration were released through that "Pink Fringe" episode. The reactionary element wouldn't have minded tearing down the church, lock-stock-and-barrel! "There was a Communist under every pew and behind most of the pulpits anyhow." And the swirl of material that was fed to our laymen was just too much for them to handle. They did not have the information to handle it, and they were frustrated. Many of these men were A. Frank Smith's closest friends, and he was determined not to violate these friendships. Every time he got back into town, often around eleven o'clock at night, he would get on the phone and call me. You could just feel the concern in his voice. He would ask about different men, and he would say, "These are my friends." And he would go around to see them. But when it got too thick, it would just crumble him to the bone. I suppose that hurt him more than any other one thing, more than all else put together.[126]

This crisis seems to reflect developments across the nation as the reaction to fifty years of domestic and international strains peaked in the early 1950s. President Truman's dismissal of General Douglas Mac-Arthur, strongly resented in Houston,[127] the stalemate in Korea, Senator Joseph McCarthy's continuing charges of Communists in the State Department—these were only a part of that whole series of events which left many Americans feeling confused, irritated, and utterly frustrated. Although the Republicans said they had "Had Enough" in 1946, they really meant it in 1952, taking control of both the Congress and the presidency. But it was Congress's many investigating committees which labored most diligently to keep the "Communist conspiracy" before the nation. "Never had the country experienced such an epidemic of investigations as it did in 1953 and 1954," and "investigations came to be the main business of Congress."[128] In early 1953 national polls showed McCarthy at his peak of public approval.[129]

As the wave of anti-Communist persuasion crested, Bishop Smith's conservative friends began pressuring him to come completely over to their side. "They were saying around town," Smith recalled, " 'It's time the old bishop got off the fence.' "[130] Accounts of the crucial confrontation vary in detail, but the pertinent points coincide. "Just after Truman had gone out of office," as Bishop Smith remembered, there was a meeting of the pastors of Houston's larger Methodist churches, several laymen from these churches who were active in the Committee for the Preservation of Methodism, and Bishop Smith.[131] As Smith later recalled the meeting, the laymen spoke first.

They were directing their shots at me, and it was proper that I should take the blame, if blame there was. And they said, "We can't understand why you haven't come out on this matter. It is time you got off the fence and came over on our side. Why haven't you denounced those men who are still in the Federation?" And I said, "These men [presumably such persons as Bishop G. Bromley Oxnam, who had resigned as early as 1947] are no longer affiliated with the Federation." Then they said, "Well, why didn't they get up in public and announce it?" And I said, "There are men sitting right here in this room who were Ku Klux members when I came to Houston [in 1922]. I never heard it publicly announced that they withdrew, but I'm not going to get up and call them Ku Kluxers now just because they were twenty-five years ago." And I could just see them drawing in their shirts.

And I said, "just because Henry Crane up in Detroit writes something you don't like in the *Adult Student*, you have no right to say to me, as some of you have, 'Why don't we put him out?' " And I said to them, "I have scars on my body that I will bear to the grave because I have refused to denounce you men. And now you turn on me and point the finger at me and denounce me because I haven't come out against the other side."

And I said, "Now, gentlemen, The Methodist Church represents a cross-section of the American citizenry. The thinking of a Methodist in the state of Maine is no more like the thinking of a Methodist in the state of Texas, economically, racially and so forth, than if they lived in two different worlds. Back home both are members in good standing. Our Methodist literature is put out for the whole church, and you will find some parts of the church that will bemoan the fact that it has too conservative stuff in it, and you are bewailing the fact that it has some radical stuff in it. Remember, it has to be representative of the whole Church. Take what you like and leave the other alone. You can't come down here and square the whole thinking of The Methodist Church with Harris County and Houston and what you believe about a thing and say anything else is all wrong. We've got to recognize that we are part of a great church that is nation-wide in membership and interests."

And I said, "Now these preachers are not as alarmed about this as you all are, and you are not going to be able to persuade them to switch over to your side in this instance. Personally, I don't think there are grounds for alarm. The seat of what you men call the radical leftist movement is in Washington. I did not vote for Roosevelt and I did not vote for Truman. I have voted the Republican national ticket ever since Woodrow Wilson. The men here who voted to keep Roosevelt and the New Deal and Truman in office are far more responsible for having created this thing you are deploring than any preacher you can put your finger on."

Well, they just dried up. And somebody said, "I guess we better go home." And I heard one old fellow say as he went out, "I thought we came down here to get some preachers' scalps."[132]

With awe and deep respect, two of the pastors who were present at this meeting remember the role Bishop Smith played. "There was danger of a wide difference developing between the clergy and the laity," Gene Slater recalls, "and Bishop Smith was trying to be a bridge, holding the two groups together. He was a steadying influence in turbulent waters, a reconciler in a difficult situation."[133] Kenneth Pope vividly remembers "the complete kindness" in Smith's voice as he spoke to the laymen. "He really cared about them."[134]

The highest tribute to Bishop Smith's reconciliatory nature came out of a related incident. Toward the close of the 1953 session of the Texas Conference, just before the reading of the appointments, the Committee on Resolutions made its report. One resolution was far from routine:

Whereas, by the wide distribution of its literature, the Committee for the

Preservation of Methodism has implied the sanction of the Texas Conference (SCJ) of The Methodist Church from the Memorial adopted by the Conference in June 1950, and

Whereas, it was not the intention of the Texas Conference to give official status to any organization by the adoption of this Memorial;

Now, therefore, be it resolved, that . . . we respectfully ask that the Committee for the Preservation of Methodism state clearly in all its material and future publications that as far as the Texas Conference is concerned it is an unofficial body.[135]

A prominent member of the committee, Hines H. Baker, was particularly offended by this resolution. Declaring that "pastors in high places of leadership" had unfairly secured this action against the committee, Baker charged that "the group of laymen . . . had no opportunity to be heard on the matter before they were so officially and publicly rebuked."[136] Bishop Smith called on his friend of almost forty years[137] but apparently failed to penetrate Baker's exasperation. Two days later, however, Baker wrote a highly personal letter to Smith, who kept it among his most prized private papers.

. . . I appreciate deeply your visit Tuesday and the generous and kindly spirit which caused you to postpone your trip to see me. . . . You have inspired me through all the years since 1916. I sincerely and earnestly value your friendship, and want to reciprocate it. . . .

Sincerely,
HINES[138]

"Frank Smith was a superb peacemaker," Mr. Baker later said. "At times I thought that he was so anxious to have peace that he really let some things get by that ought not to get by. He had to smooth me down a couple of times, but he did it with such good spirit and poise and grace that you couldn't help but appreciate it."[139]

17

Bishop Smith and His Family

WHEN FRANK SMITH WAS ELECTED a Methodist bishop in 1930,[1] he and his family had to adjust to a radically different style of life. As Mrs. Smith explained: "The children were small, and I felt like it was a breaking up of our home, even more than it turned out to be. I just thought that Frank was gone."[2] Betty, who was then six years old, remembers how the children received the news in Houston: "Mother and Dad called home about the noon hour, and I was jumping up and down, very excited. But Lula, our maid who really raised me and was just like part of the family, was upset because mother was crying. That just stuck in my head."[3]

The move out of the beloved First Church parsonage on Yoakum Boulevard and into a rented house on West Alabama was only an indication of changes to come.[4] As the pastor of Houston's First Methodist Church, Dr. Smith had time to play golf regularly at the River Oaks Country Club and to take his family on all-day outings. Frank, Jr. describes their recreation in the twenties:

We went to Galveston, to East Beach, below the sea wall and on down toward the end of the island. On at least two occasions we pitched tents and spent the night on the beach. We also went to the San Jacinto battlegrounds and crabbed down there. We'd catch those great big blue crabs, bring them home in a tow sack and cook them. We did that quite a bit. Some evenings we would go visit the Carters in their penthouse on top of the Lumberman's National Bank. Mom and Dad would play "Forty-Two" with the Carters, and I would stand by the window and look out over Houston. Main Street stopped right out here, and there wasn't too much to see.

Since Mother didn't drive, Dad spent much of his week driving her to market. Betty had a lot of ear trouble while she was a baby [born in 1924], but Mom wouldn't ride in an elevator by herself. So Dad would have to ride up to the doctor's office with her and sit and wait.[5]

In contrast, Randy Smith, who was a year and a half old when his father was elected a bishop, sketches the family's changed style of the thirties:

There wasn't much family recreation that I recall. I never saw Dad play golf or anything like that. He went fishing with me one time because he felt he ought to go with me. His favorite relaxation in the evening was to come upstairs about eight o'clock, pull up a chair and read. He had a stack of magazines there. He loved to read. He read all of the Zane Grey books. When he was traveling, he would buy a bunch of those old paperback westerns and stuff them into his suitcase until they'd just tumble out. After television came in, he liked to watch the wrestling matches. That was his evening relaxation at home.

On Sunday afternoons when Dad was home, we went for a ride. We had a regular route: we'd ride out Main Street just beyond where the Delman Theater is now—there wasn't anything beyond that except St. Paul's Church, the Art Museum and Rice. Then we'd turn back up a little road and go across to Chelsea Place, a little residential street, and over to Montrose and then cut back. I cannot tell you the number of hours on a Sunday afternoon that I sat in the car and read funny books while they went in to see Mrs. Carter or somebody. That was their entertainment.

Dad did like to do goofy things, however. I can remember going downtown with Mom and Dad to look at a flagpole sitter. Another time we went out to a parking lot and watched a hypnotist put somebody to sleep. Some man had himself buried, and he was going to stay underground for a certain time. We went out and looked at him through a little window. Dad would go out of his way to see goofy things like that.

When Dad was gone—and after Frank was off in school—Mother and I would play dominos with Granddaddy almost every night. Mr. Crutchfield lived with us the last twenty years of his life.[6]

Frank and Bess Smith worked out a number of ways to adjust to the bishop's necessary absences from home. Since Bess could not drive a car and Frank, Jr. was in college, they had to hire a driver for the family. "I guess Elbert was the first driver we ever had," Betty recalls. "He was a good driver, and Mother needed him. But we finally had to let Elbert go."[7]

Allen Brown drove for the Smiths for twenty years, beginning about 1942. As Elbert had done, Allen came early every morning, took Betty to school, drove for Mrs. Smith and on occasion for Bishop Smith, served the meals, and generally helped around the house. When Mrs. Smith needed him, he remained on into the evening. "Allen was as pleasant and good-natured a person as I have ever known," Randy declares. "All of us loved him very much, and he was a great source of humor around the house. He was always saying funny things that tickled Daddy. Daddy enjoyed having Allen around."[8] One day during World War II, Bishop Smith and Allen went by an upholstery shop to see about seat covers for the family car. The two men became interested in a Jeep that was in the shop. Much to their delight, as Smith noted in his daily journal, "Frank Abbott took Allen and me for a ride in the Jeep." Other journal entries verify the family's appreciation of Allen's services. When Allen received a call from his draft board to come before them, Bishop Smith wrote: "I don't believe they will take him on account of his hernia. If they do, Bessie will just about pass out, she depends upon him so much." The journal shows that Allen was sorely missed when he was away on his brief vacations:

Tonite Betty Ann & Gordon, Bub & three of his friends, Bessie & I all piled into the car & went to town at nine o'clock. Bessie & I went to the Texas to see "My Gal Sal"—the others went elsewhere. We got together at 11:45 & came home. . . . Allen comes back tomorrow. We will certainly be glad to see him.[9]

Many of the stories that Bishop Smith told about Allen still circulate among the bishop's friends. On one of the many occasions when Allen met Bishop Smith at the train station to take him home, the bishop asked Allen to tell him what had been happening while he was gone. Among other news items, Allen mentioned that a certain couple, longtime friends of the Smiths, had separated and were getting a divorce. "I declare, Allen," Bishop Smith commented, "that's happening so much these days, I wouldn't be greatly surprised if I came in some day and found that Bessie had filed divorce proceedings against me!" "Yes, sir," Allen replied, "that's why I keep a spare."[10]

Of the several Negro men and women who worked for the Smiths over the years as drivers or maids, Lula was the most beloved. Coming to the family in 1924, shortly after Betty was born, Lula remained with them until she died in 1941. "Lula raised our children," Mrs. Smith declared.[11] "Lula was almost like a second mother to me," Randy agrees. "I remember the morning she died. Granddaddy [Crutchfield] and I were sitting on the couch crying together, and he put his arm around me and told me that I had just lost the best friend I would ever have. I think we all felt that close to Lula."[12]

Lula lived in the garage apartment behind the First Methodist Church parsonage so that she could conveniently stay with the children when Dr. and Mrs. Smith were attending their many church meetings and fulfilling social obligations. Since this arrangement had proved satisfactory, Lula had continued to live on the place where the Smiths resided in succeeding years. "Whenever Dad was out of town, which was most of the time," Randy recalls, "Lula moved into the house and stayed with us all night, because Mother was afraid to be the only adult in the house."[13] Eventually, as Betty and Randy became teen-agers, more than baby-sitting was required and Mrs. Smith had to assume more of the responsibility. For example, she was not able to attend the Uniting Conference at Kansas City in 1939. As Bishop Smith confided to a friend: "Betty has reached the age where we cannot leave her without some responsible person to look out for her. The house is full of boys at all hours, and Lula no longer fills the bill as she did when the children were babies and we were gone for weeks at a time."[14] On the other hand, Lula continued to be of great assistance and comfort to the family. Although there was only one attempted burglary of their home while Bishop Smith was away on his constant travels, he always felt more secure knowing that Lula was with Mrs. Smith.[15] Lula, of course, was the one who had called Bishop Smith a "road lizzard."[16]

Since Bishop Smith was out of town so often, Allen had to take his vacation when the bishop was going to be home for several days and could do the chauffeuring. Sometimes these chores were sources of frustration for the bishop. Frank, Jr. remembers an occasion when his father was driving him to town on an errand. Suddenly another car turned carelessly in front of them, and Bishop Smith had to brake sharply. Momentarily pausing before driving on, Bishop Smith declared: "I wish I could cuss!"[17]

Toward the end of World War II, Bishop Smith had to borrow

Randy's car one day when the family car was in the repair shop. "I started to town in Bub's car," he explained, "and just as I rounded a corner I had a blow-out on the left front wheel. The car jumped the curb and badly damaged some shrubbery. I had to go on to town on the bus."[18] One wonders if the bishop looked a bit ruffled when he called on John T. Scott later that morning.

Bishop and Mrs. Smith were involved in a more serious accident a year later while on their way to pick up Betty at a movie theater. "A drunken woman driver, going sixty or seventy miles per hour, hit us," Smith related. "Our car was knocked twenty-five feet and crushed beyond repair. It was a miracle that we escaped with only bruises." Relieved and grateful that no one was killed or seriously injured, Bishop Smith did not bring charges against the other driver. What was perhaps another reason why he did not bring any charges is mentioned in his daily journal a week later: "I went to the Texas Safety Department this morning and got a driver's license. I had not renewed mine for several years."[19]

Even after Bishop Smith had completed his supervision of the Missouri and Oklahoma conferences and was assigned primarily to annual conferences in Texas, he still had to travel extensively outside the state. The Council of Bishops regularly met twice a year, and their special quadrennial programs—such as the Bishops' Crusade—required additional time. As president of the Division of National Missions, Smith often had monthly executive committee meetings in New York or Philadelphia, not to mention the annual board meetings, which took a week or ten days. During World War II he served on the Regional War Labor Board, adding another week or two to his annual travel schedule. Beginning in 1943, he was on the Commission on Chaplains of The Methodist Church, which met monthly in Washington, D.C. That Bishop Smith was concerned about these lengthy absences from home can be seen in the following selections from his letters and daily journal:

1940: I am at home so very little that I take the shortest line home whenever I have any time between [meetings].

1945: I am convinced that I have things reversed. I ought to stay at home two-thirds of the time and [be] away one third.

1947: I am leaving tonight for twenty-four days. I believe this is the longest period I have been away from home since I became a bishop.

1960: For thirty years I have averaged no more than four or five days per month at home.[20]

Since Bishop Smith's time at home was so limited, he and Mrs. Smith made special efforts to protect it. On a Saturday in 1944, for example, they declined two attractive invitations, one from Mrs. W. W. Fondren to attend an afternoon football game between Rice and TCU and one from Mrs. Sterling Meyer to go with her that evening to hear the famous pianist Artur Rubinstein. "Home is the best place I know to stay," Frank Smith commented.[21]

Being at home wasn't always restful, especially after Betty and Randy were in their teens. When Betty and her visiting friends stayed out until two o'clock in the morning, he objected: "I just can't sleep well till they're all in." Describing a particularly hectic Saturday night, he wrote:

We had a little blow and rain from a Gulf storm. Betty Ann did not come in till one a.m. Bub got up at 3:30 to deliver his *Chronicle* route. I tried to take him in the car, but someone had the garage keys. He went on his wheel, to be gone an hour. I sat up for his return, but he didn't get back until 7:30. His papers were not delivered to him on time.[22]

Mrs. Smith thought that her husband tended to be more lenient with the children because of his extended absences. "Frank usually brought the children some little inexpensive present when he came home," she recalled.

If there was anything the children wanted to do or something they wanted, Frank would always say: "Why, yes, that's fine." I thought children shouldn't be allowed to go to the picture show during the week. That was for weekends. But Frank would say, "Well, if they have done their lessons, why can't they go? And the children got their allowances on Saturday. By Monday morning their money would be gone, and they wanted more. My idea was that they should wait until the next allowance day, but Frank would say: "Oh, they are little, and they need some more." And he would slip them a little more money.

Frank's unanswerable reply was: "Yes, Bessie, but the children all turned out mighty well."[23]

Betty believes that their father's generosity and patience were an inverse reaction to the kind of relationship he had had with his own father. "Grandfather Smith was a very stern man, a businessman who never quite made it. He was not very close to his children. Because of him our father tried very hard to be the other way."[24]

Frank, Jr., Betty, and Randy remember their father's leniency, but they also remember his firmness. When Frank, Jr. learned to drive the family car, he was "pressed into service" to drive for his mother. "Sometimes I resented it," he admits.

I remember one instance when Dad asked me to take Mother somewhere, but I had something that I wanted to do. I was remonstrating with him, and he was telling me that he had something important to do. I was so brash that it surprised me, but I said: "Well, what I have to do is just as important to me as what you have to do is to you." He stopped and thought a minute and then said, "You know, I guess that's right." But I did drive.[25]

Randy, speaking of a similar experience, indicates that their father's tolerance had a low level when any disrespect for their mother was involved.

It was a rainy Saturday night, and Mother asked me to drive up to the drugstore and get the Sunday papers. She and Dad always read them the night before. And I smarted off to her because I was getting ready to go somewhere. That's when he finally lost patience with me. I was amazed; but I remember that I had added respect for him for having done it, because I knew that I shouldn't have been acting that way.[26]

The notes Bishop Smith wrote in his daily journal show that he made a special effort when he was at home to be with each of the children. It was difficult for the family to do things together because of the wide range of their ages: Frank, Jr. was born in 1915, Betty in 1924, and Randy in 1928. Frank, Jr. left home, for all practical purposes, when he entered Rice Institute in 1933. Married in 1939, he and Mary had their first child—Mary Tweed, the bishop's first grandchild—in 1941, the year Bishop Smith began keeping a daily journal.[27] As a result, one reads more about Tweed than about her father. There are numerous delightful glimpses of Bishop and Mrs. Smith keeping Tweed while her parents have an evening out, taking Tweed to the zoo, having a birthday party for her at the River Oaks Country Club, or just dropping by to visit her at home.[28]

Frank, Jr. appears in the journal more often during World War II. "Had lunch with Frank at the Lamar Cafeteria," Smith noted on August 7, 1942. "He is eager to get into active service. Too bad the war is cutting into the careers of all these young men, but unless the war is won their lives will be shot to pieces indeed." Frank, Jr. soon had his wish, being sworn in and receiving his commission in the United States Navy on August 27. Bishop Smith rushed home from Chicago. "This train will get me to Houston early Saturday," he wrote, "and I can see Frank before he leaves for New Orleans Sunday morning. Sorry to miss the Bishops' meeting tomorrow." In April the young man was assigned to the USS *Massachusetts* in the Pacific Fleet—"a 35,000 ton battleship only six months old." "I am sure that pleases him," Smith commented. "He has been wild to see active duty at sea. I would feel the same way if I were his age." Two weeks later this fatherly pride quickly turned into anxiety when the bishop was called out of a District Conference meeting to receive a long distance call from Mrs. Smith. Frank, Jr. was evidently sailing for the war zone. "I wired him," Smith noted. "We don't know when we'll hear from him again. We can only pray that God may watch over & bring him safely back to us." The draft of the telegram, in the bishop's large handwriting, survives in his papers:

Ensign A. Frank Smith, Jr., St. Francis Hotel, San Francisco: Hope we may hear from you before long. God bless you. Dad[29]

A long, anxious year would pass before Frank and Bess heard their son's voice again. During the summer the worried father noted: "Wrote to Frank tonite. I imagine he is in the middle of the big push being made against the Japanese this week in the South Pacific." Just before Christmas they received an encouraging letter from Frank. "Since the letter was written after the action in the Gilberts," Smith commented, "he is all right. He says he will have plenty to talk about when he sees us again."[30]

In the meantime, someone else was learning to talk. On Sunday, May 21, 1944, the bishop wrote the following brief but moving note in his daily journal: "Frank called us at 8 o'clock tonite. He sounded fine. Tweed talked to him. He had never heard her voice before. She was not talking when he left in April of 1943."

After a month's shore leave at home in Houston, Frank, Jr. took Mary and Tweed with him to Seattle, where his ship was presumably still undergoing repairs, for another month. As had happened when the young ensign first sailed in 1943, Bishop Smith was again out of town when the long distance call came. "Frank called Bessie from Seattle Wednesday nite & told her goodbye," the bishop noted. "He said there would be no use in my trying to call when I got here."[31]

Along with countless other parents, Bishop and Mrs. Smith waited out that final year of the war, carefully watching the newspapers and listening to the radio reports. In the fall, Bishop Smith took Tweed to a Houston studio where they recorded their voices in a Christmas greeting for Frank. "It is too bad that he can't be with Tweed during her babyhood," Smith noted. Following "Victory in Europe" day in the spring of 1945, the war in the Pacific intensified. Newscasts indicated that Frank's ship was in the center of the action. As expectations of Japan's surrender increased in August, the Smiths were shaken by a radio report that "a major vessel of ours" had been damaged by a kamikaze attack. "We can only hope it was not the Massachusetts," the bishop wrote. Two weeks later—ten days after Japan surrendered—they finally learned that it was not Frank's ship but the USS *Pennsylvania* that had been hit by the suicide bomber.[32]

The Smith family did not escape the tragedy of war. Charles Crutchfield, only son of Mrs. Smith's brother, Randolph Crutchfield, had lived with the Smiths for five years (1939-43) while attending Rice Institute. Since Charles's family had limited finances at the time, Bishop and Mrs. Smith had invited him to live with them where he could take advantage of Rice's fully subsidized engineering program. During that time Charles developed a close relationship with the Smiths. "The folks were fond of him," Randy recalls, "and he was like a brother to me."[33] Anyone reading the many references to Charles in Bishop Smith's daily journal would think that he was a member of the family. When Charles graduated and volunteered for submarine duty in the U.S. Navy in 1943, they were all sorry to see him go.[34] While the Smiths were in New York in September, 1944, they arranged a visit with Charles and his fiancée. Bishop Smith recorded the fateful sequence of events:

September 17, 1944: Charles & Carolyn came in this morning & had dinner with us. He looks well. He will go in two weeks to Pearl Harbor on his submarine.

April 17, 1945: Randolph [Crutchfield] wired that Charles is missing in action. I'm afraid there is no hope. He was as fine a boy as I ever knew. We can only hope for the best.

April 19, 1945: Finally reached Congressman Lyndon Johnson in Washington. He is close to Navy Dept. & will get full news for us on Charles.

April 21, 1945: Lyndon Johnson wired that there is no hope for Charles.

June 15, 1945: Arrived in New York at 10. Am at the Governor Clinton Hotel. The last time we saw Charles was in this hotel last Sept. The thought of it haunts me every time I see the corner in the lobby where we visited & then said goodbye.

When Frank, Jr. returned to his family and civilian life in October, he received a major promotion in the law firm where he had worked before the war. "Had lunch with Frank, Jr. at the Houston Club," Bishop Smith noted.

He had been made Asst. Mgr. of the firm [Vinson, Elkins . . . , Attorneys at Law], working directly under Judge Elkins. A very great honor & responsibility, but he will discharge it with credit. . . . Judge Elkins says that Frank is the most outstanding young man he has ever had in the firm. It does not surprise me.[35]

There was a strong bond of mutual respect and admiration between Frank, Jr. and his father. "Dad was a man who would discuss things with you and try to see your point of view," Frank, Jr. recalls. "I enjoyed talking with him very much. Mary and I often went over for Sunday dinner with them, and it would end up as a conversation between Dad and me."[36]

The only time of strained relationship with his father that Frank, Jr. can remember had occurred during the Depression years of the 1930s. When A. Frank Smith was elected a bishop in 1930, his salary fell from $10,000 to $6,000 a year. The church's financial difficulties in 1932 led the bishops to reduce their salaries voluntarily to $5,000. In 1933, when the Episcopal Fund was completely depleted, the bishops received no salary at all.[37] Frank, Jr. didn't know these details at that time, but he knew that his father was worried, frustrated, and uncharacteristically short-tempered.

Mother once said to me, "Your father has a lot of worries. Try to overlook it when he is this way." Dad did have problems, because he went down and borrowed money at the bank, a lot of money for that day. Mother told me that he would lie awake at night, fearful that he wouldn't be able to pay that note. He wanted us to have a happy childhood. That meant a great deal to him, and he made sacrifices in order that we could have what he thought we needed.[38]

Mrs. Betty Smith Griffin also remembers the special efforts her father made to be with her when he was at home: "Our parents bent over backwards to give the three of us a happy childhood, and my fondest memories today are of incidents that occurred during those years." Her father's study is one of those memories. "While I was not permitted to play in Dad's study, I was allowed to use his typewriter or read in his rocking chair.

It was fascinating to me to roam through his desk drawers because he kept his pencils, papers, and office supplies in meticulous arrangement. In contrast, the room itself was always a confusion of stacks of papers, magazines, mail and books." Betty even recalls at least one occasion when she was embarrassed that her father was at home. "During the 'Depression,'" she explains, "I remember my friends coming over, seeing my father there, and then asking their mothers when they got home if Betty's father was out of a job. I felt so humiliated that I would have had him move his office out of the house just to satisfy myself and my friends that he was a 'working man.'"[39]

In speaking of her father, Betty emphasizes his tolerance and patience. "Of the three children, I am the most inquisitive," she says:

I was always questioning religious beliefs—the Devil's Advocate, as Bubba says. I insisted that Dad prove God and Christ to me. But he never cut me off. He never made me feel self-conscious about my critical notions. He listened to what I had to say, and he always took time to give me his opinions and thoughts. I remember a few times when I was able to change his mind about something. . . . He was the same way about discipline. Daddy never spanked me that I can remember, but always handled situations that called for the equivalent of a spanking with a heart-to-heart talk and gentle advice. I was never afraid of my father. I felt that I could reason with him and feel good about whatever we decided. . . . I had to remind myself from time to time that others saw him in an exalted position, but Dad was just plain old Dad to me, fair, honest, funny, believable, vulnerable to teasing, and human.[40]

Of the three children, Betty was also the one who most often went with her parents to the movies. In the 1940s going to motion picture shows was, as we shall see, Bess's and Frank's favorite form of entertainment. When Betty was at home from SMU, she was always invited to join them.[41] Betty had a hearing handicap from her infancy, which demanded even more than the usual attention parents give to their daughters. Even before she was a year old, she was plagued with recurring ear infections. In those days before modern miracle drugs, lancing was the only treatment known to doctors. "They had to lance Betty's ears so many times that her ear drums just became like leather," Randy explains. "The doctors say that she didn't hear the sounds that other infants hear, and consequently she never learned to speak them."[42] "Of all the things that I have to be grateful to my mother and father for, of all the opportunities they made for me," Betty declares, "I am most grateful to them for helping me master my handicap."

Although they never told me so, I am sure that my loss of hearing was a crushing blow to them, especially because they wanted a daughter, having had two sons. I know they suffered many tests of their patience, many more frustrating moments of despair. But never once have they let my handicap defeat them. Through the years of my childhood and youth, they gave me their unfaltering love and confidence and determination for a normal life. You must remember that this was before our modern-day societies which help the handicapped. Most children afflicted as I was in those days were kept at home or sent to special schools. Mother and Daddy were truly courageous to take on the Herculean task of teaching people to accept me as well as training me to assume my place in society. I have heard it said that God gives his toughest assignments to his favorite pupils. This can certainly be applied to Mother and Daddy's mastering my handicap.[43]

With this support and encouragement from her parents, Betty was able to progress normally through elementary school. To be certain that her good grades represented more than the well-intentioned sympathy of her public school teachers, the Smiths sent Betty to a demanding private school for her junior high years. After continued success at Kinkaid, she returned to the public school system and graduated from Lamar High School.[44]

The Smiths also took Betty to hearing specialists from time to time as new developments occurred in that field. In October, 1935, for example, they took her to a Dr. Dean at Barnes Hospital in St. Louis. "The doctors in St. Louis say that Betty cannot be helped in her hearing," Smith wrote to his friend, Russell Score. The only comforting result of that consultation was that "she would grow no worse."[45]

A decade later Bishop and Mrs. Smith took Betty to see Dr. Julius Lempert in New York City. "He has obtained quite a reputation for operating on deaf people's ears," Smith explained. "We hope he might be able to help Betty Ann." But this specialist also gave a negative diagnosis. "Dr. Lempert says Betty Ann has nerve deafness & he can't help her. I expected as much. He says she will be no worse, which is good news."[46] Perhaps in order to soften possible disappointment, the Smiths planned this trip to New York City as a graduation present for Betty. Anticipating their lack of stamina to see and do everything that Betty desired—including a visit to the Stork Club—they invited her friend, Lorraine Reid, to accompany them on the two-week trip.

Bishop Smith applauded Betty's determination to live a normal life. During her first year at SMU, he wrote to her:

MY DEAR BETTY:

Tomorrow you will be eighteen years of age. . . . So here you are a grown woman, and yet it seems but yesterday that you were born. We hoped and prayed that we might have a baby girl. . . . With every passing day, we have been prouder of you. You have grown into a beautiful woman with unusual poise and intellect and personality. . . . You will make your own life from here on in largest part. We do not worry about that, however, for we know that you have ideals and force of character to back up those ideals, and that you will always do the thing that you think is right.

We think you made a wonderful record for your first term in college, and we are happy and proud.

Love,
Dad[47]

At the same time, Smith wrote in his daily journal: "Betty is a remarkable girl, & we are most proud of her. She never complains about her deafness & adjusts herself remarkably well." During the summer of her sophomore year at SMU, Betty worked at Sanger's department store in Dallas. "She showed admirable resourcefulness in getting the job," Smith commented. "It will do her good to meet the public."[48] Evidence of the success of the family's combined efforts to overcome Betty's handicap is the way in which parents of handicapped children continually seek Betty's advice "on what they should or should not do and how to keep up courage."[49]

Bishop Smith's relationship with each of his three children was unique, especially during the 1940s when he was keeping a daily journal. Frank, mature, married, and beginning his family, was establishing his career as an attorney in a prestigious law firm. Betty, the freethinker and least conforming of the three, was successfully countering her handicap while pursuing a college degree and moving toward marriage. Randy, no longer "Little Bubba" but still "Bub," was moving out of junior high into high school and on through college toward law school. Reflecting his mother's vivacious and gregarious personality, Randy was in constant motion and usually accompanied by a number of friends. Bishop Smith, as his daily journal reveals, seems to have responded with considerable patience and willingness to adjust to Randy's tempo.

Bub went to a midnite show. I got up at 2 this morning and brought him home.

Bessie and I didn't get home until eleven tonite. Took Bub and Scotty to Playland Park. A wild goose chase but they wanted to go & seemed to enjoy themselves.

Bessie and I went to the Metropolitan [movie theater] tonite. Bub had the car for a date so we came home on the bus.

Went to a neighborhood picture show tonite with Bub & Henry. It was Abbott & Costello in "Who Done It?" My first view of them—& my last. Slapstick comedy is pretty hot stuff.[50]

Bishop Smith's own brand of humor comes through in his random comments and observations concerning Bub's comings and goings:

Bub has some new clothes—yellow coat, blue pants, two-tone shoes. This is the first time he has ever shown any interest in clothes. He took his girl "Alabama" to a show tonite.

Bub went to Sunday School & Church this morning & to League tonite. He must have a girl at St. Paul's Church.[51]

The daily journal also contains a number of very human vignettes of father and son:

Took Bub to Dr. Griswold's this morn to have radium applied to his foot. He has a deep wart that had to be burned out.

This morning I took Bub and [some of his friends] to San Jacinto Monument. Bub, Marian & I went to the top, the first time I had been up there. We spent an hour in the museum. Most interesting.

Bub & I worked in the study tonite. I am answering some of our Xmas cards & Bub is drawing a map.

I called H. O. Clarke, mgr. of Ho. Light & Power. He said to have Bub come down Monday & he will give him a job [for the summer].

Bessie is in Dallas with Betty Ann. Bertie was off this afternoon, so Bub cooked some eggs & fixed supper for himself & me. He did a good job.

Bessie & I took Bub, Scotty & Henry to the San Jacinto Battlegrounds today. Ate lunch at the S. J. Inn & spent a couple of hours at the monument. We then drove down to Galveston. The boys went swimming & we ate supper on the sea wall. This was my first trip to Galveston in six or eight years.

Bub wants to go up in a plane tomorrow with his Sunday School teacher. I gave him a letter of permission, but I am hoping something happens to keep them from going.[52]

Bishop Smith wanted Randy to attend Lamar High School, perhaps because of Betty's experience there. Randy says, however, "I did not want to go to Lamar and had strong feelings about it. I think Dad had a transfer worked out, but he relented to my feelings and let me stay at San Jacinto."[53] The concerned father also wrote his son a memorable letter of advice and encouragement as Randy began his high school education. While "en route to New York," Bishop Smith wrote:

MY DEAR BUB:

I presume you will be in school by the time this reaches you. I look for this to be the fullest & happiest year you have had thus far in school. High school is always interesting. You will get more out of your work & associations.

You may think I have a lot to say about what you should do and the friends you have. . . . It is because I have such high ambitions for you, and I know what you can do. You have everything, and you can be tops everywhere. I confidently expect you to make an outstanding success in everything you undertake.

Remember this as you start in San Jacinto, a new school for you: 1st, your teachers will all know that you won the American Legion [award], and they will expect more from you; 2nd, first impressions are lasting. The opinion the teachers and students form of you between now & Xmas is probably what they will continue to think of you as long as you are in San Jacinto.

Your mother & I are mighty proud of you.

Love,
DAD[54]

Although Randy passed all of his courses that year, his achievement was well below his father's expectations. Bishop Smith was not discouraged, however, and responded calmly and confidently. "This has been a transition year for Bub, & he hasn't had much interest in his work. I imagine he will snap out of it by next year. He has all it takes to make the top in anything." The expected improvements did come in the following fall term, except in math, where Randy continued to have some difficulty. Again Smith responded understandingly: "I am afraid Bub is the son of his parents in that field. Bessie and I both flunked freshman math in college."[55]

Family crises inevitably occurred during Bishop Smith's extended absences from home. His response to an incident involving Randy affords a clear illustration of both the frustration he suffered on such occasions and the way in which he dealt with these perplexing situations. In January, 1944, the bishop was in California on a two-week speaking tour as part of the Methodist church's "Missionary Advance Program." While waiting for a long distance call to go through to Bessie in Houston—five hours in this particular instance—he began a letter to Randy.

My Dear Bub:—California is a lovely place, but it takes too long to get out here. I feel closer to China than I do to Texas. I spent the last two days in San Diego where the navy and Consolidated Aircraft have completely taken over . . .

In the midst of describing the camouflage and antiaircraft defenses he had seen, Smith was interrupted by his finally completed call. Although Bessie had a bad case of laryngitis, he heard her say that Bub had been injured in a car wreck. After the call, he returned to his letter and wrote:

I have just talked to Mother & learned of your accident. I cannot go to bed till I add this word to tell you how thankful I am that you were not seriously injured. . . . You are a careful driver, but when you are with someone else, you never know what may happen. The next time you may not get off so lightly.

I worry about you & Mother & Betty all the time when I am away. All I can do is to ask the Lord to take care of you. Watch your step. We couldn't stand it if anything should happen to you. Take care of Mother. I depend upon you to do that while I am away. You are old enough now to be the man of the house & to make things easier for her. She always takes care of everybody but herself.

I'll be seeing you a week from Sunday.

I love you,
DAD[56]

The long distance telephone system was truly the *sine qua non* of the strategy that Frank and Bess Smith developed to maintain their family. Perhaps they could have managed without it, but then the basic nature of the family would have been different too. "Frank called home almost every night he was gone," Mrs. Smith declared. "Now that sounds like an extravagance, but it was the only method he had of keeping in touch with us and of knowing what we were doing and for us to know what he was doing. Our phone bill was enormous, but we felt like it was worth it." "I don't know any better investment we ever made," Bishop Smith agreed.[57] Randy, Betty, and Frank, Jr. share this conviction. "Mom and Dad worried about what would happen to the family because Dad was gone so much," Randy explains,

and they decided that the only way he could feel a part of the family life on a daily basis and make us feel that he was a part of it was to call. He tried to call at an hour when he knew we would be there. He'd talk with us about what had happened at school that day or what we were doing. It was a short visit, but *we knew that he cared.*[58]

"Even though Dad was gone a lot," Betty remembers, "we never felt that he was gone. Mother made it a point to include him in all decisions: 'we'll talk with Daddy about that when he calls.' She helped us to sense that, in spite of his absences, he was still the head of the house."[59]

If someone were to prepare a complete concordance of Bishop Smith's daily journals, he would find that their most common three-word pattern is "I called Bessie." There are even instances when he called more than once in an evening. These multiple calls were made possible by the manner in which the interstate trains were made up. The Houston–St. Louis train stopped at Palestine and Longview to add cars from San Antonio and from Dallas–Fort Worth, usually allowing sufficient time to make long distance calls. Thus, if Bess's father was having one of his frequent spells, Frank could receive two reports during the evening. On at least one occasion, however, the trainmen were quicker than usual, and the bishop almost got left behind. "Went into hotel in Palestine to call home, and the train started off without me," Smith confessed, "but one of the crew remembered I had not returned & held it for me."[60] Bishop Smith used these long distance calls to cure a sudden siege of homesickness, to keep up with family activities, or to participate in some important family event or anniversary.

May 18, 1942: Arrived Cincinnati at 5:30 p.m. . . . Talked to Bessie before going to bed. She says Mary Tweed crawled today for the first time.

February 9, 1945: Bub told me tonite that he was one of 26 to be elected to Natl. Honor Society from his school. All our children have made this.

June 16, 1945: Today is our 31st wedding anniversary. These have been wonderful and rich years. Bess is a perfect wife & companion. I called her at noon, the hour of our wedding, but she was not at home. . . . Angie & I went to see the musical comedy "Bloomer Girl." Finally got Bessie tonite.

December 9, 1949: Talked to Bessie at 7 p.m. before leaving New York. She is at Meth. Hosp. with Betty Ann, her labor pains began this morning.

December 10, 1949: Arrived St. Louis 5:30 p.m. Talked to Bessie. Betty Ann's baby came at 10 this morn—a girl. Bessie says she's the prettiest baby she ever saw. I'm glad its a girl. They have named her Cynthia.

Although Bishop Smith won recognition as a mediator on the Regional War Labor Board, one can understand why he lost patience with telephone company employees when contract negotiations broke down.

January 11, 1946: Arrived Jackson, Miss. 11:30 p.m. Nation-wide phone strike on tonite. Outrageous when public is made to suffer in this fashion.

Family vacations in Colorado were special occasions for the Smith family. After two trips during the First Church years—to Colorado Springs in 1923 and to Chautauqua Park at Boulder in 1927,[61] the Smiths went to Boulder every summer from 1935 through 1943, skipping '42 because of the war.

According to Bishop Smith, the 1935 vacation in Boulder was brought about by two factors. "I had not thought that we would try to go anywhere this summer," he explained to a family friend, "but Betty has an annoying bronchial cough, a hangover from her flu last winter. The doctors think that a few weeks in a higher altitude would help her." In the second place, the bishop was learning the price of supervising two annual conferences closer to home.

I do not have a minute here to do the work I have to do in order to get ready for conference, etc. There are preachers and laymen here every day, and the day is gone before I get anything done. I have been home for a week, and that is what has happened every day, and the prospects for next week are still worse. So we have arranged for a cottage at Boulder. The folks can run around as they choose, and I can get my work done while we are there.[62]

"Even though Dad seemed to be easy going and gentle," Betty recalls, "there were times when he was inwardly a seething mass of tension. He needed to get away from the telephone and the office."[63]

Randy, Betty, and Frank, Jr. remember that their father always took his work with him on vacations. "Work was really his relaxation," Randy believes, "whether it was outlining sermons, writing letters, or whatever. He would set up a table and spread out his papers every morning." Generally speaking, A. Frank Smith was not enthusiastic about vacations. "The change will be good for all of us," he noted in his daily journal during preparations for a month at Boulder in 1943, "but I would enjoy being at home for four weeks." Writing from Colorado Springs on another occasion, he confessed: "I am not the best vacationer in the world, and will not object at all when the time comes for us to start home."[64]

Describing a typical day at Boulder, Betty remembers her father sitting in a rocking chair on the front porch of their cottage all morning, gathering his thoughts for sermons or planning his work for the coming months. Variety was the pattern for afternoons and evenings. There were always many friends from Houston, Beaumont, Tyler, or Dallas to visit. Bishop and Mrs. Smith both enjoyed the baths at the sanatorium in Boulder. Afternoons were also time for taking side trips: up to Estes Park to see "Uncle Angie and Aunt Bess," to Colorado Springs to see the Scores, or just to enjoy the scenery in the mountains and the St. Vrain and Big Thompson canyons. "Mom and Dad compensated beautifully on those trips," Randy remembers:

Mom loved to stop at antique places, and Dad just could not stand them. We'd pass by one in a hurry, and Mother would say, "Oh, Frank, we just passed one." And he would stop the car and back up, grumbling the whole time. Dad, on the other hand, liked historical things that Mom really didn't care about. But each let the other do his thing. Dad would stop at every historical marker, and we'd go off on some side road where you felt like you were going to drop off the edge of the earth looking for those crazy historical sites.[65]

Other afternoons the family would go into Boulder or to Denver to shop, go to movies, or eat lunch. Dinner at Bauers in Denver was a highlight of vacations. In the evenings they would go for leisurely walks, visit with friends, or see movies down at the central auditorium on the Chautauqua grounds. On Sundays there were morning and evening worship services in the auditorium, and Bishop Smith always conducted two of these community services during their stay.[66]

Sometimes these extended periods with his children had an interesting effect on Bishop Smith's vocabulary, as the following excerpts from his daily journal show:

Bessie, Betty Ann and I went to town this aft. & bummed around. . . .

We went to town for lunch & bummed around for awhile.

Tonite Bessie, Betty Ann & I went to town & knocked about till ten o'clock. . . .[67]

The summer of 1943 claims two distinctions. Bishop Smith learned to bowl, and he became intensely interested in a fortune-teller. Describing the first he wrote:

Tuesday, August 17: . . . I went to the bowling alley this aft. with Bub &

Henry & bowled two games, as far as I recall my first. I bowled 75 and 100, which the boys said was not bad for a beginner. . . .

Perhaps to prove that his performance was not a fluke, the bishop went back the next afternoon and bowled another game. "Score 92." After that, however, he was satisfied with his daily bath at the sanatorium.

The fortune-teller episode had a more lasting impact. Mrs. Smith and Betty discovered a woman in Boulder who claimed to read tea leaves. "Mother came back with her eyes as big as saucers," the children remember.

This woman had told Mother that she had two sons and a daughter, that she had lost an earlier son, and so on. Dad went over there, and the woman told him that he had just so long to live. And it worried him. The closer the time came, the more upset he got. I think when New Year's Day of that year came, he was greatly relieved.[68]

One of Bishop Smith's famous stories concerned the family's return from a vacation in Colorado, probably in the 1930s. Having been gone for a month, each member of the family had an immediate goal. Bishop Smith wanted to be dropped off at his office so he could get his mail. Then, as Elbert turned the family car into their driveway on Southmore Boulevard, the children set up a cry: "Let's go get Poppy. Let's go get Poppy." Poppy, the family cat, had been left with Lula while they were in Colorado. As a result of being out of doors more than usual, Poppy had picked up a number of fleas. Mrs. Smith insisted on taking the cat immediately to the veterinarian. The children naturally wanted to play in the yard, so Elbert drove Mrs. Smith and Poppy to the pet hospital. Meanwhile, having greeted Lula, the children saw their elderly neighbor and ran across to talk to him. The old man was hard of hearing, but he loved the children. Having seen Mrs. Smith leave in the car, he asked, "Where's your mother going?" "Oh," they replied, "she's gone to take Poppy to the doctor." "Oh, what's the matter with him?" "He's been staying with Lula and he's full of fleas." Puzzled, the old man hurried into his house and sought out his wife: "Mother, you'd better go over to the Smith's and see what's wrong. The children just told me that Mrs. Smith has taken their father to the hospital."[69]

For Betty the return from Colorado in 1939 stands out in her memories of her father.

I vividly recall our driving home that year, because Dad kept his ear glued to the car radio and H. V. Kaltenborn all the way to Houston. He was always curious about the news and kept up to date on local, national and international events, but '39 was a year of unusual tension and crisis. Dad was wise in including us as he observed the scenes, for what I learned from this front row seat—about the Roosevelt years, the Russian purges, the Jap ships loading scrap iron at the [Houston] ship channel, why one individual bested another of comparable talents, etc.—was invaluable to me. He whetted my appetite for wanting to know every side, all the pros and cons, the whys and wheres, and what was going on behind the scenes.[70]

By taking Betty or Randy with him on one of his long train trips to the East, Bishop Smith developed another opportunity to be with his children. Betty's turn came in September, 1944, when he had a meeting of the Commission on Chaplains in Washington, D.C., and a Board of Missions executive committee meeting in New York City. "Bessie, Betty Ann & I are leaving on the Southern Pacific tonite," he noted in his daily journal. "We will spend tomorrow in New Orleans and two days in Washington, then six days in New York. It is Betty Ann's first trip East, & she is greatly thrilled." Arriving in Washington a day before the bishop's meeting began, they made the most of it. By evening, Smith could properly conclude, "We pretty well 'did the town.'" Their arrival in New York was also planned to allow Bishop Smith to share a day's sight-seeing with his wife and daughter before his scheduled meetings. With his guidance they visited a variety of famous historic, religious, and entertainment centers. In the evenings when the bishop could join them, they went to three Broadway musicals including *Oklahoma*.[71]

Randy's special trip with his father came in the summer of 1947. Since only one meeting was involved, they enjoyed a more flexible schedule. The "tour guide" also shifted the emphasis to things of greater interest to a young man. "Bub and I got up at 5 AM as we reached Albany," Smith noted. "I wanted him to see the view down the Hudson River: the Catskills, the Rip van Winkle country, Hyde Park, West Point, Sing Sing, Yankee & Giant ball parks, etc. Arr. N.Y. 8 AM." After their first day in New York, Frank shared with Bessie the joys of his day with Randy. "We have made the rounds today," he wrote to her, "and Bub has been saying 'Gollee' all day long. But when I suggested that we ride the subway tonite to Hoboken & come back on the ferry, he begged off. We will see all there is to see before we leave."

The high point of the entire trip, however, began to develop when they reached Washington, D.C., and Bishop Smith called his old friend, Senator Tom Connally. The senator asked if the bishop and his son would be interested in watching the Senate decide whether or not to join the House of Representatives in overriding President Truman's veto of the Taft-Hartley labor bill. "Sen. Connally took us to the Senate Gallery where we heard the closing debate," Smith noted. "The vote was on sustaining the veto. It was over-ridden 68 to 25. A very historic occasion. We were lucky to be here." Nothing else could match the excitement of that afternoon in the Senate Gallery. Anyone reading Bishop Smith's daily diary would believe that the world of reality did not reappear until the bishop sat down at his desk three days later and looked at the mail stacked up there. "I am five weeks behind with my correspondence," he exclaimed.[72]

Apart from these special trips to the East, Bishop Smith was not able to spend much time with Betty and Randy once they left home for college. Indeed, these journeys could be interpreted as rites of passage from childhood to adulthood. Consciously or subconsciously, Frank Smith seemed to draw upon these distinctive occasions as a way of saying to Betty and Randy: "You are no longer a dependent child but an adult person in your own right. Hereafter, our relationship will be that of one adult to another." This is not to say that Bishop Smith no longer made special efforts to have time with them. His daily journal offers abundant evidence that he continued to initiate occasions for fellowship as opportunities arose. It was convenient that both Betty and Randy attended SMU, because Bishop Smith frequently went to Dallas during those years, 1941-45 and 1945-48, for meetings related to SMU's board of trustees as well as to meetings of the Regional War Labor Board. Every time he was in Dallas he arranged at least a mealtime with the current member of the family in Dallas. When the bishop went to Dallas on May 9, 1944, to consult with President Lee and the architects about proposed plans for the Perkins School of Theology, for example, Mrs. Smith accompanied him for a visit with Betty. "Bessie and I had lunch with Betty Ann at the Varsity Grill. Tonite we had dinner at the Baker Hotel & went to a show. We rode out to the University with Betty Ann on the street car. I recall vividly how we used to ride those [very same!] cars in 1916 when we lived at the University," Smith noted in his daily journal.

A number of letters that Bishop Smith wrote to Betty and Randy while they were at SMU further illuminate the kind of relationship they shared. Betty received the following letter from her father just before final exams of her first semester at SMU:

DEAR BETTY:

Excuse the pencil & the writing. I am writing on my knee at the depot in Memphis. I talked to your mother tonite & she told me you are worried about your exams. I am glad you take your work seriously, but I don't want you to be nervous or worried about it. You have a wonderful mind & if you don't make the grades you would like, just do your best & forget it. . . . We love you & are mighty proud of you regardless of grades. It won't help a bit to be nervous either before or after the exams. Just take them as they come and keep happy & get plenty of sleep. Get a coach if you need it.

I love you,

DAD[73]

Randy received this letter in response to a Father's Day greeting sent to his father in New York:

MY DEAR BUB:

I surely appreciate your letter. I shall always keep it. I have not been able to be with you and do for you as I have wished thru these years. But I have loved you devotedly, and have been increasingly proud of you. I confidently expect you to make a remarkable record in college and in life. You have everything it takes. I'll see you next Saturday.

Love,

DAD[74]

After Betty received her degree in art and journalism from SMU in 1945, Bishop Smith helped her get a job in the publicity department of Humble Oil & Refining Company. During her transition from college life to young adulthood, he wrote her these words of encouragement:

After all, life is but a matter of continuous adjustment, and whether it can be done depends upon one's inner resources and the ability to bring new interests in as old ones pass out. I do not know any person who has the ability to make such adjustments better than you have or who has more inner resources and self-reliance than you have.[75]

Betty met Don Griffin while she was working at Humble. Although there were a number of other young men actively pursuing her, Bishop Smith was not surprised when she wrote him about marriage to Don. He replied:

DEAR BETTY:

I read your letter with keen interest, and I deeply appreciate your writing exactly what you think. If Don and you feel you are suited to each other and that you would grow closer together through the years, your mother and I shall be happy indeed to welcome him into the family. . . . No parent can do a harder thing than turn a daughter over to another person when the welfare and happiness of that daughter has been a prime purpose in the life of the parent from the day the daughter was born. When the man she marries is her choice and she genuinely loves him, it gives the parent satisfaction and joy to see her started in life for herself. . . . When you and Don marry, you will have our blessing and cooperation to the end of the way. . . .

I love you and am exceedingly proud of you,

DAD[76]

Bishop Smith married Betty and Don on June 12, 1948, at First Methodist Church in Houston.[77]

Bess Patience Crutchfield and A. Frank Smith had been married only sixteen years when he was elected an itinerant general superintendent of the Methodist Episcopal Church, South. According to Methodist tradition, all ministers are itinerants, but the bishops are the most itinerant of all. During thirty of the last thirty-two years of Frank and Bess's life together, Frank was under this obligation to travel on behalf of the church. "I don't know of anything I would enjoy more," Bess once wrote to Frank, "than to live long enough that we could have some years of quiet and association together. Every minute since we married, we've been 'on a dead run.' "[78]

Their children and their friends, however, remember and celebrate the beauty and depth of their marriage relationship. "Mother and Dad were deeply in love and remained so as long as they both were alive," Frank, Jr. declares. "Their relationship was truly unique."[79] According to Bishop Paul E. Martin, who knew Bess and her family at Blossom long before her marriage to Frank, "Frank's devotion to Bess was beautiful beyond words. He wrote her every day when he was away from home, and in later years he called her every night. Theirs was one of the most beautiful romances I've known."[80] Randy Smith remembers this combination of long distance calls and special delivery letters:

Dad never missed calling, ever. And on top of that, they wrote air mail special delivery letters to one another every day. I don't know how they ever thought of so much to say. Every night a man drove up to our door to deliver a letter from Dad. And every night we drove downtown to the main post office and dropped an air mail, special delivery letter to Dad in the box.[81]

In one envelope addressed to Mrs. Smith with nine four-cent stamps stuck unevenly across the top, Bishop Smith sent the following tribute to Mrs. Smith: "Dearest Bessie:—I have just talked to you this morn. The day is always better for me when I have talked to you. Thru all these years I have been at loose ends unless I have your presence or words to give me direction & assurance. . . ." He concluded another letter by declaring: "I love you more than all the world. I wish I could make you know just how much you mean to me & to my whole life & ministry. You have been the inspiration for all I have tried to do ever since I have known you."[82]

Many passages praising "Bessie" can be found in Bishop Smith's daily journal.

June 16, 1943: This is our twenty-ninth wedding anniversary. I called Bessie tonite. No person has ever been so fortunate as I. Bessie has been perfect all these years.

August 3, 1943: This is Bessie's 52nd birthday. . . . What I owe to her is beyond calculation or expression.

January 29, 1944: I have been on the road so long that I need to stay at home and get my bearings again. It gives me new life to be with Bessie for a while.

June 16, 1945: Today is our 31st wedding anniversary. These have been wonderful & rich years. Bess is a perfect wife & companion.

November 1, 1949: I am sixty years old today . . . Time is passing. I hope Bessie can be here as long as I am & that the last years may be our best.

August 3, 1950: Rome . . . This is Bessie's 59th birthday. She has the vitality and figure of a young girl, and she is the most wonderful person I have ever known. She is life itself for me and to me.

In the early 1940s Bishop Smith became concerned about his health, complaining of spells of chest pain over his heart, which caused shortness of breath and kept him awake at night. Bess insisted that this was sufficient warning for both of them to slow down. "I am truly distressed that you are so tired," she wrote to him, "and I wish that you could have stayed at home this week to rest. I hope you are keeping your promise to me. Remember, we are starting out to outwit Father Time & live to a ripe old age. You have been everything and more in every way that a husband could be. I would be lost without you."[83]

When the condition persisted, Frank consulted a doctor. "I decided to have Dr. Ledbetter, the best heart man in town, look me over," he noted. A cardiogram showed that his heart was normal, but X rays revealed "definite arthritis" in his spine. "Dr. Ledbetter said that the pain I have had for months is a referred pain caused by the trouble in my spine." When the prescribed heat-lamp treatment did not bring sufficient relief, however, the bishop went back for a fluoroscope of his heart. "Dr. Ledbetter says my heart is absolutely normal and that my trouble is nervous tension. . . . If walking, more rest, diet, etc. will improve my breathing, I am resolved to give it a chance. It seems suicidal to go at such a pace as Bessie & I do." Frank and Bess arranged for a masseuse to give them regular treatments at home. Obviously self-conscious about all this attention to their health, Smith wrote in his daily journal: "Anyone reading this diary would conclude that Bessie & I are about to die, or that we are hypochondriacs. We are neither. We are going to doctors because we have neglected our health up to now, and we want to take care of ourselves from here on out."[84]

In addition to these regular visits to the doctor, weekly massages, and a spasmodic effort at taking long walks, Frank Smith evidently discovered that motion picture shows were relaxing for him. Furthermore, going to movies was something that Bess also enjoyed doing. The number of movies that they attended increased sharply at this time and continued at a relatively high rate through most of the decade: seven in 1942, nine in 1943, sixteen in 1944, thirteen in 1945, and ten in 1946.[85] When one subtracts the weeks that the bishop was holding conferences and traveling, the Smiths' movie attendance averages about one a week. At such a rate, of course, they did not always find the best movies.

January 2, 1942: Tonite Bessie, Betty Ann & I went to see "Hellzapoppin"—didn't like it & went next door to see Mickey Rooney in "Babes on Broadway."

September 21, 1943: Bessie & I went to the Majestic to see "Stormy Weather," all Negro cast. We then went to the Metropolitan to see "The Constant Nymph."

October 16, 1943: Bessie & I went to see a Fred Astaire show. He did very little dancing, and as an actor he is not so hot.

May 7, 1944: Tonite Bessie & I did something we never did before—we went to a picture show on Sunday. It was "The Life of Mark Twain." It was slow, however, and we left early.

June 30, 1947: Bessie & I went to see "The Yearling" tonite. Sad picture. We left before it was over.

Their favorite films were *One Foot in Heaven, Random Harvest, How Green Was My Valley, Gone with the Wind, Private Hargrove, Saratoga Trunk,* the Andy Hardy series, and the Dr. Kildare series.

Frank and Bess also enjoyed traveling together, and he took her with him whenever possible. Of all the places where he regularly attended his various church meetings, Buck Hill Falls was the one he most wanted Bess to share. The Board of Missions began holding its annual meetings there in 1943 at The Inn, a resort hotel operated by the Society of Friends high in the Pocono Mountains of Pennsylvania. In the fall of 1945, the situation at home was finally favorable. Not as experienced a traveler as her husband, Mrs. Smith had to endure his gentle childing: "Bessie stayed up till 3:00 this morning packing her bags & getting ready for the trip." On the way up they had three delightful days in New York City, shopping and seeing the sights with Angie and Bessie Mae, Joe and Lois Perkins, and Paul and Mildred Martin.

Snow covered the countryside as they made the ninety-mile train ride on to Buck Hill Falls. "I am so glad Bessie is here," Frank noted. "The Inn is a beautiful place and she has never before attended a meeting of the Board of Missions." The only inconvenience on the entire trip occurred when a mix-up in their return reservations forced Frank and Bess to share a roomette on the Spirit of St. Louis from New York to Missouri. "Tight sleeping," the bishop admitted, "but better than sitting up." The drawing room they had on the Sunshine Special out of St. Louis must have seemed unusually spacious.[86]

Another memorable shared excursion was their three-week trip to Boston for the 1948 General Conference. On the first day after their arrival, the bishops and their wives were taken on a guided tour of the area. Beginning with breakfast at the Wayside Inn, "immortalized by Longfellow," they drove to Concord and Lexington, toured the homes of Emerson, Hawthorne, Louisa Alcott, Longfellow, and Lowell, and visited the Harvard campus. After so much cultural exposure, a certain group of bishops spent the evening at a baseball game: "Angie, Arthur, Fred Corson, James Straughn & I went to see Boston Braves play Brooklyn Dodgers." On another free afternoon, "Monroe Vivion, who is here in his car, took Landrum, Clendenin, Bessie & me to Plymouth. Saw Bunker Hill Monument, John Alden's house where he & Priscilla reared 12 children, Plymouth Rock, and had supper at Toll House."

Unable to get away during the remainder of the conference, Frank and Bess decided to stay over for two more days. As Frank explained, "We will probably never be in New England again, and we want to see more historic spots before we leave." With Will and Sallie Martin, they rented a car and drove for an entire day. Frank wrote the following account:

Beautiful day. Went to Salem & saw House of Seven Gables; to Newburyport & saw crypt of George Whitefield and house where Wm. Lloyd Garrison the abolitionist was born. Had lunch at Kittery, Maine. Drove across New Hampshire, beautiful rural scenery, early American villages, to Brattleboro, Vermont; thence to Northfield, Mass., where Dwight L. Moody was born & buried. Lovely drive down Mohawk Valley to Boston.

They devoted their second day to sight-seeing in Boston, choosing those places with the greatest religious and historical interests. Bess apparently was unable to lure Frank into any antique shops.

Went thru Christian Science Mother Church. Went to King's Chapel, first Episcopal Church in Mass., and adjoining cemetery where Samuel Adams and Paul Revere are buried. Saw grave stones dating back to 1630. Took cab & went to Old State House, Revere residence, Old North Church where Revere had lanterns displayed, site of Boston Massacre & site of Boston Tea Party. . . . We had a great time at Boston. I am so glad that Bess could go.[87]

Perhaps the longest continuous time that Frank and Bess Smith had together after his election in 1930 was their three-month tour of Europe during the summer of 1950. At the request of the bishops of the three Episcopal Areas of The Methodist Church in Europe—Theodor Arvidson of Stockholm, J. W. E. Sommer of Frankfurt, and Paul N. Garber of Geneva—Bishop Smith was to visit the Methodist conferences in Europe. When they learned of Bishop Smith's forthcoming journey, the cabinets of the Texas and Southwest Texas conferences announced a gift of two thousand dollars to Mrs. Smith to enable her to accompany her husband.[88] With Bishop William C. Martin in charge of the Houston Area for three months, Frank Smith was as free of responsibility as he would ever be until his retirement.

Sailing from New York on the *Queen Mary* on June 23, Frank and Bess began a dreamlike "working vacation." They were in Norway and Sweden for eleven days, with at least twenty-four hours in Bergen, Oslo, Stockholm, and Copenhagen. Traveling south across the continent, they included Amsterdam, Rotterdam, Brussels, and Cologne in their itinerary. After a day on the Rhine River between Cologne and Wiesbaden, they toured Frankfurt and Munich and saw the Passion Play at Oberammergau. In Italy they went to Venice, Florence, Naples, Milan, and Rome, where they spent four days.

Awaiting them in Rome was a letter from Randy, asking their permission for him to marry Margaret Ann Pickett. "Mom and Dad called me from Rome," Randy recalls, "to say that we could talk about Ann's and my getting married when they got home. I knew that meant it would be all right."[89] Frank and Mary had married while Frank was still in law school, and Randy and Ann wished to do the same. "I never will be able to tell you how grateful I am to you for giving your consent to my getting married," Randy wrote to his parents. "I'm confident that everything will work out perfectly, and that I'll be able to shoulder the responsibility of which you spoke."[90]

From Italy, Bishop and Mrs. Smith crossed into Switzerland for an eight-day visit: four days in Geneva, two at Interlaken, and two at Lucerne. Four days in Paris completed their tour of the continent. Crossing the English Channel, they were in London four days before making a quick tour of Edinburgh, Glasgow, and Stratford-on-Avon. Sailing again on the *Queen Mary*, the Smiths returned to New York on September 12.[91]

When Bishop Smith performed Randy and Ann's wedding two months later, on November 25, 1950, an era in his life ended. For the first time since Frank, Jr.'s birth in 1911, there were no children at home. On the other hand, a new era had already begun with Tweed's birth to Frank, Jr. and Mary in 1941 and Cynthia's birth to Betty and Don in 1949. Bishop Smith would live to see and enjoy twelve grandchildren: Frank and Mary's Mary Tweed (1941), Karen Hannah (1947), Angie Frank III (1952), Allison (1953), and Leslie Ann (1955); Betty and Don's Cynthia (1949), Donald, Jr. (1951), Martin Randolph (1952), Lisa (1956), and Jennifer (1957); and Randy and Ann's Sherren Bess (1954) and William Randolph, Jr. (1958). Randy and Ann's Margaret Moody (1963) and David Christian (1965) were born after their grandfather's death. Although the grandchildren arrived slowly at first, nine were born in eight years. Always enjoying a joke on himself, Bishop Smith said: "After our daughter had five children in eight years, I said to her: 'Betty, you're kind of pushing marriage.' She replied, 'Well, all I've heard you talk about was a big family, and I wanted to get it over.' "[92]

Although he was writing to Frank, Jr. and Mary, Bishop Smith expressed his pride in his entire family in the following words:

The thing that means more to us than all the world is the character you have in such commanding fashion, the outstanding place you occupy in life, and the remarkable children you are rearing. Never does a day pass but that we thank God for all of you, and for the privilege of being your parents and grandparents, even as we daily ask God to bless and keep you all.[63]

18

The Houston Methodist Hospital

THE STORY OF BISHOP A. FRANK SMITH and the development of the Methodist Hospital in Houston are inextricably related. When Bishop Smith began his supervision of the Texas Conference in 1934, he found that the Methodist Hospital he had assisted in opening a decade earlier (while he was pastor of First Methodist Church[1]) had not been able to keep pace with the need for its services. The expansion and modernization program in 1928, which increased the number of beds to 140, had already been outgrown, and the hospital was turning away patients every day.[2] Dr. J. Charles Dickson, who joined the hospital's staff in 1930, remembers that Bishop Smith attended a meeting in his office to discuss the need for expansion.

This was about 1935 when Mrs. Fondren was interested in the possibility of building across on the other side of Rosalie Street. In those days the Board of Trustees only held about one meeting a year. They'd meet, elect officers and go home. We didn't have very good communication then. So we appreciated the fact that Bishop Smith was quite interested and took the time from his busy schedule to come talk with us about our problems and concerns. Over the years he helped to pull things together, because he had very free communication with the hospital trustees and with a number of the doctors.[3]

A major reason for Bishop Smith's success in relating to the trustees was the mutual respect that had developed during his eight years as pastor of Houston's First Methodist Church with such people as John T. Scott, S. F. Carter, Judge James A. Elkins, W. L. Clayton, Mr. and Mrs. Walter W. Fondren, Jesse H. Jones, Dr. Marvin L. Graves, J. M. West, R. W. Wier, and E. L. Crain. This was also true of the men who became the leaders in the 1940s and 1950s: Walter L. Goldston, Robert A. Shepherd, Hines H. Baker, R. E. ("Bob") Smith, Eddy Scurlock, W. N. Blanton, and Raymond Elledge. These men were staunch Methodists and public-minded citizens who supported worthy projects, but their personal relationship with Bishop Smith focused and strengthened those commitments.[4]

The staff doctors, on the other hand, were attracted by Bishop Smith's vision of a great medical center based on his four-year acquaintance with the internationally famous Barnes Hospital in St. Louis, a Methodist institution supported by the Methodist Episcopal Church, South.[5] The high esteem that such prominent physicians as Dr. C. C. Cody, Jr. and Dr. Marvin L. Graves had for Bishop Smith must have impressed those who were just becoming acquainted with him.[6] The bishop was also popular with the doctors because "he told the best stories on hospital rounds."[7]

While recognizing the importance of Dr. Graves, John T. Scott, and others, Dr. Hatch W. Cummings, Jr., who was associated with Dr. Graves from 1929 to 1941 and was chief of medical services at the hospital from 1946 to 1971, believes that Bishop Smith and Mrs. Fondren were the two most influential trustees in the critical years of the hospital's growth. "It's a little difficult to say which did the most in developing the hospital," Dr. Cummings explains, "because they always seemed to agree and worked together. I think he influenced her a great deal, but she had a strong mind of her own and often proposed ways of improving the hospital." It is generally agreed that Mrs. Josie Roberts, the hospital administrator from 1928 to 1953, not only ran the hospital on a shoestring but also molded the staff into such a working unit that Methodist was the first hospital in Houston to receive recognition such as certification and internships. She could not have done it, Dr. Cummings believes, without the support of Mrs. Fondren and Bishop Smith.[8]

Hines H. Baker emphasizes a third factor that was crucial in Bishop Smith's role in the development of the Methodist Hospital. "Bishop Smith's stature in Houston was not limited to Methodists or even Protestants," Mr. Baker recalls. "He had friends and admirers among the Catholics and Jews as well. He had the support and respect of the entire community. The civic leaders knew him as a broad-gauged man who was interested in what they were doing."[9] As an illustration of the bishop's standing in Houston, R. A. Shepherd recites the following incident:

Judge J. A. Elkins called Bishop Smith one day and told him, "Bishop, when you retire, I want you to come to work at First City National Bank." Bishop Smith replied: "Why, Judge, I don't know anything about banking. I couldn't hold a job down there. What would you want me to do?" "Bishop, we'll pay you ten thousand dollars a year just to walk through the lobby of the bank three or four times a day. It would be worth that just to have you down here."[10]

A more substantive illustration appears in Bishop Smith's daily journal:

May 7, 1943: Col. Bates of the Anderson Foundation told me that a great medical center is to be established here with Baylor Med. College at the center. He also said they would give building space to the Methodist Hospital if we wish.

Since 1941 Dr. E. W. ("Billy") Bertner and the trustees of the M. D. Anderson Foundation had been quietly making plans for a modern and comprehensive medical complex to be composed of both public and private institutions devoted to research, education, and health care. Early in 1943 the foundation succeeded in persuading Baylor College of Medicine to move from Dallas to Houston to become the nucleus of the Texas Medical Center. As an additional attraction, the foundation was purchasing a 134-acre tract of land and offering free sites to carefully selected medical institutions. Now, as Bishop Smith learned from the foundation's chairman, Colonel W. B. Bates, the Methodist Hospital would be offered an opportunity to become one of the first hospitals to participate.[11]

Apparently this matter did not officially come before the trustees of the Methodist Hospital until the fall of 1943. After attending the November meeting of the board, Bishop Smith noted: "It looks as tho' we may go into a campaign early next year for a million dollars or more to build a new hospital as a part of the Medical Center." At the urging of Dr. Dickson and other members of the medical staff, the board was considering a three-hundred-bed hospital. With building costs soaring every day because of the war, however, the trustees were staggered by the anticipated cost of such a hospital. In early January, 1944, Bishop Smith went to see Colonel Bates "about the possibility of the Foundation joining with the Methodist Hospital to rebuild at the Medical Center." The bishop also had a long conference with Judge Elkins concerning their financial dilemma. Eventually, the foundation offered the Methodist Hospital a challenge grant: if the Methodists would raise a million dollars, the foundation would give them a half-million dollars. This was in addition, of course, to the eight acres of land in the Medical Center tract given for the new hospital.[12]

Although the grant from the Anderson Foundation was a substantial boost to the Methodists' morale, they were still far from the amount needed to build their hospital. No one talked of giving up, but the trustees knew they had to have a major gift in hand before they could even start their campaign. Events that occurred on Friday and Saturday, March 2 and 3, 1945, provided the necessary miracle. On those two days, Mr. and Mrs. Hugh Roy Cullen gave four million dollars to four Houston hospitals: a million each to Baptist Memorial, Hermann, Methodist, and St. Luke's Episcopal. What the newspapers and general public did not know was that the Cullens had originally thought only of giving a million each to the Baptist Memorial and Hermann hospitals.

Some persons have given Bishop Smith credit for obtaining the million-dollar gift for Methodist Hospital, but the honor is properly due to W. N. ("Bill") Blanton. As the general manager and executive vice-president of the Chamber of Commerce, Bill Blanton probably knew more about what was happening in Houston than anyone else. When he heard that the Cullens were giving a million dollars to Baptist Memorial Hospital and to Hermann Hospital, he recruited the assistance of a fellow trustee of Methodist Hospital, Claud B. Hamill,[13] and these two men went to see Mr. Cullen. All of this occurred on Friday.[14] That evening Blanton broke the good news to Bishop Smith. "W. N. Blanton told me tonite," Smith noted in his daily journal entry for Friday, March 2, 1945, "that H. R. Cullen had given $1,000,000 each to Memorial & Hermann hospitals & had promised to do the same for the Methodist Hospital." Saturday morning Blanton called Bishop Smith and asked him "to go to Mr. Cullen's office to officially thank him for his gift to the Hospital." Raymond P. Elledge, chairman of the Methodist Hospital board of trustees, and Hines H. Baker, a longtime trustee, joined Bishop Smith at Cullen's office, where statements were issued to the press and pictures taken. "The Methodist Church is grateful to the Cullens for this further evidence of their keen sense of social, civic and spiritual responsibility as has been revealed in all their munificent gifts and widespread activities," Bishop Smith declared. "The entire Southwest, regardless of race or creed, is debtor to the Cullens whose philanthropies bless multitudes and whose example is an inspiration to all in the unselfish use of wealth."[15] The bishop expressed his personal reaction to the Cullen gift in his daily journal:

This means a new building program with a campaign for additional funds. We must raise another million & erect the finest [hospital] in the Southwest. [March 3, 1945]

The papers today have front page announcements of the Cullen gift to the Methodist Hospital with his picture & mine on the front page. It will help the Hospital to have this publicity. [Sunday, March 4, 1945]

Hospital Board meeting tonite. Great elation over Cullen gift. Board feels we should raise another million immediately and build a real Hospital. [Friday, March 9, 1945]

Although the newspapers overlooked Mr. Blanton's role in the Cullen gift, Bishop Smith never forgot. Sixteen years later, in a letter to Blanton thanking him for his continuing services for the Methodist Hospital, Smith wrote, "I am always keenly conscious of the crucial part you played in the securing of the Cullen gift that early set this present hospital upon its way."[16]

Bishop Smith was not alone in his evaluation of the significance of the Cullens' contribution. According to Robert A. Shepherd, who was a trustee for more than a quarter of a century and president of the board when the new hospital opened, "We could never have built that hospital if it hadn't been for Mr. Cullen's gift." With a lawyer's keen eye for details, Shepherd emphasizes the fact that Cullen gave the hospital a million dollars worth of oil *in the ground*. "By the time the payment was made, the price of oil had gone up and we received a total of $1,152,000."[17]

With the stimulus of the Cullen gift, the trustees of the Methodist Hospital planned an extensive financial campaign to begin after the war, with major gift solicitation in 1946 and a general drive in 1947. Bishop Smith's daily journal discloses his active behind-the-scenes leadership:

I went to see Hines Baker [before] the Hospital Board meeting. [July 24, 1945]

Went to see Jesse Jones at his office [Washington, D.C.]. Talked to him about plans for his Foundation which he has set up. Wants me to discuss matter with Fred Heyne who is chairman of the Trustees. . . . Called W. L. Clayton, Ass't. Sec'y. of State. [September 11, 1945]

Came by Hines Baker's office to discuss our Hospital Campaign with him. [July 17, 1946]

Went to see Walter Goldston this morning about being chairman of campaign for $1,000,000 for the Meth. Hosp. He has already given $100,000 to it & is the logical man for it. I believe he will take it. [July 19, 1946]

Spent morning in Hines Baker's office discussing set up of Hospital Campaign. Harry Wiess, Pres. of Humble Co., dropped in for a visit. [July 27, 1946]

Went with committee to see Morris Brownlee about shaping up our hospital campaign. He will do it, which is a lucky break for the hospital. [July 31, 1946]

Spent morning in town seeing Fred Heyne, Jno. T. Scott, Judge Elkins. [August 12, 1946]

Went to see Tom Monroe this aft. to talk about a gift to the Meth. Hosp. from West Foundation. [August 13, 1946]

Went to see Walter Goldston this aft. [about] Hospital Campaign. [September 25, 1946]

This aft. went to meeting of Gifts Committee on Hosp. Campaign. We are preparing to launch campaign for $1,500,000 to match amount given by H. R. Cullen & Anderson Foundation. [October 7, 1946]

Bessie & I went to River Oaks Country Club tonite. I spoke at dinner meeting on Hosp. Campaign for St. Luke's [Methodist] Church. Fine attendance. [November 19, 1946]

Went to see Mr. H. R. Cullen who with his wife has just established a Foundation worth around $160,000,000. Just dropped in for a social visit. [March 29, 1947]

Lunch with Committee to arrange for testimonial dinner for Mr. & Mrs. Cullen. Shepherd, Goldston, Nelms, Blanton, Mills on comm. [November 13, 1947]

Tonite the Methodists had their dinner of appreciation for Mr. & Mrs. Cullen at the Rice Hotel. About 1200 were there. It was one of the most representative gatherings I have ever seen in Houston. I am proud of our Methodism. [January 22, 1948]

Bishop Smith characteristically does not mention the difficulties and frustrations in such an unpredictable and ticklish operation—with one exception. At the testimonial dinner, after the designated dignitaries had spoken their respective words of praise and appreciation for the Cullens' gift, as Smith noted, "Mr. Cullen in his response made a rabid isolationist speech. . . . I am sorry, but that did not detract from the dignity of the affair" [January 22, 1948]. Presumably, since Mr. Cullen was known for his outspoken opposition to U.S. participation in the United Nations, no one was surprised. Hugh Roy Cullen was simply being himself among homefolks.[18]

Far more serious was the impact of postwar inflation on building costs. As Bob Shepherd, who at that time was chairman of the Finance Committee, explains:

Our original plans called for a 300-bed hospital, but we were unable to raise enough money to build that large a hospital. So we brought up the question in the building committee as to whether we shouldn't go ahead and build a 200-bed hospital rather than borrowing the money and going in debt for a 300-bed hospital when we didn't know whether we could even fill it up or not. We only had about one hundred patients at the old hospital at that time.[19]

Ted Bowen, who had just been appointed assistant to Mrs. Roberts, recalls additional reasons for cutting back:

Without any other motivation but the best interest of the hospital, the building committee was trying to look at the situation objectively. And they were worried about over-extended building. They knew Hermann Hospital was having problems, and we were running at a loss of about $4,000 every month. Walter Goldston and Mrs. Fondren were picking that up to keep us going. The hospital was performing more than $30,000 annually in charity services. At that point, no one could envision what this medical center was going to be.[20]

When the committee reported to the board and made its recommendation to cut back to a 200-bed hospital, the trustees reluctantly seemed to accept the unhappy necessity. There are a number of versions of the dramatic moment that followed. Some say that Mrs. Fondren had been knitting, but when the committee completed its report she began putting her knitting away. Walter Goldston, having succeeded Raymond Elledge as president of the board, was presiding. "Mrs. Fondren, the meeting isn't over yet," he said. "It is for me," she replied, "if you are going to settle for a 200-bed hospital.[21] You can build a 200-bed hospital if you want to. But I think we should build a 300-bed hospital and borrow whatever we need to build it. I can assure you that if you build a 200-bed hospital, you will not build it with any part of the Fondren money."[22] Whatever Mrs. Fondren's exact words were, all accounts agree concerning the board's response: "So we built a 300-bed hospital and borrowed the difference!"[23] "I knew it was going to cost me," Mrs. Fondren remembers with a laugh, "but I just spoke right up. When you could see the possibilities of Houston growing, you knew that a 200-bed hospital wouldn't begin to take care of the sick people."[24] Between 1948 and 1973, Mrs. Fondren and her foundation gave more than six million dollars to the Methodist Hospital, backing up her vision.[25]

Bishop Smith, of course, took second place to no one in his vision of the development of "the Great Gulf Basin." "The general growth of the whole area was something that he relished and rejoiced in, and he kept after us to take advantage of it," Dr. Stewart Clendenin says. "And he believed in the Methodist Hospital. It was a particular joy of his. And he coaxed the whole thing along until they got going."[26] Shortly after Mrs. Fondren so convincingly settled the question of the size of the new hospital, Bishop Smith met with the executive committee of the board in a "back to the drawing board" type of session. "Had lunch with Walter Goldston, Hines Baker, Bob Shepherd and Will Mills concerning need to raise million dollars more to build 300 bed hospital." Mr. Goldston rose to the occasion and pledged an additional $100,000 to initiate yet another effort to secure the necessary funds. "He is a remarkable person," Smith noted in appreciation.[27]

Joining with the leaders of the hospital board, Bishop Smith set out to find enough money to warrant the beginning of construction. He based his appeal on two basic points:

[First] We have an unsurpassed opportunity to occupy a strategic place in the new Medical Center to be developed in Houston because the Anderson Foundation has offered us eight acres of land in a very choice part of the Medical Center property, the H. R. Cullens have given us one million dollars, and the Anderson Foundation challenged us with a half million dollar matching grant.

[Second] We have an obligation to our fellow man and to our Church because the healing ministry is a vital part of the Church's mission.[28]

Those who claim that Bishop Smith never directly asked anyone for contributions to Methodist institutions should read carefully the bishop's assignment by the Big Gifts Committee: W. L. Clayton, the West family and the West Foundation, Jesse H. Jones, Mr. and Mrs. Dan Harrison, H. C. Wiess, Mrs. J. W. Neal, and J. W. Rockwell.[29] "Bishop Smith was a tremendous worker in fund raising during the difficult times from 1948 through 1951 when we had to have enough to break ground and begin building," Ted Bowen declares.[30] Bob Shepherd is equally emphatic:

Through Bishop Smith's influence we were enabled to raise the funds we needed to build our new hospital in the Medical Center, both the funds we received from the Houston Endowment, which was the Jesse Jones Foundation, and from Mrs. Fondren and the Fondren Foundation. Bishop Smith had a great deal of influence on her and her giving to The Methodist Hospital as well as to the other Methodist institutions. Bishop Smith and Will Clayton were also very close friends, and Bishop Smith personally solicited him and got his contribution, a very sizeable contribution for the hospital.[31]

While Bishop Smith was obviously effective in making direct solicitations, it is true that he preferred a more indirect approach. "Bishop Smith had a way of getting people with means into places of leadership that caused them to make a real investment," Hines Baker recalls. "He didn't ask them for any particular amount of money, but he had an influence on them to give money by interesting them in the project and inducing them to become the leaders. If they were going to do that, of course, then they had to lead out with their gifts."[32] Bishop Smith persuaded Walter Goldston to take the chairmanship of the campaign for the Methodist Hospital, for example, and Mr. Goldston contributed more than $200,000 at critical points in the campaign.

Another way in which Bishop Smith indirectly caused potential donors to make large contributions to the hospital was through his personal interest. "People gave money to the hospital," Mr. Baker says, "because he identified himself with that institution."[33] As Dr. Durwood Fleming explains, "Bishop Smith won the confidence of men like H. R. Cullen, Will Clayton, Jesse Jones and Bob Smith. They believed in his integrity and in his spirit. Maybe they didn't know much about the hospital, but because Frank Smith was there and believed in it, they gave to it."[34]

Closely related to this point was Bishop Smith's characteristic manner of showing his appreciation for these gifts and other acts supporting the Methodist Hospital. "Bishop Smith was the most appreciative person that I have ever known," Mr. Shepherd declares:

I recall many instances when I would do some small thing for the hospital, and he would take occasion to write me a note of thanks in longhand. I remember one particular note that I received from some town in Georgia where he had gone to hold a meeting. Just before he left Houston, he heard of something I had done. So after his service the first night, he went to his hotel room and penned me a note thanking me for what I had done. He never missed an opportunity to thank those who had done anything for the church or for one of the institutions related to it.[35]

Bishop Smith's personal correspondence files contain many letters from persons who appreciated this thoughtfulness. The following note from Hines Baker is a typical example: "Dear Bishop Smith: It was extremely nice of you to call on me yesterday. With all the demands on your time and the pressure of problems you have, I don't see how you manage to be so thoughtful of friends and so generous with your visits. I value your interest and friendship beyond the power I have to express."[36]

When the board of trustees let the contract for the new building on November 22, 1949, Bishop Smith believed they were marking "a milestone in Methodist history." Not even a cold and rainy day could dampen his spirits when work began three weeks later: "This afternoon we broke ground for the new $4,000,000 Meth. Hospital in the Medical Center. It will be 8 floors & 300 beds, a magnificent institution."[37] It would also be the first hospital built in the new Medical Center.[38]

Bishop Smith's pride in the new hospital was matched by the staff's and the board's appreciation for his contributions to the development of the hospital. Instead of placing the architect's sketch of the new building on the cover of the brochure for the laying of the cornerstone, for example, they had a picture of Bishop Smith printed in that position of honor. An uninformed guest would have assumed that he was the donor. When the celebration of the opening of the hospital was held in November, 1951, Bishop Smith was completely surprised to see portraits of Mrs. Smith and himself in the spacious board room together with a plaque stating that the trustees had furnished the room in their honor.[39]

As one of the thirty-seven trustees of the Methodist Hospital, how actively did Bishop Smith participate in the policy-making decisions that shaped the hospital's character and its future development? According to Dr. Hatch W. Cummings, an ex officio member of the board of trustees as president of the medical staff, "Bishop Smith was a strong force in deciding the policy of the hospital at the trustee level. He had an unusual ability to size up a situation and make a good judgment on it. He believed in growing and developing and not being timid about it, and he influenced the other trustees." With a chuckle, Dr. Cummings recalls that the bishop "used to doodle a fair amount at the board meetings, but he was always listening. When a point came up that he wanted to address himself to, he was ready to speak."[40] Ted Bowen, who succeeded Mrs. Roberts as the hospital's administrator in 1953, especially admired Bishop Smith's ability "to work out solutions, even when things looked rather difficult at the time."[41]

The trustees appreciated the manner in which Bishop Smith could ease tense situations with a humorous story. Bob Shepherd, who was president of the board when the new hospital opened, can still relate a number of the bishop's stories. On one occasion when Bishop Smith thought some of the trustees were dragging their feet on a matter, he told the following anecdote:

A preacher was exhorting his congregation on the glories of Heaven. At the crucial moment, he called out, "Now, everyone who wants to go to Heaven, stand up!" All of the congregation stood up except one member. The preacher turned to this man and said, "Brother Jones, do you mean to tell me that you don't want to go to Heaven when you die?" "Well, of course I do," Brother Jones replied. "I thought you were trying to get up a load right now."[42]

Another aspect of Bishop Smith's ministry that greatly benefited the Methodist Hospital was the Blue Bird Circle. Organized by Smith in 1923 when he was pastor of the First Methodist Church in Houston,[43] this woman's service club was concerned from the beginning with the needs of chidren and young people. It became associated with the Methodist Hospital in a major and permanent way in 1934 when it built a thirty-bed hospital—the "Little Hospital"—to house the overcrowded crippled children's ward of the Methodist Hospital. At the groundbreaking ceremonies for this original Blue Bird hospital, Bishop Smith declared: "Houston will be a better place to live because the Blue Birds have caught a vision of the spirit of God. At this beginning . . . there will be set in motion influences that will reach beyond this community and outlast the life span of all those who are making possible this enterprise." His words were to prove prophetic. In 1949 when the "Little Hospital" was reorganized as the Blue Bird Seizure Clinic in association with Baylor College of Medicine, it became the first clinic of this kind in the South and one of only three in the nation.

As plans for the new Methodist Hospital developed, the Blue Bird Circle assumed the $400,000 cost of the fourth floor and moved their clinic into the new building. The clinic broadened its field in pediatric neurology. From an annual budget of less than $12,000 and treatment of about 200 patients in 1949, the clinic grew quickly to a $120,000 budget and treatment of 1,897 patients in 1955. When the enlarged facilities of the 1960s were outgrown, Mr. and Mrs. David C. Bintliff gave $2,000,000 to enable the clinic to move into Methodist Hospital's new Neurosensory Center, where it is called the Blue Bird Circle Children's Clinic, Pediatric Neurology.[44]

The miraculous growth of the Blue Birds' "Little Hospital" to its present magnificent facilities is an indication of the expansion of the Methodist Hospital. The 300-bed unit was filled the day it opened, and by 1956 plans were under way to increase it to a 1,000-bed hospital, reaching from Bertner Boulevard to Fannin. With the addition of the Fondren and Brown Cardiovascular and Orthopedic Clinical Research Centers, the total value of the Methodist Hospital by 1973 was about $50,000,000.[45]

The 1960 *Discipline* of The Methodist Church requires that:

A bishop whose seventieth birthday precedes the first day of the regular session of his Jurisdictional Conference shall be released at the close of that conference from the obligation to travel through the connection at large, and from residential supervision. . . . [He] shall not preside thereafter over any . . . conference, or make appointments, but may take the chair temporarily in any conference if requested to do so by the bishop presiding. He may participate in the Council of Bishops, but without vote. [Par. 436.1 and 437.1]

Accordingly, Bishop A. Frank Smith was due to retire at the close of the South Central Jurisdictional Conference, Sunday evening, June 26, 1960. He apparently had mixed feelings about his retirement. As early as 1941, he and Mrs. Smith had begun to look forward to the time they would have together. They agreed to slow down their pace of living and to begin taking better care of their health. As Mrs. Smith wrote: "Remember, we are starting out to outwit Father Time & live to a ripe old age. . . . If we can just hold on until you are 72 & I 70, we can have that quiet & peace that we both want, and have our second honeymoon."[46] Ironically, it was Mrs. Smith's health that thwarted their long-range plans. "We had looked forward to Frank's retirement," she said in 1962. "We had made plans to travel and do some things that we had wanted to do and hadn't been able to do. And then I prevented that with my illness."[47] Bess's heart attack in the summer of 1953 left her in such condition that she had to lead a very restricted life. Frank, Jr. remembers that

she had to stay at sea level, so they could not go to Colorado. In fact, she couldn't even ride the fast elevator in the Humble Building. She had to go part way up, get off and wait awhile before she could get back on and go up again. She couldn't climb stairs at all. You can imagine how her opportunities were reduced. If Mr. Walter Goldston hadn't installed an elevator in the new residence on Kirby Drive, I suppose they would have had to move to a one story home.[48]

Very few people knew how much Mrs. Smith suffered from arthritis, since she persisted in getting out around town in Houston and even in going to San Antonio for the customary presentation to the annual conference.[49] "Mom and Dad joked about it," Randy recalls, "but they both suddenly found themselves just sitting there looking at one another."[50]

On the other hand, to be free from "the obligation to travel through the connection" was a welcomed release. Bishop Arthur Moore remembers a conversation with Bishop Smith about the significance of that phrase in the *Discipline* as it suddenly related to them.[51] According to Bishop Will Martin, another longtime colleague in the "itinerant General Superintendency," "Frank seemed to take his retirement as a matter of course, so far as I could tell. In fact, I rather think there were a good many of the elements of responsibility that he was glad to be rid of." Martin believes that "going out with his beloved comrade of many years, Arthur Moore, made it a more natural and normal thing for Frank to do."[52]

On the other hand, Bishop Smith was concerned about some aspects of his retirement, as he confided to a number of his friends. Dr. Lawrence Landrum and Dr. Monroe Vivion remember how Bishop Smith would tell them the number of years, months, or weeks left until he retired. "We were riding up in an elevator in 1950," Landrum recalls, " and he suddenly said to me, 'Lawrence, I've got only 520 more Sundays to go.' Ten years! And he counted down from that time on. He dreaded it like sin!"[53] Dr. L. U. Spellman cites a similar experience: "On more than one occasion Frank Smith expressed a dread of retirement. He compared himself to Bishop Sam Hay who, as Frank said, had no hobby or sideline, but whose recreation was his work, and lived out his retirement in loneliness in his hotel apartment."[54] "Frank Smith dreaded retirement," Bishop Kenneth Pope believes. "It was a dark cloud over him. He was just sure it would be a first death. His life had been the drama of the church. You take a man out of the drama where neither the lines nor the plot can, of necessity, get under his skin, and what more has he got to live for?"[55] Dr. Bonneau Murphy, who had been closely associated with Bishop Smith in the Division of National Missions for many years, agrees: " 'Bishop Frank' had been in the vortex of things so long that it was difficult for him to make the adjustment to retirement."[56] Hines Baker, who knows what it is to be retired from the presidency of a huge organization, remembers an incident that illustrates this aspect of Smith's retirement:

We were in a meeting out at the hospital. The Humble Company was trying to give a hospital that we had built down in Baytown to The Methodist Hospital. And Bishop Smith came through the room. I could see that he wanted to linger there, but the people in charge didn't invite him to sit down and participate. He dragged himself out of there, but I could see that he was disappointed. He wanted to know what was going on. People were gracious and glad to see him, of course, but he was a man without a job, really.[57]

As Bishop Smith himself often said, "When your phone quits ringing and your salary is cut in half, you know you're retired."[58]

Only within the context of Bishop Smith's dread of retirement can one appreciate what the position at the Methodist Hospital meant to him.

Several years before the bishop's retirement, according to Ted Bowen, O'Banion Williams (who succeeded Bob Shepherd as president of the hospital's board of trustees) suggested that they create a staff position that would "directly relate" Bishop Smith to the hospital when he retired. "It sounded like an excellent idea," Bowen recalls, "so we started talking with the bishop informally about coming with us when he retired, about how much we needed him and so on."[59]

As we have seen, Southern Methodist University offered Bishop Smith a "post-retirement" position in the area of development and public relations.[60] Southwestern University, Smith's alma mater, also sought his services as chancellor.[61] Since both of these university positions would have permitted Bishop Smith to continue his residence in Houston, what was the special appeal of the position at Methodist Hospital? First, since the hospital position would entail no out-of-town travel, there would be no more worry about leaving Mrs. Smith. Second, his schedule at the hospital would have the advantages of daily regularity without any pressure of deadlines or goals. Finally, and perhaps most important, the nature of the work at the hospital offered an opportunity for learning more about a challenging field and the excitement of being related to such dramatic developments taking place in health care as the cardiovascular work Dr. Michael DeBakey was doing at Methodist Hospital.

"We had only two problems, really," Mr. Bowen says. "The bishop didn't want any salary because he had the income from his retirement fund. We were prepared to offer him a sizeable salary in line with his value to us, but he was stubborn about that and would only accept a token amount." "They said if they didn't pay me a salary, it wouldn't be a real job," Bishop Smith explained, "so I told them to give me a hundred dollars a month."[62] Bowen persuaded Bishop Smith to accept sufficient housing allowance to help pay his rent at Kirby Drive. Since Bishop and Mrs. Paul Martin preferred to live in an apartment, the trustees of the episcopal residence urged the Smiths to remain in their home of ten years. Bishop Smith agreed only on condition that he pay a monthly rent of $500. Knowing of this arrangement, Bowen set the housing allowance at $2,400 annually.[63]

The other problem that arose in the conversations between Ted Bowen and Bishop Smith focused on the nature of their relationship. Bowen's parents had been members of Smith's first church at Alto, Texas, and a kind of father-son relationship developed between the two men when Bowen came to Houston in 1948. As Bowen explains:

So here I was, a young man running a health institution, and he had been running a large organization for thirty years. And he was going to come on the staff as a consultant to the hospital, primarily in the area of public relations. How would we get along together? That point worried him, and we had many long conversations about it. He would say, "Suppose I come here and you all want to get rid of me. What happens?" And I said, "Well, we would sit down and talk about it until we came to an agreement." I finally persuaded him that he would have no organizationally structured responsibility or accountability.[64]

Bishop Smith joined the staff of the Methodist Hospital on September 1, 1960, and continued until September 30, 1962, when he resigned because of ill health. He had an office "on the administration side of the hall" and a secretary. On his letterhead he was described as "Counselor." "I have no specific duties," Bishop Smith said, "but I come out nearly every morning on my half-day schedule. I've had very pleasant associations here."[65] Such a statement is typical of the bishop's customary humility. The record shows, however, that he made a remarkable contribution in a number of diverse areas during those two brief years: in his continuing role as a trustee, in his ministry to patients, in his influence on the administration and medical staff, and as an interpreter of the hospital's health care services to the respective men's and women's service groups and to potential donors in the greater Houston area. "It really was a rather schizophrenic position," Ted Bowen says. "He was still a very active member of the Board of Trustees, having been elected a life member when Bishop Paul Martin succeeded him as bishop of this area. He was also a consultant to the administration and an employee of the hospital. But he melded a conglomerate of activities together in a uniquely effective way."[66]

After beginning his usual "half-day" in a brief conversation with Mr. Bowen, Bishop Smith ordinarily made the rounds to see the many patients he knew. "I'd say he knew half of the people in the hospital on any one day," Bowen declares (that was in days of the 300-bed capacity). "He had a deep compassion for people and was very adept at picking up on emotional needs and in settling patients down. He gave them hope." As the fame of Dr. Michael DeBakey and his cardiovascular group spread, patients began coming to the Methodist Hospital from all around the world. Bishop Smith enjoyed talking with them. "It really lifted the spirits of these people," according to Chaplain Elton Stephenson, "especially if they were Methodists, to have a bishop call on them."[67]

Bishop Smith's position on the hospital staff and especially his visiting with patients might have created a difficult situation for the hospital chaplain. But Chaplain Stephenson insists that this was never the case. Bishop Smith and the religious activities staff at the hospital had established a basis for mutual respect in the years prior to his retirement, as the following examples from their correspondence show. "I appreciate, more than I can express, your thoughtfulness and your way of cooperating," Chaplain Stephenson wrote to Bishop Smith in 1956. "No hospital chaplain has more freedom to do what is right than I do because of your concern and backing."[68] A year later, Clyde Verheyden, the director of religious activities, wrote: "You have never failed, even in the midst of your busiest schedule, to make me feel that my program, my problem, was the most important thing to you at that time."[69] Stephenson is understandably proud of this handwritten note from Bishop Smith.

DEAR ELTON:
Your report, mailed to the preachers of the Texas Conference, reached me here [New York]. I have looked it over with care. It is most interesting. You are doing a grand job at the Hospital. I have never [in nine years] heard one word of criticism of you or your work.
Blessings upon you and yours,
A. FRANK SMITH.[70]

Chaplain Stephenson sums up their relationship with Bishop Smith after the bishop came to the hospital staff:

Bishop Smith was very alert to matters of protocol and insisted on maintaining his place as representing the administration. He always let people know that he was calling as a friend or as a bishop of The Methodist Church. He never did interfere in any way. He ordained me in 1947 and then appointed me as the first chaplain at Methodist Hospital in 1951. So he respected my ministry as I respected his. He shared information with us and was always just more than glad to make a call if we asked him to, regardless of the patient's status in life or denomination. He was just very, very easy to work with. We felt it was a real privilege to have been a part of his later years.[71]

The fact that Bishop Smith's office was across the hall from the chaplain's office was entirely coincidental, according to Ted Bowen, but it did make possible a very relaxed and informal relationship between them.

The office secretaries and other members of the administrative staff were very fond of Bishop Smith. "He was a great person to relate to," recalls Bowen, "and I'm sure many went to him with their problems and concerns. He was a kind of father-counselor to a lot of people. He buoyed up the whole institution while he was here."

Bishop Smith quickly established rapport with the doctors and nurses and was always happy to stop for a chat when the situation was appropriate. "The nurses just loved him," Chaplain Stephenson remembers, "and were always glad to see him on their floors."[72] From time to time, Mr. Bowen scheduled relatively informal sessions for Bishop Smith and the department heads of the medical staff. At other times the bishop spoke to the entire general medical staff, about four hundred doctors at

that time. "He could inspire our people on what he called 'plus service,'"
Bowen explains—"how to make health care more human and less cold.
He could give excellent examples of how plus care was given with
kindness, courtesy and emotional comfort. They respected him and enjoyed talking with him about the philosophy of health care." Bishop
Smith greatly admired the professional skill of the medical staff, and he
urged them to develop "a personal solicitude for the patient that may
contribute as much toward recovery as skill itself."[73] "All of us marveled
at the way Bishop Smith could express himself and hold our attention,"
Chaplain Stephenson remembers. "He really gave us some sound things
to think about."[74] Bowen agrees that Bishop Smith was effective with
any size group, "but I think his real imprint was made in talking with
two or three in the coffee bar over a cup of coffee. He helped to develop
an esprit de corps here that was long lasting."

Because Bishop Smith took so much interest in learning about the
special health care services available at the Methodist Hospital, he became an effective interpreter of the institution. "Bishop Smith took his
position here very seriously," according to Dr. Cummings, "and he could
get some things done that neither Ted Bowen nor anyone else could
have done."[75] Appreciating his interest, the doctors discussed their respective specializations with him. He especially enjoyed talking with Dr.
DeBakey about his work. "Bishop Smith really got into the health care
field," Mr. Bowen declares, "and he often said to me that it was one of
the most challenging and gratifying experiences of his life." As a result
of this eagerness to learn, Bishop Smith was able to present specific
professional needs to certain persons or groups where he had an entrée
possessed by no one else. From his perspective as the administrator of
the hospital, Ted Bowen saw the breadth and significance of Bishop
Smith's contribution more clearly than anyone else. In the following
letter to Smith, Bowen expressed his "personal appreciation for all you
are doing for this hospital":

It is true that you are helping tremendously in our fund-raising. An example
of this is the check you handed me today from Mr. Bishop. However, this
help is secondary to the fact that your very presence here in the hospital
has meant a great deal to this institution. Your interest in the patients has
reaped us many rewards. Your interest in our employees has had noticeable
effect. The very fact that you are a part of our staff has raised the prestige
of the hospital in the eyes of all who come in contact with our service. It
was a fine day for us when you decided to come with the hospital.[76]

Without depreciating the significance of Bishop Smith's services to the Methodist Hospital, those who held him dear were more grateful for the personal happiness and sense of fulfillment which he received from his work there. "Dad really cherished the opportunity that the hospital gave him after he retired," Randy Smith declares. "He told me that it was a blessing to have a place to go and hang his hat, that it gave him an opportunity to get out from under foot and to have some modicum of dignity about what he was doing during the day. That really meant a lot to him."[77] L. U. Spellman believes that the position at the hospital was a source of great comfort to Frank Smith.

It provided him a place of useful service, and it was in his beloved Houston, where he had lived for two-thirds of his ministry. I recall a conversation with him in which he told me about the elaborate office space and fixtures provided for him, all of which he thought was more than he needed or could do work to justify. But he deeply appreciated their thoughtfulness and the position.[78]

Ted Bowen credits Bishop Smith's own adaptability as being crucial. "He made a good adjustment, in my opinion, from what he had been doing to this new area of his life. I think he was as happy in what he was doing here as he had ever been in his life." Contrary to any speculation that the bishop's retirement contributed to his demise, Mr. Bowen insists: "If you retire and don't do anything, you deteriorate. But Bishop Smith was busy and happy about what he was doing. He had a tremendous time here in his period of service with us. We were thrilled at having him here, and we think he was thrilled at being here. We believe he really found his place here."[79]

Epilogue: "Crossing Over"

BISHOP AND MRS. SMITH were able to share only two and a half years of his superannuation. In mid-August, seven weeks after Frank had retired as a bishop of The Methodist Church, Bess suffered "a severe heart attack."[1] Five months later she was still confined to her bed. "Bess has been allowed to see no one save her nurses and members of the family, nor has she been allowed to come downstairs," Smith wrote to a friend. "She sits up some, but she still has to be under oxygen part of each day. Her heart muscles are weak, and heart spasms come without warning and without apparent cause."[2]

Despite the discouragement of Bess's tenuous recovery, Frank Smith continued to be a source of support to others. Bishop Paul E. Martin, who succeeded Bishop Smith in the Houston Area, gratefully recalls how Bishop Smith opened doors for him and eased the transition. Rabbi Hyman Judah Schachtel, senior rabbi of Houston's Congregation Beth Israel since the early 1940s and an ardent admirer of Smith's, remembers such an instance: "I met Bishop Smith in the doctors' lot at the Medical Center one day. 'Bishop, I understand your successor has come to town.' 'Oh, Hyman,' he said, 'you are going to love Paul Martin. There are some men who create problems just by the way they conduct themselves. But Paul Martin is a man who solves problems. You will be delighted with him.' "[3] After Bishop Martin had been in Houston for a few months, Bishop Smith wrote to him: "Dear Paul: Bess and I count you as our very own and we rejoice every day in the fact that you are in Houston. You have captured completely the hearts of the preachers and laymen alike in the Texas Conference."[4]

On Tuesday, April 3, 1962, Bishop Smith spoke at St. Luke's Methodist Church in Houston. As he and Mrs. Smith left the church, he complained of heaviness in his chest and pain in his arms and wrists. Thanks to her extensive experience with her own heart condition, Mrs. Smith recognized the symptoms and knew what to do. Fortunately, she had recovered sufficiently to accompany her husband to that morning's services. "When we got to the car," she later explained,

I gave him a nitroglycerine tablet. As quickly as Allen got us home, I gave him another and put him under oxygen. I called the Dr. [Abbe A. Ledbetter] and he took a cardiogram at once. He said Frank had a rupture of a blood vessel inside the heart in the left ventricle, "myocardial infarction."[5] . . . Frank is at home [eleven days after the attack] and getting along well. He will have to be in bed for several weeks and, much to his regret, on a very low calorie diet.[6]

The heart attack did not deprive Bishop Smith of his sense of humor and thoughtfulness of others. He responded to cards and friends through his secretary at the Methodist Hospital. "Bishop and Mrs. Smith deeply appreciate your card," Miss DePrima wrote to Marjorie Grace Beech, Assistant to President Durwood Fleming. "He is getting along fine and expects to be out in a few weeks. If he dies, he is confident it will be because of the diet imposed upon him and not because of his heart." Disappointed that he could not attend Fleming's inauguration, Smith declared that in his thirty years as an active bishop, he knew of no appointment in the church "more providential and more fitting than that which brought Durwood and Lurlyn to Southwestern."[7]

During his final four months, Bishop Smith continued to believe that he was improving. His correspondence reflects this optimism. In mid-June he wrote to Bishop Will Martin, his friend and colleague for four decades:

I am still confined to my room though I am making good progress. I have lost 27 pounds and the end is not yet in sight. My cardiogram is still ragged, but the doctors assure me that I will have a complete recovery and should be out by the middle of July. . . . You and Sally are now entering the home stretch. Yours has been a remarkable career, which has been equaled by few men in the Church [and] in which I have rejoiced tremendously. I am sure you will find your years of retirement rich and rewarding. The two years since our retirement have been the most satisfactory and the happiest Bess and I have known in the 48 years since we started.[8]

In August Smith wrote again to Bishop Martin. While admitting that his cardiogram had not "straightened out" and that he had to spend two or three hours in bed each afternoon, Smith hoped to join Martin and others at a Methodist United Funds campaign luncheon to be held in Houston.[9]

"Even toward the end, when he could have taken his human relations a little less sensitively," Bishop Kenneth Pope declares, "A. Frank Smith never lost his sensitivity to people, his complete deference, his unselfishness."[10] When Mrs. Jesse H. Jones died in August, Bishop Smith conducted her funeral. It was "against the advice of my doctor," Smith admitted, "but I had an obligation to do this, growing out of an association of 40 years. I am glad to say that I got along all right and suffered no ill effects of any sort."[11]

In what is perhaps the last letter he wrote, Bishop Smith was still being considerate. It is addressed to Bishop and Mrs. Kenneth W. Copeland and is dated October 2, 1962. The Copelands were preparing for a trip to the Far East, an "episcopal visitation" assigned by the Council of Bishops, and had sent a copy of their itinerary to the Smiths.

Bess and I have gone over your itinerary with tremendous interest. You have a wonderful trip ahead of you. . . . We never got to the Far East. That would have been my next assignment in 1954 had it not been for Bess's heart attack. We still talk in wishful terms about such a trip, but, of course, that possibility is completely behind us. . . . We will follow you in our thoughts and in our prayers from day to day. We love you a whole lot at our house and are mighty proud of you. Blessings upon you always.[12]

Responding to questions about his own health, Bishop Smith concluded: "My cardiogram has not straightened out, and I am having to observe a strict regimen.[13] I have lost 35 pounds and I am feeling very well, but it will be a long time before I am allowed to undertake any sort of engagements, either social or professional."[14]

Although Bishop Smith acknowledged the seriousness of his condition in this letter, he did not tell the Copelands about the most recent developments that were causing him concern. Why worry friends with matters he had shared only with Bess? Not even Dr. Ledbetter, their doctor since the 1940s, knew. "Mrs. Smith told me after the Bishop's death," Dr. Ledbetter later recalled, "that he had suffered a considerable amount of worry because he was gaining weight steadily for the last two weeks and yet he was dieting strictly. This was undoubtedly [due to] congestive heart failure. He was not seen at that time, incidentally, because he apparently thought he would just work harder to get himself straightened out. He died suddenly one afternoon"[15]—Friday, October 5, 1962.[16] Frank Smith's death came as he had hoped it would. "I have no desire to hasten the coming of that day," he declared to a friend a decade earlier, "but I hope when my time comes that I can go quickly."[17]

The funeral services for Bishop Smith were held in the First Methodist Church in Houston, Monday, October 8, attended not only by Methodists of the Houston Area but also by a vast multitude of friends—Protestant, Catholic, and Jewish.[18] "The esteem and affection in which he was held by members of his own church," a Houston newspaper editor wrote, "was shared by clergymen and members of all denominations and faiths and by all Houstonians who knew him as a man, as a minister and as a citizen. And all share the deep sense of loss and sadness which his death has brought."[19] Sharing in the service, Bishops Arthur J. Moore, William C. Martin, and Paul E. Martin gave tributes to their colleague, and Dr. W. F. Bryan—Frank Smith's first presiding elder—led the prayers and benediction.[20] The Methodist Hospital has published in its *Journal* a transcript of the funeral service.[21]

Words from *Pilgrim's Progress* that Bishop Smith cherished and often cited for the comfort of bereaved families and friends seem especially appropriate for the time of his own passing:

And it came to be told that Mr. Valiant-for-Truth had got himself a summons, and had this for a token that the summons was true, that his pitcher was broken at the fountain. When the import of this came to be known to Mr. Valiant-for-Truth, he called his friends about him and said: "I am going to my Father's; and though with great difficulty have I got me where I now am, yet do I not regret the great trials and tribulations which have brought me thus far. My sword I give to him that shall succeed me in my pilgrimage, and my courage and skill to him that can get them. My marks and scars I carry with me, to be a witness for me that I have fought His battles who now will be my Rewarder." When the day that he was to go hence was come, many accompanied him to the riverside, into which as he went he said, "Death, where is thy sting?" And as he went down deeper, he said, "O Grave, where is thy victory?" Thus Mr. Valiant-for-Truth crossed over, and all the trumpets sounded for him on the other side.[22]

On February 4, 1964—sixteen months after Bishop Smith's death— Mrs. Smith suffered a fatal stroke while visiting at her sister Hallie's home near Southern Methodist University.[23] Despite her weakened heart and pain from arthritis, Bess had braved a tiring trip to Dallas to participate in the unveiling of a portrait of the bishop during Ministers' Week. After the ceremonies, which were held in the A. Frank Smith Memorial Texana Room of Fondren Library,[24] she insisted on standing in the receiving line to greet hundreds of ministers and their wives, until Bishop and Mrs. Paul E. Martin persuaded her to retire.[25] Later that evening, while talking with Hallie and George, she complained of a severe headache. "We saw that she was desperately ill and called the doctor," Mrs. Pierce remembers, "but she was unconscious before we could get her to bed. She never regained consciousness. She was probably gone before the ambulance reached the hospital."[26] In death, as in life, Frank and Bess were not separated for long.

APPENDIX A

A. Frank Smith's Ancestry

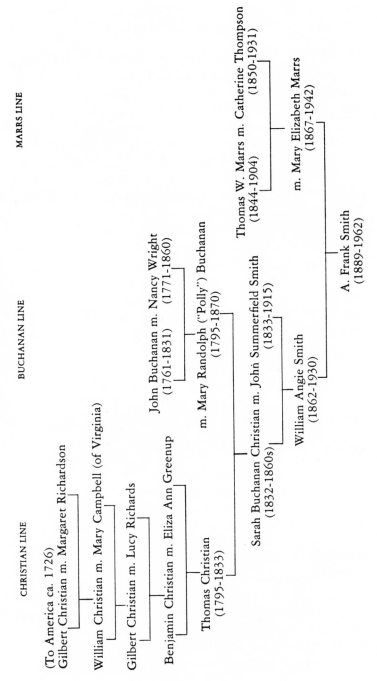

CHRISTIAN LINE

BUCHANAN LINE

MARRS LINE

(To America ca. 1726)
Gilbert Christian m. Margaret Richardson

William Christian m. Mary Campbell (of Virginia)

Gilbert Christian m. Lucy Richards

Benjamin Christian m. Eliza Ann Greenup

Thomas Christian
(1795-1833)

John Buchanan m. Nancy Wright
(1761-1831)   (1771-1860)

m. Mary Randolph ("Polly") Buchanan
(1795-1870)

Sarah Buchanan Christian m. John Summerfield Smith
(1832-1860s)   (1833-1915)

William Angie Smith
(1862-1930)

Thomas W. Marrs m. Catherine Thompson
(1844-1904)   (1850-1931)

m. Mary Elizabeth Marrs
(1867-1942)

A. Frank Smith
(1889-1962)

APPENDIX B
TAPE-RECORDED INTERVIEWS

Mr. Hines H. Baker, Exxon Building, Houston, Sept. 17, 1973.

Mr. Ted Bowen, Methodist Hospital, Houston, Sept. 21, 1973.

Bishop Kenneth W. Copeland, Houston, July 23, 1972.

Rev. Stewart Clendenin, Houston, Aug. 28, 1972.

Rev. and Mrs. Finis Crutchfield, Sr., Carlsbad, N. Mex., Jan. 24, 1972.

Dr. H. W. Cummings, Jr., Methodist Hospital, Houston, Sept. 18, 1973.

Dr. Clarence Dickson, Methodist Hospital, Houston, Oct. 26, 1973.

Dr. Durwood Fleming, SU, Georgetown, Texas, July 13 & 14, 1973.

Mrs. Walter W. Fondren, Methodist Hospital, Houston, Oct. 26, 1973.

Rev. Walton Gardner, Houston, July 23, 1972.

Mrs. Donald (Betty Smith) Griffin, Georgetown, Nov. 7, 1974.

Mrs. Harry L. (Eldora Meachum) Hughes, San Antonio, June 1, 1972.

Rev. D. Lawrence Landrum, Palestine, Texas, Jan. 17, 1973.

Bishop Paul E. Martin, Dallas, Jan. 14, 1972.

Bishop William C. Martin, Little Rock, Arkansas, Jan. 22, 1973.

Rev. O. W. Moerner, Georgetown, Oct. 10, 1973.

Bishop Arthur J. Moore, St. Simon Island, Georgia, Jan. 20 & 21, 1972.

Dr. Bonneau P. Murphy, Dallas, Feb. 16, 1973.

Dr. Alfredo Nañez, SMU, Dallas, July 20, 1972.

Mrs. J. J. Perkins, Wichita Falls, Texas, June 26, 1972.

Mr. and Mrs. George F. Pierce, Dallas, Jan. 17, 1972.

Bishop W. Kenneth Pope, SMU, Dallas, Sept. 15, 1972.

Mr. Abe Pounds, Tyler, Texas, Jan. 18, 1973.

Mr. John W. Redditt, Lufkin, Texas, Jan. 19, 1973.

Rabbi H. J. Schachtel, Congregation Beth Israel, Houston, Sept. 18, 1973.

Mrs. J. N. R. Score, Dallas, July 8, 1973.

Mr. Robert A. ("Bob") Shepherd, Houston, Sept. 18, 1973.

Bishop O. Eugene Slater, San Antonio, Aug. 8, 1972.

Mr. A. Frank Smith, Jr., Houston, Aug. 29, 1972.

Bishop W. Angie Smith, Dallas, Jan. 12, 1972, and Aug. 1, 1973.

Mr. W. Randolph Smith, Houston, Aug. 29, 1972.

Rev. L. U. Spellman, Kerrville, Texas, Apr. 16, 1972, and Jan. 23, 1973.

Chaplain Elton Stephenson, Methodist Hospital, Houston, Aug. 21, 1973.

Dr. Willis Tate, Southern Methodist University, Dallas, July 22, 1972.

Rev. Monroe Vivion, Flint, Texas, Jan. 18, 1973.

Rev. Charles L. Williams, Houston, Aug. 20, 1972.

Notes

PREFACE

1. Bishop A. Frank Smith, quoted in R. F. Curl, *Southwest Texas Methodism* (Dallas: Wilkinson Printing Co., 1951), p. 10.

2. Interview with AFS by Dr. Charles S. Braden, January 23, 1962, in Houston, Texas (hereafter cited as Braden interview). Tapes and transcripts in the A. Frank Smith Papers, Bridwell Library, Southern Methodist University, Dallas, Texas (hereafter cited as Smith Papers).

CHAPTER ONE

1. Third son of Ewan Christian, one of the deemsters or judges of the Isle of Man, William Christian was appointed receiver-general of the Isle of Man in 1648, a post he held until 1656 when he was appointed Governor of Man for two years. When the Earl of Derby attempted to introduce a new system of land tenure on Man in 1651, William led a popular uprising which won him praise from Cromwell's Commonwealth government but eventually led to his execution in 1663, following the restoration of the English monarchy. Even then his executioners were punished by Charles II, because William had been pardoned under the English Act of Indemnity. *Dictionary of National Biography*, s.v. "Christian, William."

2. It is not known which of these three sons of William was Gilbert's father. Christian family traditions all agree that Gilbert married Margaret Richardson in Ulster, Ireland, and that they brought a daughter, Mary, and three sons—William, John, and Robert—to Pennsylvania.

3. These paragraphs represent the author's efforts to harmonize three accounts of the Christian family line found in the papers of AFS: (1) "Christian Family Record," anonymous; (2) "The Christian Family History," compiled by Beulah Christian Straus, a granddaughter of Thomas Christian; and (3) "Thomas Christian Family History," based on notes Mrs. H. B. Smith made while interviewing Bettie

Burleson Brooks, "the daughter and only child of the widow of Thomas Christian and her second husband, Jimmie Burleson." Smith Papers.

4. On March 14, 1832, James Clark of Rushville, Illinois, wrote a letter to Stephen F. Austin "for the purpose of introducing to your acquaintance Mr. Thomas Christian who will hand you this letter. He is a native of Virginia [*sic*] and has resided for some years in this State in the peaceful pursuits of a farmer—I think I know him well . . . in steadiness of habits, in integrity and honour he yields to no citizen of our Country." *Annual Report of the American Historical Association for the Year 1919*, vol. 2, *The Austin Papers*, ed. Eugene C. Barker (Washington, D.C.: Government Printing Office, 1924), p. 757.

5. On April 6, 1830, the Mexican government prohibited any further colonization in Texas by Anglo-Americans. Austin succeeded in completing his quota of families by an ingenious interpretation of the law, but by "November of 1831 Austin had to admit that immigration of North Americans was totally prohibited." Rupert N. Richardson, Ernest Wallace, and Adrian N. Anderson, *Texas: The Lone Star State*, 3rd ed. (Englewood Cliffs, N.J.: Prentice-Hall, 1970), p. 55. Cf. Eugene C. Barker, *The Life of Stephen F. Austin*, 2d ed. (Austin: Texas State Historical Association, 1949), pp. 256-83.

6. Barker, *Life of Stephen F. Austin*, p. 55.

7. Thomas Christian's headright league was Abstract No. 20, Survey No. 26, according to a Christian family history written by Mrs. Sarah Gatlin Standifer (Cousin Texana), daughter of Nancy Wright Christian and granddaughter of Thomas Christian, Smith Papers.

8. "Webberville," *The Handbook of Texas*, ed. Walter Prescott Webb, 2 vols. (Austin: Texas State Historical Association, 1952), 2: 875.

9. Ibid., 1:836 and 2:908.

10. These were the three names according to AFS's account, but other versions give Standifer instead of King. Cf. John Wesley Wilbarger, *Indian Depredations in Texas* (Austin: Hutchings Printing House, 1889), pp. 7-14; and J. Frank Dobie, "The Dream that Saved Wilbarger," *Tales of Old-Time Texas* (Boston: Little, Brown & Co., 1955), pp. 34-41.

11. The granite monument is located three-tenths of a mile south of the present intersection of Manor Road, Westminster Road, and *Old* Manor Road within the Austin city limits, practically in the front yard of the residence at 5009 Old Manor Road. Old Manor Road is a three-hundred-yard section of the original Manor Road which was cut off and left dangling by the expansion of the Austin Municipal Airport.

12. Interview with Bishop W. Angie Smith, January 12, 1972, in Dallas, Texas.

13. This date continues to be debated. Dr. R. F. Curl favored 1833 in his *Southwest Texas Methodism* (Dallas: Wilkinson Printing Co., 1951), pp. 26-27. Dr. Olin W. Nail gives 1835 in his *The First Hundred Years of the Southwest Texas Conference of the Methodist Church: 1858-1958* (Austin: Capital Printing Co., 1958), p. 45. Rev. C. A. West, another distinguished historian of Texas Methodism, insists on the 1835 date. Letter to the author, March 13, 1974.

14. Curl, *Southwest Texas Methodism*, pp. 26-27. Cf. Nail, *The First Hundred Years*, p. 46.

15. It was known as the West Texas Conference before Methodist Unification in 1939.

16. Ruter to his wife, February 3, 1838: "Three weeks ago I went up to Bastrop . . ." Quoted in R. F. Curl, *Southwest Texas Methodism*, p. 27.

17. AFS, "Personal Family Notes," July, 1962, Smith Papers (hereafter cited as "Family Notes").

As superintendent of the Methodist Missionary Work in the Republic of Texas and as an ordained Methodist minister, Dr. Ruter had the authority to organize a Methodist church, whereas the lay-preacher Gilliland would not. Ruter's use of the term *society* should not be misunderstood. Although the Methodist Episcopal

Church was established by the "Christmas Conference" in 1784, the American Methodists continued John Wesley's practice of referring to members as "members in society" rather than as church members. This was not changed in the annual Minutes until 1854 in the Methodist Episcopal Church, South, and not until 1857 in the Methodist Episcopal Church. Rituals for receiving persons into the church were not adopted until 1870 and 1864, respectively. Cf. Norman W. Spellmann, "The Formation of the Methodist Episcopal Church," *History of American Methodism*, ed. Emory S. Bucke, 3 vols. (Nashville: Abingdon Press, 1964), 1:185-232, but especially pp. 221-22.

18. This identification is clouded. AFS's account states that James Burleson was an uncle of Ed Burleson, for whom Burleson County was named. *The Handbook of Texas* says that James Burleson was the *father* of Edward Burleson by prior marriage to Nancy Christian (before 1793 in North Carolina). Available accounts of the family tree do not show the interrelationships clearly, but there was a Mrs. Nancy Allison Wright who came from Scotland around the time of the American Revolution and married "the father of Ben and Thomas Christian." This woman's daughter (by her prior marriage) was the Nancy Wright (ca. 1771-1860) who married John Buchanan. Their daughter was Mary ("Polly") Buchanan (1795-1870) who married Thomas Christian. If the Nancy Christian who married James Burleson (1758-1836) was also Nancy Allison Wright Christian, she would be Mary Buchanan's grandmother. Thus Mary Buchanan Christian married her grandmother's widower when she married James Burleson! Cf. *Handbook of Texas*, 1:249-50; and Bettie Burleson Brooks's account of the Thomas Christian Family History (as recorded by Mrs. H. B. Smith), Smith Papers.

19. Bettie Burleson, the seventh child, was born of this brief marriage.

20. Originally called Glasscock, the community was for a time known as Hogeye from the favorite song of a Negro fiddler. The name was changed in 1882 to honor Robert Morris Elgin, the land commissioner who laid out the townsite. *Handbook of Texas* 1:554.

21. "Family Notes," July, 1962, p. 3. Perhaps AFS here refers to what the *Encyclopedia Britannica* describes as "the great meteor shower of Nov. 12, 1833, which was seen all over eastern North America." Although it was later established that these Leonid showers recur at thirty-three year intervals, 1833 was the peak year. *Encyclopedia Britannica*, 1973 ed., s.v. "Meteor." This 1833 shower displayed an estimated two hundred thousand meteors between midnight and dawn for any one location, many of them leaving brilliant trains and terrifying people who observed this spectacular show. *Encyclopedia Americana*, 1978 ed., s.v. "Meteor."

It does not seem likely that AFS meant to write "1835," the year that Halley's Comet paid its nineteenth-century visit to the earth's heavens.

22. "Family Notes," July, 1962, p. 3.

23. Ibid., p. 4.

24. Ibid.

25. Ibid.

26. Ibid., p. 5.

27. Ralph Wood Jones, *Southwestern University, 1840-1961* (Austin: San Felipe Press, 1973), p. 152. The school operated under the name Texas University until it was officially chartered by the state of Texas as Southwestern University, February 6, 1875.

28. "Family Notes," July, 1962, p. 6.

29. *Georgetown Commercial*, May 20, 1904. This long article concerning the death of Thomas Marrs contains a number of details that AFS did not incorporate in his family's sketch.

According to obituaries in the *Williamson County Sun* (clippings, n.d., in Smith Papers), Thomas's father, James Marrs, was born in Kentucky in 1817 and died at his home near Corn Hill on May 14, 1887. Thomas's mother, Elizabeth Ann Carl, was born in Tennessee in 1824 and died on February 20, 1886, at her home on the Youngsport Road in Glasscock Valley. There were eight children, four sons and four daughters.

30. Interview with Bishop W. Angie Smith, January 12, 1972, in Dallas, Texas. Some of the material in these two paragraphs comes from the *Georgetown Commercial*, May 20, 1904.

31. "Family Notes," July, 1962, p. 8.

32. Interview with Bishop W. Angie Smith, January 12, 1972.

33. Ibid.

34. Records for this early period are available only for students who graduated from Southwestern. Since Mary Elizabeth Marrs did not complete her college degree, it is not possible to determine the exact years of her enrollment.

35. Just how the expenses for this long journey and the additional schooling were raised is not known. Perhaps his father was willing to finance the business degree because it seemed more practical than a college degree.

36. Except where noted, the information on the Marrs family is taken from the account written by AFS in "Family Notes," July, 1962, pp. 6-10.

37. Braden interview.

38. "Family Notes," July, 1962, p. 11.

39. Ibid., p. 12.

40. Ibid., pp. 12-13.

41. Interview with Bishop W. Angie Smith, January 12, 1972.

42. Ibid. See also Braden interview.

43. Interview with Mrs. Eldora Meachum Hughes and Miss Sophie Meachum, June 1, 1972, in San Antonio, Texas. See chap. 2, p. 27, and chap. 4, p. 65.

44. Henrietta M. Larson and Kenneth Wiggins Porter, *History of Humble Oil and Refining Company* (New York: Harper & Bros., 1959), p. 11.

45. Seymour V. Connor, *Texas: A History* (New York: Thomas Y. Crowell Co., 1971), p. 317.

46. Larson and Porter, *History of Humble Oil*, p. 12.

47. Interview with Mrs. W. W. Fondren, October 26, 1973, in Houston, Texas.

48. Interview with Bishop W. Angie Smith, January 12, 1972.

49. Braden interview.

50. Ibid.

51. Interview with Bishop W. Angie Smith, January 12, 1972.

52. Ibid.

53. "Family Notes," July, 1962, p. 13.

54. Interview with Rev. and Mrs. Finis (Callie Blair) Crutchfield, Sr., January 24, 1972, in Carlsbad, New Mexico.

55. Interview with Bishop W. Angie Smith, January 12, 1972.

56. Ibid.

57. Ibid.

58. "Family Notes," July, 1962, p. 13, and Braden interview.

59. Ibid. See also interview with Bishop W. Angie Smith, January 12, 1972.

60. Most of the material in this section, except where otherwise indicated, is taken from a document AFS wrote for Dr. Charles S. Braden, which he hastily entitled "Reading and Social Habits of Childhood and Youth," Smith Papers (hereafter cited as "Childhood and Youth").

61. AFS to Dr. Charles S. Braden, August 21, 1962, Smith Papers.

62. Interview with Rev. and Mrs. Finis Crutchfield, Sr., January 24, 1972.

63. "Prayer Delivered at Inauguration of Beauford H. Jester and Allan Shivers as Governor and Lt. Governor of Texas," Austin, Texas, January 27, 1947, Smith Papers.

64. "Childhood and Youth," p. 2.

65. Ibid., p. 4.

66. Ibid., p. 2.

67. Braden interview.

68. Interview with Rev. and Mrs. Finis Crutchfield, Sr., January 24, 1972.

69. "Childhood and Youth," p. 5. On a visit to Corsicana, AFS noted in his daily journal: "I joined the Church here in 1907, and was Secy. of the Sunday School from 1905 to 1907. I went thru High School in Corsicana. My parents lived here from 1903 to 1907." Entry for Friday, October 26, 1945, Smith Papers.

70. "Childhood and Youth," pp. 5-6.

CHAPTER TWO

1. "My grandfather completely changed his attitude toward higher education in his later years and became a strong supporter of Southwestern. When it came time for me to go to college, he volunteered to send me. Perhaps he did this to requite in some measure his failure to send my father to college, though neither he nor my father ever intimated such to me." AFS to Dr. Charles S. Braden, June 26, 1962, p. 5, Smith Papers.

2. AFS, "Personal Reminiscences," handwritten in a spiral notebook, presumably in 1962, Smith Papers (hereafter cited as "Reminiscences").

3. Dr. Charles S. Braden's interview with AFS and Mrs. Smith, January 23, 1962, in Houston, Texas, Smith Papers.

4. AFS to Braden, June 26, 1962, p. 19.

5. Braden interview with AFS and Mrs. Smith.

6. Ibid.

7. AFS to Braden, June 26, 1962, p. 19.

8. *Sou'wester* (1908), pp. 101, 125, 127.

9. Interview with Rev. and Mrs. Finis Crutchfield, Sr., January 24, 1972, in Carlsbad, New Mexico. In 1903-1907 the Smith family lived in Corsicana, where Frank attended high school; they moved to Taylor before he entered Southwestern.

10. Interview with Bishop W. Angie Smith, January 12, 1972, in Dallas, Texas.

11. Interview with the Crutchfields. See also the interview with Bishop W. Angie Smith.

12. Seymour V. Conner, *Texas: A History* (New York: Thomas Y. Crowell Co., 1971), pp. 320-21.

13. "Having left the Corsicana High School in the 9th grade, I could not enter the freshman class but enrolled in the Fitting School, which was a preparatory school conducted as a part of the program of Southwestern and housed in the original University building." "Reminiscences."

14. *Bulletin of Southwestern University* 5, no. 26 (June 1908): 193 (hereafter cited as *Bulletin* [1908]).

15. Ibid., p. 31.

16. See below, p. 34.

17. *Bulletin* (1908), p. 118.

18. "Here I roomed for the 4½ years I was at SU, except for my junior year when the fraternity rented a large house on College Avenue and lived there as a group, with Misses Carrie and Estelle Reedy as our hostesses. They were sisters of Prof. Jno. H. Reedy, head of the Chemistry Dept." "Reminiscences." A good picture of the KA House is in the 1908 *Sou'wester*, p. 146.

19. Interview with the Crutchfields.

20. AFS to Braden, June 26, 1962, p. 17.

21. Interview with Bishop W. Angie Smith.

22. "Childhood and Youth."

23. Interview with the Crutchfields.

24. Ibid. See also *Bulletin of Southwestern University* 6, no. 30 (June 1909): 159; and AFS to Braden, June 26, 1962.

25. Program for Fitting School Declamation Contest, May 28, 1908, Cody Collection Scrapbook no. 15, p. 32. These scrapbooks in Cody Memorial Library at Southwestern University contain a treasure of documentation of Southwestern's history. Originally the work of Dean Claude Carr Cody, they were later continued by his son, Dr. C. C. Cody, Jr., M.D.

26. See chap. 1, p. 13.

27. AFS to Braden, June 26, 1962, p. 14.

28. Interview with Mrs. Hallie Crutchfield (George F.) Pierce, January 17, 1972, in Dallas, Texas.

29. The permanent file for AFS, Recorder's Office, Southwestern University (hereafter cited as SU file).

30. *Bulletin* (1908), pp. 32-33.

31. Ibid., pp. 144-45; interview with the Crutchfields.

32. *Bulletin* (1908), p. 34.

33. Ibid.

34. Interview with Mr. and Mrs. George F. Pierce, January 17, 1972, in Dallas, Texas. Dr. Allen had actually built the house for the Phi Delta Theta Fraternity, but when they failed to meet their financial obligations, Dr. Allen was forced to take possession of the house. The university did not then own the large tract of land between the Annex and Mood Hall.

35. *Bulletin* (1908), pp. 30-31. See also Ralph Wood Jones, *Southwestern University, 1840-1961* (Austin: San Felipe Press, 1973), pt. 2, chap. 5.

36. Letter signed by T. B. Stone as published in an unidentified Georgetown newspaper, Cody Collection Scrapbook no. 20.

37. See Robert Stewart Hyer's letter to Dr. Edwin D. Mouzon, July 1, 1908, Mouzon Papers, item no. 10,460, Bridwell Library, Southern Methodist University, Dallas, Texas; *Texas Christian Advocate* (Dallas), August 6, 1908, p. 2.

38. Jones, *Southwestern University*, p. 218; *The Handbook of Texas*, ed. Walter Prescott Webb, 2 vols. (Austin: Texas State Historical Association, 1952), 1:872.

39. See chap. 4.

40. *Sou'wester* (1909), p. 21.

41. SU files; *Bulletin* (1909), p. 49.

42. Interview with the Crutchfields.

43. *Bulletin* (1909), p. 149.

44. See, for example, Bishop Smith's entry in his daily journal concerning his friendship for Cooke.

45. *Williamson County Sun*, June 17, 1909; Program for the Freshman-Sophomore Declaration Contest, June 12, 1909, Cody Collection Scrapbook no. 16, pp. 54-55.

46. *Bulletin of Southwestern University* (Catalogue Number) 8, no. 38 (June 1911): 132.

47. Interview with Bishop W. Angie Smith; interview with Bishop Paul E. Martin; *Georgetown Commercial*, September 24, 1909, Cody Collection Scrapbook no. 16, p. 71.

48. *Bulletin of Southwestern University* 7, no. 34 (June 1910): 196. See also *Georgetown Commercial*, September 24, 1909, Cody Collection Scrapbook no. 16, p. 70.

49. Ibid., pp. 160-96.

50. SU file.

51. Interview with Dr. L. U. Spellman, April 16, 1972; interview with Mrs. J. J. Perkins, June 26, 1972; interview with Rev. O. W. Moerner, October 10, 1973. See also interview with the Crutchfields; interview with W. R. ("Randy") Smith and A. Frank Smith, Jr., August 29, 1972.

On McGinnis's career as professor at SMU and editor of the *Southwest Review*, see Charles W. Ferguson, "McGinnis: Portrait of an Individual," *Southwest Review* 45 (Summer 1960): 197-203.

52. Ibid.

53. Braden interview.

54. *Sou'wester* (1910), p. 260.

55. Interview with Eldora Meachum Hughes and Sophia Meachum, June 1, 1972, in San Antonio, Texas. Having first met AFS at Rogers, Texas, the Meachum sisters were classmates with AFS and Bess at Southwestern. Eldora married Harry Hughes, one of AFS's roommates at Southwestern and again at Vanderbilt.

56. Braden interview. In the "Memoranda" section of her college diary, Bess sketched her relationship with Arthur Henderson from its beginnings "in Prep in 1906 or '07" until "Frank commenced going with me" in February, 1910. Bess Crutchfield's "Excelsior Diary, 1911," Smith Papers.

57. "Reminiscences." AFS and Bess also carved their names in the stone walls of the Main Building's tower, where they can still be seen.

58. Program for Bess Crutchfield's "Senior Recital," Saturday, November 20, 1909, Cody Collection Scrapbook no. 17, p. 9.

59. *Sou'wester* (1910), p. 99.

60. Ibid., p. 321.

61. Ibid.

62. Ibid., p. 156; *Georgetown Commercial*, June 3, 1910, Cody Collection Scrapbook no. 18, p. 15.

63. Sketches of the faculty in *Sou'wester* (1911), p. 24.

64. *Bulletin of Southwestern University, 1911* 8, no. 38 (June 1911): 36; *Sou'wester* (1911), p. 38.

65. The Kurth name is well known to present students, through Kurth Resident Hall for Women; Kurth-Landrum Golf Course; Kurth Tennis Courts; and the Kurth Endowment for the School of Fine Arts. Ernest L. Kurth, Jr. is currently a trustee-at-large.

66. Mr. and Mrs. (Mavis Terry) Willson established lectureships at twenty-eight colleges and universities.

67. See chap. 3. Harry Hughes drowned in Japan where he and his wife, Eldora Meachum, had gone as Methodist missionaries. Harry and Eldora visited Frank and Bess at Laurel Heights Methodist Church in San Antonio just before they sailed to Japan. Interview with Mrs. Harry L. Hughes.

68. Dr. L. U. Spellman to the author, February 9, 1973.

69. "On Aug. 2, '10, I put on Frank's pin," Bess Crutchfield wrote in her college diary. This entry is in the "Memoranda" section since she did not begin keeping a daily record until March 19, 1911. A number of other significant events were also entered in this "Memoranda" section.

70. Interview with Mr. and Mrs. George F. Pierce. George courted Hallie at Southwestern.

71. Interview with Bishop Paul E. Martin.

72. *Sou'wester* (1911), pp. 341, 328.

73. Since this incident occurred in 1910-11, the sorority would have been Sigma Sigma Sigma. Theta Epsilon Chapter of Delta Delta Delta was established at Southwestern in 1912 by the merging of Alpha Delta Chapter of Sigma Sigma Sigma. See the 1912 *Sou'wester*, p. 141. The 1909 *Sou'wester* gives Bess as a pledge of Sigma Sigma Sigma, and the 1911 *Sou'wester*, p. 139, lists Lois Craddock and Bess Crutchfield as Sigma Sigma Sigma members. See interview with the Crutchfields.

74. See announcements in the *Georgetown Commercial* for September 26, November 18, December 16, 1910; February 18 and March 24, 1911. Programs in Smith Papers and in Cody Collection Scrapbook no. 18, p. 48; no. 19, pp. 33, 36, 41, 48; no. 20, p. 21. The 1911 *Sou'wester* preserves pictures of the "Trip to Mars" featuring AFS and Grace Gillett as the King and Queen of Mars.

75. See *Georgetown Commercial*, April 21 and May 25, 1911; *Bulletin of Southwestern University* 10, no. 43 (June 1912): 141.

76. Clippings from unidentified Georgetown newspaper, Cody Collection Scrapbook no. 19, p. 26. Cf. account in the *Texas Christian Advocate*, June 22, 1911.

77. Program for the Brooks Prize Debate, June 10, 1911, Smith Papers. Also in Cody Collection Scrapbook no. 20, p. 11.

78. Unidentified clipping from a Georgetown newspaper, Cody Collection Scrapbook no. 9, p. 26.

79. AFS, "Brooks Prize Debate, . . . Speech of A. Frank Smith, Second Speaker for the Negative, Alamo, 1911," typed MS (twelve pages, double-spaced), Smith Papers.

80. AFS to Braden, June 26, 1962, p. 17. Otto Moerner, Angie Smith, and L. U. Spellman—all champions in debate and oratory—agree in ranking the Brooks Prize above the Junior Orator's Medal.

81. SU file.

82. AFS to Braden, June 26, 1962, pp. 18-19. Some of AFS's friends have said this professor was Dean Cody, although AFS never said so. Records of the university indicate Frank E. Burcham, "Assistant Professor of Mathematics." *Bulletin of Southwestern University, 1912* 10, no. 43 (June 1912): 33, 84. *Minutes of the Missouri Annual Conference* show that Frank E. Burcham was treasurer of the Board of Education, a member of the Board of Finance, treasurer of the Board of Ministerial Education, and lived in Fayette, Missouri, all four years that AFS held that conference, 1930-33. Burcham is not, however, listed among either the clergy or lay delegates.

83. Official brochure for the Inaugural Banquet, Cody Collection Scrapbook no. 20, p. 32.

84. Unidentified newspaper clipping, Cody Collection Scrapbook no. 20, p. 32.

85. *Sou'wester* (1912), p. 61. Grace Gillett was editor for the senior class.

86. Bess Crutchfield's "Excelsior Diary, 1911." This entry is also in the "Memoranda" section of the diary, making it impossible to determine the year. This event might have occurred in December, 1910. The only actual daily entries are for the months of March and April, 1911.

87. AFS, "Southwestern," a six-page holograph presumably written in 1962, in the same spiral notebook with "Reminiscences," Smith Papers.

88. Program for the Texas Intercollegiate Press Association, Southwestern University, April 4-5, 1912; *Sou'wester* (1912), p. 175.

89. Braden interview. Also, W. T. Weiss and C. S. Proctor, *Umphrey Lee: A Biography* (Nashville: Abingdon Press, 1971), p. 37.

90. *Williamson County Sun*, April 11, 1912, Cody Collection Scrapbook no. 20, p. 23.

91. Interview with Dr. L. U. Spellman.

92. Bess Crutchfield's "Excelsior Diary, 1911." This entry was made in the "Memoranda" section, since the event did not occur in 1911.

93. Braden interview.

94. Ibid. See also AFS's letter to Bishop Edwin D. Mouzon, July 13, 1930. Item no. 8020, Mouzon Papers, Bridwell Library, Southern Methodist University.

95. AFS, "My Call to Preach," *My Call to Preach* (Nashville: General Board of Evangelism of The Methodist Church, 1946), p. 25.

96. This Bible is a prized possession of AFS's sons, A. Frank Smith, Jr., and W. Randolph Smith, who were thoughtful enough to show it to the author during an interview in Houston, Texas, August 29, 1972.

97. AFS left at least two very similar accounts of this incident, one in his interview with Dr. Braden, the other in his letter to Dr. Braden, June 26, 1962, p. 16. I have edited the two into one statement.

98. AFS to Braden, June 26, 1962, pp. 16-17. See also Braden interview, and my interview with Bishop W. Angie Smith.

99. Ibid., p. 17. See also the similar account in Braden interview.

100. Interview with Bishop W. Angie Smith. "Only my oldest brother was really disappointed in the fact that Frank had decided to be a preacher."

101. Braden interview. See also AFS to Braden, June 26, 1962, p. 20, and quotation from Bess Crutchfield's diary above, p. 36.

102. Interview with Mrs. George F. Pierce.

103. Braden interview. See also AFS to Braden, June 26, 1962, p. 17; *My Call to Preach*, p. 25.

104. Braden interview with AFS and Mrs. Smith.

105. Braden interview.

106. *My Call to Preach*, pp. 23-25.

107. Braden interview. See Dobie's letter to AFS, July 10, 1916 (holograph), Smith Papers.

108. Quoted by Dr. J. N. R. Score, "Bishop A. Frank Smith," *Southwestern Magazine* 33 (March 1931): 20. Score did not identify the writer beyond saying "a man who was a student at Southwestern during the period of Frank Smith's student days." It might have been Finis Crutchfield.

109. AFS to Bishop Edwin D. Mouzon, February 19, 1920, Mouzon Papers, item no. 1860. AFS kept the carbon copy, attaching it to Mouzon's letter to him, dated February 18, 1920.

110. Interviews with Bishop W. Angie Smith; with Dr. L. U. Spellman; with Rev. and Mrs. Finis Crutchfield; with Rev. O. W. Moerner; with Mrs. J. J. Perkins; and with Mr. and Mrs. George F. (Hallie Crutchfield) Pierce.

111. Nelms was appointed to the Georgetown church in November, 1910, Rev. John M. Barcus having been the pastor during AFS's first two and a half years. *Georgetown Commercial*, November 18, 1910 and March 23, 1911, Cody Collection Scrapbook no. 19, p. 32.

112. Interview with the Crutchfields. Finis graduated, of course, in June, 1911.

113. Interviews with Dr. L. U. Spellman, Mrs. Lois Craddock Perkins, Rev. O. W. Moerner, Bishop W. Angie Smith, and with A. Frank Smith, Jr. and W. R. Smith.

114. A data page in AFS's file in the Presidents' Papers, Southwestern University, carries the notation that AFS was licensed to preach by the Georgetown District Conference on May 22, 1912. E. W. Bode, a classmate and friend of AFS, who was present at this particular meeting of the District Conference, remembers that it was held in Belton, Texas. Conversation with E. W. Bode, Kerrville, Texas, spring of 1973. See also Braden interview.

115. See 1911 *Southwestern Bulletin*, p. 155; *Georgetown Commercial*, May 17, 1912, Cody Collection Scrapbook no. 20, p. 11.

116. Program for Commencement Exercises, Monday Morning, June 10, 1912, Smith Papers. See also Cody Collection Scrapbook no. 20, p. 33.

117. Newspaper clipping identified only as *The News*, June 11, 1912, Cody Collection Scrapbook no. 20, p. 24.

118. List of graduates in official printed Senior Invitations, Smith Papers.

119. Quoted by Score, "Bishop A. Frank Smith," *Southwestern University Magazine* 33 (March 1931): 19.

120. Braden interview. See also AFS to Braden, June 26, 1962, p. 17.

121. Interview with Bishop W. Angie Smith. The Smiths lived in Mart at that time, and Angie remembers going to Marlin, Texas, to hear his brother speak. See also *Williamson County Sun*, July 12, 1912, and *Dallas Morning News*, July 14, 1912. Cody Collection Scrapbook no. 20, pp. 32, 37.

122. Included among the pages of AFS's student notebook used at Vanderbilt University. AFS's handwriting was remarkably easy to read at that time. The notebook is in the possession of W. Randolph Smith.

CHAPTER THREE

1. Interview with Bishop W. Angie Smith, January 12, 1962, in Dallas, Texas.

2. Hunter Dickinson Farish, *The Circuit Rider Dismounts: A Social History of Southern Methodism, 1865-1900* (Richmond: Dietz Press, 1938), pp. 275, 285, 294.

3. John O. Gross, "The Field of Education," *The History of American Methodism*, ed. Emory S. Bucke, 3 vols. (Nashville: Abingdon Press, 1964), 3:229.

4. Bard Thompson, *Vanderbilt Divinity School: A History* (Nashville: Vanderbilt University Press, 1960), pp. 6ff.

5. William J. McCutcheon, "American Methodist Thought and Theology: 1919-60," *History of American Methodism*, 3:287-88.

6. Class of 1910: W. E. Garrison; Class of 1911: A. C. Aston, Joel B. Hendrix, Tracy L. Huffstutler, Lemuel H. Robinson. *Bulletin of Southwestern University* (Catalogue Number), Series 10 (June 1912), no. 43, pp. 318-20.

7. Braden interview.

8. McCutcheon, "American Methodist Thought and Theology," pp. 263-64, 287-88.

9. H. Shelton Smith, Robert T. Handy, and Lefferts A. Loetscher, *American Christianity*, 2 vols. (New York: Charles Scribner's Sons, 1963), 2:255.

10. Ibid., p. 256. Claude Welch and John Dillenberger, *Protestant Christianity Interpreted through Its Development* (New York: Charles Scribner's Sons, 1954), p. 189.

11. AFS, "The Dean: An Appreciation," *World Outlook* 26 (August 1936): 30.

12. Cf. John O. Gross, "The Vanderbilt Controversy," *History of American Methodism*, 3:228-32.

13. Braden interview.

14. Interview with Bishop W. Angie Smith, August 1, 1973, in Dallas, Texas.

15. Scholastic Record for Angie Frank Smith, Biblical Department, Vanderbilt University, 1912-13, 1913-14. Courtesy of the Office of the Dean, Vanderbilt Divinity School. The full list of AFS's courses is as follows:

I. *Old Testament Language and Literature*: Hebrew Language, The Patriarchal Period, The Codes, The Psalter.

II. *New Testament Language and Literature*: New Testament Language, New Testament Literature and History of the Apostolic Age, and three terms of Beginner's Greek Course.

III. *Biblical Theology and English Exegesis*: Survey of Old Testament Literature, The Gospel of John.

IV. *Church History*: Outline of Old Testament History, The Early Church, The Medieval Church, The Modern Church (Course I).

V. *Systematic Theology*: Apologetics and Theology Proper; Introduction to Theology; Anthropology, Christology, and Soteriology; Eschatology and Ecclesiology; Christian Ethics.

VI. *Practical Theology*: Homiletics, Courses I, II, and III; Homiletic Exercises, Courses I and II; General Church Polity; History of Preaching.

VII. *Practical Sociology*: Social Aspects of Christianity; The Family.

VIII. *Public Speaking*: Public Speaking; Hymn and Scripture Reading; Argumentation.

IX. *Religious Education*: Principles of Religious Education.

16. Braden interview. There are notes on a sermon that Bishop Lambuth preached at Vanderbilt in AFS's Vanderbilt Student Notebook, pp. 149-50. See also "The Dean: An Appreciation," pp. 4-5, 30-31; W. Richey Hogg, "The Missions of American Methodism," *History of American Methodism*, 3:108-9.

17. AFS, Vanderbilt Notebook, pp. 51-54.

18. Ibid., pp. 97-98.

19. Ibid., p. 98.
20. Ibid., pp. 16-17.
21. See n. 8.
22. Ibid.
23. See p. 46 above, the quotation from Smith, Handy, and Loetscher, *American Christianity*, 2:255.
24. Dillenberger and Welch, *Protestant Christianity*, p. 211.
25. AFS, Notebook, p. 41. See Dillenberger and Welch, *Protestant Christianity*, p. 212.
26. Harry Emerson Fosdick, *The Modern Use of the Bible* (New York: Macmillan Co., 1924), p. 96. Fosdick also entitled the fourth of his Lyman Beecher Lectures "Abiding Experiences and Changing Categories." See Dillenberger and Welch, *Protestant Christianity*, p. 216.
27. Program of the Vanderbilt Theological Club, Second Term, 1914, Smith Papers. See Borden Parker Bowne, *Personalism* (Boston: Houghton Mifflin Co., 1908), p. 326.
28. Interview with Mrs. Harry L. (Eldora Meachum) Hughes, June 1, 1972, in San Antonio, Texas.
29. Interview with Bishop W. Angie Smith, August 1, 1973, in Dallas, Texas.
30. Walter N. Vernon, *Forever Building: The Life and Ministry of Paul E. Martin* (Dallas: Southern Methodist University Press, 1973), pp. 8, 9.
31. AFS to Dr. Charles Braden, June 24, 1962, p. 20.
32. Braden interview.
33. The handwritten notes of this sermon are in the Smith Papers: "Notes on First Sermon ever Preached by AFS—In Meth Ch, Blossom, Tex—Xmas Sunday, 1913."
34. AFS, Vanderbilt Notebook, pp. 125-26. This incident was dated in January, 1914.
35. Ibid., pp. 126-27.
36. "Professor C. Detweiler taught in the Y.M.C.A. College across the street from Vanderbilt. Many students, particularly those in theology, took work there." Dr. Neil Housewright, Associate Dean, The Divinity School, Vanderbilt University, to the author, January 10, 1974.
37. AFS, Vanderbilt Notebook, pp. 1-6.
38. Whether this was the conclusion drawn by Professor Detweiler or by his students cannot be determined from the scant material supplied by the AFS notebook.
39. AFS, Vanderbilt Notebook, pp. 11-12.
40. Ibid., pp. 55-56.
41. Robert T. Handy, *The Social Gospel in America, 1870-1920* (New York: Oxford University Press, 1966), pp. 5, 6, 10.
42. Dillenberger and Welch, *Protestant Christianity*, pp. 232, 243.
43. Richard M. Cameron, *Methodism and Society in Historical Perspective* (Nashville: Abingdon Press, 1961), chap. 8: "The Social Gospel in Methodism," pp. 279-325.
44. Robert Moats Miller, "Methodism and American Society, 1900-1939," *History of American Methodism*, 3:389.
45. Ibid., p. 394.
46. Walter G. Muelder, *Methodism and Society in the Twentieth Century* (Nashville: Abingdon Press, 1961), pp. 48-51, 277.
47. Walter Rauschenbusch (1861-1918), Baptist minister, church historian, and professor at Rochester Theological Seminary, was the leading exponent and theologian of the social gospel in America. Robert T. Handy, "Walter Rauschenbusch," *A Handbook of Christian Theologians*, ed. Martin E. Marty and Dean G. Peerman (Cleveland: World Publishing Co., 1965), pp. 192-211.
48. Braden interview.

49. AFS, Vanderbilt Notebook, pp. 17-18.

50. Handy, *The Social Gospel in America*, p. 12.

51. AFS, Vanderbilt Notebook, pp. 111-13.

52. Program for Commencement, Vanderbilt University, June 14-18, 1913, Smith Papers.

53. "Purposes of the Biblical Department," quoted in Thompson, *Vanderbilt Divinity School*, p. 8.

54. See pp. 46 and 47, above.

55. Ivan Lee Holt, *Eugene Russell Hendrix, Servant of the Kingdom* (Nashville: Parthenon Press, 1950), p. 100. Bishop Hendrix had been chairman of Vanderbilt's Board of Trust since 1909.

56. John O. Gross, "The Bishops Versus Vanderbilt University," *Methodist History*, n.s. 2, no. 3 (April 1963): 33. Dr. Gross was the general secretary of the Division of Higher Education of the General Board of Education of The Methodist Church.

57. Ibid., p. 30. In 1910 the General Conference had elected three members to the board whom the board refused to seat on the basis that the board was self-perpetuating. And in 1913 or 1914 the bishops had vetoed the board's acceptance of a gift of one million dollars offered by Andrew Carnegie to the medical department "provided the university could prove that it was not under denominational control."

58. Ibid., p. 31.

59. Braden interview. When the General Conference met in Oklahoma City in May, the delegates voted 151 to 140 to sever all relations with Vanderbilt.

60. Quoted by Gross, "The Bishops Versus Vanderbilt University," p. 32. The Tennessee Supreme Court was partly to blame for this "blinding emotionalism," because it had included in its judgment a statement that should the General Conference "contumaciously refuse to confirm members elected" by the board or otherwise "cease to cooperate with the University" the board would then be free to "proceed independently of the General Conference to elect members to fill vacancies in its own body."

61. Ibid., pp. 33-34. See Bishop John M. Moore's statement: "To abandon or not to abandon Vanderbilt University was the issue, the very warm issue, the very strenuously contested issue, in the 1914 General Conference. I was among the 140 who voted to hold on." John M. Moore, *Life and I* (Nashville: Parthenon Press, 1948), p. 126.

62. Braden interview.

63. Gross, "The Field of Education," p. 323.

64. Minutes of the Eighth Meeting of the Educational Commission of the Methodist Episcopal Church, South, meeting in Atlanta, Georgia, July 16, 1914; as quoted in the *Bulletin of the Board of Education of the Methodist Episcopal Church, South* 5, no. 2 (July 1915): 110.

65. Quoted by Gross, "The Field of Education," p. 232.

66. Braden interview.

67. *Sou'wester* (1913), p. 172.

68. Braden interview with AFS and Mrs. Smith. This tape recording of Bishop and Mrs. Smith reminiscing is one of the most priceless items in the Smith Papers.

69. C. T. Crutchfield to AFS, November 7, 1913, Smith Papers. "Wife," of course, indicates that Mr. Crutchfield had remarried. Bess's mother died while Bess and Hallie were little girls. See chap. 2.

70. Except for an abortive effort in January, 1916, AFS was not able to complete his seminary degree. See chap. 4.

71. "Smith-Crutchfield Wedding," *Georgetown Commercial*, June 19, 1914, p. 5, Smith Papers. See also Marriage License No. 6867, recorded in Book 15, p. 218 of the Marriage Records, County Clerk's Office, Williamson County Courthouse, Georgetown, Texas. The author "discovered" the original marriage license still in

the files of the county clerk. After photocopying the documents, the author presented it to A. Frank Smith, Jr.

72. Other members of the wedding party included: bridesmaids—Leda Bass, Mary Martha Bishop, Phoebe Bishop, Kittie Cain, Wynifred Armstrong, and Ruth Smith; groomsmen—Sawnie Aldredge, Randolph Crutchfield, Harry Hughes, John H. McGinnis, John B. Milliken, and George F. Pierce; ushers—Hunter O. Metcalfe, Overton McDowell, Frank D. Nelms, and Ben O. Wiseman; soloist—Grace Gillett; organist—Ethel Elrod; violinist—Wilson David.

73. *Georgetown Commercial*, June 19, 1914, p. 5.

CHAPTER FOUR

1. Braden interview.
2. Ibid.
3. Braden interview with AFS and Mrs. Smith, January 23, 1962.
4. Ibid.
5. Braden interview.
6. Interview with Bishop W. Angie Smith, January 12, 1972, in Dallas, Texas. See also *Dallas Morning News*, August 5, 1959.
7. AFS, Student Notebook, pp. 154-55, Smith Papers.
8. Braden interview.
9. Professor H. F. Mills of Tyler Junior College to the author, August 30, 1972.
10. Interview with Rev. and Mrs. Finis Crutchfield, January 24, 1972, in Carlsbad, New Mexico.
11. Braden interview.
12. Interview with Bishop W. Angie Smith, August 1, 1973, in Dallas, Texas.
13. *Minutes of the Annual Conferences of the Methodist Episcopal Church, South for the Year 1914* (Nashville: Publishing House of the Methodist Episcopal Church, South, 1914), p. 271. The North Texas Conference met December 2-7, 1914.
14. Braden interview.
15. Braden interview with AFS and Mrs. Smith.
16. Ibid.
17. Interview with Mrs. George F. Pierce (Hallie Crutchfield), January 17, 1972, in Dallas, Texas.
18. Braden interview with AFS and Mrs. Smith.
19. *Ibid.*
20. Apparently a letter-to-the-editor, signed by J. R. Stegall. Newspaper not identified, but dated "5-5-'15" in Mrs. Smith's handwriting, Smith Papers.
21. Interview with Mrs. George F. Pierce.
22. Braden interview.
23. Ibid. Bishop Paul Martin's uncle had delivered Frank, Jr. He is probably the doctor mentioned here, although Bishop Martin's father was also practicing medicine in Blossom at the same time. Interview with Bishop Paul E. Martin, January 14, 1972, in Dallas, Texas.
24. Braden interview with AFS and Mrs. Smith. When Frank learned of this conversation, he said to his presiding elder, "She had never said that to me, hadn't complained at all. I never thought about it because I wasn't raised on a bathtub."
25. Braden interview.
26. Minutes of the North Texas Conference, 49th Session, Held at Bonham, Texas, December 1-6, 1915; as published in the *Texas Christian Advocate*, December 9, 1915.
27. Ibid., p. 2. See also *Minutes of the Annual Conferences of the Methodist Episcopal Church, South for the Year 1915*, p. 304.
28. Ibid., p. 9.
29. Braden interview.
30. Interview with Mrs. Harry L. Hughes, June 1, 1972, in San Antonio, Texas.

Announcement of the wedding was published in the *S.M.U. Times*, November 6, 1915, p. 2.

31. *Bulletin of Southern Methodist University* (Annual Catalogue for 1915-16) 1, no. 7 (June 1916): 8-10, 68.

32. Winifred T. Weiss and Charles S. Proctor, *Umphrey Lee: A Biography* (Nashville: Abingdon Press, 1971), pp. 30-35.

33. Walter N. Vernon, *Forever Building: The Life and Ministry of Paul E. Martin* (Dallas: Southern Methodist University Press, 1973), p. 11.

34. Braden interview.

35. Interview with Mrs. George F. Pierce.

36. "That which we have seen and heard declare we unto you, that ye may also have this fellowship with us; and truly our fellowship is with the Father, and with his Son Jesus Christ. And these things write we unto you that your joy may be full."

37. *Dallas Morning News*, Monday, December 13, 1915, p. 5. AFS quoted the first two stanzas of this hymn.

38. AFS to J. J. Perkins, January 31, 1946. Courtesy of Mrs. J. J. Perkins; now in Smith Papers.

39. *Bulletin of Southern Methodist University* (1916), pp. 8, 10.

40. *Texas Christian Advocate*, April 27, 1916, p. 7. See editor W. D. Bradfield's prior date for this organization: "Wednesday evening, January 19, a Church was organized for the university community." Ibid., January 20, 1916, p. 5.

41. AFS to Perkins, January 31, 1946, Smith Papers. "For this reason," Smith continued, "my name would not appear on the records, and I would not be called a former student. Actually, I enrolled in two, or perhaps three, courses and attended classes regularly for six weeks."

42. The SMU *Campus* 1, no. 20 (February 18, 1916): 1. W. Harrison Baker was editor of the *Campus*, although he did not necessarily write this article.

43. Ibid.

44. Oscar Fitzgerald Sensabaugh, "Recollections," chapter on "Dallas District," p. 5 (each chapter is numbered separately). Unpublished manuscript, Bridwell Library, SMU.

45. Doris Miller Johnson, in her history of Highland Park Methodist Church, has the name of Professor John H. Reedy at this place. If the account in the *Texas Christian Advocate* being followed here is incorrect, then it *was* Frank Smith's former chemistry professor who was elected instead of McGinnis. Both men had the same first name and middle initials. Doris Miller Johnson, *Golden Prologue to the Future: A History of Highland Park Methodist Church* (Nashville: Parthenon Press, 1966), p. 19.

46. *Texas Christian Advocate*, February 24, 1916, p. 16. Hyer's name is not given here, but it is listed by Johnson, *Golden Prologue*, p. 19.

47. Weiss and Proctor, *Umphrey Lee*, p. 32.

48. Braden interview. He should have added Bishop Mouzon!

49. Ibid.

50. Perhaps this is Hebrews 12:7: "If ye endure chastening, God dealeth with you as with sons; for what son is he whom the father chasteneth not?"

51. *Campus* 1, no. 24 (March 24, 1916): 1, 4. The parallels between these excerpts from Frank Smith's sermon and the principles of religious education as presented by George Albert Coe, the acknowledged leader of that early twentieth-century movement, are remarkable. Both the emphasis on Jesus as the great Example and supreme Educator and the concept of "salvation by education" are typical of Coe. See *The Religion of a Mature Mind* (1902) and *Education in Religion and Morals* (1904).

52. *Texas Christian Advocate*, April 20, 1916, p. 16.

53. Sensabaugh, "Recollections," "Dallas District," p. 5.

54. *Bulletin of Southern Methodist University*, General Information Catalog Number: Part I, 1959-60, p. 10. See also, Mary Martha Hosford Thomas, *Southern Methodist University: Founding and Early Years* (Dallas: Southern Methodist University Press, 1974).

55. Dr. Walter N. Vernon's interview with AFS, July 30, 1962, in Houston, Texas.

56. Bishop Mouzon held the North Texas Conference for three years: 1911-13. In 1914 he was asked to serve as acting dean of the new School of Theology at SMU. During that year, Dr. Sensabaugh and President Hyer requested the bishop to move from San Antonio to Dallas in order to be more readily available. Bishop McCoy, who lived in Alabama, held the North Texas Conference for four years: 1914-17.

57. Sensabaugh, "Recollections," "Dallas District," p. 7.

58. AFS to Perkins, January 31, 1946, Smith Papers.

59. *Dallas Morning News*, Wednesday, July 26, 1916, p. 3.

60. Minutes of the Board of Stewards, First Methodist Episcopal Church, South, Dallas, Texas, September 4, 1916, p. 228. A special word of appreciation must be given here to Mrs. Inez Alexander of the present staff of First United Methodist Church for her generous help in locating these minutes.

61. Sensabaugh, "Recollections," "Dallas District," p. 8.

62. Johnson, *Golden Prologue*, p. 23.

63. Braden interview. Originally called the North Texas Building, Atkins Hall was built by the North Texas Conference and served as the women's dormitory until 1926, when Virginia Hall was built for the women. The "Woman's Building" was then renamed Atkins Hall after Bishop James Atkins, who was instrumental in the founding of SMU. In 1965 the building was completely remodeled to be a classroom building with funds given by the Clements family and renamed Clements Hall. Thomas, *Southern Methodist University*, pp. 109, 113.

64. Although Dr. Hoyt M. Dobbs was now dean of the School of Theology, Mouzon had been elected chairman of SMU's board of trustees (succeeding Dr. Horace Bishop) and was also chairman of the Executive Committee, of the Administrative-Advisory Committee, and of the Committee on the School of Theology. *Bulletin of Southern Methodist University* (Annual Catalogue 1916-17) 2, no. 2 (June 1917): 6-7. See also *Texas Christian Advocate*, June 15, 1916, p. 8.

65. *Texas Christian Advocate*, July 6, 1916, p. 9.

66. Braden interview. Robert Wesley Goodloe later had a distinguished career as professor of Church History at the School of Theology.

67. *Bulletin of Southern Methodist University*, Annual Catalogue 1915-16 and Announcements 1916-17 1, no. 7 (June 1916): 10, 68.

68. Frank Reedy to Bishop Mouzon, July 31, 1916, Mouzon Papers, item 10,690, Bridwell Library, SMU. Reedy was among the former faculty and staff at Southwestern University whom Dr. Hyer had brought with him to SMU.

69. Holt later wrote Bishop Hendrix's biography, *Eugene Russell Hendrix: Servant of the Kingdom* (Nashville: Parthenon Press, 1950).

70. Braden interview.

71. Holt to Mouzon, September 4, 1916, Mouzon Papers, item 10,698. Mouzon's reply (a carbon copy) is attached to Holt's letter, but he does not mention either AFS or the University City Church.

72. Braden interview.

73. O. F. Sensabaugh saw the telegram from Mouzon to McCoy: "Transfer Sensabaugh and Smith to this [West Texas] conference and I will take care of them. You take Dr. Shuler and place him at Paris." Sensabaugh, "Recollections," "Dallas District," p. 9. Later, Mouzon sent another telegram asking that Sensabaugh be transferred instead to the Northwest Texas Conference, which Mouzon was also holding.

74. *Journal of the Fifty-Eighth Annual Session of the West Texas Conference of*

the Methodist Episcopal Church, South, 1916 (San Antonio: LoDovic Printing Co., n.d.), p. 27.

75. Ibid., pp. 31-32.

76. L. U. Spellman to the author, July 11, 1973.

77. *Journal of the West Texas Conference, 1916*, p. 34.

78. Charles T. Thrist, Jr., "Rebuilding the Southern Church," *History of American Methodism*, ed. Emory S. Bucke, 3 vols. (Nashville: Abingdon Press, 1964), 2:275.

79. At the time of "Roll Call" on the first day of the 1916 Session, the West Texas Conference had 138 clerical members and sixteen lay delegates present. With eight districts there could have been thirty-two lay members.

80. *Austin American*, Wednesday, October 25, 1916, p. 2. A picture of the handsome young pastor accompanied the article. Mrs. Smith was "introduced" several days later with a larger, double-column portrait. *Austin American*, Monday, October 30, 1916, p. 4.

CHAPTER FIVE

1. AFS to Dr. Charles S. Braden, June 24, 1962, pp. 2, 6, Smith Papers. AFS celebrated his twenty-seventh birthday on November 1, 1916, soon after his arrival in Austin.

2. Braden interview.

3. Ibid.

4. AFS to Braden, June 24, 1962, p. 2; Braden interview.

5. Ibid., p. 3. In an interview with Dr. Walter N. Vernon, July 30, 1962, AFS said that he had wanted to return to Alto, his first appointment. Smith Papers.

6. Braden interview.

7. Interview with Bishop W. Angie Smith, August 1, 1973, in Dallas, Texas.

8. "Varsity Methodist Pastor Preaches on 'Man with Message.' Rev. A. Frank Smith Welcomed by Congregation," *Austin American*, Monday, November 6, 1916, p. 2.

9. Mouzon to AFS, November 19, 1916, Smith Papers.

10. Braden interview.

11. See *The Handbook of Texas*, ed. Walter Prescott Webb, 2 vols. (Austin: Texas State Historical Association, 1952), 1:590-92.

12. Braden interview.

13. Ibid.

14. See chap. 3, pp. 50-51.

15. Account of a sermon by AFS preached at the University Methodist Church in a newspaper clipping, under the headline: "Confidence in God, Theme of Sermon by Methodist Minister," otherwise not identified, Smith Papers.

16. Sermon preached by AFS entitled "The Man with the Message," as reported in the *Austin American*, November 6, 1916, p. 2.

17. AFS, Notebook, p. 67. Small loose-leaf notebook in the possession of W. R. Smith, younger son of AFS.

18. *The Doctrines and Discipline of the Methodist Episcopal Church, South, 1914* (Nashville: Smith & Lamar, 1914), p. 321, par. 758.

19. This passage comes from the sermon on Hebrews 3:14 noted above.

20. From interview with Hines H. Baker, September 7, 1973, Exxon Building, Houston, Texas.

21. Ibid.

22. Ibid.

23. From sermon preached by AFS on November 5, 1916, as reported in the *Austin American*, Monday, November 6, 1916, p. 2.

24. Interview with Mr. Baker, September 17, 1973.

25. Ibid. For the later development of this relationship between AFS and Baker, see chaps. 7, 16, and 18.

26. Ibid.

27. AFS, "Hines H. Baker: Man of Faith and Action," *The Link* [Houston: Carter Oil Company] (November-December 1958), p. 21. See also AFS, daily journal, entry for May 14, 1948, and Braden interview.

28. Interview with Mr. Baker, September 17, 1973. With a chuckle Mr. Baker commented: "Maybe I shouldn't have told you that."

29. Interview with Robert A. ("Bob") Shepherd, September 18, 1973, in Houston, Texas. The relationship with Mr. Shepherd was renewed in 1934 and continued until the bishop's death. See chap. 18.

30. AFS to Braden, June 24, 1962, p. 3. See also Braden interview.

31. Interview with John S. Redditt, January 3, 1973, in Lufkin, Texas. Mr. Redditt has since passed away.

32. *The Handbook of Texas*, 1:591; 2:576; and Seymour V. Connor, *Texas: A History* (New York: Thomas Y. Crowell Co., 1971), p. 307.

33. Interview with Mr. Baker, September 17, 1973.

34. AFS to Braden, June 24, 1962, p. 4.

35. As reported in the *Austin American*, Monday, December 25, 1916, p. 8.

36. For comparative purposes, these figures are taken from the *Journals* of the West Texas Conference for 1916 and 1917 instead of from the October Fourth Quarterly Conference reports.

37. *Texas Christian Advocate*, October 18, 1917, p. 12. See also *Austin American*, October 17, 1917, p. 4. Will T. Decherd was the recording secretary of the Conference.

38. Report in an unidentified Austin newspaper: "Smith Returned to Austin Church," newspaper clipping, Smith Papers.

39. Braden interview.

40. Ibid.

41. Ibid.

42. Ibid. According to the account of the fire in the *Austin American Statesman*, Sunday, February 3, 1918, pp. 1-2, the Austin Sanitarium was located in the 100 block of East 14th Street and was owned by the Southern Presbyterian Church. Mrs. A. Frank Smith is listed among the patients rescued by the nurses from the flaming building. The fire broke out about 2:30 A.M., Saturday, February 2.

43. Braden interview with AFS and Mrs. Smith, January 23, 1962.

44. Ibid. Cf. *History of American Methodism*, 3:206.

45. Glenn Flinn, "The Wesley Foundation Work in Texas," *The History of Texas Methodism: 1900-1960*, ed. Olin W. Nail (Austin: Capital Printing Co., 1961), pp. 202-12. See also *Journal of the Fifty-Ninth Annual Session of the West Texas Conference, Methodist Episcopal Church, South, Held at Corpus Christi, Texas, October 18 to 21, 1917*, p. 79.

46. Frank Seay to AFS, December 30, 1917, and January 16, 1918, Smith Papers.

47. AFS to W. Angie Smith, December 12, 1917 (carbon copy), Smith Papers. See also letter from Bishop Edwin D. Mouzon to Rev. Sterling Fisher, Presiding Elder of the Austin District, March 27, 1918 (carbon copy), Mouzon Papers, item 4018, Bridwell Library, SMU, Dallas, Texas.

On Frank Seay, see chaps. 2, 4, 6. Dr. Hoyt M. Dobbs, later bishop, was dean of the School of Theology at SMU from 1917 to 1920.

48. AFS to Mouzon, May 22, 1918, Mouzon Papers, item 5004.

49. See chap. 3. That AFS had been trying to do this work is shown by a series of letters from Dean W. F. Tillett of Vanderbilt's School of Religion to AFS, August 10, 1916, October 18, 1916, and December 13, 1916, Smith Papers.

50. In this connection, it is interesting to note the following report made at the West Texas Conference in 1917: "The Secretary of the Department of Ministerial Supply and Training calls to our attention that . . . of our preachers, only 25.50 per

cent are college graduates; 15.18 per cent have had some courses in theology, and 5.86 per cent are graduates in theology." *Journal of the West Texas Conference, 1917,* p. 77.

51. Still quoting AFS letter to Mouzon, May 22, 1918.

52. In May, 1918, the General Conference recommended "that in order to secure continuous Episcopal supervision, the territory occupied by the Methodist Episcopal Church, South, be divided into Episcopal Districts and . . . that the College of Bishops shall assign the bishops to these districts for quadrennial supervision." *Journal of the Eighteenth General Conference of the Methodist Episcopal Church, South, Held in Atlanta, Georgia, May 2-18, 1918* (Nashville: Smith & Lamar, 1918), p. 216. Bishop Mouzon fully approved: "I am in hearty sympathy with the plan of districting the Bishops. There has been entirely too much lost motion of the Episcopacy; the present plan will add to our efficiency in confining us to a more limited territory." Mouzon to Rev. J. A. Weeks, May 24, 1918 (carbon copy), Mouzon Papers, item 4096.

53. AFS to Mouzon, May 22, 1918, Mouzon Papers, item 5004.

54. Mouzon to AFS, June 6, 1918 (carbon copy), Mouzon Papers, item 5022.

55. AFS to Mouzon, June 10, 1918, Mouzon Papers, item 5032.

56. Ibid. AFS carefully preserved this letter from Dr. Bishop in which the Southwestern president expressed his great pleasure in extending the invitation "to one of our own graduates who is early making good in a way that pleases his friends and his Alma Mater." President C. M. Bishop to AFS, June 4, 1918, Smith Papers.

57. *Williamson County Sun,* Friday, June 21, 1918, p. 1.

58. AFS to Mouzon, July 16, 1918, Mouzon Papers, item 5109.

59. Mouzon to AFS, July 20, 1918 (carbon copy), Mouzon Papers, item 5109.

60. Braden interview.

61. *Texas Christian Advocate,* Thursday, December 9, 1917, p. 2.

62. AFS to Tillett, September 11, 1918 (carbon copy), Smith Papers.

63. Dean W. F. Tillett to the Honorable Josephus Daniels, September 14, 1918 (carbon copy sent to AFS), Smith Papers.

Bishop Mouzon, in his letter to Daniels, wrote: "Mr. Smith is one of the strong young ministers of our Church. His college and university training coupled with his religious experience and sound common sense specially qualify him for service in this great hour of our country's history." Bishop Edwin D. Mouzon to the Honorable Josephus Daniels, September 13, 1918 (carbon copy), Mouzon Papers, item 1208.

64. "Thank you very much for your letter with reference to Rev. A. Frank Smith. Mr. Smith has been in to see me and we are glad to receive him into the naval service." Josephus Daniels, Secretary of the Navy, to Dr. J. L. Cuninggim, Southern Methodist University, Dallas, Texas, September 23, 1918. Cuninggim apparently gave this letter to AFS, as it is in the Smith Papers.

65. AFS kept the letter from Daniels authorizing his physical examination. It is officially stamped on the back: "Reported Sep. 23, 1918. Examined and found physically qualified. [Signed:] Phillip Leach, Captain, Medical Corps, U. S. Navy, President of the Board of Naval Examiners, Navy Yard, Washington, D.C." Josephus Daniels to AFS, September 23, 1918, Smith Papers.

66. AFS to Spann, October 2, 1918 (carbon copy). See AFS to Captain J. B. Frazier, October 2, 1918 (carbon copy). See also Braden interview and AFS to Braden, June 24, 1962, p. 4.

67. Braden interview.

68. Interview with Mrs. George F. (Hallie Crutchfield) Pierce, January 17, 1972, in Dallas, Texas.

69. According to a newspaper account, Charles's "death is thought to have resulted from influenza, as Rev. Smith was just recovering from the disease when the child died. . . . The body was taken to Dallas yesterday [Sunday] on the noon train where interment will take place today, Mrs. Smith having a sister living there.

. . . The father was hardly able to make the trip, but his friends hope it will not give him a setback." *Austin Statesman*, October 21, 1918, p. 3.

70. Texts of telegrams in Smith's handwriting to both sets of grandparents as well as to friends and relatives in Blossom, Alto, and Dallas, Smith Papers.

71. Interview with Mrs. George F. Pierce, January 17, 1972. Besides the Allens, Bess and Hallie's father was later buried there in the Greenwood Cemetery.

72. Braden interview. "That just shows you how things were run in the first World War. We didn't have a commission on chaplains and since I was under this special assignment from the secretary of the Navy, I reckon I just got by with it. Admiral Thomas, Chief of the Navy Chaplains in World War II, and some other Navy men used to say that if I ever showed up at the Navy Building, they would throw me in the brig for being AWOL." Ibid.

Documents in AFS's papers suggest a somewhat different interpretation of events. His "commission" or formal appointment as "Acting Chaplain in the United States Navy, with the rank of Lieutenant (junior grade)," signed by Josephus Daniels, Secretary of the Navy, on October 10, and sent by "Registered Mail," reached Austin on October 18, too late to be delivered. It was then forwarded to Dallas "c/o George F. Pierce, 400 University Blvd.," arriving on November 11, 1918 (according to official postmarks on the envelope). According to the letter of instructions, "Enclosed, herewith, is also a blank form of the acceptance, and Oath of Office which you will execute and return to this Department (Bureau of Navigation) immediately." The official envelope still contains not only the formal document of appointment but also the form of acceptance and Oath of Office, *still unsigned*. Smith Papers.

73. Dr. L. U. Spellman to the author, October 14, 1974.

74. During these two years, AFS received 402 new members into University Church: 129 by profession of faith and 273 by certificate and otherwise. Only Travis Park Methodist Church in San Antonio, among the churches of the West Texas Conference, exceeded this record. *Journals of the West Texas Conference* for the years 1917 and 1918, pp. 108 and 96 respectively.

75. Mouzon to John A. Kerr, November 4, 1918 (carbon copy), Mouzon Papers, item 8248.

CHAPTER SIX

1. Letter from AFS to Dr. Charles S. Braden, June 24, 1962, p. 5, Smith Papers.

2. "This session of the Conference, first appointed to San Saba, was changed to University Church, Austin, on account of a devastating drought, and again changed to Brooks Memorial Church, South San Antonio, on account of an epidemic of influenza." *Journal of the West Texas Conference of the Methodist Episcopal Church, South, 1918*, p. 20.

3. AFS to Braden, June 24, 1962, pp. 5-6.

4. Mouzon to AFS, January 7, 1919, Mouzon Papers, item 8340 (carbon copy), Bridwell Library, SMU.

5. AFS to Braden, June 24, 1962, p. 6.

6. In the Foreword AFS wrote for the history of Laurel Heights written by C. Stanley Banks and Pat Ireland Nixon, *Laurel Heights Methodist Church: 1909-1949* (Austin: Steck Co., 1949), p. x.

7. John A. Kerr to Bishop Edwin D. Mouzon, February 4, 1919, Mouzon Papers, item 8385.

8. AFS to Mouzon, February 18, 1919, Mouzon Papers, item 8409.

9. Charles Allen Smith, born January 30, 1918, had died on October 20 of that same year, just before the Smiths moved to San Antonio. See chap. 5.

10. Braden interview.

11. AFS to Braden, June 24, 1962, p. 6.

12. Ibid., p. 7.

13. Ibid., p. 6.

14. Ibid., p. 7.

15. Ibid.

16. AFS to Mouzon, March 25, 1919, Mouzon Papers, item 8432.

17. AFS to Mouzon, April 15, 1919, Mouzon Papers, item 8450.

18. Ibid. See also item 8432.

19. Robert M. Miller in *The History of American Methodism*, 3:400.

20. Quoted by Miller, ibid., 3:401.

21. AFS to Braden, June 24, 1962, p. 7. The *Journals* of the West Texas Conference show that Laurel Heights gave more to the Missionary Centenary Campaign in 1919 than all the other churches combined in the West Texas Conference gave in 1919 and 1920. *Journal* for 1919, pp. 133, 116; *Journal* for 1920, pp. 109, 112.

22. *Journal of the West Texas Conference, 1919*, p. 92. Twenty-five died during the year, making a new total of 408 members at Laurel Heights.

23. Ibid., p. 32, as stated in the Daily Proceedings. The other statement is in the "Minute Questions," p. 35.

24. *Journal of the West Texas Conference, 1918*, p. 28.

25. AFS, daily journal, "Wednesday, November 17, 1948," Smith Papers. Italics added.

26. According to a "List of Articles Which Belonged to Bishop A. Frank Smith" that were presented to Southwestern University, Smith's "Framed Certificate of Ordination as Elder, November 14, 1918" is in the university's archives. To the utter chagrin of all concerned, no one has been able to find this document. File on Bishop A. Frank Smith, Presidential Papers, Southwestern University, Georgetown, Texas.

27. Braden interview. See chap. 4.

28. AFS to Braden, June 24, 1962, pp. 6-7. "Address Delivered in Front of the Alamo, San Antonio, Texas, on First Armistice Day Anniversary, November 11, 1919" (holograph), Smith Papers.

29. See chaps. 2 and 4. Seay was one of the most promising young men on the SMU School of Theology faculty.

30. AFS to Mouzon, February 19, 1920. Mouzon Papers, item 1864.

31. Interview with Bishop W. Angie Smith, August 1, 1973, in Dallas, Texas. See also Seay to Smith: December 20, 1917, January 16, 1918, February 27, 1919; and AFS to Seay, February 18, 1919 (carbon copy), Smith Papers.

32. AFS to Mouzon, April 13, 1920, Mouzon Papers, item 3525. See also item 1862, dated January 21, 1920; and item 1864, dated February 9, 1920.

33. Ibid. The College of Bishops did eventually meet at Laurel Heights in December, 1923, a year and a half after AFS had left San Antonio. *Nashville Christian Advocate*, January 4, 1924, pp. 10-11.

34. Ibid.

35. Interview with Bishop W. Angie Smith, January 12, 1972, in Dallas, Texas.

36. Interview with Bishop Arthur J. Moore, January 20, 1972, "Epworth-by-the-Sea," St. Simon Island, Georgia. See AFS, daily journal, entry for June 15, 1942: "I love Arthur devotedly, as I have from our days in San Antonio together as fellow pastors in 1920-22." Smith Papers.

37. Since 36 is par for nine holes on most golf courses, the two preachers were still in the bogey class at best.

38. Moore to AFS, April 20, 1920, Smith Papers.

39. Arthur J. Moore, *Bishop to All Peoples* (Nashville: Abingdon Press, 1973), p. 49.

40. Interview with Bishop Moore.

41. On July 20, 1920, AFS performed the wedding ceremony for Angie and Bess Owens of Fort Worth. In October Angie had joined the West Texas Conference and was appointed to Kerrville in the San Antonio District. Interview with Bishop W. Angie Smith, August 1, 1972.

42. Interview with Bishop Moore.

43. Ibid.

44. Ibid.

45. Charles C. Alexander, *Crusade for Conformity: The Ku Klux Klan in Texas, 1920-1930*, Texas Gulf Coast Historical Association Publications 6, no. 1 (August 1962) : 3.

46. Charles C. Alexander, *The Ku Klux Klan in the Southwest* (Lexington: University of Kentucky Press, 1965), p. vi.

47. Alexander, *Crusade for Conformity*, p. 7.

48. Ibid., pp. 9, 13.

49. Ibid., p. 9; *KKK in the Southwest*, p. 39.

50. David M. Chalmers, *Hooded Americanism: The First Century of the Ku Klux Klan, 1865-1965* (Garden City: Doubleday & Co., 1965), p. 40. "Within a year, the picture had changed greatly."

51. Alexander, *KKK in the Southwest*, pp. 18-19.

52. Interview with Bishop Moore.

53. AFS to Braden, June 24, 1962, p. 10.

54. Chalmers, *Hooded Americanism*, p. 40; Alexander, *Crusade for Conformity*, pp. 29, 31. Alexander gives the names of "the best known in Texas."

55. Interview with Bishop Moore.

56. Robert Watson Sledge, *Hands on the Ark: The Struggle for Change in the Methodist Episcopal Church, South, 1914-1939* (Lake Junaluska: Commission on Archives and History of the United Methodist Church, 1975), p. 170.

57. Ibid., 171.

58. Alexander, *Crusade for Conformity*, p. 3.

59. Braden interview.

60. AFS to Braden, June 24, 1962, p. 10. See chap. 7 for AFS's position concerning the Klan in Houston.

61. *History of American Methodism*, 3:356.

62. *Dallas Morning News*, March 5, 1922, p. 11, as quoted by Linda Elaine Kilgore, "The Ku Klux Klan and the Press in Texas, 1920-1927" (M.A., Journalism thesis, University of Texas, 1964), pp. 23-24.

63. Bishop Edwin D. Mouzon to F. H. Hitchcock, August 15, 1922, Mouzon Papers, item 6042 (carbon copy).

64. George Brown Tindall, *The Emergence of the New South* (Baton Rouge: Louisiana State University Press, 1967), p. 184.

65. Winthrop S. Hudson, *Religion in America* (New York: Charles Scribner's Sons, 1965), p. 293. Cf. Ernest R. Sandeen, "Towards a Historical Interpretation of the Origins of Fundamentalism," *Church History* 36, no. 1 (March 1967) : 66-83.

66. Tindall, *Emergence of the New South*, pp. 200-201.

67. Braden interview.

68. Dr. L. U. Spellman to the author, February 9, 1973.

69. Norman F. Furniss, *The Fundamentalist Controversy, 1918-1931* (New Haven: Yale University Press, 1954), p. 17. See also John Dillenberger and Claude Welch, *Protestant Christianity Interpreted through Its Development* (New York: Charles Scribner's Sons, 1954), p. 277.

70. Robert M. Miller, "A Note on the Relationship between the Protestant Churches and the Revived Ku Klux Klan," *Journal of Southern History* 22, no. 3 (August 1956) : 368.

71. See Furniss, *Fundamentalist Controversy*, p. 15.

72. John A. Rice, *The Old Testament in the Life of Today* (New York: Macmillan Co., 1920), p. 320. In his foreword, p. viii, Rice stated: "It is hoped that this interpretation may bring relief to some who are still distressed about the results of biblical criticism."

73. See Furniss, *Fundamentalist Controversy*, pp. 86, 121.

74. *Eighty-four Golden Years: An Autobiography of Bishop Hiram Abiff Boaz* (Nashville: Parthenon Press, 1951), p. 110.

75. In the light of such excoriating attacks on Rice, one pastor from the West Texas Conference, Rev. Walter L. Barr, having "given Dr. Rice's book careful reading," commented: "I was disappointed in its being so orthodox. . . . I was looking for something 'shocking.' There is nothing new in it. Some things are said in a new way, but are in substance the things we have been studying all through the years. . . . I am willing for my boy to sit at the feet of Dr. Rice and study *The Old Testament in the Light of Today*." *Texas Christian Advocate*, September 29, 1921, p. 5.

76. Smith to Mouzon, April 25, 1922, Mouzon Papers, item 11,523. See Bishop Edwin D. Mouzon, "The Catholic Spirit of Methodism," *Nashville Christian Advocate*, April 21, 1922, pp. 7-8.

77. Bishop Edwin D. Mouzon, "Dr. John A. Rice and His Book," *Texas Christian Advocate*, July 28, 1921, p. 8.

78. Mouzon to William T. Franklin, October 4, 1922, Mouzon Papers, item 6070 (carbon copy).

79. Mouzon, "Fundamentalism and Methodism," *Texas Christian Advocate*, June 21, 1923, p. 2.

80. Mouzon, *Fundamentals of Methodism* (Nashville: Publishing House of the Methodist Episcopal Church, South, 1923), p. 24.

81. Interview with Bishop Arthur J. Moore.

82. *Journal of the Sixty-Third Annual Session of the West Texas Conference of the Methodist Episcopal Church, South, Held at San Antonio, Texas, October 19 to 23, 1921*, pp. 16, 65.

83. Interview with Bishop Moore.

84. *Journal of the West Texas Conference, 1921*, pp. 41, 67.

85. Mouzon to AFS, November 16, 1921, Smith Papers. See also the exchange between Rice and Mouzon: Rice to Mouzon, October 23, 1922, and Mouzon's reply, Mouzon Papers, item 6075.

86. Rice, *The Old Testament in the Light of Today*, p. xvi.

87. Braden interview.

88. Ibid.

89. Interview with Bishop Moore.

90. Kern to AFS, July 20, 1920, Smith Papers.

91. AFS to Mouzon, May 24, 1922. Mouzon Papers, item 11,536. Eventually AFS gave Mouzon a gift subscription!

92. Interview with Bishop W. Angie Smith, January 21, 1972.

93. *Texas Christian Advocate*, October 27, 1921, p. 9.

94. Ibid., September 15, 1921, p. 10.

95. AFS to Mouzon, January 11, 1922, Mouzon Papers, item 429.

96. AFS to Mouzon, April 25, 1922, Mouzon Papers, item 11,523.

97. Braden interview. See *Journal of the Nineteenth General Conference of the Methodist Episcopal Church, Souh, Held in Hot Springs, Arkansas, May 3-22, 1922* (Nashville: Publishing House of the Methodist Episcopal Church, South, 1922), pp. 7-8. Bishop Eugene R. Hendrix, the senior bishop, was unable to attend because of illness.

98. See Jno J. Tigert, *A Constitutional History of American Episcopal Methodism*, 3rd ed., rev. and enlarged (Nashville: Publishing House of the Methodist Episcopal Church, South, 1908), chap. 20, pp. 338-63. A much shorter account is given in *History of American Methodism*, 1:642-45.

99. For examples, see *Nashville Christian Advocate*, November 4, 1921, p. 25; November 11, 1921, p. 24; January 13, 1922, p. 24; January 20, 1922, p. 24; January 27, 1922, p. 24; March 17, 1922, p. 24; March 31, 1922, p. 24.

100. Mouzon to AFS, November 16, 1921, Smith Papers.

101. *Journal of the General Conference, 1922*, pp. 110-11.

102. Ivan Lee Holt, *Eugene Russell Hendrix, Servant of the Kingdom* (Nashville: Parthenon Press, 1950), pp. 117-18. See *Journal of the General Conference, 1922*, pp. 220-22.

103. As stated in the *Journal of the General Conference*, 1922, p. 273.

104. "The Episcopal Address," as published in the *Nashville Christian Advocate*, May 5, 1922, p. 4.

105. *Journal of the General Conference, 1922*, p. 273.

106. Elijah Embree Hoss, James Henry McCoy, Joseph Staunton Key, Walter Russell Lambuth, and Henry Clay Morrison. *Nashville Chrisian Advocate*, May 5, 1922, p. 3.

107. Braden interview; *Journal of the General Conference, 1922*, p. 166.

108. Interview with Bishop Moore.

109. Hay was elected on May 16. On May 26, Dickey wrote to AFS notifying him of his release. Bishop James E. Dickey to AFS, May 26, 1922, Smith Papers. The three other bishops elected in 1922 were William Benjamin Beauchamp, Hoyt McWhorter Dobbs, and Hiram Abiff Boaz.

110. Braden interview. See AFS to Braden, June 24, 1962, p. 8.

111. AFS to Braden, June 24, 1962, pp. 10-11. See Braden interview.

112. Bishop Sam Hay took obvious pleasure in characterizing his election to the episcopacy as "a rising up of the rough element demanding recognition." Interview with Dr. L. U. Spellman, January 23, 1973, at Kerrville, Texas.

113. Interview with Bishop Moore.

114. AFS to Braden, June 24, 1962, p. 11.

115. Braden interview. See also AFS to Braden, June 24, 1962, p. 11.

116. AFS to Mouzon, May 29, 1922, Mouzon Papers, item 6026.

117. Mouzon to AFS, June 17, 1922 (carbon copy), Mouzon Papers, item 6026. After four years over the conferences in Arkansas and Oklahoma, Mouzon had just been assigned to the Holston Conference (Virginia) and two conferences in Tennessee. *Daily Christian Advocate* 19, no. 16 (May 20, 1922): 1.

118. "San Antonio Bids Farewell to Rev. Smith," Monday, May 29, 1922. Clipping from an unidentified San Antonio paper, Smith Papers.

119. Ibid.

120. Hoax telegram, Smith Papers.

121. Hoax telegram, Smith Papers.

122. Unidentified newspaper clipping, Smith Papers. This luncheon was held on Friday, June 2, 1922.

123. "Pastor Tells of City's Romance," clipping, n.d., from an unidentified San Antonio newspaper, Smith Papers. "The leader of the day was L. E. Fite," a name honored among Methodists as well as other citizens of San Antonio.

124. Banks and Nixon, *Laurel Heights Methodist Church: 1909-1949*, p. 32.

125. Kerr to Mouzon, June 3, 1922, Mouzon Papers, item 3915.

126. Quoted in Banks and Nixon, *Laurel Heights Methodist Church: 1909-1949*, pp. 32-34 (p. 33 is a marvelous photographic portrait of the young pastor, A. Frank Smith).

CHAPTER SEVEN

1. AFS to Dr. Charles S. Braden, June 24, 1962, p. 8, Smith Papers.

2. Although the reporter's account of the sermon is very brief, it is clear that AFS once again preached his now much revised "The Man with a Message" sermon, his opening sermon in Dallas and Austin and probably San Antonio. Clipping from a Houston newspaper, Monday, June 5, 1922, Smith Papers.

3. Ibid.
The *Houston Chronicle* had announced AFS's appointment on May 25: "Rev. A. Frank Smith, pastor of Laurel Heights Methodist Church, San Antonio, is appointed

pastor of the First Methodist Church of Houston, to succeed Dr. Sam R. Hay. . . .
Selection of the Rev. Smith was made at a conference between Dr. George Waverly
Davis, presiding elder of the Houston district, Bishop John M. Moore, presiding
bishop of the Texas Methodist conference and other church leaders." Clipping, Smith
Papers.

4. Marilyn McAdams Sibley, *The Port of Houston: A History* (Austin: University of Texas Press, 1968), pp. 4, 35.

5. Ruter's manuscript journal quoted by Mrs. S. R. Campbell, "Martin Ruter,"
Biographical Sketches of Eminent Itinerant Ministers, ed. Thomas O. Summers (Nashville: Publishing House of the Methodist Episcopal Church, South, 1858), p. 340.

6. Lewis Howard Grimes, *Cloud of Witnesses: A History of First Methodist Church, Houston, Texas* (Houston: First Methodist Church, 1951), p. 23.

7. Sibley, *The Port of Houston*, p. 168.

8. Ibid., pp. 168-69. The preceding information is also based on Sibley, *The Port of Houston*, pp. 155ff.

9. AFS to Braden, June 24, 1962, pp. 11-12.

10. The First National and the City National banks later consolidated under the name of First City National Bank, whose twenty-four-story skyscraper houses the law firm of Vinson, Elkins, Searls, Connally and Smith. A. Frank Smith, Jr. is presently the managing partner of the firm.

11. George Fuermann, *Houston: Land of the Big Rich* (Garden City: Doubleday & Co., 1951), pp. 81-82, 85. Jones was a member of St. Paul's Methodist Church.

12. Jesse H. Jones, *Fifty Billion Dollars: My Thirteen Years with the RFC (1932-1945)* (New York: Macmillan Co., 1951), pp. 512-35.

13. Interview with Robert A. ("Bob") Shepherd, September 13, 1973, in Houston, Texas.

14. Jones, *Fifty Billion Dollars*, p. 353.

15. Interview with Hines H. Baker, September 17, 1973, in Houston, Texas. See chap. 5.

16. AFS to Braden, June 24, 1962, pp. 10-11. See Braden interview.

17. Quoted by Dr. J. N. R. Score in his article on AFS in the *Southwestern Magazine* 33, no. 4 (March 1931): 20. Score did not further identify the church member.

18. AFS to Bishop Edwin D. Mouzon, September 7, 1922. Mouzon Papers, item 6064, Bridwell Library, SMU.

19. Sam R. Hay to AFS, May 26, 1922, Smith Papers.

20. Braden interview. "I learned this sometime later," AFS explained.

21. Bishop John M. Moore to AFS, September 16, 1922, Smith Papers.

22. Paul B. Kern to AFS, June 1, 1922, Smith Papers.

23. Letter to Bishop John M. Moore, July 14, 1922, Mouzon Papers, item 4316. (Although this letter was signed and written on official stationery, the writer's name is withheld for obvious reasons.)

24. Carbon copy of Bishop Mouzon's reply to letter in n. 23, dated July 28, 1922, Mouzon Papers, item 4316.

25. Interview with Bishop William C. Martin, January 22, 1973, in Little Rock, Arkansas.

26. Ibid.

27. AFS to Mouzon, Mouzon Papers, item 6064.

28. Ibid.

29. AFS to Mouzon, Mouzon Papers, item 5373. These figures represent the totals for both Palm Sunday and Easter Sunday, according to a report in the *Texas Christian Advocate*, April 5, 1923, p. 5.

30. Smith to Mouzon, April 18, 1923, Mouzon Papers, item 6117.

31. See chap. 2.

32. AFS to Mouzon, September 9, 1922, Mouzon Papers, item 6064.

33. Mouzon to AFS, September 14, 1923, Mouzon Papers, item 6064 (carbon copy).

34. Mouzon to AFS, April 13, 1923, Smith Papers.

35. Both men used their full names in signing their letters to each other. Although Mouzon invariably began with "My dear Frank," his standard closing was "Fraternally yours." At times he added: "Give my love to Bess and the boy [Frank, Jr.]."

36. Mouzon to AFS, May 22, 1923, Smith Papers. AFS's telegram, of course, is in the Mouzon Papers, item 6129.

37. AFS to Mouzon, August 6, 1923, Mouzon Papers, item 8950.

38. AFS to Braden, June 24, 1962, pp. 10, 20.

39. *Houston Post*, July 24, 1922; quoted in Charles C. Alexander, *Crusade for Conformity: The Ku Klux Klan in Texas, 1920-1930*, Texas Gulf Coast Historical Association Publications 6, no. 1 (August 1962): 48.

40. Alexander, *Crusade for Conformity*, p. 17. Included in the telephones tapped by Klansmen were those of the offices of every Catholic priest in Houston.

41. Interview with Bishop William C. Martin, January 22, 1973.

42. AFS to Braden, June 24, 1962, pp. 17-18. "Foster contrived to get reports of secret Klan meetings. These he published under the byline 'Kash Kay Kale,' giving the names of some of the members. As a result the lives of both Foster and Jones were threatened." (Jesse Jones had held half-ownership of the *Chronicle* since 1908.) Bascom N. Timmons, *Jesse H. Jones: The Man and the Statesman* (New York: Henry Holt & Co., 1956), p. 121.

43. According to Charles Alexander, the "Kleagle" was a field organizer for the Klan. The head of a local Klan chapter was called "Exalted Cyclops." Alexander, *The Ku Klux Klan in the Southwest* (Lexington: University of Kentucky Press, 1965), pp. xiv-xv.

44. Braden interview. Smith only identified the Kleagle as "an ex-Kentucky sheriff, a good man, too."

45. Ibid.

46. *Houston Chronicle*, August 19, 1922, Clipping, Smith Papers.

47. See chap. 5.

48. Seth Shepherd McKay, *Texas Politics, 1906-1944* (Lubbock: Texas Tech Press, 1952), p. 112.

49. Alexander, *Crusade for Conformity*, p. 49.

50. McKay, *Texas Politics*, pp. 116-27.

51. AFS to Braden, June 24, 1962, p. 10.

52. Ibid., p. 12.

53. Ibid., p. 13. See also Braden interview.

54. Braden interview.

55. AFS to Braden, June 24, 1962, p. 13.

56. "Services Held for New Temple," undated clipping from Houston newspaper, Smith Papers. March date is taken from AFS's handwritten notes which he entitled "Address at Laying of Cornerstone of Jewish Synagogue, Beth Israel, 3-8-25, 4 P.M.," Smith Papers.

57. Barnston to AFS, August 15, 1925 (holograph), Smith Papers.

58. Grimes, *Cloud of Witnesses*, p. 120. As the Sisterhood of Temple Beth Israel expressed their appreciation—"Thanking you, sincerely, and extending the 'Greetings of the Season'"—the "Season" of course could refer to the Jewish celebration of Hanukkah. Sisterhood of Temple Beth Israel, Mrs. W. L. Griffin, Corresponding Secretary, to the Members of First Methodist Church, December 16, 1925, Smith Papers. (December could be the completion date of the new Temple Beth Israel.)

59. Ibid., p. 121.

60. Interview with Mrs. J. N. R. Score, August 8, 1973, in Dallas, Texas.

61. AFS to Braden, June 24, 1962, pp. 13-14.

62. "Our City," by MEFO. Clipping from the *Houston Chronicle*, n.d., Smith Papers.

63. Interview with Bishop William C. Martin, January 22, 1973.

64. Interview with Hines Baker, September 17, 1973.

65. Ibid.

66. *Texas Christian Advocate*, October 11, 1923, p. 14.

67. Quoted in Grimes, *Cloud of Witnesses*, p. 122.

68. AFS to Braden, June 24, 1962, p. 15.

69. *Blue Bird Circle: 1923-1973*, pp. 3-4. According to AFS's account: "I asked them to use the term Circle instead of Club because Circle is a term used by the women of the church." AFS to Braden, June 24, 1962, p. 15.

70. Ibid., pp. 4-7.

71. Interview with Bishop W. Kenneth Pope, September 15, 1972, in Dallas, Texas. For more on the story of AFS's relation to the "Blue Bird Circle" see chap. 18.

72. AFS to Mouzon, April 10, 1923, Mouzon Papers, item 5373.

73. Minutes for September 18, 1923, quoted in Grimes, *Cloud of Witnesses*, p. 125. In 1920, during Sam Hay's pastorate, the church had purchased the adjoining quarter of a block at Travis and Clay.

74. Clipping from a Houston newspaper, Smith Papers. See similar announcements in the *Texas Christian Advocate*, October 11, 1923, p. 14; and in AFS to Mouzon, November 12, 1923, Mouzon Papers, item 9219.

75. AFS to Mouzon, May 8, 1928, Mouzon Papers, item 17,607.

76. Bishop John M. Moore to AFS, January 9, 1929, Smith Papers.

77. Bulletin of First Methodist Church, January 6, 1929; quoted in Grimes, *Cloud of Witnesses*, p. 126.

78. *Houston Chronicle*, January 12, 1929, p. 2.

79. Interview with Robert A. ("Bob") Shepherd, September 18, 1973, in Houston, Texas.

80. *Houston Evening Post*, February 16, 1923. This report is on the front page of a special "Methodist Section," a remarkable sixteen-page document entirely devoted to the activities and institutions of Houston Methodism. Smith Papers.

Bishop Mouzon called this "the greatest piece of church advertisement that I have ever seen." Mouzon to Rev. George W. Davis (Presiding Elder of the Houston District), February 18, 1923, Mouzon Papers, item 6097 (carbon copy).

81. Ibid., p. 2. The Bell Home, a $45,000 three-story structure of similar construction and exterior to the new hospital, belonged to the Texas Conference but had its own board of trustees. The old Norsworthy hospital building was on the corner of San Jacinto and Rosalie.

82. Interview with Mrs. Walter W. Fondren, October 26, 1973, in Houston, Texas. Mrs. Fondren's husband was vice-president of this organizing board. The Fondrens were members of St. Paul's Methodist Church in Houston.

83. *Texas Christian Advocate*, July 24, 1924, p. 6.

In his final report before returning to the ranks as pastor of a local church, the Rev. R. W. Adams, who had directed the hospital project for four years, gave special praise to the following laymen of First Methodist Church: John T. Scott, S. F. Carter, Jesse Jones, J. M. West, W. W. Fondren, W. L. Clayton, Ed S. Phelps, R. W. Wier, and E. L. Crain. *Texas Christian Advocate,* June 12, 1924, p. 8.

The Methodist Hospital was described as follows: "One of the best furnished and equipped for its work of any in this section of the country, the hospital is now well organized in all of its workings, under the superintendency of Sam R. Hay, Jr., and with a staff of the best physicians and surgeons and the most efficient corps of nurses to be found anywhere in all our beloved Southland." *Texas Christian Advocate,* July 24, 1924, p. 6.

84. Interview with A. Frank Smith, Jr., August 29, 1972, in Houston, Texas.

85. Interview with Hines Baker, September 17, 1973.

86. Walter W. Armstrong, *Room to Grow: A History of Houston Methodist Missions, 1815-1963* (Houston: Houston Methodist Board of Missions, 1963), p. 17.

87. *Houston Evening Post*, February 16, 1923, "Methodist Section," p. 4.

88. AFS to Mouzon, November 11, 1923, Mouzon Papers, item 9219.

89. *Journal of the Eighty-Fourth Annual Session of the Texas Conference of the Methodist Episcopal Church, South, Held at Cameron, Texas, November 21-25, 1923*, p. 103.

90. AFS to Braden, June 24, 1962, p. 9. See Braden interview.

91. *Journals of the Texas Conference* for the year noted. Armstrong gives $4,400 for 1929. *Room to Grow*, p. 20. It should be noted that the amounts given for "Home Mission Specials" during these same years was approximately the same as that given for the City Board and that the amount given for "Foreign Mission Specials" was not far behind, $5,000 being the amount for both 1926 and 1928. (The stock market crash came in October, 1929.)

92. Braden interview.

93. *Houston Post*, clipping, n.d. (most likely late November or early December, 1925), Smith Papers.

94. Braden interview.

95. Interview with Hines Baker, September 17, 1973.

96. Ralph W. Jones, *Southwestern University, 1840-1961* (Austin: San Felipe Press, 1973), p. 264.

97. *Williamson County Sun*, May 11, 1923, p. 3; June 1, 1923, p. 4. See *Texas Christian Advocate*, June 14, 1923, p. 8.

98. H. L. Millis to AFS, June 9, 1923, Smith Papers.

99. See chap. 2.

100. *Texas Christian Advocate*, December 27, 1923, p. 14.

101. AFS to Mouzon, April 17, 1924, Mouzon Papers, item 12,385.

102. Interview with A. Frank Smith, Jr., August 29, 1972; Grimes, *Cloud of Witnesses*, p. 122.

103. AFS to Mouzon, December 1, 1924, Mouzon Papers, item 14,614. The previous parsonage was on Garrott Street.

104. AFS to Braden, June 24, 1962, p. 15. See Grimes, *Cloud of Witnesses*, p. 123.

105. W. A. Smith to AFS, December 12, 1925 (holograph), Smith Papers.

106. *Journal of the Eighty-Sixth Annual Session of the Texas Conference of the Methodist Episcopal Church, South, Held at Jacksonville, Texas, November 11-15, 1925*, p. 21.

107. Mouzon to AFS, November 17, 1925, Smith Papers.

108. *Journal of the Twentieth General Conference of the Methodist Episcopal Church, South, Held in Memphis, Tennessee, May 5-20, 1926* (Nashville: Lamar & Whitmore, 1926), pp. 13, 47.

109. Ibid., p. 201.

110. *The Church School Builder* (Published Weekly by First Methodist Church Sunday School) 1, no. 2 (September 9, 1927): 1.

111. AFS to Mouzon, August 6, 1923, Mouzon Papers, item 8950.

112. Interview with A. Frank Smith, Jr. and W. R. Smith, August 29, 1972, in Houston, Texas. The Depression years are included in this period, of course, as well as the first five years of AFS's episcopacy.

113. AFS to Cannon, January 31, 1928, Cannon Collection, Perkins Library, Duke University, Durham, North Carolina.

114. Robert Moats Miller, "A Footnote to the Role of the Protestant Churches in the Election of 1928," *Church History* 25, no. 2 (June 1956): 146.

115. Moore to AFS, May 14, 1928, Smith Papers. See also Bishop Mouzon's letter to AFS, May 24, 1928, Smith Papers. As Mouzon explained to Josephus Daniels: "[Al Smith's] telegram bolting the platform and his selection of Mr. Rascob

... to manage his campaign, together with Mr. Rascob's intemperate utterances concerning 'the damnable affliction of prohibition'—these things have put me where I believe that the issue is now predominantly a moral issue." Mouzon to Daniels, July 20, 1928, Mouzon Papers, item 3767 (carbon copy).

116. AFS to Mouzon, July 13, 1928, Mouzon Papers, item 3729.

117. See Bishop John M. Moore's letter to AFS, July 23, 1928, Smith Papers. See also *New Orleans Christian Advocate*, August 16, 1928, pp. 3-4; Tindall, *The Emergence of the New South*, p. 246.

118. Tindall, *Emergence of the New South*, p. 251.

119. AFS to Mouzon, November 14, 1928, Mouzon Papers, item 3722. See also Bishop Horace M. DuBose to AFS, November 21, 1928, Smith Papers.

120. Knickerbocker to AFS, February 24, 1928, Smith Papers. See also H. A. Carlton of Largo, Florida, to AFS, January 7, 1926, Smith Papers. Carlton and L. L. Evans were "both of the opinion that it will not be long until you will be elected to the episcopacy. If not in May [1962], then four years hence!"

121. Luther Bridgers to AFS, March 24, 1928, Smith Papers.

122. Ibid.

123. Candler to AFS, June 7, 1928, Smith Papers. While at Macon, AFS was a guest in the home of Bishop and Mrs. W. N. Ainsworth. See Ainsworth to AFS, April 17, 1928, Smith Papers.

124. Moore to AFS, May 7, 1928, Smith Papers.

125. Moore to AFS, May 14, 1928, Smith Papers. H. E. Jackson was a leading layman in the West Texas Conference from San Angelo, Texas.

126. *Journal of the Twentieth General Conference of the Methodist Episcopal Church, South, 1926*, p. 143.

127. See Frederick E. Maser, "The Story of Unification," *The History of American Methodism*, 3 vols., ed. Emory S. Bucke (Nashville: Abingdon Press, 1964), 3:433-38.

128. *Journal of the Twentieth General Conference of the Methodist Episcopal Church, South, 1926*, pp. 142-44.

129. Mouzon to AFS, August 3, 1928, Smith Papers. Mouzon's carbon copy is in the Mouzon Papers, item 3729. Moore to AFS, August 22, 1928, Smith Papers.

130. Moore to AFS, August 22, 1928, Smith Papers.

131. Darlington to AFS, August 23, 1928, Smith Papers. The other two committees were Doctrine, chaired by Bishop Horace M. DuBose, and Conferences and Administration, chaired by Bishop Warren A. Candler.

132. Dean to AFS, July 13, 1928, Smith Papers.

133. Dean to AFS, July 17, 1928, Smith Papers.

134. Mouzon to AFS, January 8, 1929 (holograph), Smith Papers. Rev. Felix Hill had been the Presiding Elder of the San Antonio District when Frank Smith was pastor at Laurel Heights and Arthur Moore at Travis Park. The three men had enjoyed a close friendship ever since.

135. AFS to Mouzon, March 29, 1929, Mouzon Papers, item 17,747.

136. Score to Mouzon, November 18, 1929, Mouzon Papers, item 17,943.

137. Candler to AFS, July 11, 1929, Smith Papers.

138. AFS to Mouzon, December 11, 1929, Mouzon Papers, item 17,984.

139. AFS to Mrs. Mouzon, January 21, 1930, Mouzon Papers, item 4380.

140. Horace M. DuBose, pastor 1885-86, elected 1918; Seth Ward, pastor 1895-96, elected 1906; Sam R. Hay, pastor 1901-4, 1920-22. W. Kenneth Pope would later become the fifth at his election in 1960.

141. AFS to Braden, June 24, 1962, p. 17.

142. *Journals of the Texas Conference of the Methodist Episcopal Church, South*, for the years 1922 through 1930, Statistical Tables I and III.

143. Score, "Bishop A. Frank Smith," *Southwestern Magazine* 33, no. 4 (March 1931) : 22.

CHAPTER EIGHT

1. AFS to Charles S. Braden, June 24, 1962, p. 22, Smith Papers. See also Braden interview.

2. Braden interview.

3. AFS to Braden, June 24, 1962, p. 23.

4. Ibid., pp. 20-21, 24.

5. Ibid., pp. 19, 24.

6. The four versions of "The Man with a Message": (1) as published in the *Campus* [SMU] 1, no. 20 (February 18, 1916): 1, 4; (2) as published in the *Austin American*, November 6, 1916, p. 2; (3) as published in the *San Antonio Express*, January 23, 1922; and (4) twenty-five-page holograph sermon notes entitled "The Man with a Message," Smith Papers.

7. "Too Busy," a sermon on I Kings 20:40 preached on September 20, 1925 (holograph). See also report in *Houston Post-Dispatch*, September 21, 1925, Smith Papers.

8. Ibid. Italics added.

9. Ibid.

10. Sydney E. Ahlstrom, *A Religious History of the American People* (New Haven: Yale University Press, 1972), pp. 899, 905.

11. Frederick Lewis Allen, *Only Yesterday* (New York: Bantam Books, 1959), pp. 125, 126, 127, 128.

12. Sermon on I Kings 20:40, "Too Busy."

13. "Christianize the City," report from a Houston newspaper, not further identified, n.d., Smith Papers.

14. Ibid.

15. Commencement Sermon for Central High School, based on Philippians 3:13-14, preached at First Methodist Church, Houston, May 31, 1925 (holograph). See also the newspaper clipping, undated and otherwise unidentified, Smith Papers.

16. Newspaper clippings of these sermons, Smith Papers.

17. "Man's Need of God," a communion sermon preached on November 4, 1923, First Methodist Church, Houston (holograph). AFS didn't gain much clarity by writing out this passage!

18. Ibid.

19. Sermon on "Sin, Grief, and Death," preached at the First Methodist Church, Houston, and broadcast over radio station KPRC. Clipping from *Houston Post-Dispatch*, Smith Papers.

20. AFS uses the terms *immortality* and *eternal life* as synonymns, apparently unaware of the problem involved in such an equation. See Krister Stendahl, *Immortality and Resurrection: Two Conflicting Currents of Thought* (New York: Macmillan Co., 1965); Jaroslav Pelikan, *The Shape of Death* (Nashville: Abingdon Press, 1961).

21. Sermon on "Sin, Grief, and Death."

22. Ibid.

23. Ibid.

24. *Austin American*, Monday, December 25, 1916, p. 8.

25. "The Significance of Christmas," a sermon preached at First Methodist Church, Houston, December 22, 1929, and reported in an unidentified Houston newspaper. See also manuscript sermon dated "December 26, 1920, Laurel Heights Church [San Antonio]; Xmas 1922, 1st Church, Houston; December 22, 1929, 1st Church, Houston" (holograph), Smith Papers.

26. Winthrop S. Hudson, *Religion in America* (New York: Charles Scribner's Sons, 1965), pp. 371-77.

27. Allen, *Only Yesterday*, pp. 131-32.

28. John Dillenberger and Claude Welch, *Protestant Christianity* (New York: Charles Scribner's Sons, 1954), p. 213.

29. Note the close parallel between AFS's statement, for example, and one of

American liberalism's classics, William Adams Brown's *Christian Theology in Outline* (New York: Charles Scribner's Sons, 1906, 1934), pp. 210, 258, 420.

30. J. N. R. Score, *Southwestern Magazine* 33, no. 4 (March 1931): 21-23.

31. AFS to Braden, June 24, 1962, pp. 20, 21, 24. See also Braden interview.

32. Langston G. King to AFS, November 14, 1928, Smith Papers. King was Judge of Criminal District Court No. 2.

33. W. P. Hobby to AFS, undated holograph, Smith Papers. Hobby was president of the *Houston Post-Dispatch*.

34. Braden interview.

35. Ibid.

36. Ibid.

37. Ibid.

38. Interview with Hines H. Baker, September 17, 1973, in Houston, Texas.

39. Interview with Bishop Arthur J. Moore, January 20, 1972, Epworth-by-the-Sea, St. Simon Island, Georgia. See also interview with Dr. Stewart Clendenin, August 28, 1972, in Houston, Texas.

40. Randolph and Muriel Carter to AFS, undated but almost certainly from AFS's pastorate in Houston. Smith Papers.

41. AFS, "The Minister as Director of Public Relations," *The Ministry*, ed. J. Richard Spann (Nashville: Abingdon-Cokesbury, 1949), p. 128.

42. T. Walter Moore to AFS, January 26, 1928, Smith Papers.

43. *Journal of the Texas Conference, 1970*, p. 313. See also Nell Anders, Registar, to AFS, October 11, 1927, with receipt from SMU attached, Smith Papers; Braden interview.

44. Interview with Dr. Stewart Clendenin.

45. Score, *Southwestern Magazine*, pp. 22-23.

46. Interview with Dr. Monroe Vivion, January 18, 1973, at Flint, Texas.

47. Score, *Southwestern Magazine*, pp. 22-23.

CHAPTER NINE

1. *Daily Christian Advocate* 21 (May 1930): 98.

2. Ibid.

3. From "The Episcopal Address," as published in the *Journal of the Twenty-first General Conference of the Methodist Episcopal Church, South, Held at Dallas, Texas, May 5-24 1930* (Nashville: Smith & Whitmore, 1930), p. 385. As there was no set number of bishops required, the matter was entirely at the discretion of each General Conference. The three deceased bishops were James Edward Dickey, Eugene Russell Hendrix, and John Carlisle Kilgo.

4. Ibid., p. 171.

5. *Daily Christian Advocate* 21 (May 1930): 82.

6. Ibid.

7. Ibid., pp. 82-83.

8. Ibid., p. 83.

9. Ibid.

10. *Journal of the General Conference*, 1930, p. 172.

11. Ibid., pp. 207, 208, 211, 213, 217 for reports of the first five ballots.

12. Braden interview. After six years at Travis Park, Moore had been appointed to First Church in Birmingham, Alabama, in 1926.

13. Interview with Bishop Arthur J. Moore, January 20-22, 1972, at St. Simon Island, Georgia. See interview with Bishop Paul E. Martin, January 14, 1972, in Dallas, Texas.

14. *Daily Christian Advocate* 21 (May 1930): 105. "Forney was a great story-teller," AFS declared, "but Bishop Mouzon, my father in the gospel, took offense at that and said he ought to apologize to the conference." Braden interview.

15. Score, "Bishop A. Frank Smith," *Southwestern Magazine* 33, no. 4 (March 1931): 23.

16. "Proceedings for the Thirteenth Day, Wednesday, May 24," *Journal of the General Conference*, 1930, p. 228.

17. See chap. 7.

18. Score, "Bishop A. Frank Smith," p. 23.

19. Interview with Bishop Paul E. Martin.

20. Interview with Bishop W. Angie Smith, January 12, 1972, in Dallas, Texas.

21. Interview with Dr. D. Lawrence Landrum, January 17, 1973, in Palestine, Texas.

22. Dr. Braden's interview with Bishop and Mrs. Smith, January 23, 1962, in Houston, Texas.

23. Ibid.

24. Ibid.

25. *Journal of the General Conference*, 1930, pp. 269-70.

26. Ibid., p. 197.

27. For example, most, if not all, of those receiving ten or more votes for bishop were on this committee.

28. Interview with Bishop Arthur Moore. See the statement from the Committee on Episcopacy, Bishop Cannon's statement, Bishop Candler's climactic "confession," *Daily Christian Advocate* 21 (May 1930): 98, 107-8. Bishop Moore's account is a bit more colorful.

29. *Daily Christian Advocate* 21 (May 1930): 114. The account in the *Journal* does not mention Chairman Daniel's "notice." *Journal of the General Conference*, 1930, p. 244.

30. *Journal of the General Conference*, 1930, p. 244.

31. Interview with Bishop Arthur Moore.

32. *Daily Christian Advocate* 21 (May 1930): 114.

33. Ibid., p. 115. Bishop Edwin D. Mouzon was presiding.

34. *Journal of the General Conference*, 1930, p. 245. By that time, of course, an alternate delegate had taken AFS's seat in the Texas Conference delegation.

35. "The Plan of Episcopal Assignments," as published in the *Daily Christian Advocate* 21 (May 1930): 120.

36. Braden interview.

37. Interview with Bishop Arthur Moore.

38. Ibid.

39. *The Doctrines and Disciplines of the Methodist Episcopal Church, South, 1930* (Nashville: Lamar & Whitmore, 1930), p. 469.

40. Interview with Bishop W. Angie Smith.

41. Interview with A. Frank Smith, Jr., August 29, 1972, in Houston, Texas.

42. Interview with Bishop W. Angie Smith.

43. Braden interview.

44. Bishop Edwin H. Hughes to AFS, May 24, 1930, Smith Papers.

45. AFS to Rev. W. C. Martin, June 6, 1930, William C. Martin Papers, Bridwell Library, SMU, Dallas, Texas.

46. Smith Papers.

47. *Houston Chronicle*, Friday, June 6, 1930, pp. 1, 35. Other speakers included Rev. M. M. Wolfe and Rev. A. D. Foreman representing Houston's Baptist churches; M. E. Foster, newspaperman; and Dr. William States Jacob, toastmaster.

48. Braden interview.

49. Unidentified newspaper clipping (probably the *St. Louis Christian Advocate*), Smith Papers.

50. Braden interview.

51. Braden interview with Bishop and Mrs. Smith.

52. Ibid.

53. Interview with A. Frank Smith, Jr.

54. Braden interview with Bishop and Mrs. Smith.

55. Interview with William Randolph Smith, August 29, 1972, in Houston, Texas.

56. *Journal of the One Hundred-Fourteenth Session of the Missouri Annual Conference of the Methodist Episcopal Church, South, Held at Columbia, Missouri, September 3-7, 1930*, p. 25.

57. Ibid., p. 33.

58. See chap. 7, pp. 129-30; AFS's initiative in creating a "Bishop's Gallery" at First Church, Houston, with the portraits of Bishop Sam R. Hay and his predecessors there who had been elected to the episcopacy.

59. Score, "Bishop A. Frank Smith," pp. 23-24.

60. A. C. Millar, "Bishop Smith and His First Conference," *St. Louis Christian Advocate*, September 17, 1930, p. 7. Millar sent a similar statement to the *Nashville Christian Advocate*, September 10, 1930, pp. 1, 4, 5.

61. The *Oklahoma Methodist*, October 8, 1930, p. 8.

62. *Nashville Christian Advocate*, November 14, 1930. The editor overlooked AFS's other annual conference, the Indian Mission, which he had held in September.

63. Mouzon to AFS, October 8, 1930, Mouzon Papers, item 8852 (carbon copy), Bridwell Library, SMU. See AFS's reply dated October 12, 1930, item 8853.

64. Mouzon to AFS, July 7, 1930, Mouzon Papers, item 18,182 (carbon copy).

65. AFS to Mouzon, July 13, 1930, Mouzon Papers, item 8020.

66. Mouzon to AFS, July 17, 1930, Mouzon Papers, item 8020 (carbon copy).

67. Mouzon to AFS, October 8, 1930, Mouzon Papers, item 8852 (carbon copy).

68. AFS to Mouzon October 12, 1930, Mouzon Papers, item 8853.

69. Interview with Bishop Arthur Moore. The full schedule is given in the May 6, 1932, issue of the *Nashville Christian Advocate*, p. 593.

70. "The Meeting of the Bishops," *Nashville Christian Advocate*, May 13, 1932, p. 627.

71. Interview with Bishop W. Angie Smith. The meeting was held December 16-18, 1932.

72. Arthur J. Moore, *Bishop to All Peoples* (Nashville: Abingdon Press, 1973), p. 65.

73. Interview with Bishop W. Angie Smith.

74. *Richmond Christian Advocate*, January 28, 1932.

75. *Nashville Christian Advocate*, April 8, 1932, p. 472. The six were the St. Joseph, the Richmond, the Chillicothe, the Hannibal, the Fayette, and the Mexico Districts.

76. Ibid., April 22, 1932, p. 534. At least he was scheduled to do so.

77. *Journal of the General Conference*, 1934, p. 499.

78. *Central Christian Advocate*, January 14, 1932, p. 30. The Northern Methodists were publishing their *Adovcates* at the respective printing plants of the Methodist Book Concern. Thus the *Central* was edited in Kansas City, Missouri, but printed in Chicago.

79. Interview with Bishop William C. Martin, January 22, 1973, in Little Rock, Arkansas.

80. *Journal of the One Hundred-Seventeenth Session of the Missouri Annual Conference of the Methodist Episcopal Church, South, Held at Hannibal, Missouri, August 30-September 3, 1933*, p. 31.

81. Score, "Bishop A. Frank Smith," p. 23.

82. Ibid., p. 24.

CHAPTER TEN

1. Robert Watson Sledge, *Hands on the Ark: The Struggle for Change in the*

Methodist Episcopal Church, South, 1914-1939 (Lake Junaluska: Commission on Archives and History of the United Methodist Church, 1975).

2. A favorite analogy of the defenders. *Daily Christian Advocate* 22, no. 2 (April 27, 1934): 18. The text of the Episcopal Address can also be found in the *Journal of the Twenty-Second General Conference of the Methodist Episcopal Church, South, Held at Jackson, Mississippi, April 26-May 8, 1934* (Nashville: Whitmore & Smith, 1934), pp. 359ff.

3. AFS to Moore, June 8, 1934, John M. Moore Papers, item M 712, Bridwell Library, SMU, Dallas, Texas.

4. AFS to Mouzon, September 7, 1922, Edwin D. Mouzon Papers, item 6064, Bridwell Library, SMU, Dallas, Texas. Italics added.

5. *Journal of the General Conference*, 1934, p. 191. "Memorials" is the Methodist term for petitions sent to the General Conference by individuals or organizations. The legislative committees of the General Conference report on each memorial received, individually or collectively, with the recommendation of "concurrence" or "non-concurrence."

6. *Daily Christian Advocate*, 22 (April 27, 1934): 69-75.

7. Interview with Bishop Arthur J. Moore, "Epworth-by-the-Sea," St. Simon Island, Georgia, January 20, 1972.

8. This conversation was reported to the author by Dr. L. U. Spellman, letter dated January 11, 1971. Spellman and Dr. S. L. Batchelor, clerical delegates to the 1934 General Conference and longtime friends of AFS, Moore, and Kern, were with the three bishops during this discussion.

9. As stated in the official language of the *Journal*: ". . . with a *maximum* allowance of $1,500 per year for house rent *and* clerical help and $500 per year for traveling expenses." *Journal of the General Conference*, 1930, p. 222. Italics added.

10. Arthur J. Moore, *Bishop to All Peoples* (Nashville: Abingdon Press, 1973), pp. 65-66.

11. Interview with Bishop Moore. See also *Bishop to All Peoples*, p. 64.

12. *Daily Christian Advocate* 22 (April 27, 1934): 69ff; *Journal of the General Conference*, 1934, pp. 183ff. The *Daily Advocates* give the full word-for-word debate.

13. *Daily Christian Advocate* 22 (April 27, 1934): 70.

14. See above, pp. 198-99.

15. *Daily Christian Advocate* 22 (April 27, 1934): 71.

16. Ibid., p. 70.

17. Ibid., p. 74. On the 1844 Division of Methodism, see *The History of American Methodism*, ed. Emory S. Bucke, 3 vols. (Nashville: Abingdon Press, 1964), 2:47-85.

18. Ibid., p. 75. Italics added.

19. Ibid.; or *Journal of the General Conference*, 134, p. 191.

20. *Journal of the General Conference*, 1934, p. 193.

21. Ibid., p. 298.

22. Ibid., p. 155.

23. Ibid., pp. 25-36.

24. Ibid., p. 231. Since 1792 the bishops' freedom to appoint presiding elders had been limited only as follows: "A bishop may not allow an elder to preside *in the same district* for a term exceeding four years successively." Ibid., p. 307. Italics added.

25. Sledge, *Hands on the Ark*, pp. 189, 194.

26. Interview with Bishop William C. Martin, January 22, 1973, in Little Rock, Arkansas. Having been elected in 1938, Bishop Martin had a unique opportunity to observe these developments.

27. *Journal of the General Conference*, 1934, pp. 221-22. See also *Daily Christian Advocate* 22 (April 27, 1934): 86.

28. AFS to "Rev. W. C. Martin, D.D.," May 16, 1934. William C. Martin Papers, Bridwell Library, SMU. Just twenty years before, in 1914, Smith had joined the North Texas Conference on trial.

29. Walter N. Vernon, *Methodism Moves across North Texas* (Dallas: Historical Society of the North Texas Conference, 1967), p. 270.

30. Ibid., pp. 270-76. For Bishop Boaz's interpretation see Boaz, *Eighty-Four Golden Years*, p. 193.

31. Vernon, *Methodism Moves across North Texas*, p. 318.

32. Quoted in ibid., p. 275.

33. Interview with Bishop William C. Martin.

34. See chap. 9.

35. The Smiths lived about two years each at 1514 West Alabama and 104 Avondale. Interview with A. Frank Smith, Jr. and W. Randolph Smith, August 29, 1972, in Houston, Texas.

36. An announcement in the *Nashville Christian Advocate*, October 10, 1930, stated that Bishop H. A. Boaz was moving to Houston, Texas, and would live at 2308 Southmore. "Personal" column, p. 6.

37. AFS to Mouzon, July 6, 1934, Mouzon Papers, item 14,381.

38. *Journal of the General Conference*, 1934, p. 278.

39. Ibid., p. 345.

40. Interview with Bishop Arthur J. Moore.

41. AFS to Rev. W. C. Martin, November 20, 1935, Martin Papers. See below, n. 83.

42. Minutes of the Meeting of the College of Bishops, May 1-2, 1936, Nashville, Tennessee, p. 4, John M. Moore Papers. Bishop Moore was secretary of the council.

43. Ibid., p. 5. See Moore, *Bishop to All Peoples*, p. 76.

44. Interview with Bishop Arthur J. Moore.

45. Ibid. See "Elmer T. Clark Memorial Edition" of *Methodist History* 9, no. 5 (1971), ed. Walter N. Vernon; and Bishop Nolan B. Harmon's sketch of Clark in *The Encyclopedia of World Methodism*, s.v. "Clark, Elmer T."

46. A brief history of the Bishops' Crusade, probably written by Dr. Clark, was published in the *Bishops' Crusade Pastor's Manual* (Nashville: The Bishops' Crusade, n.d.), pp. 4-5, Smith Papers.

47. Elmer T. Clark, "The Bishops' Crusade: 1937-38," *World Outlook* 26, no. 12 (December 1936): 447.

48. "The General Missionary Council in Historic Old New Orleans," ibid., pp. 448-49. The General Missionary Council was an annual meeting for information and inspiration, the first having been held in 1929 at Memphis.

49. *World Outlook* 26, no. 12 (December 1936): 462.

50. Interview with Bishop Arthur J. Moore. A large poster entitled "The Bishops' Crusade" contained the day by day schedule of both teams, including the full list of speakers at each of the forty-four rallies. Smith Papers.

51. Interview with Bishop Arthur J. Moore.

52. "Death of Dr. John R. Allen," *Southwestern Advocate*, February 11, 1937. Dr. Allen was eighty-five years old.

53. "John Robert Allen, D.D.—An Appreciation," *Southwestern Advocate*, June 24, 1937, pp. 12-13.

54. "Bishop E. D. Mouzon—An Appreciation," *Southwestern Advocate*, May 13, 1937, p. 13. A "working draft" of this article is in the Smith Papers.

55. *Bishops' Crusade Pastor's Manual*, pp. 10-12, 17. See Elmer T. Clark, *Arthur James Moore: World Evangelist* (New York: Board of Missions of The Methodist Church, 1960), p. 19.

56. "Minutes of the Ninety-First Annual Meeting of the Board of Missions . . .," *Missionary Yearbook of the Methodist Episcopal Church, South*, 1937, p. 135.

57. "We Finish But to Begin," *Nashville Christian Advocate*, May 14, 1937, pp. 612-13. See Bishop John M. Moore's report on the College of Bishops Meeting in the same issue, pp. 613-14.

58. AFS to Score, May 20, 1937, Papers of Dr. J. N. R. Score, Bridwell Library, SMU.

59. AFS to Score, August 21, 1937, Score Papers.

60. *Official Journal of the Seventy-Ninth Annual Session of the West Texas Conference of the Methodist Episcopal Church, South, Held at Travis Park Methodist Church, San Antonio, Texas, October 20-24, 1937*, pp. 30, 58-59.

61. See AFS's report in the *Nashville Christian Advocate*, January 7, 1938, p. 24.

62. Ibid.

63. AFS, "Aldersgate News," *Nashville Christian Advocate*, January 7, 1939, p. 24.

64. Ibid.

65. Quoted in the *Nashville Christian Advocate*, February 11, 1938, p. 187.

66. Ibid.

67. A partial schedule was published in the *Nashville Christian Advocate*, February 18, 1938, p. 213.

68. *Nashville Christian Advocate*, January 7, 1938, p. 24.

69. AFS to Martin, August 6, 1937, Bishop William C. Martin Papers.

70. John Wesley served one year and nine months—February 6, 1736 to December 2, 1737—in colonial Georgia as a missioner of the Society for the Propagation of the Gospel. *The Journal of the Rev. John Wesley*, ed. Nehemiah Curnock, 8 vols. (London: Epworth Press, 1909, 1938), 1:146-400.

71. "Wesley's Warm Heart and Savannah," *Nashville Christian Advocate*, December 17, 1937, p. 1614.

72. Quotations are from ibid., pp. 14-15. The other information is taken from the official program brochure, "Aldersgate in Savannah," Smith Papers.

73. All of the addresses were published under the title *What Happened at Aldersgate*, ed. Elmer T. Clark (Nashville: Methodist Publishing House, 1938). The quotation from AFS's address is taken from p. 211.

74. "An Address to the Church," *Nashville Christian Advocate*, February 4, 1938, p. 132.

75. *Birmingham News-Age Herald*, January 30, 1938, p. 10; Minutes of the College of Bishops, Memphis, Tennessee, March 31, 1938, John M. Moore Papers.

76. Program for the Aldersgate Commemoration Session of General Conference of the Methodist Episcopal Church, South, Municipal Auditorium, Birmingham, Alabama, Sunday, May 1, 1938, Smith Papers. See also the day-by-day summary of the General Conference in the *Nashville Christian Advocate*, May 6, 1938, p. 582.

77. *Nashville Christian Advocate*, May 20, 1938, p. 644.

78. "On to Aldersgate," ibid.

79. G. M. Gibson, "The Conduct of Public Worship," *Southwestern Christian Advocate*, January 28, 1932, p. 7.

80. Sledge, *Hands on the Ark*, p. 213. The Course of Study was the list of required reading for ministers seeking membership in an annual conference and ordination.

81. "Program for Aldersgate Week, May 22-29, 1938," as published in the *Nashville Christian Advocate*, April 8, 1938, p. 426.

82. The entire passage is: "In the evening I went very unwillingly to a society in Aldersgate Street, where one was reading Luther's preface to the *Epistle to the Romans*. About a quarter before nine, while he was describing the change which God works in the heart through faith in Christ, I felt my heart strangely warmed. I felt I did trust in Christ, Christ alone for salvation; and an assurance was given me that He had taken away *my* sins, even *mine*, and saved *me* from the law of sin and death." *The Journal of the Rev. John Wesley*, 1:475-76.

83. McCutcheon, "American Methodist Thought and Theology: 1919-1960," chap. 30 in *The History of American Methodism*, 3:291.

84. See chap. 2.

85. *John Wesley and Modern Religion* (Nashville: Cokesbury Press, 1936), pp. 250ff.

86. *Nashville Christian Advocate*, April 8, 1938, p. 426.

87. Ibid.

88. Interview with Bishop Arthur J. Moore.

CHAPTER ELEVEN

1. Braden interview.

2. In 1844 the Methodist Episcopal Church divided over questions related to slavery and polity. Earlier, in 1830, the Methodist Protestant Church had organized because of dissatisfaction with the episcopacy and lack of lay representation in the Methodist Episcopal Church. See *The History of American Methodism*, ed. Emory S. Bucke, 3 vols. (Nashville: Abingdon Press, 1964), vol. 1, chap. 13, and vol. 2, chap. 14.

3. AFS to Mouzon, May 14, 1924, Bishop Edwin D. Mouzon Papers, item 7793, Bridwell Library, Southern Methodist University, Dallas, Texas. Mouzon was then cochairman of the Joint Commission that had prepared the plan presented to the General Conference of the northern church meeting at Springfield, Massachusetts, in May, 1924.

4. Robert W. Sledge, *Hands on the Ark: The Struggle for Change in the Methodist Episcopal Church, South, 1914-1939* (Lake Junaluska: Commission on Archives and History, The United Methodist Church, 1975), p. 102. See also John M. Moore, *The Long Road to Methodist Union* (Nashville: Abingdon-Cokesbury Press, 1943), p. 178.

5. Mouzon to AFS, April 27, 1925, Smith Papers.

6. AFS to Mouzon, June 13, 1925, Mouzon Papers, item 16,262. R. W. Adams was the chairman of the Texas Conference "Friends of Unification," according to a list in Bishop Mouzon's papers, see item 17,082 (updated).

7. Charles C. Selecman, "Who's Who in Unification," *Texas Christian Advocate*, April 2, 1925, pp. 6, 10. See also typewritten copy in Mouzon Papers, item 17,096 (undated).

8. Typewritten minutes of the meetings of December 16 and 18, 1925, in Mouzon Papers, items 17,147 and 17,076. See also Selecman's "Who's Who in Unification."

9. Moore, *The Long Road to Methodist Union*, p. 179.

10. Report of a conversation between Bishop Mouzon and his daughter, Julia Mouzon (Mrs. J. Richard) Spann, May 19, 1931, in the Spanns' parsonage in Abilene, Texas. Mouzon Papers, item 18,481.

11. Moore, *The Long Road to Methodist Union*, p. 179.

12. Sledge, *Hands on the Ark*, p. 227.

13. *Daily Christian Advocate* (1930), p. 131.

14. The names of the members of the Joint Commission are given in the Preface of the 1935 edition of *The Methodist Hymnal*.

15. "The Joint Hymnal Commission," *Nashville Christian Advocate*, April 1, 1932, p. 439.

16. Braden interview. On the "Vanderbilt Row," see chap. 3, pp. 46-47, 55-56.

17. *Southwestern Christian Advocate*, October 12, 1933, p. 2.

18. Sledge, *Hands on the Ark*, p. 230.

19. *Proceedings of the Sixth Ecumenical Methodist Conference*, held in Wesley Memorial Church, Atlanta, Georgia, October 16-25, 1931 (Nashville: Publishing House of the Methodist Episcopal Church, South, n.d.), p. xv.

20. "World Methodist Conferences," *The Encyclopedia of World Methodism*, ed. Bishop Nolan B. Harmon, 2 vols. (New York: The United Methodist Publishing House, 1974), 1:2600-2601. The name of the conference was changed in 1951.

21. Andrew Jackson Weeks, in the "Introduction" to the *Proceedings*, of which he was a joint editor, pp. ix-x. See also *Texas Christian Advocate*, November 19, 1931, pp. 2, 7.

22. Frederick E. Maser, "Forces Making for Union," *History of American Methodism*, 3:438-52.

23. Braden interview.

24. Sledge, *Hands on the Ark*, p. 236.

25. *Southwestern Christian Advocate*, December 12, 1936, p. 4.

26. Ellison to Moore, January 14, 1938, Moore Papers, item M 877.

27. Cannon to Moore, Moore Papers. For the story of Ahitophel, counselor to King David, see II Samuel 15:12–17:23.

28. Denny to AFS, Smith Papers.

29. Sledge, *Hands on the Ark*, p. 236.

30. Ellison to Moore, February 5, 1938, Moore Papers, item M 877.

31. J. Manning Potts, "Collins Denny," *Encyclopedia of World Methodism*, 1:658-59. "His legal training remained with him throughout life and determined many of his attitudes."

32. Ellison to Moore, January 14, 1938, Moore Papers, item M 877.

33. Ellison to Moore, February 5, 1938, Moore Papers, item M 877. As Bishop Moore wrote, "Every motion made relating to adoption, and every authoritative statement and motion by the College of Bishops, was first carefully scrutinized by this committee of lawyers." *The Long Road to Methodist Union*, p. 200.

34. AFS to Leete, undated except for the word "Saturday." Bishop Leete Collection, Bridwell Library, SMU. As bishop of the Atlanta Area of the Methodist Episcopal Church, 1912-1920, and as a member of the M. E. Church Commission, Leete was particularly interested in the progress of unification. AFS and Leete had become acquainted on the Joint Hymnal Commission.

35. This is not to say that the opponents failed to put up a strong attack. Any reader of the account of the lengthy debates reported in the *Daily Christian Advocate* must sense the serious drama and tension of that critical moment. Only much later did it become clear that the dire predictions of mass exit from the Southern Church were vastly overstated. *The Daily Christian Advocate of the General Conference of the Methodist Episcopal Church, South, Birmingham, Alabama, April 28-May 5, 1938* 23, no. 3 (April 30): 3-23; no. 4 (May 2): 61-64.

36. *Daily Christian Advocate*, 1938, p. 64. After Bishop Mouzon's death, the commission had elected Bishop John M. Moore to be its chairman. Moore was also now the "Senior Bishop."

37. Ibid.

38. The voting and the appeal to the Judicial Council took place late Friday afternoon, April 29, so that the "five days" include the two-day weekend.

39. *Daily Christian Advocate*, 1938, p. 176. The account of the proceedings of Wednesday, May 4, are given on p. 136, but the text of the decision is presented on pp. 172-77.

40. Conversation between the author and Dr. L. U. Spellman, who led the West Texas Conference delegation in 1938, at Kerrville, Texas, April 4, 1975.

41. Paragraph 43: ". . . the Bishops shall announce that such rule or regulation takes effect from that time." *The Doctrines and Discipline of the Methodist Episcopal Church, South, 1934* (Nashville: Whitmore & Smith, 1934), pp. 32-33.

42. *Daily Christian Advocate*, 1938, pp. 138-39.

43. Program for "Methodist Banquet," November 29, 1938, Smith Papers. Bishop Darlington gave the "Welcome to the South" for his part on the program.

44. "Unification Session, the General Missionary Council of the Methodist Epis-

copal Church, South, Travis Park Methodist Church, San Antonio, Texas, January 3-6, 1939," Smith Papers.

45. *Missionary Yearbook of the Methodist Episcopal Church, South: 1939* (Nashville: Board of Missions of the Methodist Episcopal Church, South, 1939), p. 175.

46. *Daily Christian Advocate,* 1938, pp. 156-57. Smith's close friend, Bishop Sam R. Hay, was chairman of the nominating committee.

Ivan Lee Holt had been a member of the original commission as a clergy representative. Following his election to the episcopacy, another minister was elected to take that place on the commission.

47. "Procedure—Uniting Conference," from the Plan of Union as published in the *Journal of the General Conference, 1938,* pp. 296-97.

The time and place of this Uniting Conference were determined by the bishops and a Joint Commission on Entertainment.

48. "Preparatory Committees Appointed by the Joint Commission," appended to the *Prospectus of the Discipline of The Methodist Church* (Printed for the Joint Commission under the Supervision of the Publishing Agents of the Uniting Churches, 1939), p. 338.

49. AFS to Leete, August 9, 1938, Bishop Leete Collection, Bridwell Library, SMU.

50. AFS to Leete, August 20, 1938, Bishop Leete Collection.

51. *The Long Road to Methodist Union,* p. 209. See also the accounts in the statement by the three chairmen of the Joint Commission in the *Prospectus,* p. 11; and the "Minutes of the Joint Commission on Methodist Union, Meeting at Jackson, Mississippi, Hotel Heidelberg," January 24-29, 1939 (mimeographed document), Moore Papers.

52. AFS to Leete, "Friday" (and obviously during March, 1939, from the context). Bishop Leete Collection.

53. Although the newspapers say "sixty bishops," the *Journal* of the Uniting Conference lists the names of the fifty-two active and retired bishops present. *Journal of the Uniting Conference of the Methodist Episcopal Church, Methodist Episcopal Church, South, Methodist Protestant Church, Held at Kansas City, Missouri, April 26– May 10 1939* (Nashville: Methodist Publishing House, 1939), pp. 167-70.

54. *Kansas City Star,* Wednesday, April 26, 1939, p. 8, Smith Papers.

55. *Kansas City Journal,* Wednesday, April 26, 1939, p. 16, Smith Papers.

56. "Procedure—Uniting Conference," Article IV, *Journal of the Uniting Conference,* p. 9.

57. *Prospectus,* pp. 101-34.

58. Braden interview.

59. Ibid.

60. Interview with Bishop Arthur J. Moore, January 21, 1972, St. Simon Island, Georgia. See also letters from Jesse H. Jones to AFS, dated November 26, 1940, June 3, 1941, and June 28, 1941; and AFS's letter to "Dearest Bessie," written the day of his visit with Jones in Washington, D.C. (holograph, undated, but probably November 30, 1940), Smith Papers.

61. Interview with Bishop Moore.

62. "The delegates of the Methodist Protestant Church in the Uniting Conference shall . . . elect to the office of Bishop two ministers of their Church who, upon ordination or consecration at the Uniting Conference by the Bishops of the other two Churches, shall become effective Bishops of The Methodist Church." The Plan of Union, *Journal of the Uniting Conference,* pp. 30-31. James H. Straughn and John C. Broomfield were the two so elected.

63. Ibid., p. 30.

64. *The Organization of the Methodist Church,* rev. ed. (Nashville: Methodist Publishing House, 1953), p. 74.

As Harmon explains, the new episcopacy of the Methodist church was "a greatly modified episcopacy . . . a jurisdictionally determined episcopacy. . . . Formerly [a bishop] was a general officer of a connectional church, . . . But the jurisdictional division of the church took the election of bishops out of the hands of the General Conference and placed such elections in the Jurisdictional Conferences and these alone, and so arranged it that bishops today are to serve each within his own jurisdictional area and in that only [with carefully prescribed exceptions]." Ibid., pp. 69-73.

65. "The Council of Bishops," *Southwestern Advocate*, May 2, 1940, pp. 3-4.

66. Interview with Bishop Moore.

67. Interview with Bishop Martin, January 22, 1973, Little Rock, Arkansas. Martin was elected to the southern episcopacy in 1938.

68. *Doctrines and Discipline of The Methodist Church, 1939* (Nashville: Methodist Publishing House, 1939), pp. 2, 737. Bishop H. Lester Smith was elected secretary for that interim. This edition of the *Discipline* also lists an "Executive Committee" of the Council of Bishops composed of "the officers with Bishop A. Frank Smith and Bishop Francis J. McConnell," p. 737. See also Minutes of the Council of Bishops, April 25–May 11, 1939, Kansas City, Missouri: on May 6 Bishop Leonard moved that the two Senior Bishops be co-chairmen of the Council and alternate in presiding. Moore Papers.

69. On Monday morning, May 6, according to the Minutes of the Council of Bishops of The Methodist Church, Atlantic City, New Jersey, April 18–May 6, 1940, p. 42, Moore Papers.

The Minutes use the term "Chairman." Bishop E. G. Richardson was elected "Vice-Chairman." The announcement in the *Daily Christian Advocate of the First General Conference of The Methodist Church*, issued for May 7, 1940, p. 484, also says "Chairman" and "Vice-Chairman." Thereafter, beginning with the next meeting of the Council of Bishops (July 22, 1940), the Minutes use "President," as do the 1940 *Discipline* (pp. 2, 835) and the *Journal of the First General Conference of The Methodist Church, Held at Atlantic City, New Jersey, April 24–May 6, 1940* (Nashville: Methodist Publishing House, 1940), p. 20.

70. Braden interview.

Bishop Richardson was elected on December 11, 1941, to succeed AFS as president of the council "for the coming year." Minutes of the Council of Bishops of The Methodist Church, Sea Island, Georgia, December 9-12, 1941, Moore Papers.

According to Bishop Arthur Moore, the bishops have never set a one-year limit by formal action, but the precedent is firmly established. "The Bishops are stoutly opposed to any one man being a short of archbishop." Interview with Bishop Moore.

The office of secretary of the Council of Bishops was an obvious exception to this limitation of term of office. Bishop Oxnam served as secretary for many years.

71. Braden interview.

72. Ibid.

73. There were thirty bishops from the Methodist Episcopal Church, seventeen active and thirteen retired; nineteen from the M. E. Church, South, twelve active and seven retired; two M. E. Missionary Bishops; six M. E. Central Conference Bishops, five active and one retired; two from the Methodist Protestant Church; and three elected in 1940—making a total of sixty-two, forty-one active and twenty-one retired, as listed in the 1940 *Discipline*, pp. 833-34.

74. Interview with Bishop Moore.

75. The Plan of Union, *Journal of the Uniting Conference*, p. 31.

76. Ibid., pp. 25, 30.

77. *Journal of the Uniting Conference*, pp. 205-12.

78. Dr. Willard G. Cram was a member of the Joint Commission on Unification, a delegate from the Kentucky Conference, and the executive secretary of the General Board of Missions of the Methodist Episcopal Church, South. *Journal of the Uniting Conference*, pp. 48, 241-42.

79. Ibid., pp. 279-80, 819-30.

80. Ibid., pp. 297-98, 497.

81. Dispatch from H. Lee Millis, editor of the *Post*, dated "Kansas City, May 5," as printed in the *Houston Post*, newspaper clipping in Smith Papers.

82. *Journal of the Uniting Conference*, p. 326.

83. *Daily Christian Advocate of the Uniting Conference*, Thursday, May 11, 1939, p. 477.

84. "The Fifth Episcopal District: Louisiana, Texas, West Texas, Texas Mexican, Indian Mission," *The Daily Christian Advocate of the General Conference of the Methodist Episcopal Church, South, Held at Birmingham, Alabama, April 28–May 5, 1938* (May 6, 1938), p. 154.

85. "Report on Boundaries: The South Central Jurisdiction," *Journal of the Uniting Conference*, pp. 863-67.

86. *Houston Post*, May 13, 1939 (clipping identified in AFS's handwriting), Smith Papers.

H. Lee Millis wrote this editorial, presumably after he had returned from Kansas City, where he had been observing the Uniting Conference. Millis and Smith had been friends since their student days at Southwestern University.

87. "Procedure—Uniting Conference," *Journal of the Uniting Conference*, p. 9. The fifth task, the only one in which AFS was not closely involved, concerned the harmonizing of the Rituals of the three churches.

88. Braden interview.

89. Mrs. John H. Warnick, "John Monroe Moore," *Encyclopedia of World Methodism*, 2:1665-66.

90. "United Methodism Gathers Tonight to Honor Bishop Moore, Man Who Healed Rift in Church," *Dallas Morning News*, Wednesday, October 25, 1939; "Methodists Loose Mighty Ovation in Honor of Man Who United Them," *Dallas Morning News*, Thursday, October 26, 1939, p. 1.

Moore had been pastor of First Church, Dallas, 1902-1906, bishop of the North Texas Conference, 1922-1926, and a trustee of Southern Methodist University since 1922, serving as chairman of the board from 1932 to 1938.

91. AFS to Dr. Harry S. DeVore (Program Chairman), October 22, 1939, Moore Papers, item M 1069.

92. AFS to Moore, June 12, 1938, Moore Papers, item M 964.

Although Bishop Moore officially retired in 1938, he continued his work as cochairman of the Joint Commission on Unification at the request of the General Conference.

CHAPTER TWELVE

1. Braden interview.

2. Committee on Missions Report No. 5, *Daily Advocate of the Uniting Conference . . . Kansas City, Missouri, April 26-May 10, 1939*, p. 351.

3. *Prospectus of The Discipline of The Methodist Church, Submitted to the Uniting Conference by the Joint Commission on Unification, 1939*, pp. 135-67.

4. Ibid., pp. 178-208.

5. Ibid., pp. 208-16.

In his autobiography, Bishop Arthur J. Moore, who was then president of the Board of Missions of the Methodist Episcopal Church, South, explains the "politics" of how these three plans came to be presented to the Uniting Conference. *Bishop to All Peoples* (Nashville: Abingdon Press, 1973), pp. 93ff. See interview with Bishop Moore, January 22, 1972, St. Simon Island, Georgia.

6. In accord with the Joint Commission's "Plan of Organization" for the Uniting Conference, all legislation was channeled through eight "General Standing Committees." *Prospectus*, p. 13.

7. *Daily Christian Advocate of the Uniting Conference, 1939*, pp. 399, 401.

8. *Bishop to All Peoples*, p. 94.

9. *Journal of the Uniting Conference, 1939*, p. 810.

10. Braden interview.

11. *Journal of the Uniting Conference, 1939*, pp. 564-65; *Journal of the First General Conference of The Methodist Church, Held at Atlantic City, New Jersey, April 24-May 6, 1940* (Nashville: Methodist Publishing House, 1940), p. 613.

12. Ibid.

13. Ibid., pp. 559 and 606, respectively.

14. *Journal of the First General Conference, 1940*, pp. 709-10. "Bishop A. Frank Smith, Chairman of the Committee, being granted the privileges of the floor, spoke to the Report," p. 226.

15. *Doctrines and Disciplines of The Methodist Church, 1940* (Nashville: Methodist Publishing House, 1940), pp. 290-91 (par. 917).

16. *Journal of the First Quadrennial Meeting for Organization of the Board of Missions and Church Extension of The Methodist Church, Chicago, Illinois, July 23-25, 1940* (New York: The Board of Missions and Church Extension of The Methodist Church, 1940), pp. 9-11 (hereafter cited as *Journal of Board of Missions*).

17. Ibid., p. 23.

18. Interview with Bishop Moore.

19. *Journal of Board of Missions*, 1940, p. 29.

20. Ibid., pp. 227-28. See also *1940 Discipline*, p. 305, par. 955.

21. *1940 Discipline*, p. 306, par. 958.

22. W. Richey Hogg, "The Missions of American Methodism," *History of American Methodism*, ed. Emory S. Bucke, 3 vols. (Nashville: Abingdon Press, 1964), 3:114. Of these, 3,440 were formerly supported by the M. E. Church; 2,137 by the M. E. Church, South; and 15 by the Methodist Protestants. Ibid., pp. 126-27.

23. *Journal of Board of Missions*, 1940, pp. 227, 232.

24. Interview with Dr. Bonneau P. Murphy, February 16, 1973, Dallas, Texas. Murphy, a native Texan, member of the Texas Conference, graduate of SMU and Yale (B.D. and Ph.D.) was pastor of Houston's West University Place Methodist Church. Assigned to the Louisville office of the Section of Church Extension in 1941, he became the head of that office in 1952. When the Louisville and the Philadelphia offices were finally combined in 1956, Dr. Murphy became the first executive secretary of the Section of Church Extension, serving in that position until his retirement in 1972.

25. *Journal of Board of Missions*, p. 239.

26. Interview with Bishop Moore.

27. *The Encyclopedia of World Methodism*, s.v. "Kohlstedt, Edward D."

28. Ibid., s.v. "Ellis, Thomas David."

29. Interview with Bishop Moore.

30. *Journal of the Twenty-First General Conference of the Methodist Episcopal Church, South, Held at Dallas, Texas, May 7-24, 1930* (Nashville: Lamar & Whitmore, 1930), pp. 213, 217, 222, 225, 227. See chap. 9, pp. 179-81.

31. Interview with Bishop Moore. Moore was elected on the third ballot in that same election.

32. Braden interview.

33. Interview with Dr. Murphy

34. Interview with Bishop Moore.

35. Interview with Dr. Murphy.

36. *Journal of the Seventeenth Annual Meeting of the Board of Missions of The Methodist Church, January 8-18, 1957 . . . Including the Organization Meeting, September 13-18, 1956*, p. 37. The words "and Church Extension" were dropped in 1956.

37. *Journal of the Fifth Annual Meeting of the Board of Missions and Church*

Extension, November 29–December 8, 1944, Including the Special Meetings for Organization, July 25-26, 1944, p. 256.

38. Interview with Dr. Murphy.

39. *Journal of the Eighteenth Annual Meeting of the Board of Missions of The Methodist Church, January 7-17, 1958*, p. 180.

40. *Journal of the Sixteenth Annual Meeting of the Board of Missions of The Methodist Church, January 10-20, 1956*, p. 210.

41. *Journal of the Board of Missions, 1948*, p. 45.

42. Interview with Bishop Moore.

For the period 1942-49, AFS's daily journal is a valuable source of information.

43. *Journal of the Board of Missions, 1956*, p. 191.

44. Interview with Dr. Murphy.

45. Ibid.

46. Bishop Oxnam to AFS, September 5, 1944, Smith Papers.

47. AFS's daily journal records several serious business matters such as the Rollins & Sons suit, entries for December 4, 1943; February 18, March 15 and 16, 1944.

48. "Daily Journal of the Organizational Meeting of the Board of Missions. . . ., September 13-15, 1956," as published in the *Journal of the Board of Missions, 1957*, p. 28.

49. *Journal of the Board of Missions, 1957*, p. 267.

50. *Annual Report of the Division of National Missions, 1960*, p. 16.

51. AFS to Murphy, October 31, 1959 (photocopy in the author's files, courtesy of Dr. Murphy).

52. Interview with Dr. Murphy.

53. Interview with Bishop Moore.

54. AFS to Nañez, August 6, 1944. Alfredo Nañez Papers, Bridwell Library, SMU, Dallas, Texas.

55. "Daily Journal of the Organizational Meeting," LaSalle Hotel, Chicago, Illinois, July 25-26, 1944; as published in the *Journal of the Fifth Annual Meeting of the Board of Missions and Church Extension of The Methodist Church, November 29–December 8, 1944*, p. 257.

56. Previously, Dr. Brown had been the superintendent of the Canton and Cleveland Districts, and pastor of First Church, Akron. *Who's Who in Methodism*, ed. Elmer T. Clark (Chicago: A. N. Marquis Company, 1952), p. 90.

Regrettably, Dr. Brown was not given deserved recognition in the *Encyclopedia of World Methodism*.

57. Superintendent of the Beaumont District in the Texas Conference at the time of his election, Lokey had a Ph.D. degree in Rural Sociology from Texas A&M. *Who's Who in Methodism*, 1952 ed., p. 425.

58. "Daily Journal" of the December (annual) meeting, *Journal of the Board of Missions and Church Extension, 1944*, pp. 33-34, 252. Cropper died early in 1949, and Murphy became the top executive in the Louisville office. *Journal of the Board of Missions and Church Extension, 1949*, pp. 40, 365, 366.

59. Interview with Bishop Arthur Moore.

60. Letter to the author from Dr. Earl Kent Brown, son of Dr. Brown and professor at Boston University School of Theology, June 3, 1975. See also Dr. Brown's letters to AFS: January 24, 1945; May 22, 1956; and February 2, 1957, Smith Papers.

61. *Journal of the Board of Missions, 1957*, pp. 266-67. See also AFS's tribute to Dr. Brown before the General Conference in 1956: *Daily Christian Advocate* 5, no. 11 (May 7, 1956): 566-67.

62. *Encyclopedia of World Methodism*, s.v. "Middleton, William Vernon."

63. AFS to Perkins (undated, but Mr. Perkins's reply is dated December 9, 1948). Smith Papers.

Dr. Lee, of course, was President Umphrey Lee of Southern Methodist University.

Perkins and Smith were longtime members of the SMU board, Smith serving as chairman since 1938. See also chap. 14.

Buck Hill Falls, in the Pocono Mountains of Pennsylvania, was the location of "The Inn," a Quaker-owned resort hotel, where the Board of Missions held its annual meetings in the "Off-season."

64. See chap. 2. Lois Craddock was an active member of the Volunteer Mission Band at Southwestern, according to the *Sou'wester* (1909), p. 177.

65. Interview with Mrs. Lois Craddock Perkins, Wichita Falls, Texas, June 26, 1972.

66. Braden interview.

67. Mrs. J. J. Perkins to AFS, July 29, 1949, Smith Papers. There are also letters from Bishop Ralph A. Ward, then Resident Bishop in Shanghai, to AFS, as well as letters (carbon copies) from Mr. Perkins to the president of General Motors Corporation, in the Smith Papers.

68. Interview with Dr. Murphy.

69. Ibid.

70. Ibid.

71. Ibid.

72. Ibid. See also *Journal of the Board of Missions, 1948*, p. 336. Cropper had succeeded T. D. Ellis in 1943 as the executive secretary in the Louisville office.

73. AFS to Murphy, July 17, 1948 (photocopy in the author's files, courtesy of Dr. Murphy).

74. Interview with Dr. Murphy.

75. Interview with Bishop Moore.

76. Moore to AFS, February 10, 1946, Smith Papers. Dr. Murphy remembers that AFS always presided in Moore's absence.

77. Interview with Bishop William C. Martin.

78. Oxnam to AFS, September 5, 1944, Smith Papers.

79. Interview with Dr. Murphy. For another example of AFS's "behind the scenes" activity, see his daily journal entry for July 24, 1944.

80. Interview with Dr. Murphy.

81. Bishop Oxnam to AFS, March 25, 1946, Smith Papers.

82. Interview with Dr. Murphy.

83. Oxnam to AFS, March 25, 1946, Smith Papers. AFS had previously defended his division successfully against an Oxnam tactic. See AFS's daily journal, July 26, 1944.

84. Interview with Dr. Murphy.

85. Interview with Bishop W. Angie Smith, January 12, 1972, Dallas, Texas.

86. This is a composite of two of the many versions of the story: interview with Bishop W. Angie Smith, August 1, 1973, and interview with Bishop O. Eugene Slater, August 8, 1972, in San Antonio, Texas.

87. Interview with Dr. D. Lawrence Landrum, January 17, 1973, Palestine, Texas.

88. Interview with Bishop W. Kenneth Pope, September 15, 1972, A. Frank Smith Hall, Perkins School of Theology, Southern Methodist University, Dallas, Texas.

89. Ibid. This might have occurred in 1950 when AFS was the preacher for the Hawaii Mission, which met in Honolulu, February 13-19, 1950. Official Program in Smith Papers.

90. See the report of the meeting of the Council of Bishops (November, 1952) in the *Texas Christian Advocate*, December 7, 1952, p. 1; and par. 20 of the 1952 *Discipline*.

91. Central Conferences for the church outside the U.S. were a kind of semi-autonomous general conference, electing their own bishops, planning and administering their own programs.

92. *Texas Christian Advocate*, February 27, 1953, p. 1. See also the issue for March 20, 1953, p. 1.

93. The formal detailed itinerary supplied by the travel agent is in the Smith Papers.

94. *Texas Christian Advocate*, April 10, 1953, p. 1.

95. AFS to Martin, July 22, 1953, Bishop William C. Martin Papers, Bridwell Library, SMU.

96. Braden interview with AFS and Mrs. Smith.

97. "Daily Journal" of the Special Meeting for Organization, July 25-26, 1944, *Journal of Board of Missions*, 1944, p. 256.

See also *Journals of Board of Missions*: 1948, p. 344; 1952, p. 48; 1956, p. 36. AFS's daily journal covers only two of these reelections: July 25, 1944, and December 4, 1948.

98. Interview with Bishop Moore. For a spontaneous expression of AFS's affection for Moore, see AFS's daily journal, June 15, 1942.

99. Ibid.

100. Interview with Dr. Murphy.

101. Ibid.

102. AFS's daily journal, February 18, 1944.

103 Interview with Bishop Moore.

104. Quoted by Mrs. J. Fount Tillman, president of the Woman's Division, in her tribute to AFS at the annual meeting of the board, January, 1960, Smith Papers.

105. Interview with Dr. Murphy.

106. "To the Managers of the Board of Missions of the Methodist Church," October 16, 1959, Bishop William C. Martin Papers.

107. AFS to Nañez, January 1, 1960, Alfredo Nañez Papers. This letter is typewritten.

108. AFS to Murphy, January 9, 1960 (holograph; photocopy in the author's files, courtesy of Dr. Murphy).

109. "Daily Journal" of the Division of National Missions, *Journal of the Board of Missions*, 1960, pp. 192-93.

Dr. Bonneau Murphy obtained the following items from this memorable occasion for the A. Frank Smith Papers: a copy of Dr. Gould's commentary; a copy of the printed program; and copies of the statements made by H. Conwell Snoke, Rev. Luis Gomez, Rev. Taro Goto, Mrs. J. Fount Tillman, and President McGinnis of Alaska Methodist University.

110. "Daily Journal" of the Division of National Missions, *Journal of the Board of Missions*, 1960, pp. 207-8.

111. AFS to Murphy, January 27, 1960 (photocopy in the author's files, courtesy of Dr. Murphy).

CHAPTER THIRTEEN

1. The Indian Mission Conference was originally organized in 1884 by Bishop Thomas A. Morris at Riley's Chapel near Tahlequah, Oklahoma, as authorized by the General Conference of 1884 of the Methodist Episcopal Church. "Bounded on the south by Texas, on the east by Arkansas and Missouri, on the north by the northern boundary of Montana, and on the west by the Rocky Mountains," the conference claimed "27 local preachers, 2,992 Indian members, 133 Negro members, and 85 white members." Of the Indians approximately 1,500 were Cherokee, 1,000 were Choctaw, and 500 were Creek. Methodist work among the "Five Civilized Tribes" (Cherokee, Chickasaw, Creek, Choctaw, and Seminole) had begun in the 1820s before these and the other tribes of the southeastern United States had been forced to migrate to the Oklahoma territory during the decade 1829-39.

With the opening of the Oklahoma territory to white settlers, the conference soon lost both its Indian and its mission character, and in 1906 it changed its name to the Oklahoma Conference. Only the reestablishing of the Indians into a separate conference of their own in 1918 prevented the disappearance of the Indian work. Sidney

H. Babcock and John Y. Bryce, *History of Methodism in Oklahoma: The Story of the Indian Mission Annual Conference of the Methodist Episcopal Church, South* (privately printed, 1935), pp. 11-49, 66, 69. See also *Encyclopedia of World Methodism*, s.v. "Indian Mission (Oklahoma)."

2. *Missionary Yearbook of the Methodist Episcopal Church, South*, 1931, pp. 394-95 (hereafter cited as *Missionary Yearbook* with respective dates).

3. Ibid., 1939, p. 318. By this time, the Cherokee membership had all but disappeared.

4. Ibid., 1931, p. 394.

5. This is a composite, taken from several of Witt's annual reports, as follows: *Missionary Yearbook* 1931, pp. 388-89; 1932, p. 421; 1936, p. 102; and 1939, p. 317. During the forced migration, "More than 2,000 of the Choctaws, and fully one-fourth of the Cherokees died. All of the tribes sustained heavy losses. . . . No more cruel injustice was ever experienced by an exiled people in the annals of history." Babcock and Bryce, *History of Methodism in Oklahoma*, p. 19.

6. *Missionary Yearbook*, 1935, p. 117. See also 1932, p. 420.

7. Ibid., 1932, pp. 420-21.

8. Ibid., 1936, p. 313. See also 1937, p. 325. For a variety of reasons, the Folsom Training School at Smithville, Oklahoma, was ineffective and too expensive.

9. Ibid., 1937, pp. 327-28.

10. "The Department of Theology . . . has changed its rules so that Indian ministers and ministerial students having a high school education may enter and pursue a special course in this department." *The Minutes of the Indian Mission of Oklahoma of The Methodist Church Held at Thlopthlocco Church, Creek Nation, near Okema, Oklahoma* (September 1939), p. 26.

11. *Missionary Yearbook*, 1939, pp. 320-23.

12. *Minutes of the Indian Mission of Oklahoma, Held at Seminole Hitchitee Church, Seminole Nation, near Seminole, Oklahoma (September 1938)*, p. 35.

13. Interview with Dr. Bonneau P. Murphy, February 16, 1973.

14. AFS to Witt, July 5, 1944 (photocopy in the author's files, courtesy of Dr. Walter N. Vernon, Sr). Smith customarily began each session of the Mission with an affectionate expression of appreciation for his long association with the Indian Mission. See also *Minutes of the Indian Mission*, 1939, p. 14; 1941, p. 15; 1942, p. 18.

15. Since the South Central Jurisdiction had not elected any bishops in 1940, Bishop Angie Smith was the first bishop elected by that jurisdiction. *Encyclopedia of World Methodism*, s.v. "Smith, William Angie."

16. AFS to Witt, July 5, 1944.

17. Interview with Bishop W. Angie Smith, Dallas, Texas, August 1, 1973.

18. See chap. 1, pp. 4-5.

19. As reported to the author by Dr. Walter N. Vernon, Sr., in a letter dated August 25, 1973.

20. "The longest service ever given by two brothers to any conference in that capacity," according to Leland Clegg and William B. Oden in their *Oklahoma Methodism in the Twentieth Century* (Nashville: Parthenon Press, 1968), p. 276.

21. As related to the author by Dr. Ted Richardson during a conversation at Mt. Wesley, Kerrville, Texas, August 14, 1975.

22. *Report of the Division of Home Missions and Church Extension of the Board of Missions and Church Extension of The Methodist Church*, 1945, pp. 29-30.

23. *Minutes of the Indian Mission of Oklahoma, The Methodist Church, Held at Salt Creek Church, near Holdenville, Oklahoma, September 10-12, 1943*, p. 45.

24. *Minutes of the Indian Mission of Oklahoma, The Methodist Church, Held at Salt Creek Church, near Holdenville, Oklahoma, September 14-17, 1944*, p. 50.

25. *History of American Methodism*, ed. Emory S. Bucke, 3 vols. (Nashville: Abingdon Press, 1964), 3:506. These figures are somewhat misleading since the

1940 amount does not include the giving of the Woman's Societies, whose funds were handled through their own organizations.

26. The distribution of the $25 million is given in the *Journal of the 1944 General Conference of The Methodist Church, Held at Kansas City, Missouri, April 26-May 6, 1944*, pp. 778-79.

27. *History of American Methodism*, 3:506, 520.

28. Interview with Dr. Murphy.

29. *Missionary Yearbook*, 1932, p. 421.

30. Ibid., 1937, pp. 323-24.

31. Interview with Dr. Murphy.

32. *Annual Report of the Division of National Missions, 1960*, p. 109. The name was changed from Home Missions and Church Extension to National Missions in 1956.

33. *Changing America: Annual Report of the Division of Home Missions and Church Extension, 1952*, p. 62.

34. *Annual Report of the Division of National Missions, 1960*, pp. 108-10. See also "The Indian Mission," chap. 11 in Leland Clegg and William B. Oden, *Oklahoma Methodism in the Twentieth Century* (Nashville: Parthenon Press, 1968), pp. 275-82.

35. Formerly part of the Mexican Border Mission Conference (1845), the Texas Mexican Mission was organized in November, 1914, in Austin, Texas, by Bishop W. R. Lambuth, for the Spanish-speaking work in Texas east of the Pecos River. It was reorganized as a regular conference in October, 1930, by Bishop Sam R. Hay. "Seccion Historica," *Actas Oficiales de la Conferencia Anual Rio Grande de la Iglesia Metodista Unida, Cuadragesima Primera Sesion, 5-9 Junio 1970*, pp. 104-6; and *Encyclopedia of World Methodism*, s.v. "Rio Grande Conference."

36. Interview with Dr. Alfredo Nañez, A. Frank Smith Hall, Perkins School of Theology, Southern Methodist University, Dallas, Texas, July 20, 1972.

37. *Missionary Yearbook*, 1939, pp. 333-34.

38. Ibid., 1939, pp. 334-35.

39. Interview with Dr. Nañez.

40. Ibid.

41. *Journal of the Uniting Conference of the Methodist Episcopal Church, Methodist Episcopal Church, South, Methodist Protestant Church . . ., 1939* (Nashville: Methodist Publishing House, 1939), p. 866.

42. AFS to Martin, July 3, 1939, Bishop William C. Martin Papers, Bridwell Library, SMU, Dallas, Texas.

43. *Encyclopedia of World Methodism*, s.v. "Rio Grande Conference."

44. Braden interview. According to Dr. Nañez, the strongest objection to the name came from the people of New Mexico, the majority of whom are natives. In Texas, the majority are sons of immigrants. Letter from Nañez to the author, September 3, 1975.

45. The Rio Grande Mission Conference, an English-speaking conference, was created by the 1858 General Conference (M.E., South) to include the territory in West and Southwest Texas. In 1866 it became the West Texas Conference. *Encyclopedia of World Methodism*, s.v. "Rio Grande Conference." Dr. Nañez credits Dr. R. F. Curl with suggesting this historic name for adoption by the South Central Jurisdictional Conference.

46. While Wesleyan Institute had only a Bible Department, Lydia Patterson Institute had a School of Theology that had been recognized by the church. Dr. Alfredo Nañez to the author, August, 1975. See also *Encyclopedia of World Methodism*, s.v. "Lydia Patterson Institute."

47. AFS to Dr. Alfredo Nañez, May 27, 1942, Alfredo Nañez Papers, Bridwell Library, SMU.

48. AFS to Dr. Alfredo Nañez, September 20, 1943, Nañez Papers.

49. AFS to Gonzalez, May 1, 1943, recorded by Dr. Charles Braden.

50. Interview with Dr. Nañez, July 20, 1972. See also *Encyclopedia of World Methodism*, s.v. "Benjamin Ogilvie Hill."

51. *Annual Report of the Division of Home Missions and Church Extension*, 1945, p. 44.

52. Bishop Eleazar Guerra to AFS, March 26, 1947, Smith Papers.

53. AFS to Nañez, January 26, 1953; AFS to Nañez, July 3, 1953, Nañez Papers.

54. Interview with Dr. Nañez.

55. Statistical Summary: The Rio Grande Conference, Nañez Papers.

56. Interview with Dr. Nañez.

57. Nañez to Murphy, April 14, 1971 (carbon copy), Nañez Papers.

58. See chap. 12.

59. Interview with Dr. Nañez.

60. Interview with Dr. Murphy.

61. AFS to Nañez, December 29, 1943, Nañez Papers (italics added).

62. *Annual Report of the Division of Home Missions and Church Extension*, 1948, pp. 52-53.

63. Ibid., p. 53. According to Dr. Nañez, credit for obtaining the gift from Miss Kelsey should go to Rev. B. Y. Dickinson, who had been her pastor in Rio Grande City. Nañez to author, September 3, 1975.

64. *Encyclopedia of World Methodism*, s.v. "Lydia Patterson Institute."

65. Since Lydia Patterson Institute was only a high school, it could no longer meet the requirement of two years of college set by the General Conference for entrance into schools of theology. Nañez to the author, August, 1975.

66. Interview with Dr. Murphy.

67. *Annual Report of the Division of National Missions*, 1956, p. 56. The trustees are now elected by the South Central Jurisdictional Conference, according to the *Encyclopedia of World Methodism*, s.v. "Lydia Patterson Institute."

68. *Annual Report of the Division of National Missions*, 1960, pp. 44-51. Dr. Donald E. Redmond was chairman of the Spanish-speaking Work Committee.

69. "Statistical Summary: The Rio Grande Conference," Nañez Papers.

70. *Texas Christian Advocate*, June 5, 1953, p. 1. The Mexican Methodists elect their bishops for four-year terms.

71. AFS to Rev. Frank Ramos, March 11, 1941, Nañez Papers.

72. AFS to Rev. Ben O. Hill, May 22, 1960, recorded by Dr. Charles Braden.

73. AFS to Rev. Josué Gonzalez, May 1, 1943, recorded by Dr. Charles Braden.

74. AFS to Nañez, February 25, 1953, and March 11, 1953, Nañez Papers.

75. Interview with Dr. Nañez.

76. AFS to ———, June 6, 1959, Nañez Papers. (Names withheld by the author.)

77. AFS to Nañez, June 21, 1943, Nañez Papers.

78. Interview with Dr. Nañez.

79. AFS to Nañez, July 13, 1945, Nañez Papers.

80. Nañez to AFS, June 4, 1951 (carbon copy), Nañez Papers.

81. AFS to Nañez, June 6, 1951, Nañez Papers.

82. Interview with Dr. Nañez.

83. *Encyclopedia of World Methodism*, s.v. "Alfredo Nañez."

84. AFS to Nañez, July 15, 1959, Nañez Papers. See also January 26, 1953.

85. See chap. 12.

86. *Missionary Yearbook*, 1939, p. 334.

87. Tributes given to Bishop A. Frank Smith, Annual Meeting of the Board of Missions of The Methodist Church, Buck Hill Falls, Pennsylvania, January 20, 1960, Smith Papers.

88. Walter W. Armstrong, *Room to Grow: A History of Houston Methodist Missions, 1815-1963* (Houston: Houston Methodist Board of Missions, 1963), p. 22.

Walter W. Fondren and John T. Scott were the principal leaders of the Houston City Board, although Presiding Elder George W. Davis led in the initial reorganization.

89. Chap. 7, p. 145.

90. Interview with Bishop W. Kenneth Pope, September 15, 1972, A. Frank Smith Hall, Perkins School of Theology, Southern Methodist University, Dallas, Texas. Pope was pastor of Houston's First Methodist Church from 1949 until 1960, when he was elected to the episcopacy.

91. U.S. Census figures as published in the *Texas Almanacs* for these years.

92. Seymour V. Connor, *Texas: A History* (New York: Thomas Y. Crowell Co., 1971), p. 347.

93. Braden interview. "Why, Bessie, I don't know a better place to grow a soul," was AFS's immediate response.

94. Interview with Dr. Murphy.

95. Dr. L. U. Spellman to the author, January 1, 1972.

96. Armstrong, *Room to Grow*, p. 27.

97. Ibid., p. 21.

98. See chap. 7, pp. 140-41.

99. Interview with Dr. Durwood Fleming, July 14, 1973, in Georgetown, Texas. Fleming was the pastor of St. Luke's when Elledge, Baker, and Nelms moved their church membership from Bering to lay the foundations of that new congregation in 1945.

100. Interview with Hines H. Baker, September 17, 1973, Exxon Building, Houston, Texas.

101. Interview with Dr. Durwood Fleming.

102. Armstrong, *Room to Grow*, pp. 23, 27.

103. Interview with Dr. Fleming. Fleming himself was pastor to many of these men at St. Luke's and was active on the board for fifteen years from 1945 to 1960.

104. *Houston Post*, Sunday, August 21, 1938—as quoted in Armstrong, *Room to Grow*, pp. 24-25.

105. Armstrong, *Room to Grow*, p. 34.

106. Quoted in ibid., p. 30. Elledge was speaking to a Jurisdictional Workshop on Church Extension at the invitation of the General Board of Missions and Church Extension.

107. Braden interview. For AFS's unvarnished view of Elledge's control of the board, see his daily journal entry for Thursday, January 21, 1943.

108. Armstrong, *Room to Grow*, p. 33.

109. Ibid.

110. Ibid., p. 55.

111. Interview with Dr. Clendenin, August 28, 1972, in Houston, Texas.

112. Armstrong, *Room to Grow*, pp. 48, 55.

113. AFS, as quoted in the *Room to Grow* brochure (published by the Board of Missions and Church Extension of the Houston Districts, 1953), Smith Papers.

114. Armstrong, *Room to Grow*, p. 55.

115. Interview with W. A. (Abe) Pounds, January 18, 1973, near Tyler, Texas.

116. Armstrong, *Room to Grow*, p. 56.

117. Interview with Dr. Stewart Clendenin.

118. Interview with Dr. Monroe Vivion, January 18, 1973, in Flint, Texas.

119. *Texas Christian Advocate*, March 6, 1953, p. 1.

120. Henrietta M. Larson and Kenneth W. Porter, *History of Humble Oil & Refining Company* (New York: Harper & Bros., 1959), pp. 334, 663.

121. Interview with A. Frank Smith, Jr., August 29, 1972, in Houston, Texas.

122. Armstrong, *Room to Grow*, pp. 33, 35, 37, 39, 44, 55.

123. Ibid., pp. 35, 38, 47, 60, 62, 63.

124. Interview with Dr. Clendenin.

125. Chap. 7, p. 128. See also Bascom N. Timmons, *Jesse H. Jones: The Man and the Statesman* (New York: Henry Holt & Co., 1956), pp. 101, 119. As an expression of appreciation for Heyne's faithful services for almost half a century, Jones gave a million dollars to the University of Houston to build the Fred J. Heyne Classroom Building. Ibid., p. 377.

126. Armstrong, *Room to Grow*, p. 35.

127. Braden interview.

128. Armstrong, *Room to Grow*, pp. 47, 48, 49, 52, 53, 60. See also interview with Dr. Durwood Fleming.

129. Conversation with Jane Nelms Lansford, June 27, 1975, Georgetown, Texas. See also interview with Dr. Durwood Fleming.

130. The dedication of Dr. Marilyn M. Sibley's history of the Port of Houston is an indication of Blanton's significance in the city. *The Port of Houston: A History* (Austin: University of Texas Press, 1968), p. vii. See also pp. 194, 200.

131. Armstrong, *Room to Grow*, pp. 49, 50, 52, 56, 60.

132. Interview with Dr. Fleming.

133. Interview with Bishop W. Angie Smith. See also Armstrong, *Room to Grow*, p. 67.

134. Braden interview. See also AFS's daily journal, entry for August 20, 1949; and clipping from *Houston Chronicle*, "Neighbors of Note" column featuring Mr. Scurlock, sometime in 1953, Smith Papers.

135. Armstrong, *Room to Grow*, pp. 49, 55, 65-68.

136. Braden interview.

137. Interview with R. A. Shepherd, September 18, 1973, in Houston, Texas. For the beginning of AFS's friendship with Mr. Shepherd, see chap. 7.

138. Armstrong, *Room to Grow*, pp. 66, 68.

139. Interview with Dr. Durwood Fleming. Fleming was closely associated with the board for some fifteen years and was pastor to Hines H. Baker, Raymond P. Elledge, Loyal L. Nelms, and William N. Blanton.

140. Braden interview. According to Armstrong, fifty-six new Methodist churches were built between 1937 and 1961. In 1920, 42 out of every 1,000 persons in Houston belonged to Methodist churches. In 1961, almost 100 out of every 1,000 persons in Houston were members of Methodist churches. *Room to Grow*, pp. 23, 28.

CHAPTER FOURTEEN

1. AFS, *"The Mood of Today": A Message of the Methodist Hour, March 2, 1947* (Atlanta: The Methodist Hour, 1947), Smith Papers.

2. "Bishop A. Frank Smith became an Ex Officio member of our Board of Trustees in 1933." Marjorie Beech, Assistant to the President, to Dr. Charles S. Braden, February 28, 1963, Smith Papers.

3. "When the board decided to rebuild on the former site of the fire-demolished building, the executive committee recommended that the remaining private property between this location and the area occupied by the Administration Building and Mood Hall be purchased. . . . The cost of the building, $330,000, plus its furnishings and the sum spent on debt retirement and property purchase reached $477,000." Ralph Wood Jones, *Southwestern University, 1840-1961* (Austin: San Felipe Press, 1973), p. 268.

4. Ibid.

5. Ibid., pp. 279-84.

6. The suggestion was made by Dr. Ed Hodges, a prominent physician and surgeon in Houston, and a cousin of Mr. Wiess. Penciled manuscript by AFS entitled "Southwestern" in a spiral notebook labeled "Personal Reminiscences," probably written in 1962, Smith Papers. See also Braden interview.

7. Composite account from AFS's "Personal Reminiscences" and Braden inter-

view. See also Angie Frank Smith, "The Influence of the Gift of Mrs. Wiess," printed in a brochure entitled *The Victory Service in Honor of Mrs. William Wiess, Being Addresses Delivered at Southwestern University, Georgetown, Texas, Tuesday, June Eighth, One Thousand Nine Hundred and Thirty-seven* (Georgetown: Southwestern University, 1937), pages unnumbered, Smith Papers.

8. Dr. J. N. R. Score to Dr. Claude C. Cody, Jr., April 16, 1936 (carbon copy), Papers of Dr. J. N. R. Score, Bridwell Library, Southern Methodist University.

9. That the Score-Bergin visit came first is indicated in the following passage from a letter Score wrote to AFS: "I am glad that you know that I went to Harry Wiess and started the train of events that meant his giving the money which I trust will eventually come to the University." Score to AFS, November 23, 1936 (carbon copy), Score Papers, SMU.

10. Copy of the trust agreement dated June 26, 1936, Smith Papers.

11. Minutes of the Board of Trustees of Southwestern University, January 19, 1937; as quoted in Jones, *Southwestern University*, p. 294.

12. According to the trust agreement, Mrs. Wiess acted "by and through" her son, Harry C. Wiess, as her "duly authorized agent and attorney in fact." See n. 10, above.

13. *Southwestern University Bulletin* 35, no. 6 (July 1936): 1.

14. Jones, *Southwestern University*, p. 295.

15. AFS to Score, November 16, 1936, Score Papers, SMU.

16. AFS to Score, March 9, 1937, Score Papers, SMU.

17. The formal announcement simply stated: "Less than 200 individuals, all of them former students, patrons, or close friends of the university, comprised the list of contributors." *Houston Post*, Tuesday, March 16, 1937, pp. 1, 5.

18. Judge W. E. Orgain to President J. W. Bergin, March 19, 1937 (carbon copy sent to AFS), Smith Papers.

19. *Houston Post*, March 16, 1937, p. 5. "A formal statement relative to the gift was issued Monday by a committee composed of Dr. Claude C. Cody, chairman of the board; J. W. West, chairman of the finance committee, both of Houston; S. W. Scott of San Antonio, W. E. Orgain of Beaumont, and Bishop A. Frank Smith of Houston."

20. Ibid.

21. Jones, *Southwestern University*, p. 295.

22. The College of Bishops to Harry C. Wiess, May 4, 1937, copy in Smith Papers. See Minutes of the College of Bishops of the Methodist Episcopal Church, South, Nashville, Tennessee, April 30, 1937, p. 3, Bishop John M. Moore Papers, Bridwell Library, Southern Methodist University.

23. Will D. Orgain to AFS, March 19, 1937, Smith Papers.

24. Dr. J. W. Bergin to AFS, March 25, 1937, Smith Papers.

25. Jesse H. Jones to AFS, March 17, 1937, Smith Papers.

26. Bascom N. Timmons, *Jesse H. Jones: The Man and the Statesman* (New York: Henry Holt & Co., 1956), pp. 140-41.

27. AFS to Score, March 9, 1937, Score Papers, SMU.

28. *Williamson County Sun*, January 6, 1939, p. 3; December 1, 1939, p. 1. The library was named in honor of Dean Claude Carr Cody (1854-1923), professor of mathematics at Southwestern from 1879 to 1916 and Dean from 1906 to 1916. See chap. 2.

29. Bergin to AFS, March 25, 1947, Smith Papers.

30. Jones was made chairman of the RFC in 1933 by President Franklin D. Roosevelt, serving until 1939, when Roosevelt appointed him federal loan administrator. In 1940, Roosevelt made Jones his secretary of state. Timmons, *Jesse H. Jones*.

31. Harold L. Ickes, who was secretary of the interior from 1933 to 1946 and head of the Public Works Administration from 1933 to 1939, gained a reputation for honest and careful supervising of the huge sums spent on PWA projects.

32. See *Encyclopedia of American Biography*, s.v. "Ickes, Harold L."

33. AFS's trip to Washington occurred in December, 1938. "I spent the week before Christmas in Washington in connection with the Southwestern Library project." AFS to Score, December [after Christmas], 1938, Score Papers, SMU.

34. Braden interview. This second trip to Washington was probably in the month of February, 1939: "I had to go back to Washington three weeks ago on the Southwestern Library project, and I caught a germ while there that laid me out for ten days." AFS to Score [mid-March], 1939, Score Papers, SMU.

35. As quoted in the *Williamson County Sun*, December 10, 1938, p. 1. Application for the grant had been filed with the Fort Worth office of the PWA in September, 1938.

36. Ibid.

37. Ibid., January 6, 1939, p. 1. This edition also carried on p. 7 a feature article on AFS under the headline, "Bishop A. Frank Smith Active in Library Movement."

38. Ibid., October 20, 1939, p. 4; October 27, 1939, p. 1. As described in the first article, this colorful festivity, "one of the most treasured traditions [of Southwestern], was instituted in 1928 by the late Miss Laura Kuykendall."

39. Printed program, "Formal Opening, Cody Memorial Library Building, Sunday, November 26th, 1939, 2:30 p.m.," Smith Papers. See also *Williamson County Sun*, December 1, 1939, p. 1.

40. *Williamson County Sun*, Friday, February 13, 1942, p. 1; Jones, *Southwestern University*, pp. 301-12.

41. After receiving Dr. Bergin's retirement in November, 1941, the board elected the following nominating committee: Judge Tom L. McCullough, Dr. Jesse R. Milam, Dr. Paul W. Quillian, Dr. Edmund Heinsohn, Dr. Score, and Dr. Cody. Dr. C. C. Cody to Nominating Committee Members, January 6, 1942, Score Papers, SMU.

42. Score had been offered the presidency of Southwestern University in 1935 when AFS was on the nominating committee. At that time, AFS wrote to Score: "If you want to go to Southwestern this fall, it is yours for the asking. Claude [Cody], Jno. Bergin, Judge McCullough, Boaz and I are a committee to select a man. . . . If you are really interested, let me know." AFS to Score, August 8, 1935, Score Papers, SMU. Score's board at First Methodist Church, Fort Worth, would not agree to Score's leaving, however, since he had only recently been appointed there. See Score's letters to AFS of August 12 and September 27, 1935 (carbon copies), Score Papers, SMU. See also Jones, *Southwestern University*, p. 288.

43. Score's letters to AFS of December 2 and 11, 1941 (carbon copies), Score Papers, SMU. See also Score to Cody, September 19, 1935 (carbon copy), Score Papers, SMU.

44. Smith to Score, December 17, 1941, Score Papers, SMU.

45. AFS's daily journal, entry for Monday, January 5, 1942. Cody apparently blamed Score for the embarrassing situation in 1935 when Score had declined election. See n. 42, above.

46. AFS's daily journal, entry for Saturday, January 17, 1942. See also the entries for January 14 and 17.

47. Ibid., Thursday and Friday, January 22 and 23, 1942.

48. Score to AFS, February 12, 1942, Smith Papers. Smith had not lightly left the board meeting at Southwestern, as he later explained to Score: "I had told Mother that Bess and I would eat dinner with her at one o'clock in Austin. She has been very ill for weeks . . . and she can be up only an hour or two at a time, and I knew she would have to go back to bed if we did not get there a little after one o'clock." AFS to Score, February 16, 1942, Score Papers, SMU.

49. AFS to Score, February 16, 1942, Score Papers, SMU. Concerning Score's election, Smith noted in his daily journal: "Attended meeting of Board of Trustees

at which time Russell Score was elected President. He has a hard job but he will put it over if any man can." Daily journal, Wednesday, February 11, 1942.

50. AFS to Score, July 15, 1942, Score Papers, SMU.

51. Cody to Score, February 17, 1942, Score Papers, SMU.

52. AFS to Score, March 3, 1942, Score Papers, SMU.

53. Form letters sent to pastors, April 9, 1942, Smith Papers. Italics added.

54. For example, Score wrote to AFS: "Thank you again for coming to Fort Worth and being with me in the conference with Dr. Harris. . . . I believe you rendered a real service to Southwestern University." Score to AFS, July 16, 1942 (carbon copy), Score Papers, SMU. See also AFS's daily journal, entry for July 11, 1942; and Score to AFS, October 15, 1942 (carbon copy), Score Papers, SMU.

55. *Williamson County Sun*, Friday, October 9, 1942, p. 1. See also *Megaphone*, Saturday, October 10, 1942. Score suggested this date for his inauguration, "the beginning of the seventieth year of continuous service at Georgetown." Score to Dr. Claude C. Cody, Jr., March 2, 1942 (carbon copy), Score Papers, SMU.

56. AFS's daily journal, entry for Tuesday, October 6, 1942. Bishops Sam Hay and H. A. Boaz also participated, according to the printed program and newspaper accounts.

57. AFS to Score, Thursday [October 8, 1942], Score Papers, SMU. The full text of the Inauguration, including the addresses, was published in the *Official Bulletin, Southwestern University* 43, no. 2 (November 1942).

58. Score to AFS, October 12, 1942 (carbon copy), Score Papers, SMU.

59. Score to AFS, October 14, 1942 (carbon copy), Score Papers, SMU.

60. Ibid.

61. "The Inaugural Address," as published in the *Official Bulletin*, p. 20. See n. 57, above.

62. Cody Memorial Library and West Gymnasium were built in 1939-40. Jones, *Southwestern University*, p. 297.

63. Mrs. J. J. Perkins to Score, March 6, 1942, Score Papers, SMU. Italics added. Mrs. Perkins already had established "a fund for girls there to help some girl who could not go otherwise." Concerning Lois Craddock Perkins, see chaps. 2 and 12.

64. Score to Cody, October 24, 1942 (carbon copy), Score Papers, SMU. AFS had been a guest in the Perkins's home in Wichita Falls in August. AFS's daily journal.

65. Interview with Mrs. J. J. Perkins, June 26, 1972, in Wichita Falls, Texas. See also letter from Mrs. Perkins to the author, June 22, 1972, filed with the interview transcript.

66. Score to AFS, October 28, 1942 (carbon copy), Score Papers, SMU.

67. AFS's daily journal, entry for Sunday, November 22, 1942. See also letter from Mrs. Perkins to Score, November 20, 1942, Score Papers, SMU.

68. Perkins to AFS, November 23, 1942 (carbon copy sent to Score), Score Papers, SMU.

69. Score to AFS, October 28, 1942 (carbon copy), Score Papers, SMU.

70. Score to AFS, October 28, 1942 (carbon copy), Score Papers, SMU. See also Score to Cody, October 28, 1942 (carbon copy), Score Papers, SMU.

71. Score to AFS, November 21, 1942 (carbon copy), Score Papers, SMU. Italics added. Score wrote to Dr. Cody: "If Bishop Smith will carry through for us as he can do—and I believe he will—we can get an adequate amount of money for the Chapel we each wish to see built." Score to Dr. C. C. Cody, Jr., November 21, 1942 (carbon copy), Score Papers, SMU.

72. AFS to Score, November 25, 1942 (holograph), Score Papers, SMU.

73. AFS to Score, December 10, 1942 (holograph), Score Papers, SMU. See also Score to AFS, November 27, 1942 (carbon copy), Score Papers, SMU.

74. Perkins to AFS and Score, December 2, 1942. Both letters are in the Score Papers, SMU. AFS apparently sent his letter to Score.

75. AFS, handwritten note to Score on Perkins's letter to AFS, December 2, 1942, Score Papers, SMU. See n. 74.

76. *Megaphone*, Saturday, April 10, 1943, p. 1. See also Score to AFS, March 11, 1943 (carbon copy), Score Papers, SMU.

77. AFS's daily journal.

78. *Williamson County Sun*, Friday, April 16, 1943, p. 1.

79. Perkins to Score, November 27, 1943, Score Papers, SMU.

80. Score to Perkins, November 29, 1943 (carbon copy), Score Papers, SMU.

81. Score to AFS, November 29, 1943 (carbon copy), Score Papers, SMU.

82. AFS to Score, November 30, 1943, Score Papers, SMU.

83. AFS to Perkins, November 30, 1943 (carbon copy sent to Dr. Score), Score Papers, SMU.

84. Copies of the citations are in the Score Papers, SMU. Margaret Mood McKennon, head librarian of Cody Memorial Library and daughter of Francis Asbury Mood, prepared the citation for Mrs. Perkins.

85. Perkins to Score, June 28, 1944, Score Papers, SMU.

86. Interview with Mrs. Perkins, June 26, 1972.

87. J. J. Perkins to Dr. J. N. R. Score, December 3, 1944, Score Papers, SMU.

88. See AFS's daily journal, entry for Sunday, May 16, 1948, and Dr. Score to AFS, November 12, 1948 (carbon copy), Score Papers, SMU. See also AFS to Perkins, September 18, 1948. This is one of many letters from the correspondence between AFS and Mr. Perkins that Mrs. Perkins has generously presented to the Smith Papers in Bridwell Library, SMU.

89. AFS's daily journal, entry for Sunday, May 16, 1948. Bishop Paul E. Martin is also due credit for adding his support in favor of this additional gift. See Bishop Martin to Dr. Score, June 9, 1948, Score Papers, SMU.

90. See copy of memorandum attached to Mr. Perkins's letter to AFS, September 2, 1949, Smith Papers.

91. Perkins to AFS, September 13, 1948, Smith Papers.

92. AFS to Perkins, September 18, 1948, Smith Papers, courtesy of Mrs. Perkins.

93. Even *Mrs.* Perkins had written the previous November: "This will be all the money we will want to put into this building, and I would like to see a complete job, furnishings and all." Quoted in Score to AFS, November 12, 1948 (carbon copy), Score Papers, Presidential Papers, Southwestern University (note the different location).

94. "Tonite Bess and I went to Meth. Hosp. to see Russell Score." AFS's daily journal, Wednesday, August 24, 1949. See also Score to AFS, September 12, 1949 (carbon copy), Score Papers, SMU.

95. That this prolonged episode had become painful for AFS is revealed in a letter he wrote to Willis M. Tate four years later: "My repeated calls for more money for the chapel at Southwestern became embarrassing to me, if not to them [the Perkinses], before the enterprise was completed. The difficulty arose there because . . . rising costs and changed plans necessitated three separate gifts, and each time Mr. Perkins vowed that he was 'through.'" AFS to Vice President Willis M. Tate, August 7, 1953, Presidents' Papers, Southern Methodist University.

96. Perkins to Score and to AFS, September 6, 1949, Smith Papers.

97. AFS to Perkins, September 9, 1949, Smith Papers, courtesy of Mrs. Perkins.

98. AFS to Score, September 17, 1949 (holograph), Score Papers, SU. See also AFS's daily journal, September 17, 1949; and AFS to Score, September 9, 1949, Score Papers, SU.

The closing passage in AFS's letter to Score (September 17) responds to the following statement Score wrote to AFS on September 12: "Ruth and John think I am improving. I don't. . . . I have had spells of angina, coming in cycles, for two months. . . . You and Bess will never know how much I appreciate the attention you both showed me while I was in the hospital." Score to AFS, September 12, 1949 (carbon copy), Score Papers, SU.

99. Score to Perkins, September 22, 1949 (carbon copy sent to AFS), Smith Papers. AFS was unable to participate in the groundbreaking because of a meeting of the Commission on Chaplains in Washington, D.C. AFS's daily journal, entries for September 21 and 22, 1949.

100. *Williamson County Sun*, September 27, 1949, p. 1. See the picture on p. 6.

101. The McManus gift should be counted as part of the momentous financial foundation settled by Dr. Score in his final days of life.

102. AFS's daily journal, entry for September 26, 1949. See telegrams from Howard Knox and I. J. McCook informing AFS of Dr. Score's death, both dated September 26, 1949, Smith Papers.

103. *Williamson County Sun*, September 30, 1949, p. 1. Assisting in the service were Bishop William C. Martin of Dallas, Rev. J. W. Morgan of First Methodist Church, Georgetown, and Dr. Neal Cannon of Polk Street Methodist Church, Amarillo.

104. AFS to Perkins, September 18, 1948, Smith Papers, courtesy of Mrs. Perkins. See also Score to AFS, July 21, 1948 (carbon copy), Score Papers, SU.

105. AFS to Score, July 17, 1945. See also AFS to Score, August 21, 1945. Both letters in Score Papers, SU.

106. Telegram to Score from AFS, February 5, 1946, Score Papers, SU.

107. AFS to Score, July 17, 1945, Score Papers, SU.

108. Score to AFS, July 27, 1945, Score Papers, SU.

109. See AFS's story about Cody Memorial Library earlier in this chapter.

110. Score to AFS, March 21, 1945 (carbon copy), Score Papers, SU. See also Jesse H. Jones to AFS, March 14, 1945, Smith Papers.

111. AFS's daily journal, entry for Tuesday, September 11, 1945.

112. AFS to Score, December 13, 1945, Score Papers, SU. See also Jesse H. Jones to AFS, November 23, 1945, Smith Papers.

113. "Jesse H. Jones Scholarships," *Southwestern Magazine* 69, no. 3 (November 1950): 7. See the following correspondence between AFS and Dr. Score: Score to AFS, December 25, 1945 (carbon copy); AFS to Score, December 30, 1945 (holograph); Score to AFS, January 12, 1946 (carbon copy); and Score to AFS, July 21, 1948 (carbon copy), all in Score Papers, SU.

114. Cody to AFS, May 19, 1947, Smith Papers.

115. Jones, *Southwestern University*, p. 306.

116. See AFS's daily journal, entry for Monday, June 27, 1949.

117. Jones, *Southwestern University*, pp. 306-7. See also the original public announcement in the *Williamson County Sun*, October 7, 1949, p. 1.

118. William Carrington Finch had come to Southwestern as head of the Department of Religion and Philosophy in the fall of 1941. Since 1945 he had served as administrative assistant to Dr. Score. See "The William Carrington Finch Administration, 1949-1961," chap. 16, in Jones, *Southwestern University*, pp. 313-21.

119. AFS to Finch, October 4, 1949 (holograph), Presidential Papers, Southwestern University. See also AFS to Finch, October 28, 1949 (holograph), also in the Presidential Papers.

120. Printed program entitled "The Dedication of the Lois Perkins Chapel," Smith Papers. See also *Williamson County Sun*, November 16, 1950, p. 1; and *Megaphone*, November 17, 1950, p. 1.

121. "Dedication of Perkins Chapel," *Southwestern Magazine* 69, no. 3 (November 1950): 3.

122. AFS to Mr. and Mrs. Perkins, November 15, 1950 (holograph). Sent to President Durwood Fleming, April 30, 1965, by Mrs. Perkins. Presidential Papers, Southwestern University. Mrs. Perkins explains: "I came across the enclosed letter which brought back memories. . . . Bishop Smith seldom went on a trip without

writing us a letter. . . . I am so happy to have had a small part in making the campus at Southwestern what it is. Bess, Frank, Finis and Callie [Crutchfield] and I were there together. We were great friends." Mrs. Perkins to Dr. Durwood Fleming, April 30, 1965, Presidential Papers.

123. President William C. Finch to AFS, May 18, 1951 (carbon copy), Presidential Papers, Southwestern University. See also Jones, *Southwestern University*, p. 307.

124. Printed program entitled "Dedication of the Chapel Organ, the Lois Perkins Chapel, Southwestern University, July 14, 1954," Smith Papers.

125. Score to AFS, February 6, 1946 (carbon copy), Score Papers, SU. At that time, of course, Dr. Lee was president of SMU and AFS was chairman of the SMU board. See chap. 15. See also AFS to Score, February 13, 1946, Score Papers, SU.

126. AFS's daily journal, entry for Monday, November 8, 1948.

127. Jones, *Southwestern University*, p. 307.

128. After serving successfully for six months as acting president, Finch was elected president of Southwestern University in April and inaugurated in November, 1950. Ibid., p. 313.

129. See AFS to Dr. Finch, September 30, 1950 (holograph), Presidential Papers, Southwestern University.

130. Mrs. Fondren's reluctance was apparently due to her unhappiness over the large lecture hall, which she called "a bump on a log that completely detracts from the building." When Dr. Finch and Dr. Cody went to see Mrs. Fondren, showing her the plans and explaining the necessity of adding the lecture hall, they came away believing that she had accepted the addition. Mrs. Fondren, on the other hand, has insisted that she never agreed to the inclusion of the lecture hall.

131. AFS to Finch, April 26, 1954 (holograph), Presidential Papers, Southwestern University. See also Finch to AFS, June 17, 1953 (carbon copy), Presidential Papers, Southwestern University.

132. Finch to AFS, April 30, 1954 (carbon copy), Presidential Papers, Southwestern University.

133. AFS to Finch, May 19, 1954. See also Finch to AFS, May 21, 1954 (carbon copy). Both letters are in the Presidential Papers, Southwestern University.

134. Interview with Bishop Kenneth W. Copeland, August 23, 1972, in Houston, Texas.

135. See the report in the *Texas Christian Advocate*, May 28, 1954, p. 1; and Dr. Finch's letter to AFS dated April 30, 1954 (carbon copy), Presidential Papers, Southwestern University. The third plaque reads: "This wing of Fondren Science Hall in honor of A. Frank Smith . . . and Mrs. A. Frank Smith . . . in consecrating their lives to their fellow man, these devoted friends, wise counselors and distinguished Americans reflect the high prestige of their attainments on their Alma Mater, Southwestern University."

136. Finch to AFS, March 13, 1950 (carbon copy), Presidential Papers, Southwestern University.

137. AFS to Finch, March 21, 1950, Presidential Papers, Southwestern University.

138. Finch to AFS, January 9, 1951 (carbon copy), Presidential Papers, Southwestern University.

139. Finch to AFS, December 19, 1950 (carbon copy), Presidential Papers, Southwestern University.

140. Finch to AFS, January 4, 1952 (carbon copy); Finch to AFS, February 19, 1952 (carbon copy); Finch to AFS, September 18, 1952 (carbon copy), Presidential Papers, Southwestern University. See also Jones, *Southwestern University*, p. 317.

141. Finch to AFS, December 20, 1954 (carbon copy), Presidential Papers, Southwestern University. See also AFS to Finch, February 17, 1955, Presidential Papers, Southwestern University. Both buildings were dedicated in the spring of 1956,

according to reports in the *Texas Christian Advocate*, February 10 and April 14, 1956.

142. Finch to AFS, January 4, 1952 (carbon copy). See also Finch to AFS, November 21, 1950 (carbon copy); and Finch to AFS, February 11, 1955 (carbon copy), all in Presidential Papers, Southwestern University.

143. As listed in the *Texas Christian Advocate*, May 2, 1958, p. 1. Dates have, however, been corrected.

144. Finch to AFS, January 14, 1953 (carbon copy), Presidential Papers, Southwestern University.

145. As listed in the *Texas Christian Advocate*, April 11, 1958, p. 1.

146. AFS to Finch, January 8, 1953, Presidential Papers, Southwestern University. That "other institution," of course, was Southern Methodist University, where AFS was chairman of the board for twenty-two years, 1938-1960. See chap. 15.

147. See the *Texas Christian Advocate*, May 2, 1958, p. 1.

148. AFS to Finch, February, 1961 (carbon copy), Smith Papers. See also AFS to Finch, April 16, 1961 (holograph), Presidential Papers, Southwestern University.

149. AFS to Finch, February 14, 1961 (carbon copy), Smith Papers.

150. Interview with Dr. Durwood Fleming, July 14, 1973, in Georgetown, Texas.

151. AFS to Fleming, January 29, 1962 (carbon copy), Smith Papers. Those five former presidents were: William Carrington Finch, John Nelson Russell Score, John William Bergin, King Vivion, and James Samuel Barcus.

On April 11, 1962, AFS's secretary at the Methodist Hospital [Houston] wrote to Dr. Fleming: "Bishop Smith has asked me to write [that] he suffered a slight heart attack a few days ago [and] is confined to his room and bed for the next few weeks. . . . This will prevent Bishop Smith's coming to Georgetown for your Inaugural Ceremonies, a fact which occasions him deep and genuine disappointment and regret." Jo Ann DePrima to President Durwood Fleming, April 11, 1962 (carbon copy), Smith Papers.

CHAPTER FIFTEEN

1. Minutes of the Annual Meeting of the Board of Trustees, Southern Methodist University, June 4, 1934. At that time, the SMU board was composed of thirty-one members: nineteen elected by the Annual Conferences of the Methodist Episcopal Church, South, in Texas, Louisiana, Missouri, Arkansas, Oklahoma, and New Mexico; and twelve elected by the General Conference representing the "Church at Large." The bishops assigned to preside over the conferences in Texas were included in the twelve "at large."

2. According to Bishop Charles C. Selecman (president of SMU, 1923-1938), as quoted in the *S.M.U. News-Digest*, June 15, 1940, p. 5.

3. As told by AFS during his Fondren Lectures at SMU in February, 1955. Typescript made from a recording of the third lecture, Smith Papers. See also Bishop Selecman's statement made at the dedication ceremonies of the Fondren Library as quoted in the *S.M.U. News-Digest*, June 15, 1940, p. 5; and Mary Martha Hosford Thomas, *Southern Methodist University: Founding and Early Years* (Dallas: SMU Press, 1974), pp. 111-12.

4. See AFS to President Willis Tate, August 19, 1960, The Presidents' Papers, Southern Methodist University, Dallas, Texas.

5. As Selecman later wrote to AFS: "I claim a certain amount of credit by having diverted Brother Joe from his intention to promote Frank McNeny. It still amuses me to recall how, when I suggested your name, Brother Joe immediately went downtown and solicited the support of McNeny in your election." Charles C. Selecman to AFS, May 13, 1950, Smith Papers.

6. AFS to Tate, August 19, 1960. See n. 4, above. Henry Jackson, a prominent attorney from San Angelo, had been a trustee from the West Texas Conference since

1925. According to the Board Minutes for June 7, 1938, Jackson was present for the 9:00 A.M. roll call; but the Minutes simply record "the election of Bishop A. Frank Smith to the Chairmanship of the Board of Trustees" without further detail. Annual Meeting of the Board of Trustees, Southern Methodist University, June 7, 1938, 6: 17, 37 (hereafter cited as Board Minutes).

7. Winifred T. Weiss and Charles S. Proctor, *Umphrey Lee: A Biography* (Nashville: Abingdon Press, 1971), p. 94.

8. As typed by Mrs. Hawkins (carbon copy), Presidents' Papers, SMU.

9. See above, chap. 2, pp. 35-36, and chap. 4, p. 65.

10. "In my numerous talks with Umphrey he has told me that he would never have come to Southern Methodist had you not been Chairman of the Board." Hemphill Hosford to AFS, November 17, 1950, Smith Papers. Dr. Hosford was dean of the university and academic vice-president when he wrote this letter.

11. Program brochure for the Inauguration of the Fourth President of Southern Methodist University, Monday, November 6, 1939, Smith Papers. See AFS's first-draft holograph, also in Smith Papers.

12. AFS to Lee, December 13, 1940, Presidents' Papers, SMU.

13. Lee to AFS, December 16, 1940, Smith Papers.

14. Board Minutes, June 3, 1941, p. 4. Ultimately, the Perkinses gave a total of $175,000 to cover the architect's fee and increased costs due to wartime conditions. See Board Minutes for February 5, 1942, p. 3; and *S.M.U. News-Digest*, November 15, 1942, p. 1.

15. *S.M.U. News-Digest*, November 15, 1942, p. 1; and printed program entitled "Dedication of the Joe Perkins Gymnasium, October 2, 1942," Papers of Dr. J. N. R. Score, Bridwell Library, SMU.

16. See the *Southwestern Advocate*, October 8, 1942, p. 5; and *S.M.U. News-Digest*, November 15, 1942, p. 1.

17. AFS's daily journal, entry for October 2, 1942, Smith Papers.

18. As quoted in the *Southwestern Advocate*, October 8, 1942, p. 5.

19. L. U. Spellman to the author, July 11, 1975. Mr. Perkins expressed his appreciation more fully in a letter to AFS: "I have never seen anything go off as smoothly as did the meeting at SMU on last Friday. To say that Lois and I both enjoyed it would be to express it rather mildly. . . . You are entirely too generous in what you have to say about Lois and me." Perkins to AFS, October 6, 1942, Score Papers, SMU. (This letter was passed on to Score by AFS because Perkins closed by saying: "I regret very much that Lois and I could not be at the Southwestern exercises today" —meaning Score's inauguration.)

20. AFS's daily journal, entry for January 10, 1942. Membership on the executive committee was limited to three designated officials "and eight other members, a majority of whom shall be members of the Board." Apparently, none of the non-board members was willing to resign to make room for these two men. See Board Minutes, February 5, 1942.

21. See chap. 4, p. 60; and pp. 332ff. of this chapter.

22. See AFS's daily journal entries for January 23; February 5; June 3, 4, and 8; and Board Minutes for February 5 and June 8, 1942. McNeny threatened to resign at one point.

23. AFS's daily journal, entry for January 26, 1943. See Board Minutes for January 26 and May 31, 1943. Mr. Perkins's election to the board "from the Church-at-Large" had no apparent connection with the compromise.

24. Fred F. Florence to AFS, January 30, 1943, Smith Papers. Florence was then president of the Republic National Bank of Dallas.

25. Interview with George and Hallie Crutchfield Pierce, January 17, 1972, in Dallas, Texas.

26. Board Minutes, February 8, 1944.

27. Ibid., February 8 and April 11, 1944.

28. Located in Wichita County, the Burkburnett oil field was established when "Fowler's Folly" blew in as a 2,200-barrel gusher in July, 1918. The resulting boom, one of the wildest ever seen in Texas, caused phenomenal growth in Burkburnett and Wichita Falls until the pressure in the oil reservoir gave out. Walter Prescott Webb, ed., *The Handbook of Texas* (Austin: Texas State Historical Association, 1952), 1:247.

29. Actually, Bishop Moore's goal was four million: two million for endowment of instruction, $150,000 for a chapel, $200,000 for a library, $450,000 for dormitories, $200,000 for apartment houses for families, and one million for endowment of student scholarships. See Bishop Moore to Frank L. McNeny, April 15, 1944 (carbon copy), item M1650, Bishop John M. Moore's Papers, Bridwell Library, SMU.

30. Braden interview.

31. AFS's daily journal, entry for April 11, 1944. There is no reference to a telephone call from Mr. Perkins that night.

32. Braden interview. Since 1924, Kirby Hall had housed the library, chapel, classrooms, and offices of the seminary.

33. Braden interview.

34. Ibid.

35. Ibid.

36. AFS's daily journal, entry for May 2, 1944 (italics added). The identity of "a few friends" is not certain, but the North Texas Conference delegation included W. Angie Smith, Umphrey Lee, and Paul E. Martin. Wives would have been included at the party, of course. *Daily Christian Advocate of the Second General Conference of The Methodist Church, 1944*, 2:346.

37. AFS to Perkins, May 14, 1944. This is another of the many letters that Mrs. Perkins contributed to the Smith Papers. See also AFS's daily journal, entries for May 9 and 10, 1944.

38. AFS's daily journal, entry for Thursday, June 1, 1944. This change was not due to any lack of time, for Smith still spent a full day in Dallas "going over plans for proposed Perkins School of Theology" with Lee, the executive committee, and the architect. Nor was there any problem with the picture, for Smith described it as "magnificent." See AFS's daily journal, entry for June 5, 1944.

39. While reading AFS's correspondence, especially his daily journal, one is repeatedly impressed with this shepherd's skill in herding such a variety of sheep!

40. AFS's daily journal, entry for Friday, May 26, 1944.

41. Ibid., entry for Tuesday, June 13, 1944.

42. Ibid.

43. Braden interview.

44. Quoted in Walter N. Vernon, *Forever Building: The Life and Ministry of Paul E. Martin* (Dallas: Southern Methodist University Press, 1973), p. 117.

45. Braden interview. See also the official account in the *Journal of the South Central Jurisdictional Conference of The Methodist Church, Held at Tulsa, Oklahoma, June 12-16 1944*, p. 109.

46. Perkins to AFS, July 5, 1944, Smith Papers. Smith replied: "You owe me no thanks for designating you to escort Paul to the platform at Tulsa. That was the most appropriate thing I have ever known about, and Paul and the conference were honored in having you to do so. Incidentally, I have never known another instance in the history of the [Methodist] Church when a Bishop-elect was escorted to the platform by a layman. So you can go down in history as doing something never done before by a layman, and probably not again." AFS to Perkins, July 9, 1944, Smith Papers (courtesy of Mrs. Perkins).

47. AFS to Perkins, August 26 and November 18, 1944, Smith Papers (courtesy of Mrs. Perkins).

48. Perkins to Dr. Umphrey Lee, December 27, 1944 (carbon copy sent to

Bishop Smith), Smith Papers. The one million dollars represented half-interest in "41 oil wells in East Texas"; the three hundred thousand was in notes owned by the Tide Water Associated Oil Company.

49. Perkins to AFS, December 27, 1944, Smith Papers (courtesy of Mrs. Perkins). Mr. Perkins attached a carbon copy of his letter to Umphrey Lee to this letter. Perkins emphasized his desire that "any income from these properties be placed in the Endowment Fund for the Theological Department until we agree otherwise."

50. AFS's daily journal, entry for January 4, 1945.

51. Ibid., entry for January 5, 1945.

52. A gift of $75,000 made by the Perkinses in 1938 paid for the addition of two floors to the Administration Building which had been built in 1930, balancing Hyer Hall across the quadrangle and providing attractive space for the administrative offices of the university. See Thomas, *Southern Methodist University*, p. 108.

53. Board Minutes, February 6, 1945.

54. AFS's daily journal, entry for February 6, 1945.

55. Ibid., entry for Monday, February 5, 1945. The university had unsuccessfully sought a permit from the War Committee on Conventions of the Office of Defense Transportation. See Dean Eugene B. Hawk to AFS, January 26, 1946, Smith Papers.

56. As quoted in the *Dallas Morning News*, February 7, 1945, p. 1. See also Dean Eugene B. Hawk to AFS, February 14, 1945, Smith Papers.

57. Entry for Tuesday, February 6, 1945. Extending his congratulations to AFS, Dean Hawk later wrote: "It must give you genuine satisfaction to know that you had such a determining influence in directing the thoughts of Mr. and Mrs. Perkins. . . . I am very happy indeed that they recounted to the public and also the Board of Trustees just how they came to center their interests in [the school of theology]." Hawk to AFS, February 14, 1945, Smith Papers.

58. Mrs. Lois Perkins to AFS and Mrs. Smith, postmarked February 15, 1945 (holograph), Smith Papers.

59. AFS's daily journal, entry for Friday, May 23, 1947. Moore wrote to Mr. Perkins on May 29.

According to a master plan adopted in 1924, the SMU campus was to be developed as a series of small quadrangles surrounding the major "inner campus" formed by Dallas Hall, Hyer Hall, Atkins Hall, and McFarlin Auditorium. The theology quadrangle would be built around Kirby Hall on the northwest corner of the campus, balanced by a law quadrangle on the northeast. The artist's sketches prepared for Mr. and Mrs. Perkins had been drawn in agreement with this master plan. See James F. White, *Architecture at SMU: 50 Years and 50 Buildings* (Dallas: Southern Methodist University Press, 1966), pp. 6-7. See also the artist's conception as printed in the *Dallas Morning News*, February 7, 1945, sec. 2, p. 1; and the *S.M.U. News-Digest*, March 13, 1945, p. 1.

60. See J. J. Perkins to Bishop John M. Moore, June 3, 1947, Moore Papers, item M1882, Bridwell Library, SMU. See also Braden interview.

61. Moore to AFS, August 25, 1947, Smith Papers. Moore had comparative figures, for example, on the number of buildings and size of locations for fifteen leading seminaries, including those at Yale, Princeton, Union, Garrett, Boston, Drew, and the Southern Baptist seminaries at Louisville and Fort Worth.

62. Perkins to AFS, August 25 (*sic!*), 1947, Smith Papers.

63. AFS's daily journal, entry for Monday, September 1, 1947.

64. Ibid. See also Perkins to Bishop Moore, September 4, 1947: "Mrs. Perkins and I hope you will be at the Springfield meeting. We want you to sit in with us [as] we expect to talk this matter out somewhat in detail with Dr. Lee, Dean Hawk, and several of our Bishops . . . at which time I expect a final decision to be made upon the location subject, of course, to the action of the Executive Committee." Moore Papers, item M1892.

65. Moore to AFS (italics added), September 23, 1947 (holograph), Smith Papers. See also AFS's daily journal, entry for Sunday, September 14, 1947.

66. Vernon, *Forever Building*, pp. 118-19. Unfortunately, Bishop Martin did not give sufficient details in his "Reflections" to enable his biographer to determine the date of this trip to Wichita Falls. Perkins to Bishop Moore, September 4 (not 7), 1947, quoted by Dr. Vernon, was written in reply to Moore's letters to Perkins of August 23 and 25. Mr. Perkins does not mention the visit from Bishop and Mrs. Martin, nor does he indicate that he has seen Bishop Moore's drawings.

Also, in Bishop Martin's letter to Bishop Moore of December 28, 1947, Martin writes: "To you we all owe a great debt of gratitude for the new location of the Perkins School of Theology. You presented an exhaustive study of that matter and it made a profound impression on Mr. and Mrs. Perkins. We were happy that *we were in their home at the time your communication was received and could give our endorsement to the idea.* I think the turning point came then." Moore Papers, item M1922 (holograph, italics added).

67. The Perkinses announced an additional gift of $650,000 during Ministers' Week in February, 1946, raising their total gift at that time to $2,000,000. *S.M.U. News-Digest*, March 28, 1946, p. 1.

68. Lee to AFS, September 15, 1947, Smith Papers.

69. Hawk to AFS, September 15, 1947, Smith Papers. See also Robert W. Goodloe to AFS, September 12, 1947. Goodloe was a professor in the seminary.

70. *Encyclopedia of World Methodism*, s.v. "World Methodist Conferences." "Ecumenical" was changed to "World" in 1957.

71. Entry for Thursday, September 25, 1947 (italics added).

72. Mrs. Perkins to Bishop John M. Moore, September 4, 1947 (holograph), Moore Papers, item M1923.

73. AFS's daily journal, entry for Friday, February 26, 1947.

74. Ibid., entry for Saturday, September 27, 1947.

75. Members of this committee were: Bishop Paul Martin, chairman, Bishop William C. Martin, Mr. J. J. Perkins, Mr. J. D. Randolph, Rev. E. C. Rule, and Dr. W. W. Ward. Board Minutes, October 31, 1947.

76. AFS's daily journal, entry for Friday, October 31, 1947.

77. AFS to "Dear Lois and Brother Joe," February 11, 1949, Smith Papers (courtesy of Mrs. Perkins).

78. Perkins to AFS, February 14, 1949, Smith Papers. The three buildings named were Eugene B. Hawk Hall, Paul E. Martin Hall, and S. B. Perkins Hall (honoring Mr. Perkins's brother, an SMU trustee in the 1920s and again since 1943). Earlier, of course, the chapel had been designated Perkins Chapel.

79. *S.M.U. News-Digest*, November-December 1949, p. 1. See also AFS's daily journal, entry for Friday, November 11, 1949.

80. *Dallas Morning News*, February 9, 1951, p. 1.

81. Dwight W. Culver, *Negro Segregation in The Methodist Church* (New Haven: Yale University Press, 1953), pp. 130-31; and Weiss and Proctor, *Umphrey Lee*, p. 173.

82. Board Minutes, May 31, 1948. The juxtaposition of these motions is confusing, but Secretary of the University Phoebe Davis agrees with the author that "the far-reaching program" concerned the training of Negro ministers. Letter to the author from Miss Phoebe Davis, May 23, 1977.

83. Board Minutes, November 10, 1950.

84. The author was a member of that student council.

85. Culver, *Negro Segregation in The Methodist Church*, pp. 130-31.

86. Merrimon Cuninggim, "Integration in Professional Education: The Story of Perkins, Southern Methodist University," *Annals of the American Academy of Political and Social Science* 304 (1956): 109-15. Cuninggim succeeded Eugene B. Hawk as dean of the School of Theology in September, 1951.

87. During the summer, the Negro students wrote to the housing director requesting that they not be placed in rooms with white students for the fall semester. Weiss and Proctor, *Umphrey Lee*, p. 175.

88. An undated letter from Umphrey Lee to AFS might shed light on the bishop's memory at this point. The letter states in part: "I hope you get this before you go to Wichita Falls as I want you to know . . . I have told Brother Perkins that I was greatly troubled when I got his letter, wondering whether I should disregard my doctors or quit and let the Board put in someone who could take over at once. I told him that you insisted that I stick with my doctors and that you would assume responsibility for the matter he wrote about. Frank, I hate like everything for you to have to spend time on this. However, I should have had to tell Brother Perkins in the end that the matter had been put in the hands of the Board and that I would be a fool to try to settle the matter by administrative order. . . ." The content of the entire letter would almost positively place the writing in July or August, 1953. Lee to AFS (n.d.), Smith Papers.

89. See Cuninggim, "Integration in Professional Education," p. 113.

90. Braden interview. See also Weiss and Proctor, *Umphrey Lee*, pp. 174-75.

91. Quoted in Vernon, *Forever Building*, p. 120. According to Bishop Martin, Mr. Perkins spoke in favor of integration when the matter originally came before the board. Interview with Bishop Martin, January 14, 1972, in Dallas, Texas. While the Board Minutes indicate Mr. Perkins was present at that meeting, they record only the motions or reports presented to the board and not the discussion pertaining to those actions. Board Minutes, November 10, 1950.

92. Braden interview. According to one report, during a Woman's Society of Christian Service meeting in Wichita Falls, Mrs. Perkins had reported favorably on the full participation of the Negro students at Perkins School of Theology. "Why, what would those ladies think if the Board were to remove these boys?" Private conversation with Professor Albert C. Outler, February 11, 1977.

93. *Time*, February 19, 1951, p. 78; Bishop Charles C. Selecman to AFS, May 13, 1950, Smith Papers.

94. Interview with Mrs. Walter W. Fondren, October 26, 1973, in Houston, Texas. This was the First Methodist Church parsonage of which AFS was so proud. See chap. 7.

95. See, for example, Mrs. Fondren's remarks and the tributes paid to Mr. Fondren by AFS, Dr. Score, and others at the dedication of the Fondren Library at SMU, as published in the *S.M.U. News-Digest*, June 15, 1940.

96. Interview with Dr. Willis M. Tate, July 22, 1972, in Dallas, Texas. Vice president of development and public relations since 1950, Tate succeeded Lee in 1954 as president of SMU.

97. Mrs. Fondren announced her gift after the Fondren lecture on the opening night of Ministers' Week in 1946. See AFS's daily journal, entry for February 4, 1946; Board Minutes, February 5, 1946.

98. Quoted in the *S.M.U. News-Digest*, March 28, 1946, p. 2. Smith's full statement also praised the Perkinses for their additional gift of $650,000, which increased their total gift to two million at that time.

99. As quoted in the *S.M.U. News-Digest*, May-June, 1950, pp. 3-4. The dedication was held on May 10, 1950.

100. Board Minutes, October 31, 1947; AFS's daily journal, entry for Sunday, October 12, 1947.

101. *Mustang* 5 (May 1953): 12.

102. Florence and Hoblitzelle have been included in the recent expansion of *The Handbook of Texas*, ed. Eldon Stephen Branda (Austin: Texas State Historical Association, 1976), 3:299-300, 396-97.

103. "Florence Hall Dedication, April 21, 1951," typewritten statement, Smith Papers.

104. Florence to AFS, April 7, 1951. This was Florence's reply to Smith's letter informing him of the naming of the building at SMU. See also Florence to AFS, April 30, 1951. Both letters are in the Smith Papers.

When the Council of Bishops sent AFS to Europe in 1953 (see chap. 12), Mrs. Smith's expenses were paid by Fred Florence. Florence to AFS, January 3, 1953, Smith Papers.

105. Lee to AFS, June 3, 1943, Smith Papers.

106. Hawk to AFS, January 26, 1945, Smith Papers. See also AFS's daily journal, entries for January 21 and 22, 1945.

107. Hawk to AFS, February 14, 1945. See also Hawk to AFS, February 24, 1949, and Hawk to AFS, June 30, 1947, all in Smith Papers.

108. Story to AFS, April 27, 1951, Smith Papers.

109 Loretta Hawkins to AFS, May 10, 1953; Weiss and Proctor, *Umphrey Lee*, p. 172.

110. Weiss and Proctor, *Umphrey Lee*, p. 182; Thomas, *Southern Methodist University*, pp. 138-41.

111. John Beaty, *The Iron Curtain over America* (Dallas: Wilkinson Publishing Co., 1951). AFS's copy is in Southwestern University's Cody Memorial Library.

112. Stanley High, "Methodism's Pink Fringe," *Reader's Digest* (February 1950): 134-38; *Review of the Methodist Federation for Social Action*, prepared and released by the Committee on Un-American Activities, U.S. House of Representatives, Washington, D.C., February 12, 1952, 87 pages; *Is There a Pink Fringe in The Methodist Church? A Report to Methodists from the Committee for the Preservation of Methodism* (Houston: Ned Gill & Co., April, 1951), 44 pages (reprinted in June and August, 1951, June, 1952, and February, 1953).

113. Gerald L. K. Smith's *The Cross and the Flag* (April 1952); Gerald Winrod's *Defender Magazine* (February 1952); Bob Shuler's *Methodist Challenge* (June 1952); Colonel Alvin M. Owsley in *National Christian Journal* (Summer 1952); and *Los Angeles Times* columnist Hedda Hopper (February 1952). See Ralph Lord Roy, *Apostles of Discord: A Study of Organized Bigotry and Disruption on the Fringes of Protestantism* (Boston: Beacon Press, 1953), pp. 88-89, 383.

114. Boller's "Letter to the Editor" in the *SMU Campus*, November 25, 1953, p. 4.

115. Quoted in the *SMU Campus*, February 24, 1954, p. 6.

116. Margaret L. Hartley, "The Protestant Underworld," *Southwest Review* 38 (Autumn 1953): 342-46. Mrs. Hartley had previously written a major article concerning "The Subliterature of Hate in America," in which she shattered the "Khazar theory" basic to Beaty's thesis and effectively exposed the "superficially impressive panoply of 'scholarly' reference developed by the hate writers." Ibid. 37 (Summer 1952): 177-90.

Ralph Lord Roy, an ordained Methodist minister and graduate of Swarthmore College and Union Theological Seminary, was a doctoral candidate at Columbia University when he wrote his *Apostles of Discord*.

117. John Beaty, "How to Capture a University," Dallas: n.p., January 20, 1954, 8 pages (Dr. Decherd Turner, Librarian of Bridwell Library, obtained a copy of the pamphlet for me from American Jewish Archives, Hebrew Union College–Jewish Institute of Religion, Cincinnati, Ohio: "John Beaty, Box 2290.")

118. Carbon copy of Dr. Lee's statement of February 13, 1954, Smith Papers. See also, *SMU Campus*, February 17, 1954, p. 1.

On February 16 the SMU faculty publicly repudiated Beaty's "How to Capture a University" as being "without any foundation in fact." *SMU Campus*, February 19, 1954, p. 1.

119. Thomas, *Southern Methodist University*, p. 141; and *SMU Campus*, March 3, 1954, p. 1.

120. *Time*, April 12, 1954, p. 57. The article concludes: "Last week . . . John

Beaty was carrying on as usual. From his pen came another pamphlet, plaintively crying that the label 'anti-Semitic' was nothing but a smear aimed at people who are genuine anti-Communists. It certainly was not a tag that could possibly apply to good old John Beaty. 'I have no feelings except feelings of friendship,' said he, 'for pro-American Jews.' "

121. Lee to AFS, March 11, 1954, Smith Papers.

122. Dr. Richard M. Smith to AFS, March 17, 1954 (holograph), Smith Papers. Reports in the Dallas papers of Lee's resignation indicate that Lee was hospitalized at least by Saturday, March 13, if not earlier. *Times Herald*, March 14, 1954, p. 23 (as continued from p. 1).

123. Weiss and Proctor, *Umphrey Lee*, p. 179.

124. At AFS's instruction, Mrs. Loretta Hawkins, the assistant to the president, sent copies of Dr. Lee's resignation letter to all of the trustees with the notation that it would be presented at the spring meeting. Hawkins to AFS, March 15, 1954, Smith Papers.

125. Board Minutes, March 30, 1954.

126. Ibid. (Italics added). The statement said, in part: "As Chancellor, Doctor Lee will not be assigned to any specific duty. His unexcelled knowledge of every ramification of Southern Methodist University and his profound affection for the institution are sufficient for the Board to know that his insight, judgment and spirit will make him invaluable as Chancellor."

127. As told by Dr. Lee to his biographers: Weiss and Proctor, *Umphrey Lee*, p. 187.

128. Board Minutes, March 30, 1954. The full text of the letter is given in the Minutes. See also *SMU Campus*, April 2, 1954, p. 1.

129. Bob Shuler gave complete coverage to the lengthy resolution adopted by the ladies, February 15, 1954, in his *Methodist Challenge* 22 (May 1954): 7-8. See also *SMU Campus*, February 17, 1954, p. 1.

130. Board Minutes, March 30, 1954; *Dallas Morning News*, March 31, 1954; *SMU Campus*, April 2, 1954, p. 1; and private conversation with Professor Albert C. Outler, February 11, 1977.

131. Hawkins to Smith, March 31, 1954, Smith Papers. As the assistant to the president, Mrs. Hawkins attended all meetings of the board. Other words of praise came from Bishop Paul Martin and Fred Florence: Martin to AFS, April 2, 1954 (holograph); Florence to AFS, April 6, 1954, both in the Smith Papers.

132. Boaz to AFS, April 14, 1954, Smith Papers.

133. AFS to Hawkins, April 12, 1954 (holograph), Presidents' Papers, SMU.

134. Board Minutes, May 6, 1954. See also Board Minutes, January 25, 1933. Beaty did not resign, but he wrote no more controversial publications and made no more allegations. According to one of his supporters: "His last two years were difficult: a form of demotion was devised by instituting a new rotation system for the chairmanship of his department." Harold Lord Varney, "Southern Methodist University Pampers Leftism," *American Mercury* (January 1960), p. 18.

135. Private conversation with Margaret L. Hartley, February 11, 1977, at SMU.

136. Board Minutes, May 6, 1954.

137. The following section is based primarily upon the author's interview with Chancellor Willis M. Tate, July 22, 1972, at SMU.

138. "Just a note to thank you for your help and inspiration in my hour of decision. I have decided to accept the offer at S.M.U." Willis M. Tate to AFS, May 20, 1945 (holograph), Smith Papers.

139. Interviews with Bishop W. Angie Smith, January 12, 1972, in Dallas; Bishop Paul E. Martin, January 12, 1972, at Perkins School of Theology; Mrs. J. J. Perkins, June 26, 1972, in Wichita Falls; and Bishop William C. Martin, January 22, 1973, in Little Rock. Both Martins had been SMU trustees since 1934 and AFS since 1944.

140. Interview with Chancellor Tate, July 22, 1972.

141. Ibid.

142. Ibid.

143. For this stand President Tate later received the Alexander Meiklejohn Award for Academic Freedom from the American Association of University Professors.

144. See AFS's correspondence for March and April, 1958, Smith Papers.

145. Tate to AFS, March 24, 1958 (holograph), Smith Papers. In conversation about the Gates controversy, Tate made a comment that illustrates his point here: "There were some preachers who were kind of exercised about this [Gates's speaking on campus] who came later to realize that we were fighting their battle, that the free pulpit was at stake here as much as academic freedom. This is one reason why a university is important to a church." Interview with Chancellor Tate, July 22, 1972.

146. Tate to AFS, May 13, 1956 (holograph), Smith Papers.

147. Interview with Chancellor Tate, July 22, 1972. One of many examples of Smith's praise of Tate: "Your leadership on the campus and off is brilliant and a commanding success. We are unfailingly proud of you." AFS to Tate, November 8, 1956 (holograph), Presidents' Papers, SMU.

148. Ibid.

149. AFS to Tate, July 10, 1955, Presidents' Papers, SMU.

150. Tate to AFS, July 25, 1959, Smith Papers.

151. Tate to AFS, July 22, 1959 (italics added), Presidents' Papers, SMU.

152. AFS to Tate, August 5, 1959, Presidents' Papers, SMU.

153. Board Minutes, November 4, 1960.

154. Ibid. AFS later arranged for the signature of Fred Florence to be added to the plaque. Florence was not present at the meeting, presumably already stricken with the illness that was to take his life on December 25, 1960. See AFS to Tate, November 5, 1960 (holograph), Presidents' Papers, SMU.

155. Eugene McElvaney sent a copy of his dedicatory address for this special collection room to Mrs. Smith, postmarked May 15, 1963, Smith Papers.

156. Tate to AFS, October 31, 1960 (carbon copy), Presidents' Papers, SMU.

157. Dean Merrimon Cuninggim to AFS, December 1, 1953, Smith Papers. See also Albert C. Outler to AFS, February 21, 1955, Smith Papers. These lectures were recorded and later transcribed. Both the reel-to-reel tapes and the typescripts are in the Smith Papers. They were not published, at AFS's request. AFS to Tate, July 10, 1955, Presidents' Papers, SMU.

158. A. L. Harding to AFS, April 30, 1956. AFS's initiation was conducted in the courtroom of Florence Hall, November 1, 1956. Harding to AFS, October 25, 1956. Both letters are in the Smith Papers.

159. Boaz to AFS, May 14, 1956, Smith Papers. Concluding his letter, the old gentleman wrote: "Please remember both of us to dear Bessie and give her a big hug for us. She is largely responsible for your great success in life."

CHAPTER SIXTEEN

1. Braden interview.

As usual, AFS had his figures correct. The number of preachers who joined the Texas Conference "on trial"—"probationary members" in present terminology—during the period 1934-1960 is 419. In 1960, 338 of these were still effective, or approximately 74 percent of the 454 total effective members of the Texas Conference at that time. *Journals* of the Texas Conference for the years 1934-60.

2. Of these 189 men, 176 were still effective in 1960 when the Southwest Texas Conference numbered 319 effective members. *Journals* of the West Texas and the Southwest Texas conferences for the years 1938-60.

3. Interview with Dr. Monroe Vivion, January 18, 1973, at Flint, Texas.

4. Interview with Rev. Walton B. Gardner, August 23, 1972, in Houston, Texas.

5. Interview with Bishop O. Eugene Slater, August 8, 1972, in San Antonio, Texas.

6. Interview with Bishop Paul E. Martin, January 14, 1972, in Dallas, Texas.

7. AFS's daily journal, entry for November 17, 1949; entry for July 15, 1950 in AFS's Travel Diary, Smith Papers. See also AFS to Dr. Alfredo Nañez, March 11, 1953, Papers of Dr. Alfredo Nañez, Bridwell Library, Southern Methodist University.

8. Braden interview.

9. Ibid.

10. *Southwestern Magazine* 33, no. 4 (March 1931): 23-24.

11. Interview with Bishop W. C. Martin, January 22, 1973, in Little Rock, Arkansas.

12. Fletcher S. Crowe to AFS, October 30, 1945, Smith Papers.

13. R. F. Curl to AFS, March 24, 1954, Smith Papers.

14. Interview with Bishop W. Kenneth Pope, September 15, 1972, at Southern Methodist University, Dallas, Texas.

15. Among those who used this form were Dr. Bonneau P. Murphy and Dr. Earl Brown of the General Board of Missions; President Willis Tate and certain administrators and senior faculty members at SMU; the administrative staff and some of the doctors at the Methodist Hospital in Houston; some of the district superintendents and conference executive secretaries; and even Mr. and Mrs. J. J. Perkins.

16. Interview with Dr. Monroe Vivion.

17. See interviews with Bishops W. Angie Smith, Arthur Moore, W. C. Martin, Paul E. Martin, W. Kenneth Pope, and "pillars" of the Southern Church such as Stewart Clendenin, Finis Crutchfield, D. Lawrence Landrum, Albert C. Outler, L. U. Spellman, and Monroe Vivion.

18. Interview with Bishop W. Kenneth Pope.

19. Interview with Dr. D. Lawrence Landrum, January 17, 1973, in Palestine, Texas. See also interview with Dr. Monroe Vivion, January 18, 1973.

20. Dr. L. U. Spellman to the author, October 31, 1977.

21. Braden interview.

22. Ibid.

23. AFS's daily journal, entry for September 2, 1942.

24. Spellman to the author, February 9, 1973.

25. Interview with Dr. Stewart Clendenin, August 28, 1972, in Houston, Texas.

26. Spellman to the author, February 9, 1973.

27. Interview with Bishop W. Kenneth Pope.

28. Braden interview.

29. Almus D. Jameson to AFS, May 20, 1946, Smith Papers.

30. W. B. Oliver to AFS, June 25, 1948, Smith Papers.

31. P. E. Riley to AFS, June 30, 1948, Smith Papers.

32. Interview with Bishop Kenneth W. Copeland, August 23, 1972, in Houston.

33. William H. Wallace, Jr. to AFS, October 27, 1942, Smith Papers.

34. Interview with Dr. Monroe Vivion.

35. Spellman to the author, February 9, 1973, p. 2.

36. Interview with Dr. D. Lawrence Landrum.

37. Ibid. See also interview with Dr. Stewart Clendenin.

38. AFS's daily journal, entry for January 6, 1942.

39. Interview with Dr. Stewart Clendenin.

40. Interview with Bishop O. Eugene Slater, August 8, 1972, in San Antonio, Texas. Slater was in Houston concerning his forthcoming appointment to Bering.

41. See entries in AFS's daily journal for July 13, August 31, and November 19, 1945; December 28, 1947. See also interview with Mrs. Frank P. Wright, October 29, 1976, in Georgetown, Texas. Mrs. Wright did most of AFS's secretarial work in the latter years.

42. In a letter to Dr. Alfredo Nañez, March 2, 1960, Papers of Dr. Alfredo Nañez, Bridwell Library, SMU.

43. Interview with Dr. Landrum.

44. Braden interview.

45. Interview with Dr. Landrum.

46. Interview with Dr. Clendenin.

47. Interview with Dr. Vivion.

48. Interview with Bishop W. C. Martin.

49. See AFS's daily journal, entry for April 26, 1942.

50. Interview with Dr. Spellman. See also Spellman to the author, February 9, 1973, pp. 1-2.

51. Interview with Dr. Finis Crutchfield, January 24, 1972.

52. Interview with Dr. Vivion.

53. Interview with Bishop Slater.

54. Braden interview.

55. As quoted in the *Houston Post*, May 25, 1953, sec. 1, p. 8.

56. As quoted by Dr. Charles Braden on a tape recording of AFS's letter to "Dear Bill," no date given.

57. Braden interview.

58. Interview with Dr. Landrum.

59. Braden interview.

60. Interview with Bishop Paul Martin.

61. W. F. Bryan to AFS, October 22, 1956, Smith Papers.

62. Spellman to the author, February 9, 1973.

63. Interview with Dr. Vivion.

64. Spellman to the author, February 9, 1973.

65. Interview with Dr. Landrum.

66. Spellman to the author, February 9, 1973.

67. Interviews with Dr. Landrum and Dr. Vivion.

68. Interview with Dr. Spellman.

69. Interview with Dr. Vivion. See also interview with Dr. Landrum.

70. Interview with Dr. Clendenin.

71. An Official Board Chairman to AFS, August 11, 1945, Smith Papers.

72. Interview with Dr. Landrum.

73. Braden interview.

74. Interview with Dr. Vivion.

75. Braden interview.

76. Interview with Dr. Landrum.

77. Interview with Dr. Vivion.

78. Interview with Dr. Spellman.

79. Spellman to the author, February 9, 1973.

80. Interview with Dr. Crutchfield.

81. Rev. P. E. Riley to AFS, November 17, 1945 (holograph), Smith Papers. After holding his first session of the Central Texas Annual Conference, AFS wrote in his daily journal (Friday, November 3, 1944): "The old divisions in the C. T. Conf. caused no trouble & I hope we can bring harmony to the conf."

82. Rev. A. S. Gafford to AFS, May 12, 1948, Smith Papers.

83. AFS's daily journal, entry for Saturday, December 27, 1947.

84. "The writer of the articles was Frederick Woltman of New York, who won the Pulitzer prize for exposing communism at work in respectable organizations," AFS wrote. "Naturally his words had unusual weight." AFS to Bishop John M. Moore, January 10, 1948, Papers of Bishop John M. Moore, item M1926.

85. *Houston Press*, December 26, 1947.

86. As quoted in the *Houston Press*, December 27, 1947.

87. AFS's daily journal, entry for Monday, December 29, 1947. Woltman's

article declares that "a strong attack on America's foreign policies and a growing defense of Russia's were made. . . . The story of Mary and Jesus, the spirit of Christmas and the Sermon on the Mount, were invoked as justifications for the attack on the U.S. and the praise of the Soviet Union." The editorial praises Woltman for "laying bare the facts" but expresses "shock" at the "disclosures of what went on at that conference." "None but insidious, unprincipled leftists would have such unsurpassed gall." *Houston Press*, Monday, December 29, 1947.

88. AFS's daily journal, entry for Tuesday, December 30, 1947. "Red Activities Ignored as Methodist Group Criticizes U.S. Policies," was the headline of the newspaper article. *Houston Press*, Tuesday, December 30, 1947.

89. AFS's words in an explanation he wrote for Dr. Charles Braden, March 20, 1962, Smith Papers.

90. AFS to Bishop John M. Moore, January 10, 1948, Bishop John M. Moore Papers, M1926. According to the 1948 *Discipline*, there were fifty-eight bishops, active and retired, living in the United States. Approximately one-third of them would have belonged to the Federation.

91. The Episcopal Address, as quoted in the *Daily Christian Advocate, Proceedings of the General Conference of The Methodist Church, 1948*, 3 (April 29, 1948): 35, 45. Since all of the bishops sign the "Address," it is considered to be the work and wisdom of the entire council and not just that of the bishop designated to prepare the draft and present the final message to the General Conference.

92. AFS to Rev. O. Eugene Slater, January 16, 1948 (holograph), courtesy of Bishop Slater.

93. See the Report of the Committee to Study the Field for Social Action, *Daily Christian Advocate* 3 (April 28, 1948): 11.

94. AFS's daily journal, entry for Tuesday, December 30, 1947. The penciled, much revised notes have survived in the Smith Papers.

95. Ibid., entry for Wednesday, December 31, 1947.

96. As stated by AFS in an explanation he wrote for Dr. Charles Braden, March 20, 1962. AFS does not mention the Houston District Superintendent, Dr. Guy F. Jones, in his daily journal accounts of December 30 and 31, 1947. The *Houston Press*, however, does refer to Dr. Jones in connection with the issuing of the bishop's statement. *Houston Press*, January 2, 1948.

97. As published in the *Houston Press*, January 2, 1948. AFS eliminated a fifth point from his penciled draft which read: "I personally oppose and deplore certain utterances and actions emanating from the Kansas City meeting, as reported in the Scripps-Howard papers, and as a Methodist I repudiate any intimation that such represents The Methodist Church." Holograph notes, Smith Papers.

98. Western Union telegram, January 2, 1948, sent to AFS at the Hotel Martinique, New York City, Smith Papers.

99. AFS's daily journal, entry for Saturday, January 3, 1948.

100. As AFS explained in a letter to Rev. O. Eugene Slater, January 16, 1948. Holograph courtesy of Bishop Slater.

101. *New York World Telegram*, Saturday, January 3, 1948. On Sunday, January 4, the *New York Times*—not in the Scripps-Howard chain—published a more reserved account.

102. AFS to Leete, February 17, 1948, Bishop Frederick D. Leete Collection, Bridwell Library, SMU.

103. AFS to Moore, January 10, 1948, Bishop John M. Moore Papers, item M1926.

104. AFS to Leete, March 14, 1948 (holograph), Leete Collection, Bridwell Library, SMU.

105. Braden interview.

106. AFS's daily journal, entry for November 30, 1948. See also Braden interview.

Bishop Baker, on the other hand, had said of AFS's statement: "I think the Federation itself would be willing to endorse that." Braden interview.

107. AFS to Dr. Charles Braden, March 20, 1962, Smith Papers.

108. Eric F. Goldman, *The Crucial Decade: America, 1945-1955* (New York: Alfred A. Knopf, 1956), pp. 52-53, 121. See also Robert Griffith, *The Politics of Fear* (Lexington: University Press of Kentucky, 1970); Earl Latham, *The Communist Controversy in Washington: From the New Deal to McCarthy* (Cambridge: Harvard University Press, 1966).

109. Goldman, *Crucial Decade*, pp. 121-23. Talcott Parsons, the eminent sociologist, presents a similar thesis in "Social Strains in America—1955," *The New American Right*, ed. Daniel Bell (New York: Criterion Books, 1955), pp. 217, 223-34.

110. See Earl Latham, ed., *The Meaning of McCarthyism* (New York: D. C. Heath & Co., 1965, 1973), p. viii.

111. For a more thorough analysis of this pamphlet, see Ralph Lord Roy, *Communism and the Churches* (New York: Harcourt, Brace & World, 1960), pp. 231-32.

112. Minutes of the Council of Bishops of The Methodist Church, December 2, 1948, Methodist Historical Collection, Bridwell Library, SMU.

113. Latham, *The Communist Controversy in Washington*, especially Part II and Part III; and Robert Griffith, *The Politics of Fear: Joseph R. McCarthy and the Senate* (Lexington: University Press of Kentucky, 1970), pp. 48-51.

114. Stanley High, "Methodism's Pink Fringe," *Reader's Digest* (February 1950), pp. 134-38.

115. Roy, *Communism and the Churches*, pp. 303-5.

116. Braden interview. See Hines H. Baker to AFS, March 9, 1950, for the date of the meeting. Smith Papers.

117. Minutes of the Council of Bishops of The Methodist Church, April 17-21, 1950. AFS was chosen by the College of Bishops of the South Central Jurisdiction.

118. Ibid., April 20, 1950.

119. Interview with Dr. Landrum. Did AFS think that the district superintendents would be less subject to pressure than pastors would be?

120. Memorial Concerning the Federation on Social Action, *Journal of the Twelfth Annual Session of the Texas Annual Conference of The Methodist Church*, May 30–June 2, 1950, pp. 97-99. The draft of the original committee was revised by a second committee, also composed of ministers and laymen and appointed by AFS. Eugene Slater, R. A. Shepherd, and R. C. Terry signed the version adopted by the conference.

121. Except where stated otherwise, the information here is drawn from the printed booklet, *Is There a Pink Fringe in The Methodist Church?: A Report to Methodists from the Committee for the Preservation of Methodism*, 5th printing, February, 1953 (first printing April, 1951).

122. Braden interview.

123. L. U. Spellman to the author, February 9, 1973.

124. *Is There a Pink Fringe in The Methodist Church?*, pp. 1-4, and also the letter of introduction to the booklet.

125. Braden interview.

126. Interview with Bishop W. Kenneth Pope. See also Ralph S. O'Leary's series of articles on the Houston Minute Women in the *Houston Post*, October 11-21, 1953; and Don E. Carleton, "McCarthyism in Houston: The George Ebbey Affair," [1953], *Southwestern Historical Quarterly* 80, no. 2 (October 1976): 163-76.

127. Braden interview.

128. Walter Goodman, *The Committee: The Extraordinary Career of the House Committee on Un-American Activities* (New York: Farrar, Straus & Giroux, 1964), pp. 324-25.

129. Richard M. Fried, *Men against McCarthy* (New York: Columbia University Press, 1976), chaps. 8, 9.

130. Braden interview.

131. AFS's closest friends among the members of the committee included: First Church—Walter L. Goldston, Jr., Fred J. Heyne, R. A. Shepherd; St. Lukes—Hines H. Baker, W. N. Blanton, L. L. Nelms (all originally members of First Church when AFS was pastor there). All forty-two members of the committee are listed in their publication, *Is There a Pink Fringe in Methodism?*.

132. Braden interview. See also interviews with Bishop W. Kenneth Pope and Bishop O. Eugene Slater.

133. Interview with Bishop O. Eugene Slater.

134. Interview with Bishop W. Kenneth Pope.

135. *Journal of the Fifteenth Annual Session of the Texas Annual Conference of The Methodist Church, June 1-5, 1953,* pp. 39, 110-11. The resolution was presented by the lay delegate and the pastor of the Chapelwood Methodist Church.

136. Hines H. Baker to AFS, June 11, 1953 (holograph), Smith Papers.

137. Baker became a Methodist under AFS's ministry at University Methodist Church in Austin, establishing a relationship that was renewed when AFS came to Houston in 1922 and continued until the bishop's death in 1962. See chaps. 5, 7, and 8. AFS wrote a moving tribute to Mr. Baker in his daily journal, May 14, 1948, shortly after Baker became the president of the Humble Oil & Refining Company.

138. Baker to AFS, June 11, 1953 (holograph).

139. Interview with Hines H. Baker, September 17, 1973, in Houston, Texas.

CHAPTER SEVENTEEN

1. See chap. 9, pp. 177-81.

2. Dr. Charles S. Braden's interview with AFS and Mrs. Smith, January 23, 1962, in Houston, Texas, Smith Papers.

3. Interview with Mrs. Donald G. (Elizabeth Ann Smith) Griffin, November 7, 1974, in Georgetown, Texas. (She is referred to hereafter as Betty Smith Griffin).

4. Smith's reasons for not moving his family to Oklahoma or Missouri are noted in chap. 9, pp. 185-86. Bishop H. A. Boaz, as the presiding bishop of the Texas Conference, lived in the episcopal residence at 2308 Southmore Blvd., according to the *Nashville Christian Advocate,* October 10, 1930, p. 1332.

5. Interview with A. Frank Smith, Jr., August 29, 1972, in Houston, Texas.

6. Interview with W. Randolph Smith, August 29, 1972, in Houston, Texas. See also Betty Smith Griffin to the author, January 29, 1978, pp. 3 and 6.

7. Interview with Betty Smith Griffin.

8. Interview with W. R. Smith. See also Betty Smith Griffin to the author, January 29, 1978, p. 2.

9. AFS's daily journal, entries for Thursday, June 8, 1944; and Monday, September 21, and Saturday, August 15, 1942.

10. Interview with Dr. L. U. Spellman, January 23, 1973, in Kerrville, Texas.

11. Braden interview with AFS and Mrs. Smith.

12. Letter to the author from W. Randolph Smith, November 11, 1977; and interview with Mrs. Betty Smith Griffin.

13. Ibid.

14. AFS to Dr. J. N. R. Score, undated but clearly mid-March 1939 (holograph), Score Papers, Bridwell Library, SMU.

15. AFS's daily journal, entry for December 3, 1949.

16. See chap. 9, p. 189.

17. Interview with A. Frank Smith, Jr.

18. AFS's daily journal, entry for Wednesday, January 17, 1945. See also Betty Smith Griffin to the author, January 29, 1978, p. 10.

19. Ibid., entries for Tuesday, April 2, and Tuesday, April 9, 1946.

20. AFS to Dr. J. N. R. Score, January 27, 1940, Score Papers, SMU; AFS's daily journal, entries for April 27, 1945, and September 5, 1947; and letter to Rev. John Butterworth, December 14, 1960 (carbon copy), Smith Papers.

21. Entry for Saturday, November 25, 1944.

22. Entries for August 7 and August 30, 1942. The bishop preached twice that Sunday, nevertheless.

23. Braden interview with AFS and Mrs. Smith. See also AFS's daily journal, entry for February 8, 1942.

24. Interview with Betty Smith Griffin. See also chap. 1, pp. 13-14, and chap. 2, pp. 37-38.

25. Interview with A. Frank Smith, Jr.

26. Interview with W. R. Smith.

27. This is the journal that cannot be found.

28. For example: January 7, May 30, July 18, and August 6, 1942; April 12 and October 10, 1943; May 21, 1944; January 8, 1945; October 11 and November 1, 1947; and July 12, 1948.

29. Telegram draft written on letterhead of First Methodist Church, Caldwell, Texas, where the Bryan District Conference was meeting. AFS's daily journal, entry for Thursday, April 29, 1943.

30. Entry for Sunday, December 19, 1943.

31. Entry for Saturday, July 15, 1944.

32. Entries for Sunday, August 12, and Friday, August 24, 1945.

33. W. R. Smith to the author, November 11, 1977.

34. AFS's daily journal; the more significant entries are: January 1 and February 12, 1942; May 13, 1943; February 23 and 26 and September 17, 1944.

35. Entry for Wednesday, October 24, 1945. See also entries for November 13, 1944, July 22, 1945, and August 10, 1948.

36. Interview with A. Frank Smith, Jr.

37. See chap. 9, p. 195, and chap. 10, p. 200.

38. Interview with A. Frank Smith, Jr.

39. Interview with Betty Smith Griffin, and Mrs. Griffin to Dr. Charles S. Braden, August 8, 1962 (holograph), Smith Papers. See also Mrs. Griffin to the author, January 29, 1978, p. 9.

40. Ibid.

41. Assertion based on specific references in AFS's daily journal. Even during Betty's four years at SMU, she went to movies with her parents approximately eighteen times, including eight times in 1942.

42. Interview with W. R. Smith. Mrs. Griffin ascribes her "loss of hearing" to "a double mastoid while still a baby." Interview with Mrs. Griffin.

43. Mrs. Griffin to Dr. Braden, August 8, 1962.

44. Interview with Betty Smith Griffin.

45. AFS to Score, October 12, 1935 (holograph), Score Papers, SMU.

46. AFS's daily journal, entries for Thursday and Friday, September 6 and 7, 1945. AFS's use of "Betty Ann" here as elsewhere in his daily journal, rather than just Betty, might be due to his shorthand. He uses "B" for Bessie, so he must distinguish Betty by "B.A."

47. AFS to Betty Smith, February 13, 1942 (holograph), courtesy of Mrs. Betty Smith Griffin.

48. AFS's daily journal, entries for February 14, 1942 and July 19, 1943.

49. Interview with Betty Smith Griffin.

50. See entries for January 1 and August 18, 1942; April 2 and October 16, 1943. See also March 13, 1942.

51. Entries for April 10 and October 25, 1942.

52. Entries for January 2, 3, and 6 and August 13, 1942; June 12 and July 2, 1943; and March 10, 1945.

53. See entries for January 22, 1942 and October 5, 1943; also W. R. Smith to author, December 27, 1977.

54. Letter to "Wm. Randolph Smith," September 14, 1942 (holograph), courtesy of Mr. Smith. See also entries for May 29 and June 1, 1942.

55. AFS's daily journal, entries for June 4 and December 20, 1943.

56. Letter to Wm. Randolph Smith, January 13, 1944 (holograph), courtesy of Mr. Smith. See also AFS's daily journal, entry for Thursday, January 13, 1944.

57. Braden interview with AFS and Mrs. Smith.

58. Interview with A. Frank Smith, Jr. and W. R. Smith. Italics added.

59. Interview with Betty Smith Griffin. See also Mrs. Griffin to Dr. Braden, August 8, 1962.

60. See AFS's daily journal, entries for April 30, 1945, February 17, 1946, and May 13, 1947.

61. Interview with A. Frank Smith, Jr., and "Pastor's Letter," the *Church School Builder* of First Methodist Church, Houston, Texas, 1 no. 2 (September 9, 1927): 1.

62. Letter to Russell (Dr. J. N. R.) Score, July 28, 1935, Score Papers, SMU. Beginning in 1934, AFS was assigned the Texas and North Texas Conferences in place of the three conferences in Missouri. He continued to hold the Oklahoma and Indian Mission conferences.

63. Interview with Betty Smith Griffin.

64. Entry for July 31, 1943; and letter to "Gene and Eva B. Slater," July 18, 1952 (holograph), courtesy of Bishop O. Eugene Slater.

65. Interview with A. Frank Smith, Jr. and W. R. Smith.

66. Interview with Betty Smith Griffin.

67. Entries for August 14 and 21, 1943.

68. Interview with A. Frank Smith, Jr. and W. R. Smith. See also AFS's daily journal, entries for August 7 and 15, 1943.

69. Interview with Dr. L. U. Spellman. Spellman recalls that AFS told this anecdote to him and Rev. Walter W. Lipps when they brought AFS to Victoria to dedicate the church there. AFS's daily journal, entry for April 19, 1942.

70. Betty Smith Griffin to the author, January 29, 1978, p. 3.

71. AFS's daily journal, see entries for September 11 through 23, 1944.

72. Letter to "Dearest Bessie," June 18, 1947 (holograph), and AFS's daily journal, entries for June 15 through 26, 1947.

73. Letter to Betty Ann Smith, January 18, 1942 (holograph), courtesy of Mrs. Betty Smith Griffin.

74. Letter to Wm. Randolph Smith, June 17, 1945 (holograph), courtesy of Mr. Smith.

75. Letter to "Dear Betty," September 14, 1947 (holograph), courtesy of Mrs. Betty Smith Griffin. See also AFS's daily journal, entries for July 31 and August 24, 1945, and May 12, 1947.

76. Letter to "Dear Betty," September 20, 1947 (holograph), courtesy of Mrs. Betty Smith Griffin. See also AFS's daily journal, entry for September 18, 1947.

77. AFS's daily journal, entry for June 12, 1948.

78. Letter to "My Dearest Frank," the first of two undated holographs probably written during Holy Week of 1941, Smith Papers.

79. Interview with A. Frank Smith, Jr.

80. Interview with Bishop Paul E. Martin. See also interview with Bishop Arthur J. Moore.

81. Interview with W. R. Smith. The vast majority of the envelopes of the letters that AFS and Mrs. Smith wrote to each other are marked both "special delivery" and "air mail." Smith Papers.

82. Letter to "Dearest Bessie," January 6, 1954 (holograph); letter to Mrs. A. Frank Smith, envelope postmarked January 10, 1953 (holograph), Smith Papers.

83. Letter to "Dear Frank," the first of two undated holographs probably written during Holy Week of 1941, Smith Papers.

84. AFS's daily journal, entries for March 12, August 6, 8, 17, and 20, 1942; March 29 and 30, and October 13, 1944.

85. Ibid., 1942: January 2 and 22, February 13 and 14, April 10, June 1 and August 17; 1943: March 5, April 2, 27, and 30, September 7, 18, and 21, October 11 and 16; 1944: February 21, 26, and 28, May 7 and 13, July 28 and 31, August 4, 8, 12, 14, and 16, September 14 and 17, December 26; 1945: April 3 and 4, May 12, 22, and 26, July 12, August 4 and 20, September 8 and 17, October 1, November 28, December 22; 1946: July 4 and 27, August 2, 8, 13, 15, 16, and 27, December 6 and 30.

86. Ibid., see November 26 through December 9, 1945.

87. Ibid., see April 23 through May 12, 1948.

88. Ibid., see January 13, 1949; also AFS to Bishop William C. Martin, June 8 and 25, 1950 (holographs), Bishop William C. Martin Papers, Bridwell Library, SMU.

89. W. R. Smith to the author, November 11, 1977.

90. W. R. Smith to AFS and Mrs. Smith, undated but written in September, 1950, Smith Papers.

91. "Final Itinerary for the Right Reverend and Mrs. A. Frank Smith," American Express, June 9, 1950, Smith Papers.

92. Braden interview with AFS and Mrs. Smith.

93. Letter addressed to "My Dear Frank and Mary," March 26, 1960 (holograph), courtesy of Mr. Smith.

CHAPTER EIGHTEEN

1. See chap. 7, p. 144.

2. "The Methodist Hospital, 1924-1962: An Historical Review," *Journal* of the Methodist Hospital (September 1962), p. 3. The Methodist Hospital opened in 1924 with two units: the old twenty-bed Norsworthy Hospital and the new five-story, ninety-bed building.

3. Interview with Dr. J. Charles Dickson, October 26, 1973, at the Methodist Hospital, Houston, Texas.

4. See interviews with Dr. Durwood Fleming, July 14, 1973, in Georgetown, Texas; and R. A. Shepherd, September 18, 1973, in Houston, Texas.

5. See the articles that AFS wrote about Barnes Hospital for the *St. Louis Christian Advocate*, May 6 and 13, 1931.

6. After twenty years as professor of medicine at the University of Texas medical branch at Galveston, Dr. Graves moved to Houston and established a private practice in 1925. He was a trustee of the Methodist Hospital from 1925 to 1946 and a lifetime honorary staff member. Son of a Methodist minister, a graduate of Southwestern University ('85), Dr. Graves served as president of the State Medical Association. He was the Smiths' family doctor in the 1930s.

7. Interview with Dr. Hatch W. Cummings, Jr., Chief of the General Medical Section of the Methodist Hospital, September 18, 1973.

8. Interview with Dr. Cummings.

9. Interview with Hines H. Baker, September 17, 1973, in Houston, Texas.

10. Interview with Robert A. Shepherd, September 18, 1973, in Houston, Texas.

11. Except where noted otherwise, the sources of historical details given here are: *The Texas Medical Center*, a brochure published by the Texas Medical Center, Inc., in 1973; and interview with Dr. Cummings.

12. See AFS's daily journal, entries for November 24, 1943, January 4, 1944, and October 7, 1946. See also the form letter AFS sent to the Methodists of Houston and of the Texas Conference, dated January 18, 1947, Smith Papers.

13. The son of one of the drillers of Spindletop, Hamill is a wealthy oil man and a prominent Methodist layman. See chap. 13, p. 280.

14. Interview with Robert A. Shepherd, who received this information directly from both Blanton and Hamill. See also Ed Kilman and Theon Wright, *Hugh Roy Cullen* (New York: Prentice-Hall, 1954), pp. 225-31. The million-dollar gift to St. Joseph was made in 1949.

15. As quoted in the *Houston Chronicle* and in the *Houston Post*, Sunday, March 4, 1945. The *Chronicle* ran the full story and picture on its front page; the *Post* divided the story between its first and fifth pages, with the picture on the fifth page.

16. AFS to Blanton, April 11, 1961 (carbon copy), Smith Papers.

17. Interview with Mr. Shepherd. Shepherd, like Hines Baker, was a student in law school in Austin when he first met and came to admire AFS, then pastor of the University Methodist Church, establishing a relationship that was later renewed in Houston.

18. Kilman and Wright, *Hugh Roy Cullen*, pp. 233ff.

19. Interview with Mr. Shepherd.

20. Interview with Ted Bowen, president of the Methodist Hospital, September 21, 1973, in Houston, Texas. Bowen joined the staff in the summer of 1948.

21. Dr. Stewart Clendenin gave this version of the event to the author during a conversation at Southwestern University, October 25, 1973.

22. As told to the author by Robert A. Shepherd: "I was there when she said it!"

23. See also the interviews with Ted Bowen, Robert A. Shepherd, and Dr. Hatch W. Cummings.

24. Interview with Mrs. Walter W. Fondren, October 26, 1973, in Houston, Texas.

25. Interview with Tom Fourqurean, vice president and director of the Methodist Hospital, October 26, 1973, in Houston, Texas.

26. Interview with Dr. Stewart Clendenin, August 28, 1972, in Houston, Texas.

27. AFS's daily journal, entry for October 11, 1948.

28. Letter "to the Methodists of Houston and the Texas Conference" from AFS, January 18, 1947, Smith Papers. See also AFS's article in the *St. Louis Christian Advocate*, May 6, 1931, pp. 1-2.

29. Letter to AFS from Hines H. Baker, chairman of the Big Gifts Committee, October 18, 1946, Smith Papers.

30. Interview with Mr. Bowen.

31. Interview with Mr. Shepherd. On AFS's influence on Mrs. Fondren, see also interview with Dr. Durwood Fleming, July 14, 1973.

32. Interview with Mr. Baker.

33. Ibid.

34. Interview with Dr. Durwood Fleming. Fleming was a trustee for ten years. See also interview with Mr. Shepherd.

35. Interview with Mr. Shepherd.

36. Hines H. Baker to AFS, January 10, 1950 (holograph), Smith Papers.

37. See AFS's daily journal, entries for November 22 and December 12, 1949.

38. Hermann Hospital was completed earlier, but it is not actually on the property of the Medical Center.

39. See R. A. Shepherd, president of the board of trustees of the Methodist Hospital, to AFS, November 14, 1951, Smith Papers.

40. Interview with Dr. Cummings.

41. Interview with Mr. Bowen.

42. Interview with Mr. Shepherd.

43. See chap. 7, pp. 141-42. AFS traditionally spoke at the first meeting of each new year, and he encouraged the organization until his death.

44. For a concise history of the Blue Bird Circle, see the semicentenary booklet *Blue Bird Circle: 1923-1973*, available from the Blue Bird Circle Shop and House at 613 W. Alabama, Houston, Texas.

45. Interview with Tom Fourqurean.

46. One of two letters that Bess wrote to AFS during Holy Week of 1941, undated but datable by their contents (holograph), Smith Papers.

47. Interview with AFS and Mrs. Smith by Dr. Charles S. Braden, January 23, 1962, in Houston, Texas.

48. Interview with A. Frank Smith, Jr., August 29, 1972.

49. Conversation with Mrs. L. U. Spellman, to whom Mrs. Smith confided the truth of her condition. See also interview with Dr. Hatch Cummings.

50. Interview with W. Randolph Smith, August 29, 1972.

51. Conversation with Bishop Arthur Moore, while driving from Epworth-by-the-Sea, St. Simon Island, to Atlanta, Georgia, January 22, 1972.

52. Interview with Bishop William C. Martin, January 22, 1973, in Little Rock, Arkansas.

53. Interviews with Dr. D. Lawrence Landrum, January 17, 1973, in Palestine, Texas; and Dr. Monroe Vivion, January 18, 1973, near Flint, Texas.

54. Dr. L. U. Spellman to the author, February 9, 1973, p. 8.

55. Interview with Bishop W. Kenneth Pope, September 15, 1972, in Dallas, Texas.

56. Interview with Dr. Bonneau P. Murphy, February 16, 1973, in Dallas, Texas.

57. Interview with Hines H. Baker.

58. Interview with Dr. Durwood Fleming.

59. Interview with Ted Bowen.

60. See chap. 15, p. 340.

61. Braden interview.

62. Interview with Ted Bowen, and Braden interview.

63. Interview with Dr. Monroe Vivion, January 18, 1973; and Mr. Bowen to AFS, August 24, 1960, Smith Papers. Including a generous automobile allowance, the annual total was $4,800.

64. Interview with Mr. Bowen.

65. Braden interview.

66. Interview with Ted Bowen. Most of this section and what follows is based on the interview with Mr. Bowen.

67. Interview with Chaplain Elton Stephenson, chaplain at the Methodist Hospital since 1951, on September 21, 1973.

68. Chaplain Elton Stephenson to AFS, September 19, 1956 (holograph), Smith Papers.

69. Clyde J. Verheyden to AFS, November 7, 1957, Smith Papers.

70. AFS to Stephenson, March 22, 1960 (holograph), courtesy of Chaplain Elton Stephenson.

71. Interview with Chaplain Stephenson.

72. Ibid.

73. Quoting from a statement AFS wrote for *Methodist Staff News Notes* 8, no. 1 (February 1961): 2.

74. Interview with Chaplain Stephenson.

75. Interview with Dr. Hatch W. Cummings.

76. Ted Bowen to AFS, January 2, 1962, Smith Papers.

77. Interview with W. Randolph Smith.

78. Dr. L. U. Spellman to the author, February 9, 1973, p. 8.

79. Interview with Mr. Bowen.

EPILOGUE

1. AFS to Rev. J. Butterworth, December 14, 1960 (carbon copy), Smith Papers. Although this letter gives August 12 as the date of Mrs. Smith's heart attack, AFS wrote August 13 in two other letters: AFS to Bishop W. C. Martin, November 5, 1960, and AFS to Dr. Charles S. Braden, January 12, 1961. Photocopies of both letters are in the Smith Papers.

2. AFS to Braden, January 12, 1961.

3. Interview with Rabbi Hyman Judah Schachtel, Temple Beth Israel, Houston, Texas, September 18, 1973. See also interview with Bishop Paul E. Martin, January 14, 1972, in Dallas, Texas.

4. AFS to Bishop Martin, February 8, 1962, Bishop Paul E. Martin Papers, Bridwell Library, SMU.

5. "The Dr. who is head of the Cardiology Dept. at Methodist [Hospital] verified our Dr.'s diagnosis," Mrs. Smith added.

6. Mrs. Smith to Mrs. Lois Perkins, "Saturday" [April 14, 1962], holograph courtesy of Mrs. Perkins. For the date of AFS's heart attack, see AFS to Dr. Charles S. Braden, July 3, 1962 (carbon copy), Smith Papers.

7. Jo Ann DePrima to Marjorie Beech, April 19, 1962 (carbon copy), Smith Papers.

8. AFS to Martin, June 19, 1962, Bishop William C. Martin Papers, Bridwell Library, SMU.

9. AFS to Martin, August 24, 1962, Bishop William C. Martin Papers, SMU.

10. Interview with Bishop W. Kenneth Pope, Dallas, Texas, September 15, 1972.

11. AFS to Bishop William C. Martin, August 24, 1962, Bishop William C. Martin Papers, SMU.

12. AFS to Bishop and Mrs. Kenneth W. Copeland, October 2, 1962, photocopy courtesy of Bishop Copeland.

13. "Bishop Smith developed a considerable amount of coronary insufficiency, and it was necessary to have him under a very strict regimen because of his cardiac condition." Dr. Abbe A. Ledbetter to the author, October 4, 1973.

14. AFS to Bishop and Mrs. Copeland, October 2, 1962.

15. Dr. Abbe A. Ledbetter to the author, October 4, 1973. "The symptomatology strongly suggested that he had a ruptured aortic vessel."

16. See newspaper reports in the *Houston Chronicle, Houston Post,* and *Houston Press,* October 6, 1962. According to these accounts, AFS had suffered "a week long siege with the flu." Burial was in Forest Park Lawndale.

17. Letter from AFS to J. J. Perkins, January 29, 1952, one of the many letters that Mrs. Perkins placed in the Smith Papers.

18. See reports in the *Houston Chronicle,* October 8, 1962, pp. 1, 16, and the *Texas Methodist,* October 19, 1962, p. 1.

19. Editorial, *Houston Post,* October 7, 1962, sec. 7, p. 2.

20. *Texas Methodist,* October 19, 1962, p. 1.

21. "Special Issue Dedicated to the Memory of Bishop A. Frank Smith," *Journal of The Methodist Hospital,* n.d., Houston, Texas. This issue also contains a transcript of Bishop Paul E. Martin's tribute to AFS which he delivered to the board of trustees of the Methodist Hospital, October 23, 1962. A tape recording of the funeral services is in the Smith Papers.

22. As quoted in AFS's sermon at the funeral of John T. Scott, July 11, 1955, Smith Papers. Compare John Bunyan, *The Pilgrim's Progress,* The Harvard Classics (New York: P. F. Collier & Son, 1909), pp. 315-16.

Decherd Turner, head librarian at the Bridwell Library, first called the author's attention to AFS's extensive use of *The Pilgrim's Progress* in his funeral sermons.

23. "Clergyman's Record," Funeral of Mrs. Bess Crutchfield Smith (August 3, 1891–February 4, 1964), Papers of Bishop William C. Martin, Bridwell Library,

SMU. The service was held in First Methodist Church, Houston, on February 6, 1964, with Bishops William C. Martin, Paul E. Martin, W. Kenneth Pope, O. Eugene Slater, and Paul V. Galloway participating. Interment was in Forest Park Lawndale Cemetery, Houston. See also author's interview with Mr. and Mrs. George F. Pierce, January 17, 1972, in Dallas, Texas.

24. Although the Pierces recall the ceremony as taking place in McFarlin Auditorium, several newspaper accounts state that the unveiling occurred in Fondren Library. See *Dallas Morning News*, Wednesday, February 5, 1964, sec. 1, p. 12; and *Southwest Texas Conference News*, March 15, 1964, p. 2.

The A. Frank Smith Memorial Texana Room of Fondren Library was dedicated on May 10, 1963. Program in the Leete Collection, Bridwell Library, SMU.

25. Interview with Bishop Paul E. Martin, January 14, 1972.

26. Interview with Mr. and Mrs. George Pierce.

Index